*The Morning Chronicle's*

# LABOUR AND THE POOR

## Volume V

# THE MANUFACTURING DISTRICTS

*The Morning Chronicle's*

# LABOUR AND THE POOR

## VOLUME V

# THE MANUFACTURING DISTRICTS

# ANGUS B. REACH

*Edited By*
*Rebecca Watts & Kevin Booth*

Ditto Books
www.dittobooks.co.uk

First Published by Ditto Books 2020

© Ditto Books 2020

A catalogue record for this book is available
from the British Library

ISBN  978-1-913515-05-8  (hardback)
ISBN  978-1-913515-15-7  (paperback)

Cover Image:
Stockport
From "Lancashire: its History, Legends, and Manufactures"
George Newenham Wright
Published 1843
Image courtesy of The British Library

"Purify the air of Manchester by quenching its furnaces, and you simply stop the dinners of its inhabitants. The grim machine must either go on, or hundreds of thousands must starve."

# *Contents*

# List of Illustrations

# *Preface*

This work attempts to be a faithful reproduction of the "Labour and the Poor" letters as printed in *The Morning Chronicle*. Only obvious typographical errors and omissions have been corrected. Variations in the spelling and hyphenation of words have largely been retained. We hope any such inconsistencies prove to be of some historical interest to the reader.

As much as possible we have tried to recreate the original layout and styling of the text and all factual tables have been reproduced as closely to the originals as possible with only minimal alterations made where necessary to improve readability.

Not all letters were titled. Where missing we have added titles to the Table of Contents to assist navigation and explanation of content. The letters themselves are as per the originals.

A handful of illustrations have been added to each volume. These did not appear in the original text but hopefully provide added interest.

R. W.

K. B.

# Introduction

In 1849 a leading London-based newspaper, *The Morning Chronicle*, undertook an investigation into the working and living conditions of the poor throughout England and Wales in the hope that their findings might lead to much needed change.

The reputed catalyst for their "Labour and the Poor" series was an article written by Henry Mayhew recording a journey into Bermondsey, one of the most deprived districts of London, which was printed in September 1849. Following this it was proposed that an in-depth investigation be carried out and "Special Correspondents", the investigators, were selected and distributed around the country. The first article or "Letter" appeared on the 18th of October 1849 and the series would run for almost 2 years and 222 letters.

The well-known and respected writers and journalists recruited for the task included Henry Mayhew who was assigned to the Metropolitan districts, Angus Bethune Reach to the Manufacturing districts, Alexander Mackay and Shirley Brooks to the Rural districts and Charles Mackay to investigate the cities of Birmingham and Liverpool. The author of the letters from Wales is as yet unknown.

The "Labour and the Poor" letters were extremely popular at the time, being widely read throughout the nation and even abroad. The revelations in them caused quite a stir amongst the middle and upper classes of Victorian society. *Letters to the Editor* poured in with donations for specific cases of distress that appeared in the letters and also for the general alleviation of the suffering of the poor. A special fund was set up by *The Morning Chronicle* to collect and distribute these donations.

These *Letters to the Editor* have been included in this series, predominantly in the Metropolitan district volumes whose letters elicited the majority of responses. They provide a unique window into the thoughts and sentiments of the Victorian readership as they react to the incredible accounts of misery and desperation being unveiled.

*The Morning Chronicle's* extraordinary and unsurpassed "Labour and the Poor" investigation provides an unparalleled insight into the people of the period, their living and working conditions, their feelings, their language, their sufferings and their struggles for survival amidst the poverty and destitution of 19th century Britain. An investigation of such magnitude had never before been attempted and the undertaking was truly of epic proportions. Its impact at the time was profound. Its historical importance today is without question.

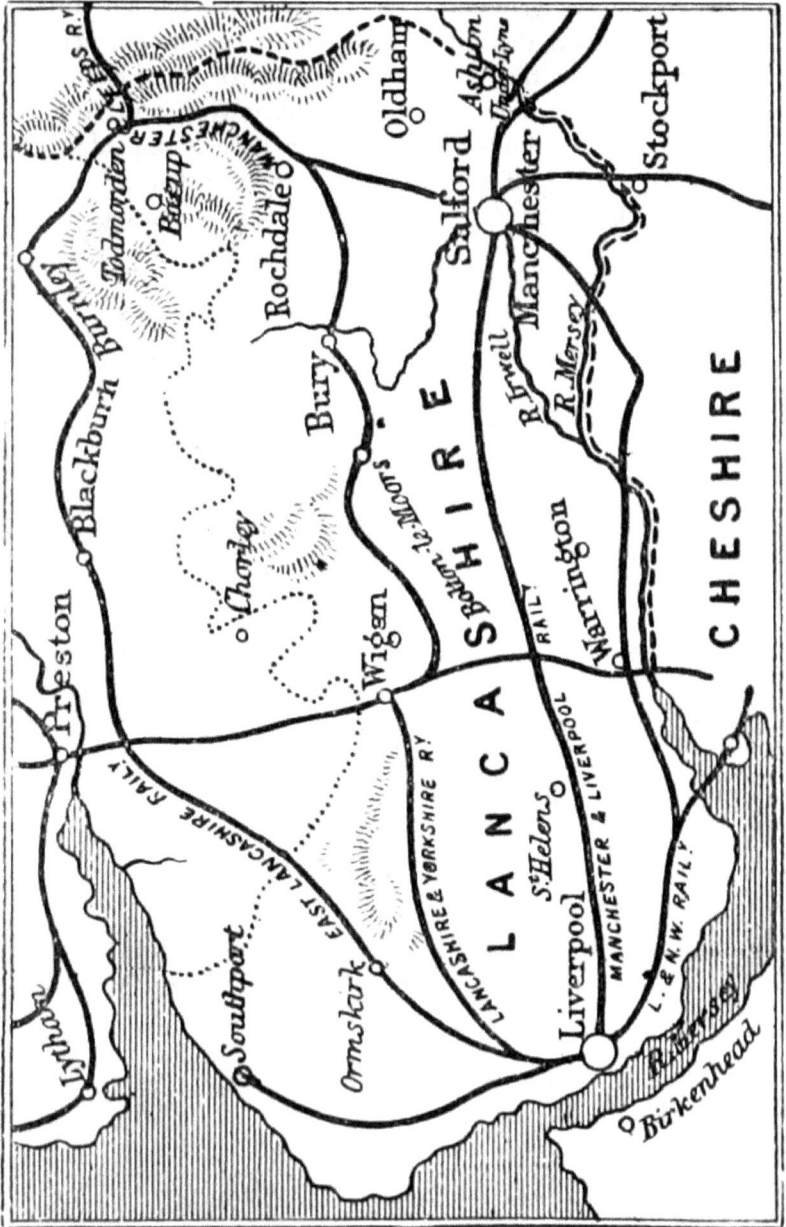

Map of The Lancashire Cotton District

*The Morning Chronicle, Thursday, October 18, 1849.*

# LABOUR AND THE POOR.

—◆—

## THE MANUFACTURING DISTRICTS.

[FROM OUR SPECIAL CORRESPONDENT.]

### MANCHESTER.

### LETTER I.

*The Morning Chronicle* has proposed to itself a great task; no less than the institution of a complete and impartial system of inquiry into the actual condition and future prospects of the labouring poor of England—the dwellers in scattered country cottages, and in lanes and alleys of the towns—the workers in our fields, our factories, our docks, our mines. In pursuance of that branch of this inquiry which has been intrusted to me, I am domiciled for the present in the great capital of the greatest department of our textile industry—amongst those "tall chimneys" which have become proverbial as the signs and symbols of that new and mighty fact—that new and mighty power—that unprecedented social and industrial development, which we call the MANUFACTURING INTEREST.

It will be for me to explore the foundation upon which that development rests; to trace its effect, in all the phases of that effect, upon the workman and the workwoman. Leaving, in a great degree, out of view those questions of commercial polity and politico-economic science which bear indirectly rather than directly and at once upon the operative, I shall confine myself to the immediate influences which encompass his life, and mould and warp his character and his social position. I shall paint the man such as the occupation which he follows, the system in which he has been brought up, the district and the social condition of the community of which he forms an item, have made him. I shall accompany the labourer to the loom, to the mine, to the forge. I shall describe his toil and the circumstances under which it is performed. I shall also visit the workman in his home. I shall describe the economy of the lodging-room, the cellar, the cottage. I shall investigate the bearing of the system of gregarious toil upon family ties and sexual relationships. I shall narrate to what extent the factories tend to cheer, and to what extent they tend to sadden, the hearth of the artizan who toils amongst them. I shall follow his children to the school and to the mill. I shall inquire how far an undue precocity is nurtured by their early toil and their early wages; I shall observe how far that precocity tends to very early marriages, and consequently to a very early disruption of family bonds—a very early cooling of family affections. I shall inquire diligently and impartially into the vital statistics of the manufacturing system. I shall examine into the effect of factory labour upon the health and life of the factory labourer. I shall investigate the sanitary conditions under which he works at the mill—the sanitary conditions under which he lives at home. I shall likewise diligently inquire into his religious and theological opinions. I shall analyse, first, his educational, then his moral and intellectual standing. I shall examine into what forms his ordinary reading; I shall hear the lectures which please and instruct him; I shall witness the amusements which he favours; I shall accompany him, as with his family he goes to breathe the fresh air of the fields, or to take part in the rational and elevating diversion of the concert-room.

Nor shall I forget most particularly and most diligently to inquire into what have been the consequences of, and what are the opinions of, the factory operatives—men and women—as regards recent factory legislation. To obtain full and accurate information upon this head is, indeed, one of the most important objects of my mission. It has appeared to the wisdom of Parliament that an industrial system, unprecedented and anomalous in its features, should be dealt with by laws which even their warmest advocates admitted to be anomalous, if not unprecedented. The Ten Hours Bill has now been in operation for more than a year and a half—a period amply sufficient to test its practical popularity. That the toil of women and children, away from their households and their homes, ought to be jealously watched by a guardian Legislature, is what few even of the most rigid free-traders in labour are disposed to deny. Premature toil in youth brings premature age on manhood. The child who is overtasked when the vital energies are still feeble and the bones still pliant, will never grow up daring of spirit or stout of frame. The woman who perfectly understands all which belongs to the tending of mules and spindles, but knows nothing of domestic duties, is ignorant of the very rudiments of the art of cooking a dinner, and has yet to learn how to make a shilling go farthest in the market, will seldom make the fire-side more pleasant than the public-house, or foster and encourage those home habits and home tastes which form one of the very best social characteristics of men of Anglo-Saxon blood. The Legislature has, therefore, providently ordained that the child shall have its due season of recreation and instruction; that the mother shall be so circumstanced as to prevent the possibility of the woman sinking hopelessly into the mill-labourer—into the position of one whose home is rather among looms and spindles than within her threshold and beside her hearth. So far the great question of free trade in labour seems of comparatively easy solution; the difficulty still looms ahead. If the Legislature takes care of the child and the woman, may not the man take care of himself? Leading-strings are useful, but leading-strings too long worn become as fetters. It happens to be the nature of the factory system that, more or less, all its processes must go on simultaneously. The engine, the loom, the mule, and the hands of men, women, and children, must all labour together. Consequently, the ten hours maximum of toil for "women and young children" becomes virtually the maximum of toil for all. The labour of the adult—the industry of the free Englishman—is thus attacked. Abstractedly, his liberty is taken from him; for to say to a man that he shall not work when he wishes to work, is to enslave him as much as to compel him to labour when he wishes to rest. This is the strict political economy and abstract reasoning of the question. But many other elements may be taken into view in its solution. Has political economy no exceptional cases? Is sentiment to be utterly ignored, and a coldly correct system of reasoning—which would deal with men and women as Euclid deals with perfect squares and isosceles triangles—to hold on an eternal and unbroken course? Such questions can only be answered by a strict investigation of the exceptional circumstances and conditions to which they apply.

Such, then, being the state of matters, it becomes of the utmost importance that the sentiments of the factory population upon the Ten Hours Bill, now that they can speak from experience, should be known. This point I shall expressly inquire into. I shall endeavour to ascertain whether any, and if any, what moral, social, and physical advantages have resulted from the diminution in the hours of toil. I shall inquire how the workman and the workwoman spend their additional time of leisure—whether evening schools are better attended—whether reading-rooms have more occupants, and libraries more subscribers. I shall also investigate fully the circumstances of the pending attempt to elude the Ten Hours Bill, by means of what is called the "shift" or the "relay" system. I shall inquire whether that system has not been originated by the ingenuity of the small proportion of the workmen, and the larger proportion of the masters, who opposed the Ten Hours Bill; and I shall take pains to ascertain whether the present efforts of the minority of the factory population be not rendering nugatory the recent triumphs of the majority.

Such, in brief recapitulation, are the points to which my researches in the cotton districts will be directed. I undertake the task with a determination to be impartial; but animated with the strongest desire to see the labourer elevated in the social scale. I believe the abyss between our highest and our lowest classes to be unnaturally wide. I believe that the shaft of the social column places an undue distance between the Corinthian capital and the basement which bears up all. I fear that the spirit which animates society has in it too much of cold formality, of class selfishness, and of a systemic want of sympathy with struggling labour. Doubtless political economy sprung not before it was wanted into the world. It cleared men's minds of stifling masses of ignorance and prejudice. It pointed out to us the highway to national wealth, and, by consequence, to social prosperity. It taught us to see many things; but none more clearly than that to which we were longest and most unwittingly blind—our own interests. But although political economy brought those great blessings in its train, still, like all earthly things, it was not a gift of unmingled good. Misunderstood or perverted, it spread abroad a hard, dry, bargaining spirit—a spirit well adapted for carrying on to the utmost advantage the operations of production and of exchange—but a spirit hostile to the growth and development of that genial and hearty appreciation of class by class, which ought to form, if not the clamps by which society is bound together, at least the mortar which gives the fabric additional adhesiveness and additional smoothness. It was the consciousness of this mutual, and mutually deadening, want of genial warmth and of chivalrous sympathy operating on a few quick and generous, yet essentially unpractical, and in some cases impracticable, minds, which a few years ago produced that political and literary school which, running from one extreme to another, proposed to overturn the fabric of society, in order to remould it upon something like the feudal system, imbued with something like the patriarchal spirit. Far be it from me to uphold the slightest phase of the least monstrous of these chimeras. But still, is there not something in the tone of the philosophy of which

I speak worthy of the ear of the most economical of statesmen? Do we not lack a brotherly and a mutually cherishing spirit? Might not the "cold charity of man to man" be somewhat warmed and quickened? The extremes of our society are awful and threatening. We are the richest and the poorest nation upon earth. Cheek by jowl stand palaces odorous with perfume and cellars deadly with typhus. Capital and labour look upon each other with suspicious eyes. The owner of the former characterizes the holder of the latter as one of the "dangerous classes"—only, perhaps, to be characterized in turn as one of the tyrannous classes. Let us rest assured, that if one definition be correct, the other is not utterly destitute of truth. If society were properly constituted, need there be any class "dangerous" to the classes above it? It is not the poor—in the ordinary acceptation of the term—who are "dangerous." It is not even the simply destitute who are "dangerous." It is those who are destitute, without, as they conceive, any fault of their own, yet find no sympathy expressed for them—those who are destitute, yet perceive no apparent marks of pressure on classes the interests of which they have been long told are bound up with theirs, and who do not see the signs of that pressure and that embarrassment, simply because of the cold barrier which subsists between the two orders—because of the lack of communication, of frankness, of cordiality, of personal intercourse, which separates the man who deals in capital, from the man who deals in labour.

Without, then, attempting to alter or to remodel the fabric of society, we might advantageously do much to better the spirit of society, and to gather in nearer to a common centre the outposts of society. This must be effected by raising the position—that is to say, raising the standard of the comforts and the education, of the labouring man. How such a change is to be effected will, judging from all indications, soon become the question of questions. Social reforms are getting to be the most pressing of all politics. Land was at first the power which swept everything before it. It was the first form of capital. Then capital, popularly so called, enjoyed its triumphs, swayed the national mind, and altered the national polity. Is not that other species of capital—unaccumulated capital—that is to say, labour—also to possess its time of favour and advancement? The question may indicate imperfect knowledge, and lead to error; but it will be asked, and it must be answered. Among races of men whom we flatter our vanity by designating savages, there does not exist the continued privation and the animal ignorance which place their degrading stamp upon masses of our own labouring population. While this continues to be so, are we safe? Wonderful has been our recent escape from the fever of convulsion which fixed upon almost all Europe, and most highly does that escape speak for the manly endurance, the sturdy good sense, the admirable good feeling of the working poor of England. But the very fact that we have experienced so signal a deliverance ought surely to induce us to seal up those sources whence danger may arise. If we are thankful to the people, who, feeling dire poverty and beholding boundless wealth, never sought, like their continental neighbours, to get up a convulsion and a scramble, ought we to persevere in that cold system of exclusion and neglect which makes poverty doubly bitter, seeing that it is manifestly spurned and outcast? Because no labourer here called out, "A bas les riches," are we to persevere in calling, "A bas les pauvres"? It may be answered that the one cry is as little heard as the other; and I believe that a sounder and a healthier and a more catholic spirit than England has seen for many years is stirring, and will shortly walk abroad.

Most Englishmen are, either from actual observation or reiterated description, familiar with the general appearance of what are called the manufacturing districts. The traveller by railway is made aware of his approach to the great northern seats of industry by the dull leaden-coloured sky, tainted by thousands of ever smoking chimneys, which broods over the distance. The stations along the line are more closely planted, showing that the country is more and more thickly peopled. Then, small manufacturing villages begin to appear, each consisting of two or three irregular streets clustered round the mill, as in former times cottages were clustered round the castle. Roads substantially paved with stone, so as to support the weight of heavy waggons, wind among the fields. Canals, with freights of barges, intersect the country; and the rivers, if they be not locked and dammed back, and embellished with towing paths upon the banks, run turbid and thick—charged with the foulness of the hundred mills they have aided in their course. Presently the tall chimneys begin to figure conspicuously in the landscape; the country loses its fresh rurality of appearance; grass looks brown and dry, and foliage stunted and smutty. The roads, and even the footpaths across the fields, are black with coal dust. Factories and mills raise their dingy masses everywhere around. Ponderous waggons, heavily laden with bales or casks, go clashing along. You shoot by town after town—the outlying satellites of the great cotton metropolis. They have all similar features—they are all little Manchesters. Huge, shapeless, unsightly mills, with their count-less rows of windows, their towering shafts, their jets of waste steam continually puffing in panting gushes from the brown, grimy wall. Between these vast establishments, a network of mean but regular streets, unpicturesque and unadorned—just the sort of private houses you would expect in the vicinity of such public edifices; and around all this, and here and there scattered amongst all this, great irregular, muddy spaces of waste ground, studded with black pools and swarm-ing with dirty children. Some dozen or so miles so characterized, the distance of course more or less according to the point at which you en-ter the Queen of the cotton cities—and then, amid smoke and noise, and the hum of never-ceasing toil, you are borne over the roofs to the terminus platform. You stand in Manchester.

There is a smoky brown sky overhead—smoky brown streets all around—long piles of warehouses, many of them with pillared and stately fronts—great grimy mills, the leviathans of ugly archi-tecture, with their smoke-pouring shafts. There are streets of all kinds—some with glittering shops and vast hotels, others grim and little frequented—formed of rows and stacks of warehouses; many mean and distressingly monotonous vistas of uniform brick houses. There are principal thoroughfares, busy and swarming as London central avenues—crowded at once with the evidences of wealth and commerce—gay carriages and phaetons—clumsy low built omnibuses, conveying loads which a horse must shudder to contemplate—carts, and waggons of every construction, high piled with bales and boxes. There are crowds of busy pedestrians of every class which business creates—clerks, and travellers, and agents—bustling from counting-house to counting-house, and bank to bank. There are swarms of mechanics and artizans in their distinguishing fustian—of factory operatives, in general undersized, sallow-looking men—and of factory-girls, somewhat stunted and pale, but smart and active looking, with dingy dresses and dark shawls, speckled with flakes of cotton-wool wreathed round their heads.

This city—this great capital of the weavers and spinners of the earth, the Manchester of the power-loom, the Manchester of the League, *our* Manchester—is but a thing of yesterday. Yet the nucleus of the town is as ancient as the walls of our most ancient cathedral cities. From the time to which the memory of man goeth not to the contrary, a hamlet stood where Manchester now stands. It was a borough since the first year of the fourteenth century. When Henry

VIII. was upon the throne Manchester was spoken of as the "best builded, quickest, and most populous town of Lancashire." For indeed the shadow of coming events fell curiously early on the banks of the Irwell. In the reign of Elizabeth, Manchester had already acquired a fame for its "coatings"—in all probability a species of woollen stuff. Cotton from the Levant was wrought into fabrics here before the Protectorate. In 1650 the trade of Manchester comprehended "woollen fringes, fustians, sackcloths, mingled stuffs and tapes, whereby not only the better sort of workmen are employed, but also the very children by their own labour can maintain themselves." The town was then a meanly-built straggling place, with a principal street, the greater part of it composed of quaint projecting gables, sloping down to the banks of the Irwell. Divers hamlets lay around it, on the shores of the main stream and the two tributaries, the Irk and the Medlock, which here join it; among these were the villages of Salford, Pendleton, and Hulme. The manufacturers of those days pursued their calling in rude and patriarchal guise. Each family, with its apprentices, wrought on its own account. The master of the household was the master of the factory, and when he was not labouring among his dependants, he was guiding, through the hills of Lancashire and Yorkshire, a string of pack-horses, laden with his fabrics, which he hawked as he went along. Sir Richard Arkwright was the man who laid the foundation of *our* Manchester. Since the introduction of roller-spinning the city sprung up as though by magic. A man, only a very few years dead, recollected the people crowding to admire the first tall chimney built in Manchester, and had seen the Liverpool coach set forth at six in the morning, in good hope of its reaching its destination not very long after six o'clock at night. Considerably within two-thirds of a century the scattered villages of Manchester, Salford, Hulme, Pendleton, Chorlton, and two or three others, became the vast cotton metropolis which has lately succeeded in swaying the industrial and commercial polity of England.

Perhaps no species of labour has been more enthusiastically lauded, and none more spitefully attacked, than that which the cotton-factory system originated. That system has been spoken of as the glory and the shame of England. It has been described as the sinews and as the canker of our land. To hear one party, we might imagine that, in their view, the whole end, and aim, and object of life was the production of cheap calico. To listen to another set of partizans, one might believe all millowners to be Molochs—all mills temples for the immolation of children. Mr. Southey described the factory system as "a wen, a fungous excrescence on the body politic;" and a devout Protectionist journal prayed for the day when the plough would turn up the grass growing over Manchester. Let it be our care to study whether there may not be a middle and a wiser course of opinion between the extremes of either sect of rhapsodists. It would have been admitted, even by Sir James Graham, when he contrasted the "dewy call of incense breathing morn" with the "dismal clank of the factory bell," that it is still possible that a man, with a family to feed, might prefer the smoke of Manchester, with twelve shillings a week, to the bright dawn and the green fields of Wiltshire with six. No one questions the manifold evils, the manifold abominations, of the life of great cities. Happy, no doubt, should we be to see every man enjoying himself beneath his own vine and his own fig-tree. Happy, no doubt, should we be, were it possible, to clear for ever the blue sky from smoky pollution, and enfranchise the swart artizan from toil which racks his limbs from before sunrise until after sundown. But what can we do? A stubborn ring-fence of facts girdles us. Here are vast masses of people absolutely dependent upon the labour which bristles with so many forbidding points. Purify the air of Manchester by quenching its furnaces, and you simply stop the dinners of its inhabitants. The grim machine must either go on, or hundreds of thousands must starve. There, in a word, is the stern inevitable answer to all who in this matter would allow sentiment to get the better of common sense. But are the pure sentimentalists right even in their view of the matter as it stands? Is the factory operative a less happy man than the rural labourer who toils with the sweet breath of heaven and the glories of God's creation about him? Perhaps the inquiry now opening in your columns may convey an instructive answer to the question. There is a curious practical difference between the word "country" literally applied, and the word "country" signifying landscape. Are we not sometimes too apt to take it in its latter sense? When we look at the sunlit panorama of hill and vale and glade and stream, we are not always apt to remember that, in these scattered cottages, so picturesquely situated, there grovels poverty more keen and grinding, and suffering as hopeless and as intense, as in ever a cellar or garret of Manchester or Bolton. If the operatives about me here be stunted, is there not a sort of equipoise in the grim gauntness you too often see in the country? In truth, the repulsiveness of the factory system is upon the surface; the advantages lie beneath. Manufacturing towns are so essentially, so abominably, ugly, smoky, and dirty, that it really is no wonder people turn from them with something like horror. It never seems to have struck the capitalist of the north that appearances are of the least account. On the contrary, he seems to build his mills in the express hope that each succeeding huge brick box will rival its predecessors in intensity of ugliness. So with chimneys. No earnest, or persevering, or systematic attempt ever seems to have been made towards the consumption of the smoke and the purifying of the air. It is my real belief that nine-tenths of the superficial unpopularity of the manufacturing system would be got rid of, were the manufacturers to set heartily to work to purify and beautify their towns. The small per centage of profit sacrificed for this object would be well laid out. It would rescue its spenders from the imputations of narrow-minded and sordid insensibility to all which is beautiful and refined, which we so often hear them contemptuously charged with. Not, perhaps, that those who are best acquainted with the institutions of Manchester would most willingly credit such accusations; but I repeat that the eye demands its homage, and that ranges of mills with their pillared porticos, their stately façades, and their minaret or column-like chimneys, would, in the estimation of the world, divest the manufacturing system of much of the odium, by freeing it from much of the ugliness, attached to it.

The moral ugliness and the moral beauties of that system, I shall examine in their proper places. Where great bodies of people, the vast proportion of them labouring poor, are crammed together, crime must abound. So it was since human nature was human nature. The temptation to crime and the facility of its commission increase together. But the same causes which make the few dishonest, tend to make the many intelligent; clever and daring thieves belong to communities of clever and daring men. The warped branch has yet something in it of the grain of the goodly tree. In a coloured table of crime which lies before me—one of those ingenious modes of painting statistics which the present statistical age has invented—the metropolis is the most darkly-shaded district. Next to it comes the iron country; then the cotton region; and treading close upon their heels—closer, perhaps, than most people imagine—we have, as the next deepest in criminality, the rural districts. If we represent the amount of manufacturing crime during the year 1847 by the figure

18, we shall find the proportion of agricultural offences to stand as high as 14—a proportion which will be of startling magnitude to the many who naturally connect rustic beauties with rural innocence, and take but little account of the fact, that the agricultural labourer endures more habitual and more pinching hunger and cold, amid his fair fields and woods, than the factory operative amid the dust and smoke of his alley and his mill.

But such comparisons, more especially if made with invidious import, are worse than idle. England is a manufacturing and agricultural community, and will continue so.

Whether or no there be anything essentially unnatural in the manufacturing system—whether or no its very existence be a plague spot on the land—involves a controversy which only very idle men would willingly pursue. The thing itself, is a great fact—*un fait accompli*—an "established innovation." Whether a philosopher, if he could plan out the track for an infant nation to pursue, would devise so that the happiness of a great part of that nation should be rigidly dependent upon the extent of the table of its manufactured exports, we have not now to inquire into. Whether we had any business to set ourselves up as the spinners and weavers for half, and more than half, of the civilized, and a fair slice of the savage, world, is now a question beside the mark; the deed, for good or evil, has been done. The prosperity, and of course the happiness, of the north of England depend upon the continually increasing number of yards of cotton or woollen purchased by Europe, Asia, Africa, and America. If we do not spin and weave for the greater part of the world, our furnace fires must grow cold, our looms stand, and our operatives starve. Let us be thankful that Political Economy has opened our eyes to the necessities of our position. Let us be thankful that we have succeeded in taking measures which have created and will create markets, and have cheapened and will cheapen food. Now it is for Social Economy to play its part—to investigate diligently into the condition, the comforts, the mode of work and of life, of our factory population, and to devise and to urge every possible means for the amelioration of their lot, in their mills and in their homes—for the elevation physically and morally, of that most toilful, most enduring, most intelligent race of our population—that race amongst which the general vigour and enterprise of England seem to be especially condensed—that race which shows by so many tokens that in its veins runs the ruddiest Anglo-Saxon blood, and which, even in its rude *patois*, spoken by the forge and the loom, keeps still alive the antique phraseology of William Wicliffe and Geoffrey Chaucer.

# LABOUR AND THE POOR.

## THE MANUFACTURING DISTRICTS.

[FROM OUR SPECIAL CORRESPONDENT.]

### MANCHESTER.

### Letter II.

Since I wrote my introductory letter I have visited and minutely inspected three cotton mills—two of them spinning establishments—one of them a spinning and weaving factory. These three mills I selected as likely to afford fair average specimens of the condition of the textile industry of Manchester. The first establishment which I visited was the great spinning and weaving factory of Messrs. Birley, situated on the small stream of the Medlock, in the district of Chorlton-upon-Medlock. This establishment, including a manufactory of MacIntosh cloth, which adjoins it, and which is the property of the partners, consists of several huge piles of building, separated from each other by streets, but connected by subterranean tunnels, in which iron tramways are laid down for the speedier and easier conveyance from ware-room to ware-room of the raw material. Nearly two thousand hands are regularly employed in this vast industrial colony, and the machinery with which it is filled is impelled by several steam-engines, some of them of small power—a couple working with the strength of 70, and one with the force of 150 horses. Like the great majority of mills in Manchester, Messrs. Birley's establishment works fairly ten hours a day. The thread spun there is of the coarser quality, and is principally intended to be woven into cloth for the foreign markets—a statement which leads me to a general remark, which must be constantly kept in mind in all our inquiries into the cotton-mill system. Manufactories of this species of fabric are divided into classes, according to the fineness or tenuity of the threads into which they spin the raw fibre of the cotton. The mills producing the most delicate threads, such, for example, as those requisite in the manufacture of lace, are called "fine spinning mills." The motion of the machinery in these mills is slowest, and, as a general rule, the wages of the operatives are highest, the thread being more valuable, and a greater degree of care and attention being requisite for its production. There are, then, "fine" spinning mills, "coarse" spinning mills, and a variety of establishments producing thread of intermediate degrees of fineness, which I may term medium mills. The factory of the Messrs. Birley spins, as I have said, coarse threads and the coarser ranges of the medium varieties. This factory has been long established, and being the largest in Manchester, may fairly be considered as one of the largest, if not the largest, in the world. A former partner in the mill was one of the magistrates in command at the riot nicknamed Peterloo.

The second mill which I visited is a much smaller one. It is situated in Canal-street, Oldfield-road, and has been driven by the same steam-engine for half a century. This factory is the property of Messrs. Harney and Tysoe—gentlemen who exert themselves to the utmost to promote the social comfort and improvement of their workpeople. In the admirably ordered establishment which they possess, are workmen who have toiled for the same masters for more than forty years; and twenty years ago, a spinner, who had been in the service of the same partners for thirty-two years, was carried to the grave by six of his comrades, who had laboured beside him for more than twenty years. This is a "fine" spinning mill. The partners are steady adherents of the teetotal system, and lose no opportunity of inculcating the advantages of temperance upon their workpeople. The hours of labour are ten.

The third mill which I have inspected is one of a medium size, and is spinning fine and medium threads, some of the former so exquisitely attenuated as to furnish more than 15,000 yards to the pound weight. Cotton, however, can be spun to a much greater fineness still. The factory at present in question is the property of Messrs. Gardner and Basley, who are also the owners of a country mill upon the line of the Bolton Railway. Both of the mills work ten hours a-day, according to act of Parliament.

In inspecting the two latter establishments which I have mentioned, every facility was afforded me for forming an accurate judgment of the condition of the workpeople. Messrs. Harney and Tysoe laid their wages-book before me, and were at pains to educe the exact average of the earnings of their people. Mr. Basley also gave me every information as to the wages in every department of his establishment; and in both mills I was invited to put any question to the operatives which I might desire. This last privilege I was not slow of using. The workpeople conversed freely with me in the mills, and I have had ample opportunities in other quarters of holding personal conference with operatives of all grades in the cotton manufacture, and of all varieties of opinion respecting the conditions under which it is, or ought to be, carried on. I propose, therefore, in this letter to give as elaborate a picture as I can of the economy of a cotton mill—of the various sorts of labour performed—of the appearance and condition of the various labourers engaged upon it, and generally to state my honest, and I hope not quite uninformed, views with reference to the toil of the multitudes who work the raw produce of the cotton plant into those cheap and beautiful fabrics so widely dispersed over the world.

The first thing, then, which strikes the observer as an essential and fundamental part of the factory system, is the comparative lightness of the actual labour—the comparatively small amount of physical strength required in any of the processes. In truth the engine is the worker. The operative is the superintendent of the engine's labours. In the earlier and ruder stages of textile industry, the labourer was required to furnish all the motive power, much of the mechanical skill, and all the superintending intelligence. Now, the engine relieves him altogether in the first respect, while the exquisite perfection of the machinery supersedes the necessity for not a small degree of the mechanical adroitness which was formerly kept upon the constant stretch. The guiding intelligence which overlooks with skilled and vigilant care the motions of wood, iron, and thread—prompt in a moment to stay and rectify a false movement—to repair in a moment an unavoidable accident—in fact, as it were, to supply a soul to the wondrous mechanism of engine, spinning frame, and loom—this guiding intelligence it is which the workman is now called upon to supply. So far from being degraded to the level of the machines amongst which he works, he rather seems to elevate them to his own perceptive and reasoning powers. Steam and machinery are the real factory operatives—the nominal factory operatives are really the factory superintendents. This great fact is, I think, the first and obvious feature which the slightest practical acquaintance with the system impresses upon the inquirer. I repeat, that the amount of physical strength—the actual wear and tear of the muscular fabric in a cotton factory—is astonishingly small. Probably in no mechanical employment is animal force more utterly at a discount than in the operations of a cotton mill. He who digs, he who hammers, he who saws, lavishes upon his labours a continuous degree of muscular energy. He has not only to direct, but to impel. The factory operative finds three-fourths of his work done to his hand. Watchfulness, intelligent attention, and manual quickness to repair and supply accidental defects, are what he requires. The question then comes to be, whether or no this species of labour necessarily wastes and consumes the frame by its irksomeness and continuity more than ruder kinds of work—by the absolute ex- haustion which they produce. The affirmative of this proposition was the ground taken by Mr. Sadler's factory committee in their report, and is the ground taken still by the keener opponents of the factory system. I cannot yet venture to speak positively, but I can venture to state my belief, that that ground will be found untenable. What species of labour is not irksome? Find that out, and nine-tenths of the human race will willingly bind themselves apprentices to acquire it. Daily toil of an uniform and unchanging character, as in the nature of things all toil to be steadily valuable must be, does necessarily in- volve a certain degree of irksomeness. The ploughman over his furrow, the blacksmith over his anvil, the sailor upon his watch, will each— so long as human nature continues to be human nature—long for the conclusion of his task. So, also, do the spinners and the weavers who work by hand; and so, doubtless, often must the spinners and the weavers who work hand-in-hand with steam. Irksomeness, in a greater or a less degree, is inseparable from labour. He who divides the one from the other eludes the primeval curse.

What we have, then, to inquire is, whether or not the labour of which especially I speak appears to be of a character so peculiarly irk- some, so peculiarly exhausting, that nature shrinks away from it with a stronger abhorrence than it would feel for other forms and modes of industry? This is a question which has been often asked, and as often answered by the assailants of the factory system in the affirmative. We have been told that labour carried on in great *ateliers*, by great bod- ies of operatives disciplined to work in steady conjunction with the uniform movements of machinery, is in itself something anomalous and unnatural. That it is something novel in the world's history, all may admit; that it is an organisation of human and mechanical power requiring to be strictly watched and judiciously checked, is what few will deny; that it possesses, so far as the consumer is concerned, palpa- ble and immense advantages, is unquestioned on all hands; and that it may be so conducted as to benefit the producer, as well and as much as the consumer, is an assertion which I believe to be capable of clear and unquestioned demonstration.

Let us, then, in the first place, consider what cotton-spinning really is. I do not purpose attempting anything like an accurate mechanical account either of the machines or of the several processes. I shall merely sketch the various operations in general terms, so as to give the reader an idea of the exact nature of the toil required at the hands of the operative.

The cotton is first unpacked from the bales, and the different qualities mixed together, so as to produce a material of uniform character. The labour requisite here is quite unskilled. A superintendent fixes the various qualities, and the operatives tumble and mix them together. This labour is always carried on in the basement storeys of the mills, and the wages paid for it are the smallest given to adults. The cotton is now ready for the operation of the first series of machines to which it is subjected. These serve roughly to tear the material, and partly to cleanse it from dust, dirt, and all coarse impurities. The mechanism used is a number of what are called blowing-machines, and the labour consists in little else than supplying these with the rough, dirty cotton, and gathering it up as the material emerges, cleansed and purified, from the operation of the revolving cylinders to which it has been subjected. Men and boys are generally employed at this work, and their wages may be taken as ranging from 7s. 6d. to 8s. 6d. We are still, the reader will perceive, dealing with little skilled labour. The atmosphere of the blowing-rooms is, perhaps, the most unpleasant and injurious to be encountered in a cotton mill. The air is impregnated with flying dust and impalpable filaments of the cotton wool, which the workpeople unavoidably breathe. In "fine" mills, the machinery works slower, and the dust and fibres are not so thickly blown about as in the "coarse" mills, but the latter have generally the advantage in point of temperature and airiness. Great improvements in the ventilation and construction of this portion of factories have recently been made, and various ingenious contrivances are in use for the purpose of carrying off into the open air as much as possible of the flying down and dust.

We now come to the card-room, where the cotton, already partially cleansed, is thoroughly purified and torn into uniformly fine filaments, which pour forth from the cylinders in smooth layers or sheets, and are wound upon revolving drums. The material at this stage of its progress is in the state familiarly known to us as "wadding."

The labour here requisite consists almost entirely in supplying the machines with the half-cleansed material, in withdrawing the drums as each becomes encompassed with its fleecy burden, and in taking from the spots where they lodge the coarser fragments of the wool rejected by the machine. Men and boys are the operators, and their wages run from 4s. to 15s. in the fine mills, and to about 13s. or 14s. in the coarser spinning establishments.

We now approach a new category of operations, in the first of which the germ of the spinning process is visible, and in which women and girls are almost exclusively employed. The cotton has been already reduced to a pulpy state—if I can apply the word to a dry material—to a pulpy mass of down-like wool. It is now subjected to the operations of the "drawing frame," and after passing round cylinders, their circular surfaces formed of fine wires, as thickly set as bristles in an ordinary clothes brush, and revolving so closely to each other that the material educed is a mere film, like cobwebs—this gauzy substance—if I can call substance that which appears more like a shadow—is collected from the broad surface of the cylinder, and condensed, as it were, by passing through small holes, from whence it descends, in a species of loosely-adhering yarn, into tin tubes placed to receive it. I may class together the next several processes, all of which are superintended by women and girls, and all of which are modifications of the same operation. We have brought the cotton to loosely-adhering yarns, called "card rovings." The object is now to condense, as it were, several of these together, managing that the material shall be so compacted by each operation that a yarn made up of three loose yarns shall be closer in fibre and smaller in bulk than any of the constituent parts taken singly. Let me illustrate this by a simple metaphor. Imagine three broad shallow rivers uniting and becoming one narrow deep one. The process is again and again repeated, in the skillet frame, the bobbin frame, the coarse jack frame, and the fine jack frame, the yarns gradually, of course, becoming finer, while they are being combined one with the other, running off from whirling pirns or bobbins, and being twisted more and more compactly in each successive frame. It will be evident that with each new degree of fineness acquired by the fabric the manipulation required becomes more delicate, and the motion of the machinery becomes faster. It is the duty of the operatives to watch that none of the threads or yarns break, and in case of such a catastrophe at once to catch up the broken thread, and by a dexterous twist of the fingers unite the parted continuity. They also take away the bobbins as each acquires its proper load of thread, and renew the exhausted ones from which the coarser yarns are run off. I have mentioned five machines or frames used in this process, and I repeat that they are generally if not always "tented" (mark the old Saxon phrase) by women. The wages earned by the "tenters" of the first three frames may be from 7s. to 8s.—a sixpence more or less. The coarse and fine jack frames produce higher earnings. Women labouring at the former have about 9s., and girls 7s.; the female operatives at the latter can clear from 10s. to 11s. and 11s. 3d. per week. In estimating these wages, I take the finer class of mills. It is quite impossible to give any literally exact statement of wages, as almost every shade in the coarseness or fineness of the yarns manufactured produces a corresponding variation in the rate of pay.

Carding, Drawing, and Roving

We have now brought our thread to the last and most important stage of its process—to the mule, which spins it out to its finally required degree of tenuity, and gives it the last compactness of twist. There are two sorts of mules in use in Manchester. First, there is the ordinary mule, used for "fine" work, requiring a spinner, two piecers, and a scavenger. In this machine, the spinner, by a wrench of a lever, gives the mechanism those alternate motions backwards and forwards which draw out and twist the threads. The piecers, either girls or boys, are his aide-de-camps; they walk along with the mule as it advances and recedes, catching up the broken threads and skilfully re-uniting them. The scavenger, a little boy or girl, crawls occasionally beneath the mule when it is at rest, and cleans the mechanism from super-fluous oil, dust, and dirt. The self-acting mule, which is used to any extent only in the coarse mills, dispenses with the services of a spinner. The man who attends it bears, in some mills, the significant appella-tion of the "cypher." The piecers are required, however, just as in the ordinary mule.

This is the process in a cotton mill in which there is most muscular exertion requisite. That exertion, however, merely consists in walking. The distance thus traversed every day has been very variously esti-mated. I remember Lord Ashley used to find plenty of calculators who put it at more than a score of miles a day. More reasonable esti-mates vary from seven to eleven miles; and from the inquiries which I have made, and the rude calculations which I have been trying to frame, I should be inclined to put the distance as much nearer the former figure than the latter. Be the work what it may, however, the place of a spinner is one of the prizes of the cotton trade. The ordi-nary wages of this class of operative varies from £2 to £2 5s. and £2 10s. per week. His piecers earn, say on the average, 11s. per week, and the tiny scavenger clears his or her half-crown. The wives of the spinners never work in the mill; and this I believe to be a very strong incentive, over and above the high wages, to induce the men to struggle for the post; so at least they have told me over and over again. The spinner is quite a patron in his way. He employs his own piecers and his own scavenger, generally selecting the younger members of his family for both offices.

I have now gone over the several operations performed in the pro-cess of eliminating the coarsest and the finest thread from the raw, tangled, and filthy cotton wool. I have shown that these operations are really performed by machinery, and that the workman does lit-tle but superintend the machinery, supply it with material, and re-move that material when the mechanism has done its duty. Vigilant attention, and a greater or less proportion of manipulating dexterity—the degrees of either being exactly reflected by the amount of wages paid—are the great, indeed the only, requisites for the toil. That toil appears to me to be neither especially severe nor irksome. The atten-tion, indeed, is kept upon the stretch, but the faculty is not such a high one as, in the case of adults at least, to be very easily wearied, while the manual operations, every now and then requisite, are of that light

Mule Spinning

and dexterous class which diversify the labour without fatiguing the labourer. The average of wages I have been at pains to ascertain. A very careful calculation, made from the books of Messrs. Harney and Tysoe, gives as the result an average over men, women, and young persons, of 11s. 3¾d. weekly. This is probably a somewhat high average, as the mill spins fine, and children under thirteen years of age are not employed. In Messrs. Gardner and Basley's factories, which spin rather coarser threads, the average is from 10s. 6d. to 11s. Taking, then, all the mills, coarse and fine, now working at ten hours, according to act of Parliament, I believe that I am justified in estimating the average wages at nearly 11s. per week. And here let us bear in mind that, in speaking of the average of wages, we are apt frequently to take the head of a family as the sole recipient, his household looking to him for support. Here the case is different. Take a man, his wife, and his children working in the mills, and the average wage is 11s.— not earned by one for the support of all, but earned by each for the support of each, or by all for the support of all.

I have described at some length the operations of a cotton-mill, considered generally with reference to the operators. Let me now try to convey a correct idea of the operators themselves at their work. In the majority of mills, labour begins at six o'clock a.m., throughout the year. In a certain number, the engine during the dead winter months does not start until half an hour later. As a general thing, however, operative Manchester is up and stirring before six. The streets in the neighbourhood of the mills are thronged with men, women, and children flocking to their labour. They talk and laugh cheerily together. The girls generally keep in groups with their shawls twisted round their heads, and every few steps, in the immediate vicinity of the mill, parties are formed round the peripatetic establishments of hot coffee and cocoa vendors. The factory bell rings from five minutes before six until the hour strikes. Then—to the moment—the engine starts, and the day's work begins. Those who are behind six, be it but a moment, are fined two pence; and in many mills, after the expiration of a very short time of grace, the doors are locked, and the laggard, besides the fine, loses his morning work.

Breakfast hour comes round at half-after eight o'clock. The engine stops to the minute, and the streets are again crowded with those of the operatives who live close by the mills. A great many, however, take their breakfasts in the factory, which, as a general rule, supplies them with hot water. The practice of the people taking their meals in the mill, though I believe contrary to the letter of the law, is quite necessary, owing to the distance which many of the workpeople live from their place of labour, and to the short time—only half-an-hour—allowed for the meal. Its constituents are generally tea and coffee, with plenty of bread and butter, and in many cases, a slice or so of bacon. At five minutes to nine the factory bell sounds again, and at nine the engine starts again. The work goes on with the most perfect method and order. There is little if any talking, and little disposition to talk. Everybody sets steadily and tranquilly about his or her duties, in that calm methodical style which betokens perfect acquaintance with the work to be done, and perfect skill wherewith to do it. There is no hurrying or panting and toiling after the machinery. Everything appears—in ordinary phrase—to be "taken easy;" yet everything goes rapidly and continuously on. The men commonly wear blue striped shirts, trowsers, and slippers; the women generally envelop themselves in coarse pinafores and loose jackets tying round the throat. Spinners and piecers go about their work generally barefoot, or with such an apology for *chaussure* as forcibly reminds you of the old story of the sedan chair with the bottom out. Were it not for the honour of the thing, they might just as well go entirely unshod. I fear that I cannot say much for the cleanliness of the workpeople. They have an essentially greasy look, which makes me sometimes think that water would run off their skins, as it does off a duck's back. In this respect the women are just as bad as the men. The spinners and piecers I have mentioned fling shoes and stockings aside, but I fear it is very very seldom that their feet see the interior of a tub with plenty of hot water and soap. The floor which they walk upon is as dark as the darkest mahogany, from the continued oily drippings with which it is anointed; and it is really painful to see a pretty girl with toes and ankles the exact colour of the dingy boards. Efforts have been made for the establishment of baths for the working classes in Manchester, and several millowners have actually erected conveniences of the sort, but the operatives in too many cases absolutely declined making use of them, and, as a general rule, can with very great difficulty, if at all, be made to appreciate the advantages of clean skin and free pores.

The atmosphere in which the work is conducted I found to vary much in different mills. In the fine factories a higher temperature is requisite than in the coarse, and the old mills are generally built upon defective ventilating principles, or rather upon no ventilating principles at all. Very considerable attention, however, is paid in all the factories to keeping up a supply of pure air; the object being attained by scientific means in the newer mills, and aimed at through the medium of open windows and swinging panes in those of an earlier date. The atmosphere in Messrs. Gardner and Basley's establishment was remarkably fresh and agreeable. Of course the air in which they work exercises a marked effect upon the appearance of the people. This is a subject which I shall treat of at length in a subsequent letter; but I may be here permitted to remark upon the more obvious physical characteristics of carders, spinners, and weavers. In the first place, I do not remember seeing one male or female adult to whom I would apply the epithet of a "stout" man or woman. There is certainly no superfluity of flesh in the factories. When I say this, I do not by any means intend to insinuate that the people are unhealthily or unnaturally lean; they are generally thin and spare, but not emaciated. By such occupation as is afforded in the various branches of cotton spinning, much muscle cannot be expected to be developed. There is no demand for it—the toil does not require it—it would be useless if it existed. I cannot, therefore, term the appearance of the people "robust." They present no indication of what is called "rude" health. They are spare, and, generally—so far as I can judge—rather undersized. At the same time their appearance cannot rightly be called sickly. Their movements are quick and easy, with nothing at all of languor expressed either in face or limbs. The hue of the skin is the least favourable characteristic. It is a tallowy-yellow. The faces which surround you in a factory, are for the most part lively in character, but cadaverous and overspread by a sort of unpleasant greasy pallor. Now and then you observe a girl with some indications of roses in her cheeks, but these cases are clearly the exceptions to the rule; and amid the elder and matronly women not a single exceptional case of the kind did I observe. Altogether, the conclusion which a very careful examination of the physical appearance of the people led me to was this, that the labour cannot be said to exercise a seriously stunting or withering effect upon those subjected to it—that it does not perhaps make them actually ill, but that it does prevent the full development of form, and that it does keep under the highest development of health. Men and women appeared to be more or less in a negative sanitary condition. At any rate, what is called the "bloom of health" is a flower requiring more air and sunshine than stirs and gleams athwart the rattling spindle.

While we are making these observations, however, the dinner hour approaches. In Manchester everybody, master and man, dines at one o'clock. As the chimes sound, all the engines pause together, and from every workshop, from every industrial establishment—be it cotton, silk, iron, print works, or dye works—the hungry crowd swarms out, and streets and lanes, five minutes before lonely and deserted, are echoing the trampling of hundreds of busy feet. The Manchester operative in prosperous times needs never want, and seldom does want, a dinner of what he calls "flesh meat." This he sometimes partakes of at home, sometimes at a neighbouring cook-shop; occasionally he has it brought to him at the mill. A favourite dish with the operatives is what they call potato pie—a savoury pasty made of meat and potatoes, well seasoned with pepper and salt, and roofed in with a substantial paste. Many of the men, after despatching their dinner, which they do comfortably in half-an-hour, spend the other moiety of their leisure in smoking or lounging about, until the never-failing bell proclaims that time is up, and that the engine and its attendant mechanism are ready to resume their labours. The work than proceeds until half-after five o'clock, at which hour all labour finally ceases; the periods of toil having been from six o'clock until half-past eight o'clock, from nine o'clock until one o'clock, and from two o'clock until half-past five o'clock, making an aggregate of ten hours. This arrangement, however, although very general, is by no means universal. Some of the mills do not open until seven o'clock and half-past seven o'clock, while a few prefer commencing at eight o'clock, after their people have breakfasted, and making but one stoppage during the day. There seems, however, to be a general, and I think a very well-founded, opinion, that this division of the ten hours is a bad one, inasmuch as it protracts the time of working until late in the evening, and casts the additional leisure, which it was the object of the Ten Hours Bill to secure to the workpeople, into the middle of the day, when they cannot well be expected to settle down to those domestic pursuits and means of self-improvement, which I am assured they are most eager to seize and avail themselves of, when they have a reasonable space to come and go upon between the closing of the mills and bedtime.

I stood to-day at the principal door of Messrs. Birley's establishment, watching the hands take their departure. It was curious to observe how each sex and age clung together. Boys kept with boys, men with men, and the girls went gossiping and laughing by in exclusive parties of their own. I chanced to overhear a proposition confidentially made by one of these young ladies as she passed me to a comrade. There was not much in it, to be sure; but the proposal, at all events, showed that the fatigues of the day had by no means the effect of preventing a personal brushing-up for the evening. "I say, Jane," said the damsel in question, "I tell you what—you come home and braid my hair, and then I'll braid yours." The out-door dress of the men is comfortable and respectable. Velveteen jackets and shooting coats seem to be in great favour, with waistcoats and trowsers of dark fustian cloth. The people are uniformly well shod, and their general appearance is that of unostentatious comfort.

Generally, then, I am bound to speak favourably of what I have as yet seen of the factory system. I have not been without discovering many blemishes existing in different departments, of all of which I shall speak in due time. In general terms, I may say that I could wish the mills to be built with greater attention to the circulation of air than even the best of them at present exhibit—I could wish the height of the rooms to be increased—I could wish a greater degree of cordiality and familiarity to subsist between employers and employed—I could wish to see the people pay more attention to personal cleanliness, since I believe that their looks and health would thereby be equally improved. And I could also wish—although I confess I do not see my way practically to the accomplishment of the aspiration—that matters might be so devised as to permit the mothers of young

children to be more at home than they are at present—an arrangement which would tend to diminish one of the most deep-founded
objections to the factory system, and which, happily for the infants
of the rising generation, would preclude the necessity for the administration of many a stupifying dose of Daffy's Elixir and Godfrey's
Cordial.

# LABOUR AND THE POOR.

---

## THE MANUFACTURING DISTRICTS.

[FROM OUR SPECIAL CORRESPONDENT.]

## MANCHESTER.

## LETTER III.

Manchester may be roughly divided into three great regions. The central of these—lying round the heart of the Exchange—is the grand district of warehouses and counting-rooms. There the fabrics spun, wove, printed, and dyed at the mills, are stored for inspection and purchase. There the actual business of buying and selling is carried on. There are banks, offices, agencies innumerable. The far outskirts of the city, again, form a sort of universally-stretching West-end. Thither fly all who can afford to live out of the smoke. There are open handsome squares, and showy ranges of crescents and rows, and miles of pleasant villas peeping out from their shrubberied grounds. Between these two regions—between the dull stacks of warehouses and the snug and airy dwellings of the suburbs—lies the great mass of smoky, dingy, sweltering, and toiling Manchester. It is from that mid region that the tall chimneys chiefly spring, and it is beneath these—stretching in a network of inglorious-looking, but by no means universally miserable streets, from mill to mill, and factory to factory—that we find the homes of the spinners and the weavers, whose calicoes are spread abroad over three-parts of the garment-wearing globe.

I have already mentioned the monotonous aspect of that large mass of the cotton capital wherein are lodged the great proportion of her working children. I have described the streets as being, with few exceptions, two-storied rows of unadorned town houses, so small that they ought, perhaps, to be rather called town cottages. Since then I have studied their economy outwardly and inwardly, and I think I am now in a position to give a fair account of the dwellings of the Manchester cotton-working population. It is not, however, easy to generalize upon the subject. The streets of some districts are very far superior to those of others, although the inhabitants of all belong very much to the same class, and the rents paid are tolerably uniform. The old districts are, as might be expected, invariably the worst. They contain the largest proportion of cellar dwellings, of close, filthy courts, of undrained lanes, and of rows of houses built back to back, without any provision for ventilation, and with very little for cleanliness. Still, a tolerably extensive inspection of the worst localities of Manchester has not revealed to me alleys so utterly squalid and miserable as many I could name in London; and certainly the filthiest court which I have penetrated is decency itself compared to the typhus-smelling wynds and closes into which I have adventured in Glasgow. In the older parts of the borough of Manchester itself, along the great thoroughfare called the Oldham-road, and in the Ancoats district—the latter entirely an operative colony—are situated some of the most squalid-looking streets, inhabited by swarms of the most squalid-looking people which I have seen. Outlying portions of the borough of Salford are also very miserable, full of streets unpaved, undrained, strewn with offal and refuse, and pierced with airless *cul-de-sacs,* rendered still more noisome by the quantities of ill-coloured clothes hung to dry from window to window. The township of Chorlton—a more modern one—is decidedly better; but of all which I have yet seen—I am of course referring strictly to the operative *quartiers*—the district of Hulme (pronounced Hoom) presents the most cheering spectacle, not only on account of its comparatively broad and airy streets, but from the progress which it evinces in the plan of construction of the houses. Hulme is a new district. A very few years ago, a great portion of the space now covered with humble but comfortable streets was open fields.

The house of the Manchester operative, wherever it be—in the old district or in the new—in Ancoats or Cheetham or Hulme—is uniformly a two-storey dwelling. Sometimes it is of fair dimensions, sometimes a line fourteen feet long would reach from the eaves to the ground. In the old localities there is, in all probability, a cellar beneath the house, sunk some four or five feet below the pavement, and occupied perhaps by a single poor old woman, or by a family, the heads of which are given to pretty regular alternation between their subterranean abode and the neighbouring wine-vaults. In the modern and improved *quartiers,* the cellar retires modestly out of sight, and is put to a more legitimate use as a home for coals or lumber. Nothing struck me more, while visiting and comparing notes in the different operative districts of Manchester, than the regularity with which the

Exterior of a Manchester Cellar

better style of house and the better style of furniture went together; it being always kept in mind that, so far as wages are concerned, the inhabitants of one locality are almost, if not quite, on a par with those of another. But the superior class room seemed, by a sort of natural sequence, to attract the superior class furniture. A very fair proportion of what was deal in Ancoats was mahogany in Hulme. Yet the people of Hulme get no higher wages than the people of Ancoats. The secret is that they live in better built houses, and consequently take more pleasure and pride in their dwellings.

The worst class of houses, not being cellars, commonly inhabited by the "mill-hands," consist each of two rooms, not a "but-and-a-ben," but an above and a below, the stair to the former leading directly up from the latter, and the door of the ground-floor parlour being also the door of the street. In some cases the higher story is divided into two small bedrooms, but in the superior class of houses there are generally two small, but comfortable, rooms on the ground-

Interior of a Manchester Cellar

floor, and two of corresponding size above. The street-door in these
tenements opens into a narrow passage, from which the stairs to the
bedrooms also ascend. The window of the ground-floor room, opening to the street, is always furnished with a pair of substantial outside
shutters, and the threshold is elevated from the pavement, so as to
admit of very emphatic stone door-steps with flourishing scrapers,
both of which, by the way, are generally to be found in a very com-
mendable state of purity. A local act of Parliament, obtained a few
years ago, and providing that every house built after its enactment
in Manchester should be constructed so as to possess a back door
opening into a small back yard, has been of immense advantage to
the newer portions of the town. The unhealthy practice of building
houses back to back was thus at once put down. A free current of
air was permitted to circulate in the rear as well as in front of the
tenements, and ample space was obtained for the necessary cesspools,
ash-pits, &c., &c., while convenient approaches for the cleansing of

such receptacles from the back were everywhere formed. Take, for example, a part of Hulme, which I inspected the other day in company with Mr. Taylor, the exceedingly intelligent manager of Mr. Birley's mills. Between every street were two rows of the best class of operatives' houses, each with four rooms and a cellar a-piece; and between each of the rows, running the whole length, was a paved courtway, with a gutter in the centre, formed by the back walls of the yards of the tenements on either side; the walls in question being pierced with apertures, through which all sorts of domestic refuse could be easily got at and conveyed away with as little annoyance to the inhabitants as may be. Certainly the plan was a vast improvement upon the old style of building. Still more might have been done. Most of the streets were provided with regular drains and gratings. In the case of new streets, I believe, the corporation insists upon these necessary appendages being completed within two years after the completion of the street (it would be as well, one would think, to make the whole business simultaneous); but the drains in question, as I am informed, only carry away the surface water and slops flung into the gutter in the central back passage, all sorts of foul refuse having to be removed by manual labour. The construction of water-closets is yet a desideratum, even in the best class of the operatives' houses; while in the old districts the accommodation in this respect is deficient in the extreme, and that which exists filthy in the extreme. This is a matter which, in discussing seriously and earnestly the social condition of the people, it would be weak and foolish to shirk. There will be little female virtue where, in the very nature of things, there can be little delicacy or decent reserve. In town and in the country, in low lodging-houses and in squalid clusters of agricultural cottages, the evil is the same. The sexes, at all times and at all hours, are huddled together, simply from want of room and accommodation to bestow them separately, and thus follow the inevitable results of brutalized men and hardened and shameless women—of childhood precociously knowing in everything which children ought not to know, and by consequence precociously licentious and precociously criminal.

I visited several of the better class houses in Hulme, and shall sketch, in a few lines, the parlour of the first which I entered, and which may be taken as a fair specimen of the others. The room was about ten feet by eight, and hung with a paper of cheap quality and ordinary pattern. In at least two of the corners were cupboards of hard wood, painted mahogany fashion, and containing plates, tea cups, saucers, &c. Upon the chimney-piece was ranged a set of old-fashioned glass and china ornaments. There was one framed print hanging from the wall—a steel engraving of small size, reduced from the well-known plate of the "Covenanter's Marriage." Beside this symbol of art was a token of allegiance to science, in the shape of one of the old-fashioned tube barometers, not apparently in the most perfect state of order. There were two tables in the apartment—a round centre one of ordinary material, and a rather handsome mahogany Pembroke. Opposite the fire-place was one of those nondescript pieces of furniture which play a double part in domestic economy—"a bed by night, a wardrobe all the day." The chairs were of the comfortable old-fashioned Windsor breed; and on the window-ledge were two or three flower-pots, feebly nourishing as many musty geraniums. The floor was carpetless—a feature, by the way, anything but characteristic. In the passage, however, was laid down a piece of faded and battered oil-cloth. The general aspect of the place, although by no means a miracle of neatness, was tolerably clean and comfortable. The landlady, a buxom dame of fifty, or thereabouts, does not work in the mill herself, but her sons and daughters, two of the latter married, all do. She was perfectly ready to submit her dwelling to our scrutiny, and expressed a strong hope, in anything which might be said of her or her family, that special mention might be made that "they were all for the Ten Hours Bill in that house."

In the majority of the streets inhabited by operatives the front room on the ground floor is used both as parlour and kitchen. Sometimes a second room, of small dimensions, opens back from it, and when such an apartment exists, it is generally seen littered with the coarser cooking and washing utensils. I have described the principal "public" room in a house of the first class in Hulme; let me sketch the generic features of the tenements in the older, worse built, and in all respects inferior quarter of Ancoats. Fancy, then, a wide-lying labyrinth of small dingy streets, narrow, unsunned courts terminating in gloomy *cul-de-sacs*, and adorned with a central sloppy gutter. Every score or so of yards you catch sight of one of the second and third class mills, with its cinder-paved courtyard and its steaming engine-house. Shabby-looking chapels, here and there, rise with infinitesimal Gothic arches and ornaments, amid the grimy nakedness of the factories. Now a railroad, upon its understructure of arches, passes over the roofs; anon, you cross a canal, with wharfs and coal-yards, and clusters of unmoving barges. In most cases the doors of the houses stand hospitably open, and young children cluster over the thresholds and swarm out upon the pavement: you have thus an easy opportunity of noting the interiors as you pass along. They are, as you will perceive, a series of little rooms, about ten feet by eight, more or less, generally floored with brick or flagstones—materials which are, however, occasionally half concealed by strips of mats or faded carpeting. A substantial deal table stands in the centre of each apartment, and a few chairs, stools, and settles to match are ranged around. Occasionally, a little table of mahogany is not wanting. Now and then you observe a curiously small sofa, hardly intended for a full-grown man or woman to stretch their limbs upon; and about as often one side of the fireplace is taken up with a cradle. Sometimes there is a large cupboard, the open door of which reveals a shining assortment of plates and dishes—sometimes the humble dinner service is ranged on shelves which stretch along the walls; while beneath them are suspended upon hooks a more or less elaborate series of skillets, stewpans, and miscellaneous cooking and household matters. A conspicuous object is very frequently a glaringly-painted and highly-glazed tea tray, upon which the firelight glints cheerily, and which, by its superior lustre and artistic boldness of design, commonly throws into shade the couple or so of tiny prints, in narrow black frames, which are suspended above it. A favourite and no doubt useful article of furniture is a clock. No Manchester operative will be without one a moment longer than he can help. You see here and there, in the better class of houses, one of the old-fashioned metallic-faced eight-day clocks; but by far the most common article is the little Dutch machine, with its busy pendulum swinging openly and candidly before all the world. Add to this catalogue of the more important items of *meublement* an assortment of the usual odds and ends of household matters, deposited in corners or window ledges or shelves—here a box, there a meal or flour barrel—now and then a small mirror gleaming from the wall—now and then a row of smoke-browned little china and stone-ware ornaments on the narrow chimney-piece—in general a muslin window-screen, or perhaps dingy cotton curtains, and not unfrequently a pot or two of geraniums or fuchsias rubbing their dry twigs and brown stunted leaves against the dim and small-paned lattice. Picture all these little household appliances, and others of a similar order, giving the small room a tolerably crowded appearance, and you will have a fair notion of the vast majority of the homes of the factory operatives, such as they appear in the older and less improved localities of Manchester. The cellars are, as might be expected, seldom furnished so well. They appear to possess none of the minor comforts, none of the little articles of ornament or fancy furniture which more or less you observe in the parlours. The floors seem damp and unwholesome, you catch a glimpse of a ricketty-looking bed in a dark airless corner, and the fire upon the hearth is often cheerlessly small, smouldering amongst the unswept ashes.

Decidedly the worst feature of the house tenements is the (in some districts) invariable opening of the street-door into the parlour. One step takes you from the pavement to the shrine of the Penates. The occupant cannot open his door, or stand upon his threshold, without revealing the privacy of his room to all by-passers. This awkward mode of construction is objectionable in other respects, as tending, for example, to be a fruitful source of rheumatic and catarrh-bestowing draughts. But, as I have stated, the new houses are almost invariably furnished with a decent lobby, a characteristic which of itself places them fifty per cent. above those built after the old fashion.

Saturday is generally the great weekly epoch of cleansing and setting things to rights in the homes of the Manchester workpeople. The last day of the week may, indeed, be generally set down as a half holiday amongst all the industrial population, exclusive of artizans and tradespeople. At the ordinary dinner hour, there is a vast stir amongst the denizens of counting-houses and warehouses, many of whom have country establishments to visit upon the Saturday, and one o'clock sees a simultaneous starting of scores of heavily-laden omnibuses bound for every suburb and village of and round Manchester. The mills knock off work at about two or half after two o'clock, and if you visit the class of streets which I have been attempting to describe an hour or so thereafter, you will marvel and rejoice at the universality of the purification which is going forward. Children are staggering under pails and buckets of water, brought from the pump or the cock which probably supplies a small street. Glance in at the open portals, and you will witness a grand simultaneous system of scouring. The women, of course, are the principal operators—they are cleaning their windows, hearthstoning their lintels, scrubbing their furniture with might and main. The *pater familias*, however, does not always shirk his portion of the toil. Only last Saturday I came upon two or three lords of the creation usefully employed in blackleading their stoves.

Every evening after mill hours these streets, deserted as they are, except at meal times, during the day, present a scene of very considerable quiet enjoyment. The people all appear to be on the best terms with each other, and laugh and gossip from window to window, and door to door. The women, in particular, are fond of sitting in groups upon their thresholds sewing and knitting; the children sprawl about beside them, and there is the amount of sweethearting going forward which is naturally to be looked for under such circumstances. Certainly the setting of the picture is ugly and grim enough. A black, mean-looking street, with a black unadorned mill rising over the houses, and a black chimney pouring out volumes of black smoke upon all—these do not form very picturesque accessories to the scene, but still you are glad to see that, amid all the grime and dinginess of the place, there is no lack of homely comforts, good health, and good spirits.

The rents paid by operatives in Manchester vary from 3s. to 4s. 6d., and in some cases 5s. per week. This is for an entire house. Cellar dwellings fetch—I give the statement upon the authority of Mr. P. H. Holland, surgeon, whose report upon the sanitary condition of Chorlton was published in 1844—from 1s. to 2s. weekly, according to size. There is, however, I am happy to understand, upon all sides, a growing disinclination to those unwholesome abodes; but as their rent is low, a period of stagnation in trade often forces the people to occupy them. In 1844 Mr. Holland calculates that in Chorlton one cellar in every six was empty. The number of cellars, as compared with that of houses, was then one in twenty-eight. Mr. Holland adds, "they (the cellars) are much disliked, and justly so. They are always badly lighted and ventilated, and generally badly drained." In Chorlton Mr. Holland calculates that about one-third of the working population live in houses constructed back to back, and consequently without any thorough ventilation. About one-eighth live in "closed courts, or streets which are little better than courts." Now Chorlton being neither a very new nor a very old district, may be taken as giving not a bad idea of the general style of the working homes of Manchester. The proportion of people living in unventilated, undrained, and unwholesome buildings, in the districts traversed by the St. George's-road, the Oldham-road, and Great Ancoat's-street, must be much more considerable, while in such districts as Hulme the case is reversed.

Manchester, like most great manufacturing and commercial cities, is scantily supplied with water, and that which is to be procured is not by any means universally transparent or tasteless. The streams which traverse the town are incarnations of watery filth. A more forbidding-looking flood than the Medlock, as it may be seen where it flows beneath the Oxford-road, it would be difficult to conceive. The black fœtid water often glistens with the oily impurities which float upon its surface, and the wreathes and patches of green froth which tesselate it prove the effervescence produced by impure gases. For any household purpose whatever, the water of this uncovered sewer is quite out of the question; and the contents of the larger stream of the Irwell are not much better. Manchester, therefore, obtains its water partially by means of pipes, partially by means of wells and pumps. The last satis-factory statistics which have been published upon the subject are those contained in the "Manchester Police Returns," compiled by Captain Willis, the head of the constabulary force, for 1847. By these returns it appears that the number of "Streets, squares, alleys, &c., within the borough of Manchester," was, at the date in question, 2,955. The number of dwelling-houses was 46,922. Of these there were "supplied with pipe water in the interior, including shops," 11,190; while not less than 12,776 "houses, &c.," derived their water from a common cock or tap in the street. The number of houses which reaped no advantage, either from pipes conducted into their interiors, or from taps in the streets, was nearly as great as the amount of dwellings provided for in either of these ways, being 22,956. The number of dwelling cellars in the borough was 5,070. Of these only 1,108 were provided with pipe water. Upwards of 1,968 had the advantage of a common tap, and 1,994 were entirely dependent upon other means of supply. The wa-ter sold by the Waterworks Company is derived from a tunnel called Gorton's Brook, which is principally land drainage. So intensely im-pure is the atmosphere over Manchester, that the rain water is unfit even for washing until it has stood for some time to purify and set-tle. Many of the poor who have no cisterns to allow the water to rest in, and, probably, no room for them even if they had, carry the fluid to be used for washing and scouring from the canals, and are frequently so economic in their use of it that they keep a bucket-full until it stinks. Mr. Holland has "frequently detected the practice by the abominable smell produced in a patient's sick room." Generally the landlord of a set of houses sinks one or more wells, covering them of course with pumps, for the use of his tenants. The right to draw water from these sources is purchased by the neighbours at the rate of from 6d. to 1s. per quarter. Sometimes they come as far as a quar-

ter of a mile to a favourite pump, or have the water carried home
to them, paying for its conveyance a penny for every three gallons.
Where stand pipes or public taps are erected, the charge by the water
company is about 10s. a year for every house, the inmates of which
use the convenience. Of the petty thefts which occur in Manchester,
however, none—although they do not appear in the police returns—
are so common, as larcenies from taps and pumps. Many people, too,
who do not choose to steal their water, obtain it nearly as cheaply by
begging for it. The "pressure" is kept on by the Waterworks Company
for a few hours each day, Sunday excepted; and, consequently, cisterns
and tanks are necessary when the quantity of water required for the
day's consumption is at all large. In the course of a year or two, however, it is probable that Manchester will be bountifully and cheaply
supplied with water. The works now in the course of construction
to conduct a fresh stream of the pure fluid from Glossop will, when
completed, vie with many of the most superb aqueducts of antiquity.
I may add here, that the pumps attached to factories are frequently
made use of by the workpeople. Messrs. Harney and Tysoe have sunk
a well, for the use of which one penny per week is charged, the small
sums thus collected going to the mill library fund, for the purchase of
books. Another gentleman, Mr. Ashton, a very extensive millowner
at Hyde, one of the suburbs of Manchester, has, at his own expense,
introduced water into no less than 320 labourers' houses belonging to
him, at the total cost of about £1 per tenement. The rent he charges
for this convenience is the moderate sum of one shilling per annum—
a weekly sum of three-pence being charged for the water itself. Since
the introduction of this system, Mr. Ashton informed the Health of
Towns Commissioners that the houses, and especially the back-yards,
were very much cleaner, and that the change was very observable in
the persons of the people themselves. Mr. Ashton is for a compulsory
supply of water, to be introduced to every tenement, however humble. The system of taps or public pumps he describes as being fraught
with all sorts of danger to morals.

Upon the whole, then, I am rather inclined to look hopefully upon
the condition of the dwellings of the operatives of Manchester. At
all events, there is an evident disposition to improvement. The corporation are rigid in enforcing the observance of the Local Building
Act; and as Manchester is still rapidly increasing, the proportion of
better-class dwellings is becoming every day greater. I believe, too,
that a very powerful stimulus has been given to increased neatness at

home by the additional evening leisure time which the Ten Hours Bill has insured to the women. "I have time now to clean my house, and I do it, too, every evening," is the phrase I have heard repeated an hundred times by the tenter and female weavers. "Before, I was so tired that I could do nothing but just eat my supper and go to bed," they generally added. I fear, indeed, that anything like a thorough reform of that great portion of operative Manchester—built upon a bad plan, or rather upon no plan at all, save, perhaps, that promising a yearly return of the greatest number of shillings in the pound—is at present out of the question. It is not, however, I know, beyond the powers of the people, if they be sober and industrious, to keep almost clear of the cellar dwellings. Building societies are a very common means of investing the savings of wages, and I believe that the people are beginning to see that the better the dwellings are, the cheaper in proportion can they be rented. For an additional third of what a cellar costs, a decent house, with several rooms and respectable conveniences, can be procured. The millowners in Manchester have paid, until recently, little or no attention to the state of the dwellings of their workpeople. They have maintained that if the labouring rooms in the factory were tolerably sweet and wholesome, that was all which they had to do with the matter; that the homes of their workmen and workwomen were the exclusive concern of the dwellers in them—a doctrine which, if not perfectly correct, was, at all events, exceedingly convenient. But the question comes to be, whether, in such a system as the factory one—a system in which an employer can exercise almost as great a degree of moral influence over great masses of the employed as the captain of a man-of-war can do over his crew at sea—whether, in such circumstances, the employer is not—morally at least, if not politico-economically—bound to attempt by his intelligence and enlightenment as much as possible to guide and direct the efforts and the energies of the new social development which he has himself aided in calling into being, and which is rising with so strange and anomalous a rapidity around him. It is to be presumed, that all sorts of property confer their duties—mills, and steam-engines, and warehouses, and printed calico, as well as fields and woods; and if a landowner is not held to perform his duty unless he pays some attention to the social and sanitary state of the labourer upon his ground, so I cannot see that the manufacturer is to be excused from a similar obligation. That ideas of this class are now making way, both in field and city, I am happy to believe. Unhappily, the bulk of Manchester arose during a period in which they had no existence—during which master and man more commonly regarded each other as mutual enemies rather than as mutual dependants, whose best interest it was to be mutual friends. A vast population suddenly sprung up round the mills. This population had to be housed, and they fell into the hands of unchecked speculators, who ran up mobs of filthy and inconvenient streets and courts, utterly unheeding, or perhaps profoundly ignorant of, the sanitary and social guilt of their doings. In the cases of the country mills, I am told that the case is very different. There the cottages of the labourers are in many, if not in most, instances the property of the millowner, and the isolated and disciplined character of the population render it exceedingly easy to exercise a wholesome social influence over them. I promise myself pleasure from a visit to one of these communities.

In Manchester, however, the constant flux and reflux of poor population, seeking successfully or unsuccessfully for work, and provided with wretched and demoralizing accommodation, renders the city hardly a fair test of the social condition created by the factory system. The late Dr. Cooke Taylor, the Rev. Mr. Parkinson, and other writers upon the manufacturing system, whose views lean strongly in its favour, urge this consideration forcibly and frequently. Country mills they hold only to afford a fair test of the social and moral effects of manufacturing labour. But they seem to be right only in part. It must never be forgotten that the tendency towards centralization—towards forming great popular nuclei—must always exist in more or less force in manufacturing districts. Local circumstances favouring the production of any species of material, will always be sufficient to draw together towns. How, indeed, else have Manchester, Leeds, and all the great cities of textile industry sprung up into such vast and sudden greatness? Admitting, then, that the tendency of manufactures is to accumulate population upon given points, I believe that the moral duty of master manufacturers is to see that that population be, in essential things, properly cared for. At all events, whether it be their duty or not, it is very clearly their interest; and so much is this understood, that I believe—could a new Manchester be built next year, we should see a widely different city from the old—one which, built for the accommodation of a population receiving in ordinary times good wages, would furnish them, at cheap rates, with clean, wholesome, well aired, ventilated, and drained dwellings. At present, I see from the last police returns that the number of low lodging-houses in Manchester, where the "sexes sleep indiscriminately together in one room," is no less than 169. The number in the year before was still greater. The number of houses for the reception of stolen property known to the police was, by the last returns, 131—showing, I am sorry to say, an increase upon the number of any former year back to 1843. The thieves in Manchester, however, as I am informed by Captain Willis, the exceedingly intelligent and courteous chief-constable of the borough, are principally a class who make their living regularly by dishonest means, and who are in no ways connected with or produced by the manufacturing system, further, of course, than that they naturally resort to places where great accumulation of labour produces great accumulation of property. This branch of the subject, however, in another letter. What I am at present urging is, the necessity and the policy of an increased degree of communication and interchange of mutual good offices between the millowners and their people.

"I have worked, sir," said an intelligent "card-room hand" to me— "I have worked in that mill, sir, these nineteen years, and the master never spoke to me once. I think if he did I would be gratified like, and go on working with better heart." "The masters," said another man, from another mill, "are afraid that if they speak to us they will be losing their authority; and so they say the overlookers and the managers must see to everything; but we would often like to speak to the masters themselves. We could often tell them a many things."

I said before, however, and I repeat now, that matters in this respect are decidedly upon the mending tack. The tone of masters and men in their business relationship is, I am assured on all hands, incredibly improved. Unions, trade combinations, and strikes have gone greatly out of fashion. The men shake their heads doubtfully if you bring up the subject, and refer—many of them did, at least, in my communications with them—to a long list of defaulting secretaries and treasurers who had levanted with the funds of too many of the combinations. Besides, a system of amicable conference upon the subject of wages is springing up. Some time ago, a deputation of four of the female weavers in a very large mill, the name of which I am not at liberty at this moment to give, waited upon the partners, and presented the following memorial, very neatly lithographed:—

"Respected Sirs—We, the workpeople in your employ, approach you with great respect, and beg most respectfully to solicit an advance of wages of ten per cent. During the recent depression of trade, we patiently submitted to the reductions then made—reductions which we could ill afford to endure; and now that trade has revived, we trust you will restore to us the full amount of the reductions to which we were then subjected. In making this application we are not unmindful of the fact, that the interests of masters and men are so interwoven that one cannot suffer without the other. Notwithstanding our opinion upon this point, we believe the time has come when we are justified in making this application, and hope to find to it a ready response."

A long argument was the result. The Price Current in that day's *Manchester Guardian* was appealed to, and calculations gone into to show the impossibility of raising the rate of wages without paying the increase out of capital. The result was, that the deputation professed itself satisfied, and withdrew, acknowledging that the partners were in the right.

"Four years ago," said the manager of the mill in question, "it would have been a turn-out and a strike." But under the most favourable circumstances, it is difficult to look upon the factory system without discovering some flaw; and I am strongly inclined to believe that the worst feature of the system is, not the moderate employment of children, not the moderate employment of young women, but the employment in the mills of women with young families. Dinners may be cooked and homes made tidy by hired labour, but no attendant, such as they can procure, can compensate for the absence of nursing mothers. Some women remain out of the mill for several months after an accouchement—others go back as soon as they have gathered strength; but nearly all are compelled to leave young children under the charge, perhaps, of a little brat of a girl, who is paid 1s. or 9d. a week for doing the baby with "Godfrey," and keeping the other children from the fire on one hand, and from beneath the wheels of vehicles on the other.

"There are a many more accidents happen through the mothers being away from home, than happens through the children being in the mills," was the sensible observation of the "card-room hand" whom I have mentioned. The imperfect nature of the superintendence exercised by the "little girls" in an accommodating neighbourhood may be inferred from the extraordinary number of "lost children" who every day get astray in Manchester. In 1847 the police restored not less than 2,064 of those missing little responsibilities to their disconsolate parents, while the number recovered by means of a hue and cry raised by the parents themselves was 2,284, making a total of 4,348 children, or about 18 a-day, wandering away from their homes, through the carelessness of those entrusted with the charge of them.

Into the subject of the early marriages and the early breaking up of families, occasioned by the youthful age at which a sufficiency of wages can be earned, I have not left myself room in this letter to enter. Both subjects will be considered under future heads of the inquiry; but I may add, that, from the information which I have received, I do not think it is at all usual for the girls to leave their parents' houses until they are married, except in the cases where fathers or mothers in law do not prove kind. But whatever may be the extent or the evil tendency of the system, there can be little doubt that the latter is likely to be modified, and is, indeed, in the process of modification, by the excellent influence of the shortened hours of work upon the people. I have personally conversed with at least two dozen young men and women who have learned to read and write since the passing of the Ten Hours Bill. Night schools for adults are now common; most of these have libraries attached to them. The men and boys learn reading, writing, and cyphering; and the women and girls, in addition to these branches of education, are taught plain, and are in many instances teaching themselves fancy needlework.

I have seen, no later than yesterday, and in its proper place I shall have occasion more minutely to advert to it, a most gratifying exhibition, illustrative of the good use to which the young women put their evening time. Upon a hint that samples of the industry of over-hours would be acceptable, I was invited the next day to inspect a counter in a mill near the Oxford-road, which was actually heaped up with specimens of crochet work, knitting, netting, sampler sewing, and a whole series of copy-books.

Their fair owners were perfectly unanimous in informing me that the crop I saw before me was the harvest of the Ten Hours Bill.

Manchester is known as being of late years a decidedly musical place. Since the passing of the Ten Hours Bill a great Monday night concert for the operative classes has been in successful operation. I visited it the other night. The musical attractions to be sure were rather mild—a small organ, a piano, an amateur chorus of some thirty voices, assisted by a few professors of only local celebrity. But the programme comprised selections from Handel, Meyerbeer, Rossini, and Bishop; and if these were at the best only respectably performed, they were listened to with the most reverent silence, and then applauded to the echo by an assemblage of between two and three thousand working men and women, who had respectively paid their threepence for admission, and who took up nearly the entire area of the Free-trade Hall.

The first encore was won by Handel's beautiful melody, "Oh, had I Jubal's Lyre;" and to prove how catholic were the sympathies of the audience, they broke out into raptures when the vocalist, upon being recalled, substituted for the Handelian melody "Jeannette and Jeannot." If the concert were not a musical phenomenon, it was at all events a moral one.

# LABOUR AND THE POOR.

—◆—

## THE MANUFACTURING DISTRICTS.

[FROM OUR SPECIAL CORRESPONDENT.]

### BOLTON.

## LETTER IV.

I proceed with my notices of the effects of the factory system upon the social condition of the labourers employed by it. I have already described the toil of the mills and the general characteristics of the dwellings in the several districts of Manchester inhabited by the cotton workers; and I have dwelt upon these subjects at greater length, inasmuch as I felt that they involve the very foundations upon which all speculation relative to the social state and social prospects of the factory operative must necessarily rest. For, if the toil in the mill be inevitably unwholesome and oppressive—if the inevitable effect of the mills be to rear cities, the dwellings of which must be constantly overcrowded and unhealthy—then undoubtedly the social state of the cotton operative must everlastingly remain low and unhappy. I believe, however, and every day confirms me in the belief, first, that the labour of the mills may be carried on so as to be neither unwholesome nor oppressive, nor, in too great a degree, anti-domestic; and, secondly, that a population of mill-labourers may be so lodged, and ought to be so lodged, that the sanitary conditions of their homes will be at least equal to the sanitary condition of their working places. In elucidating these points I have sought to describe what the mills actually are—what the houses of the mill population actually are—and I have begun to consider the bearing of the toil in question, and of the homes in question, upon the general social state of the people. Let us pursue the subject.

There exists no means of ascertaining with statistical exactitude the average period in the lives of parents and children, throughout the cotton districts, when home is broken up, and the members of the family dispersed. The results of the inquiries I have instituted in different quarters are contradictory and unsatisfactory. There are—if

I may use the phrase—a great number of shades of family disruption. Sometimes the scattered members of a household remain in constant communication with each other. Sometimes only occasions of sickness or death bring them together. Sometimes they sicken and die without any mutual knowledge, and without much mutual regard, each isolated member of the family having become part and parcel of a new circle of social relationship. In fact, it would appear as if, in the manufacturing districts, everything moved quicker than in other parts of the world. The child toils sooner, attains physical development sooner, marries sooner, has children in his turn sooner, and, in the present sanitary state of matters, dies sooner. But over and above this natural precocity—this crowding together, as it were, of the ordinary epochs of life—it may be observed that an existence of constant labour, and not unfrequent privation, has an universal tendency to diminish the time during which the family tie subsists in all its cohesive powers. The members of a family living in comfortable ease, continue bound together far longer than those of a family struggling to live. This rule is as natural as it is universal. In the latter case each child, as it grows up, must necessarily labour for itself. The family income is not earned by a common head, nor does it flow from a common source. The circle becomes a sort of joint-stock company, and as that great and universally prevailing law of self-preservation comes gradually into play, the force of habit and of affection weakens, while that of individual interest strengthens, and as surely as the different personages of the company begin to perceive that they are contributing, either in money or in comfort of situation, more to the family than the family contributes to them, so surely do they withdraw from the association to labour in isolation, or to form new and more profitable social combinations for themselves.

The operation of this law is very strongly marked in the cotton district. But its existence is universal, and that which the factory system does is simply this: By the early period at which it enables children to earn enough to live upon, and by that precocity which it developes, the factory system brings a universal and natural law into early force, and at the same time concentrates population, so that the operation of that law, and indeed of all other social laws, is shown so distinctly that people are very apt to mistake the clearness of medium through which the working of the law is observed for a special exaggeration of the powers of the law itself.

The age at which the administrators of the new poor-law calculate that they have to provide for individuals, as items in the population, and not considered as members of a family, is, in the manufacturing districts, sixteen. I am assured, on the very highest authority, that nothing in Manchester is more uncommon than a child after the age of sixteen systematically contributing to the support of his or her parents, or parents doing anything for the support of a child above that age. The family tie may, therefore, be considered—allowing three children to each family—as broken up about twenty years after the marriage from which the children spring. "Nothing," says my informant, a gentleman of high official standing, "nothing can be more warm and keen than the affections of parents throughout the cotton districts for children, so long as they continue children, and nothing more remarkable than the lukewarm carelessness of feeling which subsists between these parents and their children after the latter are grown up and doing for themselves." In this respect the instinct observable in the lower animals is strongly developed in the classes of which I speak. Affection lasts in its strongest degree only so long as helplessness subsists. It is as in the case of the birds—the young one, when fully feathered, flies away, and parents and nest are forgotten together. If, in the manufacturing districts, the flight takes place unduly early, it is because the plumage appears unduly early also. The process itself is universal in all classes and all countries. And let me here remark, that no mistake can be greater than any supposition that these early household disruptions are—amongst the manufacturing operatives—made matters of sentimental grief. I have the best authority for stating that nothing of the kind occurs. Parents and children look upon early separation as the natural course of events. The father and mother have left their own homes soon—their children, they know, will follow their example, and they are neither disappointed nor surprised when the event takes place. Occasionally the catastrophe is precipitated, especially in the case of girls, by a second marriage of either of the parents. It is, I believe, rare to find children living with a stepmother or stepfather. As a general rule, it may be safely asserted that comparatively few family disruptions take place which do not lead to early marriages, or which are not occasioned by the system of early marriages. The one tendency, in fact, is closely and inevitably connected with the other; so much so, indeed, that they may be described as different phases in the operation of the same great system.

We may then take it for granted that the factory system tends to a speedier recurring break-up, and a speedier recurring formation of families, than is to be observed in the lower classes of society in general. We may also safely add, that the tendency of continuous and struggling labour is always to that speedy disruption and speedy reforming of social relationships; but that the factory system facilitates the working of the tendency by supplying the necessarily early wages. The evils of this state of matters, and the advantages of it, are easily pointed out. The early cooling of domestic affections, even when these are replaced, as they are in the case of the children, by new connections, must be allowed to be one of the evils of a state of society the members of which are engaged in a continued struggle to live. Burns felt the force of the hard but inevitable law when he wrote his "Poortith Cauld." From the operation of that law spring the evils of a population increasing with more than politic rapidity, and pressing with more than advantageous force upon the means of subsistence and the demand for labour. Another evil, of a more purely physical nature, is a terrible and a progressively serious one. The children of parents not come to the full vigour and development of their strength, must be a weakly and a stunted race, and they in their turn will produce weakly and stunted successors. To this cause rather than to the unwholesome nature of the labour of factories must be referred the unrobust appearance of a factory population. It is not what takes place in the mills, but what takes place out of the mills, which gives the factory worker the blanched face and weakly—or if not weakly, at least not vigorous— looking frame which he generally exhibits. He is too often the child of children, and, delicate and feeble at his birth, he has been too often neglected, and drugged with those deleterious compounds which hush the cries of the infant, while the mother pursues her occupation by the drawing frame or the loom.

The advantages, on the other hand, of the early marriage system, as it subsists in the factory districts, is its natural tendency to check that amount of indiscriminate sexual intercourse which otherwise would assuredly have the effect, not merely of demoralizing vast and populous districts, but of absolutely crushing morality altogether. The factory system accumulates great masses of population—it has a peculiar forcing effect upon the physical energies of youth—it causes the sexes to labour together, and brings them into hourly communication. Amid a population, generally ignorant, generally untrained to habits of self-denial, and upon whom the bonds of abstract morality cannot be expected to lie very heavily, what must, in the natural course of things, be the effect of such a combination of circumstances? Were it not for the early marriage system, and the consequent easy disruption of family ties, the practical result would be a state of society from the contemplation of which all right-minded persons would shrink.

Thus, then, we see one evil checking and abating another. The question comes to be, can anything be done which shall be potent to remodel the social condition from which both evils spring? Of this I have little hope. All states of society must have their drawbacks. Here we find, in the centre of our empire, a vast and a rapidly increasing population, massed together in great towns, and earning, on the whole, high wages. While man is man, and passions are passions, these causes will produce the effects of early marriage—early household disruption. To put down the causes of the evils, would be simply to destroy the population which the evils afflict. The source whence the grievance comes is the source whence the people and their means of subsistence come. The things must to a certain and a great extent co-exist. But if the evil cannot be destroyed, it does not follow that in its worst phases it cannot be abated. What is wanted seems to be an increase in the attractions of home, and an improvement in the intellectual and educational condition of the people. While there is little comfort by the hearth of parents, children will naturally be the less loath to quit that hearth. While the name of home is associated only with stifling and overcrowded dwellings—while the necessities of the condition of daily life are such as to brush away that bloom of feminine delicacy and reserve, the existence of which naturally tends to counterbalance the promptings of gradually developing passion, and while an untrained and ignorant population continue—as all untrained and ignorant populations will continue—to obey the promptings of animal nature and of obvious convenience, rather than considerations of good, more distant and less distinctively observed, so long, I repeat, as this is the state of matters—so long will the evil of which we speak exist in perfectly undiminished force.

The remedies thus indicated are undoubtedly very inefficient to the absolute rooting out of the social disease. But a perfect state of society is what no one ever saw, and no one ever will. We have vast populations crowded into small industrial spaces; from their labours a stream of comfort is perpetually flowing forth over the whole world of consumers. But these labours are conducted under the necessary conditions of an artificial social system, which has its deep shadows as well as its bright lights. It will, however, I apprehend, be readily and generally admitted that the creation of additional home comforts, and the institution of an intellectual standard, high enough to eliminate and foster the moral qualities, while it checks mere animal instincts, would have a not inconsiderable effect in strengthening and vivifying the family tie, and preserving for a longer period than they now exist the filial affections, untouched by that other species of love, which sooner or later must, to a certain extent, take their place, but which it is for the interests of society should not be too soon developed.

The evils of which I speak are partially the produce of the factory system, but they are invariably exaggerated by the factory system working in large towns. There is a degree of what we may call pure factory vice—and there is also a degree of what we may call pure great-town vice. I admit that the tendency of the factory system is to create great towns, but I deny that it is its inevitable result. I deny, therefore, that all the evils of great factory towns are to be charged upon the factory system, and the assertion brings me to that branch of my subject in which I promised to touch upon the features and condition of the rural factory population.

A "rural factory!" To how many will the phrase seem a contradiction in terms! In the minds of how many are even the best features of the cotton-mill associated with the worst features of a squalid town. And yet, thickly sprinkled amid the oak-coppiced vales of Lancashire, with the whitewashed cottages of the workpeople gleaming through the branches and beside the rapid stream, or perched high on the breezy forehead of the hill, are to be seen hundreds on hundreds of busily working cotton mills. In the vicinity of these there are no fetid alleys, no grimy courts, no dark area or underground cellars. Even the smoke from the tall chimneys passes tolerably innocuously away—sometimes, perhaps, when the air is calm and heavy, dotting the grass and the leaves with copious showers of "blacks," but never seriously smirching nor blighting the dewy freshness of the fields and hedge-rows, through which the spinner and the weaver pass to their daily toil.

I visited the other day the country factory of Egerton, belonging to the Messrs. Ashworth, and situated a few miles to the north of Bolton. The railway from Manchester to the latter town spans ten miles of open breezy country, dotted here and there with mills and calico works snugly nestled in the valleys—amid meadow and pasture land and pleasant hardwood coppices—the eye not failing here and there to catch the antique outline of a clumsily picturesque farmhouse, which has looked forth from amid its sheltering trees since the days when Bolton was a petty hamlet, and Manchester a handful of straggling streets. The former town is as bad a specimen of a nucleus of cotton manufacture as can be conceived. It is an old spinning and weaving station, and the great mass of the houses are built in the oldest and filthiest fashion. Cellars abound on every side, and I saw few or none unoccupied, while the people appeared to me to be fully as squalid and dirty in appearance as the worst classes are in the worst districts of Manchester. Bolton is inhabited by what in this part of the country is known as an "old" population—a population which in a great degree preserves hurtful old prejudices and filthy old fashions, which have little hold in the more modern seats of industry. In common with Stockport, the town of Bolton was awfully afflicted by the stagnations of business in 1842 and 1847. In the latter year, the unemployed population was supported at a weekly cost of from £400 to £500. And even at present, when trade is reasonably brisk, the weekly amount of poor-rates is nearly £230. The last poor-law returns, dated Somerset House, July 17, 1849, inform us that the number of inmates of the Bolton workhouse on the 1st of July, 1848, was 418; while no less than 7,371 individuals had, up to that date in that year, received out-door relief.

The road to Egerton is full of beauties. It winds along the valley of the Egret, a tributary of the Irwell, amid pleasant meadow land, green grassy ridges, and sheltered ravines and dells running wantonly amid the humbled hills. The oak seems an especial favourite of this hardy soil. Here and there are flourishing coppice-woods, green with the scolloped leaf of our national tree; and now and then you mark the grand branches and lichen-grown boll of a fine gnarled old fellow who has shed his leaves an hundred times. Every mile or so down in the valley beside the running stream lies a factory of some sort or other, often half-hidden by the sheltering trees; and further up the hill, upon the green slope, you mark the decent row of substantial stone-built cottages, where the "hands" live. Churches with neat spires, and the more unpretending tabernacles of dissent, plain, capacious buildings, with "Sion" or "Bethesda" deeply-carved over their simple lintels, bespeak the different shades of religious feeling of the district; while the handsome garden-circled mansions which you frequently pass remind you that the proprietors of the wealth-producing establishments around are rarely, if ever, absentees. Little or no corn is grown here-abouts. The ground is meadow land, for the pasture of horses and kine. Beneath the surface lie thick strata of coal, as the rude-looking mechanism, reared upon mounds of cinders and presided over each by a short smoking chimney, will not fail to testify. The river, you will observe, is frequently damned back into ponds or "lodges," in order that the power which it supplies may be as much as possible husbanded, the mills here working by force both of hot water and cold; and the entire picture which we have been trying to reproduce is set in a frame of dusky hills, many of them heather-covered and haunted by moor game.

The village of Egerton principally consists of a long street running along the highway. The Messrs. Ashworth's Mills lie beneath it, at the bottom of a rather deep and wooded valley, and thither we will descend.

Factories, as I have, perhaps, too often remarked, abound little in architectural graces, but the country mills appear to far more advantage than their town brethren, inasmuch as all of them are clean-looking, some brightly whitewashed, and others, in certain parts of the country, built of substantial grey stone. The mills at Egerton are of this last description. They are propelled by steam and water power, and a huge wheel for the latter purpose, sixty feet in diameter, is really one of the sights of Lancashire. The number of hours worked at this establishment is eleven a day, and the time of labour at present commences at six o'clock. The general arrangements of cotton mills are very similar, but I can confidently speak of the excellent arrangements of the Messrs. Ashworth's establishment. The large card-roving and drawing room on the basement story is fully eleven feet from floor to ceiling, and perfectly ventilated. The temperature was a few degrees higher than that of the atmosphere, but perfectly clear from the slightest degree of closeness or smell. The windows, too, are very large, and provided with full arrangements of swinging panes. The labour which was proceeding in this airy and well-arranged *atelier* was clearly of a nature which could have no prejudicial effect upon health; and the women looked very obviously better than those in the town mills. Their faces, in hardly a single instance, wore that thoroughly blanched hue which is an almost unvarying characteristic of the city cotton spinners; while many of the girls had very perceptible roses in their cheeks. Their working dresses were scrupulously neat, and upon the shoulder of each was embroidered the name of its proprietor.

Water Wheel, at Ashworth's Cotton Mill

The Messrs. Ashworth are in the constant and excellent habit of mingling familiarly and kindly with their workpeople, all of whom they are personally acquainted with. They do as much as they can to discourage the working of married women with young families in the mill—a practice which I confidently hope to be able to stigmatize as being, beyond cavil, infinitely the blackest plague spot on the whole of the manufacturing system. Not above four women of the class in question labour in the Messrs. Ashworth's Egerton mills. The average wages in the country mills are a trifle below those paid in towns, but rent and provisions being usually lower in the rural districts, there is little virtual difference. Seven-eighths of Messrs. Ashworth's people live in cottages built upon their employers' land, but this is left to their free option. The rent of these cottages varies from 1s. 6d. to 3s. 6d. weekly. For the latter rent a labourer can possess a substantially-built stone cottage, containing a good parlour and kitchen, two or three bed-rooms, a cellar, and a small garden. The latter advantage is not, however, much in request among the Egerton workpeople. The amount of rent quoted is the sum total payable for the occupation of the house. It is generally deducted from the wages; but the tenancy being, as I have said, purely optional, there is no objectionable approach to the truck system in the transaction. I wish, however, I could say that this practice prevails universally. The case of certain mills in Bolton has been brought under my notice, in which the charge of a complement of spinning mules—the best operative situation in a cotton mill—is always clogged with the condition that the spinner shall live in a house belonging to the employer. In the workpeople's own phraseology, "a key goes to each set of mules." Now, although I do not mean to say that the houses are not worth the rent charged, yet a spinner may be unmarried, and have no occasion for four or five rooms. I heard it stated, indeed, that in one instance, in Bolton, a young man so situated sub-lets his house for sixpence a week to an individual who keeps pigs in it.

To return, however, to the Egerton mills. The cottages are not supplied with water in the interior, but there is plenty in the vicinity. The three-shilling houses have a bedroom less than the first class cottages. There is a news room attached to the mill, in which twelve papers, besides periodicals, are taken. For its support the operatives who frequent it pay a penny per week. There is also a library, numbering about 300 volumes. The children under thirteen years of age go as usual to school, and play one half of each day, and work the other half.

The village of Egerton, although inhabited solely by a factory population, is as sweet, wholesome, and smokeless as it could be were its denizens the most bucolic hinds of Devon. I wandered up and down its straggling streets. The houses are furnished much in the same fashion as those of the middling Manchester class; but every article of household use looks better, because cleaner and fresher. Here is no grime nor squalor. The people are hard-working labourers, but they live decently and fare wholesomely. There is no ragged wretchedness to be seen, no ruinous and squalid hovels. There are two taverns in the village—quiet, decent places. One of them, called the Globe, boasts of a sign which, I trust, may not lead astray the geographical wits of the rising generation of Egerton, seeing that the hydrographer has drawn the outline of Europe as encircling the South Pole. This by the way, however. There are no dram shops in Egerton, and no pawnbrokers. None of the people in the mill belong to any trades' combination, and there has been no turn-out since the village was a village. In the country around, hares and rabbits are plenty, but no poaching is heard of. The few agricultural labourers in the vicinity get on the average 12s. a week. For this they frequently labour 15 hours a day. They live in the farm-houses with their employers. Altogether, the village of Egerton presents a gratifying spectacle of the manufacturing system working under favourable auspices. I was perfectly delighted with the healthy and ruddy looks of the young children. While I was lounging about, a caravan came toiling up hill, and the news of the arrival of the wonder-laden vehicle having quickly spread, the youngsters came swarming out of every cottage to wonder and admire—fine chubby, red-faced, white-headed urchins, the pictures of health and good feeling. This very gratifying result I attribute partly to the pure air, but mostly to the mothers seldom or never labouring in the mill. It is, as I shall afterwards prove, the neglect of very young children at home, while their mothers toil in the factories, which causes nineteen-twentieths of the infant deaths in Manchester. The people of Egerton are described to me as being very healthy, and epidemics are rare amongst them. The late Dr. Cooke Taylor, in one of his able and interesting works on the factory system, gives a gratifying account of the morality of the mill population of the district, taking as an index to the general feeling of respect for property the case of the garden of the Messrs. Ashworth, which, although it was full of the finest fruit, perfectly unprotected, and passed every day by the mill hands, young and old, never suffered so much as the loss of a cherry or a flower. This statement, from my own observations, I can readily believe. There are a number of country mills excellently ordered in the valley of the Egret. Conspicuous amongst those is the establishment of Mr. Bazley, the president of the Manchester Chamber of Commerce. This gentleman has constructed ranges of admirably built cottages, each of them supplied with water in the interior. A lecture-room, capable of accommodating 400 or 500 people, is one of the principal public buildings of this excellent operative colony.

Returning to Bolton, I proceeded to visit the mill and the cottages belonging to Messrs. Arrowsmith and Slater, upon the outskirts of the town. The gentlemen in question have taken the lead in Bolton in providing good accommodation, at reasonable rates, for their workpeople, having built two comfortable ranges of cottages, respectively called after Mr. Cobden and Mr. Bright, in which their spinners reside. Indeed, at present, Mr. Arrowsmith lives in one of these cottages himself. The houses are of two classes; the better sort have each a good front parlour, a light and spacious kitchen, a commodious pantry, a back yard with proper out-house conveniences— and above, two bed-rooms. In the inferior class one room serves for parlour and kitchen, the second apartment on the ground floor being a sort of scullery or laundry. There was a small but handy range for cooking, by each fireplace. The rent for a dwelling of this sort is 4s. 1d. per week, a sum which includes gas and water, both of which are laid on. In the cottage which I visited, dinner was just being got ready, and a dish of more savoury smelling Irish stew I have seldom encountered. On a slope stretching away from "Cobden-terrace," is about an acre and a half of ground laid out in unfenced gardens, one of which belongs to each cottage. This summer, Mr. Arrowsmith gave his people prizes of engravings for the best shows of vegetables and flowers. The wane of autumn is a bad time for inspecting a garden, but I saw enough to satisfy me that the ground had been very carefully tilled, and a good harvest of vegetables reaped from it. I may add, that upon the occasion of a recent strike in Bolton, the turn-outs, although they tried hard, only succeeded in stopping for about two hours Messrs. Arrowsmith's and Slater's mill.

In investigating the cotton trade and the condition of the cotton workers in Lancashire, I must not forget the important process of emblazoning the pure calico with those fantastic patterns which suit

the taste of different purchasers in different markets. There is something curious while walking through the stacks of coloured stuffs with
which the rooms of a great warehouse are heaped, in the reflection
that in the course of a year or so the piles of fabric which surround
you will form the clothing and household drapery of half the nations
of the East and South. This piece of gaily-tinted cloth will cover a
divan in a Turkish harem—this other will flutter across the desert in
the turban of an Arab sheik. Here is the raw material of a garment
which will be stitched by Hindoo fingers—there a web which will be
"made up" by a Chinese tailor; while beside it there may perchance
be the staple of the flowing robe which the Tahiti girl will doff when
she laves her limbs in the pellucid depths behind the coral reefs of
the South Sea. As a general rule, the Mediterranean and Levantine
nations prefer the most glaring patterns. The manufacturer can never
make his reds, oranges, and yellows, too bright for the taste of the
Archipelago, the Smyrniote cities, and the fashions prevalent among
the African subjects of France.

"So you find a market in the military colony?" I said to a calico
printer.

"Yes," was the reply; "the French are an ingenious people. They
go first and do the fighting, and we come quietly after them and sell
our calicoes."

In what strange places do the circling waves of a diplomatic misunderstanding break. Possibly the only result of the difference between
the Porte and the Czar will have been, that it created a temporary
slackness in the demand for calico, printed in staring colours and uncouth patterns, in the works round Manchester.

One of these, situated upon the stream of the Medlock, before
it descends to Manchester, I have recently visited. It is the calico-
printing establishment of Messrs. Wood and Wright, and the great
courtesy of the former gentleman I am pleased to have an opportunity
of acknowledging. The process of calico printing may be described as
a modification of dyeing, combined with an adaptation of the process
of letter-press machinery. The old block printing system, performed
by hand, is becoming extinct. In the establishment of Messrs. Wood
and Wright, at Bank-bridge, the block printers do not earn, upon
the average, more than 8s. per week. Their wages, when in full employment, are much higher, but they are seldom in full employment.
The lowest wages paid to adult men in the establishment, working
full hours, are 16s. per week. The machine printers make about 35s. a

week, and the children employed in folding the stuffs, and in a variety of light duties, earn from 3s. 6d. to 5s. a week. There is one species of labour employing boys in the printing process, which certainly ought to be performed by machinery, and which is, without doubt, the most wearying and irksome species of toil which I have seen in Lancashire. It consists simply in turning a wheel, which causes cylinders to revolve in a dye-pit beneath. Here is a species of labour at once degrading, stupifying, and exhausting. It is paid for at the rate of 5s. a week, of twelve hours' daily toil. The boys, as might be expected, plied their tasks lazily and listlessly. The superintendent of the department said that they were brisk and active, and merry enough when released in the evening. It may be so, but I am bound to state that these boys were the only species of labourers whose condition I pitied since my arrival in Lancashire. The calico-printing process involves in certain rooms a necessity for a very high temperature and a moist atmosphere, necessarily more or less impregnated with the fumes of chemical combinations. In one apartment in particular the steam of the boiling water gushed out in such profusion that the place seemed a mass of hot mist. The breathing was at first impeded, but in a second or so became free enough. The hand-block printing room was, however, the most unpleasant, and I should think the most injurious, not so much on account of the actual temperature or the fumes of the colouring matter, as by reason of the vast quantity of newly-printed calico hanging up to dry, and completely stopping anything like a free circulation of the air. The bleaching and washing rooms were as healthful as may be—although the work must be rather a cold one in cold weather. Hot and steaming as are many of the processes, however, I could not ascertain that any evil sanitary consequences had been observably developed. At least, the workpeople themselves said that they had no reason to complain; and of this I am certain, that a greater number of fat jolly-looking personages than have been employed for years in Messrs. Wood and Wright's establishment I never saw. There is but a very insignificant proportion of women employed in calico printworks, and their duty chiefly consists in such coarse needlework as is required for stitching together the pieces.

I have already referred to the Manchester police returns in illustration of the social effects of the manufacturing system. A gratifying feature which one of the tables so furnished presents, is the regular yearly diminution of crime in the borough of Manchester since the year 1842. That year was one of severe manufacturing distress, and the number of apprehensions which it furnished was 13,801. In 1843 the number had fallen to 12,127, in 1844 to 10,702, in 1845 to 9,635, in 1846 to 7,629, in 1847 to 6,587, and in 1848 to 6,277, being a decrease of about 40 per cent. in six years. During this time, too, Captain Willis informs me that the police have been getting more and more vigilant, and that at present they work in perfect harmony with the townspeople, who have great confidence in them. "Not the value of a cabbage-stalk," he added, "is now stolen without it being reported to the police." A question which I was desirous of putting to this excellent authority was, whether the factory system, as a necessary consequence, fostered any particular species of crime. His reply was decidedly in the negative; but he added that the warehousing system, from the value and portable nature of the property left lying about in great ranges of rooms was to a certain degree prolific of theft. In 1848 there were apprehended in Manchester 6,277 persons, male and female, the total population being for the same year 299,445. Of the 6,277 persons in question, 97 only were spinners, and 656 male and female weavers, piecers, carders, &c., making a total of 753 factory hands employed in the great staple manufacture of the place. Of the other prisoners, 1,073 were of "no trade"—at all events, of no honest one; 172 were mechanics and engineers—a rather large proportion; 65 were calico printers, 132 were coachmen and carters, 266 were reputed thieves, and 920 were prostitutes. These general results, I think, amply bear out Captain Willis's statement. The species of crime which prevails the most is, of course, that of larceny, and the species of larceny which flourishes the most is that "in dwelling-houses, warehouses, shops, and out-houses." There is, according to Captain Willis, a considerable floating criminal population in Manchester, a considerable fixed criminal population, and a smaller number of persons who are known both to work and steal.

There are very various opinions afloat as to the extent of female immorality in the mills. It is the sincere conviction of a millowner in a town about thirty miles to the north of Manchester—a gentleman who has devoted a great deal of attention to the study of the social state of the cotton operatives—that there is hardly such a thing as a chaste factory girl—at least in the large towns. But this is an assertion the correctness of which is generally, and I believe with truth, denied.

The fact is, as I am assured, that there exists among the mill girls a considerable degree of correct feeling—sometimes, indeed, carried to the extent of a species of saucy prudery upon these subjects. They keep up a tolerably strict watch upon each other, and a case of frailty is a grand subject for scandal throughout the whole community. Dr. Cooke Taylor narrates that in a register of instances of seduction kept by a millowner, it was found that the guilty parties never belonged to the same factory. They met, not at work, but casually, and in other ways. The number of bastardy warrants granted by the Manchester magistrates in 1848 was 53. Under these, two persons were discharged, eight summarily convicted, and 39 cases "amicably settled." There appears, however, to be no doubt whatever that prostitution is rare among the mill girls. In the Manchester Penitentiary, in 1847, the number of female inmates who had worked in mills amounted to only one-third of the number who had been domestic servants.

Speaking generally, the exceedingly quiet and inoffensive character of the Manchester mill population cannot be too highly estimated. "After ten o'clock," says Sir Charles Shaw, the late head of the police, "the streets are as quiet as those of a country town." The statement may be a little, but not much, exaggerated. The mill operatives are in general a most inoffensive and long-enduring people. How admirable has been their conduct in recent times of stagnation and distress. "I have visited Manchester," says Dr. Cooke Taylor, "at seasons when trade was pre-eminently prosperous. I see it now (1842) suffering under severe and unprecedented distress, and I have been forcibly struck by observing the little change which the altered circumstances have produced in the moral aspect of the population. Agricultural distress soon makes itself known. 'Swing' on this side of the water, and 'Rock' on the other, write the tales of their grievances in characters which no man can mistake, and seek redress by measures strongly marked with the insanity of despair. But suffering here has not loosened the bonds of confidence. Millions of property remain at the mercy of a rusty nail or the ashes of a tobacco-pipe, and yet no one feels alarmed for the safety of his stock or machinery, though in case of an opera-tive *Jacquerie* they could not be defended by all the military force of England."

Similar sentiments I have heard expressed on all sides by those whose mental powers admirably qualify them for judgement, and whose position, while it brings them closely and habitually in contact with the poor, preclude the possibility of partiality either on one side or the other. In truth the Manchester operative is amongst the most industrious and patient of citizens. He toils cheerfully, and is day by day learning to read more, and to think more. If he has a turn for study, he devotes himself, in a few cases, to mechanical science—in the great number to botany. The science of plants is, indeed, a passion with the Manchester weaver. It is as common here as pigeon-fancying in Spitalfields. Every holiday sees hundreds of peaceful wanderers in the fields and woods around, busily engaged in culling specimens of grasses and flowers; while, generally harmless and industrious as the present generation are, there is good hope for expecting yet better things at the hands of their successors.

*The Morning Chronicle, Monday, October 29, 1849.*

To the EDITOR of the MORNING CHRONICLE.

Sir—Under the significant title of "Labour and the Poor," I read that it is your intention to investigate with an impartial eye the physical, moral, and domiciliary aspect of factory life—to narrate as you may find it the daily life of the factory operative, his toil, his remuneration, his amusements, his social and religious habits, and the bearings of his labour on his intellectual and physical powers.

The comprehensive summary which your correspondent's introductory letter embraces opens up a wide and chequered chapter of human life. We need not travel to the antipodes for startling contrasts and social anomalies in human existence. We have—God knows!—within our own compact island depths of misery and degradation, with their opposites of wealth and supineness—dreary regions of toil and cadaverous exhaustion, with sunny slopes of luxuriant ease and mental repose—sufficient to deepen the shadows and tinge the rosy hues of light on the canvas of the moral painter.

Your commission, with its duties, appears to me singular, but momentous. Does the nation require to be enlightened afresh as to the condition of her sons and daughters of toil? Is it necessary to exhibit in new forms the actual life and destinies of our labouring classes? Are the habits and customs of another hemisphere better known to our ruling powers than are the habits and customs of the millions who swarm in our cities, and hamlets, and rural districts? Is property slumbering over its duties, and watchful only to maintain its rights? Does the deep calm which at present presides over the districts of toil betoken the healthy state of the body politic, or is it the portentous hush of the gathering storm?

These interrogations are naturally suggested by the mission on which you are now bent. I hail with infinite satisfaction this germ of an opening spirit of inquiry in high places into the multifarious condition of our labouring poor. It is a move in the right direction—it is a duty demanded of us by our common Christianity.

It must be gratifying to the promoters of this commission to know that much interest has already been awakened among our factory operatives by the letters of your correspondent.

I speak from an intimate knowledge of their opinions, for my lot is cast among them, and my avocations lead me into close fellowship with them. Their curiosity was much excited to know the object of your correspondent's enquiries; and on the appearance of the introductory letter, a buzz of eager questions was asked from loom to loom, if he or she had read the "Letter." (You must know that many of the women are great readers of the newspapers.)

I have visited the penny news-rooms, the Temperance-hall, and the public tap-room, and found the subject of the letter the principal topic of criticism. According to the temperament of the individual was the subject treated. The sullen looked upon it with suspicion—a few grey beards pronounced their opinion that "*nought*" would come of it. The young and sanguine wondered if this was to be the commencement of a new agitation; and the high-spirited wished the gentlefolks would mind their own business, and "show up" the extravagance and waste of their lives, which burden the poor with taxes.

Such are a few of the running commentaries which an hour's ramble of an evening elicited.

You have already obtained a great point—you have awakened public attention. You have directed the eye of the nation to the most interesting, though sorrowful, portion of her people; and in the revelations which are yet to come from the pens of your correspondents, data will be served for many a tale of human suffering and endurance, and, we trust to God, ample materials collected for the better understanding of the solemn question of the social amelioration and improvement of the labouring classes.

I am, &c.,

ONE WHO HAS WROUGHT AT THE LOOM.
Manchester, Oct. 25, 1849.

# LABOUR AND THE POOR.

——◆——

## THE MANUFACTURING DISTRICTS.

[FROM OUR SPECIAL CORRESPONDENT.]

## MANCHESTER.

## LETTER V.

In this communication I propose to direct the reader's attention to the sanitary condition of Manchester and the cotton spinning districts—to try to discriminate between the mortality which is peculiar to those districts, and that which is common to all—between the mortality which is the effect of the system of working in mills, and that which is the effect of living in large and ill-built towns—between the mortality which, both in factory districts and great towns, can be put an end to, and the mortality which in factory districts and great towns is inevitable.

Manchester occupies a bad pre-eminence in the statistics of death; and Manchester is the metropolis of cotton spinning; *ergo*, it has been a good deal the fashion to argue that death and cotton-spinning go together. It will be my object, on the contrary, to show that there exists no such necessary partnership—that it is death and ill-built towns—death and the abuses of cotton-spinning, which really and actually stride *pari passu*. And herein is involved one of the most profound and terribly urgent of the social problems which it is given us to solve on behalf of our poorer brethren. We have no actual statistical data for ascertaining exact proportions, but the inquiring student who duly pores over that extraordinary book, annually written by the Registrar-General, and who confirms its pages from those repertories of mud and filth—airless alleys and ricketty hovels which he will find scattered in grimy towns and bleak or sunny fields—the student who fails not to consult these sources of information, will not, perhaps, disagree with me, when I assert that the difference between the sanitary condition under which the rich and the poor Englishman lives is as great as that which subsists between the Englishman and the Hindoo, or between the Englishman who dwells in the cities of the nineteenth century and the Englishman who dwelt in the cities of the fifteenth century. The unhealthiest parts of England are more than twice as fatal to life as the healthiest parts. As a general rule, and speaking in rough numbers, the country is about ten per cent. healthier than the town. But it may be asserted with fearlessness, that the unhealthiest parts of towns are more than ten per cent. more fatal than the healthiest parts. The chances of life, therefore, are greater in the open square, as contrasted with the typhoid alley, than in the breezy country, as contrasted with the smoky town. "The difference in salubrity," says Mr. Macaulay, "between the London of the nineteenth century and the London of the seventeenth century is very far greater than the difference between London in an ordinary season and London in the cholera." Measuring health by space, instead of time, it may be truly said that the difference in salubrity between a district where the rich live exclusively, and a district where the poor live exclusively, is as great as between the former district in an ordinary season and the same district in the cholera. It is a tendency of manufacturers to accumulate masses of the poor, as it is of our system to accumulate masses of the rich and poor. But is it the inevitable consequences of either system that the accumulations which they produce shall be as unwholesome, as though it were a law of nature that, wherever two or three thousand were gathered together, there should a plague dwell also? This is a proposition of which few will deny the falsehood. It was said that the poor should never be out of the land; but it was not said that chronic plagues, cutting short the lives of the poor, but in a great degree sparing the rich, should never be out of the land. It has been broadly contended that the power of the politically ruling classes of this land will never really be safe until the social felicity of the labouring classes shall have been augmented. And what a mass of curable social misery is there exhibited in the columns of the Registrar-General's report. If we take the deaths in towns as one in forty-five of the population, while the deaths in the country are one in fifty-five, we may estimate the disproportion as being still greater between the deaths of the rich and those of the poor. Both disproportions, particularly the latter, are, I believe, greater than in the order of things they need be. Give the towns those improvements in drainage, ventilation, and construction which can be, and which ultimately will be, secured to them, and we add in some cases five, in others ten, in others twenty, in others near an hundred per cent. to the health, the life, and therefore the sum of the social felicity of England.

To no portions of the kingdom do these remarks apply with so much force as to the unhealthiest. I may instance the district of Bideford—one person only dies in every sixty-two. One person in fifty is not a higher proportion than is to be found in scores of English towns. In Liverpool one person dies every year out of every twenty-nine of the population. In Manchester one person dies out of every thirty.

Manchester is the metropolis of cotton-spinning, but in Liverpool barely a hank of yarn is run off the mule. Manchester has a tribe of cotton-spinning satellites around it. In all of them the mortality is lower than in itself. In Salford one annually dies out of 34, in Bolton one out of 37, in Rochdale one out of 38, in Preston, a purely cotton-spinning place, one also out of 38. There is, I believe, no district in Lancashire of which the statistics regarding life are given by the Registrar-General which does not include town mills as well as country mills. It is not, therefore, easy to get at the relative mortality of the country and the town mills; but the mortality of Lancashire— an almost purely manufacturing county—is yearly one out of every thirty-nine of the population, precisely the same as the proportion in the town of Worcester, only one per cent. over that of Bath, and six per cent. over that of Cheltenham.

So far, then, it would appear that it is not merely the factory system which makes Manchester so insalubrious. The statistics of the Registrar-General corroborate the evidence which I have personally collected, and the observations which I have personally made. I have already, in describing the exact nature of factory toil, stated that it was a species of labour, light and easy of performance, seldom or never calling forth the full employment of all the energies, and allowing frequent periods of rest. The charges of over-crowding the people in factories, arise from simple and sheer ignorance of what a factory is. In the most crowded department of a mill, the people cannot be placed nearly so closely as the passengers are in a first-class railway carriage, and for the simple reason that the vast proportion of each room is occupied by machinery. The ventilation and the temperature of factories have next to be taken into consideration. As a general rule, I believe that the air which mill-labourers breathe at their work is far better than the air which they breathe at home; and in this respect the condition of the mills is year by year improving. It is instructive, for example, to compare the amount of window-glass—in other words, the extent of the arrangements for admitting light and air—in the more recently built mills, with those subsisting in the mills of older standing. The fact is, that the better the air, the better do the people work; and of this truth millowners are now fully aware. As a general rule, the worst ventilated mills being the old ones, are also provided with old machinery, and the obvious result is, that neither in amount nor quality of production can they compete with the newer mills. The owners of such establishments struggle under disadvantages so great as often to make them the first, at periods of depression, to go to the wall. Within the last three weeks, the price of raw cotton has considerably advanced, and two old-fashioned factories in Manchester have failed. In the mill-windows, ample arrangements for swinging panes for admitting air are now almost universally made; and in by far the greater number of work-rooms which I have visited, the air, if it did not smell wooingly, was at all events perfectly inoffensive. In certain mills—those spinning five threads, or, as they are technically called, "high numbers"—an elevated temperature, say from 70 to 80, is required, and constantly kept up. In these rooms, attention to the ventilation is of course extremely requisite; but if this attention be, as it can be, duly enforced, the mere height of the temperature is not a matter of much sanitary consequence, except, perhaps, in relation to a certain forcing effect which it seems to exert on children, and also as regards the tendency it produces in the people to attempt to keep the thermometer up to a corresponding degree at their own homes.

I have before me a great number of tables, giving calculations of the amount of health and sickness prevalent, not only in the mills of Lancashire, but amid labourers employed in many occupations. These tables in general go to prove the existence of a very high degree of health in the cotton mills; a degree indeed which, taken without some modifying circumstances, would, in my opinion, clash very materially with what we know to be the mortality of the cotton region. For example, the average number of days' sickness per man in the "Lancashire mills" is stated at 5.35 per annum. And the average number of days' sickness of the "East India Company's servants," in England, I presume, is put down as 5.4 per man. Now the mortality of Lancashire, making allowance in the one direction for children not yet in the mills, among whom mortality is excessive, and in the other for the richer classes among whom mortality is comparatively small, the mortality amongst adult mill-labourers must, I apprehend, be greater than that of the East India Company's servants.

The apparent discrepancy can be easily accounted for. In the first place the cotton labourer is not required to perform very toilsome work. A man must be really and seriously ill, if he cannot attend to a carding-frame or a self-acting mule. In the second place, he is paid by the piece, and he will exert himself very strenuously rather than knock under and forfeit his wages. I have occasionally seen in a mill men going languidly about their work, suffering from headache or stomach derangement. Had these labourers heavy toil to pursue, they would have been physically unable to master it, and had they been paid by a regular weekly wage, independent of the quantity of work turned off, they would, and rightly, have considered that they were telling no lie in reporting themselves as ill, and unfit for work.

I have thus stated considerations which, rightly viewed, will strengthen rather than weaken the credibility of the actual facts given by the tables in question, although to a certain extent they will impart to these facts a new colouring. What I believe is, that cotton spinning in the mills does not produce more actual sickness than the tables show; but what I do not believe is, that the domestic arrangements and social and sanitary evils of the great towns, where so large a portion of the spinners live, do not produce more sickness than the tables show. These tables support my view of the case strongly; but unless I had stated the modifying circumstances detailed, my fear would have been, that, contrasted with the condition of matters shown in the bills of mortality, the tables, like those dangerous things, over-favourable witnesses, would have supported my case *too* strongly. That the tables would literally apply to very many of the country mills, I have not a doubt; but that they literally apply to mills the workers in which live in closely-crowded, undrained, unventilated, and filthy houses, is what I have my doubts of.

With these remarks I copy that part of the tables referring to males. The apparent period of sickness of the females is greatly swelled by what the Manchester Statistical Society very naïvely, and somewhat characteristically, term the time "lost" in accouchements:—

| | Average duration of sickness per annum for every person employed. Day and decimal parts. | Average duration of sickness per annum for every person sick. Day and decimal parts. |
|---|---|---|
| Under 11 | 2.46 | 13.58 |
| From 11 to 16 | 3.81 | 14.58 |
| 16 to 21 | 4.42 | 16.43 |
| 21 to 26 | 4.91 | 18.27 |
| 26 to 31 | 6.88 | 22.14 |
| 31 to 36 | 3.85 | 12.19 |
| 36 to 41 | 4.13 | 13.05 |
| 41 to 46 | 5.09 | 14.25 |
| 46 to 51 | 7.18 | 30.31 |
| 51 to 56 | 3.47 | 13.10 |
| 56 to 61 | 12.68 | 11.05 |

The reader will not fail to perceive that the comparatively small per centage of *cases* of sickness, contrasted with the comparatively long duration of the *periods* of sickness, corroborates what I stated as to the class of minor maladies not forcing the people to leave their work.

The Manchester Statistical Society, in their "Analysis of the Evidence taken before the Factory Commissioners," go on to give the average number of days' sickness among the operatives engaged in various branches of industry:—

| | Days' Sickness per man. |
|---|---|
| In the Staffordshire Potteries up to the age of 61 | 9.03 |
| Silk mills | 7.08 |
| Woollen ditto | 7.08 |
| Flax ditto | 5.09 |
| Cotton ditto in Glasgow | 5.06 |
| Among the East India Company's servants | 5.04 |
| Labourers in Chatham Dockyard | 5.38 |
| In the Lancashire cotton mills | 5.35 |
| Ditto    ditto, under 16 years of age | 3.14 |

These results are striking, and I suspect that to many they will be new. The ghastly stories of men choked wholesale by devil's dust, and children pounded with "billy rollers," cannot yet be quite reckoned amongst the superstitions which have passed out of date. I have stated certain modifying circumstances which may be fairly taken into account in judging of these figures; but I apply these circumstances almost altogether to the town mills; in other words, I make allowances for the state of health caused, not by the mills, but by the town homes of the people. The mortality of the cotton districts, in my belief, is the mortality of defective domestic—not the mortality of defective working, arrangements. Take the case of a sick club for adults, established at Messrs. H. and A. Ashworth's, at Egerton, referred to by Dr. Cooke Taylor. In 1843 the club numbered 66 members, all mill-workers. Of these, nine only were sick and one died during the year. In a sick club at Bolton, mentioned in the evidence taken by the Factory Commissioners, and which comprised factory hands and artisans in nearly equal proportions, only a little more than one-fourth of the cases of sickness, and one-fifth of the deaths, during the year before the inquiry, were those of the mill subscribers—proving, if it proves anything, that of two classes of persons living at their homes, under tolerably similar circumstances, the members of the class which passed a great proportion of its time in factories were healthier than the members of the class which laboured as well as slept in their own dwellings.

Official testimony to the sanitary harmlessness of the process of cotton spinning I might multiply to any extent. I will, however, only give a few instances:—

"Factory labour is decidedly not injurious to health or longevity, compared with other employments."—*Reports of Inspectors of Factories. R. Rickards, Esq.* 1837.

"I am of opinion that the effect of factory labour has been greatly exaggerated, and that it has not been as injurious as it has been represented, or, indeed, so much so as many other occupations not under legislative control."—*Leonard Horner, Esq. Report, July* 21, 1834.

"As the occupation of children in the mills is so light as to cause no bodily fatigue, they would pass their eight hours there as beneficially for their health as at home, indeed in most cases far more so."—*Leonard Horner, Esq. Report, July* 21, 1834.

"With some few exceptions, I found the mills and factories remarkably clean and apparently well regulated; and nothing came under my notice that could lead me to suppose that the operatives, whether adults or young persons, or children, were unhealthy or so severely oppressed by labour as has been strongly represented."—*R. J. Saunders, Esq. Report, Dec.* 28, 1833.

The opinions of two medical gentlemen of Manchester, with whom I have conversed upon the subject, come to this:—That the insalubrity of Manchester and of the Manchester operatives is occasioned, not by the labour of the mills, but by the defective domestic arrangements for cleanliness and ventilation. Each of the gentlemen in question has peculiar opportunities of observation. One of them, Mr. Golland, surgeon, is one of the medical officers of the police and the poor-law authorities; the other, Dr. Johns, M.D., is the registrar for one of the most populous operative districts of the town.

Before me lie several Reports, made to the Health of Towns Commission, on the sanitary state of the manufacturing districts. Little, if any, mention is made of the mills in these documents. But the reporters enter, with great minuteness of detail, into the home mode of living of the people, and deduce therefrom the cause of mortality and death.

Thus, Mr. Golland, in his report on Chorlton-on-Medlock, proves that the mortality varies amongst the same class receiving the same wages in proportion as they inhabit second or third-class houses, and second or third-class streets. In first-class streets in Chorlton, the mortality is 1 in 46, a lower rate than the mortality of Brighton; in third-class streets, it is 1 in 27, a higher rate than that of Liverpool. Again, in houses of the first class, the Chorlton mortality is 1 in 52, a proportion nearly as small as the mortality of Windsor; in houses of the third class, the mortality is 1 in 29, a proportion higher than that of the borough of Manchester. I shall give one more additional proof of the fact of the intimate connection between mortality and unhealthy dwellings. In the comparatively small town of Leicester, the average age at which death takes place in well-drained streets is 25½ years; in tolerably drained streets, 21 years; in undrained streets, 17 years; while the average number of persons carried off by epidemics in the well-drained streets is 1-12th, in the undrained streets 1-6th.

A vast proportion of the mortality of Manchester is that of children; but of children, be it observed, under the age to labour in the mills. Out of every 100 deaths in Manchester, more than 48 take place under five years of age, and more than 51 under ten years of age. In some of the neighbouring towns—particularly Ashton-under-Lyne—the proportion is still more appalling. There, by a calculation made embracing the five years ending with June 30, 1843, it appeared that, out of the whole number of deaths, 57 per cent. were those of children under five years of age.

It is, of course, generally known that the first five years of life are the most fatal in all districts; but upon comparing a series of cotton spinning districts in the North with a series of purely rural districts in the West and South, I find that, while the infant mortality in the former is about 50 per cent., speaking in round numbers, that of the latter is only about 33 per cent. In this difference of proportion is to be found the great evil of the factory system as it at present exists, an evil committed not by the work of the mills, but by the work of the mills drawing individuals in certain conditions from their homes. To this I shall come almost immediately.

The result of my observations hitherto is, that labour in factories is not to any important extent necessarily unhealthy, that the people employed in factories breathe better air than at their own homes, that they are neither overcrowded nor overworked; but it also appears to me that in the vast proportion of cases the operatives are crammed into filthy, overcrowded, and insufficiently-drained habitations; and that from thence, and not from the factories, the high mortality springs. There are two classes of towns—the very old and slow-growing ones, and the very new and fast-growing ones—afflicted by similar sanitary evils. In the former, the dwellings of the poor were constructed before such things as ventilation or drainage were heard of; in the latter, the dwellings of the poor were constructed so hurriedly that ventilation and drainage were unheeded. The consequence is, that chronic and epidemic diseases linger round and smite each alike. Compare the cholera returns of Bristol with those of Liverpool, and of Salisbury with those of Manchester. For the new towns, however, there is more hope than for the old. There are energy and capital in the one class, which are wanting in the other. During the last few years the corporation of Manchester have been busy flinging open *cul de sacs*, and running airy streets through overcrowded neighbourhoods. Parks are being provided with gymnastic apparatus for children; and an ample supply of the purest water is slowly but surely making its way from the distant hills.

I now return to the dismal topic of infant mortality, the undue proportion of which arises from the neglect of mothers who are compelled to leave their young children at home while they labour in the mill. This I hold to be the blackest blot on the factory system. Whether it can be remedied is a question which I will not attempt to answer. "Pregnant women," says Dr. Johns, "frequently continue their work up to the very last moment, and return to it as soon as ever they can move about." "In Ashton-under-Lyne," says Mr. Coulthard, "it is no unfrequent occurrence for mothers of the tenderest age to return to their work in the factories on the second or third week after confinement, and to leave their helpless offspring in the charge of mere girls or superannuated old women." The same authority mentions the case of a nurse "suckling three of these children," and so exhausted as to be "unable to walk across the room," while the children were "almost unable to move their hands and feet." The inevitable result of this system is the reckless and almost universal employment of narcotics. First, the child is drugged until it sleeps, and too often it is drugged until it dies. There is a notion abroad that laudanum, as a stimulant, is frequently used by adults in the manufacturing districts instead of spirits. Upon this subject I have made inquiries, which have convinced me that the practice, if it exists at all, does so only in exceptional cases. Medical men have generally said that little or nothing of the kind came under their observation. Druggists are exceedingly shy and reserved upon the whole subject of narcotic dosing, and indisposed to admit that laudanum is commonly given in any cases except those in which it is medically necessary. The truth is, however, that in England opium-eating, or drinking what De Quincey calls "laudanum toddy," is an anti-social vice, practised in secret, and of which its practisers are ashamed. The man who thinks no harm of admitting that he takes his glass of wine, or his tumbler of grog, or his pint of porter, will be sorry to make any such confession in favour of preparations of the poppy. If he gets drunk on opium pills, he will keep the failing to himself. In the case of infant drugging, although the subject is generally mentioned with reserve both by those who sell and those who employ the medicine, the practice is too notorious and universal to be for an instant denied. Still, says Mr. Coulthard, writing of Ashton—and his experience corroborates my own—"both buyer and seller are aware that they are doing wrong, and try to mystify the facts." The truth is, there is not a more thoroughly household word through the cotton spinning towns than "Godfrey." Indeed, just as the gin-loving race of London delight to call their favourite beverage by dozens of slangy affectionate titles, just as there is "Cream of the Valley," and "Regular Flare-up," and "Old Tom," so there is to be found in the druggists' shops in the lower districts here, "Baby's Mixture," "Mother's Quietness," "Child's Cordial," "Soothing Syrup," and so forth, every one of these lulling beverages being a sweetened preparation of laudanum. In Ashton these abominable doses are actually sold at many of the public-houses, and I think it highly probable that the same practice may exist in Manchester. In the former town, the weekly sale of the narcotic drugs in question, by 15 vendors, was on the average 6 gallons 2 quarts 1½ pints. In Preston, as it appears from the report of the Rev. J. Clay, 21 druggists sold in one week of:—

|  | lbs. | ozs. | drs. |
|---|---|---|---|
| Godfrey's Cordial ... ... ... | 23 | 5 | 5 |
| Infant's Preservative ... ... | 18 | 4 | 0 |
| Syrup of Poppies ... ... ... | 16 | 9 | 0 |
| Opium ... ... ... ... ... | 1 | 1 | $6\frac{1}{2}$ |
| Laudanum ... ... ... ... | 7 | 8 | 2 |
| Paregoric ... ... ... ... ... | 0 | 9 | 0 |
| Making a total of Narcotics of ... | 68 | 1 | $5\frac{1}{2}$ |

Appended to the return made by the largest of these twenty-one vendors is the following note:—"Such preparations are only given, he believes, to enable the mother to work at factory." A small quantity of laudanum is noted as sold for adult consumption, but the proportion is quite trifling.

When we take into consideration this horrible system of juvenile "hocussing"—this feeding infants upon loathsome syruppy laudanum rather than their mother's milk—when we duly ponder on the state of filth in which children left inefficiently attended must live (and the nature of the superintendence they receive is well illustrated by the fact already adduced, that more than 4,000 go annually astray and get "lost" in the streets of Manchester)—and, finally, when we take into consideration such facts as those stated by the registrar of Deansgate, in Manchester, when he tells us that, in one district, nearly 200 children died in a year "without any reasonable attempt having been made to save them"—the miserable little wretches having been soothed and stupified in their sickness by opiates—when we endeavour to realise in our minds in its full horror this foul and unnatural state of things, can we feel either shocked or surprised at the deliberate declaration of the registrar, that, in Manchester, in the course of seven years, there perished 13,362 children, "over and above the mortality natural to mankind?" Yes: 13,362 "little children brought up in unclean dwellings and impure streets—left alone long days by their mothers—to breathe the subtle sickly vapours—soothed by opium, a more cursed distillation than hebenon—and when assailed by mortal disease, their stomachs torn, their bodies convulsed, their brains bewildered, left to die without medical aid, which, like hope, should come to all, the skilled medical man never being called in at all, or only summoned to witness the death and sanction the funeral!"

There are two exciting causes for this mass of infantine misery. First, but in a comparatively small degree, the unhealthy state of the houses; secondly and mainly, the neglect and all the concomitant evils consequent upon the mothers of children of tender age passing their days in the mill.

Herein—I cannot too often repeat it—lie, in my solemn conviction, the bane and the disgrace of the cotton system. If we are to have any legislative interference in the factories at all, is not this the point to which interference ought to be directed? Whether the evil be curable or irremediable, I pretend not to say. I have brought together an array of facts bearing upon it, and I leave those facts to suggest, as different minds may view them, whether or not it would be advisable in factory legislation to make any difference between "women" and the mothers of young children, even to the extent of relaxing the restrictions upon the daily work of the former, if thereby we could increase the time apportionable to the domestic duties of the latter.

The mortality in Manchester is greater than in the neighbouring factory towns, because it is a common centre to which tramps and vagrants resort, and to which immigrants flow from the agricultural districts, these last being very frequently in such bad health as to be incapable of longer pursuing field work. Out of 17,406 persons admitted into the Manchester Asylum for Houseless Poor between February, 1838, and February, 1839, there were 9,870 actually relieved. Of these, 3,500 only belonged to Lancashire, 1,700 were Irish recently arrived, and the vast majority of the whole were strangers in search of work. To such overflows all great capitals of industry will probably be ever more or less exposed, and such overflows will ever add to the due amount of sickness and of death. But let there once exist a universal system of healthful sanitary regulation, and even the typhus generated by masses of poverty crowded together in search of work may be modified and kept under control. We have heard old legends of victims built up in the thick walls of ancient donjon keeps cited as proofs of feudal tyranny. The day, let us be thankful, is dawning upon us when capitalists who run up ranges of streets, terraces, and crescents, will be made aware that, in rearing cities without drains and water supplies, without light and air, they are committing crimes blacker than those of ever an old castellan of them all—that they are sacrificing, not one life, but scores of lives—that they are piling up fabrics of disease—building in, with the very walls, masses of deadly typhus and cholera.

How curiously one-sided have our sanitary advances been! Our paupers and our criminals are, as a matter of notoriety, far better off than our honest and struggling labourers. Contrast the wards of prisons and of unions with the dwellings in the "Angel-meadow" of Manchester, where "20 or 30 persons live in houses in which there is not accommodation for one-third part of the number." Doubtless the cause of the difference is not far to seek. Criminals and paupers, when massed together, are handy to deal with. The very same thing on a greater scale is true of towns. They supply the material for association, and association, humanly speaking, can do anything. In our shipping—in the sanitary condition of our marine—we have done great things. Read Smollett's account of a man-of-war in his day, and compare it with the state of one of Sir Charles Napier's experimental squadron. Scurvy, with its foul features of ulcerated glands and bleeding gums, was once the disease of the sea. Commodore Anson, the link between the race of the discoverers and that of the Buccaneers, lost, in a voyage of ten months, 626 men out of 961. The first fleet of the East India Company lost 100 men out of 528, between England and Table Bay. The men had "scurvy, dysenteries, and putrid fevers—their limbs dropped off—they swooned and died." In the year 1780 the Channel fleet sent 11,732 sick men to Haslar, "1,457 had scurvy, 240 dysentery, 5,539 fevers." Sir James Saumarez truly said at the time that "neither men nor ships could keep the sea for two months." Yet, before that period Cook had sailed round the world with 112 men. The voyage occupied three years, and he brought back his crew only five short, and of these five a single person had died from disease. Cook's plan was soon generally adopted. Clean, sweet ships, pure water, plenty of air, good provisions, vegetables, and lemon juice now abound in our fleets, and the result is that we hear of ships of war coming from the antipodes, after being four years in commission, without the loss of a single hand by a disease. So much for the sea. How stands the land? In many of our towns it is very probable that there are courts and alleys just as foul as any ship of Cook's time; cellars and garrets just as filthy, overcrowded, and unwholesome, as when the first East India fleet sailed. Fever and dysentery abound there now, just as they did half a century ago. And yet there is no real reason why we should not eradicate typhus in our towns as we have eradicated scurvy in our ships, for the one class of disease can be attacked as successfully as the other.

# LABOUR AND THE POOR.

———◆———

## THE MANUFACTURING DISTRICTS.

[FROM OUR SPECIAL CORRESPONDENT.]

## MANCHESTER.

## LETTER VI.

The substance of the remark with which I open this communication must be kept steadily and keenly in sight by those who would acquire from my letters a true insight into the social condition of the great capital of the cotton cities. The Manchester which I am describing is the Manchester of prosperous times. True, there has not been any recent fever of production; there has been no sudden and imperious demand for calicoes, such as in the olden times, before Ten Hours Bills were heard of, would have kept the steam-engines throbbing, and the mechanism whirling for fifteen or eighteen hours out of the twenty-four; but there has been for some time a fair and steady trade; the workpeople have for some time earned fair and steady wages, and the butcher and baker have happily had the power of being reasonable in their demands. But good times in Manchester hang—so to speak—on a fibre of cotton. In Birmingham, where a hundred trades employ a hundred different guilds of handicraftsmen, the stagnation of any one branch of employment affects only one working family out of a hundred working families. Here, universal well-doing, or universal suffering, depend solely upon the one article of cotton—upon the supply of the raw material—upon the demand for the manufactured fabric. The whisper of a hostile tariff amid the markets of the East, the rumour of a worm or a blight in the plantations of Alabama or Louisiana, is sufficient, by checking the demand of the warehouseman on the one hand, or raising the prices charged by the cotton broker on the other, to produce, in a week, short time and short wages— to change, as by the waving of a wand, the industrial and consuming power of a vast community. In most towns, in periods of operative distress, the pressure is partial, and little, if any, of it is seen upon the surface. All trades cannot be bad at the same time. Here, speaking in general terms, the distress of one operative is the distress of all. Let there come a glut or a panic in that one grand item of cotton, and straightway the smoke ceases to pour from the tall chimney; the great halls, crowded with complex machinery, are silent and lone; and, lingering round the corners of courts and alleys, groups of wageless workmen curse the chance which keeps them idle and their children hungry.

No account of the operatives of Manchester would therefore be correct in which the attention of the reader was not specially called to that sadly often-recurring period of calamity which throws the whole social machine out of gear, and flings back, from time to time, the generally advancing tide of social comfort and improvement.

I now proceed to notice the general, moral, and educational condition of the Manchester operative—to state my impressions and the data upon which I found them—of "mind among the spindles." I have already, in general terms, noticed the almost universal testimony borne by those who know the Manchester "mill hand" best, to the mild and inoffensive character and bearing of the cotton population. The colliers and metal workers throughout the north, indeed, profess to hold the men of the loom and the mule in great contempt, as a set of spiritless milksops—as soft and pliable as the woolly fibre which they twist. And truly there can be little doubt but that the men who habitually deal with bobbins and threads must form a very different race to the sturdier and more turbulent spirits whose lot is cast among sledge-hammers and pick-axes. A turn-out of the cotton workers is a very different, and, generally speaking, a far less riotous affair than a strike in the districts of iron and coal. Occasionally, no doubt, there have been deeds of crime and lawless violence perpetrated by Manchester turn-outs. The persecution of the "knobsticks," as the workmen were called who, during a strike, were willing to labour at lower wages than those which the union sanctioned, and to obtain which the stand was made—the persecution which on one or two occasions these poor wretches underwent, was at once cowardly and cruel. They were set upon in lonely places, and beaten and ducked by mobs. Their feet were wounded by blows from iron-spiked sticks, and blinding vitriol was flung into their eyes. Still it must be recollected that these atrocities were committed by the most fanatical rabble of the mills, during a period of intense excitement—during a struggle between labour and capital which was as for life and death, while the attacks were made upon men who were esteemed by their persecutors as enemies to their order and traitors to their peers.

As a general rule, the men of cotton are essentially a peaceful and moral-force generation. They are greatly under the influence of leaders, whose mental powers they respect. There are not a few of the weavers and spinners whose capacity for thought is considerable; and these again have to deal with a population whose faith is one of their most distinguishing moral attributes. The cotton-mills of Manchester abound with hard-headed, studious, thoughtful men, who pass brooding, meditating lives, sometimes taken up in endeavours to sound those profound social problems which lie at the bottom of the relations between capital and labour; sometimes, again, occupied with the various phases of physical and mechanical science; and not unfrequently sturdy theologians, profoundly versed in the subtleties and casuistries of all warring schools of Calvinism. In this respect, indeed, the Lancashire temperament is not unfrequently akin to that which so plentifully prevails to the north of the border. I have conversed with many operatives of the class which I have sketched, and generally left them with a very considerable respect for their self-acquired attainments, and their earnest if not enthusiastic tone of character. Such men often rise to be overlookers in their respective mills, and in many instances pass their evenings in teaching adult classes of their fellow labourers. As a general rule, they are nearly all either professed or virtual teetotallers, and as such are greatly given to that cant of temperance which denounces as a folly and a crime the most harmless degree of social indulgence. I had one long conversation with a man who was a good specimen of the class in question. He is now an overlooker in a mill in Hulme. He told me he had been a thoughtless scamp in his youth, and that he had led a vagrant sort of life, thinking of nothing but sensual pleasures until he became a man. Then he began to reflect upon the degrading life which he was leading, and to ask himself what was the use of his having a soul if he did not strive to elevate it; so, setting to work, he found—in his own words— that he was "endowed by God with a great capacity for study." He liked mechanical science the best, and now it was a great pleasure to him to strive to make his children fond of reading, and to educate and enlighten his fellow-workmen. He was at the head of a small library, principally scientific. "Did they admit novels?"—"Yes," with a melancholy shake of the head, "they found that they could not get on without something of that kind—the people liked stories." My friend, however, did not seem by any means "up" in the fiction department of his library, for he mentioned the "Pickwick Papers and other works by Eugene Sue." He highly approved of the cheap summer trips which the railways were giving the people. He had thus been able to "take his good woman one hundred and twelve miles from Manchester," and explained the country to her as they went along. Sometimes, in the department of which he was overlooker, they worked so fast that they got a-head of the others, and had half a holiday. They were lucky in this respect lately. It was a fine day, and he had taken not only his own family, but all the workers in his department, out in a body to enjoy themselves in the fields, "a far better place than the public-house."

Another intelligent operative I encountered in his own house, just as he returned from work. The room was cheery and clean. Two little girls, with fat dimpled legs and arms, sat on a stool before the fire. The plates and pot-lids shone as brightly as old china or armour from the white-washed walls. The wife bustled with the tea-things, and the good man sat him down in his rocking chair—that delicious piece of furniture of which the Yankees borrowed the idea from Lancashire, and now impudently take credit for having invented.

My friend was a Ten Hours Bill man: "The people had health, and time, and spirits now to clean their houses, and teach themselves something useful. The cotton folks were improving. Oh, yes, they were; the next generation would be better than the present. No one ever thought of schools for children when he was a child. No; he had wrought many and many a time for twelve hours a day when he was not eight years old. The children were lucky now to what they were in them old times. There were good evening classes too for the men and women, only he was afeard that a good many of them, particu- larly the boys and girls, were too fond of going to the music saloons, where they did not hear no good, and did not do no good. He had gone to one himself lately." A look from the wife. "Oh, of course only to hear what was going on—only that—and he was disgusted, he was. Nigger songs," and, with a significant wink, "other songs, and nonsen- sical recitations and trash—and girls dancing on the stage, with *such* short petticoats. Oh, places like them wasn't no good. But there was the Monday night concerts—*there* was music—there was the place for a working man to have a night's rational amusement."

In prosecuting my Ten Hours Bill inquiries, the results of which I shall give in another letter, I picked up a good deal of information respecting the evening pursuits of the rising generation. Girls and young men, by the score and the hundred, appear to be learning to read, write, cypher, and sew. Some had friends in America, and they wanted to send them the news. Others were the oldest in the family, and it behoved them to set their little brothers and sisters a good example. The girls made their own clothes, too—"clothes of all sorts—paletots and visites, and they were very fond of sampler work." I have seen a great many of these samplers. In nine cases out of ten they commemorate the death of a relation—very often of a brother. They exhibit a tombstone and a weeping willow, with a verse of poetry or a sentence from the Bible beneath. The poetry was commonly of the "afflictions sore long time I bore" school, favoured by the national churchyard muse. They copied it, they said, from books or from old samplers, but sometimes they composed it themselves. No young lady would however plead guilty to any of the elegiac effusions which were exhibited. The men had frequently learned to write since they were grown up. They were anxious to read well also, that they might avail themselves of the libraries. The lads were in a great proportion of cases members of night schools. One stout young fellow whom I asked if he was learning to read, replied, "No, he professed—the fiddle," and presently introduced a couple of youths who professed the fiddle likewise. Their musical preponderating over their literary tastes, the trio had clubbed together to engage the evening services of a master, and having got over the preliminary difficulties, they now met every night to practise and improve.

I have visited a great many children's schools—factory and mixed schools, and the first and last thing which struck me in connection with them was, that the factory children were decidedly smarter looking and more intelligent than the non-labouring juveniles. "They're not backward, sir," said the excellent and intelligent master of the Lyceum in Great Ancoats-street, "especially at mischief." In the All Saints National School, Chorlton, there were no factory children. The master described the boys as being principally the sons of small tradesmen and artisans. They appeared unintelligent, noisy, and indifferent. The master spoke despondingly of the prospects of education in Manchester. The system he thought was too slight and superficial to produce much practical effect. There was, of course, *a degree* of anxiety on the part of parents that their children should be educated, or his "scholars would not be there." This teacher appeared intelligent and conscientious, but he had evidently small faith in his prospects of success.

From his school I went straight to another, entirely a factory one, and situated in the most densely-peopled part of operative Manchester. The Lyceum is close to Union-street, and Union-street is a locality which merits a word or two of special description. As Lancashire is to England, so is Manchester to Lancashire; and as Manchester is to Lancashire, so is Union-street to Manchester. The locality is the very incarnation of the spirit of the district. A more perfectly ugly spot you shall not find between sunrise and sunset. Fancy a street one side of which is all mills, huge square piles of mills, with six, seven, and eight tiers of foul and blackened windows, the grimiest, sootiest, filthiest lumps of masonry in all Manchester. Through the thick, sunless air comes the throb and the boom of many steam-engines, and the lowly clattering whirl of hundreds of thousands of revolving pirns and bobbins. Look in at the lower ranges of filth-encrusted windows. What multiplying revelations of endless carding frames, and draining frames, and tenting frames. Above, ponderous masses of hammered iron, limbs of toiling engines, appear ever and anon to rush to the open window, glance abroad, and then retreat to their dens. On the other hand lies a canal—the Rochdale Canal—a ditch of muddy water, very much like rotten pea soup. Curious, old-fashioned, highly-springing bridges span it. On the further side are tumble-down houses, smouldering edifices, sinking into their foundations of muck and mire—filthy wharfs, littered with dung, and bricks and rubbish-heaps of splintered stones lie along its course. Blacksmiths' forges are established in rickety old tenements, with every pane of glass in their casements long since dashed away. Mean streets, and patches of black waste ground, with mouldering fences and fetid pools, back these wharfs and ruinous forges; and a dingy fringe of second-rate mills, with puffing steam gushes, and everlasting volumes of smoke, shut in the cheerless picture.

Close to this dreary but characteristic street are the Lyceum Factory Schools. The establishment boasts of a News-room and a Library. In the former, a quiet comfortable room, a fair assortment of the London and local journals are taken. The Library is one of three thousand volumes. In the day-time, the children from the neighbouring mills receive there their three hours' modicum of instruction; at night adult classes meet in the same rooms. The children are charged threepence and fourpence a week, according as they remain half the day or the whole day in the school. Adults pay two shillings a quarter for classes, library, reading-room and all. The afternoon studies were proceeding when I entered the noisy room. Before me, ranged with their slates upon benches, or standing round chalked rings on the floor, were some three-score of the little carders and scavengers from the dreary mills of Union-street. A set of more animated dirty faces, and brighter twinkling eyes, you would find nowhere. The little fellows were tolerably ragged, to be sure—and some of them shoeless—but full of life, fun, and devilry. One class were copying, upon their frameless slates, the word "Britannia" chalked upon a large black board. I asked them what was the meaning of Britannia. They looked at each other, shuffled their feet—half-a-dozen were about to speak, when one urchin roared out—"Britannia? Why, to be sure, 'Britannia rules the waves.'" And there was a great laugh at the appositeness of the quotation. Another class were spelling, under the care of an "apprentice teacher," a singularly fine-looking and intelligent boy. The pupils spelt very fairly a variety of dissyllabic and trisyllabic words. A third class were reading a simple account of the discovery of America. The school was not so crowded as usual, because one of the steam-engines in Union-street had broken down.

"And what has the steam-engine to do with it?" I naturally asked.

"Everything," was the reply; "when an engine ceases here everything ceases—there are no wages, no fees, no schools."

Each spinner is obliged by the Factory Act to pay for the education of his piecers and scavengers. The fees are sometimes collected in the mills, but occasionally the boy is entrusted with the amount himself, the consequences of which piece of faith are not unfrequently a day's truant-playing, and a terrific debauch on unripe apples, toffy, and gingerbread. Mr. Clay, the principal master of the Lyceum, informed me that he had great difficulty in instilling anything like a moral sense into the children—particularly as respects lying. They saw no moral degradation in the idea of a falsehood. It was only inconvenient to be found out. The boys, too, were obstinately dirty, and he had often to send them home to wash themselves. In summer he told me that they seldom wore shoes. Mr. Clay is confident that a vast deal is being effected for the factory population by the education now provided for them.

"Do you lose sight of the children when they leave school?" I asked. The answer was cheering—

"No—especially the girls—for they come back so often to the library for books."

Mr. Clay teaches a night adult class. He has grey-haired scholars, and sometimes mothers bring their children. This class had "decidedly increased" since the Ten Hours Bill. The worthy teacher was anxious to impress upon me that the young men and women attending the evening schools were kept very carefully apart. "I sometimes tell the young women that they only come to pick up sweethearts; but I take care that the one set has gone before I dismiss the other."

The Manchester Mechanics' Institution is supported by decidedly a better class than the average of mill operatives—that is to say, by workmen exercising a more skilled species of labour, and by shopmen. In the pianoforte class there are thirty-five pupils, generally trades-people's daughters. The library is a good one. The books principally inquired for are, first, novels and romances; secondly, voyages, travels, and biographies; thirdly, philosophic works. Books in foreign languages are rarely demanded.

Every London publisher knows that Lancashire furnishes no unimportant part of the literary market of England. I was very desirous of ascertaining, therefore, the species of works most in demand amongst the labouring and poorer classes. The libraries in the better parts of the town are of course stocked in much the same way as the libraries in the better parts of London. I wished to ascertain the species of cheap literature most in vogue, and accordingly applied to Mr. Abel Heywood, of Oldham-street, one of the most active and enterprising citizens of Manchester, who supplies not only the smaller booksellers of the town, but those throughout the county, with the cheap works most favoured by the poorer reading classes. The contents of Mr. Heywood's shop are significant. Masses of penny novels and comic song and recitation books are jumbled with sectarian pamphlets and democratic essays. Educational books abound in every variety. Loads of cheap reprints of American authors, seldom or never heard of amid the upper reading classes here, are mingled with editions of the early Puritan divines. Double-columned translations from Sue, Dumas, Sand, Paul Feval, and Frederic Soulie jostle with dream books, scriptural commentaries, Pinnock's Guides, and quantities of cheap music, Sacred Melodists, and Little Warblers. Altogether the literary chaos is very significant of the restless and all devouring literary appetite which it supplies. Infinitely chequered must be the *morale* of the population who devour with equal gusto dubious Memoirs of Lady Hamilton, and authentic narratives of the "Third Appearance of John

Wesley's Ghost," duly setting forth the opinions of that eminent shade upon the recent speeches of Dr. Bunting.

So much for the *primâ facie* aspect of Mr. Heywood's literary warehouse. I was courteously furnished with details of his business, which throw an unquestionable light upon the tastes of the operative reading world of Lancashire.

That species of novel, adorned with woodcuts, and published in penny weekly numbers, claims the foremost place. The contents of these productions are, generally speaking, utterly beneath criticism. They form, so far as I can judge, the English reflection, exaggerated in all its most objectional features, of the French *Feuilleton Roman*. In these weekly instalments of trash Mr. Heywood is compelled to be a large dealer, as will appear from the following statement:—

| | |
|---|---|
| Angelina<br>Almira's Curse<br>Claude Duval<br>Eardley Hall<br>Ella the Outcast<br>Gentleman Jack<br>Gambler's Wife<br>Gallant Tom<br>Lady Hamilton<br>Mazeppa<br>Mildred<br>Old Sanctuary<br>Royal Twins<br>String of Pearls<br>The Brigand<br>The Oath | Average 6,000 weekly sale. All this mass of literary garbage is issued by Lloyd, of London, in penny numbers. |

Of similar works, published also in numbers at 1d. per week, Mr. Heywood sells:—

| | |
|---|---|
| Adam Bell ... ... ... ... | 200 |
| Claude Duval (Dipple) ... ... | 400 |
| Court of London ... ... ... | 1,500 |
| Gretna Green ... ... ... ... | 460 |
| Love Match ... ... ... ... | 750 |
| Mysteries of London ... ... | 1,000 |
| Nell Gwynne ... ... ... ... | 700 |
| Perkin Warbeck ... ... ... | 100 |

Of the penny weekly journals, some of them, such as *Barker's People*, political and democratic, but the greater number social and instructive, the Lancashire sale is:—

| | |
|---|---:|
| Barker's People ... ... ... | 22,000 |
| Reynolds's Miscellany ... ... | 3,700 |
| Illustrated Family Journal ... | 700 |
| London Journal ... ... ... | 9,000 |
| Family Herald ... ... ... ... | 8,000 |
| Home Circle ... ... ... ... | 1,000 |
| Home Journal ... ... ... ... | 1,000 |
| Penny Sunday Times ... ... | 1,000 |
| Lancashire Beacon ... ... ... | 3,000 |
| Plain Speaker ... ... ... ... | 200 |
| Potter's Examiner ... ... ... | 1,500 |
| Penny Punch ... ... ... ... | 360 |
| The Reasoner ... ... ... ... | 160 |
| Chat ... ... ... ... ... | 200 |

Of these publications the *Lancashire Beacon* and the *Reasoner* are avowedly infidel. I have not had an opportunity of seeing the latter, but in the number of the former which I perused, I found nothing more fatal to Christianity than abuse of the Bishop of Manchester. The Lancashire mind is indeed essentially a believing, perhaps an over-believing one. Fanaticism rather than scepticism is the extreme into which it is most likely to hurry. In Ashton-under-Lyne Johanna Southcote's bearded followers still meet under the roof of the New Jerusalem. In remote districts astrologers still watch the influences of the planets; and all quackeries, moral and physical—the remedies of Professor Mesmer or of Professor Holloway—equally find a clear stage and very great favour.

But to return to the cheap book trade of Lancashire. Of the better class of weekly publications, generally selling at 1½d., Mr. Heywood makes the following returns:—

| | |
|---|---:|
| Domestic Journal ... ... ... ... | 600 |
| Eliza Cook's Journal ... ... ... | 1,250 |
| Chambers' Journal ... ... ... ... | 900 |
| Chambers' Information for the People | 1,200 |
| Hogg's Instructor ... ... ... ... | 60 |
| People's Journal ... ... ... ... | 400 |

The cheap double-columned edition of Dickens' and Bulwer's books, sell as follows:—

| | |
|---|---:|
| Dickens ... ... ... ... ... | 250 |
| Bulwer ... ... ... ... ... | 200 |

The sale of *Punch* is 1,200. The *Family Friend* sells 1,500 monthly, at two pence; the *Family Economist*, 5,000 monthly, at one penny.

Mr. Heywood informed me that the sale of cheap books has decidedly not increased in consequence of the Ten Hours Bill. The same assertion was made by another extensive, though a much smaller, bookseller in the vicinity of Garrett-lane. The department of the literary trade which alone seemed to have received any impetus from recent legislation, was the sale of copy books, which improved. The only classification of the purchasers of cheap literature which I found it practicable to make was, that the comic or *soi disant* comic publications were usually patronised by clerks and shopmen, while tales were inquired for by the working classes, commonly so called. It is, indeed, by the links of a story that the operative taste seems to be most bound. For the encouragement of literary speculators, I may add that every cheap book is sure of a sale in Lancashire—*at first.*

At the library of the Mechanics' Institute, and at that of the Ancoats Lyceum, I was informed that the Ten Hours Bill had decidedly made no change in the reading habits of the subscribers.

In educating the poor the workhouses have unfortunately a great part to play—now more, now less, according to the pressure of the times. From the scholars who frequent either small private schools, often held in close, unventilated, and incommodious rooms, and the scholars who resort to the larger and better seminaries, supported by, or in connection with, the great Educational Association, and with local funds—from each and all of these scholars a weekly sum of pence is exacted. The fees of some schools are as low as 2d.; the terms of others, for the more advanced children, mount to 7d. But the pauper can neither have his two-pennyworth nor his seven-pennyworth of learning—those who feed and clothe must teach him, or he grows up a savage in his ignorance. Where manufactures have massed together vast populations so rapidly that the growth of the toiling crowd has far outstripped the decent and healthful accommodation which ought to be provided for it; and where, consequently, operative life is short, and sickness frequent and severe—in such social conditions the extent even of chronic pauperism must be considerable. But besides, the administrators of the Poor-law know well the perpetual crowd of hangers-on, which as it were floats round the skirts of northern industry—a crowd of nondescript composition, the supernumeraries of the cotton-spinning cities—men and women who are content to live by a little labour and a good deal of charity—who pulsate backwards and forwards, as the shades of trade vary, between the work-house and the mill. So, therefore, it happens that great hosts of children are always dependent upon the rate-payers for education as well as food. On the 1st of July, 1848, there lived in the Manchester union 1,206 children under sixteen years of age; in the Salford union 253; in the Chorlton union 255. On the same day there lived in the town, as out-door paupers of the Manchester union, 7,048 children under sixteen years of age; as paupers of the Salford union 3,220; as paupers of the Chorlton union 1,603. This plain statement indicates at once the amount of juvenile pauper ignorance with which the Poor-law administration has to grapple—that of the children resident in the workhouse—and it indicates too, the far greater amount of juvenile pauper ignorance over which the Poor-law administration can exercise little if any control—that of the out-door pauper population. Making the proper deductions for children under a teachable age, it is the opinion of Mr. Browne, the Government inspector of parochial union schools for the North of England, that the number of out-door pauper children receiving "little or no education," is not under 100,000—being ten times the number of the children in the workhouses.

This fact only requires to be plainly and broadly stated. Of course the ignorance of these young English savages is dense and deplorable. The statement of the schoolmaster at the Canal-street Workhouse in Manchester, that only one in twelve of the children who came into that establishment could repeat the Lord's Prayer, proves the fact only in a very modified degree; for the reports of the school inspectors, as to the frequency with which children can prate a form of words compared with the rarity of their understanding the meaning, warrant me in asserting that perhaps not one in twenty-four could give any intelligible account of the meaning of the prayer, or of the source from whence it came.

The children in workhouses throughout the manufacturing districts commonly attend school from nine to twelve o'clock in the forenoon, and from two to half-past four or five in the evening. In some workhouses the school-room is in the building. In others the children go to school beyond the union walls—sometimes to national schools, where "it is possible that the teachers do not always take the same pains" with the young paupers as with the other scholars—sometimes (I am still quoting Mr. Browne's Report for 1847-8) to schools "of a very inferior description, where the teachers are either negligent or incapable." As a general rule Mr. Browne finds the children sent to school out of the workhouse "ignorant and ill instructed." But, indeed, the species of education generally afforded in the workhouse schools is very low and unsatisfactory. In twenty-five workhouses in Mr. Browne's district the teachers were paupers. Occasionally these men and women are neither precisely paupers nor independent persons. They live in the workhouses on the rates, but receive a small salary. Some of these teachers are, as might be expected, grossly incompetent—unable to write a decent hand or to spell an ordinary word. Those who have sunk into the workhouse from a good position, requiring fair educational attainments, are often morally unfit to be entrusted with the rearing of youth. In the Burnley workhouse, the teacher combined the duties of a porter with those of the schoolroom. The mistresses are frequently inefficient. One schoolmistress believed that Saul and Paul were identical; another described the miracles of Christ as having been wrought before Pharaoh. Neither of these persons are now teachers. The position of a workhouse instructor is, however, described as being by no means an enviable one. It is a post of much confinement, of frequent collision with the union authorities, and generally of such a nature that no master who can procure a situation elsewhere will accept it. The schools, therefore, continues Mr. Browne, "are likely to remain stationary when a certain point has been reached—by no means advanced—and below that where education may be expected to make a lasting impression upon the child, and consequently to operate as a check upon pauperism." But, in many instances, ground has yet to be got over before even the lowest educational point—worthy of the name—is attained. For example, in Alston, a boy who had been a scholar for two years, could not tell how many two and three made. In a Durham school, the "only boy who showed any intelligence" believed that there were fourteen hours in the day, and that the sun rose in the west, but did not know the name of the country. At Gateshead a scholar said that Yorkshire was the capital of England. At Sedgefield, in the workhouse school, "none knew the Queen's name nor the capital of England." In Kirkby Moorside, the Queen's name was understood to be "Anna." In the Pickering workhouse school, "our Saviour was stated to have been crucified by order of the Virgin Mary." At Stokesby, "an island was a place where there's no person to see." In Bradford Idle, the last three Gospels were understood to have been written by "Shadrach, Meshach, and Abednego;" and an island was described as "a great city;"

in Kirkham Fylde, it was a "place where nobody lives." In Hasling-
den, none could say in what county they dwelt; and in Preston, by a
most singular confusion of ideas, "prophecy" was defined as "fortune-
telling."

In a great many of the workhouse schools, however, education,
though of a low species, is actually progressing, and the teachers, according to their capacity, strive to do their duty. The larger towns
generally, as might be expected, take the lead, and in these the inspector frequently found competent and intelligent masters and gradually
improving pupils. In many instances the remark is "inefficient, but
promising," and teachers are often spoken of as earnest and pains-
taking. The two great cities of Lancashire support two great pauper
educational establishments, which may in some respects be reckoned
models. Manchester has its Swinton and Liverpool its Kirkdale. In
the infant school attached to the former establishment, the children
could point to Washington and Iceland on the map. They named the
books of the Testament, and understood what a thermometer was. In
the girls' school, five-sevenths of the pupils could read the New Testament. They were also taught to sew, knit, cut out, wash, iron, and mangle. In the boys' school, the reading was "fair," and a "certain standard
of education attained by many," so that "material progress may be expected." The industrial training consisted of tailors' and shoemakers'
work, and clogging, and the general discipline was "excellent." At the
Kirkdale establishment, the boys' school was efficient; but the infant
and girls' schools were less satisfactory, and the progress of the learn-
ers slow. The girls sew and do household work, being out of school
one week in three.

I have endeavoured in the foregoing columns to collect together
at least some portion of the facts which, in surveying the moral and
educational condition of cotton-spinning Lancashire, come most naturally to the surface. I know that beneath that surface there lies dormant a terrible mass of unmoved stolid ignorance, and strongly developed animal passion and instinct. But from the machinery which is at
work, from the ideas which are making way, I believe that that mass
will be, sooner or later, shaken and probed to its inmost depths. Education is but yet opening its trenches and arranging its batteries. The
social and sanitary pioneers which must precede education, have but
just begun in earnest to advance. I believe that we must have a comfortable and a cleanly living people before we have an educated or a
moral people; and, odd as the conjunction may seem, I believe that

neither church nor school will do what each is capable of doing until drains are dug, water laid down, and men's homes are sweetened and purified, and rendered fit not only for the preservation of due physical health, but of due social decency and modest reserve.

# LABOUR AND THE POOR.

———◆———

## THE MANUFACTURING DISTRICTS.

[FROM OUR SPECIAL CORRESPONDENT.]

### ASHTON-UNDER-LYNE.

## LETTER VII.

In selecting the minor cotton towns round Manchester, which I think it my duty to visit, I try to fix upon those which present local peculiarities and distinct social characteristics. In general, indeed, these towns wear a monotonous sameness of aspect, physical and moral. The rates of wages paid are nearly on a par—the prices of the commodities for which they are spent are nearly on a par—the toil of the people at the mills, and their habits and arrangements at home, are all but identical. In fact, the social condition of the different town populations is almost as much alike as the material appearance of the tall chimneys under which they live. Here and there the height of the latter may differ by a few rounds of brick, but, in all essential respects, a description of one is a description of all.

In searching, however, for minor shades of social distinction, I find some two or three characteristics which separate Ashton-under-Lyne from its spinning neighbours—and which may excuse me for making it the main subject of a letter. Ashton is occupied by a "new" population, and, in some respects, it is as much a model cotton-working town as any we have. The nucleus of the place is indeed old, filthy, and dilapidated in the extreme; but nine-tenths of the town owes its existence immediately to the power-loom, and, in nearly all that large proportion, the houses are more comfortable, the streets more open, and better drained than in the great majority of industrial Lancashire towns.

Ashton lies about seven miles from Manchester, and directly "under" the "Lyne" of that long healthy ridge of hills called the "Backbone of England"—a chain which, under the local name of Blackstone Edge, separates Lancaster from York, and then runs northward through Westmorland and Northumberland, until it loses itself among the undulations of the Scottish Cheviots. Ashton is built upon the banks of the Tame, a stream rising in the Yorkshire moors. The country around is level and bleak, the soil marshy and cold. In 1841, the population of the town was 24,000; at present it is over 34,000. The mills about Ashton are very generally the property of large capitalists, who can afford, and often do afford, to employ their people at full hours when a period of temporary slackness in trade obliges those masters whose command of capital is less at once to curtail their producing operations. In this respect Ashton is the reverse of Oldham. In the latter town small capitalists abound. It is not, indeed, uncommon there for several masters to unite to rent a mill, and sometimes to unite to rent even the floor of a mill. These employers conduct their operations in the hand-to-mouth style which naturally follows from such a state of things. They spin, moreover, generally speaking, the coarse and inferior kinds, of thread, and the slightest check in the demand falls at once upon the workman. There is no shield of capital to stand between the humble producer and the immediate fluctuations of the market. From what reason I know not, but no returns of the pauperism of Oldham are given in the last tabular statistics presented by the Somerset House Board to Parliament; but I was informed by Mr. Tipping, the active and very intelligent relieving officer of Ashton, that an estimate had been constructed, showing the relative amount of pauperism at Oldham to be nearly double that at Ashton. The latter union contains a population of 101,000, and includes one or two small hamlets. The amount at present paid by the guardians is about £125 weekly for out-door relief, while there are in the workhouse about 200 inmates. I may add that the locality has been very slightly visited by cholera—only about thirty deaths having taken place throughout the union.

The population of Ashton have the reputation of being turbulent and fanatical. A policeman was killed in a disturbance here lately. The most ultra-political and theological opinions run riot amongst the population. The only manifest opposition which I have observed to the late day of humiliation was in Ashton, where the dead walls were covered with placards denouncing the "Humbug," but adding, and Heaven knows with much truth, that the people want feasts quite as much as fasts. Ashton, too, is still the stronghold of the Southcote faith. A handsome row of grocers' shops, with long-bearded men behind the counters, was pointed out to me as a sort of colony of the people who still hold the strange creed in question. There is a "New

Jerusalem," too, in which the faithful still meet. It is a substantial stone building, with the words, "The Sanctuary of Israel," flanked by two Hebrew mottoes, carved upon the wall. Indeed, what La Vendée was to Louis XVI., Ashton was to Johanna Southcote. Her labourers there mustered sturdiest, strongest. They proposed to enclose the town within a square wall, and actually did build four large houses— three of which are still standing, and which were intended to form the corners of the barrier. The chief disciple in Ashton was a Mr. Wroe. He established a "Treasury of the Lord," constituted himself the treasurer, and supplies poured in fast from those who wished to have an investment at once in earth and Heaven. Many families were thus ruined at Ashton. At length the leader of the sect, having fallen into bad odour with his brethren, was tried in the New Jerusalem, whither repaired the chief man of the congregation, armed with a horsewhip. Before the reading of the list of imputed iniquities was half over, the accused tried to bolt out of the chapel. The denouncer followed his pastor, whip in hand; but Wroe having partisans, his pursuer was seized, a battle royal ensued, pews and seats were splintered, beards torn out by handfuls, and at length the police were obliged to clear the New Jerusalem. Notwithstanding the scandal of such events, the Faith was not overturned, and, as I have hinted, the flowing beard of a "Johanna," as a disciple is called in Ashton, is still very common in the streets.

In Ashton, too, there lingers on a handful of miserable old men, the remnants of the cotton hand-loom weavers. No young persons think of pursuing such an occupation—the few who practise it were too old and confirmed in old habits, when the power-loom was introduced, to be able to learn a new way of making their bread. The Ashton hand-loom weavers live, almost to a man, in the old, filthy, and undrained parts of the town. I begged Mr. Tipping, the relieving-officer, who was good enough to be my cicerone, to enable me to see what he would consider a fair specimen of the class. We repaired, therefore, to one of the oldest portions of the place, called Charleston. The streets thereabouts were filthy and mean, the houses crumbling, crazy, and dirty. We threaded a labyrinth of noisome courts and small airless squares, formed generally of houses of a fair size, but miserably out of repair, slatternly women lounging about the thresholds; and neglected, dirty-faced children sprawling and roaring in the gutters. The door of one of these houses stood open, showing a steep, dark staircase, black with mud. The plaster had fallen in lumps from the wall, showing the lath beneath, and the coating which remained seemed covered with a dark greasy slime. Up this staircase we proceeded, and at the top turned into a bare room, the picture of squalid desolation. The chamber was a large one, but hardly an article did it contain which could be by courtesy denominated furniture. The principal objects were the loom and the bed. The latter had, to my eye, the appearance of a large square frame about seven feet long, and at least four broad, filled with sacking, upon which lay a single blanket recently given by the workhouse, and a chaos of miserable articles of dress—bundles of rags, in fact, which appeared to be used as additional coverings. Upon lines stretching across the room hung tattered morsels of under-clothing. There were one small round deal table and two or three broken old chairs, but the whole place was littered with an indescribable chaos of dirty odds and ends, bits of broken pewter spoons, fragments of plates—here a rusty old breakfast knife, there a dry blacking-bottle, there a strip of stained and torn calico. On a low chair, by the small fire, sat a woman, looking one bundle of dingy tatters, bending over the hearth, and busily employed in some job of needlework, while she rocked herself to and fro to lull the child which clung to her bosom. Another child was sprawling on the floor, playing with a large brown and white rabbit, which scampered about the place, frisking among the treddles of the loom. By the latter stood the weaver. He was a gaunt, big-boned man, with a stony glare in his eyes, and a rigid unimpassioned looking face, on which was stamped the most unequivocal marks of a stolid, hopeless, apathetic despair. The man was preparing hanks from which to produce a mingled web of linen and wool. He went about it like one half torpid, and who works from mere instinct, without energy and without hope.

I asked him what were his usual wages?

"Not five shilling a week."

"Your trade is a bad one now?"

He made no reply for a moment, but presently said, in a low drawling tone, and with a sort of strange smile on his face, as if he enjoyed the recital of the very hopelessness of his condition—

"Look here—I'll have to weave eighty yards of cloth in this piece. It will take me eight or nine days, and I shall have seven shillings for it. I walked to Manchester and back to the master's to fetch the yarn, and I shall walk there and back with the cloth when I am paid."

Here was a journey on foot amounting to nearly thirty miles, and nine days' work at the loom, for seven shillings!

The family consisted of four. They all slept together in the bed of sacking and rags. The rent of the room was one shilling per week, which the parish paid. Some of the hand-loom weavers are better off, because they have sons and daughters who work in the mills; but, taken all together, they are a wretched and hopeless set. Potatoes and bread, with a little miserably weak tea, form, of course, the only articles of nutriment which they ever taste.

The trade of the hatter was once a flourishing one both in Manchester and Ashton, but owing to the demand for silk hats instead of beavers, the occupation is now at a low ebb, and hundreds to whom it once afforded subsistence have enlisted in the army. We went from the old hand-loom weaver's to the house of a man who had been a beaver hatter, but who now gained his bread by winding silk for the construction of the new style of hats. The house was in a muddy lane, half the dwellings of which were ruinous and uninhabited. We found the husband presiding at a winding apparatus, which his son, a boy of five years of age, turned. The room in which the machine was bestowed, opened from the kitchen and sitting chamber. The aspect of things here was much brighter than at the last house. The man used to earn at his old trade 5s. or 6s. a day. He now earned, one week with another, 12s. Some days he made 3s., some days 2s., but he had often to "clem"* for want of work. However, as I have said, his average earnings were 12s. a week. It is his house I wish principally to notice. It was a sort of compromise between a house, properly so called, and a cellar. The lane without was undrained and unpaved, and the mud lay more than ankle deep all along it. From this vile thoroughfare you entered the house by a door, certainly not two feet in width, and down a high step, which brought the stone-flagged floor a good eighteen inches beneath the level of the lane. The consequence was, that the place was reeking with damp. There was tolerably decent furniture—a clock and other little matters; but the air of both the rooms had that wet earthy smell peculiar to underground places—and the moisture welling up marked with obvious stains the outlines of the flagstones which formed the floor. For this house the occupant paid £5 a year. It was an unwholesome place, he said, but he could not get sufficiently beforehand with the world to move to a better. The wife told me that she had never had a day's health since they lived there. Nothing but

---

* The authoress of "Mary Barton" thus explains the word, and illustrates its antiquity:—*Clem,* to starve with hunger. "Hard is the choice when the valiant must eat their arms, or *clem.*"—Ben Jonson.

coughs and colds that she could not get rid of, and asthma settling on her chest. The poor woman was evidently in a critical pulmonary state. The wet cold air was killing her.

There are very few weavers out of work at Ashton, but I desired my guide to take me to the house of one. It was situated—I am still talking of the old part of Ashton—in a sort of broad *cul de sac*, so broad that it might almost be called a square. There may have been altogether thirty or forty houses composing it; and near one end of the open space was situated a great ash-pit and three or four privies, common to all the inhabitants, and ingeniously placed so as to be by far the most conspicuous objects in the place. In the low room of the house which we entered, two men, father and son, one of them in the prime of life, the other perhaps between sixty and seventy, were seated on either side of the hearth, listlessly peeling potatoes. On a small table beside them were the remains of breakfast—a coffee-pot, a dirty cup or two, and a filthy pewter spoon. The younger man had been sixteen weeks out of work. He looked wretchedly ill and languid; indeed, as he said, he had never been well since he was "down with the cholera." His wife was working in a mill. She earned about 9s. a week. He had been flung out of work owing to his having refused to submit to what he considered an unjust abatement of 5s. There was nothing absolutely squalid in the appearance of the room. Its worst feature was the listless, soddened look of the two men as they pursued their unfitting household toil. The old man had 2s. a week from the union, and went errands, or did any such odd job as he could obtain. The family amounted in all to seven.

At the dinner hour, in a cotton town, you have always ample opportunity for catching the general characteristics of the appearance of the population. "You can take stock of the workpeople," as a mill-owner phrased it to me, when they come flocking out of the factories. The appearance of the Ashton operatives is, I think, on the whole, superior to that of their Manchester brethren, and more akin to that of the population of the country mills. It may have been that my visit being on a Monday had something to do with the matter; but certainly the operatives, especially the women and girls, looked very much cleaner, both in skin and clothes, than the spinners and weavers of Manchester. Most of the girls wore necklaces of some sort—generally imitation coral, and both men and boys almost universally rejoiced in a species of round white felt hats, in Manchester called "wide awakes," and here dignified by the curious title of "bobbin nudgers."

The system of the millowners building and letting out comfortable cottages to their workpeople prevails as much, or even more, in Ashton than in any town in Lancashire. It is common, particularly in the outskirts, to see every mill surrounded with neat streets of perfectly uniform dwellings, clean and cheerful in appearance, and occupied by the "hands." The first of these snug little colonies to which we went was that attached to the mills of Messrs. Buckley. Here are ranged in rows and squares, some of them with gardens attached, a little town of dwellings, regularly planned, and each house let, according to the number of rooms which it contains, at 3s., 3s. 9d., and 4s. 6d. If a garden be attached, a few shillings annually are charged in addition. The Messrs. Buckley, I am informed, live among their people, and are in the habit of familiar intercourse with them—facts which operate as very great checks upon drunkenness and all sorts of disorderly behaviour. "If a master," says Mr. Tipping, "never puts eyes on a man from Saturday till Monday, he may be drunk all that time with impunity; but here any conduct of the kind can't fail to be noticed, and so the man at once gets a hint that if he doesn't mend his manners he may look out for other employment." "Such a thing as an application for parish relief from the people hereabouts," Mr. Tipping added, "is scarcely ever heard of." The cottage gardens were, when I visited them, one and all fluttering with linen drying upon lines and hedges.

We afterwards proceeded to visit a street of cottages, erected by the Messrs. Kershaw, for their people. The outer doors led at once into the sitting rooms—a style of building which I was sorry to see persevered in. Otherwise the houses were all that could be desired. The floors were paved with flag stones, but perfectly free from moisture, and generally sprinkled with white glistening sand. In each there was a parlour, a kitchen opening from it, and a yard and proper conveniences behind. The kitchen grate was furnished with a good range, including an oven and an ample boiler; and water from a neighbouring spring was laid on, with a sink and all its due apparatus. There were two bed-rooms up stairs. For a house of this kind 3s. 6d. per week was charged. The rent used to be 3s., the tenants paying the local rates; but the change has lately been made with their full concurrence. In the first house which I entered I found a respectable-looking woman, a widow. She was peeling potatoes for dinner. Two of her sons worked in the mill—one was a spinner, the other a piecer under him. The first earned 25s., the second 7s. a week. In many of the houses in this row, I was very glad to perceive an apparatus for converting yarn into hank, which was worked by the wife at home. A good hand could, I was informed, make 10s. a-week at this process, and I was assured that a woman could easily earn 4s., and have, at the same time, ample leisure for attending to her household duties and taking care of her children.

The last mill cottages which I visited were those built by the Messrs. Mason and Sons. The first thing which these gentlemen did, in laying out the ground, was to spend £1,000 in drainage, by which the refuse from every house is carried down into the river. The cottages are of two kinds—four and six roomed. For the former, 3s. per week is charged; for the latter, 4s. 3d. per week. The inhabitants of the better class of houses are, therefore, voters. I inspected one of the four-roomed class. There was a lobby, and the stairs leading to the bedrooms were nicely carpeted. The front room was furnished strictly as a parlour; but the back one, or kitchen, which opened into a flagged yard, was obviously the ordinary sitting room.

I went over two mills in Ashton—one, working ten hours, that of the Messrs. Redfern; the other, working twelve, that of the Messrs. Mason and Sons. In both of these factories I was encouraged to examine the people upon any points I pleased. The results of my conversations with them I shall detail in my letter upon the Ten Hours Bill. The manager at Messrs. Redfern's factory told me that one of the women, whom I had at random selected for examination from the weaving shed, was worth more than £100. At the Messrs. Mason's I was furnished with a note of the wages weekly paid to the different classes of spinners in their employment, giving an average of more than £2 2s. to each spinner, and a general average for adults, in all the branches of employment, including skilled and unskilled labour, of £1 2s. 5d. It must be distinctly observed, however, that piecers are not included in the calculation. The Messrs. Mason work twelve hours, but employ no relays of children or women. They find it quite practicable to carry on the business of a great cotton-spinning establishment for two hours a day with the help only of adult males—a fact to which it is important that its due weight should be attached.

I have before alluded to the sporting propensities of the hand-loom weavers. I learn that, in better times, the same spirit actuated the cotton, flax, and woollen hand-loom weavers of Ashton. There is, or used to be, a capital pack of harriers kept in the vicinity, and the Ashton weavers, armed with huge leaping-sticks, by the help of which they could take hedges and ditches as well as the boldest rider of the hunt, were usual attendants on the pack. The mill system has, however, utterly extirpated every vestige of the ancient sporting spirit. The regularity of hours and discipline preserved seem, by rendering any such *escapades* out of the question, to have at length obliterated everything like a desire for, or idea of, them. The taste for botany, common to the district, seems, however, nearly as strong in Ashton as in Manchester. I observed a public-house, kept by an enthusiast in the science, called the "Botanical Tavern."

Taking leave of Ashton for the present, let me try to describe a curiously characteristic place of amusement which I visited the other day in Manchester. I was anxious to see and judge of for myself one of the music saloons, of which I had heard so much, and so, ascertaining that the Apollo in the London-road presented a very good specimen, I waited until Saturday night should exhibit it in its greatest glory, and then set off for the hall of jollity and harmony. The London-road, on Saturday night, has very much the appearance of Tottenham-court-road, in the metropolis; at the same period of the week. It is full of cheap shops, devoted to the sale of ordinary household matters. Stalls, covered and uncovered, heaped over with still coarser and cheaper wares, abound. Gas flares and blazes amid the joints in the butchers' open shops. Faintly burning candles, enclosed in greasy paper lanterns, cast their dim and tallowy influence over tables slimy with cheap fish, or costermongers' barrows littered with cabbages or apples. The gin-shops are in full feather—their swinging doors never hang a moment still. Itinerant bands blow and bang their loudest; organ boys grind monotonously; ballad singers or flying stationers make roaring proclamations of their wares—the Mannings forming last Saturday evening the burden of their lays. The street is one swarming, buzzing mass of people. Boys and girls shout and laugh, and disappear into the taverns together. Careful housewives—often attended by their husbands, dutifully carrying the baby—bargain hard with the butchers for a halfpenny off in the pound. In a cheap draper's shop, a committee of young women will be examining into the merits of a dress which one of them has determined to buy; while, in an underground pie-shop, a select party of juveniles will be regaling themselves upon musty pasties of fat pork. The pawnbroker is busy, for pledges are being rapidly redeemed, and flat irons, dirty pairs of stays, candlesticks, Sunday trowsers, tools, blankets, and so forth, are fast being removed from his shelves. The baker has chalked on a black board, in his boldest characters, "Down again to even money—a four-pound loaf for fivepence!" Here a woman is anxiously attempting—half to drive, half to lure home her drunken husband; there a couple of tipsy fellows are in high dispute, their tobacco pipes in their hands, and a noisy circle of backers urging them on. From byways, and alleys, and back streets, fresh crowds every moment emerge. Stalls, shops, cellars are clustered round with critics or purchasers—cabmen drive slowly through the throng, shouting and swearing to the people to get out of the horse's way; and occasionally, perhaps, the melodious burst of a roaring chorus, surging out of the open windows of the Apollo, resounds loudly above the whole conglomeration of street noises.

A bright lamp over an open door points out the entrance to lovers of harmony and beer. Here there is a check-taker, helped, and no doubt superintended, by a policeman, who will not allow drunken people to pass. An intimation stares you in the face that, in order to "keep the company select," a charge of twopence is made, on the payment of which a ticket will be given, entitling the bearer to twopennyworth of refreshment up stairs. Having complied with the terms of this reasonable proposition, you mount a broad steep staircase, and presently find yourself at the extremity of a long narrow room. On the occasion of my first appearance on the scene, the place was densely crowded by men and women, and the air was one rolling volume of tobacco smoke. I thought that to obtain a seat was out of the question, but a bustling personage, whom I soon found to be the landlord, was very busy packing away his guests into the smallest possible compass; and, at length, he accommodated me with six inches of a bench, and about two square inches of a table on which to place the tumbler of porter—and not bad it was—to which my twopenny coupon entitled me. I have said that the room was long and narrow. The walls were covered with paper representing carved woodwork. About midway on one side was a small bar, where the landlady was drawing ale and beer, the only liquors for which the house was licensed. Along the length of the apartment ran curiously narrow tables, with benches on either side, placed so close to each other, and occupied by such a dense swarm of people as to make it all but impossible for the female waiters to hand the malt liquor about, and accordingly the tumblers were often passed along from hand to hand. At the upper end of the place was a curiously small stage, with a regular proscenium, built *secundem artem*, but so low that the performers' heads almost touched the "flies." Upon the stage was what is technically called a "set scene" of a cottage and a landscape. Beneath was an orchestra, consisting of two or three fiddles and a pianoforte. Of the audience, two-thirds might be men, the others were women—young and old—a few of them with their children seated in their laps, and several with babies at their breasts. The class of the assembly was that of artisans and mill-hands. Almost without an exception, men and women were decently dressed, and it was quite evident that several of the groups formed family parties. When I entered, a man, dressed in the conventional "nigger" costume, was singing one of those really pretty airs which have of late gained such popular renown, and singing it, too, with more feeling for the melody and less regard for the slang part of the business than are generally exhibited by London performers of a similar class. The audience joined in the chorus *con amore*, so that, just as I entered, nearly two hundred voices, male and female, were entreating Susanna not to cry for the minstrel who was "going to Alabama with his banjo on his knee."

I stayed nearly an hour, heard half-a-dozen songs, and witnessed a couple of dances. The former were chiefly of that class happily characterized by Mr. Thackeray as the "British Brandy-and-Water School." One of the whole number was objectionable, from its double *entendres*, but it was vehemently applauded and uproariously enjoyed. The only female performer was a little girl about twelve, who sang a "Medley song," and danced a *pas* to correspond. The other saltatory artist was a young man who, dressed as a soldier, went through a sort of parody of the manual exercise, and then, swinging round, exhibited himself with a mask tied to the back of his head, and his rear "made up" for the front of a theatrical sailor, in which character he performed a most energetic hornpipe.

"He's a clever chap, is that," said a little dirty-faced man to me.

"Indeed!"

"Aye, is he. Why, sir, he works in factory with me."

There was no answering such conclusive criticism. I asked the connoisseur whether the other performers were also factory hands? No; they were all mere "arteests," save the hornpipe man. So far as I saw, the company were quite as decorous as could be expected for a convivial assemblage of their rank. There was plenty of loud speaking, and now and then coarse speaking; but there was nobody drunk—an assertion which, however, I fear would hardly stand good a couple of hours afterwards; while the only person who seemed inclined to be riotous and unruly was a middle-aged woman who had taken more porter than was good for her; and, what appeared to me worse, was successfully encouraging two young girls, whom she had brought with her, to do the same—vehemently expressing all the time her admiration at the masculine beauties of the bass singer, and repeatedly demanding (with reference to the gentleman in question) whether I had "ever seen such a lovely nose on a face?"

Another evening I went to a favourite musical place in another part of the town, at the corner of the Oldham-road. Unhappily I had mistaken the harmonic night; but the landlord, to whom I explained my business, showed me the curious arrangements by means of which he manages to have the same performance in two rooms at once. There are two spacious apartments directly over each other. The floor of the upper, and the ceiling of the lower, are perforated with a great square aperture like a hatchway in a deck. This vast trap can be covered or revealed by two flaps, which, when they are lifted, are secured back to back in the centre. In the upper room, upon a little platform on the brink of the gulf, the vocal performers stand, so as to be seen by all the audience in their own room, and by about one-half of those in the lower room, in which again, just beneath the feet of the artists, is placed an extremely handsome barrel organ, the front consisting of plate glass, and exhibiting its musical snuff-box-like machinery, and which can be seen by all the guests in the lower room and a few of those in the higher room. Thus the musical attractions are made as impartial as possible. The organ cost £194. The landlord wound it up for my benefit, and it went off with good effect into the overture of *William Tell*.

On my way home that night, I looked into two additional places of popular amusement. One was a sleight-of-hand exhibition in a small room up a rickety flight of stairs. The charge was 2d., and the benches were occupied principally by young men and women, evidently mill-hands. One boy, not above sixteen, sat between two girls, with an arm round each of their necks; while the Sultanas, who were evidently jealous, exchanged scowling glances as they cracked the hazel nuts which all three were occupied in demolishing. The others of the company sat quietly enough. There were two elderly women, in faded shawls and limp bonnets, gravely discussing how the magical tricks were performed. Near them sat two young women, nursery maids apparently, with young children on their knees, and a sprinkling of grown-up men, with folded-up carpenters' rules protruding from their pockets, and bespeaking their occupation, formed a party of their own. There was music, in the shape of a flageolet and fife, blown by two men seated at the end of the audience benches, while a lout of a boy in shoes, with wooden soles an inch thick, danced a Lancashire clog hornpipe, keeping up a monotonous rattle with his wooden-shod feet. At first I looked upon the young gentleman as an amateur, his performance being conducted in the audience part of the room; but, from the unvarying clatter which he produced during any interval between the sleight-of-hand, I found he was one of the *artistes* of the establishment.

The last place of "amusement" which I visited was a gratis concert-room, but frequented by a better class than the attendants at the Apollo, many of the persons present being evidently mechanics from the neighbouring Atlas Iron Works. There were also women in the room, all of them apparently, in their own fashion, respectable. The room was a comfortable one, with oil paintings, one representing the Vale of Tempe "in Italy." There was a piano and some wretched sentimental singing, during which the *habituées* grimly smoked and drank their spirits and water. I soon beat a retreat from such dull quarters.

# LABOUR AND THE POOR.

◆

## THE MANUFACTURING DISTRICTS.

[FROM OUR SPECIAL CORRESPONDENT.]

### OLDHAM, AND THE LOW LODGING-HOUSES OF MANCHESTER.

### Letter VIII.

In this letter I shall give an account of the operatives of Oldham, in so far as they seem to differ from the average cotton population of Manchester and the surrounding towns. In Oldham, as I have stated in a previous letter, there are a great number of small capitalists renting floors or small portions of factories. These employers have themselves generally risen from the mule or the loom, and maintain in a great degree their operative appearance, thoughts, and habits. In Oldham, many of the coarser operations performed upon the coarsest sorts of cotton are carried on—numerous mills are "spinning waste" as it is called—that is, working up for the commonest purposes the material rejected as refuse by the factories engaged in producing the finer and medium degrees of goods. The stuff subjected to the operation of these Oldham mills, immortalized by Mr. Ferrand as "Shoddy" and "Devil's dust," is specially produced in its manufacture. Those helots called the "Low Irish" are to be found in considerable numbers at Oldham, and I shall shortly describe their homes and haunts. Then, proceeding back to Manchester, I shall entreat the reader's company into some of the districts inhabited by the exceptional population of the great cotton city—into the cellars and lodging-houses occupied by cadgers, thieves, and nondescript outcasts of all kinds.

The visitor to Oldham will find it essentially a mean-looking straggling town, built upon both sides and crowning the ridge of one of the outlying spurs which branch from the neighbouring "backbone of England." The whole place has a shabby underdone look. The general appearance of the operatives' houses is filthy and smouldering. Airless little back streets and close nasty courts are common; pieces of dismal waste ground—all covered with wreaths of mud and piles of blackened brick and rubbish—separate the mills, which are often of small dimensions and confined and crowded appearance. The shops cannot be complimented, the few hotels are no better than taverns, and altogether the place, to borrow a musical simile, seems far under concert pitch. I observed, as I walked up from the railway station, melancholy clusters of gaunt, dirty, unshorn men, lounging on the pavement. These, I heard, were principally hatters, a vast number of whom are out of employment. Another feature of the place was the quantity of dogs of all kinds which abounded—dog-races and dog-fights being both common among the lowest orders of the inhabitants.

The union of Oldham includes eight townships, and comprises a population of about 85,000 souls, 50,000 of whom actually live in the town itself. The operations of the union only commenced in 1847. During that year as much as £262 was spent in out-door relief in a week. The amount at present paid is about £112 per week for out-door relief, and there are about 450 paupers in the workhouse, which is, however, very inadequate to the wants of the population. The union is often obliged to pay for beds at common lodging-houses for the vagrants and destitute tramps whom they cannot take into the house. The acreage of the union is 11,000, and, like the neighbouring district of Ashton, it has escaped with about thirty fatal cases of cholera.

One of my first cares was to ascertain, so far as I could, the difference in the tone of relationship subsisting between the class of operative capitalists in Oldham and the workpeople, as compared with that existing between the mill hands and the larger and more assuming capitalists of greater towns. This is exactly one of those delicate social points with reference to which the passing visitor is compelled to seek for information at second hand. The particulars which I received from the different sources to which I applied differed widely. By two or three intelligent persons, life-long residents in Oldham, I was assured that the class of operative-employers were by far the most popular with the mill hands. "These masters," I was informed, "are just the same as if they were the fellow workmen of those they employ. They dress much in the same way, they live much in the same way, their habits and language are almost identical, and when they 'get on the spree' they go and drink and sing in low taverns with their own working hands." I inquired in what sort of houses these masters lived? "In houses a little better and larger than the common dwellings, but managed inside very much in the same way." "Do they educate their sons as gentlemen?" "They seldom do. They may give them a better education than the sons of common men; but they wish them to supply their own places, and to be just like what they themselves are." My informants added, that although masters and men often caroused together, yet, on occasions of difference arising between them, the masters would get dreadfully abusive, and terribly bad blood would ensue. This latter piece of information, as well as a little experience of human nature, inclined me rather to credit the opposite view, urged among others by Mr. Clegg, the courteous clerk to the union, that the larger capitalists, the men who had not themselves been operatives in the memory of the existing generation, were the class of millowners most generally and most continuously popular:—

"Their establishments are the larger and the better regulated. The work there is more regular, the rooms often better ventilated and more pleasant, and all sorts of minor conveniences for washing, shifting clothes, &c., better ordered than in the smaller mills."

Oldham is tolerably well supplied with water, by means of pipes, from the adjoining hills. Most of the springs in the town have been dried up by the coal mines hitting the same strata as those in which the water runs. The pit population are generally reckoned inferior, morally and intellectually, to the mill population. The wages of the former have materially suffered from the Ten Hours Bill, the factory engines not requiring the same amount of fuel. The wages earned by a good pitman at present cannot exceed, if it amounts to, a guinea a week. In this district the women never work, and never have worked, in the collieries.

Under the guidance of two intelligent relieving officers, I set out to see some of the characteristic manufactures and some of the characteristic population of the place. It was about noon, and the people were pouring out from the mills on their way home to dinner. I observed that the women almost universally wore silk bandanna handkerchiefs fluttering round their heads. "It has always been so in Oldham," I was informed. "They would pinch hard rather than go with a plain cap instead of a silk handkerchief." Presently I overtook two little girls, the eldest not above eight years of age, each carrying a baby some three or four months old in pick-a-back fashion, the infant being snugly enough wrapped up, and only its head protruding from beneath the cloak of its bearer. These girls, I was informed, were nurses, paid for taking charge of the children while their mothers laboured in the mills. I accosted them.

"So, you have these children to nurse? What do the mothers pay you?"

"Oh, please sir, they pay us 1s. 6d. a week for each baby."

"And where are you taking them now?"

"Oh, please sir, to their mothers. They come out of the mills now, and we carry the babies down to meet them, and the mothers give them suck, when they're at dinner."

"And so you take the babies in the morning, and nurse them all day till dinner-time, and then take them to their mothers, and then fetch them back, and at last take them home at night?"

"Yes, sir, that's what we do; but sometimes, you know, the babies have little sisters, as old as us, and then they are nursed at home."

The first manufacturing process which we saw was the cleaning of "shoddy." Unlike any stage of the preparation of cotton which I had seen, this was carried on in an isolated building, situated in the midst of a piece of doleful-looking waste ground. There was a small steam-engine at one extremity, which turned five or six "devils," or coarse and primitive-looking blowing machines, each being placed in a compartment of its own, somewhat like the stall of a stable, and attended by a single guardian, whose business it was to feed the machine with handfuls of the coarse dirty cotton. The door was in each case open, or the dust and flying fibres from the machine would have rendered the air unbreathable. As it was, I could not but pity the gaunt-looking men who tended the devils. I questioned them, but they seemed loath to complain, admitting, however, that the flying "dust and stuff" gave them pains in the chest and terrible hacking coughs and asthma. One of them only remarked, "we don't get old men, sir, at this work." They were paid from 8s. to 12s. per week. The refuse of each devil was consigned to the next coarser machine. The products of the better sort of machines are wrought up into quilts and coarse sheeting; those of the next coarser kind are worked into a coarse paper; from those of the third coarser kind are spun candlewicks; the product of the lowest sort of devils is the material with which flock beds are stuffed; and the refuse from these, heaps of oily seeds and broken and tangled fibres, inseparably mashed up with dirt, is sold for manure. Each shed or stall in this concern was let out for £25 a year, the landlord finding the motive power. The engine spun ceaselessly on; and the asthmatic labourers, each in his stall, between a heap of impure cotton and the whirling devil, pursued amid the dense and fibre-laden air, his monotonous and unwholesome toil.

From thence we went to visit two factories, in one of which are spun very coarse threads, intended for the Indian market, and in the other of which are manufactured candlewicks. The proprietors of both politely accompanied me in my rounds. They had been working men, and were, in language, manner, and dress, very much akin to the people they employed. In the coarse spinning mill—a small airless building—I found an apparently chronic system of dirt and neglect prevailing. The stairs were ricketty and filth-encrusted, and the drawing and spinning rooms not only hot, but what is much worse, chokey, and stifling, and reeking with oil. The women employed exhibited, in a palpably exaggerated degree, the unwholesome characteristics of the appearance of the Manchester mill-workers. They were not so much sallow or pale, as absolutely yellow, and their leanness amounted to something unpleasant to look at. The mill was of the old construction, and had no means of ventilation. The wages of the people ranged a shilling or two beneath the average of the medium Manchester rate.

From this place I had but a few paces to walk, partially through narrow courts and by a ricketty, wooden bridge over a green pool of stagnant water, to the mill where candlewicks were manufactured. The establishment consisted of but a single room, not more than six feet high. Here the cotton refuse used was cleaned, drawn, and spun. The heat, the stink, the flying dust were almost overpowering. At one end of the room stood a blowing machine of the rudest construction, and the mules and drawing frames were built to correspond. The boy who principally attended the "devil" was covered from head to foot with the clinging fibres of floating wool. I exaggerate not one jot—on the contrary, I use the metaphor simply to describe the fact—when I say that the outline of his figure was clothed as it were with a halo of downy tissue. From this the state of the atmosphere may be imagined. The labour of the piecers was the most severe I have yet seen. The coarse knotty threads were continually breaking, and the attendants were therefore eternally hurrying about reuniting them. The different pieces of mechanism were so very closely crammed that it was difficult to walk between them, without the risk of being injured by the unboxed wheels and cranks which worked around. The floor was soppy with the rankest oil; the small windows were almost obscured by coatings of woolly fibre which clung to the interior of the casements, as snow sometimes does to the exterior of panes and sashes; and the bare joists and rafters were furred with the same downy-like substance, as stakes set in the sea are clothed with clustering weeds.

Altogether the place was unfitted for human beings to work or breathe in. When you looked through the beams, and flying straps, and revolving wheels, you saw the toiling slatternly workpeople as through a fog of fibry dust and floating cotton particles. I asked the principal spinner which he preferred, the Ten Hours Bill or the twelve, and he gave his vote unhesitatingly for the latter: "Couldn't afford to do with ten hours wages." The mill, however, if I remember right, only works ten hours a day. The wages of the spinners ranged from 9s. to 11s. per week.

I afterwards went over two small mills, compartments of which are rented by different individuals. Both were dirty, and constructed in the old-fashioned unventilated style. The workpeople looked more gaunt, yellow, and slatternly than they are in the average of factories; but I saw nothing calling for any special notice, over and above what I have said of the coarse spinning mill already alluded to. The candlewick making establishment was, out of all sight, the most repulsive working place I have seen in Lancashire.

Understanding that here and there, scattered in cellars or perched in garrets, were a few old men who still wove cotton by the hand-loom, I requested to be introduced to one of the practitioners of this fast expiring trade. We accordingly descended a narrow flight of area steps, leading beneath the surface of a mean back street, and discovered two stone-paved rooms, dark and squalid; one of which served for the common apartment; the other, a mere closet, was almost entirely occupied by one of the old-fashioned treddle looms. In the first room was some coarse deal furniture, and one of those low broad beds raised about a foot above the floor, and covered with truckle, which by their shape generally appear intended for accommodating at a pinch perhaps four persons. Two dirty children were lying fighting and squalling upon the floor. The woman of the house was a sturdy dame of some sixty years. The man, who was at his work, had a gaunt, skeleton-like face and head, and thin white hair. By way of beginning the conversation, I remarked that the "pegging stick" which he had just laid down—that is, the stick used to jerk the shuttle—was beautifully constructed. I had never seen such another. It was fluted and wreathed, exactly suiting the grasp of the fingers and thumb, "Constructed!" said the weaver—"constructed, indeed! Why, man, I did that myself. I wore them hollow bits in the hard wood with my own flesh, in the long working days of fifteen years. I aye loved to weave better nor to play in the road. I've not been an idle man, sir."

I asked what he paid for his rooms? The rent for the two was 1s. 9d. a week. What were his wages? He was old, and soom'mut failed now, and with his wife to wind for him, he could only get 4s., work as hard as he might. They had parish assistance, however; and, besides, his daughter worked at factory. Those were her children I had seen in the other room.

"By the way," said one of my companions to the old woman, who now joined us, "has your daughter affiliated that last child of hers yet?" The parents did not think she had.

"So the children are illegitimate?" I observed.

"Yes," said their grandmother. "You see they're by different fathers, and she (the daughter) don't know which she would be happiest wi', and so she don't marry nyether."

The old man took the opportunity of observing quietly that, for himself, he did not trouble his head about them things, and that young people would be young people. Very soon after these naïve declarations, both the old people began to boast of the excellence of their bringing up, and their regular attendance at church. I inquired into their domestic arrangements more particularly. The daughter fed herself and her two children, and paid her parents some trifling sum a week for lodging and attending to the children while she was at the mill. I tried to get at the literal particulars, but there were so many charges and counter charges, and deductions and sets off, of pennies and twopences, that I gave up the financial part of the business in despair. They seldom or ever saw meat, but lived on oat-cake, potatoes, porridge, and a little coffee; a pitcher of dark-looking liquid, which stood upon the table by the loom, held treacle beer, a sickly tasting stuff. The man said that even if he could get meat his stomach was so feeble he could not digest it. He lived upon slops. His trade, he began to tell me, was a thriving one in his young days. "When old George III. was king, he could make £2 2s. a week easy. Twenty years ago he could make 20s. Now, without the parish, he would starve. He thought that altogether the people who worked in factories made nearly as much, taking them in families, as they could have done in the old time before the power-loom. But they spent the money in drink, instead of laying it by. They went much too often to the 'hush houses' (low beer-shops, frequently unlicensed). Also the young men had pigeon matches and dog fights, and gambling and drinking on the Lord's-day. Indeed, last Sabbath morn he had been awakened by the whole family in the next cellar fighting together." I had some difficulty in getting a reply to the question—whether the working people altogether lived upon as good food and had as much of it as when he was a boy? At length he said, after much pondering, that he thought the people now-a-days "lived full as well."

From the old weaver's cellar we went to visit some similar dwellings, situated in a group of close undrained and unpaved courts. These were occupied almost entirely by elderly women, who made precarious livings as laundresses. Several of these cellars, though miserably poor, were kept beautifully clean, and the little ornaments and paltry pictures ranged about the walls often showed a touching struggle between pinching poverty and a decent desire to keep up appearances. One cellar was, however, of a different stamp. We approached it along a foul subterraneous passage, and, on opening the door, a stench so abominable burst forth, that even my companions, accustomed to scenes of want and filth, recoiled, and called to the people in the room to open the single swinging pane in a window of about six—each pane being about four inches by three—looking out into a sort of slit rather than pit, dug down to the level of the window sill from a back court. The place was almost dark. It contained three low beds, covered with ragged, unmade wisps of bed clothes. A woman and a little girl sat upon stools cowering over a morsel of fire, and drinking tea, or some decoction which passed as such. In one of the beds lay a third female, moaning in her confinement. She was a married woman; her husband had left her, and she was now brought to bed of a child by another man. This woman was a millworker. All the occupants of the room professed themselves unconscious of any smell whatever; but one of them having gone out for a moment, admitted on her return that the sewer was "rather bad to-day." It turned out that a drain, passing from some other part of the town, ran underneath the house, the stone flags were here and there broken, and through the slimy soil beneath, the fœtid gases rose bubbling up, in such strength as to render it physically impossible for me to draw breath in the apartment. Yet the inmates had every aperture through which the fresh air could come carefully stopped, and complained when the door and window, or rather pane, was opened of the cold. The rent paid for these cellars is from 1s. to 1s. 9d. a week.

Our next visit was to the "low Irish" *quartier*. We first entered a kitchen, where a haggard man and woman were seated at tea. Above, the relieving officer told me, was an old man dying upon bundles of rags on the floor. He would not consent to be carried to the workhouse, and so he had 2s. a week where he was. Upon the floor of the kitchen were ranged a number of nicely tied brooms or brushes, made of fresh-smelling furze, or, as the people here call it, "ling," which grows in abundance on the neighbouring hills, and the cutting and forming of which into besoms constitutes almost the only work of the Irish adult population of Oldham. The man before us had, however, been a millworker, but his chest could not stand the flying cotton dust, so he had to take to besom-making instead. It occupied him, he said, one day to go to the hill, cut the ling, and carry it home; another day to make the besoms, and the rest of the week was taken up, with the assistance of three of his children, in hawking them about for sale. A dozen fetched half-a-crown once, but the price was much lower—not one-half that now—so that in good weeks he could only make about four shillings. Two of his children worked in a factory, which helped them on a little. The worst was, however, that, as he heard, they were to be prevented from cutting ling because of destroying the cover for the grouse. What would become of him, if it was so, God only knew. The bread which he and his wife were eating, and upon which they chiefly lived, was made of oatmeal, baked soft, like the cakes called "barley scones" in Scotland, and of heavy and doughy texture. At another house, occupied by an Irish family, which was filled with the sharp, pungent smoke of the refuse ling used for firewood, a man, grimy, unshaven, and half clad, and yet who had in his face and proportions the making of a model stalwart Irish peasant, recapitulated the sad rumour that the ling cutting was to be stopped. He had to walk eight and a half miles for the ling, and carry home as much as he could on his back. One of the cutters "got a month (a month's imprisonment) the other day. Oh, begarra! but it was hard on the poor the gentry was." This man had been fifteen years residing in Oldham. He came from the county Sligo. We now proceeded to visit one of the Irish lodging-houses. A description of one will nearly serve for all. In the low kitchen, amid some wretched rickety furniture, and pots, pans, and broken plates, was littered huge heaps of the ling, among which lay sprawling, as they bound it into shape, three or four strapping young men, talking Irish to each other, and to the wretched drabs of ragged women who were cowering by the fireplace. In this room there were two beds. In a back room, a similar manufactory was going on, and in it, among all sorts of wretched household litter—broken tubs, cracked jars, and pots full of all manner of filthy slops—was another bed—merely a bundle of rags shaken down upon a substratum of the all-pervading ling. There was a back yard, with an ashpit reeking of abominations. Up stairs were two little rooms. In one were three or four beds; in the other and larger, six. I examined the sheets; they were drab colour with unmitigated filth. The beds were made up on crazy bedsteads, fastened together with knotted ropes, and sometimes propped with big stones. The bed-posts, broken of different heights, sloped hither and thither. It was late in the day, but the beds had not been made—I question whether they ever are—nor the slops emptied. Sixpence a bed was the nominal price per night; so that three tramps could, as they often do, sleep together for twopence each; but the price varies with the influx of lodgers, sometimes sinking to a penny, to a halfpenny, indeed to anything which the poor creatures have. In the lower room was a daub of an oil painting in four compartments, representing four events in the career of a criminal—the robbery, the apprehension, the trial, and the execution. Near it were paltry prints of the Virgin, and of saints exhibiting burning hearts; and beside them was a sort of allegorical chart, called "A Railway to Heaven, with a Tunnel through Mount Calvary." The lodgers were nearly all hawkers of besoms. The men I had seen working in the house would be next day miles off, upon Saddleworth, gathering fresh material. Sometimes more than thirty people, men and women, slept in the three rooms which I have described. We went over more than a dozen of similar places—some a little better, some a little worse, than I have described. The owner of each house was always anxious to explain that half of the people we saw in the low rooms, cowering round the fire, wretched soddenlike men and women, were not lodgers, but merely "naybours, sure, that comes in to see yez;" and usually upon our descent from the bedrooms the kitchen would be all but cleared of its occupants.

The poor-law authorities of Oldham are making exertions to improve the sanitary state of the worst districts of the town, but the Irish puzzle them excessively. "No sooner," I was informed—"no sooner do we try to make the houses a little decent and wholesome, than the people leave them, and flock to other localities, to be driven thence with a like result." Fever—the "Irish fever"—that is, the most malignant species of spotted typhus, frequently breaks out. A very promising young medical man was swept away by it in Oldham a short time ago; and if the people resident in the dens I have described have, comparatively speaking, escaped the cholera, most certainly they owe more to their luck than their management.

Before going to see the vagrant lodging-houses in Manchester, I proceeded to inspect the model lodging-house recently established there. It is situated in the low and populous district of Ancoats, and was once the suburban mansion of the proprietor of a large neighbouring mill. It was curious to contrast the splendid sweep of the staircases, the mahogany doors, the rich cornices, and massy marble chimney-pieces of many of the rooms with the style of the new fittings-up and the appearance of the inhabitants. We first went into the common dining-room. It was filled with plain clean deal tables and benches. It was after the general dinner hour in Manchester, and the few who had taken that meal in the house were gone. Two decent-looking young men only remained, smoking their pipes by the fire. In the "larder" are 40 cupboards, shut in by doors of perforated zinc, and so situated as to be exposed to a cool thorough draft. Each lodger pays 1s. for his key, and when he leaves the money is returned. The lodgers cook their own meals in the kitchen, where fuel and cooking apparatus is found them. Two men were engaged by the range in frying beef-steaks, when I was in the room. The apartment was perfectly sweet and cleanly. The dishes were washed in an adjacent scullery. The bed-rooms were somewhat like the wards of hospitals, but the beds were placed fully six feet apart from each other. They are spread on compact iron bedsteads; the material is flock, and there are coarse but clean linen sheets, blankets, and a coverlid. By the head of each bed is a square box for the occupant's clothes. Many lodgers, however, had trunks of their own besides. In one of the bed wards, partitions six feet high have been built, inclosing each bed, and forming a series of little chambers, each about the size of what is called a state-room on board ship. As these partitions are screens rather than walls, the ventilation is not materially interfered with, while a proper degree of isolation is produced. It is probable that this arrangement will be made general. The superintendent, a very obliging person, showed me four beds in one of the upper rooms, which were being arranged for four young men of a religious turn, who wished to be accommodated together. Let me not omit that there are washing-rooms, with plenty of water, copper basons, and jack towels, a bath-room, where the lodgers can have each, in turn, a plunge into hot water, and a large enclosed yard behind, which is to be made into a gymnasium. The establishment has been open only eight weeks. It commenced with fifteen or sixteen lodgers, and has gone on slowly increasing its number. The accommodation provided is at present for forty. The charge to each lodger is 2s. a week. For this he has a comfortable bed, conveniences for washing, cooking, eating his meals, and perfect and wholesome cleanliness. The charge for a single night is 4d. Many of the lodgers only sleep in the house, taking their meals abroad. The occupants are principally mechanics. There are blacksmiths, joiners, ribbon makers, three mill hands only, a schoolmaster, and a doctor.

Having thus seen the decent and wholesome lodging which a poor man may have for a sum which amounts to a very little more than the sixth of the average weekly earnings of an adult in Manchester, I proceeded to visit the lodgings which many of the poor, but generally speaking, of course, the exceptional classes, earning precarious livelihoods, do occupy.

The lowest, most filthy, most unhealthy, and most wicked locality in Manchester, is called, singularly enough, "Angel-meadow." It lies off the Oldham-road, is full of cellars, and inhabited by prostitutes, their bullies, thieves, cadgers, vagrants, tramps, and, in the very worst sties of filth and darkness, by those unhappy wretches, the "low Irish." My guide was a sub-inspector of police, an excellent conductor in one respect, but disadvantageous in another, seeing that his presence spread panic wherever he went. Many of the people that night visited had, doubtless, ample cause to be nervous touching the presence of one of the guardians of the law.

We first went into an ordinary "low lodging house." The hour, I should state, was about nine o'clock at night. A stout man, partially undressed, was sitting, nursing a child, upon the bed of the outer room, and the landlady emerged from the inner apartment, whence followed her a great clack of male and female tongues. The woman spoke with profound deference to my companion, and began to assure him that the house was the best-conducted in all Manchester. Meantime we had entered the inner room. It was a small, stiflingly hot place, with a large fire, over which flickered a rushlight, or very small candle, stuck in a greased tin sconce. There were eight or ten men and women seated on stools and low chairs round the fire. They had been talking loudly enough a minute ago, but on our entrance they became as mute as fishes, staring stolidly into the fire, and only casting furtive glances at my companion, and nodding to each other when his back was turned. Hot as the place was, most of the women had shawls about their heads. They were coarse-looking and repulsive— more than one with contused and discoloured faces. The men were of that class you often remark in low localities—squalid hulking fellows, with no particular mark of any trade or calling on them. The women were of the worst class of prostitutes, and the men their bullies and partners in robberies. The beds up stairs were very much of the class already described as found in the Oldham low lodging-houses—broken and rickety bedsteads, and clothes which were bundles of brown rags. These couches were placed so close that you could only just make your way between them. The regular charge was fourpence a bed. The landlady stoutly asserted that only two were allowed to sleep in each bed, but as to the sexes she was "noways particular—lodgers was lodgers, whether they was men or women." In the room in which we stood, and which might be about fourteen feet by twelve, more than a score of filthy vagrants often pigged together, dressed and undressed, sick and well, sober and drunk.

These lodging-houses are under the superintendence of the police, and only a certain number of beds are allowed to be in a room. But the law is continually violated. "Shake-downs" are made on the floor, and threes and fours crammed into the same bed. In another lodging-house my companion suddenly exclaimed to the landlady, "Why, here's a bed more than you are licensed for," pointing to a bundle of straw enclosed in a piece of coarse sacking, and set upright in a corner. "Guide us a'," answered the woman, in the richest *patois* of the Canongate, "guide us a', what's the body havering about? It's my ain bed, man. Ye wad na hae me sleep on the stanes? But we'se remove it, if that be a';" and so saying she caught up her couch, and trundled it down stairs.

"Where do you generally sleep?" I said. "Oh, just ony gate. It depends on whether the hoose is full—but or ben, or in the passage, or ony gate."

The nominal price of fourpence for a bed I found to be everywhere the same, and the general disposition of the bed-rooms was equally identical. They consist simply of filthy unscoured chambers, with stained and discoloured walls, scribbled over with names and foul expressions. Sometimes the plaster had fallen, and lay in heaps in the corners. There was no article of furniture other than the beds—not even, so far as I saw, a chest. Still the worst of the places was quite weather-tight.

One street in this quarter is entirely composed of lodging-houses, and is well known to the police throughout the kingdom. It was called Blakely-street, but now goes by the name of Charter-street. There is a tavern here, with a coloured lamp like that of a doctor's, called the "Dog and Duck." This is the house of call for the swell mob of Manchester and the superior class of "prigs." When I entered the parlour, which differed in no respect from that of an ordinary low-class tavern, and which was hung with boxing prints, there were only two men present, drinking ale, and playing dominos for handfulls of coppers. In a beer-house close at hand there was a large assemblage of men and women, most of the latter like those I have already sketched, but a few whose faded finery proclaimed that they had formerly held a higher position in their wretched class. A number of bare-footed boys were drinking here. The rattle of dominos was heard on every side; the yellow dips which lighted the room burned with a sickly flicker amid the draughts and the thick tobacco smoke. Ensconced in the seat of honour by the fire was a villanous-looking black man without shoes, who said that he had just come to town, having "cadged it from Stafford;" and in a corner sat two pedlars, each upon his box. As we were leaving the house a boy about thirteen or fourteen, smartly dressed, with a tassel dangling from his cap, entered.

"Well, young'un," said my companion, "whose pockets have your hands been in this evening?"

The boy stared coolly at the inspector. The light from a lamp fell upon his face, and I never saw a worse one—little deep sunk eyes and square bony jaws, with a vile expression. "What do ye mean talking about pockets to me? I don't know nothing about pockets," and turning on his heel he entered the house. The boy had been twice convicted, and several times in trouble. He walked Market-street at night, often in partnership with a woman.

There were few or no Irish in the houses we had just visited. They live in more wretched places still—the cellars. We descended to one. The place was dark, except for the glare of a small fire. You could not stand without stooping in the room, which might be about twelve feet by eight. There were at least a dozen men, women, and children, on stools, or squatted on the stone floor, round the fire, and the heat and smells were oppressive. This not being a lodging cellar, the police had no control over the number of its inmates, who slept huddled on the stones, or on masses of rags, shavings, and straw, which were littered about. There was nothing like a bedstead in the place. Further back opened a second cellar, strewn with coals and splinters of wood used for making matches. Here, upon shavings, bits of furze, and intermingled rags and straw, lay two girls asleep in two corners. The party in the outer room had a few handfuls of nuts and apples, with which they intended—it was the 31st of October—to "keep" All Hallow's Eve. Half the people who lived in the den had not yet returned, being still out hawking lucifers, matches, and besoms. They were all Irish, from Westport, in the county Mayo. They lived on potatoes, meal, and sometimes broken victuals begged. There was no fever there, and there had been no cholera—"Glory be to God." "Sure they was poor people, but they was daysint and did their best." After leaving, a woman followed me into the street to know if I had come from Westport to find out anything about them, and was greatly disappointed at being answered in the negative.

The last place we visited is, I am told, the "worst cellar in all Manchester." The outer room was like that of others which I had seen, but following a woman who held a light, we proceeded into the inner cellars. They were literally vaults, three of them opening from one to the other. The air was thick with damp and stench. The vaults were mere subterranean holes, utterly without light. The flicker of the candle showed their grimy walls, reeking with fœtid damp, which trickled in greasy drops down to the floor. Beds were huddled in every corner: some of them on frames—I cannot call them bedsteads—others on the floor. In one of these a man was lying dressed, and beside him slept a well-grown calf. Sitting upon another bed was an old man maudlin drunk, with the saliva running over his chin, making vain efforts to rid himself of his trowsers, and roaring for help. In the next cellar two boys were snoring together in one bed, and beside them was a man sleeping in an old battered hat for a nightcap. "Is he undressed?" I said. The police officer, for answer, twitched down the clothes, and revealed a stark naked man, black with filth. The smell in this room was dreadful, and the air at once hot and wet.

"What's this you have been doing?" said my conductor to the landlady, stooping down and examining the lower part of one of the walls. I joined him, and saw that a sort of hole or shallow cave, about six feet long, two deep, and a little more than one high, had been scooped out through the wall into the earth on the outside of the foundation, there being probably some yard on the other side, and in this hole or earthen cupboard there was stretched, upon a scanty litter of foul-smelling straw, a human being—an old man. As he lay on his back, his face was not two inches beneath the roof—so to speak—of the hole.

"He's a poor old body," said the landlady, in a tone of deprecation, "and if we didn't let him crawl in there he would have to sleep in the streets."

I turned away, and was glad when I found myself breathing such comparatively fresh air as can be found in Angel-meadow, Manchester.

# LABOUR AND THE POOR.

## THE MANUFACTURING DISTRICTS.

[FROM OUR SPECIAL CORRESPONDENT.]

### MANCHESTER.

### LETTER IX.

In pursuing an inquiry like that in which I am engaged, it must unavoidably happen that facts and phases connected with the social features which I endeavour to dissect come to light, or at all events thrust themselves forcibly upon my attention, after the despatch of the letters in which the features in question have been more particularly treated of. The Factory System is a sea which cannot be explored but by patient and long-continued soundings. I have already tried to fathom some of its depths, and explain some of its sets and currents. But the longer I study it, the more clearly do I perceive the relation and connection of these social ebbings and flowings, and the more determined do I feel to allow no finical apprehension of marring a pre-conceived arrangement of topics to prevent me from giving to the public *all* the facts with reference to *all* the features of Manufacturing life, which continued experience in the search enables me, day by day, to seize and drag to light.

In this letter, then, I shall detail what further information I have collected with reference to subjects already partially disposed of, and what particulars I have ascertained regarding ground still untrodden. Without any very strict view to a symmetrical order of arrangement, but rather having respect to the abstract value of the facts and information presented, I shall begin with some account of the Sunday-school system as it exists in Manchester, many of my observations being also applicable to the system as it exists in the manufacturing districts generally.

The Sunday-schools of the industrial North form not only a vast moral and educational engine, but a curious and characteristic social fact. The system originated by Mr. Raikes, some seventy years ago,

took deep root in Lancashire, and grew with the growth of manufacturing industry. The serious cast of the Lancashire mind, and its
earnestness and zeal, acting upon the facilities afforded by the order
and discipline which it is the very nature of the factory system to in-
stil, formed a soil in which the Sunday-school system took very deep
root and bore very rich harvests. I rather understate than overstate the
numbers when I say that in the Sunday-schools of Manchester may
be found from 40,000 to 50,000 scholars, and from 4,000 to 5,000
teachers, inspectors, and visitants. In 1832, the fiftieth anniversary of
the foundation of the system was celebrated by a day of jubilee, and
upon that occasion no less than 32,000 medals were disposed of, to
be worn by members of the Sunday-scholars procession which de-
filed through the streets of Manchester. "Were it not for the Sunday-
schools," I have been over and over again assured, "Lancashire would
have been a hell upon earth." Long before educational committees of
the Privy Council and British and Foreign Societies were heard of,
long previous to the era of Institutes and Athenæums, the Sunday-
schools were sedulously at work, impregnating the people with the
rudiments of an education which, though always rude and often narrow and fanatical in its teachings, was yet preserving a glow of moral
and religious sentiment, and keeping alive a degree of popular intelligence which otherwise would assuredly have perished in the rush
and clatter with which a vast manufacturing population came surging
up upon the land. The early patrons and early champions of Sunday-
schools are now dying fast away. The great world has never heard of
them, but yet amongst a large and influential class in the north they
have left immortal memories. Often and often have I lately had occasion to see the walls, both of drawing-rooms and humble kitchen-
parlours, hung with portraits of grave sober-clad men, whose names
I had never heard of, and who were yet pointed out to me as among
the greatest and most glorious of Englishmen. Local poets, too, have
hymned the departure of locally famous Sunday-school worthies. To
those who know nothing of the excellent man commemorated, there
is something which almost savours of the ludicrous in such a couplet
as—

> "———Oh was it not
> The meek and earth unblazoned name of Stott."

Yet Mr. Stott was a hero in his way. He was for half a century the foremost champion of the Lancashire Sunday-schools. When he com-

menced his labours he had to struggle against all the chimera terrors
with which the first French Revolution peopled England. If he assembled a knot of children on the Sunday afternoon, he was accused
of preaching Jacobinism to the rising generation. If he caused the
children to walk in orderly procession from the school-room to the
church, he was drilling them in military tactics, preparatory to the outbreak of an operative Jacquerie. Yet Mr. Stott worked steadily on. He
began with two score pupils. In the school which he founded, I last
Sunday saw two thousand six hundred. Sunday-schools in Manchester, as I have said, form not only a great educational engine, but a
great social fact. Nearly every school has its library, and besides the
library, many have their sick and burial societies. At Whitsuntide, the
yearly week of rest in Manchester, nearly every school enjoys its gala
and its country trip. Many of the richest and most prosperous men
in Manchester will tell you, that to the Sunday-school, which taught
them to read and write, and inculcated honesty and sobriety, they now
owe their villas and their mills. Sunday-schools, as they are worked
in Lancashire, more than any set of institutions which I know, tend
to bind different classes of society to each other. Men in the middle
ranks of life very commonly act as teachers, or at all events take a practical interest in the proceedings, and acquaintanceships first formed
in the class-room, lead, in very many cases, to subsequent and often
life-long business connections. It often happens that families are for
generations connected, as pupils or teachers, with the same Sunday-
school. "A great number of the children before you," I have been repeatedly told, "are the children of old scholars, and a great many of
our teachers were themselves scholars in the classes which they now
instruct."

The education afforded in the Manchester Sunday-schools is, of
course, of an elementary and religious character. The pupils are first
taught to read; then scriptural extracts, or the Scriptures themselves,
are put into their hands, and instructions in psalmody are diversified
by familiar moral and doctrinal addresses and examinations into the
contents of the chapter or passage last studied. This general description applies pretty well to all the Sunday-schools connected either
with the Church or with Dissent. Most of the schools, however, meet
upon week days and week evenings, when secular instruction is communicated, consisting principally of reading, writing, cyphering, and
a little geography. The Sunday education is purely gratuitous. For that
which goes on upon working days a small fee, varying from 2d. to 6d. a

week, is commonly charged. Many Sunday-schools have adult classes for men and women. I have repeatedly seen grey-haired scholars. In general, the ages of the pupils vary from eight to twenty, the girls commonly remaining in connection with the school longer than the young men.

There are in Manchester, connected with the Church, about fifty Sunday-schools. Upon Whit-Saturday every year the pupils of most of these schools walk in procession through the streets; and turning to the file of the *Manchester Guardian*, I copy the names of the twelve schools which last year brought the largest number of pupils into the field. These are:—

| | |
|---|---:|
| St. Paul's, Bennett-street | 2,600 |
| St. Paul's, German-street | 1,400 |
| St. Stephen's | 800 |
| St. George's, Hulme | 777 |
| St. Simon's | 580 |
| St. John's | 560 |
| St. Michael's, Miller-street | 550 |
| The Cathedral School | 500 |
| St. Ann's | 500 |
| St. James's | 500 |
| All Saints' | 450 |
| St. Mathias', Salford | 400 |
| Making a total of | 9,617 |

The number of scholars attending the other schools ranges, with one or two exceptions, above 200 a-piece, and the sum total may be taken, on a rough calculation, to be somewhere about 25,000.

Besides the Church schools, there are in the Manchester district two "unions," as they are called, or communities of dissenting Sunday schools, termed respectively the Manchester and the Salford Union.

I have before me various published returns relative to the Manchester union, but I am informed that their details are so incorrect that I can only venture upon giving general results. The religious denominations in connection with the union are six—Independents, Baptists, Wesleyan Association, Primitive Methodists, New Connection, and Welsh Calvinists. The number of schools is 28, with a total of 9,658 scholars. The average morning attendance is 4,527; in the afternoon the average is 6,525. The libraries connected with these schools contain a total of 16,527 volumes, and almost every school has its sick and burial society.

The Salford union consists of schools in connection with the following religious bodies:—

| | | |
|---|---:|---|
| Wesleyan Methodists, 1 school | 783 | pupils. |
| Primitive Methodists, 1 school | 293 | „ |
| Independents, 6 schools | 3,167 | „ |
| Association Methodists, 3 schools | 657 | „ |
| New Connection Methodists, 1 school | 246 | „ |
| Baptist | 386 | „ |
| Total | 5,532 | „ |

Besides these, there are schools in connection with bodies of Welsh and Scottish Calvinists. The exact numbers taught by the Roman Catholic Sunday-schools I have not been able exactly to come at, but there are six or seven chapels, each having numerously attended schools connected with them. The above rough data will, I think, prove that my general estimate of the number of children attending Sunday-schools in Manchester does not overshoot the mark. And, I may add, that more than half of these children attend school during the week likewise. Before proceeding to give a more particular account of the schools which I visited, I would wish to state—as showing the extent to which the moral restraint exercised by these institutions goes—that when, on the famous 10th of April, a great Chartist meeting was being held, under circumstances of intense public excitement, within three minutes' walk of the largest establishment of the kind in Manchester, the number of pupils in attendance was only six beneath that of the previous day. This school is that of St. Paul, Bennett-street, the one founded by Mr. Stott, and that to which—taking it as a good example of the Church schools—I last Sunday paid a very lengthened visit.

The Bennett-street Sunday-school is a vast plain building, fully as large as an ordinary sized cotton-factory, and exhibiting four long ranges of lofty windows. The number of pupils at present on the books is 2,611, and the average attendance 2,152. The number of Sunday scholars who learn writing and arithmetic, two evenings a week, paying for their paper, pens, and ink, &c., is 260. The number attending the daily schools, and paying twopence per week, is 350. The members of the School Funeral Society amount to 1,804, and of the School Sick Society to 400. The total amount of relief afforded by these societies since their commencement is upwards of £7,285. I may add, that, in one evening in each week, the female scholars are instructed in plain sewing and housewifery.

I have said that the building is composed of four stories; the girls occupy the two highest, the boys the two lowest. As to ages, the former ranged from little things of five and six, brought by their elder sisters, to well-grown young women. Many of them were the children of small shopkeepers and mechanics, the others were mill hands. Every girl there was decently attired, and many of them were neatly and tastefully dressed. They sat in classes, engaged, according to their progress, in reading Scripture or Scriptural extracts. One roomful was preparing to go to church, and practising choral versions of the responses, easily and gracefully arranged. The girls, however, did not sing with anything like the spirit and effect which the boys beneath threw into a concluding hymn. Perhaps the chanting of the responses presented more difficulties than the more familiar rhythm of one of Dr. Watts's hymns. Descending to the most crowded of the boys' rooms, I found that all the classes had just concluded reading the chapter in St. John giving an account of the interview of Nicodemus with Christ, and that one of the teachers, installed in a reading desk, was questioning the scholars upon the chapter. As a general rule, the questions were answered intelligently and readily—the demand for a definition of the word "Pharisee" being the greatest stickler propounded. At the courteous invitation of Mr. George Lawton, the superintendent present, I selected a class to hear them read, pitching upon one composed of boys of medium age—say from 12 to 14. They read, without exception, fluently and correctly—the only marked feature in the performance being the invariable pronunciation of the letter "U" in "up," for example, as if the word were spelled "oop." But this is a common peculiarity of teachers, as well as scholars. Glancing around the class, which was composed in the main of commonplace-looking boys, dressed, some of them, in fustian, others in coarse cloth, and generally sallow-faced, thin, and rather undersized, as Manchester urchins too often are—I thought I would like to know something about the social position of each, and accordingly, with the sanction of the master, examined the boys *seriatim.* The following are the results:—

1. Is ten years of age. Works ten hours a day in the card-room, and makes 5s. 10d. a week, which he gives his parents. They allow him fourpence or sixpence for pocket money. Can read and write.

2. Is fifteen years of age. Is in a greengrocer's shop all day, for which he gets half-a-crown a week. Goes on week nights to the Lyceum school. Can write a little.

3. Is fourteen years of age. Works six hours and a half a day at a boiler-maker's. Only goes to the Sunday-school. Has 3s. a week. Gives it to his mother. Can write.

4. Is fourteen years of age. Also works in an engine-shop twelve hours a day for 3s. Can write, because he was taught at Sunday-school.

5. Is thirteen years of age, and works in a machine-shop from six in the morning till eight and nine, and sometimes ten o'clock at night. Has 4s. a week. Would rather work fewer hours; but his father sends him, and takes the money.

6. Is fourteen years of age. Can write. Works at weaving, and makes 5s. 6d. a week, working ten hours a day, and gives it to his aunt, who keeps him.

7. Is sixteen years of age. Works at factory, and has 6s. 2d. a week. Can write.

8. Is ten years of age. Works at a foundry for 13 hours a day, and earns 2s. 6d. a week, which his parents take.

9. Is ten years of age, and in a warehouse from half-past eight in the morning until eight o'clock at night. Can write. Learned to write here. Can make 3s. a week.

10. Is fourteen years of age. Works at factory, in a spinning-room. Has 5s. 9d. a week, and his father gives him 2d. a week pocket money. Can write a little. His father pays his fees at a night school.

11. Is fifteen years of age. Works at a factory, and makes 14s. or 15s. a week. Pays it all to his father, who sometimes gives him a shilling or so. Works from a quarter past five a.m. until seven p.m.

12. Is twelve years of age. Works for his father, who is a painter, and who gives him 6d. a week to spend. Goes to a night school, for which his father pays 5d. a week.

13. Is eleven years of age. Works in a stone-yard for twelve hours a day. Has 4s. a week. Goes to a night school.

14. Is thirteen years of age. Works for 4s. a week at a "making-up" place. His father and mother give him 6d. a week for pocket money. Buys "a many things."

15. Is eight years of age, and does not go out to work. Goes to school Sundays and week days.

16. Is eleven years of age. Works in a foundry from seven o'clock a.m. until eight or nine o'clock. Has 2s. 6d. a week.

The reader will perceive, from the above particulars, that boys are commonly employed in branches of trade, many of them of a laborious nature, for several hours a day longer than the term during which they could be legally employed in factories; and that for a much smaller amount of wages than they would earn in the different processes of the cotton trade. In this one class were boys earning from 6s. to 7s. in factories, whilst those employed as workers in iron did not make much more than half the money. It must be borne in mind, however, that the future prospects of the young mechanics are better than those of the young spinners and weavers. Mr. Lawton, who has passed much of his life amid factory children, and has devoted much of his attention to the moral results of the factory system, expresses his fears that changes for the worse are gradually being accomplished by it. The great moral evil upon which he looks with dread is the gradually increasing preponderance of children in the mills. The tendency of every improvement in machinery is to dismiss adult labour, and it seems to be possible that factories may one day be worked almost entirely by children. Already the children hold a vast proportion of the sinews of war. They can stop a mill whenever they please; and the result of this precocious independence is, of course, the utter relaxation of all bonds of domestic and, in many cases, scholastic control. Within Mr. Lawton's recollection, a spinner working in the mill, often with his family about him, received their wages and kept them under proper control. Now, the self-actors have in a great measure dispensed with the necessity for skilled adult labour in that department of manufacture. Mr. Lawton thinks that the cotton population, particularly the females, has generally deteriorated in appearance within the last few years. The young women dress in a more loose and slatternly fashion, but he has often been pleased at being able to single out the Sunday school girls by the comparative neatness and propriety of their attire.

In the afternoon I visited a very large Dissenting Sunday-school, connected with the Independent body—that attached to the Hope chapel, in Salford. In this school it is not uncommon to see assembled, on one Sunday, three generations of the same family—children, their parents, and their grand-parents. There are three large school-rooms for the youthful scholars—from those who are mere children up to those of 18 or 20 years of age, and separate rooms for the adult scholars of both sexes. The male adult class is managed by Mr. William Morris, the principal partner in a very large cotton-working establishment—some features of the internal economy of which I shall presently allude to. Mr. Morris, who is one of the most respected citizens of Manchester, and who is justly proud of having worked himself up "from the ranks," takes the deepest practical interest in Sunday-school and temperance movements, and is a distinguished advocate of both causes. He passes many hours every Sunday, surrounded by his adult class, in the Hope chapel. The total number of pupils taught in those schools is about 1,200, and the average afternoon attendance is about 924. There are 160 in the infant class, and about 600 above fourteen years of age. More than 100 of the pupils are married persons. The absentee children are visited by the teachers. In the day school connected with the Hope chapel there are about 300 scholars. To the sick relief fund there are about 100 subscribers, and to a clothing charity about 530. This school raises annually about £50 for missionary purposes. The number of adult scholars taught separately is about 250.

In the library there are nearly 1,000 volumes, consisting principally of books of a serious character, and including a number of religious and controversial novels. The books in the Bennett-street school library are of the same general class, and number about twice as many. Upon neither of these libraries did the Ten Hours Bill produce any perceptible change.

In general intelligence and acquirements the children of both the St. Paul's and the Hope schools seemed pretty much upon a par. The children from ten to twelve years of age were able to read with tolerable fluency and correctness. After hearing one of the reading classes, I proceeded to examine into the social position and standing of the scholars, as at the Paul's school, and with the following results:—

GIRLS.

1. Is fifteen years of age. Works in a silk mill, and earns 3s. 5d. per week, which she gives to her parents. Can read and write.

2. Is fifteen years of age. Works in a weaving room, and earns 5s. 2d. a week. Her parents allowed her the odd twopence for herself, and she put a penny of it weekly into the missionary box.

3. Is thirteen years of age, and earns 2s. 3½d. per week at winding cotton. Has no pocket money.

4. Is sixteen years of age, and works as a piecer. Her wages are 8s. a week. Gives the money to a married sister with whom she lives, except twopence or threepence for herself. Can read and write.

Two girls, respectively seventeen and nineteen, who earned 10s. each as weavers, would not tell what they did with the money.

BOYS.

1. Is ten years of age. Works at a brick-croft as long as there is light. Has 2s. 6d. a week.

2. Is sixteen years of age. Works at a dye-house, where he has 6s. 6d. a week. His mother gives him 3d. or 4d. every Saturday night, and he spends it in sweet stuff. Can't read much.

3. Is twelve years of age. Works with a joiner for 2s. a week. Is learning to read. Works more than 12 hours a day very often.

4. Is fifteen years of age. Works with an umbrella frame maker, and has 1s. 6d. a week, which he pays to his father. Has no pocket money.

5. Is fourteen years of age. Makes 5s. a week at a bleaching field. Gives the money to his parents, and has 6d. a week to do what he likes with. Buys fruit and sweet stuff.

6. Is fourteen years of age. Can read well. Works at a brick-croft from dark to dark, for which he has 5s. a week.

7. Is sixteen years of age. Can read and write. Earns 12s. a week in a silk factory, and gives it to his old mother, except 6d., which he spends himself.

8. Is fifteen years of age. Works at a bleach field, where he has 14s. every fortnight. Gives it to his aunt. Is going to a night school, to learn to write, as soon as possible.

9. Is fourteen years of age, and has 4s. a week at a warehouse. Is allowed 3d. for pocket money. Can read and write.

10. Is seventeen years of age. Makes 6s. a week as a piecer. Gives it to his mother, except 4d., which he keeps to himself.

The remark as to the length of employment of "children and young persons" in occupations not connected with factories, made *apropos* of the pupils of the Bennett-street school, stands also good in the present case. I am informed that very young children are frequently employed in the brick crofts, or fields, for fourteen hours a day in summer, and that the number of them has increased since the Ten Hours Act came into operation. I have no reason to doubt the accuracy of the statements made by the Sunday scholars as to their giving their wages almost entirely to their parents; and the inference which one would naturally draw from the fact, knowing what we do of the general practice, is, that the Sunday-school system has, to some extent, the effect of discouraging the generally speedy rupture of the family tie. I now pass to another subject, only pausing to remark that the ages of the boys, as stated by themselves, astonished me. From their appearances I should have thought them, on an average, at least three years younger than they represented themselves to be.

I have already alluded to the practice, too common in the cotton districts, of dosing infants with narcotic medicine to keep them quiet while their mothers are at their daily work in the factories. In my former communication, I stated that the druggists were exceedingly shy of giving any information upon the point; but it is one of such great interest and importance, that I resolved, *coute qui coute*, to obtain a body of evidence upon the subject. With this view I have waited upon many medical men, examined a great many elderly factory hands, male and female, and called at no fewer than thirty-five druggists' shops.

The information given to me by medical men was general in its character, and may be summed up in the evidence elicited from Mr. John Greg Harrison, one of the factory medical inspectors, and a gentleman carrying on a very large practice amongst the operative classes.

"The system of drugging children is exceedingly common, and one of the prevailing causes of infant mortality. Mothers and nurses both administer narcotics; the former, however, principally with the view of obtaining an undisturbed night's rest. The consequences produced are imbecility, caused by suffusion on the brain, and an extensive train of mesenteric and glandular diseases. The child sinks into a low torpid state, wastes away to a skeleton, except the stomach, which swells, producing what is known as pot-belly. If the children survive the treatment, they are often weakly and stunted for life. To this drugging system, and to defective nursing, its certain concomitant—not to any fatal effect inherent in factory labour—the great infant mortality in the cotton towns is to be ascribed."

Dr. Harrison added, that the practice of procuring abortion was sadly common, particularly among unmarried women, and among married women living separated from their husbands. A person in Stockport is notorious for the extent of his practice in this way, instruments, and not drugs, being the usual means employed.

To return to the narcotic part of the subject. From evidence given me by mill hands themselves I select the following cases, observing that they merely serve as samples of the ordinary stories told me by those who were sufficiently candid to speak out upon the subject.

An intelligent male operative, in the Messrs. Morris's mill, in Salford, stated that he and his wife put out their first child to be nursed. The nurse gave the baby "sleeping stuff," and it died in nine weeks. The neighbours told his wife how the baby was dosed, but the nurse denied that the child had ever got anything of the kind. They never sent a child out to be nursed again. For that one they paid 3s. 6d. a week, and the weeks that the nurse washed for it, 4s. The mother had to get up at four o'clock and carry it to the nurse's every morning; but the distance was too far for her to suckle it at noon, so the child had no milk until the nurse brought it home at night. The nurses are often old women, who take in washing, and sometimes they have three or four children to take care of. The mother can often smell laudanum in the child's breath when it comes home. As for mothers themselves, they give the "sleeping stuff" principally at night, to secure their own rest.

Another operative in the same mill gave the following evidence:— He had put out one child to nurse, and he and his missus had sorely rued it ever since. The child, a girl, had never been healthy or strong, and the doctors told them, when she was 14 months old, that she had been dosed, and how it would be with her. They paid 5s. a week to the nurse. His wife then earned 15s. a week in a mill. At present he thought that 4s. was about the average paid for nursing children. The nurses very often take in washing, and put the infants to sleep by drugging them. He had six children, and they were all hearty except the first.

A female weaver, in a mill in Chorlton, stated the case of a little girl who was nursed by a neighbour of hers, and who got "sleeping stuff." The child seemed to be always asleep, and lay with its eyes half open. Its head got terribly big, and its fingernails blue. The mother took the child from the nurse and carried it to the doctor, who said it was poisoned. The mother went on her knees crying, and said she had never given the child anything; but it died very soon after. The witness was a married woman, but had never had any family. She had often heard tell of the effects of "sleeping stuff," and how it killed the poor children.

Another woman, employed in the weaving room of the same mill, had put out all her children to nurse, and had lost none of them. But she had a good kind nurse—a married woman—not one of the regular old nurses who made a trade of it. She had often heard of children getting "sleeping stuff." It made them that they were always dozing, and never cared for food. They pined away, their heads got big, and they died. She carried her own child every morning to the nurse, rising for this purpose a full hour before she went to the mill, because the nurse lived some way off. The nurse did not rise at the same time, but she (the mother) put the baby into bed to her and left it there till the evening. She did not suckle it in the course of the day, because the distance was too far to go. All her children were thriving.

I now come to the druggists. With one or two honourable exceptions, these individuals either point blank denied that the drugging system existed, or declined giving any information whatever. More than one of the proprietors of the most noted "Godfrey shops" in Manchester were amongst the latter class, while of the others, who repudiated the traffic entirely, several of them had their windows crowded with announcements of different forms of the medicine which they were cool enough to declare they did not deal in.

My inquiries extended to the use of laudanum in different forms by people of all ages, and I transcribe the evidence of those druggists from whom I received any information worthy of the name.

A highly-respectable druggist in Salford states as follows:—"The use of laudanum as a stimulant by male and female adults is not at all uncommon. His sales in that way are, however, small. He disposes of about a shilling's worth weekly, in pennyworths. Some of his customers will take a teaspoonful or a teaspoonful and a half of laudanum; and in bad times, when they have no money, they come and beg for a dose. The sale of crude opium has, he thinks, diminished in his part of the town. When people come for laudanum, to use it as a stimulant, he sells it mixed with tincture of gentian, in the hope that it may do them less harm. Children are drugged either with Godfrey's Cordial or stronger decoctions of opium. Every druggist makes his own Godfrey, and the stronger he makes it, the faster it is bought. The medicine consists of laudanum, sweetened by a syrup, and further flavoured by some essential oil of spice. Mothers sometimes dose their infants, but the nurses carry the practice to the greatest extent. The mother takes the infant from the warm bed at five o'clock in the morning, and carries it to the nurse's, where it is left till noon, and often drugged to keep it quiet."

Among the druggists who were obviously disingenuous upon the point, I may particularly mention one, not far from the Rochdale-road. He tried to pooh-pooh the whole thing. "He sold nothing of the kind, at least next to nothing—nothing worth mentioning. Oh, no. The fact was that a great deal of nonsense was talked upon the subject. Isolated cases might be found, but to say that there was anything like a general practice of drugging children was to raise a mere bugbear." Now, during our conversation, which occupied about five minutes, my cool and candid friend actually suited the action to the word by handing over the counter, to two little girls, three distinct pennyworths of the very drug the demand for which he was resolutely denying! I would have given something for that gentleman's power of face. I think it could be made useful.

Another druggist told me of a common feature in this hocussing system. The women go to shops where the "cordial" is made weak, and where a certain quantity—say half a teaspoonful—is prescribed as a dose. Afterwards they go to shops where the mixture is made stronger, and without making any further inquiry buy the drug, and give the child the old dose. "Yet some of the druggists," said this gentleman, "put twice or thrice as much laudanum into their Godfrey as others."

By a druggist carrying on an extensive business in a low neighbourhood in Ancoats, inhabited almost exclusively by a mill population, I was informed that personally he did not sell much narcotic medicine, but that it was tolerably extensively vended in small "general shops," the owners of which bought the drug by gallons from certain establishments which he named. He informed me also that he was in the habit of making Godfrey without putting laudanum into it—a system, from all I hear, very much akin to making grog without spirits. He affirmed, however, that the carminative ingredients, used for flatulence, constituted an important element of the medicine, and one for which it was frequently bought. He expressed his belief that the drugging system was gradually going out, and that the "old women" and midwives, who were its great patrons, were losing their hold upon the mill population. Recipes, which had been handed down in families for generations, and which often contained dangerous quantities of laudanum, were occasionally brought to him to make up, but he found little difficulty in convincing their possessors of the noxious character of the ingredients, when he was sometimes allowed to change their proportions. Sometimes a half-emptied bottle of cordial would be brought, in order that more laudanum might be put into it— a request which he always met by pretending to comply with it, and sending the applicant away with the contents of the phial increased by a few drops of harmless tincture. The mortality among infants in Manchester this gentleman attributed not to narcotics, but to careless nursing and insufficient and unwholesome suckling. "When women work nearly all day in a hot and close atmosphere, and live for the most part upon slops, their milk does children much more harm than good. Infants are suckled hastily at dinner time, while the mother is eating her own meal, and then they are left foodless until well on in the evening. The consequence is a train of stomach complaints, which carries them off like pestilence. Children who had been drugged with 'sleeping stuff' he could recognize in a moment. They never seemed fairly awake. Their whole system appeared to be sunk into a stagnant state. He believed that when such doses were administered, nurses were chiefly to blame; for mothers often came to him with their ailing children, asking, in great trouble, whether he thought that 'sleeping stuff' had anything to do with the child's illness. The proportion of illegitimate children carried off through inefficient nursing was terrible. As to adults, he knew that a good deal of opium and laudanum was taken by them. Women were his chief customers in that way. He had seen a girl drink off an ounce-and-a-half of laudanum as it was handed to her over the counter. Most of these people had begun by taking laudanum under medical advice, and had continued the practice until it became habitual." While we were talking, another druggist entered the shop, and confirmed the main points of the above statement. He added, that "when he was an apprentice, twenty years ago, in a country place, principally inhabited by hand-loom weavers, his master used to make Godfrey in a large boiler by twenties and thirties of gallons at a brewst. He believed that the people did not drug their children half so much now-a-days. Coroners' inquests were good checks. Almost all the laudanum he sold was disposed of in pennyworths. A great number of old women took it for rheumatism."

I beg, however, to direct particular attention to the following evidence, given by a most intelligent druggist carrying on a very large business in a poor neighbourhood surrounded by mills, and a gentleman of whose perfect candour and good faith I have certain knowledge:—

"Laudanum, in various forms, is used to some extent by the adult population, male and female, and to a terrible extent for very young children. I sell about 2s. worth a week of laudanum, in pennorths, for adults. Some use raw opium instead. They either chew it, or make it into pills and swallow it. The country people use laudanum as a stimulant, as well as the town people. On market days, they come in from Lymm and Warrington, and buy the pure drug for themselves, and 'Godfrey,' or 'Quietness,' for the children. Habitual drunkards often give up spirits and take to laudanum, as being cheaper and more intensely stimulating. Another class of customers are middle-aged prostitutes. They take it when they get low and melancholy. Three of them came together into my shop last night for opium to relieve pains in their limbs. These women swallow the drug in great quantities. As regards children, they are commonly dosed either with 'Godfrey' or 'Infant's Quietness.' The first is an old-fashioned preparation, and has been more or less in vogue for near a century. It is made differently by different vendors, but generally speaking it contains an ounce and a half of pure laudanum to the quart. The dose is from half a teaspoonful to two teaspoonfuls. Infant's Cordial, or Mixture, is stronger, containing on the average two ounces of laudanum to a quart. Occasionally paregoric, which is one-fourth part as strong as laudanum, is used. Mothers sometimes give narcotics to their children, but most commonly the nurses are in fault. The stuff is frequently administered by the latter without the mothers' knowledge, but is occasionally given by the mothers, without the fathers' knowledge. I believe that women frequently drug their children through pure ignorance of the effect of the practice, and because, having been brought up in mills, they know nothing about the first duties of mothers. The nurses sometimes take children for 1s. 6d. a week. They are very often laundresses. Half-a-crown a week may be the average charge of the nurse, and the 'nursing' commonly consists of laying the infant in a cradle to doze all day in a stupified state produced by a teaspoonful of 'Godfrey' or 'Quietness.' Bad as the practice is, it would not be so fatal if the nurses and parents would obey the druggists' instructions in administering the medicine. But this is what often takes place. A woman comes and buys pennorths of 'Godfrey.' Well, all is right for five or six weeks. Then she begins to complain that we don't make the 'Godfrey' so good as we used to do; that she has to give the child more than it needed at first; and so nothing will do but she must have 'Infant's Quietness' instead, for, as she says, she has heard that that is better, *i.e.* stronger. But in process of time, as the child gets accustomed to the drug, the dose must be made stronger still. Then the nurses, and sometimes the mothers, take to making the stuff themselves. They buy pennorths of aniseed, and treacle and sugar, add the laudanum to it, and make the dose as strong as they like. The midwives teach them how to brew it, and if the quantity of laudanum comes expensive, they use crude opium instead. Of course numberless children are carried off in this way. I know a child that has been so treated at once; it looks like a little old man or woman. I can tell one in an instant. Often and often a mother comes here with a child that has been out to nurse, to know what can be the matter with it. I know, but frequently I dare hardly tell, for if I say what I am sure of, the mother will go to the nurse and charge her with sickening the child; the nurse will deny, point blank, that she did anything of the sort, and will come and make a disturbance here, daring me to prove what of course I can't prove legally, and abusing me for taking away her character. The children also suffer from the period which elapses between the times of their being suckled. The mothers often live on vegetables and drink quantities of thin ale, and the consequence is that the children are terribly subject to weakening attacks of diarrhœa."

Hearing in several quarters of the "little shops" which retailed "Godfrey," I looked out for such an establishment, and in a back street in Chorlton, surrounded by mills, I hit upon what I wanted—a shop in the "general line," in the window of which, amongst eggs, candles, sugar, bread, soap, butter, starch, herrings, and cheese, I observed a placard marked "Children's Draughts, a penny each." There was a woman behind the counter, and on my making inquiries as to whether she sold "Godfrey," or any similar compound, she replied that she had not for six months. The draught announced in the window was purgative.

"Then you used to sell 'Godfrey'?"

"Oh yes, we used to make it and sell it for children, when they were cross; but the people did not think ours strong enough."

"What did you make it of?"

"We took a pennorth of aniseed, a quarter of a pound of treacle, and a pennorth of laudanum (a quarter of an ounce). Then we stewed down the aniseed with water, and mixed up the whole in a quart bottle."

"And so this stuff was too weak?"

"Aye, that it was. I could have sold it fast enough if I made it stronger; but I daren't do it, for fear of getting into trouble."

"Do you ever give it to your own children?"—there were several sprawling about the back parlour.

"Yes. But I never put a pennorth of laudanum into the bottle that I give it to them out of."

"But very strong stuff is generally used?"

"Indeed it is; you may know the children that get it at once—if you have any experience in them things—they're so sickly, and puny, and ill-looking. It's a shocking thing that poor people should be obliged to give their children such stuff to keep them quiet."

I have taken some pains to ascertain in what way the mill operatives conduct the purchase of the tea and sugar which form so large a portion of their nourishment. I find that these are very generally purchased in pennyworths at small chandlers' shops. The customers commonly buy on credit, paying on the Saturday night for what they have had during the previous week; but frequently requiring longer trust. They are always very particular in having a good pennyworth—that is, in having the draught of the scale in their favour; so that, with the credit demanded and the risk run, the profits of the vendor would be small indeed, were it not that he usually sells at 6s. a lb. tea which the regular dealers sell at 4s. a lb. Thus the poor mill operatives pay higher by 33 per cent. for their tea than their masters. In order to get rid of this disadvantage, the Messrs. Morris have started a co-operative society in their Chorlton mill, the working of which was explained to me. The mill is mapped out into twelve districts, the overlooker of each of which is furnished with a slip of paper, properly ruled and headed, in which each operative enters the amount of tea, at 5s. or 4s., black, green, or mixed; the amount of coffee, at 1s. 4d., 1s. 8d., and 2s.; that of cocoa, at 8d. and 1s.; and that of chicory, which he or she may require during the week. The quantities of tea are reckoned in quarter pounds, those of coffee in half pounds. The different papers being filled up are carried to the Secretary of the Association, who casts up the sum total, and the people having paid for their week's supply when they received their wages, the amount, together with the order for the next week's consumption, is sent to a large wholesale house, which of course supplies a good article at wholesale price—that is to say, deducting half-a-crown in every pound of the nominal rate. Thus the average weekly supply costs about £20, and it is received for about £17 10s. The saving to the hands effected by this rate of discount, since the institution of the association, three years ago, is calculated at £251 11s. 11d., and the saving from the 28th of March to the 7th November of the present year has been no less than £69 7s. 1d. The collectors throughout the mill levy twopence on every pound sterling subscribed, and out of this fund they make good to the wholesale house the deficiencies of any defaulter.

Similar systems, upon a larger scale, and embracing all sorts of provisions, have been tried, but found not to answer. "Not," says Mr. David Morris, "from any defect in the system itself, but because the workpeople mistook its object, tried to become dealers in the goods and to keep stocks on hand." The Tea and Coffee Association works admirably. At its starting, Mr. David Morris became responsible to the grocery house for the goods delivered, but that establishment is now quite content to give the operatives themselves credit, without any such collateral security.

I cannot quit the Messrs. Morris's establishment without mentioning the exertions which they have made for the ventilation of their mills, particularly in the card-room department. I saw one elderly woman who said that under the old system she was so asthmatic that she used every week to lay by a shilling to buy a bottle of physic to enable her to breathe. Since the ventilators have been at work she has never taken one drop of her medicine, and actually keeps the last phial, half full, as a trophy!

In my notices of the sanitary condition of the cotton metropolis, I ought not to omit mention of the strenuous exertions being made by the corporation of Salford to improve that portion of Manchester—for Salford is as much a part of Manchester as Southwark is of London—which is committed to their charge. The last yearly report (as yet unpublished) of the Nuisance Committee of Salford has been courteously shown to me by Mr. David Chadwick, the borough treasurer, and from it I condense the following account of the vigorous sanitary reforms being carried on by the authorities:—In the borough there are about 12,000 premises of all kinds. Of these, there were last year inspected no less than 11,075, out of which 7,870 were found to require "cleaning and improving." Notices were served in all these cases, and of the notices 4,438 have been already complied with. Of 1,372 cellar dwellings examined, 152 have been "cleaned and improved." The nuisance committee report upon the large number of offensive cesspools. Of these, 1,348 have been materially improved, 107 were taken down and re-constructed, and 648 had their walls raised from three feet and under to six feet. During the last year there were paved, drained, and cleansed in Salford eighteen streets and courts; and operations are proceeding in four more; whilst there have been constructed 3,134 yards of sewerage. The number of slaughterhouses in Salford is thirty-three, and they have all, "with the approbation of the butchers," been put under a stringent code of sanitary law. Notices have been served upon 243 persons keeping pigs in cellars, for the removal of the animals, and a vast number of piggeries, kept in back yards, have been cleaned and improved. Under so vigilant a system of sanitary police, the reader will not be surprised when he learns that during the recent cholera visitation, those localities which at former periods of pestilence suffered most have been as healthy as any in the borough. Still much remains to be done, there still being in Salford no less than 232 streets requiring, either partially or entirely, to be drained and paved.

In returning last Sunday night, by the Oldham-road, from one of my tours among the druggists, I was somewhat surprised to hear the loud sounds of music and jollity which floated out from the public-house windows. The street was swarming with drunken men and women; and with young mill-girls and boys, shouting, hallooing, and romping with each other. Now, I am not one of those who look upon the slightest degree of social indulgence as a downright evil, but I confess that last Sunday night in the Oldham-road astonished and grieved me. In no city have I ever witnessed a scene of more open, brutal, and general intemperance. The public-houses and gin-shops were roaring full. Rows, and fights, and scuffles were every moment taking place within doors and in the streets. The whole street rung with shouting, screaming, and swearing, mingled with the jarring music of half-a-dozen bands. A tolerably intimate acquaintance with most phases of London life enables me to state that in no part of the metropolis would the police have tolerated such a state of things for a single Sunday. I entered one of the musical taverns—one of the best of them. It was crowded to the door with men and women—many of them appearing to belong to a better station in life than mill hands or mechanics. The music consisted of performances on the piano and seraphine. In the street I accosted a policeman, telling him of my surprise that music should be allowed in public-houses on Sunday evenings. Such a thing was never dreamt of in London.

"Oh," quoth he, "there is an understanding that they don't play nothing but sacred music."

"Sacred music," I said; "well, it is the first time I ever heard the 'Bay of Biscay,' and the 'Drum Polka' invested with the title."

# LABOUR AND THE POOR.

———◆———

## THE MANUFACTURING DISTRICTS.

### [FROM OUR SPECIAL CORRESPONDENT.]

### THE TEN HOURS BILL.

### Letter X.

I approach this subject with the less hesitation, as it is beyond my province to attempt to solve any of the profound social and economic questions which it involves. In this one subject-matter there are indeed bound inextricably together the deepest, yet the most delicate considerations connected at once with the rights of property, the rights of labour, and the degree to which it is good and expedient that society as a whole shall, for the ultimate benefit of peculiar classes affected by peculiar conditions, and carrying on their pursuits under peculiar circumstances, infringe upon the general law by which each individual is competent to dispose of his or her labour in the best market. It will be my object to show, so far as I have been able to elucidate the subject, how the latest restrictive enactment upon factory labour has worked—to state what I consider to be the feeling of the people upon the subject, supported by evidence collected by myself and by others—and to show how the additional hours of evening leisure are commonly spent; and also to explain how the law upon the subject is evaded, and what are the views of the workpeople with respect to these evasions.

First, then, let me state distinctly what the restrictive laws respecting factories are. The first act passed upon the subject came into operation in 1833. It defined the ordinary "factory working-day" as extending from half-past five in the morning to half-past eight in the evening—a period of fifteen hours; and within these limits it was lawful to employ "young persons" at any hour, so long as they only worked for twelve hours each day. The act of 1844 placed women in the category of "young persons;" and the act of 1847 limited the labour both of women and young persons from twelve to ten hours. The law, therefore, as it at present stands, affects three classes of workers immediately and avowedly, and one class indirectly, and by a side-wind. The first three classes are children, young persons, and women. The last class is that of male adults. Children are persons between the ages of eight and thirteen. They are permitted to work daily for 6½ hours, and are obliged daily to go to school for three hours. The phrase "young persons," signifies boys and girls between the ages of thirteen and eighteen. They are restricted to working ten hours a day; and the same rule applies to women of all ages. The class whose labour is left nominally free is that of male adults; but as, in nine cases out of ten, the manufacture of cotton cannot be carried on without the simultaneous efforts of men, women, and young persons of both sexes, it is clear that the maximum number of hours of toil prescribed for any one class will, generally speaking, be the maximum number of hours for all.

This system has been more or less in operation—I use the phrase because the law has been more or less evaded—for two years; and it becomes important to ascertain what have been so far its effects upon trade, and upon the condition, social and moral, of the worker.

As regards the first of these inquiries, I learn, upon the highest authority, that the law has not yet been fairly and fully tested. The spinning and weaving trade, since the passing of the bill, has attained to fair average prosperity, but there has happened none of those sudden and vast demands for goods which the fluctuations of the market sometimes create, and which must be provided for as rapidly as the call comes, or the execution of which we must leave to our unfettered rivals on the Continent or at Lowell. It has often happened that sudden orders for cotton goods have come upon the Manchester millowners, to execute which the engine has been kept in motion for fifteen hours a day. This cannot, one would think, legally happen again. "So much the better for the workpeople," will be said. "Men and women are not to be wrought to death to satisfy the lust of cotton lords for gold." But then, if the order be not executed by us, it will possibly be executed by others. The consequence will be, that we lose so much of the capital out of which wages are paid and mills built. I have heard of instances in which new factories, giving employment to new hands, have been created out of profits accruing during such periods of over time. Had the Ten Hours Bill then existed in force, these additional factories would not have been built. Now, I do not pretend to hold the balance between these conflicting considerations; I wish to state the practical *pros* and *cons* as practical men put them to me. I repeat, however, that the Ten Hours Bill has not as yet been called upon to weather the storm, while I may add that there is no immediate appearance of any such tempest. Several mills, which were not long ago working eleven and twelve hours by relays and other means, have come down to ten hours; and I have just been told by the managing partner of a very large spinning and weaving house in Manchester, that his establishment will be working short time before the year is out.

It is clear that in such circumstances as these the Ten Hours Bill becomes a dead letter. The markets themselves enact a far more rigorous law. In times of slackness of trade, then, the bill is neither felt nor needed by master or man; in times of moderate and equable demand its pressure upon capital may be considered as comparatively trifling. It is in periods of sudden demand only that the restrictive power will be felt in its full strength. Now, I have conversed with many gentlemen directly or indirectly connected with the cotton trade, and I have found that, viewing these periods as the exception rather than the rule, it was a very general opinion among them that the bill— taking one season with another—will practically exercise less restrictive power upon the employer than it is theoretically endowed with; while, in many instances, as it has been remarked to me, tending, as it will, to modify the effect of any mere partial spirt of demand, it will also modify anything like reactionary slackness—a consummation devoutly to be desired by those who think that a general period of ten hours' labour is better for both employer and employed than twelve hours one half the year, and eight the other.

In ascertaining the views of the workpeople, I have, previously to going for information to the fountain-head, asked the opinion, on this point, of many gentlemen whose positions have brought them into long and intimate connection with the operatives. I think that I fairly sum up the substance of what was communicated to me by these authorities, when I say that in their opinion the great bulk of the working-class are listless and apathetic upon the subject—viewing the advantages and disadvantages of the Ten Hours Bill as pretty nearly counterbalancing each other. The agitation for the bill, I have been told, was, although well got up, in reality very partial, and generally conducted by a comparatively small number of individuals in each locality. As a common rule, the workers in the country mills valued the proposed restriction less than their town brethren, probably because they had not so many tempting opportunities for the disposal of their evening time. One point, however, my informants almost universally conceded—and what they stated is strongly verified by my own observations—that it is the best-conducted, the most thoughtful and well-informed workmen in each mill, who have been most earnest in the ten hours' agitation, and who are now most zealous in the support of the present law. To men whose deepest enjoyment is the quiet pursuit of some branch of study in their own homes, and who are earnestly labouring at the task of self-enlightenment—time, in the early part of the evening, is money. To men, on the contrary, who make their way from the mill to the public-house, time is not money, for, even should the factory work until eight o'clock at night, they have ample leisure for getting drunk, and more money for the purpose than they could have earned by shorter hours. Now, as the comparatively unintelligent preponderate, in melancholy weight, over the comparatively intelligent body of the operatives, the alleged apathy of a great mass of the workpeople can be very easily and naturally accounted for. I remember, when these views were upon one occasion stated to me, observing that of all the workpeople I had yet questioned, every single individual avowed his satisfaction with the Ten Hours Bill. "Yes," said my informant, "that is likely enough, but there is no enthusiasm among the bulk of them on the subject. If you wish to know the difference between a real and deep-felt, and a partial and factitious agitation, you should have seen and contrasted the agitation for the Ten Hours Bill and the agitation for the Charter."

From what I have ascertained, I believe that a large proportion of the working people fully believed that their wages would not be reduced by the Ten Hours Bill; and a smaller proportion still believe that the reduction which has taken place cannot last, and that the ultimate effect of the Ten Hours Bill will be to keep up wages. This notion is founded upon a piece of political economy taken up unhappily at the wrong end. A weaver at Ashton-under-Lyne, who held the comforting dogma and was especially loath to give it up, stated to me what had been his own belief, and the belief of a great body of his fellows, nearly as follows:—

"You see, sir, that wages depends among other things on the prices our masters get for the goods. Well, the prices depends upon the proportion between the buyers that want the goods, and the quantity of goods there is for them to buy from. If two buyers come after the same bale of calicoes, the price will be high; but if two masters run with a bale each after one buyer, the price will be low. You see all that."

"Yes, certainly; it is quite clear."

"Very well, then; the working men thought it stood to reason that, if we diminished production, we'd alter the proportion between the lot of goods and the number of merchants as came to buy 'em, so that there would be less of one while there would be as many as before of the other, and that, in consequence, the prices would rise and the masters would be able to give us as much wages for ten hours as they used to do for twelve."

"Yes, but don't you see that if you were right, and that if you carried the rule out, you ought to get as much for working one hour as you did for twelve; because, there being only one-eleventh of the old quantity of goods produced, they would, according to your theory, be worth eleven times the old price. You forget that when things get dearer the number of people who can buy them diminishes."

The poor weaver shook his head dolefully, and allowed that they had been sadly disappointed, and that he feared that they had been in the wrong. "But for all that, sir," he added, "I would rather have the ten hours' work, even though we don't have the twelve hours' wages."

The unsound politico-economic doctrine held by the Ashton weaver, was, I am informed, exceedingly general during the ten-hours' agitation, and is—as I have hinted—not yet quite overturned, even by the practical arguments weekly urged at the pay-table. In some cases these arguments, indeed, owing to particular circumstances, are of greater or less weight, because the reduction of wages under the Ten Hours Bill has been not at all uniform. And this brings me to another part of the subject.

Is it possible, by the increased energy and sharpened attention which a shorter period of toil may reasonably be supposed to produce, and also by the speeding of the machinery, that the amount of production in ten hours can be forced so closely up to that of twelve hours, as only to leave a trifling per centage of difference between them?

This question is very differently answered. The more sanguine ten hours' men are loud in their assertions that the gradual march of improvement in machinery will very speedily make up all, or nearly all, deficiencies, or that at all events, if the quantity of work turned off be not quite so great, the quality will be better. On the other hand, millowners reply that they have been always working as rapidly as their machinery would let them, and always producing an article suffi-ciently good in quality to command the market price. I have, however, ascertained beyond cavil, that in a great proportion of mills the en-gine *has* been speeded, and the quantity of work per hour *has* been in-creased since the Ten Hours Bill. This increase, however, cannot have been to any important extent, as the amount of wages—the labourers being chiefly paid by the piece—demonstrates. That overwork, how-ever, as regards the time occupied at the mule or the loom, produces in the end consequences unprofitable, not only to the workman, but the master, the following curious facts will put in a striking light. Some years ago a firm in Manchester received a large and pressing order for calico. The emergency was stated to the workpeople, and by general consent a working day of fifteen hours was agreed to. The results, in the words of the manager of the factory, were as follows: "The first week we got a fair extra quantity of goods; the next week the extra amount fell off by one quarter; the third it fell to one half, and in the fourth week of labour at fifteen hours a-day, less was turned off than the average production of a week of twelve hours a-day."

The reduction of wages made by the mills working ten hours may be generally stated as one-sixth upon the whole amount given. This, however, is but a rough estimate, as the effects of the change have been differently felt in different departments of labour. The principle upon which the masters proceeded was generally this. They slightly reduced the rates of wages for all work, in order to make up for the loss of interest upon capital involved in the enforced idleness of the machinery, and then they struck off from the new rate one-sixth of the amount, corresponding with that sixth part of the labour which was given up. In many cases the reduction at first amounted to no less than 25 per cent.—a terrible slice out of a man's income. Thus in some places hands earning 10s. a week were reduced 1s., being at the rate of 10 per cent. for the fall in the rate, and then further reduced 1s. 6d. for the diminution in time, making a cruel total of 2s. 6d. out of a weekly 10s. I have stated, however, that the reduction, as it soon began prac-tically to operate, turned out to be by no means uniform. First, there are a certain number of hands, principally the less skilled labourers, who are paid by the week. Their wages were of course reduced with those of their brethren, and have continued reduced, while, owing to the speeding of the machinery and other circumstances, the degree of remuneration in the higher departments has to a certain extent rallied. From all I can learn, the women in the different roving and drawing departments have suffered less than almost any other class, owing, I presume, to a greater degree of capability possessed by the machinery which they tend for being speeded. A card-room hand in a mill in Chorlton told me that there were "five jack tenters" in his factory, who earned as much in ten hours by working hard as they used to do in twelve. In other departments, speeded machinery and harder and closer application to the toil have also made a certain difference. It is exceedingly difficult as well as dangerous to generalise upon a subject the extended data of which have not yet been anything like fully collected; but perhaps it is not far from the mark to take the average fall of wages produced by the Ten Hours Bill as from 16 to 20 per cent.

Such, then, having been the consequences of the bill upon the most material point in connection with the social condition of the people—their wages—we have now to inquire how the blow has been borne—whether or not the great majority of the workmen are satisfied with their diminished hours and diminished wages, or whether they would like to go back to the old system of more money and more work. The matter is to so great an extent a labourer's question, that the feelings of the people themselves are of the most primary consequence in forming a judgment. I have therefore, in every mill which I have visited in Manchester, Bolton, Ashton, and Oldham, taken opportunities of personally learning the opinions of the workpeople from their own lips, and in their own phraseology. I have also conversed with cotton operatives at their homes, in the streets, in the taverns, and in my own apartments. I have thus examined probably near one hundred persons, and the result is, that, with two exceptions—that of a young woman, a winder in Manchester, and that of a spinner in the coarse mill I have described at Oldham—I was told by one and all that they preferred the ten hours' system to the twelve hours, even if they only got ten hours' instead of twelve hours' wages.

From a crowded note-book I select the following answers, not because they are peculiar in any degree, but, on the contrary, because they furnish fair specimens of the different classes of replies, and the different classes of reasons given for the preference alleged by the witnesses. The people examined were card-room hands, drawing and roving frame tenters, spinners, and weavers. I first take the

MEN.

1. Prefers ten hours, and for two reasons—on account of the time it gives children to be educated, and on account of the additional time which it gives women, especially mothers, to be at home. Would have

been a different man himself if he had got schooling when he was young. But he worked fourteen hours a day before he was ten years of age.

2. Likes the ten hours, fine. Thinks that it is better for trade than twelve; because if they'd been working twelve last summer, they would be working regular short time now.

3. Thinks the Ten Hours Bill a blessed thing for the poor people. They have time now to clean themselves and their houses, which they hadn't well to do before—they were so tired.

4. Hopes the great people in Lunnon will not allow that relay system to go on, for it's very tyrannous to the poor.

5. Would like, of course, that his wages had kept the same, but thinks it wouldn't be reasonable like to expect as much for working ten hours as for working twelve.

6. If he must tell his opinions, would say that he is for the Ten Hours Bill, because he considers ten hours long enough for any man to labour. His health is better since the ten hours, and he has more energy to do soom'mut of an evening. All the workpeople who dare tell you what they think will say as he says.

7. Was a great deal better and a great deal happier since the ten hours.

8. Could write his name now, which he had learned since the ten hours. His mother used always to be pressing him to go to school, but he never could see that he had time for it until the ten hours.

9. Was all for the ten hours. Would be very much pleased if he could have the old wages, but the additional time and comfort at home was pretty nigh worth the money.

10. Went to a night school since the ten hours to learn writing, which he wanted to very much. Would not go back to the twelve hours for anything. He thinks that the change did good, and hears that the brewers are complaining that they haven't so much custom as they had. [This piece of information is very apocryphal.]

11. The Ten Hours Bill disappointed them very much in the wages; but even if it never gave them more than they had, would prefer it to the twelve hours.

WOMEN.

1. The Ten Hours Bill was the greatest thing as ever came into operation. Every woman in the shed (the weaving room) will tell you the same as me. Thinks everybody in the mill prefers the ten hours, all but one man.

2. Can do her washing now, which she always put out before, and saves money that way. The Ten Hours Bill is a good thing, and she'll always say so.

3. Has learned crochet work, "a many patterns," since the Ten Hours Bill. Thinks it a great improvement, for she has time to do lots of things about the house she couldn't look at before.

4. Goes to a night school to learn writing since the Ten Hours Bill, and likes it very much (copybook produced).

5. Makes her own dresses, "polkas and visites as smart as you like." Would decidedly not go back to the twelve hours—even though she did make more money then than now.

6. Likes the ten hours very much, because she does her house-work after she gets home. Her place is much more comfortable than it was before, and she is glad to say her husband thinks so too.

7. Believes that ten hours' work a day is enough for any Christian. At least, it's enough for her, and she don't care who knows it.

8. Likes ten hours better than the old plan, because it gives her more time to look about her before she goes to bed at night.

9. Was too much knocked up in the twelve hours' time to do any house-work; but it's quite different now, and hopes it may continue.

10. Is sure it's a great blessing to a woman to get home to her children sooner than she used. All the women in her street are for the ten hours.

Here is the evidence of twenty-one witnesses selected perfectly at random from the mass of notes in my memorandum book. The girl who preferred the twelve hours, gave, as her reason, that she earned more money—sometimes 2s. a week more—on the old plan, and that she did not see any good the two hours in the evening did her. Four of the spinners employed by the Messrs. Mason and Sons, of Ashton, a firm working twelve hours a day, when questioned by me, gave their votes for the Ten Hours Bill. The elder Mr. Mason informed me that a spinner recently came to him from an eleven hours' mill, seeking for the additional hour's employment, and alleging that, with the family he had to support, twelve hours' wages were absolutely necessary for him. The Oldham coarse spinner said the same thing to myself. That there must be numerous similar instances I cannot doubt. All I can say, is, that in the perfectly random investigation which I made, the results have been, *verbatim et literatim*, what I have stated.

The factory inspectors have, since the passing of the Ten Hours Act, instituted a similar and very extensive inquiry, and the results are detailed with great minuteness in their two last reports, the particulars of each individual examination being fully given. I extract from the report for the half-year ending October, 1848, the general tabular results, premising that in different parts of the country the feelings of the operatives appear to vary upon the subject, so that in one sub-inspector's district, 30 per cent. were for eleven hours, while in another more than 91 per cent. were in favour of ten hours.

"The Appendix contains the evidence of 212 operatives, whose opinions I myself (Mr. L. Horner) ascertained, and of 941 conversed with by the 5 sub-inspectors, together 1,153 persons; and the following are the general results:—

"1. That of the 1,153, 713 or 61¾ per cent., prefer 10 hours' work; that 147, or 12¾ per cent., prefer 11 hours' work; that 293, or 25½ per cent., prefer 12 hours' work; and thus 860, or 74½ per cent. are against returning to 12 hours.

"2. That of 651 men, 441, or 67¾ per cent., prefer 10 hours' work; that 96, or 14¾ per cent., prefer 11 hours' work; that 114, or 17¾ per cent., prefer 12 hours' work; and thus 537, or 82¾ per cent., are against returning to 12 hours.

"3. That of 502 women, 272, or 54¼ per cent., prefer 10 hours' work; that 51, or 10 per cent., prefer 11 hours' work; that 179, or 35¾ per cent., prefer 12 hours' work; and thus 323, or 64 1-3d per cent. are against returning to 12 hours.

"4. That of 90 men, receiving only from 5s. 9d. to 10s. 10d. of weekly wages, 45 (or 50 per cent.) are in favour of remaining at 10 hours' work.

"5. That of 256 women, receiving only from 4s. 6d. to 8s. of weekly wages, 141 (or 55 per cent.) are in favour of remaining at 10 hours' work.

"6. That of the 57 mill-owners conversed with, 20 expressed their belief that the majority of their people prefer 10 hours' work, although getting less wages; 22 that 11 hours would be preferred, and 15 that 12 hours would be preferred.

"7. That of the 97 agents conversed with, 50 expressed their belief that the majority of their people prefer 10 hours' work although getting less wages; 34 that 11 hours would be preferred, and 12 that 12 hours would be preferred.

"8. That of the 57 masters, 42 (or 76 per cent.), and of the 97 agents, 85 (or 87 per cent.) thus expressed their belief, that the majority of the people would be against returning to 12 hours' work."

There cannot be the slightest doubt, however, let the opinions of the majority of the workpeople be what they may, that those millown-

ers who choose to work twelve hours a day find no lack of hands to enable them to keep their mechanism in motion for the extra time. Now,
admitting that this may partially be caused by the great competition
for employment, particularly in the spinning department, where the
introduction of the self-actors is gradually displacing skilled labour,
still I think that the fact tends strongly to corroborate the views of
those who maintain that the aversion to twelve hours is, if general,
by no means either deep or zealous. The men were stigmatised as
"knobsticks," and attacked, and often maimed for life, who took employment from masters paying reduced wages; but there is not the
shadow of a hostile demonstration on the part of the ten-hours' majority against those of their comrades who work or have recently worked
in the twelve-hours factories. On the contrary, there is no doubt whatever that the "relay" system is not unfrequently carried on by the
women and young persons employed in ten-hours' mills, proceeding,
as soon as they are released, to help in the over-time operations of a
twelve-hours' establishment—an arrangement which, if it be objectionable in most respects, seems at least to have this recommenda-
tion, that it enables the operatives in some degree to proportion the
amount of labour which they perform to their physical capabilities or
their pecuniary circumstances.

The important question of how the additional evening's leisure is
spent has been to a certain extent answered by the replies given by the
witnesses whom I have examined. The point will be further elucidated
by additional testimony which I shall presently adduce. In the meantime I may state that it is the opinion of two of the largest booksellers
in Manchester dealing in cheap publications—one of these gentlemen being Mr. Heywood, of Oldham-street—that the sale of books,
newspapers, and periodicals has not increased since the Ten Hours
Bill, at least in any degree which can be attributed to that bill. There
has been an increase in such sales within the last two years, but an increase has been going steadily on since a period far more remote, and
it has in no perceptible degree been influenced by the recent factory
legislation. In the number of copybooks sold, however, a very decided
increase has taken place. The price of these books was formerly 2d.:
the demand being now greater, they are sold for 1½d. The testimony
of the chief booksellers as to the *statu quo* condition of their trade
is corroborated by that of librarians. The secretary to the Mechanics'
Institute reports that the Ten Hours Bill has not visibly affected the
number of subscribers to the library of that institution; and the li-

brarian at the Ancoats Lyceum makes a similar statement. There is, however, no doubt that the number of adults attending night schools has materially increased, although there exist no means of ascertaining the exact proportion.

The fact is, as I have already hinted, that the sober, diligent, and well-disposed of the workpeople profit most by the additional evening leisure. A man who did not want to learn or improve when he worked twelve hours a day cannot be expected to have his disposition changed by an alteration in the length of the working period to ten hours. Those who expected that the new law would of itself be likely to produce a beneficial moral change in the population will most probably be disappointed; while, from all I hear, there can be no doubt but that the law is operating, and must operate, so far as to create opportunities and facilities for that beneficial moral change which were not previously in existence.

In the spring of the present year, when the extensive spread of the relay system began to threaten the practical existence of the Ten Hours Bill, a short time committee, composed entirely of working men, was formed in Manchester for the purpose of collecting evidence upon the working of the bill. The secretary of this committee accordingly entered into an extensive correspondence with the operatives in the various cotton towns, both in Scotland and the North of England, and a mass of the replies received has been submitted to me. The evidence contained in these letters is obviously of an *ex parte* nature. The writers are uniformly working mill operatives, and the leading champions of the Ten Hours Bill in their several localities. Their testimony must therefore, be taken *cum grano;* but at the same time I have considered it right, by making some extracts from the correspondence in question, to show the views entertained by the leading supporters of the Ten Hours Bill, among the factory hands, now that that bill has been nearly two years in operation. With these remarks I proceed to extract some of the most characteristic points of the correspondence, premising that the whole of the letters are of the same general stamp, varying only in expression and matters of local detail. The dates range over March, April, and May of the present year. For obvious reasons I withhold the names of the writers.

OPERATIVE EVIDENCE ON THE TEN HOURS BILL.

1. GLASGOW.—"We are waiting with the greatest anxiety to hear what Sir George Grey is going to propose. I never saw such anxiety

manifested to keep the Ten Hours Bill whole and entire as at the present time. Heretofore, we had some trouble with the women when we were agitating for it, but now they are the most strenuous advocates for the bill. For instance, in the factory where I work, they have got up a subscription to pay the expenses of the short time committee, and although their wages have been reduced 12½ per cent., every woman gave her penny. There are nine factories here working irregularly, and many more are ready to follow, if the system be not put a stop to."

2. HEYWOODS, IN LANCASHIRE.—"I can assure you that the general opinion of the factory workers here is, that they are satisfied with the bill, and to show how they are spending their time, they have got a number of gardens. Where there was one previously, there are ten now, and the people take great delight to spend their time in these gardens, not as labour, but as recreation."

3. BURNLEY.—"I am happy to inform you that we are all right in Burnley as regards the Ten Hours Bill. We have had a committee sitting these two months, who have opposed all the masters in Burnley running more than ten hours, and in one or two instances successfully."

4. STALEYBRIDGE.—"A public meeting of overlookers has been held, and a committee formed, who have authorized me to correspond with you. You will see, therefore, that we are up and doing."

5. STOCKPORT.—"With regard to the opinions of the operatives, I think there never was a time when they were more enthusiastic in favour of the Ten-hours Bill. The number of masters breaking the law amounts to fifteen. They are working by shifts, and resorting to all manner of base practices to evade the law. And many and bitter are the curses which their workpeople bestow on them."

6. TODMORDEN.—"I have talked with some men who refused to agitate for the bill, but who now declare that sooner than work twelve hours they would certainly become agitators."

7. ENFIELD, NEAR PRESTON.—"All hands are in favour of ten hours a day. In Accrington all the masters are working ten hours. In Oswald Twistle Mr. Walmsley is running his self-acting mules twelve hours per day, but the minders are in favour of ten hours per day."

8. MOSSLEY.—"All the mills here are violating the provisions of the Ten Hours Bill in one shape or another. They run more than ten hours a day, yet make a pretence of keeping within the law by means of the relay system, but the females and young persons in our mill work more than ten hours a day—some more than twelve, and in some of the mills the spinners are obliged to work more than fourteen hours. The members of our association at these mills beg and pray for the committee to interfere, for they say that their constitutions are undermined by the labour which they have to perform."

9. OLDHAM.—"They all want the ten hours question to be put on the motive power. There are several mills in our district working twelve hours a day."

10. HEBDEN-BRIDGE.—"The masters are red-hot for the persecution of those workpeople that may stir in this matter. They have with few exceptions commenced the relay system, and the females would rather return to twelve hours and be paid for it, than work the relay system, which causes them to be 13½ hours from home, although they do only ten hours' work. The masters know this, and put them to as great inconvenience as possible, in order to get them to cry out against the Ten Hours Bill."

11. ASTLEY BRIDGE.—"There are a school and library established here. The school is open three nights a-week; and last quarter it had 95 members, besides the committee, chiefly factory operatives. The piece hands have not felt the reduction of time much. The females attend more to their domestic duties, and the men are more comfortable than before."

12. BURNLEY (Second Letter).—"The young people are generally employing their leisure hours very profitably; many adults employ their leisure time in cultivating land or gardens. Wages have fallen about 1s. 6d., except in mills, where the machinery is rapid. Females have attended better to their domestic duties, and the men have been in consequence more comfortable."

13. GLASGOW (Second Letter).—"Twenty factories are breaking the law and setting it at defiance. The effect of the bill has hitherto been in the right direction, but it has not yet had time to prove its usefulness. The committee consider that the women generally pay more attention to domestic duties than formerly. Many of them employ their time in sewing and knitting, and the young attend school more than they used to do. The time allowed during the day by relay systems is quite lost to the worker; and it causes young people to wander in the street, and be introduced to bad company, because few, if any of them, can go home during the short interval."

14. STALEYBRIDGE (Second Letter).—"The men are often employed instructing their fellow-labourers or cultivating small plots of ground. The women are more engaged in their households. The weekly hands have only ten hours' pay, but the piece hands are getting more money, according to the time, than they used to earn."

15. PRESTON (Second Letter).—"One mill here has piecers who go to work in it for two hours, after having worked in other mills for ten. Many of the people employ their two hours in schools, one of which is attended by 300. A great improvement has taken place in the health of the workpeople, and a vast number have learned the arts of reading and writing, and the improvements in the homes of many factory workers

would not be believed, except by those who were well acquainted with the facts."

I now proceed to give a short account of the relay system already so often alluded to. It would appear that those millowners who please find no more difficulty in running their steam-engines through the provisions of the Ten Hours Act, than Mr. O'Connell used to find in driving a coach and six through the stipulations of other legislative enactments. The factory inspectors have tried hard to obtain convictions against those millowners who, as they contend, have violated the act of Parliament, but without success. In every case, with I think a single exception, the informations have been dismissed, the magistrates declining to convict upon the ground of the confused and equivocal wording of certain of the restrictive clauses.

The hands who are worked in alleged violation of the law are the women and young persons. The factory day extending from half-past five a.m. until half-past eight o'clock p.m., workpeople can be employed during the whole of these hours, provided the period of each person's labour in the same mill is not extended over ten hours. It is therefore evident that, by employing two sets of hands, two mills, having an understanding with each other, could work fourteen hours per day, simply by the interchange of their hands, each set working in each mill only seven hours per day, the alteration being effected after the dinner hour, common to both sets. This is a possible arrangement, but I do not hear that it has been carried out in the exact way in which I have put the case. I proceed, therefore, to the shifts most commonly practised. The first mode of proceeding involves the necessity of a ten-hours and a twelve-hours mill existing tolerably near each other. The general hour of commencing work is six o'clock a.m. As this, however, is quite optional, the twelve-hours mill will not commence until half after six. Each establishment then works the ten hours fairly out, allowing the same time for breakfast and dinner. The early mill has finished the day's work at half-past five o'clock, the late mill has not finished until six o'clock, by which time the necessary young persons dismissed from the ten-hours' establishment have arrived, and are ready to relieve the young persons and women in the twelve-hours' establishment, which may, therefore, keep on working until half-past eight o'clock. In these cases the young persons in the ten-hours' mill really work ten hours or more, and the young persons in the twelve-hours' mill work only ten hours. This is one of the modes in which the relay system is carried on.

Another way of doing the business is more properly called the "shift" system, and is managed with the same set of hands in the same mill. The principle upon which the plan proceeds is the possibility of keeping the machinery going during the absence of a small proportion of the women and young persons, the individuals composing which proportion are successively and in rotation dismissed from the mill for one or two hours per day, at different periods of the day, and then called in to resume their work and allow of the temporary absence of the next division. There are various ways of accomplishing this device, some of which are excessively complicated and difficult to be understood by anybody who has not a thorough knowledge of the factory system. Let me try, however, to state the details of one case of the kind—premising that one of the clauses of the Factory Act requires that all meal-times, at all mills, shall be the same. A. and B. are "young persons" within the meaning of the act. The work of both is thus arranged:—

A.

| Work hours. | Meal hours. |
|---|---|
| From 5.30 to  8    | ... From  8    to 9.30 |
|  „    9.30 to 12.30 ... |  „   12.30 to 2.30 |
|  „    2.30 to  5    | ... „    5    to 6.30 |
|  „    6.30 to  8.30 | |

Total work 10 hours.

B.

| Work hours. | Meal hours. |
|---|---|
| From  5.30 to 9    | ... From 9 to 10.30 |
|  „   10.30 to 2    | ... „   2 to  4 |
|  „    4    to 6    | ... „   6 to  7.30 |
|  „    7.30 to 8.30 | |

Total work 10 hours.

An attentive examination of the above table will show how it may be contended that the meal hours of A and B are the same, because the respective times allowed partially include each other. Thus, A's breakfast time, 8 to 9.30, includes half an hour of B's breakfast time, 9 to 10.30; A's dinner time, 12.30 to 2.30, includes half an hour of B's dinner time, 2 to 4; and A's tea time, 5 to 6.30, includes half an hour of B's tea time, 6 to 7.30. The object of the arrangement is this:—

| B. | | | A. | | |
|---|---|---|---|---|---|
| Is in the factory and does A.'s work during A.'s absence. | | | Is in the factory and does B.'s work during B.'s absence. | | |
| | o'clock. | o'clock. | | o'clock. | o'clock. |
| From | 8 to | 9 | From | 9.30 to | 10.30 |
| „ | 12.30 to | 2 | „ | 2.30 to | 4 |
| „ | 5 to | 6 | „ | 6.30 to | 7.30 |

In this way A and B, working only ten hours a-piece, and having their meals nominally at the same hours, are in reality in attendance for fifteen hours, during which time the machinery is moving, with the exception of the regular hours for meals specified by law. This system of relays, or shifts, has been compared to a coach professing to change horses every hour, and then starting with four steeds, two pulling, and two trotting alongside, ready to form the relay when the first stage is accomplished, the two original workers then taking their places until their spell of pulling comes round in turn.

The evil which has been most complained of to me respecting this relay system is, that the young men and girls employed in it do not go home during their times of absence throughout the day, but rather resort to public-houses together, or lounge about in the streets. The women say that they cannot "settle themselves" to do anything at home, when they have to go back to the mill again, and they complain that virtually, and so far as domestic duties go, their time is as much lost to them as if they were labouring the whole twelve or fourteen hours, as the case may be, while they are receiving but ten hours' wages—the factory paying them only for the hours during which they work, not for the hours during which they have to knock about in attendance. I would also remark, that this relay or shift system puts an end at once to the facilities for adults attending schools, as the only hours at which they can or will attend are after working is over in the evenings.

It is a common thing to hear the operatives say that the only Ten Hours Bill which cannot be evaded would be a ten hours restriction upon the work of the steam engine—a proposition, however, which would interfere obviously and directly with the freedom of adult labour. The last decisions by various benches of magistrates, fortified by the advice of counsel, have been against the rigorous interpretation sought to be put by the Factory Inspectors upon the clause in the bill, which, they contend, provides that in reckoning the number of hours which any person has worked in a mill, these shall be reckoned from the commencement of the first hour at which the first person began to labour in the mill.

As I was anxious to ascertain the actual effect of the cutting down of time, and consequently of wages, upon the physical comforts of the mill hands, I applied to a great many butchers, to know whether the sale of meat had materially fallen off since the short time commenced. The universal answer which, without a single exception, I received was in the affirmative. The sale of meat fell in a marked manner immediately after the Ten Hours Bill came into operation, and has not, or only in a very slight degree, rallied. Yet meat has been cheaper by 1d. and 1½d. per lb. than for years previously. "The Ten Hours Bill," said one butcher, "cut at the luxuries of the poor, and the principal of these luxuries is meat." "Families," said another, "that used to buy four pounds a week, now buy only two or three. They say they must have tea and sugar, and bread, and they must pay their rent and get clothing, and then they have nothing left for the butcher." I could multiply replies like these to any extent, but the two given above are specimens of the whole.

And so the matter stands.

With this communication I take leave of the cotton districts. I have sought to describe the condition of the factory population— physical, social, and moral. I have described their toil, their homes, their places of amusement, and, so far as I could elucidate them, their own views and feelings respecting their condition, their masters, and themselves. I have tried, in viewing the social and physical evils which I saw around me, to discriminate between those which spring from factories and those which spring from the large towns wherein factories are so often located; and if I have stated a fact or suggested a train of thought which may lead either to a practical improvement in the condition of the industrious swarms by whom I am now surrounded, or even to a better and more correct appreciation of their merits or demerits, then I apprehend that one at least of the purposes of these letters will have been accomplished.

My next communication will be dated from the Silk districts.

# LABOUR AND THE POOR.

—◆—

## THE MANUFACTURING DISTRICTS.

[FROM OUR SPECIAL CORRESPONDENT.]

### MACCLESFIELD AND THE SILK TRADE.

### LETTER XI.

I am writing at a window commanding the crowded market-place of a quaint, old-fashioned town. The houses are irregular and massed together in picturesque clumps, their outline serrated by crazy chimney-stacks and high-peaked gables. Opposite to me is an old, buttressed Norman church—a gilt crown placed loyally above the weather-cock, and a gilt mitre placed religiously above the crown. The market-place is built on the top of a hill—for steep lanes slope down from it in all directions, and through their openings you catch pleasant glimpses of distant heathy hills. A majority of the crowded shops display in their windows richest silks of the gayest patterns—gown-pieces, waistcoat-pieces, and handkerchiefs of all hues and sizes. The market is crowded with stalls, and booths, and tents, and these are surrounded by chaffering customers. The wares displayed are here and there peculiar. Amid great heaps of vegetables and fruit, piled in pyramids upon the pavement, are the stalls of vendors of blacking—for here is manufactured the material which polishes the boots and shoes of a great part of Lancashire. One family make and sell near half a ton weekly. Close to the blacking-merchant is a quack, with his portable furnaces and retorts, distilling his remedies before a gaping crowd of on-lookers. Next to him sits, in his canvas-roofed tent, a bread-merchant—home-baked wheaten loaves on one side of his shop—round doughy cakes of oatmeal, sold at a penny a piece, piled up on the other. Hard by is a stall filled with hares, rabbits, black game, and plovers; and just before it stands a man with a huge inverted umbrella, filled with coarsely-made brown stays. The aspect of the people is on the whole comfortable, and well-to-do. The vendors are generally country folks, burly farmers, or knowing pedlars. The buyers are the people of the town, amongst whom the lower class of females appear decidedly better dressed and better looking than the factory women. Nevertheless, most of them do work in mills. A short turn through the old-fashioned town, with its narrow streets and its ranges of stairs from one elevated plateau to another, will reveal many factories, similar in appearance to the cotton mills, but smaller in size, and crowned with chimneys, which, though tall, are yet not so tall as most of those with which we have been lately dealing.

These are silk mills; the population is a population of silk throwsters and weavers; for I have been describing the principal features of the market-place and the market-day in Macclesfield, the capital of the silk trade in England.

Macclesfield is situated among the Cheshire hills. The population of the township was, by the last census, 56,035, and it has since increased, but by no means rapidly. The number of persons in the receipt of parish relief, on the 1st of January, 1848, was 2,974. The value of life in Macclesfield is about 1 in 38—a proportion similar to that of the majority of the smaller cotton towns. The number of marriages in 1846, according to the rites of the church, was 532; otherwise, 42. Of the 1,148 persons thus united, 350 women and 178 men, making a total of 528 persons, or rather under 50 per cent., signed with their marks—the proportion between the ignorance of the men and the women being nearly in a similar ratio. Of the persons in question 115 women, or nearly 20 per cent., were under age, and 46 men. The legitimate births during 1846 were 2,223, and the illegitimate 238—the proportion being about one to eight. Out of 825 deaths, 214 were those of persons under one year of age—a proportion very much smaller than the average of the cotton towns. These broad facts afford landmarks in making our first advances towards estimating the condition of the Macclesfield silk manufacturing population. It is a population increasing in a much slower ratio than that of the cotton towns. Thus the female inhabitants of the neighbouring township of Stockport rose between 1831 and 1841 from 36,000 to 44,000; while those of Macclesfield increased only from 25,000 to 28,000.

The manufacture of silk may be said to be the only one in Macclesfield. There is but a single cotton-mill in the town. Silk has been the staple of the place for more than half a century. Before that time Macclesfield was but a paltry village. "We took the trade," said a manufacturer to me, "from Spitalfields, and now the country places about are taking it from us; and with every successive stage of the expansion of the manufacture the wages seem to come down." About one-half of the labouring population of Macclesfield work at home, and the other half in the mills. The home-labourers are exclusively weavers, and include a large proportion of men; the mill-labourers are principally engaged in throwing, doubling, and other processes, analogous, in a certain degree, to the drawing and spinning of cotton-mills—in preparing the threads which are intertwisted by the loom. By far the largest proportion of the mill population is female, the weavers who work looms in the mills being inconsiderable in number, compared with those who work at home. I may add, that the amount of silk thread spun in Macclesfield is much greater than the amount woven there. The warp and the shute, being prepared for the loom, are sent out all over the silk-weaving districts of Lancashire and Cheshire, for the process to be completed. The wages earned in and out of the mills in Macclesfield do not materially vary. The throwsters and spinners in the mills have the most regular work. The weavers can earn higher wages when in employment, but their looms stand idle upon the average fully three months in the year. A weaver may, one season with another, make from 10s. to 12s. a week; a female throwster or doubler in the mill from 8s. to 9s. The rate of wages, hours of work, species of employment, and other particulars will, however, be best understood from the following details of the different branches of the silk trade, gathered from personal observation of every department and of every process, and from the personally collected testimony of the workpeople.

I premise by stating that I took great pains, in traversing the silk district, to ascertain whether accounts of the distress in Spitalfields seemed to have reached or to have affected the country weavers. In general, I found that the people knew very little and cared very little about the matter. It was only the state of their own district in which they appeared to take any interest. There did not seem to be any general ideas prevalent upon the causes of the distress of the metropolitan silk-weavers. My details upon the subject were listened to with an apathetic "Aye, indeed—well, they do seem very poorly off, to be sure." I frequently put the question as to what my listeners thought could be the reason why a trade which was comparatively good in one part of England should be so bad in another; but heads were invariably shaken, and a stolid "Well, I dunna know, indeed, sir," formed the most frequent response. One man, indeed, said he supposed Government intended to root out the Spitalfields weavers altogether; and another was of opinion that much of the Spitalfields distress was caused by there being no throwing mills in London, and the weavers being thus rendered dependent for their supplies of thread upon Italy and France. Such answers were, however, the exceptions to the rule. Nine-tenths of the people knew nothing and cared nothing about Spital-fields, or their brethren there—the apathy in that respect being very different from the mutual understanding and the constant mutual correspondence kept up between the unions and operative associations of the various cotton towns.

I have said that the silk-mills are generally smaller than the cotton factories. They are also generally cleaner, and filled with a purer atmosphere. There is no necessity for keeping the temperature of any of the rooms above 50°; and nothing analogous to, or resembling, the flying dust and floating film which abound in certain stages of the cotton manufacture is to be found. The machinery of a silk-mill is altogether simpler, slower, and less overwhelming in its power and vastness than that which spins thread from the cotton-wool. The work is cleaner too, and, in many respects, is well fitted for females, who are enabled to dress with far more neatness and propriety than the girls in the cotton factories. In several of the silk-mills which I have gone over, the girls were dressed rather in the style of milliners' apprentices than of ordinary female operatives; and if good looks may be taken as a test of satisfactory physical condition, I have no hesitation in saying that the general physical condition of the young women employed in throwing and winding silk is excellent. Very few married women work in the silk-mills—the quantity of labour to be performed at home being so considerable, that a natural and generally understood arrangement comes almost insensibly into force, and tends to keep within their own dwellings those whose absence from them would be most undesirable and domestically unprofitable. The Ten Hours Bill applies to silk factories, with certain modifications as to infant labour—a child being there accounted "a young person" at eleven years of age, instead of thirteen—a concession made by the Legislature, on account of the healthier and cleaner species of employment carried on in the silk-mills. What that employment is I shall now shortly describe.

There are in the silk-mills no operations analogous to the cleaning and carding of the cotton-mills. The first stages of the manufacture have, so to speak, been already performed by the worm which spins the cocoon. The raw fibres of silk are imported from France, Italy, or China, in compact bundles, which are sorted and arranged, according to the fineness and quality of the material, by women. The labour thus employed is, of course, physically very light, but the post is one of some responsibility, and demanding considerable acquaintance with the varying qualities of the silk. The wages paid to the sorters may be stated at 10s. a week. The silk is next plunged into hot water—the operation being generally managed by men, who are also employed in different odd jobs about the mill, and who may make from 15s. to 20s. a week. After this purification comes the first process of manufacture. It is the simple one of transferring the thread from the circular pieces of framework, upon which the sorter has put it, to bobbins. The winding is effected, of course, by steam power, the bobbins and wheels being arranged upon long frames, attended by women and girls. Each woman has the charge of four and a half of these frames, and she has an assistant girl under her. The work consists principally in shifting the wheels and bobbins when they respectively get empty and full, and in re-uniting the fibres which may chance to break. The dunter, as the principal operative is termed, gets about 7s. 6d. per week, and the little girl, her assistant, from 5s. 6d. to 6s. The temperature in these winding-rooms is generally agreeable, and, as I have said, the appearance of the females is prepossessing. Although their wages are so decidedly lower than those paid in the cotton-mills, the silk girls seem, as I have said, to belong to altogether a superior and more refined class of society than the female cotton workers—an appearance to be accounted for by the cleaner and more wholesome nature of their work. In several of the rooms which I visited, the girls' bonnets and shawls were neatly arranged along the walls; the machinery worked almost noiselessly, and there was a curious absence of the clatter and systematic hurry-skurry which marks the interior of a cotton-mill. The next process is that of cleaning. Here we have a similar system of frames and female attendants, the latter being, however, almost entirely girls. The silk is wound from one bobbin to another, passing through an implement very like an all but closed pair of scissors, which clears away all sorts of extraneous dirt and filaments. The labour of the girls is purely of a superior tending species, their charge being to renew the broken threads, and to keep up a due supply of bobbins. The wages earned are from 6s. to 6s. 3d. per week. It will be seen that the work exacted from both these classes of females is exceedingly light and simple. Still, as in the cotton processes, they require to be continually upon their legs. The thread is next carried to the doublers. The term explains the na-

ture of the operation, which is in a certain degree analogous to the
drawing process in cotton manufacture. The superintendents of the
frames are still young women; and their work requiring more attention and more skill than those demanded by the inferior operations,
their wages average 7s. 6d. The thread is now ready for being spun,
or, to speak more correctly, twisted—an operation generally known as
throwing. The apparatus used for this process differs materially from
the cotton mule, having no backward or forward motion. Each machine is a compact series of spindles, bobbins, and wheels, ranged one
above the other, so as to necessitate the spinner or throwster availing
himself of a triangularly-built ladder, placed upon small wheels, in
order to enable him to superintend the working of the higher ranges
of spindles. The motion of these is excessively quick, making, in many
instances, not less than 3,000 revolutions in a minute. The spinner,
in attending to the lower tiers, has a good deal of unpleasant stooping work to perform, and the atmosphere of the room has, generally
speaking, a sickly oily odour. Each spinner is attended by a boy, who
pieces, as in the cotton-mills. The men earn about 12s. a week—some
a little more, some a little less—and the boys about 6s. 6d. All these
estimates of wages, I ought to mention, are to be understood as applying to ten hours' daily work. The thread, having been spun, is now
taken to the dyers, where it is tinted with any hue desired. On its
being brought back, a series of reeling and winding operations, very
similar to those already described, is gone through. These are, as formerly, conducted by young women and girls, but their wages range
higher than those of their predecessors, averaging from 7s. 6d. to 8s.
per week. A number of purely technical processes—depending upon
the sort of pattern which is to be woven—are gone through before
the silk is finally ready for the loom. No description of these would
be at all intelligible; but I may add that one of them, called "bear-
warping," is the highest species of labour performed by women in silk
mills, and brings them not less than 12s. per week. Another operation,
called "coupling and knitting," also connected with the arrangement
of the silk for the pattern-weaving looms, is conducted by women and
little girls. The work here is light, and little skilled, consisting principally of passing threads through the constellations of holes in the
pattern cards, masses of which are to be seen hanging from the top of
Jacquard looms. The young women earn only 5s., and the little girls
not above 3s. A superintendent, who also works, has 10s. per week.

We now pass to the weaving department. Very little silk, and that only of the coarsest kind, is woven by power. A small quantity of bandannas are thus turned out in Macclesfield; but in the production of the higher class of silk fabrics, and in all fancy goods, the delicacy and intelligence of human labour is requisite, and the Jacquard is never beholden for its motion to the steam-engine. A silk-weaving shed, filled with Jacquard looms, is a curious-looking place, somewhat reminding one of a forest of apparently tangled rigging, so multitudinous are the upright and horizontal beams, and so perplexingly complicated are the threads, cards, and strings, which stretch from one to the other. Most of the silk-mills in Macclesfield weave as well as throw upon the establishment. Indeed, the masters discourage the domestic weaving, particularly with reference to the finer sorts of fancy goods. They wish to have the men more under their eye than the former would be at their own homes; and they urge that they are much more sure of the work being turned out of hand at the time appointed. The coarser sort of weaving is, however, almost universally performed away from the mill. I have visited Macclesfield at rather an unpropitious time for seeing the Jacquard weavers at their work—the winter fashions having been completed, and the labour upon those for the spring not yet commenced. In the large weaving shed of Messrs. Brodrick and Brinsley only one or two Jacquards were in operation—the rest were waiting to be filled for the spring fashions. A Jacquard weaver in full work, at a superior piece of goods, can still earn as much as 35s. a week; but taking the year round, including his seasons of enforced idleness, his wages, at least so far as Macclesfield goes, may be stated as averaging 10s. to 11s. In this estimation, masters and men very generally agreed. I inquired whether, in seasons of slackness of work, the weavers labouring in the mill had the preference in respect to what work there was. The answer was, "Decidedly not. In such times, they all fare alike." Still several of the domestic weavers informed me that they thought that the men who worked in the mills had more regular employment than the home operatives. The former class have, at all events, rather higher wages, because they decidedly do obtain the greater proportion of superior work. I may add here, that the spinners or throwsters are generally young men, and that adult males are employed in this capacity in only a few of the mills. It is no uncommon thing for a throwster, when he grows up, to take to weaving, in which case he has to pay from £5 to £10 for being taught. These men have frequently a local reputation for their ingenuity in useful branches of minor mechanics, and about Macclesfield they are famed for making mouse-traps and analogous pieces of domestic machinery.

From the mills I proceeded to inspect the habitations and work-places of some of the domestic weavers. A street of medium appearance having been pointed out to me as being solely occupied by silk hand-loom weavers, I visited five of the houses, taking them at random. In each I was cordially received, and readily furnished with all the information for which I asked. The houses inhabited by the Macclesfield hand-loom weavers are very generally similar in construction, having been mostly all built with an eye to the staple manufacture of the place. They consist, in nine cases out of ten, of five rooms: two on the ground-floor, one serving as sitting-room and kitchen, and the other as a scullery. On the first floor are generally a couple of bedrooms—those into which I peeped were clean and neat; and then ascending a ladder, and making your way through a trap-door, you reach the loom-shop, which is always located in the garret, and which is exclusively devoted to the operation of weaving. In the first house which I visited, the lower room was fitted up much in the same style as that which prevails in the medium class of operatives' houses in Manchester. The eternal rocking chair stood by the fire; there were small prints hung upon the walls, mingling with shining pot lids, and placed around ranges of shelves filled with crockery and all sorts of minor household matters. One of the bedrooms up stairs was furnished, the other was littered with portions of the apparatus of looms. The garret was a lofty and airy room, the roof rising in a sort of peak—it was a corner house—to the height of about ten feet. The window extended longitudinally, almost the whole length of the room, reminding me of the "long lights" described as abounding in Spitalfields by my Metropolitan colleague. In the apartment there stood, I think, five treddle-looms and a Jacquard, and a young man and two girls were at work. The male weaver informed me that he was making silk for handkerchiefs. He was a journeyman, and he paid 5s. a week rent for the Jacquard at which he was seated. He paid this rent to the undertaker. The undertaker was the man who rented the whole house, to whom the looms belonged, and who also found work for the journeymen and apprentices. In short, the undertaker seemed to act as a sort of middleman between the weavers and the masters. The latter gave him out the prepared silk, on his promising that it should be returned within a certain time woven—and then he in turn distributed the material to the workers, bargaining for the completion of the job by the stipulated period, but not interfering with the hours of labour, which, except in the case of apprentices, are at the option of the weaver. The undertaker sometimes worked, and sometimes contented himself with acting as a sort of agent. Very often he had a family who worked for him. If he had not, he took apprentices, and let out his looms to journeymen. The weaver to whom I was speaking said that he could make, when in full work, 23s. a week, but that was only for the best species of weaving which he had to do. Besides, he was generally out of work altogether for about three months in the year. Striking an average, he thought he could earn about 10s. a week the year round. For this he generally worked twelve hours a day. Although the rent of a Jacquard was 5s., other looms could be rented for 3s. 6d. Apprentices generally served five years, and received one half of their earnings. This man was decidedly of opinion that machinery had done no harm to his trade. The second weaver whom I visited was unintelligent, and gave little or no information. The third was an old man, and disposed to be frankly communicative. He believed that the Macclesfield silk-weavers were better off than the generality in the country places—in Middleton, for example—because in Macclesfield the better sort of fabrics were generally produced. He himself was making silk for handkerchiefs. He considered that the weaving of eight dozen a week was very fair work, and he was paid 2s. 1½d. per dozen. He was thus earning rather less than 17s. per week. For this he toiled sometimes 12, sometimes 13 hours a day. He had work, he thought, for two-thirds of the year. Machinery, in his estimation, had greatly injured the trade. Why else was it that 30 years ago he could earn as much in one week as he could do now in three, working very hard, too? He thought, upon the average, that people worked twice as hard now as they did when he was a boy. The work was more "drierd" (more continuously difficult) than it was in the old time. People were more easily satisfied with silks then than now. At present they were hard to please. And everything went so much on fashion, and fashions changed so fast, that it was difficult either for master or man to suit the market. The lowest sort of silk weaving was the manufacture of greys, for bandanna handkerchiefs. The weavers were paid 5s. 1d. per cut for this sort of silk twenty years ago. Now they couldn't earn more than 2s. 6d., with harder work, because the "shute" (the thread carried across the warp by the shuttle) was finer and required greater care. The lowest amount of wages made by a weaver he put down as about 7s. 8d. to 8s. Working figured goods with the Jacquard, they could make a considerable deal of money, 24s. or 26s. a week; but the Jacquards were standing half the year. The man whose information I am recording was an undertaker, and his journeymen paid him 3s., 3s. 6d., and 5s., for loom rent. He went on to say, that the frequently recurring periods of stagnation in trade kept the weavers poor during the time they had full work. They were busy sometimes, but they were poor always. Twenty years ago the people lived better than now. They had plenty of substantial food, but at present, where one got it a dozen missed it. The people in the mills were better off, particularly the throwsters, than the people out of them, because the mill hands had more regular employment. It was the sudden changes in the taste for fancy articles that made the sudden fluctuations in the demand for goods, and occasioned a great deal of the poor weavers' poverty. Mayhap the master would give an order for a certain pattern. Well, all at once the taste would pass away, and the silks would lie upon the shelves. Soom'mut new was always coming up, and that made the changes from the busy times to the slack times. The trade was very uncertain—so uncertain, that the masters were afraid to speculate so much as they would if they could sell their goods steadier, and therefore they gave small orders—great ones might be left upon their hands. He thought that, one with another, the weavers in the mill might earn 12s. or 14s. a week; working at home he would not put the average higher than 10s. a week. The house in which he lived had four rooms, besides the loom-garret. He paid £10 a year rent for it, besides taxes. It had good drains, and there was water laid on—all complete and handy.

On my way down stairs I looked into the different rooms, and found things tidy and (in a homely way) comfortable. It was a Saturday—the weekly washing and scouring day in the North, and the stone floor of the kitchen was undergoing a thorough polishing. In the next house which I entered, I found in the loom garret only a young man of about eighteen, a smart intelligent lad. He was working at "greys," a coarse kind of silk stuff, which is printed and made into bandannas. "He could manufacture six cuts a week, and the price for each cut was 2s. 4½d. He did not, however, receive all he earned. He was an apprentice to the undertaker who rented the house. He had been bound for three years, and he now received 2s. 3d. of what he made. For the first two years of his apprenticeship he had received only one-half. Many of the undertakers tried to get apprentices bound for seven years, but people didn't like that. The work was terribly irregular, or it would not be bad work—but when folk was busy, it behoved them to save up money against they had to go 'play.' He had been three months playing, and several times six, seven, and eight weeks. The trade was generally slackest towards midsummer." "What did the men do when they played?" "Why, they did not do no work." "How did they pass their time?" "Oh, different ways, according to fancy. They were a great deal in the streets. They took walks, and went to each other's houses, or anywhere. Some of them had dog-fights, but they were the lowest sort. Only the lowest sort had dog-fights in Macclesfield. There might be pigeon-matches, but he had never heard much tell of them. As for himself, he liked to read and play the fiddle." "What did he think was the cause of these stagnations in the trade?" "Well, he had heard say as they were caused by over-production. More goods was made nor people wanted. Then the masters couldn't sell what they had on their shelves, and of course they didn't want for more, so the looms stood idle. It was a necessity. The weavers there about didn't eat very much flesh meat. Certainly, as a general thing, not every day. Some would have it though, whatever came of it. They would think the world couldn't go on if they hadn't flesh meat to dinner. But a great lot lived poor in that town. A great lot, too, were fond of fine clothes, particularly the young women, and they would have their backs gay although their bellies pinched for it."

The Macclesfield Mechanics' Institute is a flourishing establishment. The great majority of the members are silk-weavers. They have recently been making considerable additions to the building, and they have a library containing more than 2,000 volumes. The secretary spoke in high terms of the general standard of intelligence of the silk population. Of their marked superiority in appearance to their neighbours, the cotton-workers, there can be no doubt. The nature of their occupation is not only more conducive to personal cleanliness, but to the development of those minor symbols of health which are to be found in the presence of clear skins, bright eyes, and good complexions. One is inclined to wonder at the co-existence of, comparatively, so low a rate of wages, with the outward evidences of, comparatively, so fair a state of social comfort. And wages, I am informed, are, unhappily, likely to sink even still further. The weavers living in remote country districts are gradually absorbing much of the work which used to be exclusively performed in Macclesfield. As the silk towns of the

North served Spitalfields, so, I am assured, the rural districts are serving the silk towns of the North.

*The Morning Chronicle, Saturday, November 24, 1849.*

To THE EDITOR OF THE MORNING CHRONICLE.

SIR—I shall feel obliged by your dividing the two sovereigns enclosed, between the young woman who sat up for three weeks to work for her parents, and the old man who slept in a sort of cave hollowed out of the side of the wall—the latter mentioned in your paper of Saturday; the other case the day before.

I am, sir, yours truly,

K. B.

# LABOUR AND THE POOR.

—◆—

## THE MANUFACTURING DISTRICTS.

[FROM OUR SPECIAL CORRESPONDENT.]

### THE SILK-WEAVERS OF MIDDLETON.

## Letter XII.

Somewhat more than five miles from Manchester, and midway upon the high road to Rochdale, lies, in a pleasant hollow, surrounded by ridging hills, and watered by the stream of the Irk, the ancient village of Middleton. Although near the centre of the charmed circle within which the steam-engine, the three-decked mule, and the power-loom are alone potent, and almost as it were beneath the heel of the cotton capital—still the prevailing spirit of the region has passed but lightly over Middleton. Standing on the gravestone-clad hill, beneath the antique belfry of the Norman church, you see in your immediate neighbourhood but a few scattered stragglers from the host of tall chimneys which muster on the horizon. Beneath you, perched upon gardened banks or nestling in petty ravines, lie the scattered streets of an old-fashioned village, the high-gabled and irregular tenements built of wood which was leafy three centuries ago, interspersed with ranges of modern red-brick two-storied cottages. There is a gas-work rising, spick and span new, close to where the long grass is waving on the ruins of a brave hall; and a Manchester omnibus stands at the door of a tavern which may have seen the esquire ride forth to fly his hawks. There is nothing of the suburban character about Middleton. The cits of Manchester do not resort there. The place has a stamp of its own. Some of the oldest and purest blood of the Lancashire yeoman keeps its current still unmixed by the hearths of this village. Needwood and Charnwood sent forth no tougher bows nor longer shafts than twanged along the banks of the Irk, and amid the coppices of Birtle and Ashworth. On the northern window of the church transept are emblazoned the effigies of the Middleton Archers, who, like Hubert's grandsire, drew good bows, not indeed at Hastings, but on Flodden Edge. There, upon the coloured glass, march, like the merry men of Robin Hood, the staunch Middleton Archers, all of a row, with their long light Saxon hair, and their retainers' liveries of blue. Each carries his unslung bow upon his shoulder; over each bow is painted, in antique letters, the name of its owner, and every one of these names is still borne by an inhabitant of Middleton. It was curious, indeed, after the multitude of brown bricken Sions, and Ebenezers, and Bethesdas, to which I have lately been accustomed, to find myself standing upon the brazen memorials of buried Crusaders, amid mullions and quatrefoils, carved by Norman chisels, and beneath mouldering standards and rusty spears, which were probably shaken and couched in the wars of the Roses. And in moral as well as physical attributes is the stamp of the old age strong upon this Lancastrian hamlet. A great deal of what was generally believed in England under the Tudors is believed in Middleton and its neighbourhood to this day. Indeed, says the courteous and accomplished Rector, "the people are but too apt to disbelieve what they ought to believe, and to believe what they ought to disbelieve." The fortune-teller abounds, and his oracles are as gospel. The astrologer still casts nativities and projects schemes, and the culler of simples is careful to pluck his herbs only during the waxing of the moon. Upon a dead wall I saw a placard announcing that the "Sacred Drama of Joseph and his Brethren" would be performed by certain Sunday-school pupils. Most unfortunately the date of the representation was past, or I would have astonished you by a critique upon something in the nature of a mediæval *mystery* seriously enacted almost amid the smoke of modern Manchester.

From what I have stated the reader will be prepared for a population pursuing some distinct and ungregarious species of occupation. He is in the right. The "folk o' Middleton," to use their own vernacular, are almost all silk handloom weavers, pursuing their craft in their own houses, preserving an independent and individual tone of character, intermarrying to the extent of breeding scrofulous disease—clannish and prejudiced and peculiar as all such septs are—keeping up even amid their looms a great degree of the rural and patriarchal tone of by-gone times—a few of them handling the plough and the hoe as well as the shuttle and the winding-wheel, and the entire community great favourers of the old English manly sports. "When the Hopwood hounds pass the village (says the Rev. Mr. Dunsford, the rector), there is always a goodly train of sportsmen, on foot, in attendance."

On my arrival in the village I inquired where I could best see the weavers at their work, and was directed to the "club-houses." Do not imagine however a satin-weaving Pall-mall. Turning from the high road, which is also the main street, I climbed a roughly-paved lane skirted by commonplace, mean houses, some of them little shops, and presently I heard on all sides the rattle of the shuttle. Still the aspect of the place was half rural. Trees here and there bowered the cottages, and the noise of the flail mingled with that of the loom. The "club-houses" were a double row of two-story cottages constructed by an old club or building society, whence the name, and not dissimilar in general arrangement to those I have so often described as forming the operative homes of Manchester. They were reared upon the face of a steep hill, and the surface of the street between them being level, the ground-floors on the lower side of the way are unavoidably underground-floors. You descend to them by means of a roughly-paved area, extending the whole length of the street. The general aspect of the place was certainly humble enough; and the day being a dismally wet one, everything looked cheerlessly sloppy. I entered a house at random; as usual, the street door was the parlour door, that is to say, the door of the parlour, and kitchen, and hall. Two apartments opened from the principal one, the small one to the back being a sort of scullery and store-room, piled up with dirty dishes and household utensils, waiting to be washed; the other, a room nearly, if not quite, as large as the dwelling chamber, was the "loom-shop," where business is conducted.

First, of the living room. It was a sort of country cousin to the same class of apartments in Manchester, furnished a good deal after the same fashion, in rather a rougher way to be sure, but wanting the grime and smoke-dried air, and the close, hot smell of the town operatives' lodging. In the corners were niched the invariable cupboards. From the wall ticked the invariable clock; beside it hung little miniature-sized engravings in black frames. On the high chimneypiece were tiny pieces of nick-nackery, china and glittering ware, in the usual cottage style, and on each side of the fireplace hung the usual polished pot-lids. There was good substantial furniture in the place; strong useful deal tables, an old-fashioned chest of drawers, chairs of different patterns—some of them antique, high-backed affairs, the wood carved into innumerable lumps—others like the ordinary Windsor pattern; and by the fireside the never-to-be-too-highly-honoured rocking-chair. The floor was stone-flagged, sanded, and clean; and I must not omit to mention that on either side of the grate stood excellent cooking ranges—a feature almost universal in the Middleton weavers' cottages. Altogether, the place was by no means uncomfortable, inspiring neither the idea of privation nor unwholesomeness. I was met on the threshold by a decently-dressed middle-aged woman, who ushered me into the loom-shop, where sat busy at his work her lord and master. The work-room boasted but an earthen floor, scratched and scraped by half a dozen cocks and hens, which were jerking their necks about beneath the mechanism of the four looms which the chamber contained. The loom arrangements were barbarously primitive. There was a hole scooped in the earth beneath the treddles, and the weaver sat, like the craftsman of Hindostan, half buried in the earth, which, however, seemed as dry as Sahara. The walls were fairly whitewashed; and the stretching oblong window, or rather range of windows, separated from each other by a two or three inch broad strip of wall, furnished the "Long Light," already so often alluded to. Of the four looms in the apartment two were at work, one of them wrought by the husband, the other by the wife. Before the former, on the loom, was stretched a piece of blue satin— the rich texture of the stuff contrasting well with the rude woodwork in which extended that glossy mesh of purple threads. I had some difficulty in drawing this weaver into conversation. He was not sullen, but not intelligent. While I stood by his loom, his wife took her place at hers, and began to labour upon a piece of brown silk shot with blue.

The man lamented over the fall of wages. Twenty years ago he used to make twice as much as now. He didn't know how it was. He supposed it was the masters. They was hard on the poor man. They was very grievous in their 'batements. When the weaver carried his work home, the master or the agents wor very clever to see flaws in it. They wouldn't see none, not them, if they wor a-selling it to a customer; trust 'em for that. And wages was falling still. For a piece he would have got twenty shillings and sixpence for eighteen months ago, he could hardly get sixteen shillings now. It wasn't so bad with some sorts of silks. It all depended on the fashions and the run there was in the market. It would take a very clever weaver to make 10s. a week as a general thing, but there wor some good pieces as paid well, if the weavers could get plenty of work at them. He wrought, himself, ten hours a-day, or twelve, just as he was in the humour—some days more nor other days. If he wor lazy beginning in a morning, he made up for it at night. Sometimes, in course, he stopped the loom and went for a walk—why not? I inquired whether the house belonged to him? No, he wished it did. A vast heap in them parts lived in their own houses—more nor in any town of Lancashire. The children (by the way, they were feeding the poultry with crumbs of bread left from the dinner table)—the children were just brought up to their father's trade. There was 'naought' else for 'em to do.

The woman told me that she was weaving silk for which she was paid 6½d. per yard, and she could make only two yards by a hard day's work.

In the next house I visited, the man—a stalwart well-looking fellow—had just taken a piece of silk off the loom and was folding it on the table. He had to carry it to Manchester to be paid for his work. I admired the beauty of the stuff. "Aye, aye, but there be always soom'mut to find fault wi' when I take it whoam, that they may bate me down." He worked long hours—just as long as any factory hours. If he didn't begin so soon in the morning he kept at it longer at night. He *was* independent in that way, however. Yes, that *wor* soom'mut. They often wove in these parts till ten o'clock in the long winter nights. A good weaver couldn't make more nor 8s. or 9s. a week. There wor some sorts of odd work as paid far better—perhaps a dozen, or it might be fourteen shillings; but they had seldom such a price. Wages wor falling—that was over true. He thought it was the fault o' the machinery.

I said that they were not so ill off at Middleton as at Spitalfields.

"Aye, aye; but it's a poor sort of work, and I dinna doubt but they want to banish silk weavers from Spitalfields. It's too low and too poor a life for the fine folks o' Lunnon."

I crossed the street, and made my way into one of the lower situated houses. The general arrangements were nearly the same as those I have already described, in the first dwelling that I visited. In this house a stout, burly-looking fellow, with a decided Milesian look, was smoking at the ingle corner; and a gaunt, pale-looking, middle-aged woman was seated on a low stool, rocking her lean body backwards and forwards, and pulling away at a pipe with great gusto. In the work-room were four looms. A rather nice-looking girl of fourteen was working one—a sallow, unshorn, lean man another. The latter was producing beautiful figured silk. He was paid for it 9d. per yard, and could weave three yards a day. The price within his recollection would have been 2s. a yard, "Worn't that enough to make a man bitter at his work?" For other sorts of silk 4d. a yard was paid, and he well remembered when it was 1s. 3d. What was the cause of this? "Lord! He didn't know; I ought to know better nor him." Were there more people weaving now than when he was a boy? "Aye, that there wor— twice as many."

I had several times asked whether there was any weaver among them whom they thought especially a clever man, and one who knew the history of the trade. Public opinion pointing with many forefingers to a certain door, I tapped thereat, and the latch was raised by a venerable old lady adorned with a pair of silver spectacles on her nose, and a pipe in her mouth; she looked somehow like a nice indulgent grandmamma—she had such a kind old-fashioned face; but I could not help staring at it, for never in my life had I seen an elderly lady's countenance embellished at once with a pair of silver spectacles and a clay pipe. The master of the family was a very intelligent, chubby old man, with grey hair, a pair of twin spectacles, but no pipe. After ascertaining that I was "not in the trade," and that I knew as much about the secrets of "dents" and "shute" as about the mysteries of Eleusis, he made me extremely welcome, and we had a long gossip together. In his workroom stood four looms, one of them the invention of the celebrated weaver of Lyons. When I entered, the master of the house was instructing a girl in the management of the loom. He straightway left his pupil, and, having heard my errand, launched headforemost into a sea of silk-weaving reminiscences.

I shall not attempt to classify the topics which I found scribbled in my note-book. In conversations with working men it is almost impossible to keep them to the point, and perhaps a more vivid idea is given of the colloquy, and especially of the principal interlocutor, by putting on paper his chat, rambling and disjointed as it was uttered.

"Remember better times? That do I well. Twenty-six years ago we had 13d. a yard for what we have 3½d. now. It's the machinery—the machinery as has done it—for see that Jacquard, and the silk in it (there are many hundred Jacquards hereabouts)—well, the weaving of that silk used to be 3s. a yard. What is it now? Why, 1s. 3d. About thirty years ago we were mostly cotton weavers hereaway. But the power-looms flung us out of work, and we were nigh starved. Then, sir, there came gentlemen from Lunnon, from Spitalfields (of course as you come from Lunnon you know Spitalfields), and they took down silk here and they set us to work on it. We was very glad to get the chance. But the masters was using us to bate down the Spitalfields weavers. Some of them, sir—the weavers I mean—came down here, but their old masters wouldn't employ, no, not never a man on them, because they would want their old wages and old rules. That was the way, sir, that silk weaving became so general hereaway. Well, but we was soon served just as we had served the Spitalfields folk. There's a place called Leigh, not far from here, where there was then a heap of hand-loom weavers as wrought cottons and such like. Well, after some time, our masters didn't give us our due, and so we combined and had a strike. What did the masters do but took the work to Leigh from Middleton, just as they did from Spitalfields to Middleton, and the weavers at Leigh wrought at one ha'penny a yard less than we did. To be sure they was glad to get the work at almost any price. The wages are not very different now, but there are grievous and unjust abatements. The masters are some of them honourable good men— but some of them are very tyrannous. They were very tyrannous in this way at Leigh, and a committee of the weavers collected information as to abatements, and printed it in a book. [I have the pamphlet before me.] Very often, sir, there was one-and-sixpence and two-and-sixpence unjustly 'bated out of a week's work. The poor people could not live under it. They couldn't."

At this point we adjourned to the parlour. Grandmamma, with the pipe, swept up the hearth. A nice tidy girl sat peeling apples, apparently for a pie. Another weaver, a sturdy, good-humoured looking fellow, flung himself into a cosy elbow chair, with his legs over the arms, and we resumed our talk somewhat in this fashion.

"What rent may you pay now for this house?"

"Seven pounds a year, and a good many folks pays six."

The room was comfortable, and comfortably and substantially furnished. In an open corner cupboard sparkled two antique silver salt-cellars. I am always glad to see such things in a poor man's house. They were possibly heir-looms. The old weaver resumed.

"Some folks live in their own houses—but I don't. This better nor factory work? Aye, that it is. You see you keep your children at home about you, and you don't lose control over them. We live very friendly like. There be all sorts here, but we're good folk the'gether. When the children are ten or twelve years old we put them to the loom, but we must attend them, you know, and teach them. It takes long to make them perfect in the trade."

"Perfect in the trade!" exclaimed he of the elbow chair; "there's naought on us perfect in the trade. We are aye learning."

The *pater familias* gravely coincided, and went on. "There's many drawbacks to a weaver's work. Sometimes it takes a week to gate a loom" (prepare it for a web of particular fineness). "I heard say that in Spitalfields all that is done at the master's charge, but here we do it ourselves. How do we live? Well; there's not much flesh meat eaten. There would be a deal more if we could get it. But there's tay (the Lancaster peasant invariably pronounces the word *more Hibernico*), there's tay, and bread, and bootter—that's ready cooking."

"Tay!" interrupted the younger weaver; "hot water and a little sugar, ye mean. It's not tay."

"Well," resumed his elder; "in this family we only have an ounce of tay a week; but I'll just tell you how we live in homely Lancashire sort. Well, we have tay and bread and bootter morning and afternoon. At dinner we have potatoes, and perhaps a little meat. Here's in this house a family of four or five, as it may be. Well, at the end of the week we buy two or three pounds of beef, and that's all the flesh meat we have till next week. So we make it into as many dinners as we can scheme. We cook may be half a pound at a time, to give the potatoes a flavour like. But what's that for eating? Why, my share at meal-times is not bigger nor my thumb. So I often throw it in and take a fried ingan and two or three drops of vinegar to relish the potatoes. That's about our general way of living. To be sure we may get a lift in spring time when the spring fashions come; but very often we've been getting into debt in the winter; and first, you know, we must keep our credit; and then there's clothes want renewing. Teetotallers here? Aye, there be a few on 'em; but we're all very moderate."

"We wouldn't be so very moderate if we could afford a little drink better," said the second weaver.

"I like my glass of ale myself," resumed the first, "and I like good coompany, and a good joke and soom'mut to laugh at, I do. I like to sing a song too." How the conversation turned round I do not remember; but the next entry I have upon my note-book is, that the old gentleman was fond not only of a good song, but that he was especially fond of reading the "Skootchings" which Cobbett used to give to people he didn't like. Then we got back to convivial matters, and so gradually to the subject of the *morale* of the village.

"We've got a rural police here. But, Lord! we haven't no more use for them nor you have for water in your boots. There's three policemen, and the devil a thing they have to do but to walk about with their hands in their pockets, like gentlemen. Why, they haven't had a job this three months; except, may be, when a chap gets droonk-like. The sergeant, as they call him, thinks it's quite ridiculous. He says he never saw such people. If he offends one he offends all. We like each other so well, and we turn out after dinner and have a great talk about politics, and what they're doing in Lunnon, and smoke our pipes. We often have long discussions—we're great chaps for politics, and we just go into each other's houses and talk. I like to be idle myself sometimes— I dare say you do, too. Yes, of course you do. Well, then, when I feel idle, I go and walk about in the fields may be, and work harder to make up for it after."

I quite regretted being obliged to tear myself from my garrulous friend, who, I doubt not, would have talked till midnight with very great pleasure.

The next weaver I saw I was introduced to by the worthy rector. He was the patriarch of the village—a fine-looking old man of eighty-two—with the remains of a well-cut massive set of features and curling white hair. He was feeble, and at times wandered in his speech. His dame was still a stout hearty body, enjoying a green old age; and busily employed when we called in scouring the flagged floor with hearthstone, a bucket, and a mop. She must have seen seventy winters, but she worked as vigorously and spoke as briskly as a damsel in her teens; her white hair all the while streaming from under a narrow frilled calico nightcap—the ordinary head-dress of the Middleton matrons.

The patriarch sat before the fire and bubbled of times present and past. "The first silk ever woven in Middleton was made into bandanna handkerchiefs. Sixty years ago and better he had woven such himself. Some folk farmed then—others wove cotton. After the bandannas, came twills and sarsnets and satins. Wages were lower, much lower now, than in the old times."

"But did the people then live better than they do now?"

Somewhat to my surprise the old man said, "No, sir; no, they live better now. They have tay and coffee liken—(observe the lingering Saxon idiom)—tay and coffee *liken* the gentlefolk. I had coffee to my dinner this day, sir. They had porridge and milk then instead; and often, sir, they had to go three miles to fetch the milk. But still they didn't work in the old days as now. They ran after the hounds, or went a-shooting and a-sporting in the fields nigh three days a week, and many had farms and tilled them likewise."

"I suppose you drink a glass of beer sometimes," said the rector. "You can brew it yourselves, in this capital range."

At this the buxom old dame took up the word.

"Well, sir, some on 'em does, but others drink it at the hush houses—that is, sir, the places where they keep it *withouten* being licensed. But we have naought to say to such like. Oh, there's a much drinkin'—too much—folk com round door by door and ask, 'Will we buy a knife?' and if we say, 'Aye,' why, then, they out with a bottle of smuggled whisky and sells it. That's the knife, sir."

Leaving the octogenarian and his dame, Mr. Dunsford said he would show me a house built by an industrious and intelligent weaver, entirely out of his own savings—a house which, in the phraseology of the district, "all came through the eye of the shuttle." We crossed the Irk by a slippery wooden bridge. "That," said my companion, "that is, for its size, about the hardest worked brook in England." There had been many hours of heavy rain, and the flood was rushing turbulent and strong. It looks as if it had been a likely trout stream long ago, but the gudgeon is now the only tenant of its waters. Verily the gudgeon must be a long-enduring fish—patient of foul things—an ichthyologic Job. The house we went to see was a neat and substantial cottage, built on the summit of a steep garden-planted bank. The industrious family who dwelt in it were its architects, and a snugger kitchen or a neater parlour, in a small way, might not easily be found. Over the dresser was ranged a fair collection of useful books.

To the Rev. Mr. Dunsford I am indebted for some interesting notices of the "Middleton folk," touching matters on which a stranger could not, during a hurried visit, well gain information for himself. The people are very generally careless and indifferent about the education of themselves or their children, taking the latter from school as soon as they can be useful at the loom. Writing is the attainment which they most prize, and most excel in. The art is a mechanical one, and Mr. Dunsford is convinced that the symmetrical order and due slope of the threads constantly stretching before their eyes exercise no little effect in producing good penmen from amongst weavers. The young people marry early, and although long periods of betrothal are common, they almost invariably take each other for better for worse without a stick of furniture or a shilling of saved money. The bride and bridegroom then go to live in the house of the parents of one of them; or frequently one takes his or her meals and remains during the day with his or her own friends; the other doing the same thing at another house, and the couple coming together again in the evening. During this time they pay for "loom room," or in other words, hire a loom a piece, and pay also for their board. Sometimes the father thus becomes a sort of capitalist—letting out, in a large family of sons and daughters, as many as half-a-dozen looms. Generally, by the time the first child is born, the young couple have saved something towards furnishing a dwelling for themselves—and that the more often, inasmuch as their notions of setting up housekeeping are very modest. If they have a bed, a chest of drawers, and a corner cupboard, they think that in all the essentials of furniture they are set up. The bed-rooms are generally neat, clean, and tidy, beyond what might be looked for. The hand-loom system here appears, so far as family is concerned, to exercise exactly the opposite effect of the factory system. The Middleton weaver keeps not only his sons and daughters, but often his sons and daughters in law, long about him; while the children who are too young, and sometimes the adults who are too old for the heavy labour of the loom, turn the winding wheel, and prepare the glistening silk for the frame. They are great politicians the good folks of Middleton, and occasionally given to lazy fits, during which smoking, sauntering, and chatting listlessly are the amusements most in vogue. The women very frequently smoke, but it is always with some pseudo-medical excuse. They feel a "rising" or a "sinking," or a headache, or a toothache, or any ache, or no ache at all. A curious indication of the prevailing shade of radical politics in the village is afforded by the parish register, the people having a fancy for christening their children after the hero of the minute. Thus, a generation or so back, Henry Hunts were as common as blackberries—a crop of Feargus O'Connors replaced them—and latterly they have a few green sprouts labelled Ernest Jones. A very small proportion of the weavers only labour in the fields; but in many farm-houses around there are looms which the women work during the long winter evenings. The Spitalfields hobby of pigeon fancying is not uncommon, particularly among the young men; and pigeon matches, which give rise to a good deal of gambling, are frequent. The birds are taken some miles away, and then flown back to their homes. *Apropos* of the betting propensity, there was a bagatelle table in the quiet tavern where the omnibus from Manchester deposited me, above which was inscribed the following *naïve* and ingeniously-worded proclamation:—"No gaming allowed on this board. Any person having a wager or wagers on this board, the landlord shall seize it, and spend it in liquor."

I mentioned to Mr. Dunsford the complaints which I had heard of the masters being grievously tyrannical in abating the nominal wages given, on account of alleged imperfections in the work. Most of these stories, he said, like other stories, had two sides to them. He had known weavers work for years for a firm without any abatement being made, or at least any that was not admittedly just. Many of the abatements, so called, were fines for broken contracts for work not being finished at the stipulated time. Still he did not doubt but there were often cases of real hardship in the system—cases in which shabby and screwing agents sought, by extreme ingenuity in finding or fancying flaws, to bate down the fair price of the work. In the pamphlet published by the Leigh weavers' committee upon the subject, one fact most damning to the masters, if true, is broadly asserted—viz., that the weavers who are abated the most, and who, consequently, were the abatements justly made, must be the worst workmen, received by far the greatest share of labour from the employers. Many of the cases reported by the committee in question seem harsh and cruel to the last degree. As regards the amount of these abatements, I may mention, quoting at random from a great mass of tabular statistics, that out of £265 10s. 8d. of wages nominally earned by 171 weavers, £45 12s. 3d. was abated on account of real or alleged imperfections in the fabric, being an average of 5s. 4d. clipped from each man's pay.

By the time I had completed my tour of inspection, lights were gleaming from the "loom shops," and in the wooden-roofed market-place gas jets flared amid the meat, and on the eager faces of chaffering customers. Two Manchester omnibuses, each with three horses, and an indefatigable horn-blowing conductor, stood at different inn doors, and I naturally selected the lightest laden. Although the rain was coming down in bucketfulls, and the interior of the vehicle I had chosen was all but empty, the other was thronged outside and in. I mentioned the matter to my only *compagnon de voyage*. "Oh," he said, "you don't know how queer they are, the weaver folk of Middleton. They have a line of omnibuses belonging to a man they like, and won't go in the other people's busses not if you paid them: they'd walk through all this rain and dirt to Manchester first. Sometimes they hoot the people who ride in t'other bus, and if we were each of us Middleton tradesmen, and to be seen where we are, why we'd never sell another ha'porth to a weaver of them all!"

*The Morning Chronicle, Thursday, November 29, 1849.*

# LABOUR AND THE POOR.

—◆—

## THE MANUFACTURING DISTRICTS.

[FROM OUR SPECIAL CORRESPONDENT.]

### THE RURAL CLOTH WORKERS OF YORKSHIRE.

SADDLEWORTH.

## Letter XIII.

The name of Saddleworth is applied to a range of wild and hilly country, about seven miles long and five broad, lying on the western confines of Yorkshire, and including one spot from which a walk of ten minutes will carry the visitor across the boundaries of four counties, into Lancashire, Cheshire, Derbyshire, and Yorkshire. To all intents and purposes, however, Saddleworth lies in the latter county— its heathery hills and deep valleys dividing the woollen from the cotton cities, and being themselves peopled by a hardy, industrious, and primitive race, engaged in the manufacture of flannel and cloth— sometimes in mills, sometimes by their own hearths—in which latter case the business of a dairy farmer is often added to that of a manufacturer, and the same hands ply the shuttle and milk the cows. Saddleworth is now intersected by the Leeds and Huddersfield Railway, and, as a consequence, is beginning to lose much of those primitive characteristics for which it was long renowned. Until recently there was no regular means of transit from many of its valleys to the more open parts of the country. Goods were conveyed by the Manchester and Huddersfield Canal; and many a small manufacturer and comfortable farmer grew grey amid the hills, without having ever journeyed further than Oldham and Staleybridge on the one hand, and perhaps Huddersfield, or at furthest Leeds, upon the other. The rail has, however, thrown open the wilds of Saddleworth to the world. Mills, driven by water and steam, are rising on every hand, and the old-fashioned domestic industry carried on in the field and the loom-shop is gradually dying away.

I entered Yorkshire by way of Oldham. To some extent the domain of cotton seems to be invading that of wool, for, as my vehicle slowly toiled up the steep ascents of the many ribs which branch from the "backbone of England," the driver pointed out to me several old woollen-mills which are now cotton factories. Leaving the straggling streets and abounding tall chimneys of Oldham behind, we enter a bleak, hilly country, high, naked, and sterile. All around rise great lumpish ridges of hill, divided by loosely piled walls into cold-looking pasture fields, and clothed here and there with substantial stone-built cottages. The agricultural labour requisite hereabouts is light; but the few labourers are well off, making from 12s. to 15s. a week. We passed several of the poor Oldham besom makers, whose trade and dwellings I have already described, returning from the moors with vast bundles of dripping "ling" upon their backs; and at length, after a tedious ascent, attained a bare, wild summit, from whence bursts upon the view one of the finest panoramas of hill and valley to be found in England. Beneath you opens out a stretching vista of irregularly-running glens, hemmed in by bristling ranges of heather or fir-clad hills. Here slopes pleasantly to the sun a fair expanse of green pasture—there runs a ridge, grey with rock or purple with heather. The eye wanders over clumps of oak and through straggling woods of sombre fir—from cottage to cottage, and hamlet to hamlet, and mill to mill—the former often perched high upon the hills, where the green of the pasture begins to give place to the brown sterility of moss and moor, and the latter invariably nestled in the very bottom of the glen, each beside its lakelet of clear water, dammed up from the rapid stream of the Thame. It was a wild, stormy morning, with lowering clouds, now breaking, now gathering before the strong wind, which drove great masses of whirring vapour along the high mountain ridges, lashing the ground at intervals with such rattling bursts of hail and rain as only fall among the hills—and anon lulling, while a bright sun gleamed forth, lighting up the blue correys of the hills, flooding with its radiance the great belts of fertile green, and shining bright upon the dripping surface of grey sloping rocks.

All around—hill and glen, oaken coppice and fir-wood, green pasture and heathy ridge—is Saddleworth.

Before proceeding to notice in detail the physical and social condition of the woolworkers of Yorkshire, it will tend to the clearer understanding of much of what I have to say if, at the outset, I succinctly describe the general process of manufacture, which, in many instances, is performed from beginning to end in mills, and which is occasionally carried on partly in mills, partly in the homes of the workmen.

The raw material, having been unpacked from the bales in which it arrives, is delivered over to the sorters. The duty of these men is to pick out and arrange the different classes and qualities of the wool, according to the length and fineness of the fabric. Their labour can only be performed by daylight, and their wages of course vary not only with the season, but with the different classes of raw material submitted to their manipulation—a mill manufacturing fine broad cloth which needs more expert judges of the wool than one producing the coarser and inferior stuffs. Thus, in a mill in Saddleworth manufacturing the blanketing which is used in certain parts of cotton machinery, the sorters earn from 15s. to 20s. weekly. In a mill in Huddersfield producing the finest cloth the same class of workmen can make about 25s. a week in winter, and 27s. in summer. The next operation is one requiring merely unskilled labour, and is generally entrusted to women. It consists simply of picking the impurities out of the wool, and is paid for at about the rate of 1½d. per lb. The filthiest sort of wool is sometimes sent to the gaols to be picked, where the operation is performed for about 1d. per lb. In the vicinity of the country mills superannuated old women frequently earn 2s. or 3s. a week by picking. In the towns the process is performed in the mills, and an active hand may make from 6s. to 7s. a week by the operation. After being sorted and picked, the wool undergoes a series of washing, and sometimes of dyeing operations, according to the intended colour of the stuff into which it is to be wrought. As is more or less the case in all processes of the kind, the rooms in which they are carried on reek with the steam of hot water and the smells of melting dye stuffs. Some of the dyes used for fancy coloured goods are exceedingly unhealthy. A foreman in a mill at Huddersfield told me that he had frequently helped to carry out workmen who had fainted amid the stench. As a general rule, however, the emanations from the vat do not appear to exercise any particularly injurious effect upon the workmen, who are moreover a good deal in the open air. Dyers and washers make from 16s. to 18s. a week.

We now come to the first of the operations having reference to the preparation of the fibre. This is exactly analogous to the stage of cotton manufacture performed by the "devil"—the machine which tears the wool to pieces being termed the "willon." There is a little, but not much, dust and flying fibre evolved by the process. The wool,

it will be observed, has been previously in the dyeing-vat, and during the next few stages of the manufacture the faces and hands of
the workpeople assume much the same tint as will be exhibited by
the cloth which they are preparing. The willon requires but a single
attendant—generally a boy—who feeds it with the coarse material,
and bears to the carding-machine the torn and softened filaments.
His wages may average from 6s. to 7s. per week. The woollen carding-
machine differs materially from that used for cotton—the "cards" produced by the former being rolled out sideways from the implement in
distinct portions, each about a yard long, and forming, as it were, rope-
like cylinders of woollen fibre. The feeder of the carding-machine—a
boy or girl—earns about as much as the feeder of the willon. It is
now the turn of the "slubber" to play his part. The duty of this workman is, by means of his slubbing frame—an apparatus somewhat like
a spinning mule—to draw out the thick "cards" into slender threads.
Each slubber is attended by two piecers, whose duty it is to renew the
products of the carding machine as the slubbing frame successively
exhausts them. This office is anything but a sinecure, as the slubbing
frame draws out into yarn the cards as fast as the piecer can supply
them. The slubber, who is always a man, can make from 18s. to 20s.
a week. The piecers, who are often his children, have from 4s. 6d. to
6s. each. The process just described is, it will be remembered, exactly
analogous to "drawing" in the manufacture of cotton. The wool having now been converted into yarn, has next to be spun. This operation
is very similar to the same process in the cotton trade, but as it is not
held to require the same jealous watchfulness or the same delicacy of
manipulation, the wages paid are considerably less, few or no woollen
spinners making more than £1 per week. In some mills, mules similar
to the self-actors of Lancashire are being introduced, attended to only
by young persons, who may make from 11s. to 14s. a week, and superintended by a man, who has frequently two or more rooms under his
charge. In other cases, each spinner has two mules to attend to, with
one or more piecers to each, according to the number of spindles. The
thread having been thus prepared, is now taken to the loom. For plain
stuffs the shuttle is generally driven by steam, but in the case of many
kinds of cloth, and of all kinds of fancy goods, handloom-weaving is
preferred, if indeed it be not absolutely necessary. The average earnings of power-loom weavers may be stated at 12s. a week. They are
sometimes men and sometimes women, and each weaver has, as a
general rule, charge of two looms. The appearance of a cloth-weaving

room is very different from that of a cotton "shed." The looms are larger, heavier, and clumsier in appearance, and the shuttle traverses the twelve or fourteen feet, which it has frequently to cover, with a far more deliberate motion than the glancing jerks of the cotton shuttle, flying through the fast growing webs of calico. The stuff having been woven, is subjected to the action of steaming hot water and the "fulling" hammers, which cause it to shrivel up almost to one half of its former dimensions. The wages earned by the artisans who labour in the steaming atmosphere of the fulling mill are from 18s. to 21s. The next process is exclusively performed by women. It is called "birling," and consists of picking out of the cloth, with a sort of tweezers, all the little knots and inequalities which may be apparent upon the face of the fabric. In the country, this operation is very generally performed at home. In towns, it is executed in the mills, the cloth being spread upon a wooden frame placed at an obtuse angle to the window, and three or four women, closely jammed together, being seated on benches before each frame. This is almost the only department of the trade in which married women are extensively employed away from their homes. In the birling room of a Huddersfield mill, I heard more giggling, and saw more symptoms denoting a relaxed state of discipline, than I had previously observed in any department in any of the textile industries. It was clear, from the atmosphere, that some of the women had been smoking, but the pipes were, of course, instantly smuggled away on our entrance. The cloth having been "birled," now undergoes a variety of operations included in the general term "finishing," the object being to render the surface as velvetty smooth as possible, and to obtain that beautiful glossy face for which broad-cloth is remarkable. Men and boys are employed in these operations. The wages of the former may range from 18s. to 20s., and those of the latter from 5s. to 7s. It was the introduction of improved machinery in one of the operations under question—that of cutting smooth the face of the cloth—which produced the Luddite outbreak. In stating the general wages paid for the finishing processes, I ought not to omit that the "hot-pressers" are highly paid, their wages often amounting to 30s. a week.

I have thus sketched in general terms the process of woollen manufacture in its principal phases. He who sees a woollen mill preparing plain or slightly coloured stuffs will have a very different opinion of the cleanliness and pleasantness of the operation from the visitor who watches the stages in the production of broad cloth. When the wool is dyed of a deep colour previously to being carded, slubbed, and spun, the aspect of the mill and of the workpeople is grimy and filthy in the extreme, and the atmosphere of the various rooms is more or less charged with sickly-smelling odours produced by the dye-stuffs. Mills manufacturing the lighter and coarser species of stuffs are, on the contrary, clean-looking and agreeable to all the senses. In none of the rooms where the textile operations are being performed is any particular degree of heat required. In the dyeing and some of the finishing operations alone the temperature is necessarily high.

The first woollen mill which I inspected was that belonging to the Messrs. Whitehead, in Saddleworth. It is a country factory, beautifully situated in the deep cleft of a wooded glen, and scattered round it are the cottages of the workpeople. As is generally the case with respect to country mills, the average rate of wages is somewhat below that paid in towns, from which the foregoing estimate has been constructed. The Messrs. Whitehead send their Buenos Ayres wool to be picked in the prisons of Manchester, that species of raw material being so coarse and dirty that it is difficult to find free labourers to meddle with it. A great deal of the ordinary picking is, however, done by the women in their cottages in the neighbourhood. The Messrs. Whitehead also put out their "birling," and many married women make a practice of "birling" a sufficient quantity to pay their rents, devoting the rest of their time to household duties. The domestic manufacture in this part of Saddleworth, which nearly adjoins the cotton districts, is fast dying away, and large old-fashioned houses attached to small farms are now being let at one-half and one-third the rents they formerly produced.

One interesting branch of the Messrs. Whitehead's manufacture is the construction of flags. They dye, spin, and weave the bunting, which is cut into proper pattern, and sewn together either in their mill or in the cottages around. The flag makers are exclusively women. Although the industry is one principally carried on in seaport towns—the wives and widows of sailors being frequently the persons employed—there is many a yard of bunting manufactured amid the hills of Yorkshire by people who never saw a ship or the ocean. It seemed strange so far inland to come upon a room hung with gaily-tinted bunting, the forms and colours of ensigns and union jacks painted upon the tables, and collections of the patterns of national and signal standards displayed upon the walls. The bunting, after being cut into due form, is firmly sewn together. And there is a regular fixed scale of prices paid to the workwomen for the different descriptions of flags. For a scarlet ensign, five yards long, with the Jack in the corner, 2s. 1d. is paid; for an ensign of four yards, 1s. 11d.; for a Union Jack of four yards, 2s. A good sewer can make at this work from 8s. to 10s. a week. They seldom commence operations until eight a.m. The best workwomen in the Messrs. Whitehead's establishment earned the week before my visit 10s. 10d., and the week before that 12s. 3d. A great number of the flags are, however, manufactured at the homes of married women, who give part of their time to this species of industry. On referring to their books, the Messrs. Whitehead informed me that 3s. might be the average earnings of a workwoman of this class. Selecting at random a name, I found that the owner had in three weeks earned respectively 3s. 10d., 3s. 1d., and 3s. 8d.

From the mill I proceeded to visit some of the cottages of the workpeople. Without a single exception, I found them neat, warm, comfortable, and clean. They consisted almost universally of a common room, serving as parlour and kitchen, a scullery behind it, and two or more bedrooms upstairs. The main rooms were, I think, as a general rule, larger than those I have lately been accustomed to see. The floors were stone flagged, nicely sanded. Samplers and pictures uniformly ornamented the walls, and the furniture was massive and old-fashioned; the chairs with rush bottoms and high well-polished backs. One characteristic feature of these cottages was universal. It consisted of a sort of net stretched under the ceiling, and filled with crisp oat cakes. These formerly constituted almost the only bread consumed in the district, but home-baked wheaten loaves are now coming into general use. Indeed almost every family in Saddleworth bakes its own bread and brews its own ale—a capital nutty-flavoured beverage it is. The composition of the oat cakes is, however, held to require a peculiar genius, and when a matron gets a reputation in that way, she frequently bakes for half a village. In the first cottage I entered I found a rosy-cheeked girl occupied in "birling." Her father worked in the mill; her mother had her household to attend to, and did a little "birling" besides. The matron, upon her appearance, informed me that the house had five rooms, and that the weekly rent which they paid for it was 3s. 4d. The girl could, by devoting the whole of her time to the work, make 7s. or 8s. per week by "birling." It was common for married women to birl enough to pay the rent, which they could do, and get ample time to attend to their families. Very few married women worked in the mills. They found no difficulty in getting as much work as they wanted at home. In the second house which I saw there were also five rooms, and the rent was 3s. 1d. per week. Besides this, the occupants paid 6d. a week for gas, which they could keep alight until half-after ten, and on Saturdays and Sundays as long as they pleased. The woman of the house was a fine, fat, hearty-looking dame of sixty, the very picture of health and matronly enjoyment. There was a bed, with curtains, in a corner of the room. Who the occupant was I do not know—he did not think proper to show himself, but ever and anon a voice from amid the blankets joined vigorously in the conversation. The old lady corroborated the statement I had heard as to the small proportion of married women who preferred working in the mills to "birling" at home. The use of oat cake, she said, was gradually decreasing, and she produced a substantial home-made wheaten loaf as a specimen of the bread coming into favour. She could remember when the people ate nothing but oat cakes. These were then made four times as thick as now. The people used to eat a great deal of cheese. Indeed, they used to live on cheese, oat cake, porridge, and butter milk, but now-a-days nothing but tea and coffee would do for them. They took a good deal of porridge yet, however, for breakfast; but generally they had some meat for dinner, perhaps some bacon, perhaps some beef. At all events, they had plenty of porridge and bread and potatoes. The price of meat was a little dearer than when she was a girl. Good mutton could not be had now under 6d. a lb., but she thought, on the whole, that people lived just as well now as they did forty years ago.

At one end of a straggling village, called Upper Mills, I entered a small factory in which carding and slubbing are performed. The place was rudely and clumsily built; the stone stairs were dirty, and the joists and beams of the house bare and exposed. In the principal room I got into conversation with the slubber, who stopped his mechanism to give me what information he could. His wages averaged about 18s. a week. He worked ten hours a day. The little piecer was his daughter, and her wages were 4s. 2½d. Another of his daughters worked under his eye as a carding-feeder. Her wages were 5s. 10d. The united earnings of his family were better than 30s. a week, and of course they lived pretty comfortably. He paid only 2s. 3d. a week for a "very decent cottage," with a buttery (the old word is still in use in Saddleworth), a kitchen, and two bedrooms. For breakfast, they had all porridge and milk, and for dinner they had generally a little meat, with bread and potatoes, and home-brewed beer. His wife did nothing save her household work. The carding-feeder, an intelligent girl about 16 years of age, observed that the prices of provisions had very much fallen within the last two years. Meat, which used to be 7d. per pound, could now be had for 6d., and flour, which used to be 3s. per stone of 12 lbs., might now be bought for 1s. 10d. Tea and coffee were also cheaper. They generally bought a quarter of a pound of tea for 15d. weekly, and one pound of coffee for 1s. These groceries were purchased at Mosley, a small town not far from Staleybridge, to which one of the family went weekly for the purpose. If they were to buy tea and coffee at Upper Mill they would have to pay 18d. and 14d. for it respectively, instead of 15d. and 1s., and they would not get such a good article for the higher as they now did for the lower price.

I had the good luck to light upon a courteous gentleman, a manufacturer at Upper Mill, who was born and bred in the district, and who understands the people and their habits thoroughly. In the mill owned by this gentleman no adult male receives less than 15s. a week, and many young men, from 16 years of age to 20, earn between 12s. and 14s. He gives out a good deal of birling to be performed by the married women at their homes, and pays them 4s., 5s., and 6s. a week for their work. As a general thing, he thought the weavers in mills might earn about 14s. a week, the slubbers about 18s., and the spinners from 18s. to 20s. There was no child employed by him earning less than 3s. Some children had 3s. 6d., others 4s., others 5s. The process of "finishing" in the cloth trade paid well. Boys of twelve years of age in his mill were making 10s. and 11s. a week, and the principal hands had from £1 1s. to 30s.

Understanding that the "hand spinning jenny" is still extensively used in Saddleworth, I requested my informant to take me where I could see this, to our present notions, primitive instrument at work. I found that there were plenty going all round us. The wool is generally willowed, carded, and slubbed in the mills. The domestic manufacturers then carry the yarns home, spin them upon the hand jennies, and weave them in the same apartment.

"Do you see," said my conductor, "that jolly-looking old fellow, loading a horse with a pack of goods? Well, he's rather a good specimen of the domestic manufacturer of Saddleworth. I warrant you he's worth not less than two or three thousand pounds! We'll go and see his place."

The general appearance of the village, I should say, is that of a straggling, yet substantially-built hamlet—the oblong ranges of windows running along beneath the eaves of many of the houses, denoting the nature of the occupation carried on within them. Sometimes they stand alone, backed by steep banks of grass and stunted trees; sometimes they are clustered together with narrow courts and passages leading from the high way. Up one of these courts we proceeded, and after passing through one of the usual parlour kitchens, ascended a ladder to the work-room. Here were two looms and two hand-jennies; each of the latter may have had about forty spindles. They are worked upon the general principle of the power mule—the muscle of the operative, however, supplying the place of the steam-engine. In fact, the whole machine looks somewhat like a toy power mule. One of the looms and one of the jennies only were at work when we entered, being urged respectively by a son and daughter of the old proprietor, who however speedily made his appearance, and took his place at the vacant jenny. The operator with this machine performs the whole of the work, acting as piecer as well as spinner. The labour, however, cannot be called severe, for the travelling frame is exceedingly light, and a very weak arm is sufficient to propel it. The girl told me that she was making about 8s. a week. Before the introduction of power mules she could have made nearly twice as much; but wool spinning would soon be performed altogether by steam and machinery, because steam and machinery could do it much faster and much cheaper than men or women. The weaver said he could sometimes make 15s. a week—that was when he got a good web; but the average with the cloth hand-loom weavers was considerably lower. Porridge and milk made the best of their fare, with butter-cakes and meat "when they could catch it." The workroom where these people wrought was airy, but not by any means particularly cleanly.

From this place we proceeded by a steep path up the hill side to a cluster of old-fashioned houses called Saddleworth-fold, and which were the first, or amongst the first, stone buildings erected in the district. They are occupied by several families, who are at once spinners, weavers, and farmers. The hamlet was a curious irregular clump of old-fashioned houses, looking as if they had been flung accidentally together up and down a little group of knolls. Over the small latticed windows were carved mullions of stone, and in a little garden grew a few box-wood trees, clipped into the quaint shapes which we associate with French and Dutch gardening. The man whose establishment we had come to see was a splendid specimen of humanity—tall, stalwart, with a grip like a vice, and a back as upright as a pump-bolt, although he was between 70 and 80 years of age. We entered the principal room of his house; it was a chamber which a novelist would love to paint—so thoroughly, yet comfortably, old-fashioned, with its nicely-sanded floor, its great rough beams, hung with goodly flitches of bacon, its quaint latticed windows, its high mantel-piece, reaching almost to the roof, over the roaring coal fire; its ancient, yet strong and substantial furniture, the chests of drawers and cupboards of polished oak, and the chairs so low-seated and so high-backed. An old woman, the wife of the proprietor, sat by the chimney-corner with a grandchild in her lap. Her daughter was engaged in some household work beside her. In this room the whole family, journeymen and all, took their meals together. Porridge and milk was the usual breakfast. For dinner they had potatoes and bacon, or sometimes beef, with plenty of oat bread; and for supper, "butter-cake," or porridge again. The old man had never travelled further than Derby. He had thought of going to London once, but his heart failed him, and he had given up the idea. He did not at all approve of the new-fangled mill system, and liked the old-fashioned way of joining weaving and farming much better. He could just remember the building of the newest house in Saddleworth-fold. He thought the seasons had somehow changed in Saddleworth, for snow never lay upon the ground as it used to do, and the scanty crops of oats here and there sown did not ripen so well. The daughter having in the meantime placed oat cake and milk before me, the patriarch observed that until he was twenty he had never tasted wheaten bread, except when his mother lay in. In the room above us were two or three looms, and as many spinning jennies. They produced flannel and doeskin. Weaving and spinning formed the chief occupation of his family—they attended to the cows, of which he had four, and to the dairy, in their leisure time. He paid his sons no regular wages, but gave them board, lodging, and clothing, and "anything reasonable" if they wanted to go to a hunt or a fair or "sooch-loike."

I may as well state here that the country weavers of Saddleworth are, like Nimrod, mighty hunters. Every third or fourth man keeps his beagle or his brace of beagles, and the gentlemen who subscribe to the district hunt pay the taxes on the dogs. There are no foxes in Saddleworth—the country, indeed, is too bare for them to pick up a living; but hares abound, and occasionally the people have "trail" hunts—the quarry being a herring or a bit of rag dipped in oil dragged across the country by an active runner, with an hour's law. A few, but only a very few, pursue the sport on horseback—the weavers, who form the great majority of the hunt, trusting to their own sound lungs and well-strung sinews to keep within sight of the dogs. Even the discipline of the mills is as yet in many instances insufficient to check this inherent passion for the chase. My informant, himself a millowner, told me that he had recently arranged a hunt to try the mettle of some dogs from another part of Yorkshire against the native breed. He had tried to keep the matter as quiet as he could, but it somehow leaked out, and the result was, that several mills were left standing, and that more than 500 carders, slubbers, spinners, and weavers formed the field. The masters, however, are often too keen sportsmen themselves to grudge their hands an occasional holiday of the sort. The Saddleworth weavers must be excellent fellows to run. A year or two ago, a gentleman, resident there, purchased a fox at Huddersfield, and turned him loose at Upper Mill, a spot almost in the centre of the hills. There started on the trail upwards of 300 sportsmen on foot. Reynard led the chase nearly to Manchester, a distance of about twenty miles, and then doubled back almost to the place where he was unbagged, favouring his pursuers with an additional score of miles' amusement. Of the 300 starters, upwards of 25 were in at the death. My informant had reason to remember the chase, for it cost him the bursting of a blood-vessel. In passing through the little village of Dubcross I observed a quaint tavern sign, illustrative of the ruling passion. On the board was inscribed, "Hark to Bounty—hark."

From Upper Mill I proceeded to a village called Delph, where there are only a very few mills, and round which is scattered a thick population of small farmers and hand-loom weavers. The cottages of many of these people are perched far up among the hills, on the very edge of the moors. As a general rule, the houses are inferior, both in construction and cleanliness, to those nearer the mills; and I should say, although the accounts I received were often most puzzlingly contradictory, that the run of wages is decidedly lower. In several of these remote dwellings I found beds of no inviting appearance in the loom room; and broken windows were often patched with old hats and dirty clothes. The hand-jenny spinners, when in employment, earn, as a pretty general rule, about 8s. a week. The weavers, as I have said, may and often do make 15s. and 17s. per week; but, taking the year round, and the good webs with the bad ones, 10s. in many parts of Yorkshire would be too high an average. As a general rule, the Saddleworth weavers seem to be better off than those upon the lower grounds round Huddersfield and Halifax. Among the hills dairy farms are, as I have said, very common; but the nearer we get to large towns the more rare does the union of occupations become. High up on the hill side above Delph I counted from one point of view a couple of dozen cottages, in each of which the loom was going, and around each of which the kine were grazing. It was a glorious sunny afternoon, and amid the fields, and by the road side, the weavers with their wives and children were many of them stretching out their warps upon a rude apparatus of sticks to dry them in the genial air. The gay tinting of many of these outstretched meshes of thread, glancing along the green of hedges, or the cold grey of stone walls, made quite a feature in the landscape. The workpeople were very chatty and communicative. With two in particular I had long conversations, after which I accompanied them to their houses. The first was a slatternly place— one of those in which dirty beds lay unmade in the workshop. The weaver complained of the uncertain nature of his work, and spoke bitterly of the power-loom, which would, he was afraid, in the long run beat him and his comrades out of the field. Wages, within his own recollection, had sunk one-half. He lived upon potatoes, porridge, oat-cake and milk, and meat "when he could catch it"—a common phrase hereabouts. Trade was not very brisk at present, but it was much better than it was, "because" wheat and meat were cheaper. I asked him whether dear bread and bad trade always came together. His answer was, "I never knowed it otherwise with the weavers. Look, sir, when everything to eat was terrible dear, two years ago, what happened to us? Why, we could not get no work at no price, and all the weavers hereabouts that hadn't farms were forced to turn out and work at the railway tunnel under Stannidge. If it wasn't for that I don't know what would ha' becoom of us."

Another weaver, a very intelligent man—much more so indeed than most of his class, for he had travelled much, and been twice in America—gave me some curious information. He confirmed what the old man at Saddleworth-fold had stated, as to the non-ripening of the oats sown now-a-days, and spoke sensibly enough about machinery. "Machinery," he said, "had been a great advantage to the weaver as long as it was pretty simple and cheap, for then he could use it for his own behoof." His mother had told him that in her younger days the distaff was the only drawing implement in Saddleworth. The carding was performed by the women with a rude instrument placed upon their knees, and the old-fashioned wheel, with its single spindle, was the only spinning apparatus known. "Look, sir," he continued, "at that yarn. It was stretched out by the road side to-day. In those days, it would have taken a dozen of people, with a dozen of wheels, more than a week to spin it. Now my mistress can make it with the hand-jenny in two days and a half, and a power mule could spin it in a forenoon." He feared that it was but natural that the power mule would supplant the hand mule, just as the hand mule had supplanted the spinning wheel. It was during the time that machinery was in the medium state, when any industrious man could obtain it, that the weavers of Saddleworth flourished most. At one time he had paid a journeyman £35 a year besides his board, lodging, clothing, and washing, and they did not use, in those times, to work more than five or six hours a day. They were too often out following the hounds. Now his average wages were not above 10s. a week, although he could sometimes make nearer 20s. His wife worked the hand-jenny, and could make, when in full work, about 15d. a day. Thirty years ago she could have easily earned 18s. a week. He kept a cow, and paid £7 10s. of rent for the requisite land. His family consumed most of the dairy produce, selling very little. The ordinary price of buttermilk was about 1d. for three quarts; of blue, or skim-milk, 1d. for three pints; and of new milk, about 2d. a quart. Milk of all kinds was sent down during the summer-time, in great quantities, by many of his neighbours, who kept donkeys to carry it, to Staleybridge, Oldham, and other cotton towns, where the factory hands consumed it as fast as it could be sent in.

Adverting to the work and food question, I asked him whether the high prices a year and a half ago had exercised much influence on his trade. He answered nearly as follows:—

"Did they not, indeed? Why, when corn is very dear we have next to no trade at all. It stands to reason. The fabrics we make be mostly for the home market—the best and most nat'ral of all markets, sir; and if the poor people have to spend all they earn to pay for their food and to keep the roofs over them, why, they can't buy no good warm clothing. Two years ago flour was 3s. 6d. a stone, and oatmeal was 3s. 2d., and potatoes was selling as high as 2s. 6d. a score. Then, sir, there was next to no work. I was better off than many, but even in our house it was hard living I assure you; and a great lot of the weavers had to go work along with t' navvies on the railroad."

I am happy to say that this honest man appeared to be in better case when I saw him. His house was beautifully clean, and his wife was preparing a comfortable stew for dinner. One of his children was recovering from scarlet fever, and two plump fowls were being boiled down to make chicken broth for the invalid. They had had fifteen fowls, of which ten had been thus used up, and they expected every day to get a fresh supply of poultry.

Comfort such as this must, however, by no means be taken as the rule. The weavers in the upland districts who have farms, and those in the lower grounds who, although they possess no land, have got advantages of a particular class from the vicinity of the country mills—these two classes are generally decently off, and live wholesome and tolerably agreeable lives. But there are districts, principally in the neighbourhood of the large towns, where competition keeps the wages miserably low, and where hard labour brings in but a hard and scanty subsistence. Some districts of this kind I shall touch upon in my next letter.

# LABOUR AND THE POOR.

—◆—

## THE MANUFACTURING DISTRICTS.

[FROM OUR SPECIAL CORRESPONDENT.]

### THE CLOTH DISTRICTS OF YORKSHIRE.
### THE HUDDERSFIELD FANCY GOODS, AND THE DEWSBURY "SHODDY" MILLS.

### LETTER XIV.

The town of Huddersfield is a species of minor capital of the broad and fancy cloth working districts of Yorkshire—Leeds being taken as the general manufacturing metropolis of the county. In Huddersfield and its neighbourhood, however, a very important proportion of the cloth working of the entire district is carried on, and much of the fine-textured stuffs, conventionally known as "West of England goods," is spun, woven, and finished on the banks of the Colne. The township of Huddersfield contains rather more than 36,000, and the district comprehended by the Huddersfield Union is peopled by somewhat more than 108,000 inhabitants. The number of paupers at present accommodated in the several workhouses of the Union amounts to about 250, and the amount of out-door relief granted during a single week in the beginning of the present month was £186. In the year 1846, out of 939 couples who married, 378 men and 696 women signed the register with their marks. The value of life in Huddersfield, as stated in the Registrar's General Report, is 1 in 49 as regards males, and 1 in 52 as regards females; showing a degree of mortality less by nearly 10 per cent. than that of Chorley, the healthiest of the cotton towns.

The population of Huddersfield and the surrounding districts are almost entirely engaged in the manufacture of wool—the scattered cotton and silk spinning and weaving establishments which may be found here and there being merely exceptions to the general rule. By far the greater part of the woollen manufacture of Huddersfield is carried on, in all its stages, in the mills. When weaving is put out, the work is generally executed by country people living within a circuit of some half dozen miles. The species of fabric so manufactured, is commonly that distinguished, in its different kinds, as fancy goods. The Ten Hours Bill applies to woollen factories just as it does to cotton mills. In the woollen districts, however, there seems to have been no attempt made to get rid of its restrictions. No mill, so far as my inquiries have extended, has sought to work by means of the relay system; and in the vast majority of instances, at least so far as regards the woollen in opposition to the worsted trade, no children are employed until they are above thirteen years of age.

The town of Huddersfield belongs to one ground landlord—Sir John Marsden. No building leases are granted, and the inhabitants are therefore, *pro tanto*, tenants at will. The town has sprung up almost entirely within the last sixty years. Previous to that time it was but an insignificant cluster of irregularly built lanes. The small manufacturers around brought in their wares upon pack horses, and on the market-day exposed them for sale on the churchyard-wall. When the Cloth Hall was opened, many of these humble producers had not sufficient capital to rent a stall. Although thus comparatively a new town, Huddersfield is by no means a well-built town. The houses inhabited by the working classes have, until very recently, been constructed back to back, or rather as double houses, a partition running from the ridge of the roof perpendicularly downwards. The consequence of this system is, that the more humble portions of the town—that is to say, three-fourths of it—are either exceedingly deficient in necessary conveniences, or the structures in question are erected in front of rows of houses, in positions perfectly destructive of anything like decent or seemly reserve. A local act has, however, been lately obtained, applying to Huddersfield the provisions of one of the Health of Towns Bills, and under this act, the borough commissioners are proceeding with energy and vigour to remedy, so far as they can effect it, the sanitary grievances of the township. A scheme is in agitation for the opening up of an important continuation of the main street, and it is hoped that in the construction of the new quarter which will thus spring into being, proper sanitary regulations will be observed.

I have already sketched the principal features of the long staple woollen manufacture—my information being derived from a careful inspection of several of the mills, great and small, in Huddersfield and in the surrounding district. The processes of converting the wool into broad cloth or fancy goods are carried on both in and out of the mills, but the strong tendency of the trade is to concentrate itself in the factories under the eyes of the proprietors, who very generally complain of the dilatoriness of the home workmen and the uncertainty of their completing their tasks by the stipulated time. The workpeople, on the other hand, maintain that they suffer from the caprice of the employers in bestowing work, and from the frequency with which they are compelled to make repeated journeys to the warehouses or mills before they obtain the yarn which they are to spin and weave in their own homes.

The houses inhabited by the factory hands of Huddersfield consist in most cases of a large parlour-kitchen opening from the street, with a cellar beneath it, and either two small bedrooms or one large one above. In some instances a scullery is added to the main apartment. The general style of furniture is much the same as that which distinguishes the operative dwellings of the cotton districts. If there be any difference, I should say that that of Huddersfield seems the more plainly substantial of the two. The clock and the corner cupboards, and the shelves glittering with ranges of dishes and plates, are to be found as universally as in Manchester, and a plentiful supply of good water is in general conducted into every house.

Taking wages as the test of social condition, the operatives of Huddersfield may be considered as very fairly situated. Children below thirteen years of age are seldom employed in the mills, and the average earnings of those over that age may be 5s. weekly. The earnings of the women may vary from 7s. or thereabouts—obtained by those who pick and boil—to 9s. or 10s. or thereabouts, obtained by those who weave. The average may be about 8s. 6d. The average wage of the women is raised by the number of their sex who work at the loom, as the average wage of the men is depressed by the same cause. Slubbers, carders, spinners, dyers, fullers, raisers, and finishers may average about 18s. a week. Taking into account the number of adult males employed as weavers, both by power and hand, the general average sinks, and may be placed at from 14s. to 15s. per week. Admitting these estimates to be generally correct, the average wage earned by adults in Huddersfield may be placed at 11s. 6d. a week—an amount very similar to the general run of wages in the cotton districts, while the average earned by all sexes and ages may be estimated at something more than 9s. I have said that the Huddersfield cottage houses are generally constructed back and back, and that a common arrangement is their division into a cellar or store place, a kitchen-parlour, and a large bedroom above it. The rents paid range from £7 to £8, or about 3s. per week.

The yarns given out by the mills to be spun and woven at the homes of the workpeople, are taken to the rural districts around, or to the remote suburbs of Huddersfield. At a little village called Paddock, about a mile from the town, a number of looms are generally going. Proceeding there, I entered upon a series of domiciliary visits. The general arrangements of the houses were similar. The looms invariably occupied the first floor. In some cases one and two uncurtained beds, almost invariably left unmade, were placed in corners. In other instances, the sleeping arrangements were upon the ground floor, or within a third chamber roughly partitioned off from the loom apartment. In the first house I entered, one loom only was at work. The weaver was manufacturing a rough greyish cloth for a peculiar sort of great coat. It was a web by which he could earn 17s. a week. He had not always so good a job, and with his wife to wind for him, he did not on the average earn so much as 10s. a week. There were four in family—his wife, himself, and two children, too young as yet to be of any use to their parents. In answer to my inquiries as to what they lived upon, the weaver said that, as dinner must now be almost ready, I had better go below and satisfy myself. I did so, and found that the fare for the family consisted of two huge pig's pettitoes, with bread and potatoes. The weaver's wife said that dear times "was always a candle that burned at both ends with them," for when bread, potatoes, and meal was at the dearest, work was always the scarcest. "Aye," said her husband, who had in the meantime descended to dinner, "we've found that oot long ago."

In another house I found that only two people resided, a man and his wife. They had no family. The bedroom was, in this instance, partitioned off from the loom room. It was carpeted with a strip of drugget, and looked decent, if not comfortable. There were two looms here for the husband and wife. The man, who was busy, stopped his shuttle to speak to me. For the cloth which he was weaving he could have got seven years ago 10d. a yard—the price now paid was only 4½d. When he had pretty regular work his average weekly earnings were about 10s. For this he frequently worked from six o'clock in the morning until eight o'clock at night. Last summer trade had been bad with him, and one week with another he had not much above 8s. The earnings of his wife generally amounted to about 3s. 6d. per week. Taking an average, he thought that their united earnings might be about 12s. 6d. or 13s. a week. This was when trade was tolerably good. Sometimes they could not make more than 10s. a week between them. He paid for his house £8 10s. per annum. The poor rates were 6s. 3d.; the highway rates, 3s. 3½d.; and the charge for water, 5s. The woollen hand-loom weavers about Huddersfield were very ill off. "If they have young families," said the woman, "that is, families over young to help them by working in the mills, they don't get half enough to eat." "It was not often, however, that the mills would take the children until they were thirteen years of age, and legally able to work ten hours a day. They might then earn from 5s. to 6s. a week as piecers." I told the weaver that I had heard a great deal about slack work and dear food coming together in his trade, and asked him if he had ever noticed anything of the kind.

"It would be queer, indeed, if I hadn't done that," he said. "We had a long spell of high prices since 1846, and I'll tell you what was the consequence to me. For sixteen months I had only four webs, at 34s. a piece. Not a bit of work more than that came into this house."

"Why," I said, "did you live upon £6 16s. for near a year and a half?"

"We did, sir. God knows how—but somehow we did; and flour was then 4s. a stone. The flour you can get now for 1s. 11d."

"I don't call it living," said the wife. "We kept ourselves alive, but that was all."

There are a considerable number of "low Irish" in Huddersfield, but the effect of the sanitary reform measures in process of being carried out, is to drive them forth from the borough into the adjacent townships, where they cannot be hindered from pigging together on the floors of garrets and cellars by dozens and scores. The sanitary act applied to Huddersfield, gives the local board of works power to regulate the number of persons to be accommodated in each common lodging-house, and, as a consequence, the Irish population within the borough is rapidly diminishing. I paid a visit to several of their haunts—these being principally the uncleansed alleys and fever-smelling *cul-de-sacs* in the higher parts of the town.

The first domicile which—accompanied by Mr. Joshua Hobson, the very efficient and courteous clerk to the Board of Works—I visited had been a lodging-house, and had only been very recently cleared out. The occupants of the two rooms of which it consisted were an old woman, her two daughters, and a tolerably numerous array of grandchildren. In a corner of the lower room, a flock bed with a dirty rug was rolled up. The grandmother slept here. When the place had been a lodging-house she slept down in the cellar. We descended the stairs to inspect the dormitory. It was lightless and airless—the earthern floor and stone walls were sopping with fœtid damp, and the smell clearly showed that the place was used as a cesspool as well as a cellar. In this noisome hole the family kept their supply of drinking water. The bed-room above the common apartment might measure about 16 feet by 12 feet. It contained two beds—mere frames covered with brown rugs, which lay in wisps just as the occupants of the couches had left them. In this room, when the dwelling was used as a lodging-house, upwards of twenty people were accustomed to sleep, huddled together upon rags flung on the floor. The common room was furnished with a few coarse household articles, lying littered about in squalid disorder. Broken plates, dirty knives, forks, pewter spoons, and such like, were scattered on tables, chairs, and the filth-encrusted floor; and amongst them was piled a heap of frowzy-smelling rags, mouldy bones, old iron, and empty medicine phials, the produce of the last day's excursion of the landlady of the domicile. I could wring little from her as to the ordinary profits of her trade as a rag collector. She had been prevented from keeping the swarm of lodgers which her house had formerly accommodated, and seemed to be exceedingly sore upon that, and indeed upon most other subjects.

The next house we entered was also rented by a woman. Her husband had gone to America, and she expected that he would shortly send money for her to go out and join him. In the meantime she was principally supported by his remittances, and by taking in lodgers at as many pence a night as they could afford to give her. The house, although it was tenanted by two almost idle women—the landlady and her sister—was in a slatternly state of filthiness, the rickety furniture scattered about the room—the dirty children roaring on the floor—broken crockery, containing the heads and tails of rank-smelling herrings, the fragments of breakfast, left unheeded on table and chair—and the single window a mass of dust and mud stains. Neither of the women of the house had any particular occupation. They stowed away what lodgers they could get, and vegetated on from day to day in the midst of filth and stenches, the major part of which a forenoon's work would remove.

Next door to this place was a cellar-dwelling. Access to the apartment—if it can be called one—had formerly been obtained by means of a flight of stairs from the ground floor of the house above;

but these had been blocked up, and as there was a small sunken area on the outside, an extra door, or rather hole, not four feet high, had been broken in the wall, and through this the inmates crawled backwards and forwards. This den—the place was about eight feet by six—was inhabited by a man, his wife, and several children. The man was a mason's labourer, and in constant work, earning 14s. per week. The woman did the house work, as she said. Filthy plates, and tubs full of foul-smelling scum and slops lying everywhere about, testified how diligently she performed her duties, which were rendered more onerous by the children of a neighbour being committed to her care, while the mother was absent upon a country expedition, exchanging pots and pans against old iron, glass, bones, and rags. For taking charge of the children in question the woman received from their mother fourpence a day. While we were talking, a stout-built fellow, the model of a stalwart navvy, lounged into the cellar and seated himself on the window sill. This man seemed a perfect specimen of good-natured laziness. He worked, he said, when he got a job. He could then make 15s. a week, but there wasn't much doing in his way at present. His wife was out gathering rags and bones. I asked him whether he could not get work at any of the factories? He burst into a loudish good-natured laugh, as he replied, "Bedad, sir, and is it me fingers yer would like to see snipped off entirely by them blissid machinery. Sure I can handle a hoe or a pick; but them mules and looms is a pig with another snout intirely."

I was anxious to ascertain the particulars of the pot and rag trade, by which so many of the Huddersfield Irish live, and after some trouble and much collation of the facts deposed to by the gatherers, with those affirmed by the rag merchants, I ascertained that the business is usually conducted as follows:—

The rag-gatherer comes in the morning to the rag-merchant's shop, and obtains a number of coarse earthenware pots, pans, and pipkins upon credit. With these he or she sets out on the expedition, very often making a circuit of more than a score of miles—offering at every promising house the earthenware in exchange for rags, white or coloured, bones, or old glass. The products of the swapping is brought to the rag-merchant, who gives about 1½d. per lb. for white rags, from 6d. to 7d. per stone for coloured rags, and 4d. per stone for old iron. The day's transactions are then settled between the rag-collector and the rag-buyer, the latter paying the former the balance produced by the value of the rags, offal, &c., over the value of the pots. Sometimes, on very lucky days, the balance amounts to 1s. 6d. A very few pence, however, more frequently settles the account; and it is not very uncommon for the balance to be—for the rag-collector—on the wrong side of the book altogether. The number of English who pursue this traffic is inconsiderable, and they seldom or never make the lengthened circuits which the Irish are in the daily habit of traversing. Many of the latter hawk salt about, with tapes, staylaces, buttons, and all the usual *et ceteras* of cadging pedlars.

"Och, indeed, sir," said a woman to me, "it's a hard life intirely. Sure you may walk till you're foot-sore, and after, and knock at twenty doors, before you knock the value of a brass farden out of any of them."

In one of the courts of one of the Irish quarters—a place, by the way, reeking with abominations, but which the authorities are energetically improving—I observed one house, poor indeed in appearance, but notably clean. On entering it I found that the inhabitants were English, the only English people in the court. They had lived there for more than thirty years, and always paid their way. I found them, however, in deep poverty, and their story was affecting. The family consisted of five—an old man, his old wife, their daughter, her husband, and the infant of the latter couple. The grandfather had worked all his life in a woollen mill, but he was now, in the estimation of the masters, too old to be employed. He had gone from mill to mill in Huddersfield, begging in vain for work. His wife was quite past all labour, and the family were entirely supported by the daughter's husband, whose earnings amounted only to 13s. a week. The old man, the women said, was wearing himself away fretting at the idea of being a burden upon the husband of his daughter. The latter was to go into a mill the moment the infant could be left with its grandmother. "It was cruel," she said—speaking of her husband, and struggling to keep back her tears—"to see a hearty man trying to work hard day after day on nothing but bread and a little milk." The contrast between this poor family and their lazy Irish neighbours was very striking and very painful.

The Huddersfield Mechanics' Institution is, out of all sight, the best conducted and most useful establishment of the kind I have seen in the north of England. In too many towns, the mechanics' institute really means a cheap news-room, with an occasional trashy concert for the subscribers. In Huddersfield the case is very different. The Mechanics' Institution there is a vigorously working and most effective educational establishment, supported not so much by occasional galas, and factitious and incidental contributions, as by the steady assistance of a large body of working men. The names upon the books, as fortnightly and quarterly subscribers, are about 1,000; and since 1844, upwards of 2,860 persons have partaken of the advantages of the institution. I was surprised and delighted, when conducted through the establishment and shown the great number of young men diligently and methodically pursuing different courses of study. In one room, the members were engaged in constructing maps, the drawing roughly executed to be sure, but zeal and intelligence everywhere most strikingly manifest. There exists, in connection with the institution, a school of design, very efficiently superintended, in which I found about twenty pupils of every age from 12 to 40, but all of them of the working class, busily employed in drawing from the antique. On another night in the week the class meets for instruction in mechanical art. Altogether, the Huddersfield Mechanics' Institute is a model which may be most advantageously studied by many similar establishments of much greater pretensions and much smaller performance.

The small town of Dewsbury holds, in the woollen district, very much the same position which Oldham does in the cotton country. The reader will remember that an essential feature in the manufacture of the latter town is the spinning and preparing of waste and refuse cotton. To this stuff the name of shoddy is given, but the real and orthodox shoddy is a production of the woollen districts, and consists of the second-hand wool manufactured by the tearing up, or rather the grinding, of woollen rags by means of coarse willows, called devils; the operation of which sends forth choking clouds of dry pungent dirt and floating fibres—the real and original "devil's dust." Having been, by the agency of the machinery in question, reduced to something like the original raw material, fresh wool is added to the pulp in different proportions, according to the quality of the stuff to be manufactured, and the mingled material is at length re-worked in the usual way into a coarse and little serviceable cloth.

There are some shoddy mills in the neighbourhood of Huddersfield, but the mean little town of Dewsbury may be taken as the metropolis of the manufacture, and thither I accordingly proceeded. The first mill I visited was that belonging to the Messrs. Blakely, in the immediate outskirts of the town. This establishment is devoted solely to the sorting, preparing, and grinding of rags, which are worked up in the neighbouring factories. Great bales choke-full of filthy tatters lay scattered about the yard, and loaded waggons were fast arriving and adding to the heap. As for the mill, a glance at its exterior showed its character. It being a calm, still day, the walls and part of the roof were covered with the thick clinging dust and fibre, which ascended in choky volumes from the open doors and glassless windows of the ground floor, and which also poured forth from a chimney, constructed for the purpose, exactly like smoke. On a windy day I was told that the appearance of the place would be by no means so bad, as a thorough draft would carry the dust rapidly away to lee-ward. As it was, however, the mill was covered as with a mildewy fungus, and upon the grey slates of the roof the frowzy deposit could not be less than two inches in depth.

We went first into the upper story, where the rags are stored. A great wareroom was piled in many places from the floor to the ceiling with bales of woollen rags, torn strips and tatters of every colour peeping out from the bursting depositaries. There is hardly a country in Europe which does not contribute its quota of material to the shoddy manufacturer. Rags are brought from France, Germany, and in great quantities from Belgium. Denmark, I understand, is favourably looked upon by the tatter merchants, being fertile in morsels of clothing, of fair quality. Of domestic rags, the Scotch bear off the palm; and possibly no one will be surprised to hear, that of all rags Irish rags are the most worn, the filthiest, and generally the most unprofitable. The gradations of value in the world of rags are indeed remarkable. I was shown rags worth £50 per ton, and rags worth only 30s. The best class is formed of the remains of fine cloth, the produce of which, eked out with a few bundles of fresh wool, is destined, as broad cloth, or at all events as pilot cloth, to go forth to the world again. Fragments of damask and skirts of merino dresses formed the staple of middle class rags; and even the very worst bales— to my eye they appeared unmitigated mashes of frowzy filth—afford here and there some fragments of calico, which are wrought up into brown paper. The refuse of all, mixed with the stuff which even the shoddy-making devil rejects, is packed off to the agricultural districts for use as manure. I saw several unpleasant-smelling lots which were destined to fertilize the hop-gardens of Kent.

Under the rag wareroom was the sorting and picking room. Here the bales are opened, and their contents piled in close, poverty-smelling masses, upon the floor. The operatives were entirely women.

They sat upon low stools, or half sunk and half enthroned amid heaps of the filthy goods, busily employed in arranging them according to the colour and the quality of the morsels, and from the more pretending quality of rags carefully ripping out every particle of cotton which they could detect. Piles of rags of different sorts, dozens of feet high, were the obvious fruits of their labour. All these women were over eighteen years of age, and the wages which they were paid for ten hours' work were 6s. per week. They looked squalid and dirty enough, but all of them were chattering, and several singing, over their noisome labour. The atmosphere of the room was close and oppressive; and although I perceived no particularly offensive smell, we could not help being sensible of the presence of a choky, mildewy sort of odour—a hot, moist exhalation—arising from the sodden smouldering piles as the workwomen tossed armfuls of rags from one heap to another. In this mill, and at this species of work—the lowest and foulest which any phase of the factory system can show—I found, for the first time, labouring as regular mill hands, Irish women.

The devils were, as I have said, upon the ground floor. The choking dust burst out from door and window, and it was not until a minute or so that I could see the workmen, moving amid the clouds, catching up armfuls of the sorted rags and tossing them into the machine to be torn into fibry fragments by the whirling revolutions of its spiky teeth. So far as I could make out, the place was a large bare room—the uncovered beams above, the rough stone walls, and the woodwork of the unglazed windows being as it were furred over with clinging woolly matter. On the floor, the dust and coarse filaments lay as if, to use the quaint phrase of a gentleman present, "it had been snowing snuff." The workmen were of course coated with the flying powder. They wore bandages over their mouths, so as to prevent as much as possible the inhalation of the dust, and seemed loath to remove the protection for a moment. Not one of them, however, would admit that he found the trade injurious. No, the dust tickled them a little, that was all. They felt it most of a Monday morning after being all Sunday in the fresh air. When they first took to the work it hurt their throats a little, but they drank mint tea and that soon cured them. I asked whether there was not a disorder known as "shoddy fever"? The reply was, that they were all more or less subject to it, especially after tenting the grinding of the very dusty sorts of stuff—worsted stockings, for example. The "shoddy fever" was a sort of stuffing of the head and nose, with sore throat, and it sometimes forced them to give over work for two or three days, or at most a week; but the disorder, they said, was not fatal, and left no particularly bad effects. This was the statement, generally corroborated, of a person who had worked for years in the horrible atmosphere which I have described. In another mill, two Irishwomen who fed the devils told me that they had been working there, one sixteen and the other eighteen months, and had experienced no perceptible change in their health. In spite of all this, however, it is manifestly impossible for human lungs to breathe under such circumstances without suffering. I myself was exposed to the atmosphere in several mills for perhaps ten minutes altogether, and the experiment left an unpleasant, choky sensation in the throat, which lasted all the remainder of the day. An intelligent woman in Batley Car, a village near Dewsbury, told me that the rag grinders were very subject to asthmatic complaints, particularly when the air was dull and warm. According to her, the shoddy fever was like a bad cold, with constant acrid running from the nose, and a great deal of expectoration. It was when there was a particularly dirty lot of rags to be ground that the people were usually attacked in this way, but the fever seldom kept them more than two or three days from their work.

In Batley I went over two shoddy establishments—the Bridge Mill and the Albion Mill. In both of these rags were not only ground, but the shoddy was worked up into coarse bad cloth, a great proportion of which is sent to America for slave clothing. In one of the mills in question, the two rag grinders at work were the Irishwomen whom I have mentioned. They laboured in a sort of half-roofed outhouse, the floor littered with rags and heaped with dust, the walls and beams furred with wavy down-like masses of filament, as though they had been imbedded in clusters of cobweb, while the air, stirred by the revolving cylinders and straps, was a perfect whirlwind of pungent titillating powder. Through this the women, with their squalid, dust-strewn garments, powdered to a dull greyish hue, and with their bandages tied over the greater part of their faces, moved like reanimated mummies in their swathings: I had seldom seen anything more ghastly. The wages of these poor creatures do not exceed 7s. or 8s. a week. The men are much better paid, none of them making less than 18s. a week, and many earning as much as 22s. As I have mentioned, the amount of dust produced is different with different classes of rags. I may add, that when the better sort of material is consigned to the teeth of the "devil," a quantity of coarse rank oil which is thrown upon it, so as to cause the fibres to adhere better in the slubbing process, effectually lays the dust. There is no objection to the use of this oil, as I understand, in the grinding of any species of rags—always excepting the expense.

After the rags have been devilled into shoddy, the remaining processes are much the same, although conducted in a coarser way, as those which I have already detailed in my description of the manufacture of woollen cloth. The wages hereabouts run, I am assured, quite as high as in the neighbourhood of Huddersfield, and some classes of workmen earn still more. Dinner time came round when I was in one of the mills, and as many of the people had their meals carried to them, I had a good opportunity of observing the general style of the fare. Meat pies, with thick under-baked crusts, appeared to be the staple dish. The meal was despatched in the most primitive style. I observed one woman helping herself to potatoes with one of the broad-bladed shears used for cutting rags. The weaving is, for the most part, carried on at the homes of the workpeople. I visited several at Batley Car. The domestic arrangements consisted, in every case, of two tolerably large rooms, one above the other, with a cellar beneath—a plan of construction called in Yorkshire a "house and a chamber." The chamber had generally a bed amid the looms. The weavers were, as usual, complaining of irregular work and diminished wages. Their average pay, one week with another, with their wives to wind for them—*i.e.*, to place the thread upon the bobbin which goes into the shuttle—is hardly so much as 10s. a week. They work long hours, often fourteen per day. In one or two instances I found the weaver a small capitalist with perhaps half a dozen looms, and a hand-jenny for spinning thread, the workpeople being within his own family as regular apprentices and journeymen.

On my return to Dewsbury I applied to Dr. Hemingway, a gentleman who has a large practice in the district, for some precise information touching the "shoddy fever." The substance of the statement which I received is as follows:—

The disease popularly known as "shoddy fever," and which is of too frequent occurrence hereabouts, is a species of bronchitis, caused by the irritating effect of the floating particles of dust upon the mucous membrane of the trachea and its ramifications. In general, the attack is easily cured—particularly if the patient has not been for any length of time exposed to the exciting cause—by effervescing saline draughts to allay the symptomatic febrile action, followed by expectorants to relieve the mucous membrane of the irritating dust; but a long continuance of employment in the contaminated atmosphere, bringing on as it does repeated attacks of the disease, is too apt, in the end, to undermine the constitution, and produce a train of pec- toral diseases, often closing with pulmonary consumption. The doctor added, that ophthalmic attacks were by no means uncommon among the shoddy grinders, some of whom, however, wore wire gauze spec- tacles to protect the eyes. As regarded the effect of the occupation upon health, Dr. Hemingway is of opinion that, on a rough average, it may shorten life by about five years, taking, of course, as the point of comparison the average longevity of the district.

"Shoddy fever" is, in fact, a modification of the very fatal disease induced by what is called "dry grinding" at Sheffield; but of course the particles of woollen filaments are less fatal in their influence than the floating steel dust produced by the operation in question. The value of life in the Dewsbury district is about 1 in 47. It is always to be distinctly understood that the rag grinders constitute an exceedingly trifling minority of the workpeople employed. The operations which succeed that in which the devil plays the most prominent part, seem to be just as healthy as in those mills which prepare from the finer wools the finer cloths.

# LABOUR AND THE POOR.

---◆---

## THE MANUFACTURING DISTRICTS.

[FROM OUR SPECIAL CORRESPONDENT.]

### THE "STUFF" DISTRICTS OF YORKSHIRE.

#### HALIFAX AND BRADFORD.

### LETTER XV.

The manufacture of long-fibred wool differs from that of short-fibred wool in almost as many and as important respects as the general wool manufacture differs from the general cotton manufacture. From the short-stapled wool are wrought all kinds of cloths—properly so called—and all the tribe of the warm fleecy stuffs, from winter shawls to blankets. The long-stapled fleeces form the raw material of what is technically known as the "stuff" or "worsted" trade. To this branch of industry we are indebted for the twilled and untwilled fabrics, which may, for the convenience of the general reader, be described as belonging to the merino family. Strictly speaking, the latter term is applied only to stuffs twilled on both sides. Coburgs and Paramattas are twilled on one side, and *moussline de laines* and Orleans stuffs are untwilled. This twilling process is a technical peculiarity in the weaving, with which I have nothing to do. All the fabrics which I have enumerated belong to the same industrial family, are manufactured out of the same general class of long-stapled fleeces, and (still speaking in a general way) at the same places and by the same stages of manufacture. The classes of "stuff" fabrics indicated above are those principally used for female attire. To the list, however, I may add another group of fabrics, manufactured from the long-stapled wool, and which may be conveniently indicated as damasks and moreens.

I should not have adverted to these details—belonging, as they do, rather to the technicalities of manufacture than to the social and physical condition of the manufacturer—but that some general knowledge of what a man makes, and how he makes it, seems indispensable if we would judge correctly of his social position and the circumstances of his daily life. Some such explanations are in this case the more necessary, inasmuch as I have a shrewd guess that there are thousands of well-educated and tolerably informed people who will very probably associate the idea of worsted with the single production of warm winter stockings.

The worsted or stuff manufacture is, therefore, a branch of the woollen trade carried on in different districts, and under different social conditions, from that branch of the same trade which gives us broadcloths and blankets. Nothing is more remarkable than the unknown influences which so often determine the flow of a particular branch of textile industry to a particular locality, and in no more striking instance is this mysterious tendency manifested than in the woollen trade—using the word in its general sense—of Yorkshire. In Huddersfield and Dewsbury hardly an ounce of long-stapled wool is to be seen. In Halifax and Bradford hardly an ounce of short-stapled wool is manufactured. Leeds is the general industrial metropolis of the county, yet Huddersfield boasts that it is attaching to itself, from the larger town, the finer sorts of broadcloth; and Bradford can point to dozens of masters and hundreds of workmen who have recently made their way from the banks of the Aire, and flung their capital and their industry into what is now indisputably the metropolis of the worsted trade of England. Huddersfield and Bradford, therefore, each in its own way, contend that they are gradually absorbing very important proportions of the enterprise and industry of Leeds.

Such being the present state of matters—Halifax being an old worsted-weaving, and Bradford a new worsted-weaving town—let me shortly allude to the features which, in the most marked manner, distinguish the process of "stuff" making from that of "cloth" making. In each the wool is sorted, picked, and torn into easily-yielding filaments by the whirling teeth of the "willow." In the cloth trade, the carding machine and the slubbing frame next play their parts. At the commencement of these latter processes, the worsted manufacture parts company, and proceeds by different stages. After being willowed and crashed, instead of being consigned to the carding-machine, the material—at least in the case of 90 lbs. out of every 100 lbs.—is delivered to the wool comber, whose labour I shall, in its due place, describe. I ought to add here, that there has been lately introduced a sort of card-roving machine, very much like that which is used in the cotton trade, and which tears the wool into filaments, then brushes it, by a jerking motion, from the last cylinder, and collects the broad cobweb-like tissue into lengthened "slivers," like those produced by the hand-combers. The coarser sorts of wool only, however, are as yet subjected to this process; and the impression is strong among the hand-combers that it will not, in any formidable degree, compete with their already poorly-paid industry. The woollen-slivers, or card rovings, have now to be drawn, and afterwards spun—the operations being, in principle, precisely those which I have already detailed in describing the process of cotton manufacture. In the stuff manufacture, however, no mule, with its extended ranges of spindles, and its advancing and retiring motion, is used. The thread is spun upon stationary frames, somewhat in the same manner as silk, and the only adult male labour put in requisition for the process is that of superintendents or overlookers, each of whom may have a dozen of frames committed to his charge. In the weaving department, the power-loom is used to a greater extent than in the manufacture of cloth; the nature of the threads—which, to some extent, are akin to cotton—determining the mode of manufacture. When "stuffs" are woven, they may—except, perhaps, for the operations of the dye-house—be considered as ready for sale, such fabrics not involving the multiform finishing processes necessary in the production of glossy broadcloth.

So much for the technical differences between the production of woollen cloths and stuffs. In these differences are involved matters tending to produce, to a very considerable extent, different social phases amid the workpeople. Stuff manufacture is a much cleaner trade than woollen manufacture. Stuff mills rival, if they do not surpass, silk mills in cleanliness, and coolness, and sweetness of atmosphere. The dye is rarely applied until the fabric is turned out of the factory. There is little or no oil used in, or evolved by, the process. No high temperature is requisite, at least so far as the mills go; and altogether the work carried on in the stuff factories is well calculated to exhibit in the most favourable light the physical condition of the labourers. Notwithstanding all this, however, the stuff manufacturers are worse off than the woollen manufacturers, when tried by the grand test of the labourer's condition—his wages. In the stuff-mills there are employed, at the very least, a score of women, boys, and children, to one man. The adult males employed at the machinery are either the few who are overlookers, or the rather larger number who are forced to compete with women and girls at the power-loom. The great bulk of the male worsted population work at the unwholesome, easily-acquired, and miserably paid for—because easily learned—labour of wool-combing. Thus the average of wages is kept lower than in the cotton and cloth, and about as low perhaps as in the silk districts. The average wages of adult male workmen engaged in the stuff trade cannot be above 10s. a week, at the most liberal estimate. That of women ranges closely up to them, for a female weaver will earn as much, or more, than a male comber. And as for the children, the average of the wages which they receive is kept down by the great number of "half-timers"—boys and girls under thirteen years of age, who are employed. Exclusive of half-time workers and young persons, the average weekly wages of male and female adults may be reckoned as from 8s. 6d. to 9s. 6d.—lower by about 2s. 6d. than the average wages in the cotton districts, reckoning in both cases on a time of fair prosperity, and a period of ten hours' daily toil.

Halifax and Bradford are, as I have said, the centres of the stuff manufacture. The former town possesses, however, other industrial resources than that of the staple trade. The mayor, Mr. Crossley, for instance, is the chief partner in an immense carpet manufacturing establishment, employing about 1,500 hands, principally adult males, and paying about £1,000 weekly in wages. Besides this and other establishments of different kinds, the worsted manufacturers of Halifax prepare so great a variety of the staple production, that periods of distress fall in general lighter upon them than on their Bradford neighbours. The latter town is, perhaps, more quickly and keenly affected by the variations of trade than any other manufacturing depôt in England. The masters are generally reputed as bold speculators; and the millowner who ventures his money freely, hazards, of necessity, the wages of his people as well as his own profits. In Halifax, however, things are conducted more slowly and quietly. Compared with Bradford, the place has a touch of antiquity in its aspect and its tone. So far as appearance goes, no two towns can be more dissimilar. Halifax is an ancient borough, girdled by an *enceint* of mills and mill-hands' dwellings. Bradford seems spick and span new from the centre to the circumference. There are points in the town of Halifax, from which the gazer will be put in mind of the quaint cities of Normandy and Bavaria—Rouen or Bamberg—so steep and narrow are the streets, and so picturesque the plaster walls streaked with chequering beams of blackened wood—the numerous street-turned gables—the ledge-like stories, each overhanging the other—and the grey and time-tarnished hue of the great coarse slates which form the high crow-footed and ridgy roofs. There is a fine Norman church, rising, wan and weather-stained, from its field of graves; and an odd, old-fashioned, nondescript building, in the centre of the town, traditionally called the Castle, and from the battered pinnacles of which watchers were wont to guard the approaches to the borough—against what habitual foemen tradition does not seem to be by any means clear.

Mr. Smith, of Deanston, in a sanitary report made about 1837, describes Bradford as being the dirtiest town in England. Mr. Smith must have written ere he extended his researches to Halifax. At all events Bradford is rapidly improving. The corporation is busy paving and draining; but that of Halifax has as yet been able to do nothing. I ought to add that both towns have received their municipal charters within the last two years, and that Halifax is now, or has been until very lately, unprovided with any funds to carry on a sanitary campaign. The sooner, however, that it begins, the better. Few towns in England are better situated for being effectually drained. Mainly placed on the side of a steepish hill, with a rapid stream running at the bottom, Halifax ought to be a miracle of cleanliness, instead of, as it is, a marvel of dirt. The state of the low back streets and of the dwellings which compose them, I shall presently sketch.

The first factory in Halifax which I visited was that of the Messrs. Holdsworth. It is a vast establishment, weaving all manner of stuff goods, situated upon the outskirts of the town, and surrounded by the dwellings of the workpeople. The active and energetic chief of the firm conducted me through the works. The weaving shed is one of the noblest structures of the kind I have ever seen, perfectly lighted, not only by ordinary windows, but by means of a species of serrated roof, the perpendicular portions of which are glass. That the arrangements for ventilation are excellent, was sufficiently proved by the perfectly fresh state of the atmosphere, and the workpeople laboured with spirit and energy. There were a few Jacquard looms in the shed, but the greater number were of the ordinary kind. There might have been about one man present to every ten women and girls. The wages of the former average 10s., those of the latter 8s. weekly.

In estimating the remuneration of workpeople, I am frequently puzzled to reconcile the statements of the operatives and those of their masters, and yet I believe both to be grounded on fact. Where the amount of wages fluctuates with the skill of the workman and the quality of the fabric wrought, two parties looking at the question from different points of view will almost invariably state results each of which is capable of being supported by figures representing the sums earned or the sums paid, but neither giving a really fair view of the case. The master will frequently strike an average from what his best hands working at the best jobs may earn. The labourer will just as frequently base his calculations upon what the most ordinary hands working on the most ordinary jobs do receive. In neither case can you complain of absolute want of truth, but in both cases you will have to lament an equal absence of candour. In visiting the homes of the poor, accompanied by relieving officers, I have been again and again cautioned by my guides not to accept as literal truth the statements which were made to me. "All the class upon the confines of pauperism—the class which are in daily risk of becoming paupers— will understate their incomes purposely for me to hear, and will per- haps afterwards appeal to what I cannot deny that I heard them state." This was the warning given by a most active, intelligent, and, as I be- lieve, kind-hearted relieving officer in Bradford; and I think that I am bound to repeat it here. My only aim is to hit the truth. I shall give the statements made to me by labourers and masters, guarded by the rules of belief which I have myself been able to educe, as well as by the caution of non-interested parties.

To return to the workpeople of Messrs. Holdsworth's factory. The vast majority of weavers were young women. In neatness and propri- ety of dress they rivalled the silk spinners, and shawls and bonnets were hung along the walls, as I have described them in Macclesfield. In a smaller spinning room, the machinery ran quicker—so quickly, indeed, as to cause a perceptible tremor in the building, and here the wages of the workwomen ranged somewhat higher. To be removed to the quick spinning room was to be promoted. In the carding, draw- ing, and spinning departments, the mechanism was almost exclusively looked after by young women and girls, at the low wages of 5s. and 5s. 6d. The men employed were overlookers, and earned from 15s. to 22s. The ventilation in these rooms was hardly so good as in the weaving shed, but still I cannot say that there was much to complain of. The girls looked hale and hearty, and Mr. Holdsworth was energetic in calling my attention to their plumpness, a quality which in a large majority of cases they certainly possessed to a very fair degree. The dinner hour arrived during our inspection. As a considerable propor- tion of the women live too far from the mill to go home to their meal, arrangements are made for enabling them to take it upon the spot. A sort of small cookshop is established near the furnace of one of

the steam-engines, and thither every girl who pleases brings her dinner, ready cooked, but disposed in a dish so as to allow it to be readily
warmed up again. I stationed myself in the dinner-bar at noon, and so
had an opportunity of seeing nearly 300 of the messes prepared, and
they were handed out through a sort of buttery-hatch to each applicant as she shouted the number of her carding-machine, her spinning-
frame, or her loom. The dinners consisted almost invariably of a portion of baked meat with potatoes, and in a few instances mushrooms.
A great number had coffee and tea in little tin flagons. Altogether
the dinners seemed substantial and nourishing. I was gratified by the
appearance both of the consumers and the fare consumed.

Afterwards I visited, alone, the cottages of several of the
workpeople connected with the mills. As a general rule the dwellings
of the Lancashire operatives are better than those of their Yorkshire
brethren. In the superior class of cotton-workers' houses you will
find a parlour, a kitchen, and two bed-rooms. In Yorkshire the
tenements are almost invariably double, and the equally constant rule
of construction is—a common room serving for parlour and kitchen,
a cellar below, and a bed-chamber above. The Yorkshire apartments
are perhaps larger than those of Lancashire, but the domestic conveniences afforded are very inferior. The houses attached to the Messrs.
Holdsworth's establishments are fair specimens of the ordinary
construction throughout the towns of the county. Hearing that there
were one or two hand-loom weavers manufacturing damasks in the
place, I found out one of them. The lower room was not absolutely
squalid—but that is the best that can be said of it. Up stairs in the
loom room was one of those unmade, brown, frame-like beds, which
I have so often seen. The weaver rated his average earnings at from
8s. to 9s. With the best sort of work, and plenty of it, he could earn
15s., but the trade was dying out. His wages used to be double what
they were now. The rent he paid was £5 a year. I may observe that
stuff handloom weaving seems likely to sink into the condition of
cotton handloom weaving, the quality and tenseness of the threads
of each fabric approaching each other pretty closely. In the other
houses which I visited I found the furniture generally coarse, and
sometimes scanty. The absence of convenient accommodation, so
far as my experience goes, tends invariably to the production of
household slovenliness. Give people a good house, and there is a
far higher chance that they will become good housekeepers than if
they live in a dwelling so constructed that they can take little pride

in its accommodations or its arrangements. Local acts are passed providing for the construction of tenements with free ventilation from the front to the back door.

From the Messrs. Holdsworth's mill I proceeded to another—that of the Messrs. Ackroyd. The average wages paid in this establishment were thus stated to me by a very intelligent overlooker. The adult males, not including the weavers, might have about 17s. a week. Female adults might average, in the spinning and drawing rooms, about 6s. or 6s. 3d. Young persons, from 13 to 18, about 4s. 9d.; and children from 8 to 13, working five hours a day, from 1s. 9d. to 2s. 3d. In the weaving department my informant thought that the average rate earned by men and women might be somewhat above 8s. per week. As in the case of the former mill, the factory in question was kept as clean as possible. It was dusk when I went through it—a period which may account for the atmosphere not feeling quite so fresh as did that of the last-mentioned establishment.

I have said that the streets of Halifax are disgracefully neglected. The remark applies especially to the courts and *cul de sacs* inhabited by the very poor—including, of course, the Irish—and locally termed "foulds." I inspected several very closely, and found them reeking with stench and the worst sort of abomination. The ash-pits and appurtenances were disgustingly choked, ordure and filthy stagnant slops lay freely and deeply scattered around, often at the very thresholds of swarming dwellings—and among all this muck, uncared-for children sprawled by the score, and idle slatternly women lounged by the half dozen. The "low Irish" in Halifax are hawkers and rag collectors, like nearly all the brotherhood in the North of England. I talked to several in their cellars. One old woman, who had been more than thirty years in England, talked dolefully of the decline of the hawking trade. She had frequently, in her youth, she said, made 20s. out of one house. She carried about "chaney and such like." But the poor people now seldom earned more than a shilling, or eighteenpence at the very most, for a hard day's work. This woman kept lodgings in a cellar. Two strapping fellows sat smoking by the smouldering fire. The beds were greasy mattresses partially covered with foul rags and rolled up in corners. In another cellar, which was almost totally dark, and for which its occupant paid 9d. a week, a grey-headed negro—an old man-of-war's man—had lived for seventeen years. He seldom or never stirred out—vegetating there in a world of dirt and darkness. All the "foulds" which I penetrated were of the same class. The vilest filth lying unswept and seemingly unheeded—the most noxious stenches filling the air—the grimy houses and ordure-covered stones swarming with a foul, a lazy, and—worse than both—a seemingly contented population. The corporation of Halifax have a perfect Augean stable to clean, and the sooner they set about it the better for the health and character of their town.

Of course there are a great number of wool-combers in Halifax, but the account which I shall give of these workmen in Bradford will suffice for both.

Let us now proceed, then, to the latter place. In an architectural point of view, the best features of Bradford consist of numerous ranges of handsome warehouses. The streets have none of the old-fashioned picturesqueness of those of Halifax. The best of them are muddy, and not too often swept. Mills abound in great plenty, and their number is daily increasing, while the town itself extends in like proportion. Bradford is, as I have said, essentially a new town. Half a century ago it was a mere cluster of huts: now the district of which it is the heart contains upwards of 132,000 inhabitants. The value of life is about 1 in 40. Fortunes have been made in Bradford with a rapidity almost unequalled even in the manufacturing districts. In half a dozen years men have risen from the loom to possess mills and villas. At present, stuff manufacturers are daily pouring into the town from Leeds, while a vast proportion of the wool-combing of the empire seems, as it were, to have concentrated itself in Bradford. I was struck by the accent in which many of the wool-combers addressed me; and, in answer to my inquiries, I had frequently a room-full of workmen exclaiming, "I'm from Leicestershire"—"I'm from Devonshire"—"I'm from Cornwall"—"I'm from Mount Mellick, in Queen's County."

As I have hinted, the Bradford employers are, in the slang of the manufacturing districts, accounted "high-pressure men." I have been told that a mere spirt of rapid demand is sufficient to cause loom-shed after loom-shed to arise. The fabrics manufactured being also of the same general class, their sale increases and diminishes simultaneously, and the consequence is, that every shade of variation in the market means hundreds of dinners the more or the less in Bradford. A town of this class is just one of those on which, in prosperous seasons, the flood of agricultural pauperism bears down. Trade is at present exceedingly brisk in Bradford—so brisk that even stables are put into requisition to contain the wool, for lack of warehouse room.

The number of persons, therefore, receiving parish relief is compara-tively small, and, excepting an isolated case or two, I am told that not a single native of the town is upon the books. The paupers are mainly Irish and English agricultural labourers who have not as yet learned to be useful in their new sphere. In the last period of commercial stag-nation, about two out of every five labourers in Bradford were out of employment. A test, consisting of shovelling and wheeling earth, was established, and about 1s. 6d. per head was weekly paid to all unable to find work. The revival of trade was marked by the most gratifying social tokens. The masters, following the example of the Mayor, gave either dinners or holidays, and railway trips, to all their hands. Up-wards of £2,000 was thus expended during the last summer, and the addresses of thanks presented in all instances by the working hands were so worded as to afford gratifying proof of the good feeling be-tween employer and employed.

With the exception of a few of the main thoroughfares, which are bustling, and characterized by good shops, and in many cases by the handsome ranges of warehouses which I have alluded to, Bradford may be described as an accumulation of mean streets, steep lanes, and huge mills—intersected here and there by those odious patches of black, muddy, waste ground, rooted up by pigs, and strewn with oyster-shells, cabbage-stalks, and such garbage, which I have so often noticed as commonly existing in manufacturing towns. Since Mr. Smith, of Deanston, passed sentence upon Bradford, the corporation, although they might have done more, have not been idle. Upwards of thirty streets and lanes have been paved and drained, and some of the worst Irish colonies have been materially improved. I was taken to see one locality which had been the worst in Bradford, and which was once a constant well-spring of fever. It has been opened up, drained, paved, and regularly cleansed, and is now not fouler than an average dirty lane. The houses of the workpeople are very inferior. They are one and all constructed back to back, or rather built double, with a partition running down from the ridge of the roof. This is the case even in rows and streets at present building. "The plan," said my informant, "is adopted because of its cheapness, and because it saves ground rent." Cellars are very numerous in Bradford, and not one operative family in a hundred possesses more than two rooms—"a house and a chamber." In respect of dwelling accommodation, the worst feature of the stuff and woollen towns is, that they seem to be making little or no progress. In the cases of ranges of houses, even of a comparatively superior class, the privies are built in clusters, in a small space, left open behind, instead of each being placed in a quiet, decent situation, close to the house to which it belongs. Bradford, like Halifax, is well situated for drainage. There is ample fall, and the "Bradford Beck," a rapid stream, which flows through the town, would, if arched over, make a capital main sewer. This brook at present runs the colour of ink. The relieving officer, with whom I inspected the town, showed me a spot where the foul water washed the grimy walls of half a dozen steaming mills. "There," he said, "when I was a boy, I used to catch trout in as bright a stream as any in Yorkshire." The two towns in England, indeed, which within the last half-century have sprung up most rapidly, form an odd pair. They are Brighton and Bradford.

We proceeded first to see some of the low Irish haunts. As usual, the great majority of the adults are hawkers, but a few of them are wool-combers. Of these I shall have something to say presently. Rags, and in some cases brushes, form the staple of their trades. Instead of exchanging pots and mugs, the collectors frequently barter salt for rags, the terms being always pound for pound. Sevenpence a stone was the market value of mixed rags—sixpence a stone that of bones. The average earnings of the hawkers they stated as from 1s. to 1s. 6d. a day. The general appearance of their houses I have frequently sketched. They almost always consist of a single room—generally a cellar—a low, dark, foul-smelling place, with rough stools and a broken table or so lying about; coarse crockery, either unwashed or full of dirty water; knives without handles, and forks with broken prongs; bits of loaves smeared over by dirty hands; bundles of rags, buckets of slops, and unmade beds huddled on the stone or earthen floor in corners. There always seems to exist a sort of community of dwellings among these people, which I never find among their English neighbours. The doors invariably stand open, and when I inquire about the sleeping accommodation I am invariably told that half the people whom I find crouching round the fireplace smoking are only "naybours." Sometimes I find a room almost empty, but before I am there a minute it is sure to be filled by the aforesaid naybours, who, having nothing to do, come stalking in to learn what my visit portends. In a lodging-house which I saw, there was bed room for 16, at 3d. each; that is to say, there were four frames, covered with rags and rugs, in the lower room, and the same accommodation in the higher. The single men slept by themselves. Married couples and single women occupied the other apartment jointly. There could not, when I called, have been less than a dozen men and women smoking round the fire. In an adjacent cellar the scene was perfectly savage. The floor was earth, covered with splints of wood produced in match making. The articles of furniture were two—a rough wooden trestle, on which were placed a broken brown plate and some herring-bones—and a square box, like a small coffin, in which lay an infant. A woman, with a skin so foul that she might have passed for a negress, was squatted on the ground—and a litter, I cannot call them a group, of children burrowed about her. The woman could barely talk English; yet she must have been more than a dozen years in the country, for the eldest boy, an urchin fully as old, told me that he had been born in Lincolnshire. In a corner lay a litter of brown rags—the family bed. The rent paid for this place was 8d. a week.

As I have stated, the greatest part of the labour of male adults through the worsted districts consists in combing wool. In Bradford I was told on good authority that there are about 15,000 wool-combers. These men sometimes work singly, but more often three or four or five club together and labour in what is called a shop, generally consisting of the upper room or "chamber" over the lower room or "house." Their wives and children assist them to a certain extent in the first and almost unskilled portions of the operation, but the whole process is rude and easily acquired. It consists of forcibly pulling the wool through metal combs or spikes of different lengths, and set five or six deep. These combs must be kept at a high temperature, and consequently the central apparatus in a combing room is always a "fire pot," burning either coke, coals, or charcoal, and constructed so as to allow three, four, or five combs to be heated at it—the vessel being in these cases respectively called a "pot o' three," a "pot o' four," or a "pot o' five." When coals are burned, the pot is a fixed apparatus like a small stove, with a regular funnel to carry away the smoke. When charcoal is used the pot is a movable vessel, without a funnel, the noxious fumes too often spreading freely in the room. Scattered through the chamber are frequently two or more poles or masts, to which the combs, after being heated, are firmly attached while the workman drags the wool through them until he has reduced it to a soft mass of filament—when he educes the substance as it were, draws it by skilful manipulation out of the compact lump into long semi-transparent "slivers," which, after certain minor operations, are returned to the factory to be subjected to the "drawing machines." The general aspect of a combing-room may therefore be described as that of a bare chamber, heated to nearly 85 degrees. A round fire-pot stands in the centre; masses of wool are heaped about; and four or five men, in their shirt sleeves, are working busily.

The first wool-combing apartment which I entered contained five workmen. There was a coal fire-pot in the centre, with a regular communication with the chimney. The heat was great, but modified by the windows being left open. The entire house consisted of the working room, and a cooking, sitting, and sleeping room beneath. The rent was 1s. 9d. It belonged to one man, to whom the rest paid each 4d. weekly. For this the landlord provided the necessary fire. The arrangement of a common room has reference principally to economy in fuel. The masters who give out the wool to be combed pay a certain amount, called "fire-brass," wherewith to provide the necessary fuel. The "fire-brass," when paid in money, is about 1½d. for every 24 lbs. of wool. When charcoal is employed, it is usual, however, for the masters to give fuel instead of money. The estimate of wool-combers' wages given by the five workmen in this room was, that they amounted, on an average, to 8s. or 8s. 6d. per week. In Halifax the chief labourer in a similar room said that some hands might occasionally earn 12s. a week, but for this they laboured 15, 16, and 17 hours out of the 24. He put the average at about 9s. a week. This comber afterwards corrected his original statement so far as to add, that in the 12s. a week he included the earnings of the wife, who frequently "picked and handfulled" the wool. Wool-combers' hours are, I believe, proverbially long. The men in Bradford said they were sometimes forced to work most of the night. Low as their wages are, they were recently still lower; but since the revival of trade in the district, the wool-combers have raised the amount of their remuneration upwards of 3s. by three successive strikes. The combers have now to compete with machinery. Each machine will do about ten times the work of a hand labourer, but it employs several hands, two of whom get good wages. These machines are in general, however, only used for the coarsest work, and did not seem to excite any great apprehension among the workmen. Wool-combing is the only branch of manufacturing industry which I have yet met with supporting a fair proportion of adult Irish males. A number of them have been bred to the employment at Mount Mellick, in Queen's County. The mass of the wool-combers of Yorkshire includes natives of almost all the southern counties of England. One and all, they were loud in their denunciations of the accommodation provided for their labour.

In the south the masters used to provide shops for the work. Here the men had to labour in their houses, and often to sleep in the room in which they toiled. They put it to me, whether the hot air I was breathing was fit for human beings to sleep in. "But the furnace, the 'pot,' is extinguished at night?" I said. "Never," they replied, "from Monday morning till Saturday night. It is always left with a smouldering glow of fire. But they're much worse off than us, those who use charcoal."

In this I fully agreed, and started off to see a "charcoal pot." I had not far to go. In an adjacent street I lighted upon a man working at mohair over a charcoal stove. The pot was funnel-less and uncovered, and the noxious fuel glowed with a subdued bluish light. I was not sensible of any odours, but an immediately commencing headache told that there was something atmospherically wrong. The wool-comber was a gaunt, sickly-looking man. His wife entered the room when we were speaking, and joined in the conversation. He said that combing mohair was a bad work. Mohair was a desperate thing to float and cling. He had often to brush away the fibres as they gathered round his lips, but he knew that he breathed some on 'em. The wife said that the work made her husband sick, often and often. But it was regular, and what could they do? The charcoal was a terribly bad thing, he knew that. Why did he not use coal? Why, because the master would not allow him. The master thought charcoal best for combing mohair. He got no "fire-brass," only charcoal. Sometimes it was stronger like than other times. Then it made him sickish, and he would have to go out into the air for a while. He worked from six in the morning till ten at night. He knew it wasn't wholesome, but "what could he do?" There being a bed in the room, I asked who slept in it. "Some of the children." They had seven; five of them slept in that bed. "But, of course," I said, "you put out the charcoal?" The reply was, "Well, not exactly; but there's only a spark or so left burning, and the window's a little down."

"But surely your children suffer from such an atmosphere?"

"Well, yes. Some odd times there is one of our little ones comes down in the morning very sickish, but 'what can we do?'"

Three of this man's children worked in the mills, earning among them 12s. a week. One of them, the eldest girl, was ill with scrofulous sores on her legs, for the cure of which the poor creature had recently swallowed ten boxes of quack pills.

I next visited a squalid cellar; and this time, taught by experience, I was at once sensible of the subtle vapours of the charcoal pot. A man, his wife—a miserable, broken-hearted looking woman—an old grand-dame, and two little children, were at their dinner. It consisted of coffee and bread. The place was underground. All the family slept in it, and all night long the charcoal pot glowed beside them. These people were Irish, and miserable creatures they were.

"Where's your daughter?" said my companion.

"Gone, gone," answered the mother. "She gets 6s. a week, and so she went plump over the door and left us."

"After all," said the poor father, "perhaps it's as well. When children grows up, their keep and their clothes take their wages fully."

The mother shook her head in obvious bitterness of spirit. They had a son who had served them in the same way.

"But surely," I said, "he comes to see you sometimes?"

"Niver, sir. He's ould enough to take care of himself, and he niver comes near us—niver."

In another cellar, or at least a sort of compromise between a ground-floor and a cellar, I found five combers at work. I congratulated them upon having a coal, instead of a charcoal, pot. The difference in the air was very striking, coming as I had done immediately out of the fumes of charcoal. The atmosphere here, although hot enough and impure enough, had a sweet genial taste—if I may use the word—compared with the charcoal-laden air. The latter felt at once hot, acrid, and bitter. The terms may be unphilosophical, but they convey an idea of the actual sensation. In reply to my remark, the oldest man of the party said he could never stand the charcoal. It made him sick and giddy. But some masters had a prejudice in favour of it, and obliged their men to use it. Theirs was a poor trade. They had long, long hours, and they did not make more nor 8s. or 9s. a week.

I asked whether the new machine affected them much?

"It don't do us much good, any way," replied one.

"There's worse than the new machine for Englishmen," said another, "and that's the ship loads of them Irish that's coming among us, and pulling down the wage."

"There's no doubt of that," a third went on; "they don't live like Englishmen, them people."

"But if you dislike them so much," I said, "why do you teach them your trade?"

"We don't," said the first man. "No Englishman would, I hope."

"I'll tell you how it's done, sir," continued another. "There's old Irish hands here, and the new ones goes to them. Then the old ones gets a lot of work out from five or six masters, and gives it to the new ones to do, teaching them the way, and perhaps doing the job over, if so be their scholars spoils the work; and so them persons, who are a sort of middle men like, pocket most of the wages that their countrymen earns."

"Aye," said the first comber, "and they doesn't sleep in beds, but on the wool."

"I heard tell," remarked the former speaker, "of a house where five-and-thirty on them pigged together on the floor."

Notwithstanding this display of animosity, my guide informed me that, on occasions of differences between the masters and the workmen, English and Irish pulled together in the most brotherly fashion.

During my investigations at Bradford I had more than one opportunity of seeing how the parochial authorities in agricultural districts pack their paupers off to the manufacturing regions. I select two cases. The first was that of a widow from a purely rural part of Yorkshire. She had a large young family. Her husband had been an agricultural labourer at 15s. a week in summer, and in winter he broke stones on the road for 15d. a day. On his death, the family became chargeable. The parish immediately offered to pay the expense of removal, and gave the family £1 1s. if they would go to Bradford. They consented, and several of the children being sickly and subject to fits, so as to be unable to work in the mills, they have been mainly supported by Bradford ever since. The woman who told me these particulars said, that she knew many families who had been sent to Bradford from the same locality in the same way.

The other case is that of a poor Irishwoman, one of the cleanest, tidiest, and best specimens of her country people, in that walk of life, I have ever seen. Having heard of her case, she came out of the mill where she worked to speak to me, and conducted me to her chamber. A poorer one, and yet a cleaner one, I never saw; the deal table had been scoured until it shone again—there was a faded bit of carpeting on the floor, and not a speck of dust from wall to wall. I had never witnessed a more striking instance of cleanliness taking away all the squalor of poverty. In the room were three children. The eldest, a girl of seven, was rocking the cradle of the youngest, and attending to the proceedings of her other little sister.

"This is my housekeeper," said the mother, "and I can trust her and feel easy about the younger ones when I am at my work." The story of the family I shall relate nearly in the mother's words:—

"My husband and me lived at Minstun (an agricultural district of Yorkshire). He was a hand-loom weaver. Wages were very low, and times were very hard with us. We were at Minstun ten months, and in that time we tasted flesh twice. My poor husband had a consumption on him, and little by little he was forced to give up work. The farmers and the neighbours were very hard-hearted to us. They never sent as much as a ha'p'orth of milk even to the dying man. When he was gone, the parish offered me and my four children 1s. to pay the rent every week, and 1s. to live on. If we didn't like that, they said, we might go to Bradford, and they would give us 30s. to move. They didn't give us 30s., but they gave us 29s., and we came here. If they had only given us 3s. a week I would have stayed. I have a little boy, and I brought him to the mill, and told them all about us. The people at the mill were very kind, much kinder than the farmers. They took the little boy and set him to easy work, and gave him 2s. a week. Then the manager said I might come into the mill and see him, and try if I couldn't learn to do something myself. So I got to know how to pick lumps out of the slubbings, and first I got 5s. 6d., and last week I was raised to 6s., so we have now 8s. a week. Well, first I lived in a room belonging to the mill, with an outside stair, and I paid 1s. rent. But I was afraid of the children breaking their necks there. The only other place I could get near the mill was this. There are two rooms here, and the rent is 2s. I know it's too much for the like of me to pay; but think of the children. Well, sir, the parish are very good to me, and give me 3s. a week—2s. for the rent and 1s. for coals—and we live and clothe ourselves on the other 8s. We live chiefly on bread. I get a stone and a half of flour every week, and I bake it on Sundays. Then we have a little tea or coffee, and sometimes we have a little offal meat, because it's cheap. A good gentleman gave me the furniture I have and the bed in the other room. It cost altogether 15s. Everybody has been very kind to me, and the neighbours come in often to look after the children when I'm at work. I was born in Shandon parish, in Cork; and oh! I wish there were mills there for the poor to work in. It would be a blessing to them indeed."

# LABOUR AND THE POOR.

—◆—

## THE MANUFACTURING DISTRICTS.

[FROM OUR SPECIAL CORRESPONDENT.]

### THE WOOLLEN AND FLAX DISTRICTS.

#### LEEDS.

## Letter XVI.

Leeds, as most people are aware, is the manufacturing capital of Yorkshire, as Manchester is of Lancashire. Each city is surrounded by a group of satellites, in some of which the enterprise and vigour of industry displayed excel even those of the district capitals. In the West, Staleybridge is popularly accounted a more "go-a-head" place than Manchester; and Blackburn takes the lead in point of speed of machinery. So, in the East, Huddersfield piques itself on producing finer broadcloths than Leeds; and Bradford boasts that it is absorbing the stuff manufacture of the larger town altogether to itself. Leeds, however, can very well afford to bear the prosperity of its young and growing rivals. It is, and will probably long continue to be, the real emporium of the cloth trade—while the preparation and spinning of flax is a branch of industry which belongs exclusively to itself.

A cluster of mud-huts stood where Leeds now stands as early as the signing of Magna Charta; and it was a considerable spinning and weaving place in the time of James I. His son granted municipal privileges to the town. The market days were then, as now, Tuesday and Saturday; and then, as now, the country manufacturers thronged in with their cloth, and exposed it for sale, not indeed in a porticoed hall, but on the parapet of the antique bridge which spanned the Aire. The Yorkshire, like the Lancashire mind, was grave, and somewhat Puritanic, in its instincts, and Cromwell invited Leeds to send a representative to the House of Commons. The Protectorate passed away, and Leeds thereafter continued unenfranchised until the Reform Bill.

In the reign of Charles II. the population of the district of Leeds is estimated, by Mr. Macaulay, at 7,000. In 1801 the population of the township was 30,669. In 1831 it was 71,602. In 1841 it was 88,741; and it is now estimated as amounting to fully 100,000. The population of the parish of Leeds is 15,000. The value of life in Leeds—imperfect as its sanitary arrangements are, and grievously neglected as great and thickly-peopled ranges of its outskirts are left—is greater by a very considerable degree than in Manchester. While upon this subject, it may not be amiss for me—as this is the last time I shall have the opportunity—to bring together the figures showing the rates of mortality in the principal cotton, woollen, and commercial towns in the North of England. In the cotton districts I take representatives of all the types of cotton towns—the same in the woollen districts—and then I strike a mean between the value of male and female life, as given by the Registrar-General's returns:—

### COTTON TOWNS.

In Blackburn there are living to one
death . . . . . . . . . . . . . . . . . . . . .  39  persons.
„ Bolton  . . . . . . . . . . . . . . . . . . . .  37    „
„ Ashton and Oldham  . . . . . . . . . .  37    „
„ Preston  . . . . . . . . . . . . . . . . . . .  38    „
„ Manchester  . . . . . . . . . . . . . . . .  30    „

Showing the mean number of deaths in the cotton towns to be one for every 36 1-5th of the population.

### WOOLLEN AND WORSTED TOWNS.

In Huddersfield there are living to one
death . . . . . . . . . . . . . . . . . . . . .  50  persons.
„ Dewsbury  . . . . . . . . . . . . . . . . . .  47    „
„ Halifax  . . . . . . . . . . . . . . . . . . . .  47    „
„ Bradford  . . . . . . . . . . . . . . . . . . .  40    „
„ Leeds  . . . . . . . . . . . . . . . . . . . . .  38    „

Showing the mean number of deaths in the woollen and worsted towns to be one for every 44 2-5ths of the population. Taking the two great shipping ports of the two counties, we find that the proportion of deaths is reversed. In Liverpool, one person dies out of every 29. In Hull, one person out of every 35. Still, the latter place seems the worst, in a sanitary view, in Yorkshire. In Sheffield, one person dies to every 36½ of the population. So that Leeds stands, in its own county, the third from the bottom of the list.

By the census of 1841, there appear to have been in Leeds 34,002 inhabited, and 2,419 uninhabited buildings. The latter at present include about 15 churches of the Establishment, containing sitting room for about 20,000 persons—and upwards of 30 dissenting places of worship, affording seat room for about 30,000. Of these latter the Wesleyans possess six chapels—the New Connexion Methodists, 3—the Association Methodists, 2—the Primitive Methodists, 2—the Teetotal Methodists, 1—the Independents, 5—the Particular Baptists, 1—the General Baptists, 1—the Society of Friends, 1—the Presbyterians, 1—and the Unitarians, Swedenborgians, and Inghamites, 1 each. A new Established Church is at present being built by the Messrs. Marshall. Most of the places of worship named above have, as in Lancashire, Sunday schools attached to them. The number of scholars is estimated at about 12,000. In Leeds, as in Manchester, a great proportion of poor-law relief is out-door. At present trade is brisk, and but for the recent visitation of cholera, which threw a great number of widows and orphans upon the parish, the pressure upon the rates would be light. As it is, the amount of out-door relief weekly administered is about £350.

Leeds has little or none of that hothouse appearance which to some extent distinguishes Manchester. It seems, in its physical peculiarities, a more substantial and slower-growing town than its high-pressure cotton neighbour, and it possesses none of the metropolitan attributes of the latter. Leeds has no public parks. With here and there an exceptional spot, the suburbs extend, in mean, clumsy, straggling streets, out into the bare country. There are no such fair ranges of villas as those which, in many quarters, skirt the busy portions of Manchester; and the dwellings of the labouring class, to which I shall speedily call particular attention, are, in point of appearance—and of symmetrical outward and convenient inward arrangement—decidedly inferior to those of the cotton capital. A locality on which I cannot but bestow a few descriptive words is the Cloth Hall—or rather, the Cloth Halls—for there are two for different kinds of stuff in Leeds. The manufacture of cloth has always been to a greater or less extent domestic. Out of the vast quantity of yarn or thread manufactured from the flax in Leeds, very little is converted into cloth in the town. The weavers live scattered in the neighbouring villages, working for different masters, who, on Tuesdays and Saturdays, by themselves or their agents, expose the goods for sale in the Cloth Hall. The business is carried on with that curious taciturn regularity, amounting to a sort of industrial discipline, which specially characterises the buyers and sellers of the North. The Hall which I visited is a plain brick building forming a quadrangle, in which the grass grows, and which was crowded with carts ready to take away the goods. The building consists simply of four long corridors forming a square. Two narrow tables run the whole length of each corridor. A stance about three feet long is apportioned to each manufacturer, and his name and residence are inscribed upon the table between the painted boundaries which divide him from his neighbours. The hour arrives, a bell rings, the doors are flung open to purchasers, and there, ranged all down the long bazaar—or "streets" as they are called—stands each vendor, silent and erect behind the counter, with his goods heaped up before him. There is a sort of Oriental taciturnity and reserve in the whole aspect of the affair. No man solicits custom. No man wishes to be informed what he can tempt the buyer with next. The merchant walks slowly down the "street." If his eye fall upon a parcel of goods, the vendor silently unfolds the cloth to show its gloss and texture. If the lot does not suit, not a word is spoken; if it does, the price is merely named, and the transaction is concluded in an instant. Five minutes before the close of an hour the bell rings again. The clock strikes in due time, and the market is ended. A fine is imposed upon any manufacturer who lingers even five minutes after the stipulated time is up. Of those connected with the woollen trade, only cloth merchants are admitted into the market; no stapler, for instance, is allowed to be present for a moment.

So much for the sale of cloth. I have already described its manufacture in my letter upon Huddersfield and Dewsbury. It will, perhaps, be for the advantage of the reader, before I touch upon the sanitary and social condition of the population of Leeds, that I describe the process of manufacture of what I may call the second staple of the place—the dressing of flax, and the spinning therefrom of linen and tow yarns and threads. There are about a dozen flax establishments in Leeds, the largest of which is the celebrated mill of the Messrs. Marshall—a concern employing from 1,200 to 1,500 hands, and paying about £600 a week in wages.

As in the worsted trade, the vast majority of the hands employed in the flax mills are women and children; but, unlike the worsted trade, there is no such branch of industry as wool-combing to employ the male adults. In Leeds, a considerable proportion of the husbands and brothers of the female flax-workers find employment in the cloth trade; but it is not easy to ascertain how the numbers of boys employed in some of the mills—that of the Messrs. Marshall for example—are provided for after they have out-grown their labour in the heckling

of flax and the carding of tow. As in the case, however, of all manufacturing processes, they are needed and they appear. They perform
their spell of duty, and are then absorbed into other occupations. Of
course, the work being so managed, the average of wages paid in flax-
mills is a low one. As in the case of worsted, but unlike the cases of
wool and cotton, the weavers gain the highest pay; but the quantity
of linen woven in the Leeds flax-mills is very small. The threads are
often exported, and of those woven in this country, Barnsley, in Yorkshire, takes and works up into fabric the greatest quantity. The flax
manufacture, in all its stages save one, is a cleanly and healthful occupation. The objectionable process is the necessary one of heckling—
analogous, so far as the difference in the staple material will permit of
comparison, to the willowing of wool and the cleaning and blowing
of cotton. The dust produced in the heckling process is very considerable, and it is a dust of a most injurious character—hard, subtle,
fine and penetrating. Even in the best-ventilated and most carefully
regulated mills, it flies in clouds, which dim the extremities of the
room; and I have experienced an effect from it, which not even shoddy
dust produced—a smarting and a watering of the eyes. The heads and
shoulders of the workpeople are plentifully strewn with this sharp dry
powder; and although in well-ordered mills the machines, &c., are
cleaned thrice a day, an hour's work is sufficient to coat them again
with a dun layer of dust and filament. In coarse spinning establishments, and in the process of evolving the large loose yarn made from
tow, there is another unpleasantness of a minor nature. Flaxen threads
are always conducted in the spinning process through hot water—and
when the threads are large, loose, and spongy, the whirling motion
of the spindles on which they are wound flings the moisture about
in all directions. Splashboards of different constructions are in use,
and in some establishments the tenters wear thick leather aprons; but
the result is always to make the place sloppy, and the air, particularly in winter, disagreeably and unhealthily damp. These drawbacks
excepted—and the second is very partial in occurrence as well as minor in nature—flax dressing and spinning may be counted as amongst
the healthiest and cleanliest of factory processes.

The sorters first operate upon the flax. They are male adults, and
their labour is skilled. They therefore earn the fair wage of from £1
1s. to £1 5s. The boys who assist them, and who are learning, are paid
about 5s. The next process is "breaking." The boy who tends the necessary machine feeds it with the raw material, which, passing between

the crushing wheels, emerges bruised and pliable from the tremendous pressure. One boy is sufficient to look after each machine, under the eye of a superintendent. The former earns about 4s. 6d.; the superintendents, I may add, throughout the different operations, are paid from 20s. to 25s. weekly. The heckling comes next. Here great numbers of children are employed. They screw the bunches of flax tight to iron rods, which, being placed in the centre of a complicated and powerful piece of machinery, the flax is subjected to the shining steel teeth or heckles, which, set in a circular frame-work, revolve rapidly, and rend and comb the substance just as the float-boards of a paddle-wheel strike the water. The refuse flax thus torn away is tow; the remainder, combed into soft smooth locks, is called "line," and ultimately forms the thread of linen. This is the dusty and unhealthy process which I mentioned. It is usually conducted almost altogether by children, girls and boys. In the heckling room in Messrs. Marshall's mill about 130 children are employed. Some of the girls there wore handkerchiefs over their mouths in the manner of the shoddy grinders. A number of "half-timers"—children from eight to thirteen years of age—work at this process in the mill in question. I was struck by their appearance, not only as presenting the greatest number of young children labouring in a body which I have yet seen, but as exhibiting a greater amount of labour performed—of continuous active exertion going on—than I have yet found requisite in any branch of any manufacturing process. There is hardly a moment of inactivity. The flax has to be taken up in locks, screwed into its frame, placed on the heckling machine, taken off, and the supply constantly renewed. When I say that the young children—toiling so quickly and dexterously, amid the flying dust and the whirling mechanism, every limb and every finger in rapid and continuous play—had a strange elfish appearance, which I have never before remarked in any department of juvenile industry, I only use the expression to convey an idea which struck me forcibly as I beheld the scene of labour. The wages paid to these young labourers are small enough in all conscience. The half-timers do not earn above from 1s. 6d. to 1s. 8d. a week. The elder children make double the amount. They are, of course, superintended by overlookers.

The first of a long series of "drawing" operations comes next, identical in principle with the drawing processes which I have so often had occasion to describe. The flax is drawn into what I may call a set of ribbons, each narrower and thinner but more compact than the preceding, until it becomes a mere strip of exquisite fineness, when it is loosely twisted upon large bobbins—having thus arrived at the state of yarn. All these drawing processes are superintended exclusively by girls and women—one to each frame. The work is very light. Indeed, so far as any muscular exertion goes, the tenters are really idle half their time. I have seen the majority of them seated and quietly watching their frames, without at all neglecting their duty. It is only, indeed, any accidental flaw in the material, or irregularity in the mechanism, which calls them into action. The wages of these girls are from 5s. to 5s. 6d. per week. The yarn has now to be spun. The operation is performed, as in the case of worsted, upon frames. The atmosphere of the spinning-room is kept warm by the quantity of hot water through which the threads are passed; but the temperature is not so high as in fine-spinning cotton factories. It may range from 76° to 80°. The spinners, like the drawers, are all women and girls. A young person of from fifteen to eighteen years of age is preferred, as having the finest touch for the repair of broken threads. The wages of the spinners are sometimes, but not always, a shade higher than those of the drawing-frame tenters. The reelers, who work by the piece, and whose duty it is to reel the threads off the bobbins into skeins and hanks, form the next set of workpeople. They are generally grown-up women, and the most expert and industrious amongst them can make about 8s. a week. The simple reeling frame being driven round by hand, the labour of its attendants is not regulated by the motion of the steam-engine, and they frequently continue their toil while the rest of the hands are at dinner. The winders are, however, obliged, in beginning and leaving off work, to conform to factory hours. I have said that comparatively little linen cloth is prepared in Leeds, and that still less is woven by power in the mills. In the Messrs. Marshall's establishment the small amount of weaving performed is entirely carried on by women, their wages being stated to me as ranging from 8s. to 9s. per week. The reader will recollect that in the heckling process the tow is separated from the "line." The former is then carried to another department, where it is carded, drawn, and spun into coarser threads. The wages earned by the workpeople are almost the same as those paid in the finer department of the trade. The dust in the tow-carding room is very considerable, and the floating filament abundant and annoying. No allowance whatever is made to the hands employed in the heckling and tow-carding rooms in consideration of the unpleasant and unwholesome nature of their occupation. Indeed, I cannot find, in the whole range of textile manufacturing industry, that an advanced rate of wages is given for any unhealthy occupation, nominally or really, on account of its injuriousness. In all the flax-mills which I have seen, provisions, more or less ample, are made for ventilation. Where swinging panes are adopted, however, the workpeople are too often apt to shut them. In Mr. Morfitt's flax-mill I found that the hands in the spinning room had voluntarily deprived themselves of fresh air because the day was boisterous and rainy. Mr. Marshall's establishment is scientifically ventilated—a fanner, driven by an eight-horse-power engine, being employed to fan the air up through gratings in the floor into the large room.

This large room is one of the sights of Leeds, and a sight amply worth seeing. Having some short time ago had occasion to add very largely to their original establishment, the Messrs. Marshall conceived the idea of constructing a mill in which all the processes of flax manufacture, save those of sorting and heckling, should be conducted on one level and in one vast hall. This design they carried out. The hall occupies two acres, the roof is supported by 66 iron pillars, and the whole is lighted by 66 glass cupolas. The *coup d'œil* of this vast apartment, crowded from wall to wall with busy machinery, tented by hundreds of active and healthy-looking young women, is a very fine as well as a curious and interesting spectacle. The atmosphere, except in the spinning portion of the room, is perfectly cool and pleasant. The cleanliness preserved is perfect. The girls, I was informed, take a pride in scouring and keeping bright the portion of stone floor over which each presides. The frames are provided with boxes, where the girls keep those articles of dress which they lay aside for working costume when in the mill. The dinner hour arrived when I was in the room, and there was a general production and application of clothes and shoe-brushes preparatory to leaving the establishment. The roof of this vast room is as curious in its way as the interior. It is perfectly flat, and covered with grass—the cupolas rising from the green expanse like so many fairy tents of crystal.

Among the few weaving establishments in Leeds is an old riding-school, which has been converted into a loom-shop, and gives occupation to nearly 100 weavers and winders. The place is of course merely a shell crowded with hand-looms. The stuff woven is woollen, with occasionally a mixture of cotton. The weavers are men, women, boys, and girls. Some of the latter wind for their grown-up relatives. These weavers work for a large firm, and have pretty constant work. Their

Interior of Marshall's One-Storied Flax-Mill at Leeds

average wages may be about 10s. or 10s. 6d. a week. About 1d. in the shilling is paid to the winder, and the rent for each loom is 3d. per week. The hours of labour are regular and long—from six a.m., until half-past eight p.m., allowing half-an-hour for breakfast, an hour for dinner, and half-an-hour for tea. In summer the hours are from five a.m. until eight p.m. When whole families work in the establishment, the superintendent tries to group each of them together. Parents will bring their children, and pay for a loom for them to learn at, and when they can do a little coarse work they begin to receive a small salary. As I stood between two looms, the foreman told me that the job on the one would bring in about 8s. 6d., and the other about 12s. a week. The best webs were given out as impartially as possible. Their house employed many domestic weavers, but when work was slack those under the immediate control and inspection of the firm had the preference.

"Since bread and food have been so cheap," continued the foreman, "almost all of us who are industrious may have a bit of meat for dinner every day. But when provisions were twice as high, when flour was 4s. a stone, we had no better wages than now, and not half so much work. I have seen this room half empty—half the looms standing—because the prices of everything to eat were so high that people had no money to buy aught else; but now every one of us has as much work as he can put his face to."

This man, an exceedingly intelligent person, went on to condemn the common Yorkshire system of providing only two rooms in a working man's house, as being neither decent nor wholesome. "It might do," he said, "for the Irish, who would always live together by families to save house rent, but it ought not to be tolerated by Englishmen."

From something which I heard in this establishment, I proceeded to the neighbouring row of cottages recently erected. These had each a common room, a bedroom, and a cellar loom-shop. In the first which I entered two Irishmen were weaving a coarse sacking, and the wife of one of them was winding in the bare, scarcely-furnished room on the ground floor. The tenant of the house told me that the row was all alike, and belonged to the gentleman for whom he was working. The two looms were fixtures; of course, therefore, he could not rent them without renting the house. The rent was stopped every week out of his wages. Whatever they were, much or little, the rent must always come out of them before he got the money. He believed the work was given to him just to enable him to pay the rent (which was 3s. weekly), and thus to make a good return for the money invested in the houses; otherwise, it would be cheaper for the master to get the stuff woven by power. His wages, with his wife to wind, were very small, not averaging above 9s. or 10s., at the highest. From another source I learnt that many of the poor weavers inhabiting houses built upon a similar plan, and with a similar view, had suffered most severely during the last season of depression. It often happened that their wages were entirely absorbed by their rent, while the parish refused them assistance on the very reasonable plea, that a man who was paying 3s. of weekly rent could not be said to be an object of charity. Thus these poor people had no means of obtaining work, except from a quarter which would give it them only on condition that they paid back all or the greater part of their remuneration in rent. In good times, of course, a weaver need not be so hard driven; but if a master, having work for ten men, and being also the landlord of ten houses, says to twenty men seeking employment, "I shall give my work to the ten who will consent to live in my ten houses, and pay me a high rent for them," then assuredly the scheme, if it does not actually amount to the truck system, is a very close imitation of it. I admit, with pleasure, that the houses were decided improvements on the general run of labourers' dwellings in Leeds. Indeed another row which I visited—newly built, and devoted to cloth hand-loom weaving—were most excellently arranged; roomy, airy, and in every respect comfortable; but, with regard to them, the same, or at all events a similar, system was in operation. The house in the row in question in which I found the most intelligent tenant was fitted up somewhat like the silk-weavers' cottages at Macclesfield. The loom-shop was on the attic floor; the looms in operation were four, of which three were fixtures belonging to the house; and the tenant had of course the preference when work was slack over those weavers who wrought for the landlord, but who did not live in any of his houses or work by his looms. I have said that the house was most excellent; it contained a half cellar, or rather area, sitting room, a kitchen, with sink and water laid on, a ground-floor parlour, and two bedrooms. The rent was 5s. 6½d. per week, and it must be paid the first thing out of the weekly earnings. In answer to my questions, the weaver said that the distinct understanding was, that if by any chance, in any week, he only earned 5s. 6½d., then the whole of his earnings during that week must go to pay the rent. His family worked for him. If he had no family, he would let out the looms, which were constructed for weaving broadcloth, at 1s. each. For the best jobs he could earn from 13s. to 14s.; the inferior sorts of work produced about 10s. In his house they laboured from six a.m. until seven p.m.; and they very often did not take more than a quarter of an hour to dinner. They mostly had a bit of meat for dinner every day, but many had to make tea and coffee and bread serve them. "Sir," concluded the weaver, "don't you think that a skilled, hard-working, sober man, with a family to feed, ought to be able to earn a pound a week, if everything was as it should be? There's few Englishmen would grudge hard labour if they felt that they were so paid for it that they could live wholesomely and bring up their families in decency and independence."

This house-trucking system is not confined in Leeds altogether to cottages fitted up with looms, and of which the loom is in reality a part. In connection with at least one mill, I shall not specify its nature, a similar system prevails. The proprietor has built a number of cottages for his labourers, and these cottages *must* be occupied. Of course all the mill-hands do not live on their master's property, because the number of cottages is comparatively inconsiderable—but not a hand will get employment in the factory should he refuse to occupy any of them which may become vacant. I think I mentioned a somewhat similar case in Bolton, when to each mule a house-key was attached, which the spinner was bound to pay rent for. Now in many instances I have had to praise the style of cottage erected by the millowner for his people, and to praise, also, the spirit in which the undertaking seemed to be conducted. Masters and men have assured me that the renting, on the part of the working people, of these cottages was perfectly voluntary. There the houses stood ready. They were superior to the ordinary run of operative dwellings; they were conveniently near to the mill, and they were cheap. As a natural consequence they never wanted occupants. If, however, on the other hand, the holding of a cottage be made in any case compulsory upon any mill-hand, the result is simply that he is obliged to take out a part of his wages in goods—these goods in the present instance consisting of house-room. This is a matter to which public attention may well be directed. In all the cases which I have specified the master holds in his own hand the fund from which his rent is paid; and in hard times, let others suffer as they may, he—at all events so long as any wages at all are paid—is certain of the interest and profit on his own building speculation. As to the truck system in general, from all the inquiries which I can make, I learn that virtually it is abolished. Railway excavators were perhaps the last class which, as a class, suffered from it. Here and there, no doubt, relics of the practice still linger—the parties being small manufacturers, often located in out-of-the-way country places, where the occasional difficulty of obtaining commodities gives some semblance of excuse for the practice. But even in these instances the offence is so disguised, there are so many links of agency employed, and so many quirks and quibbles resorted to, that the difficulty of making out a legal case is almost insuperable. Instances have occurred in the Bradford district, but the authorities have in vain endeavoured to prove legally what no one doubted morally. For all practical purposes, however, the "Tommy-shop" may be considered as finally shut up in the manufacturing districts.

There are two classes of operatives' houses in Leeds, and the first and worst species includes fully three-fourths of the workmen's tenements in the borough. These are the two-roomed dwellings known as the "House and Chamber" class of abodes. In nine cases out of ten they are inferior to the cotton workers' houses in furniture, cleanliness, and neatness. I have been in the dwellings of many of the flax hands, and found them not only poor and uncomfortable, but in frequent instances squalid. The clothworkers, having higher wages, are very generally better off; and the quarter which they principally inhabit— the west part of the town—is, of the operative districts, decidedly the best, in point of building, paving, draining, and cleansing. Still even their dwellings are not what they ought to be; and, altogether, I am compelled, after a minute and searching survey of the town, to say that the domestic condition of the working population of Leeds seems to me lower than that of any manufacturing town which I have yet investigated. Between Leeds and Huddersfield the difference in favour of the latter is palpable and distinct, and yet a great portion of the workpeople of both towns labour in the same branches of trade, and receive the same, or nearly the same, amount of remuneration. The very low wages paid in the flax trade, the consequence of girls and children being chiefly—indeed, for all practical purposes, exclusively—employed, seems to me to tend strongly towards dragging down the standard of living and of domestic comfort, even of the better-paid artizans. At all events, be the cause what it may, the clothworkers of Leeds, although they live in better dwellings, and in greater comfort than the flax workers of that town, do not live in such good dwellings, or in such great comfort, as the clothworkers of Huddersfield. In all my peregrinations in the manufacturing capital of Yorkshire, I have not discovered a single operative dwelling with a back and front entrance, and consequently a thorough current of air. One man, indeed, said that he thought double houses were more wholesome than single ones, because they were snugger and warmer. "One heats the other," he said; "like sleeping two in a bed." The illustration sums up the argument against the practice. In a large proportion of the houses in question, the family, except when all are grown up, sleep together in the higher room. Beds in the lower rooms are, however, not uncommon. The furniture seldom shows the commonly existing neat comfort, or the less frequently occurring pretension, which mark Manchester tenements of different grades. A parlour-kitchen can be made, after its own fashion, a very cheerful apartment. Many a one have I recently visited, in which the gleam of a good fire was playing on polished pot-lids and glancing crockery, arranged tidily and orderly upon the well-scoured racks, the floor either carpeted with a decent drugget, or nicely and brightly sanded—many a house of this class, I repeat, I have lately entered, in which the sensation of comfort was very decidedly in the ascendant. But in Leeds, I have found, as a general rule, domestic utensils coarser and scantier, and the spirit of neatness and good housewifery manifested on rarer occasions and in a slighter degree. The second and better class of houses, which form the minority, possess a sunken parlour-kitchen, half the window of which only rises above the pavement. Above this apartment are placed two rooms in the ordinary manner. The sunken story is not quite a cellar, and in many instances I found it dry, warm, and cheerful. When it exists the ground-floor room is very generally half unfurnished, the family making the lower apartment their ordinary living place. Good cooking-ranges are abundant. Water is seldom introduced into the houses; the stand-tap system being the usual one, each cock serving a greater or a smaller number of houses, according to the comparative poverty of the locality. The rents range, for the medium class of dwellings, from 1s. 6d. to 3s. weekly. The houses letting for the former sum are often ricketty old places, in bad repair, and with small close rooms. In almost every case the house-door is the parlour-door. Even in the very superior house rented at 5s. 6½d. by the cloth weaver, a visit to which I have above described, there was no lobby, the door only separating the best room in the house from the street.

An institution in Leeds has recently been opened in connection with the workhouse, a visit to which gave me very high gratification. It is the industrial school for pauper children; and an establishment more perfect in its architectural arrangements, and, so far as I could judge, in its system of discipline and training, I never saw. The industrial school, a handsome Elizabethan structure, stands in the midst of six acres of land belonging to it, on the brow of a declivity, removed by about half a mile from the smoke and foulness of the town. It has now been open rather more than a year. The average number of pupils may be stated at 150, and as yet only two deaths have occurred in the establishment. During the prevalence of cholera in Leeds, not even a case of diarrhœa occurred in the industrial school, and when I visited it, although I found a few children in the infirmary, none were so ill as to be in bed. A circumstance, however, indicating a sanitary feature of the district, is, that the institution possesses two rooms with particularly constructed blinds, for cases of sore eyes. Although neither of these apartments were darkened on my visit, three or four of the children in the infirmary wore green shades. Mr. Hisk, the master of the establishment, thinks that these cases are very frequently of scrofulous origin. Nothing can exceed the exquisite neatness and cleanliness which pervade the establishment, to its most insignificant corner. The children themselves, under the superintendence of paid servants—for very properly no adult pauper is suffered to come within the walls— perform the household duties. The object is to bring up the pupils for domestic servants and apprentices. The girls learn to cook, scour, wash, iron, sew, and make their own dresses. The boys do the rougher cleaning work, and, under the superintendence of a gardener, raise the greater part of the vegetables consumed in the institution. The trades taught the boys are shoemaking and tailoring, so that the school will speedily be, so far, self-supplying. All the boys are exercised in spade husbandry. Of course it is the elder boys who are taught mechanical trades. The younger ones go to school every day, and the tailors, shoemakers, washers, ironers, &c., have three days' school and three days' work. I visited the tailoring, shoemaking, and sewing-room. In the first the average number of boys who had worked during the previous week, was seven. The amount of work done was twenty articles, such as jackets, trowsers, and waistcoats repaired, three new jackets made, and one waistcoat. In the shoe-making room, the average number of workers had been six. They had repaired eighteen pairs of boys' and girls' shoes, made five new pairs, and an odd one. Two pairs were in progress. In the sewing-room, the number of girls employed had been six or eight. They had made ten shirts and mended fifteen. They had mended twenty-six chemises and ten bed-gowns; mended thirty-four pinafores and made a dozen; bound seven pairs of shoes, run seven pairs of stockings, and darned about 145 pairs. About a dozen boys have been already apprenticed, and a dozen girls sent out to service. They are doing well, and applications for the children come in faster than the establishment is as yet able to supply them. Certainly there will seem to be less durability in early impressions than is generally be-lieved, if the boys and girls brought up in the Leeds Industrial School fall into habits of slovenliness and sloth. The dietary adopted is, in its essential parts, that of the workhouse, consisting of meat thrice a week, and soups and puddings on the off days; but in all essential features care is wisely taken to place no obvious pauper stamp upon the institution, and to banish, as much as may be, the workhouse as-sociations from the children's minds.

A popular co-operative institution in Leeds, similar to none which I have seen, is worked in a building called the "People's Mill," close to the Messrs. Marshall's factory. The "People's Mill" grinds corn of all kinds, and supplies to its large circle of proprietors flour and grain, perfectly unadulterated, and as near cost price as the actual working expenses will permit. The number of members is about 3,000, and the vast majority are working men. Each pays £1 1s. entrance money. There is no yearly subscription. The average amount annually saved to the subscribers was computed by the managing miller, whom I found upon the premises, as about equal to each member's subscription—that is to say, the flour in the mill can be had so much cheaper than the same flour in the shops as to save an ordinary family about a pound in the year. The great advantage, however, looked to is the purity of the article. No member is allowed to hold more than one share, or to receive more flour than is necessary for the consumption of his own family; and any member selling bread made of the society's flour is, for a second offence, expelled. The only similar institution in Yorkshire is at Hull.

The cotton-town practice of dosing children with narcotics does not prevail to any great extent in the woollen or worsted districts. Still it does more or less exist. The relieving officer at Bradford told me that he had broken many a bottle of Godfrey; and in Leeds paregoric is not unfrequently sold by the small general dealers. Narcotic drugs are more or less taken by adults in *all* manufacturing towns, and in Leeds opium-chewers (often women) are not unfrequent. A medical gentleman in large practice among the poor informed me, that in times of manufacturing distress he has seen people reduced to a state bordering on *delirium tremens* for want of means to purchase the usual laudanum dram. The same gentleman added that Ophthalmia was not unfrequently produced by the excessively penetrating and irritating nature of the dust in flax-heckling and tow-carding rooms. The substance in question also produced a throat complaint similar to "shoddy fever." There is indeed a shoddy trade in the flax districts as well as in the cloth. Old ropes are untwisted as old rags are unpicked, and the unravelled hemp is heckled and wrought again into a coarser sort of sacking. The dust produced by the old hemp heckling is, as may be well conceived, stifling.

*The Morning Chronicle, Monday, December 10, 1849.*

# THE MORNING CHRONICLE

ON

## "LABOUR AND THE POOR."

The demands constantly made to obtain the early Numbers of THE MORNING CHRONICLE containing the Letters on "LABOUR AND THE POOR," in the Metropolitan, Agricultural, and Manufacturing Districts, have induced the conductors of that Journal to direct the Republication of those Letters in

## SUPPLEMENTS

(containing Twenty-four Columns each), to be given twice a-week, commencing on Friday, the 21st of December.

The sole object of these Supplements being to enable the Public to obtain the complete Series, they will be discontinued as soon as the Letters which shall have been published previous to the 21st of December have been republished, as parties desirous to possess the Letters that will be published after that date will have it in their power to do so, by ordering, from the 21st instant, copies of the regular daily publication of THE MORNING CHRONICLE, in which the Series will be continued.

The Supplements will be supplied GRATIS with THE MORNING CHRONICLE of the days on which they appear; and all persons desirous of Completing their Sets are requested to forward their orders to the Publisher of THE MORNING CHRONICLE, 332, Strand; or to their respective News-agents.

---

*The Morning Chronicle, Tuesday, December 11, 1849.*

### HUDDERSFIELD.

—◆—

To the EDITOR of the MORNING CHRONICLE.

Sir—In the letter of your Special Correspondent for the Manufacturing Districts respecting Huddersfield, inserted in your paper of Monday (which I have only just seen), there are one or two trifling inaccuracies, which it may be well to correct—trifles are to some people matters of great moment.

The name of the owner of the ground on which by far the greater part of Huddersfield stands is Sir John William *Ramsden*, Bart., not *Marsden*, as your Correspondent has it. Probably this may be but a typographical error; but even these, in a series of letters likely to be so often appealed to as those now appearing in *The Chronicle*, may be worth correcting. The hon. baronet abovenamed is the son of Charles Ramsden, Esq., once M.P. for Yorkshire. He sat in Parliament for the county when the Reform Bill was passed, and afterwards for Malton.

As Sir J. W. Ramsden, Bart., is a minor, the estates of which he is owner are managed by trustees and a guardian; the Earl Fitzwilliam and the Earl of Zetland being trustees, and Lady Ramsden the guardian.

Your correspondent has fallen into error in saying that in Huddersfield "no building leases are granted." I can easily see how this error has arisen, for conversations in the public streets may easily be misapprehended. The fact is, that in Huddersfield, building leases, or leases of plots of ground with which the lessees can do almost as they please, are granted; and such leases are, in fact, leases in *perpetuity:* not leases, as in London, for terms certain, and then all the buildings erected falling into the hands of the owner; but leases for sixty years, renewable every twenty years, on a fine certain, the fine being one year's rent. Perhaps, about one-third of the town may be held on lease; the other two-thirds are built on ground *held at will* at a small annual ground-rent; the only security the parties possess for their buildings being the *good faith* of the owners of the estate: and yet the buildings so situate are regularly bought and sold, bequeathed and mortgaged; the only *deed* of either owner or mortgagee being the inscribing of the name of the party concerned on the rent-roll of the ground landlord. A very cheap way of effecting both mortgages and transfers!

One reason why leases are not sought for more extensively no doubt is, that as the rent fixed in the lease is *for all time*, if the holders of the lease please, it is necessarily higher than it is in the case of tenancies *at will;* because the latter can be increased at the "will" of the landowner.

Another fact, as bearing strongly on the object of the mission of your Special Correspondent—the ascertaining the actual condition of the working-class—ought to be set forth. In no town in the kingdom of equal size are there as many *workers* owners of dwellings as in Huddersfield. It is a pride and a boast among this class to be able to say that they have a house or houses (and some who labour daily have many) of their own. To accomplish *this*, habits of frugality and saving are much encouraged, and building and money clubs abound. The party building has not to purchase the land, so that expense is saved, and the ground rent is easy, and only comes twice a year. When a man has paid for some time into a club he can get out his "share" on the personal security of bondmen, or by "booking" the officers of the club, along with himself, in the rent-roll, for the house he erects with the money, until the club is paid off; and thus a dwelling is easily acquired, and paid for with its own rent. To a very considerable extent this has been done by the working men in the township of Huddersfield.

Another phrase of your Correspondent, where he says that "Huddersfield is by no means a well *built* town," is rather calculated to mislead, or rather to give wrong impressions as to the nature of the buildings in Huddersfield. The fact is, the neighbourhood of Huddersfield abounds with stone of the finest and most endurable qualities. The town, therefore, as far as materials and labour go, is well-built—not a town in the kingdom better—and few can come up to it. The brick-built dwellings of Manchester, Leeds, or London are not at all to be compared to those in Huddersfield, for either substantiality or appearance. But of the *arrangement* of the town, of the utter want of system exhibited, of the numerous courts and alleys, of the back-to-back dwellings, of the great dearth of necessary conveniences—of the very, very inferior character of the main of those that are erected—of the fact that from this unwise back-to-back arrangement those places which from their very name ought to be *private* are necessarily the most *public* spots of the whole localities, and of the deteriorating effect that this reprehensible arrangement has upon the character of the dwellers, I confess that I am ashamed to speak. Your Correspondent has not too strongly stated the fact, nor too strongly condemned it. I always feel, as my daily avocations take me amongst these irregularities, to devise and suggest means to abate the abominations that everywhere abound, that the past managers of the Ramsden estates have much to answer for in permitting such gross mal-arrangement on property over which they had the exclusive control; and I cannot but re-echo the hope of your Correspondent, that in the new parts of the town about to be opened out for building purposes far different arrangements from those indicated will obtain.

Before I conclude I must express the strong sense that myself and others in this town entertain of the important duty to society the conductors of *The Chronicle* have imposed on themselves, and are so ably and so satisfactorily performing by means of their intelligent and truthful "Commissioners," and by the publicity they give to the important body of facts collected for the first time in our history as to the actual condition of "Labour and the Poor." Though the inquiry, from its very nature and from the time that can be devoted to it, must necessarily be hurried, and in some degree superficial, yet more accurate information as to the actual condition of those who labour for their bread will be known than could possibly be known before; and the way will be prepared for a more general and more systematic inquiry into the social condition of the producing classes than time and opportunity will permit at present. For this service to humanity the conductors of *The Chronicle* are deserving of all praise.

I am, sir, yours respectfully,

JOSHUA HOBSON,

Clerk to the Board of Works under the Huddersfield Improvement Commissioners.
Huddersfield, Dec. 5.

*The Morning Chronicle, Thursday, December 13, 1849.*

# LABOUR AND THE POOR.

—◆—

## THE MANUFACTURING DISTRICTS.

[FROM OUR SPECIAL CORRESPONDENT.]

### LEEDS.

## Letter XVII.

The corporation of Leeds is, I understand, about to spend a very large sum, about £30,000 or £40,000, in the formation of an extensive system of paving, drainage, &c., in hitherto neglected portions of the borough. Never were sanitary reforms more imperatively called for. The condition of vast districts of the opulent and important town of Leeds is such as the very strongest language cannot over-state. Virulent and fatal as was the recent attack of cholera here, my wonder is that cholera, or some disease almost equally fatal, is ever absent. From one house, for instance, situated in a large irregular court or yard—a small house containing two rooms—four corpses were recently carried. I looked about and did not marvel. The whole vicinage was two or three inches deep in filth. This seemed to be the normal state even of the passable parts of the place. In the centre of the open space was a cluster of pigsties, privies, and cesspools—bursting with pent-up abominations; and half a dozen paces from this delectable nucleus was a pit, about five feet square, filled to the very brim with semi-liquid manure gathered from stables and houses around. This yard lies on the south side of the Aire, not more than a gunshot from Leeds Bridge.

The east and north-east districts of Leeds are, perhaps, the worst. A short walk from the Briggate, in the direction in which Deansgate branches off from the main entry, will conduct the visitor into a perfect wilderness of foulness. Conceive acre on acre of little streets, run up without attention to plan or health—acre on acre of closely-built and thickly-peopled ground, without a paving-stone upon the surface, or an inch of sewer beneath, deep trodden-churned sloughs of mud forming the only thoroughfares—here and there an open space, used not exactly as the common cess-pool, but as the common cess-yard of the vicinity—in its centre, ash-pits employed for dirtier pur-poses than containing ashes—privies often ruinous, almost horribly foul—pig-stys very commonly left *pro tempore* untenanted, because their usual inmates have been turned out to prey upon the garbage of the neighbourhood. Conceive streets, and courts, and yards which a scavenger never appears to have entered since King John incorpo-rated Leeds, and which in fact give the idea of a town built in a slimy bog. Conceive such a surface drenched with the liquid slops which each family flings out daily and nightly before their own threshold, and further fouled by the malpractices of children, for which the par-ents and not the children deserve shame and punishment. Conceive, in short, a whole district to which the above description rigidly and truthfully applies, and you will, I am sorry to say, have a fair idea of what at present constitutes a large proportion of the operative part of Leeds. I have seen here and there in Bradford spots very nearly, and in Halifax spots quite as bad; but here it is no spot—the foulness over large sections of the town, particularly towards the suburbs, consti-tutes the very face and essence of things. I have plodded by the half hour through streets in which the undisturbed mud lay in wreaths from wall to wall, and across open spaces, overlooked by houses all around, in which the pigs, wandering from this central oasis, seemed to be roaming through what was only a large sty. Indeed, pigs seem to be the natural inhabitants of such places. I think they are more common in some parts of Leeds than dogs and cats are in others; and wherever they abound, wherever the population is filthiest, there are the houses the smallest, the rooms the closest, and the most over-crowded. One characteristic of such localities is a curious and signif-icant one. Before almost every house-door there lies, of course until the pig comes upon the deposit, a little heap of boiled-out tea leaves. Although all the domestic refuse is flung out, you hardly ever see bones, but the teapot is evidently in operation at every meal. Here and there, I ought to add, the visitor will, even in the midst of such scenes as I have tried to sketch, come upon a cluster or a row of houses better than ordinary, and through the almost invariably open doors of which he will see some indications of domestic comfort; but such buildings are the exceptions—and, exceptions as they are, they rise out of the same slough of mud and filth, and command the same ugly sights as their neighbours. There is, I believe, a Nuisance Commit-tee in Leeds. I inquired whether they were aware of even the most

flagrant of all these sanitary enormities. Had their attention, for instance, been ever drawn to the practice of keeping pigs, or rather of
letting the pigs keep themselves, in crowded neighbourhoods? "Yes,"
I was answered, by a gentleman much interested in the subject—"Yes,
I have reported these things over and over again, until I was sick and
tired of reporting; but, you see, nothing has been done."

Referring to the opening sentence of this communication, it is to
be hoped that Leeds is on the eve of a sanitary revolution, and that
what is true of the town to-day will be but historic a twelvemonth
hence. Things are at present so palpably bad, that even a small outlay
would make an immense change for the better. Even if it be impracticable to construct at once a thorough system of house sewerage, or
to lay down at once miles of substantial paving, it would be surely
easy, by means of the police, to compel the observance of something
like ordinary human decency in the habits of children, to clean out
and render available revolting cesspools, and to make a devastating
razzia amongst those foul nuisances—in a crowded and often a fever-
smitten locality—the pigs and pig-sties.

In one respect Leeds is superior to most of its great industrial
neighbours. Owing to its more easterly position it is not so exposed
to descents of vast masses of Irish poverty as are the towns of Lancashire; and owing to the second staple of the place being flax, a certain proportion of the Irish who do reach Leeds have been more or
less trained to industrious habits, amid the wreck of the linen manufacture in their own country. In Leeds I have, for the first time, found
considerable numbers of Irishmen steadily working at the loom. Most
of them had learned the work at home, and had followed the track
when it left their shores. They had all the same story to tell, of work
scanty and wages low, compared with what they had been in Dublin. I
found many of these weavers employed upon the coarsest sort of stuff,
such as sacking and canvass. One of them said, that forty of his countrymen whom he knew were working in Leeds, and that they sent
their children to the flax mills. The Irish, however, he added, who
came from parts of the country which had never been manufacturing, kept their children very often at home, and bred them up to any
sort of little trade which they themselves followed. This is a species
of education which I suspect is very often equivalent to breeding up
the children to no trade at all. In one house, for instance, I found an
old Irishman, in the receipt of parish relief, with his grand-daughter,
a stout girl of 13 at the very least, seated by the fire. "The poor thing,"

said the old man, "wasn't fit to go to one of them mills. Why, sure they would, may be, maim her. Childer was maimed there every day." I asked whether she went to school? "Not at present," was the reply; "but she has been ever since she was three years of age, till lately." I was rather surprised to hear, as a pendant to this statement, that the scholar did not know her letters.

Three of the ordinary trades of the Irish in Leeds are rag-picking—such as I have described it in Batley, near Dewsbury—untwisting old ropes, and mat-making. Men and women generally work at the latter employment; but the women almost invariably hawk the produce about for sale. I visited two cellars in one of the Irish streets, in each of which I found a man and woman preparing mats. A sentence of description will suffice for both apartments. They might be about seven feet square, littered with old bagging, Russia mats, old ropes, and shavings—furnished with rickety deal tables, and two or three chairs more or less dilapidated, and a bed, in one case, spread on a low frame, in the other, rolled up in a corner. The cooking apparatus, in both cases, consisted of a single pot. Miserable as these abodes are, they were clearly superior to the Irish cellars in Manchester and Oldham. The people in the second cellar were rather better off than those in the first, because the wife had a "good connection" in the mat-selling business, and could more generally realise fair prices for her wares. In both instances the people gave me every information about their trade, and I subjoin the substance of their statements, which in the main agreed.

"We make two sorts of mats—rope mats which are the best sort, and stitched mats. Both of these mats are principally made of a stuff called 'dewit.'" This dewit was a substance like long clusters of coarse hemp. "We buy it for 3s. a stone. We then dye it brown with catechu; we dye it by boiling a stone of it, with 1½d. worth of catechu, and then we rinse it out with clean water and a little alum, and hang it up to dry." The side of each room was clothed with clusters of the stuff in question. "We have next to get ropes for the rope mats, and old sacking and shavings and twine for the stitched mats. The ropes cost about 1s. 3d. per stone. The old bagging comes to about 1¼d. per mat, and the twine and Russia matting to a trifle more. We use shavings when we can get them for nothing. To make a good-sized rope mat, like what we sell for a gentleman's door, takes six or seven pounds of rope, and from a pound to a pound and a half of dewit. We generally count, working up the waste of one with another, that 16 lbs. of dewit will make three rope mats. Stitched mats do not take more than half that quantity, but they require, besides the sacking, twine and garden mats."

The rope mats are made upon the principle of weaving. The strands of untwisted ropes are stretched across a frame, exactly like warps, and then the workman, passing a stronger rope in the manner of a woof across them, binds into the twisted cord-locks of the dewit, which forms the superficies of the mat. In the stitched sort the dewit is fastened by coarse needlework to the sacking. One of the mat workers I saw was an old man. He could, he said, once have made four or five rope mats a day. Now he could not make more in a week. The stitched sort required a day to make two, and another day was generally requisite to sell them. The woman in the first cellar stated, in regard to the sale, as follows:—"I sell the mats we make here, and it's very hard work—much harder than making them, and very uncertain. The prices I get depend mostly altogether upon whether it's poor houses or rich houses I sell at. There is no regular price for the mats. I take what I can get, and if we're very hard up I take very little. I get as little as 6d. and 4d. for each of the stitched mats, and as little as 1s. or 1s. 2d. for the rope mats. The last day I was out selling I went four miles into the country with four mats, three of the cheap sort and one of the best. I walked all day. Sold two and brought home two. I sold the dear one and one of the cheap ones, and had only 15d. for both. The time before that, I went out at seven in the morning, and never broke my fast. That day I sold three of the bag sort for 1s. 7d."

The woman in the next cellar hawks larger and superior mats in better neighbourhoods. She was a buxom dame from Sligo, with broad shoulders and a quick tongue. Her statement was to this effect:—"I sell the mats for as much as I can obtain. I have no fixed price. I ask as much as I think there is a chance of getting, and then bate. If I make a good day's sale in the morning I sell cheaper in the afternoon. Sometimes we're very poor and have only a little bread and coffee; but sometimes, when we're in good luck, we want for nothing. It all depends on the chance of sale. One day last week I walked to Tadcaster with mats. It is fourteen miles there and fourteen miles back. I took six mats with me, and sold five. They came, one with the other, to 5s. The highest price I can ever get for a rope mat is about 2s. or 2s. 4d. The sacking mats may fetch 6d. a piece." In answer to further inquiries about the sacking which they used, I was told that the main part of it came from India, containing sugar. I observed that it seemed very clean. "Oh, indeed, sir," said the woman, "and it's well it may be clean. Sure they mashes it about and boils it before we gets it, to take out the sweet stuff, to make treacle of. Sure, and it's few people would eat treacle if they knew what a deal of it came out of. I used to like a sup of it in my tay, but I'm cured of that now, any how."

I visited several cellars and wretched dwellings in the vicinity, inhabited by the Irish and the lowest class of English labourers, male and female, many of whom were engaged in the miserable occupation of unpicking old ropes, so as to prepare the oakum for being ground up again and wrought into shoddy, canvas, and sacking. This species of labour is so unutterably wretched that it can only exist as eking out the pittance procured by the industry of the principal supports of the family. The first woman upon whom I lighted, and who professed to follow this miserable trade, I found ill in bed. It was indeed a squalid household—the floor, dirty stone—the mean furniture, scanty and broken—the smashed window panes stuffed with rags—and an emaciated woman, ghastly as death, lying shivering on a flock bed on the floor, covered principally with a dress and a faded shawl. She told me that she could earn just 4d. by unpicking a stone of ordinary ropes, and that she was too weak to pick more than three stones a week. The family lived principally on parish relief. She did not mean to say that a better hand than she was could not make more by opening ropes. She could not work at it longer than from eight o'clock in the morning until four o'clock in the afternoon. It was a terribly dusty work. The house would be all covered with dust. The labour was awfully hard upon the fingers, particularly when the ropes were "green." For this kind of work, however, she was paid a penny a stone additional.

I was anxious to see the process actually going on, and presently I came upon a household in which, poor as were its physical attributes, the moral debasement and apathy which it disclosed were still more terrible. In a bare, stone-paved room, a principal part of the furniture of which consisted of tubs and apparatus for washing, sat three young children cowering over a spark of fire, and slowly and painfully tearing tough ropes to pieces with their weak, bony, little fingers. An intelligent girl, about eight or nine years of age, seemed to have the control of the other children, who were younger, and for whom she spoke, labouring away all the time. I ought to observe that I was accompanied by a relieving-officer, and that the father of the family had been receiving parish relief for seven years:—

"Where's your mother?"—"Gone out to try to get some washing to do."

"Where's your father?"—"In the Fleece—that's a public-house. Ah, mother told him he had better not go to-day, for you (to the relieving-officer) would be very likely to come round, but he wouldn't stay."

"What does your father do?"—"Sweeps the streets, sometimes."

"But does not he help you to pick these ropes?"—"No; *he* wouldn't do that. He makes *us* do that."

"What do you get for picking?"—"Fourpence a stone, but I give it all to my mother."

"Do you go to school?"—"Only on Sundays. I must work, you know. I can't read yet. But my little brother goes to school on week-days. Parson pays for him, only sometimes they keeps him at home to help in picking. He can't read either."

"And is not the other little boy your brother?"—"Oh no; he only comes in to help us to pick."

"Do you like picking?"—"No, because it makes me poorly. The dust gets into my eyes and down my throat, and makes me cough. Sometimes, too, it makes me sick. I can't keep at the work very long at a time because of that."

"You say you give all you earn to your mother, does she never let you have a penny for yourself?"

The poor child hung down her head, hesitated, and then stammered out—"sometimes."

"And what do you do with it?"—"I buys bread."

In another house, very close to the last, I found three children left alone, but in idleness. The place was a mass of filth. The scanty furniture, broken and flung carelessly about—the unmade bed a chaos of brown rags—cracked and handleless cups, smeared with coffee grounds, on the floor—amid unemptied slops, and beside a large brown dish, full of fermenting dough, upon which dust and ashes were rapidly settling as it stood at the fireside. The uncleaned window and the dim light of a winter's afternoon made the place so dark, that it was with difficulty I made out these details. There were here three little savages of children—their hair, tangled in filth-clotted masses, hanging over their grimy faces. Their clothes were mere bunches of rags, kept together by strings. A wriggle of their shoulders, and they would be free from all such incumbrances in a moment.

I asked them if they ever went to school?—"Never."

"Can you tell your letters?"—A mere stolid stare of ignorance.

"How old are you?" I asked the eldest girl.—"Don't know."

"Do you know what is the Queen's name?"—"No."

"Did you ever hear of anybody called the Queen?"—"No."

"Where were you born?"—"Don't know."

The relieving-officer said he believed all the family were Irish.

"Did you ever hear of a place called Ireland?"—"No."

"Or of a place called England?"—"No."

"Or of a place called Yorkshire?"—"No."

"Do you know the name of this town?"

After a pause, this question was answered. The eldest girl did know that she lived in Leeds; and this knowledge, with the exception of matters belonging to the daily routine of existence, seemed positively to be the only piece of information in the possession of the family. In two other houses, in both of which the inmates were receiving parish relief, the ignorance was almost equal. None of the children knew the Queen's name. In each of these instances I must observe that the reason of the families being upon the parish was simply a temporary stoppage of the husband's employment in a mill. In neither case could the mother read. The relieving officer who was with me spoke of the improvident habits common among the Leeds operatives. A man who had been earning 20s. a week in a cloth mill for very many years, and had only his wife to support, came recently upon the parish ten days after he had been out of work. The officer added that he knew of many similar cases. I was struck during the course of my rambles in the Irish quarters in Leeds at the frequency with which pictures of the "Liberator" hung upon the walls. Wherever the cottage or the cellar was filthiest and meanest—where potatoes to be eaten and rags to be picked lay mingled upon the floor—the features of Mr. O'Connell looked blandly down upon the squalor; and, in one or two instances, I found his effigy supported by a repeal map of Ireland—the south and the west coloured a vivid green, and the "Black North" tinted to a sable corresponding with the title.

A number of the cases of poverty which I was taken to see, were those of wives with four or five children, deserted by their husbands. Others were the sad ones of old working men who had outlived their capability for labour. One of these individuals lived certainly in the blankest poverty I ever saw. In his room there was a bed, not worth, I should suppose, eighteenpence as old rags, and one solitary broken chair. The floor was sinking, and the laths showed in great patches, plasterless and bare. The occupant was an unshorn, little, old man. He said, "I have nothing to do. I want to work, but they say I am too old. The parish pays 1s. a week for the rent of this room. I live on bread and water."

"Then why did you leave the workhouse?" said the relieving officer.

"Because I wanted my freedom," said the old man, sitting down on his one broken chair. The sentiment must have been strong, to survive amid such misery. He had been a weaver, but had not flung a shuttle for near a dozen years. He had walked well nigh through Yorkshire trying for work, and got none. Since he had been out of employment as a weaver, he had been a bricklayer's labourer, and had earned as much as 17s. a week; but now he was too old for that, too old for anything. But he would not go into the house. No; he would have his freedom, and his bread and cold water. Another man, who would be in a similar position were it not for the kindness of his family, observed to me—"They say I'm past work. I'm not. I could work yet— only a little perhaps—but I could work. But things have come to that pass in this land, that lads and lasses have men's work."

The wages of hand-loom weavers in the woollen and worsted districts have puzzled, and do still puzzle me, sorely. I doubt not that the reader has often noted many apparent contradictions, or at all events very great variations, in the amounts stated as realized. But the truth is that, as I cannot generalise from contradictions, I am obliged sometimes to report contradictions. In the course of one day's inquiry at Leeds I have had at least a dozen sums stated to me, by a dozen weavers, as a fair average of the weekly gains of their craft. The working foreman of the loom-shed noticed in my last letter, said that every industrious weaver could eat meat daily. Since then I have been again and again assured that if a hard-working weaver got porridge he might think himself well off. One man will tell you that he can hardly earn 6s. a week; another, in the next street, and weaving much the same sort of goods, will put down his gains as twice that sum. Here you will find a workman denouncing the power-loom as the cause of universal distress. His neighbour will probably opine that as much can be made by the weavers who tent the power-loom as could be earned by a workman fabricating by hand the coarse stuffs which the power-loom commonly makes, even if the machine in question had no existence. No later than yesterday, a gentleman, who possesses an intimate acquaintance with operative life in Leeds, told me that 15s. was, in his belief, the very highest sum which the best weaver could clear at the best work. The very next house we entered, the workman stated that he commonly earned 17s. and 18s. per week. The fact seems to be that there is an endless variety of prices paid for different sorts of goods—an endless variety in shades of industry and skill—and an endless variety of temperaments, inclining men to make the very best or the very worst of their cases. In the cotton trade, the power-loom of course reigns supreme. In the stuff trade it is largely, but not, by any means, exclusively employed. In the woollen trade it plays a very subordinate part; and in both manufactures, as a general rule, it makes those kinds of fabrics for which the worst price would be paid were they wrought by hand. It is really a puzzling case, when the weaver says pitifully, "Twenty years ago a man could make 26s. a week at this work, and now he can only make 8s.," to go into the next street and there to find a workman engaged on what appears to be the same stuff, or at all events is very similar, and who avows that he is actually earning the alleged wages of twenty years ago. That the average wages of weavers of all kinds—cotton hand-loom weaving I reckon as extinct—have greatly fallen, there can be no doubt; but the standard from which they have sunk, and by which they are judged, is almost always the high one of the war prices. It is commonly known, that wages in England in 1810 were at least double the amount of wages in 1790. But poverty and toil appear to be in their nature fearfully chronic and immoveable. Two hundred years ago it would seem as if the cry of the hand-loom weavers was precisely what it is now. Even then the workmen complained that the good days of high pay were gone, and that modern masters and modern competition were grinding the faces of the poor. Mr. Macaulay quotes some verses of a song which was sung about the streets of Leeds in the reign of Charles II. *Mutatis mutandis*, the same burden yet rings mournfully in our ears. The popular poet represents the master clothier of Leeds speaking as follows:—

" In former ages we used to give,
So that our work folks like farmers did live.
But the times are changed, we will make them to know.
    *        *        *        *        *        *        *

We will make them work hard for six pence a day,
Though a shilling they deserve if they had their just pay.
If at all they murmur, and say 'tis too small,
We bid them choose whether they'll work at all.
And thus do we gain all our wealth and estate,
By many poor men that work early and late,
Then hey for the clothing trade!"

Such were the plaints of labour nearly two centuries ago. It is sad
and solemn to think that on the very day preceding this on which I
write, I heard men of the same craft, working in the same place, utter
the same complaint—raising the old cry against the hardship of a lot,
which, as one labourer feelingly said to me, "makes a man work like
a slave, but don't allow him to live so well as a slave."

The number of women in Leeds, and in other manufacturing
towns of all sorts, who make their living by their needles, is very
small. The work of the mill is far shorter and easier than that of the
sempstress; and in the case of the few who do ply the needle, the vicinage of the mills keeps their wages somewhat above that starvation
point below which they have elsewhere sunk. I discovered, however,
one most miserable case. The woman in question had been a stay-
stitcher working at the lowest and coarsest sort of stays—generally
small brown ones for children. When I saw her she was ill in bed—a
white, ghastly-looking creature. Three people lived in the room beside herself—a decrepit father and mother, and a grown-up brother
fast dying of consumption. The stay-stitcher occupied the only bed in
the room. It was of that miserable sort I have so often described, and
there was another similar couch spread on the floor in a corner. The
little strip of carpet on the dirty floor was as ragged as a net; the poor
half-broken furniture, and cooking and eating utensils, such as they
were, lay scattered about in that strange disorder which I have learnt
to believe does not always indicate slovenliness, but the disregard and
carelessness engendered by utter and abject misery. The small window
was fast closed against the cold, and in consequence the air was foul
and stifling. The woman told me that she had been paid for stitching
stays 4d., 6d., and 8d. a pair, according to their size. But there was
little more work in the largest than in the smallest kind, although the
price was double. To make a pair of small ones took her a long day's
work. Often and often she had kept at it till twelve at night. Some
weeks she made 3s., some weeks 4s. She did not intend, however, to

resume the trade when she recovered. She intended to take in shoe binding. She could only do the slippers, however—particularly carpet slippers. The prices were 1d. per pair, and it would take her a hard day's work to finish half a dozen pair. She did not understand mill work. Of course this family were mainly supported by the parish, from which they drew about 6s. a week.

Shoe binding is better paid than slipper binding—the work required being neater, and demanding more skill. One woman, a binder, whom I questioned, worked at low-priced shoes. She was only paid 15d. a dozen; and she calculated that she could make 8d. a day, if she were fully employed. This woman had four children—one by her husband, who had been transported, and three by another man since that event. The parish gave her 1s. 6d. per head per week. Not far from this person I found another shoe-binder, employed on the best sort of work. Here was a tolerably comfortable home. The husband and wife sat on each side of the fire plying their tasks. He made shoes for one master, and she bound shoes for another. She was paid sometimes 2s. 6d., sometimes 3s., sometimes 3s. 6d. per dozen, and she could earn in "good weeks" about 6s. or 7s. She found her own silk and thread, and had constant work.

I visited the only two slop-workers I could hear of. One was receiving public charity, the other was the wife of a weaver, who stated that he earned 17s. a week. The former made in substance the following statement:—She laboured at fustian and corduroy trowsers, working-jackets, and working-sleeved waistcoats. All these garments were lined with cotton. For making a pair of trowsers she had 10d. and her thread found her. She could make a pair in a day. By a day she meant from seven o'clock in the morning till ten o'clock at night. For lined jackets and sleeved waistcoats she used to get 15d. each, but the price had been reduced lately. Sometimes she made drawers, for which she was paid 4d. a pair. They had buttons and button holes all complete. Work as she might, she could not finish two pair in a day, and the utmost she could make in a week, with the very hardest labour, was 5s. The second slopworker was principally employed upon boys' dresses. These she made of three sorts and sizes. The first, and smallest size, consisted of a jacket and trowsers, the latter buttoning over the former. For such a suit, generally of corduroy, she received 1s. 4d., and she could make one in a day. The second-class suit consisted of a jacket, waistcoat, and trowsers. For this she was paid 2s. 6d., and to make it took a good day and a half. The third-class suit consisted of a surtout with skirts, a waistcoat, and a jacket. For this she was paid 3s. 6d., and she took more than two days to earn it. These were the main articles of dress which she sewed, and she cut them out herself. She sometimes, however, made moleskin jackets and waistcoats, such as are worn by engineers. These, from the nature of the stuff, are very hard work. For a waistcoat of this kind, with sleeves, she was paid 1s. 3d. For a double-breasted waistcoat, without sleeves, she was paid 9d. Her hours of work were from seven in the morning until ten, eleven, or twelve o'clock, as the case might be. She found her own thread. In all the garments which she made she put regular lining.

In the course of my wanderings through Leeds, I encountered two or three women engaged in a rather curious trade, a description of which I am not able to give with technical accuracy, though I can easily make clear the object in view. Like most occupations, the cloth trade has its share of tricks, one of which consists in passing off an inferior for a superior kind of cloth by some legerdemain practised in the dyeing process. The deception, were it not for the ingenious device I saw being practised, would, however, I was told, be exposed at once by the peculiar action of the dye employed upon the selvage of the cloth. The object, therefore, is to dye the cloth without dyeing the selvage upon its borders, and for this purpose the piece is delivered to a woman, who "selves" it—that is to say, who rolls up the selvage into a circular cylinder all round the cloth, and then covers it with a sort of envelope, tightly stitched and perfectly water-proof. The whole is then plunged into the dye-vat, and after being duly taken out and dried, the sewing is unpicked, and the selvage unrolled precisely in its original state. The women employed in this adroit trickery have about 10d. per piece for sewing up the selvage, and 2d. per piece for unpicking it after the cloth comes from the dyers' hands. A good work-woman will earn from 5s. to 6s. a week; but the work is seldom regular. One of the women engaged in it had been "playing" for three weeks before she got the piece upon which I found her labouring. The parish, of course, is in the meantime supporting her and her sick child.

The Leeds Mechanics' Institution is a prosperous and vigorous working establishment. It counts four life members, 143 proprietary members, 379 subscribers at 15s. yearly, 455 at 12s., and 583 members paying 10s., 8s., and 5s., annually. The number of day scholars is 94, and the mutual improvement class includes 210—making a total of 1,868 members. The statistics of this Institution are collected with more ease than is at all usual in similar establishments, and I am therefore enabled to present some interesting general results. For the last year the number of pupils entered in the arithmetic and mensuration class has been 35—average attendance, 22; writing and book-keeping, 34—average attendance, 23; grammar and geography, 14—attendance, 11; drawing, 45—attendance, 30; analytical chemistry, 11—attendance, 9; manufacturing chemistry, 4—attendance, 4; French evening class, 17—attendance, 12; ditto ladies', 4—attendance, 4; German class, 9—attendance, 9. The library contains 7,026 volumes. The issues of books in the past year, including periodicals, make a total of 57,174 volumes. These issues, with reference to the species of works in demand, are classed as follows:—Books on theology, were given out 1,784 times; on philosophy and education, 3,089 times; on politics and statistics, 572 times; on history and biography, 9,129 times; on voyages and travels, 3,074 times; poetry and the drama, 1,887 times; works of fiction, 15,675 times; fine arts and literature, 4,450; mathematics, 483; mechanics, 651; chemistry, 997; natural philosophy, 995; medicine and dietetics, 533; bound periodicals, 4,926; foreign works, 172; unbound periodicals, 8,256—making a grand total of 57,174. The features which may be noted in this return are—the great demand for works of fiction, and the small demand for works of any character in any language save English. The total number of lectures delivered last year was 39. They embrace a wide range of subjects—literary, historic, economic, scientific, and artistic. In connection with the institute there is a school of design, attended by an average of 11 male and 13 female pupils in the morning, and 30 male pupils at night. The annual Government grant to this school has lately been raised from £80 to £150, in addition to which some ninety volumes of works connected with the arts have been sent down by the Council of the Government School of Design, to form the nucleus of an Art library. It is quite impossible to overrate the importance of these seminaries throughout the manufacturing districts. In every respect, save the single one of drawing patterns, our manufacturing population seem to carry all before them. The industrial spirit is abroad in its strength, but the art spirit is weak and cold. It was humiliating in the calico districts to see the abject dependence of English manufacturers upon French pattern designers. In too many instances a notion seemed to prevail that to invent beautiful and tasteful forms was the province of the French, while to stamp them upon cotton cloth was the business of the English. It is to be hoped that the influence of the numerous Schools of Design now springing up in the North may tend in some degree to counteract that hard-headed contempt for everything but what is exclusively practical and "business-like," which stamps so uninviting an impression upon the surface aspect of the manufacturing system. The Leeds Mechanics' Institution is at present some four hundred pounds in debt; but a series of exhibitions and explanations, by Mr. Frederick Warren, the well-known lecturer upon the cotton trade, of his working models, which is about to take place on behalf of the institution, will, it is hoped, remove the greater portion of its liabilities.

Before leaving the manufacturing districts, it may not be amiss that I should devote a few words to the life and toil of the men who, before the era of railroads, were chiefly concerned in the conveyance of heavy goods from place to place, and who still transport by water-carriage a very considerable proportion of our manufactured and mineral wealth—I mean the bargemen engaged in navigating our inland canals. The railway passenger will be familiar with the aspect of these men and their boats. The canal and the rail often run together for many a mile, each crossing the other in its windings. Thus, as the train puffs across the viaduct, the passenger may often mark the shining course of the canal, glittering in its long serpentine undulations beneath him, the unruffled clayey water, the mud-trampled towing-path, and the green meadows sloping on either hand to the brink, with here and there a fringe of willows or rushy plants rising from the water. Gliding along these tranquil channels come barges, which, creeping slowly but surely along, make their gradual way from Lancashire to Surrey, and from the Thames to the Severn. The boats are long, narrow, and deeply laden. A tarpaulin covers the cargo stowed amidships; and sometimes in the bow, sometimes in the stern, sometimes in both bow and stern, rise one or two funnels—the number being according to the size of the boat—smoking cheerily, and proclaiming that the cabins of captain and crew lie beneath. As a general rule, a single horse draws these boats along, the driver being frequently seated complacently upon its back, with both feet towards the water. This individual belongs to a class often talked of but seldom seen. In the slang of the canals he is called the "Horse Marine." The "marine" is, indeed, his regular trade appellation. Sometimes a man, or a couple of men, lounge idly on the barge's deck—occasionally a woman taking a "trick" at the helm is the only person visible. Let us descend into the after cabin of one of the larger class of barges—one carrying from forty to fifty tons. It is a hot, choky, little box, between four and five feet high; near the scuttle is a stove. On either side run berths made after the usual fashion afloat. One is very generally constructed broad enough to contain a couple of persons; the other has often only room for one. Beneath them are lockers which serve for seats, and at the stern, just forward of the rudder, opens the little cupboard, wherein the "sea stock" is deposited. Even with the scuttle open you will probably find the air close and oppressive, but the captain will generally tell you that two, sometimes three, people sleep there with the hatch on. "We move it so as to make a chink, if we feel it over hot." The larger boats are generally navigated by a captain and two "mates," and helped, of course, by the "marine." The average wages of the captain amount to about 22s.—those of the mates and the marine to 18s. weekly. The captain has often his wife on board, but sometimes one of the mates gives his "missus" a trip, the skipper on these occasions gallantly giving up the use of the cabin and sleeping with the other mate in the forecastle. Only one lady, however, is allowed to be on board at a time. The usual speed of the barges is from two to three miles and a half an hour. The "fly" barges, which are commonly the larger sort, proceed night and day, never stopping, except at the locks, and to deliver goods. Each horse performs a stage of from twenty to twenty-five miles. The marine in charge of the relay knows when the barge will be up, "to an hour or two"—a latitude reminding one of the very old coaching days. The smaller barges have only a single horse, which goes the whole journey. These boats "tie up" at nights. The bargemen always sleep on board. The marine looks after his steed, and sleeps ashore. There do not seem to be any regular watches on board these barges, as at sea. The turns of duty depend upon circumstances and varying arrangements. Three hours is reckoned a fair spell at the helm, and if there is a woman on board she always steers when the men are at their dinners. In passing a lock, however, all hands must be on deck, by day or night. The foregoing sketch would seem to indicate that the inland bargemen lead a life of fair comparative comfort.

I now, for the present, leave the great subject of our textile industry. I have endeavoured to describe its different developments, and the different physical, moral, and social phases of each development. I have tried to ascertain with correctness the amount of wages paid to each separate class of operatives, in each separate manufacture. I have striven to paint truly the effect of each scale of remuneration upon the workman, as regards his appearance, his domestic accommodation, and his domestic comfort. I have not neglected to inquire into the effects of each branch of occupation upon his health; nor whether it tended to rear up any particular social characteristics or social anomalies. These, when I found them, I have striven fully and accurately to display. I have detailed, without pretension to technical or scientific accuracy, the industrial processes which I saw, always viewing them strictly in connexion with the labour which they called forth, and the labourer who furnished it. I have described the homes of the workpeople, the sanitary characteristic of each manufacturing town, and the general aspect *en masse* of each manufacturing population. I have tried to discriminate between factory evils and large-town evils. I have, so far as the nature of my work permitted, glanced at the principal educational engines which I found at work; and—of course, principally keeping my attention fixed upon the great staple manufactures—I have not altogether neglected the condition of the few who ply casual and exceptional trades, ranking beneath the level of the prevailing species of labour. It now becomes my duty to direct attention to another, and a not less important, field of toil. I proceed to the occupation of a class of men upon whose operations our whole industrial system depends—the men whose labour primarily causes the piston to move and the tall chimneys to smoke. Leaving the cotton works of Lancashire, and the woollen manufactures of Yorkshire, I turn to the colliers and the collieries of England, beginning with the great mineral fields of Durham and Northumberland.

*The Morning Chronicle, Monday, December 17, 1849.*

# LABOUR AND THE POOR.

—◆—

## THE MANUFACTURING DISTRICTS.

[FROM OUR SPECIAL CORRESPONDENT.]

## THE COAL-FIELD OF NORTHUMBERLAND AND DURHAM.

## LETTER XVIII.

In this letter I propose to give an introductory sketch of the occupation furnished by the raising of coals from the mines of Northumberland and Durham—describing the mineral field itself—touching upon the statistics of the trade during its progress to its present condition, and adding such an outline of mining operations as will enable the reader the better to understand those minute details connected with the working of coal-pits—the daily life of the Hewers, Putters, Drivers, and Trappers, and the ventilation of mines, so far as the subject seems to be sanitary, rather than purely scientific—into which, in subsequent communications, it will be my duty to enter.

In the north-eastern corner of England lies that great carboniferous deposit which supplied in 1845 eleven-twelfths of the entire mass of coal burned in the grates and furnaces of the kingdom. The boundaries of the great northern coal-field are mapped out with some distinctness to the north and west, but their southern limits are vague and unsettled, and the eastern frontier of the mineral region lies deep within the German Ocean. Speaking in general terms, the Northumberland and Durham coal-field is bounded to the north and south by the Coquet and the Tees. The Coquet is a Northumbrian stream, rising amid the southern slopes of the Cheviots, and joining the ocean some twenty miles north of Tynemouth. The Tees separates Durham from Yorkshire. Between these rivers run the Tyne and the Wear, draining the broadest and richest portions of the coal-field, and on their banks lie scattered the oldest, deepest, and most extensive pits. Like almost all coal deposits, the strata forming the Newcastle-field "dip" to a common bottom, somewhat in the manner of a basin, and of this basin the centre, and therefore of course the deepest point, lies

near the sea coast hard by Sunderland. Here are situated the deepest
mines, one of which, that of Monkwearmouth, is the most profound
excavation in the world, sinking more than 1,500 feet beneath the
level of the sea. The centre of the coal basin being thus near the ocean,
and the line of coast running a pretty accurate transverse, it follows
that, so far as we know, the land and the sea divide in two pretty equal
portions the great northern coal-field. Twenty miles westward from
Tynemouth, the lower strata, forming of course the under edge of the
basin, begin to rise up into day; and it is probable that twenty miles to
the eastward of Tynemouth, the other extremities of these strata heave
themselves upwards to the bottom of the ocean. The landward portion
of the coal-field thus forms a sort of half oval, attaining its greatest
breadth not far from the point where the Tyne intersects its inland
boundary. The length of the Newcastle-field, or, at all events, of the
workable portion of it, is about 44 miles, and the greatest breadth
about 20. A glance at a geological map will show the great slice of the
shires of Northumberland and Durham within which the coal strata
extend. This slice includes about one-third of the seaward face of the
first county, and at least two-thirds of the seaward face of the second. From its northern extremity, at the mouth of the Coquet, the
coal-field strikes gradually inland, running at an acute angle with the
coast. From its southern angle, about Barnard Castle, on the Tees, the
precious mineral runs seaward, almost at right angles to the coast line,
being hereabouts more or less overlapped by vast layers of magnesian
limestone—beneath which, however, it is now demonstrated that the
coal extends to an unknown distance to the southward. Following the
landward boundaries of the basin topographically, they may be described as commencing on the Coquet, and passing southwardly and
westerly in the vicinity of the Northumbrian towns of Acklington,
Morpeth, Prestwich, Callerton, Heddon-Ovingham, Mickley, and
Newlands. Here the Tyne divides Northumberland from Durham,
and passing into the latter county we find the coal line stretching past
Heyleyfield, Wolsingham, and Redburn to Barnard Castle, where it
forms an angle, and runs in an undulating line, past Bishop Middle-
ham and Castle Eden, to the sea. Coal strata, indeed, extend to the
southward of this last stretch of boundary, but the workable part of
the field lies north of it. The reader will thus perceive that the northern
coal-field is an irregular but (on the whole) oval space—the greatest
portion of it to the west of high-water mark, and that portion watered by two great rivers, bounded by two less important streams, and

containing the smaller shipping stations of Amble and Blyth, and the greater shipping depôts of Shields and Newcastle on the Tyne, Sunderland upon the Wear, Hartlepool, and Stockton.

I have said that the coal strata dip in a basin-like shape, and that the centre of this basin, and therefore the centre of the coal-field, lies near Sunderland. It will follow as a general rule that the deepest pits have been sunk upon the sea coast of Durham. Following the shore from the northern to the southern extremity of the field, the depth to which pits have been sunk so as to command good seams is as follows:—In Northumberland, the Coquet pits average 80 fathoms, the Cowpen pits 100, the Hartley 50, and the Whitby 60. In Durham, at South Shields, coal is brought from a depth of 200 fathoms, at Monkwearmouth from a depth of 263 fathoms, at Marten Winning from 220, and at Castle Eden from 150 fathoms. Several of the southern and eastern collieries are situated upon the overlapping strata of magnesian limestone, which here intrudes into the coal-field. It was long thought that where the limestone began, the successful search for coals would end. This was the favourite scientific theory of which Professors Sedgwick and Buckland were the chief expounders. Practical miners, however, have demonstrated the fact to be otherwise. At Hetton 156 feet, at Monkwearmouth 200 feet, and at Haswell 280 feet of solid limestone were pierced through before the adventurers arrived at coal seams extensive enough to be profitably worked.

The basin-shaped strata of coal are divided from each other by great layers of sandstone and bituminous clay. On a rough calculation, there may be about eighty distinct beds of coal, one lying beneath the other, and all of them, as a general rule, dipping in a similar direction. Out of about 1,700 feet penetrated, it is calculated that the various layers of coal make up an aggregate bed of 24 feet in depth. The different strata are of all degrees of thickness, from more than six feet to less than six inches. Of course the very thin strata count practically for nothing; they cannot be worked. Of the principal layers, that called the High Main, from which the original Wallsend coals were dug, is about 6 feet in thickness. The Low Main is 6½ feet; the Bensham seam is 4 feet; and the Coalyard seam 3 feet. These layers of coal must not be supposed to extend in uniform sheets across the whole field. Great convulsions of the earth have broken and scattered them—flung them up at one point, and ground them down at another. Indeed, it often happens that with the change of level the quality of the coals changes also. Thus, in the valley of the Tyne a particular seam, called the Low Main, furnishes a species of coal used for furnace purposes, having a splinty fracture, little bitumen, yielding a rapid though not a lasting heat, and depositing a quantity of white ashes. This is the class of mineral called steam coal; but the vein which furnishes it, in passing south, acquires another quality, takes another name, and under the titles of Hetton, Lambton, Stewart's, &c., commands the highest price as a household coal in the London market. As a general rule, the deeper a seam runs the higher becomes the quality of the coals. In spite of this, however, it often happens that a seam running still lower furnishes an inferior species of mineral. So far as the nature and quality of the coals, the production of the Newcastle field, can be topographically arranged, I have reason to believe that the following classification may be relied on:—The main seams of the Tyne, the Wear, and the Tees, and the Hetton seam of the second river, furnish the coals best adapted for domestic purposes. The best gas and coke coals come from the mines to the south-west of Newcastle, in the vicinity of Durham and Chester-le-Street. The Northumberland coals, as well as the Low Main of the valley of the Wear, are those best suited for steam purposes.

The probable duration of the supplies afforded by the coal-field of Northumberland and Durham is perhaps to us not a very practical, but it is a very interesting question, and a communication professing to give a general prefatory view of the coal trade would hardly be complete without some reference to it. In 1829 and 1830 two parliamentary committees sat upon the coal trade, and calculations as to the probable duration of the supply from the Durham and Northumberland field were laid before each. Dr. Buckland was one of the estimators. He admitted that his calculations were "vague and conjectural," and he founded them upon a basis which has since been practically demonstrated to be erroneous. Dr. Buckland believed, that beneath the masses of limestone which formed the old south-eastern boundaries of the basin no coal would be found, and he fixed the probable duration of the supply to the northward and westward at about 400 years—taking the quantity of the mineral to be annually brought to the surface at the amount dug up during the year previous to his calculation. Other and more practical estimators fixed a far longer date to the era at which the Northumbrian and Durham mines will become unworkable. Mr. Buddle estimated the average thickness of all the coal seams in Durham at twenty-five feet eight inches, and of all those in Northumberland at twenty-one feet—the calculation, taking it in connection with the comparative extent of each field, giving an average thickness of twenty-four feet over the whole coal basin. But of this 24 feet, a considerable proportion is made up of beds only a few inches, or perhaps a foot or two, thick, and therefore practically unavailable. Mr. Hugh Taylor, a gentleman of vast practical experience, estimated the depth of coal over the whole field as eight feet of available mine—a calculation, which, taking the vend of 1829, would give us 1,727 years ere we shall have exhausted the Great Northern field. Later calculations have somewhat shortened the period, because they are founded upon the supposition of an increasing vend. An estimate, drawn up on high practical authority, computes the extent of the coal area as 924 square miles. The mean thickness of the mineral is taken at eighteen feet. To make allowance for what are called "denudations"— that is, spots where strata have broken entirely off—three feet are allowed, leaving the net thickness fifteen feet. But still further deductions have to be made for minor obstacles, such as "dykes" and "troubles," by which the level of a seam is suddenly changed, and also for the impossibility in all cases of working out the entire mass of coal. For these drawbacks the estimator gives up one-third of his calculated available thickness, leaving finally a depth of ten feet of coal extending over a superficies of 924 square miles. The produce would be about 9,107,000,000 tons of coal. From this, there being subtracted 1,517,900,000 tons as already excavated, the result would be about 7,590,000,000 tons, which, at the consumption of 1837, would give us a supply for 1,450 years. Let the precise period, however, be what it may, the majority of calculators estimate the time during which the yield of coals in the Newcastle field is likely to last as over one thousand years.

I have mentioned various irregularities in the lie of the strata. These are known to miners as "faults," "troubles," "hitches," and "dykes." Sometimes a vein of stone suddenly intersects the seam. Sometimes it breaks off short, and then continues at a different level either above or below. Two principal dykes, or sudden breakings off and changes of level, intersect the northern coal-field, both of them running in a general easterly direction. The great dyke flings the seams principally worked near Newcastle and North Shields, including Wallsend, perpendicularly down to an extreme extra depth of 130 fathoms—so that two collieries may be working the same seam within a quarter of a mile of each other, but at a difference in depth of from 90 fathoms to 130 fathoms perpendicular. The low level extends on the northern side of the dyke. The other principal phenomenon of the sort is the Hemerth dyke, south of which the main seams suddenly rise 25 fathoms. These dykes are considered to be, on the whole, advantageous rather than otherwise to the miner. Sometimes, indeed, the great convulsive movements of the earth, of which they are the tokens, have sunk masses of coal to an impracticable depth, but they have as often upheaved seams to within a working distance of the surface. The Great Dyke has been useful in preventing the Wallsend seam from "cropping out"—that is, appearing at the surface; in which case masses of coal now available would have been long ago wasted by the action of the elements.

The operations of the pitmen are, of course, frequently impeded by springs of water, which, were it not for the system of pumps continually kept at work, would gradually fill up and "drown" the mine. In some pits the quantity of water present is trifling. Throughout the extensive workings of the Gosforth Colliery, embracing dozens of miles of under-ground galleries, only a few gallons per minute distil. Other pits are very watery. Mention was made before a parliamentary committee, of a mine, the weight of water lifted from which was just eighteen times that of the coals. At Friars' Goose Colliery, 1,000 gallons per minute are pumped out, or above 6,000 tons per day—the weight of the coals extracted being from 250 to 300 tons per day; and when the Haswell Pit was being sunk beneath the magnesian limestone, the engine power drew from the earth no less than 27,600 tons of water daily. These springs, if arising from below a certain depth, are uniformly salt. Where the impregnating matter lies is a mystery, as no indication of rock salt has ever been discovered near the coal-field. In some mines, however, the water which trickles far down amid the coal seams is three times as salt as the sea. This is the case in the St. Lawrence Colliery. At several of the pits the saline springs are so copious that salt works have been established in the vicinity. At Birtley Colliery, near Chester-le-Street, a runnel of hot salt water was discovered in 1794, producing about 1,100 gallons per hour. At Lambton Colliery, to the south, and at Walker Colliery, close to the Tyne, salt works are also in operation.

The temperature of coal mines rises in proportion to the depth— the deepest pits being of course the hottest. Much necessarily depends upon the efficacy of the ventilating apparatus; but the following statement of temperatures in and about the Jarrow Pit gives an idea of the general average proportions of atmospheric heat at different depths:—

| | | |
|---|---|---|
| At the surface | 46 | degrees. |
| At the bottom of the shaft, 146 fathoms | 61 | „ |
| Returned air, after having traversed the workings | 75 | „ |
| Engine boiler house, 700 yards from the shaft | 144 | „ |

All coal pits are ventilated upon the simple principle of creating a draught of air, by means of a great furnace kept constantly blazing near the bottom of one of the shafts. The details of the contrivances in use I shall state when—after having, as I am now striving to do, given the reader a general idea of what the coal district and the coal trade are—I come to describe, in all their minutiæ, the appliances and working of a pit.

In sinking a coal mine, the object of the engineer is not, as might be at first supposed, to come upon the seam at its highest elevation. On the contrary, he digs his shaft where he has reason to believe the bed dips most deeply. Having reached the coals, he then works upwards, and gains the advantage of inclines, down which his laden waggons run to the bottom of the shaft. The old manner of working the seam, and that still practised in Scotland, is called the "long-wall" system—in which the miner digs almost the whole mass of coals out, supporting the roof of the hollow thus formed with wooden props, so long as he is digging in it—and then, when his portion of the seam is exhausted, withdrawing the props and leaving the undermined soil to collapse behind him. The manner of working adopted in the Newcastle and Durham field is the withdrawal of the mineral in passages crossing each other at right angles, and between which square masses of coal (called "pillars") are left. The seam is thus honeycombed, and when the process is complete throughout its whole extent, the miner retraces his steps, and cuts away as much of the pillars as he can with safety to himself, leaving the roof to fall in, and the exhausted part of the mine to become a series of crumbling caverns, often filled with stagnant masses of fire-damp.

The accidents in mines, produced by atmospheric causes, are usually most numerous in warm weather, because the temperature of the air of the pit being then more equable, the difficulty of causing a column of fresh air to descend is very much increased. Out of seventy accidents, causing the loss of nearly 1,000 lives, there have occurred:—

In the winter months . . . . . . . . . . 8 explosions.
In the spring months . . . . . . . . . . 13 „
In the summer months . . . . . . . . 20 „
In the autumn months . . . . . . . . 30 „

Total . . . . . . . . . . 71 „

In all deep mines, and more especially in working at a distance from the shaft, the Davy-lamp is uniformly used. It will, however, astonish many persons to learn that during the 18 years previous to 1816, when the safety-lamp was introduced, the loss of life in the counties of Northumberland and Durham, by explosions, was 447—whereas during the 18 years subsequent to 1816 the amount of life lost in the same way was 538—the difference being accounted for by the working of many "fiery collieries," previously inaccessible—by the neglect and carelessness of the workmen themselves in the management of their lamps—and by the too frequent relaxation of ventilating measures that were previously rigidly carried into effect.

With respect to accidents of all kinds in collieries, I transcribe a table given among the results of one of the parliamentary inquiries into the subject, detailing the number of fatal accidents during the year 1838, and applying to fifty-five mining districts:—

By falling down shafts . . . . . . . . . . . . . . . . . 63
Breaking of ropes . . . . . . . . . . . . . . . . . . . . . 1
During the time of ascending and descending
    shafts . . . . . . . . . . . . . . . . . . . . . . . . . . . . . 10
Drowned . . . . . . . . . . . . . . . . . . . . . . . . . . . 22
Fall of stones and coals . . . . . . . . . . . . . . . . 97
Various injuries in coal-pits . . . . . . . . . . . . . 43
Explosions of gas . . . . . . . . . . . . . . . . . . . . . 88
Explosions of gunpowder . . . . . . . . . . . . . . 4
By trams and waggons . . . . . . . . . . . . . . . . 21

Total . . . . . . . . . . . . . . . . . . . 349

For the purposes of ascending and descending into mines, wire ropes are now coming into general use, and an ingenious invention, which I shall afterwards describe with the fulness which its importance deserves, has lately been patented, the object being to prevent loss of life in case of breakage of the rope drawing the buckets up the shaft.

As a general rule, the mines in the coal district of Northumberland and Durham are worked by lessees, either companies or individuals, who rent the royalty—including everything beneath the surface—from the proprietors. The lessees have generally power to vacate the colliery by giving a year's notice. They are bound to leave the pit in an open and tenantable state, and they are liable for all damage done to the surface in the course of working. The principal coal-pits worked by and for behoof of their owners are those belonging to the Marquess of Londonderry and the Earl of Durham. The engagements made with pit hands are always by the month, with an occasional stipulation for a certain number of days' work, greater or less, according to the season and the state of the market. The Miners' Union in the Newcastle district was almost totally overthrown by the great strike of 1844, which exercised a very important influence upon the trade.

The rise and extent of the great traffic in question—the amount of capital which it uses, and of labour which it employs—I shall now statistically sketch. As early as the thirteenth century a royal charter enabled the "good men" of Newcastle to raise and dispose of coals, and the revenue of the town, principally derived from the sale of the mineral, soon amounted to £200 a year. In the course of the next century, vain efforts were made to put coal-burning down, on account of such fires lading the air with noxious vapours; and prohibitory duties were placed upon the export of the mineral to all continental ports, save Calais, then, of course, an English garrison-town. The coal-pits, however, continued to increase and flourish; and as the ancient forests were consumed, "fears," pretty well grounded, began to be entertained that "sea-cole will be good merchandise ewen in the Citie of London." In the reign of Elizabeth the price of coals in London was 9s. per chaldron of six bolls. This was a monopoly price—for the right of working coals in the North was then possessed by an incorporated guild of "hostmen," whose proceedings caused frequent parliamentary interference. At this time the duty on exported coals was 5s. per chaldron. In 1615 the coal trade employed 400 sail of ships, one-half of which carried the mineral to the Thames; and as early as the reign of James I. the coal duty of the town of Newcastle produced to the corporation a revenue of £10,000 per annum. In the time of Charles I., coals for the first time became the almost universal fuel of London; and one of the most unpopular acts of the King was granting a new monopoly in the article. The selling price in London under this charter was 17s. per chaldron in summer, and 19s. in winter. There were now employed in the collier trade 2,000 seamen, being not quite a fourth of the whole number in the kingdom. The trade suffered cruelly in the wars of the Commonwealth; and it was not until the Restoration that Sunderland became an important place. In 1676 the coal shipping of the Tyne

was estimated at about 80,000 tons, of which a considerable proportion was foreign-built. Waggons and waggon-ways, the rude form
of railroads, had already come into operation both above and below
ground; and the right of way from a pit to the "staith," or wooden
wharf, where the coals were shipped, was rented at the dear rate of
£20 per annum per rood. During the rise of the trade, it was harassed
by duties, perpetually fluctuating, and by monopolies which, by increasing the price, diminished the consumption. At the beginning of
the last century, coals sold in London for 18s. 6d. per chaldron, and
the Masters of the Trinity House estimated that 600 ships—able to
carry on an average 80 Newcastle chaldrons—were necessary for the
conveyance of the mineral between the Tyne and the Thames. There
were at this period about 1,500 "keel" or barge men employed upon
the former river. In 1714 the first rude steam-engine north of the Tyne
began to work, and within a few years the new machines were in common use for pumping water from the seams. The mines now began
to grow individually great and important. Some employed from 600
to 700 carts, and from 300 to 400 pitmen. The engines were gradually improved, and the piston rods gradually lengthened; and, in 1764,
the coast trade from the Tyne was 20,000 chaldrons, and the foreign
trade 40,000. In this year, 3,727 vessels coal-laden cleared from the
river, and 99 steam engines on the Newcomen principle were at work
throughout the valleys of the Tyne and the Wear. In 1772, no less than
5,585 ships, carrying 330,200 tons of coal, left the former river. The
wages of seamen at this period, for the London voyage, were £3 10s.
The beginning of the present century witnessed some of the greatest
fluctuations which have occurred in the trade, with reference to both
masters and workmen. In 1804 there was a mania for coal digging,
and a general scramble for workmen. Previously to that time, it had
been usual to bind pitmen for the twelvemonth, and to give them two
or three guineas as binding or bounty money, at the season at which
the annual engagement took place. In 1804 the binding money rose
to twelve or fourteen guineas per man on the Tyne, and to eighteen
guineas on the Wear. Drink flowed abundantly on all sides, and the
pit districts were the scene of one vast orgie—the regular wages being raised at the same time upwards of 40 per cent. The consequence
was a speedy overflow of labour. Workman of all kinds flocked to obtain employment in the pits, and gradually the wages settled down to
their former level. No binding money whatever is now paid. In 1810,
the Durham water sale collieries employed 7,011 men, and the land

sale collieries 382 men. The keelmen on the Wear amounted to 750; the casters, trimmers, and fillers, to 507; and the same classes of individuals, employed by the Durham collieries upon the Tyne, were reckoned at more than 2,000. In 1816, the introduction of the safety-lamp led, as I have stated, to the renewed working of many "fiery" pits, formerly considered unapproachable; and in 1826 the pitmen's Union was founded. The progress of the trade about this period will appear from the following statement of chaldrons exported from the Tyne and the Wear:—

NEWCASTLE.
In 1810 there were exported ... 649,552 Chaldrons.
In 1820 there were exported ... 801,309 „
In 1828 there were exported ... 784,407 „

SUNDERLAND.
In 1810 there were exported ... 372,622 Chaldrons.
In 1820 there were exported ... 430,397 „
In 1828 there were exported ... 532,508 „

In the next year Newcastle was the second port in the kingdom, reckoning 987 ships of 202,379 tons; while Sunderland had 624 ships, of 107,628 tons. In 1832 occurred one of the great pitmen's strikes, the consequence of which was the introduction of a vast quantity of hitherto rural labour into the trade. To this era a number of good authorities look back as the point subsequent to which the amount of labour in the trade became permanently too great for the demand, and the quantity of coal raised too great to allow of the profits formerly made by the traffic. In 1844, a second great and ineffectual turn-out took place, the yet existing effects of which are principally displayed in the still dissolved colliers' union. The number of collieries and of colliers in the counties of Durham and Northumberland, as reported to the Coal Trade Office at Newcastle in 1844, was as follows:—In the valley of the Tyne, including the Blyth pits, there were 66 collieries, employing 16,515 hands; on the Wear, there were 31 collieries, employing 13,172 hands; and on the Tees 22 collieries, employing 4,211 hands.

The engineering progress of the coal trade went hand-in-hand with its commercial advancement. The early wooden waggon-ways followed the natural undulations of the country. The waggons had wooden wheels studded with nails, and accidents were constantly occurring from their breaking away down the steep hills, up which they were dragged with great difficulty and labour. Cast-iron rails were introduced in 1767, and some ten years later metal tramways were employed underground. Coals were first pulled to the surface by horse machines called "gins," and the drainage was effected by chain pumps, wrought by horses or water power, and sometimes by strings of buckets working on the principle which may be now seen in dredging machines. By 1720, engines for draining, wrought by steam, had come into common use. It was about the middle of the last century that coals began to be screened, so as to divide the smaller sort from the more valuable lumps. Hewers' wages at this period ranged from 1s. 6d. to 1s. 10d. a day; they now vary from 3s. to 4s. The hewer, as the reader will afterwards understand, is always paid by the piece, and about a hundred years ago the recompense for hewing was about 1d. per peck of coal worked. The putter, who then conveyed the coal to the bottom of the shaft, made about 10d. a day—the wages of little boys working as "trappers" at the present time. The pits, until the application of steam, were mere surface scratches, compared with the depth to which they now extend; sixty fathoms was the utmost depth then attained. Ventilation was neither understood nor attended to, and accidents by explosion were of constant occurrence. In 1732, furnaces for the promotion of a ventilating draught were first kindled in the Fatfield Colliery; and in 1756 the first air tube was erected at North Biddick. Women were occasionally, but not commonly, employed underground; but they laboured in great numbers at the pit heaps, and at the staiths, emptying the waggons into the keels. The standard price for such work was from 1d. to 1½d. per ton. The first application of steam to pumping purposes was after a most curious round-about fashion. The steam-engine first pumped water into a cistern; this running out turned a water-wheel; and the revolving water-wheel drew up the brimming buckets from the pits. The genius of Watt put an end to this rude contrivance, and about 1796 the first steam-engine, in the modern sense of the term, was erected on the Northumbrian bank of the Tyne, below Newcastle. With deep pits, contrivances for ventilation became a necessity, and means were found of splitting the descending current of air so as to fling it simultaneously into different levels and corridors, instead of the old practice of sending one current through the whole mine. In some pits, about the beginning of the present century, the air travelled thirty, forty, and fifty miles before it rose again to mingle with the atmosphere. The consequence was that this current of air was almost unbreathable long before it had completed its circuit. Instances have, indeed, been known of the main current having arrived at the "up cast" shaft so loaded with inflammable gas that it fired when brought into contact with the furnace blazing there. Many improvements were from time to time made in the ropes by which the communication between the top and bottom of the shaft is kept up. Gunpowder was introduced for blasting, and, the main passages having been sufficiently enlarged, horses were let down to draw the trains of tubs to the shaft. From the year 1780 the improvements in mining engineering were constant. Cast iron tramways were introduced underground; shafts were divided into compartments by wooden or iron tubbing, and the build and rig of keels were so much improved as to enable them to make five, instead of three, tides per week to the most distant collieries. Inclined planes were also put into requisition, along which the full waggons running down drew, by their own weight, the empty ones up. About 1813 or 1814 the first rude locomotives were used to convey the coal from the pit to the staith. This invention produced a revolution in the trade, causing great fields of inland coal to be worked which had hitherto been neglected, owing to the difficulty of transport. In 1825 a coal railway was opened from Stockton to Whitton-park Colliery, and now vast quantities of coal are carried to Shields by the Stanhope and Tyne and the Brandling Junction Railways. About twenty years ago, the corves, or baskets in which the coals had formerly been carried, gave place to square tubes fitted with wheels, and carrying from six to eight hundredweight. The wire-rope invention came into notice in the same year, and shortly thereafter the pitmen began to be conveyed up and down the shafts in baskets, instead of dangling in a loop after the old fashion.

The first parliamentary inquiry into the coal trade which has taken place in comparatively recent times was that of 1800. It was principally directed to the subject of combinations in the trade to keep up the price of coals. These combinations, in their modern shape, originated in 1771, and the committee recommended stringent measures for their repression. Before this committee, it was stated that a pitman's wages had increased 50 per cent. within the last ten years.

In 1829 another parliamentary inquiry was instituted. The trade was then open, the "regulation," or combination, of coalowners having broken up in the previous year. Before this committee it was stated that the waste from screening, and the consequent rejection of the small coal, amounted to no less than one-fourth of the whole products of a mine. Among the facts elicited by this inquiry were the following: that the capital then employed in the Tyne collieries, independent of shipping, amounted to 1½ millions of money; and it was reckoned that the collieries then open were capable of producing twice the quantity of coals required. The number of men employed in the trade, directly or indirectly, was stated as follows:—

|                  | Tyne.  | Wear. |
|------------------|--------|-------|
| Above ground     | 3,463  | 2,300 |
| Below ground     | 8,491  | 6,700 |
|                  | 11,954 | 9,000 |

| | |
|--|--|
| In round numbers | 21,000 |
| Employed on board colliers (men and boys) | 15,000 |
| As keelmen, boatmen, trimmers, &c. | 2,000 |
| In London and on the coast | 7,500 |
| Total of men and boys employed by the Newcastle and Durham coal trade | 45,500 |

The consumption of coal in England and Wales was estimated at 3,500,000 tons yearly for manufacturing purposes, and 5,500,000 for household purposes. These are the inland-dug coals. The additional quantity carried coastwise was estimated at 3,000,000 of tons, making a grand total of 12,000,000 of tons.

In the year 1830 another parliamentary inquiry took place, but as it chiefly related to the commercial and monetary affairs of the trade, I pass it over, as I do a subsequent investigation which was instituted in 1836, and in which the committee again reported against the policy of permitting combinations for limiting the sale, and of course raising the price, of coals.

In the June of 1839, a local committee was formed at South Shields for the purpose of investigating the causes of and the remedies for accidents in collieries. Just before this body commenced their investigations an explosion had destroyed 52 lives in the South Hilda pit, near Shields. The committee ascertained that, within the last twenty years, no fewer than 680 miners had been killed in the districts of the Tyne and Wear by the ignition of inflammable gases. The committee described the general effect of an explosion in a northern coal pit. They detailed its consequences as deranging and disfiguring every avenue, extinguishing every light, and blowing to pieces, by the concussion, the doors and traps requisite for the general ventilation of the mine. The consequence often was, that the survivors of the explosion, even when well acquainted with the topography of the works, could not make their way out to the pit shaft in time to escape the baneful "after-damp" or azotic acid gas, which, almost as soon as the thunder of the explosion is stilled, comes rolling forth, and speedily fills great districts of the mine. This committee ascertained that the number of fatal explosive gases generated in coalmines is three—light carburetted hydrogen, heavy carburetted hydrogen, and sulphuretted hydrogen. These gases explode at the flame of a lamp, or by contact with metal heated to a red heat. Carbonic acid gas is commonly generated by explosion. It abounds in old and deserted workings. Lights will not burn in it. The miners call it "stythe," "choke damp," and "black damp," and a single breath of it, in an undiluted state, kills. For the prevention of explosive accidents in mines, regular and scientific ventilation is what the committee strongly recommend. No lamp has ever been, or can ever be constructed, which is absolutely safe in an explosive atmosphere. The committee considered that, generally speaking, the ventilating currents were not large enough, and did not move fast enough through the mines; and the remedy suggested was an increase in the number of shafts. The committee further recommended the erection of an instrument, in all mines, for measuring the speed of the ventilating current, and cited, without actually adopting, Mr. George Stephenson's opinion, that the ventilation of mines ought to be put under parliamentary regulation. They strongly deprecate the present system of leaving the ventilation of collieries "to chance and the unassisted efforts of individuals."

In 1840, the commission for inquiring into the condition of women and children in mines commenced its labours. The investigation was followed by the legislative enactment for the regulation of mines and collieries, now in force. Under this Act no woman, on any pretence whatever, can be employed under ground in any manner whatever. No boy can be employed until he has completed his tenth year, and no apprenticeship can last for a longer period than eight years. No person can have the charge of shaft machinery under the age of 15 years, and no payment of wages made at a public-house is valid. These are the main provisions of the act, which does not, as in the case of factories, prescribe the length of the working day.

I have repeatedly mentioned the great strike of 1844. It commenced on the 5th of April of that year, on which day nearly the whole of the underground workers in Northumberland and Durham ceased to labour. It was the fourth great industrial disturbance which took place in the district since 1826. The strike had been long debated and was deliberately resolved on. At first it was believed that the turn-out would be general over the kingdom, but a meeting of delegates was held in March at Glasgow, at which it was decided that no such movement should take place. Delegates representing 23,357 miners voted for the general strike, but delegates representing 28,042 miners were of a contrary opinion. As, however, it was represented that the organization of the Durham and Northumberland pitmen was complete, it was resolved that in that section of the kingdom, underground labours should be suspended on the 5th of April; but that the other districts should not be called upon to contribute to the expenses of the turn-out. The demands of the colliers were principally as follows:—They sought for payments every week; for six-monthly engagements sure; to be guaranteed five days per week at 3s. a day; to be paid by weight; hewers not to be called on to *put;* day's work to be limited to eight hours, at 3s. In case of accident, they required to be paid 10s. a week, with medical attendance. In case of death, 5s. per week to widow or children for twelve months, and £5 for burial. The terms of the owners were chiefly as follows:—They would give no guarantee for work or wages; term of engagement to be for twelve months, terminable on either side at a month's notice; pay once a fortnight; and hewers to put or do any work required. On the commencement of the strike great bodies of special constables were sworn in; but the conduct of the people, except in a few exceptional instances, was perfectly peaceable. Little or no injury was done to person or property. Every day great meetings were held, and exciting speeches delivered. Many conferences with the masters failed to bring about any amicable result. A religious feeling came to be strangely mixed up with the movement. The Ranters' chapels were crowded, and the success of the strike was prayed for from the pulpit. The people went to chapel and held prayer-meetings, as they said, to "get their faith strengthened." The local preachers were frequently their fellow-workmen. These were often persons gifted with a rude energy and picturesque fluency of language, and their influence was almost unbounded. The men sustained themselves during the strike by various expedients. There were some who had saved money, in anticipation of it, and all began with a fortnight's wages in hand. When these were spent, and the short credit which the small shops could afford to give was exhausted, the pawnbrokers for a time supplied the funds, and in many cases the wedding rings of the wives were the last valuables parted with. The next resource was found in the funds of the benefit clubs, which were broken up. But contributions from the other coal districts came in sparingly and slowly, and the condition of the colliers at length became desperate. Meantime the coal-owners were moving heaven and earth to obtain labour. Men were sent for from Staffordshire, Derbyshire, and Wales, and great numbers were taken from other species of work and sent into the pits. Hardly one colliery was entirely stopped even for a short time. The number of hewers generally employed in the districts of Tyne, Wear, and Tees is 6,000. On the 1st of June, the third month of the strike, 1,386 hewers were at work; on the 15th, 2,656 were at work; and on the 6th of July, 3,975 were in the pits. From the beginning of June the combination melted rapidly away. The influx of strangers intimidated even the most resolute, and towards the end of July there was a rush for employment—the strike was at an end, and the union utterly prostrate and overthrown.

The principal move of the union, previous to the strike, was to impose a restriction upon labour by which each hewer bound himself to earn as little as possible above 3s. a day. The average amount of earnings before the restriction was 3s. 9½d. per day, so that the men submitted to a voluntary loss of about 9½d. a day. Although the union, as I have said, is shattered, there are pits in which the men still restrict their labour. These cases may now, however, be said to be exceptional.

The consequence of the strike was disastrous to coal-owners and coal-workers. The former lost upwards of £200,000 by the four months of partial cessation from labour. The number of the latter was greatly increased by the immigration from other coal districts. Before the strike it was calculated that there were 30 per cent. more labourers in the market than the number requisite to perform the work; and since the resumption of labour, strangers in many cases occupy the places in the cottages and the pit of old hewers, who have been forced to seek employment in the new iron works springing up upon the moors of Durham, Northumberland, and Yorkshire.

# LABOUR AND THE POOR.

—◆—

## THE MANUFACTURING DISTRICTS.

[FROM OUR SPECIAL CORRESPONDENT.]

## THE COAL-FIELD OF NORTHUMBERLAND AND DURHAM.

WHAT A COAL PIT IS.

## Letter XIX.

The traveller who enters the coal country from the manufacturing districts will be struck by the complete change of features presented to him. I have, in the opening letter of this series, sketched the first glances which a railway passenger catches of the cotton country. Let me try, in a few rapid words, to describe the *primâ facie* aspect of the great northern coal region. And first, the visitor will be struck by the comparative paucity of towns. The tendency of textile industry is always to the accumulation of human dwellings. The tall chimneys love to rise in clusters, and every few miles along the line of rail the train passes within gunshot of groups of huge factories, strung together by closely-built rows of mean cottages. But in the coal district the case is different. In traversing that undulating region, the spectator will cast his eyes over vast ranges of country, of peculiarly soft and wavy outline, dotted with those buildings and scaffold apparatus which denote that beneath each of them a mine shaft sinks into the earth, but totally unmarked by that luxuriant crop of towns which the power-loom has called into being. The collier population is scattered because the pits are scattered. Millowners may be next-door neighbours; but when we recollect that the underground corridors of a mine may extend miles and miles from the bottom of the shaft, it is evident that the coal adventurers must give each other ample elbow-room. A "pit row" of cottages, therefore, situated near each shaft, affords accommodation for the population whose daily duty calls them to descend it. Far and near, on slope and hollow, their usually dumpy chimneys hardly peering above black piles of small coal and massive scaffoldings, are to be seen the erections characteristic of the region, and telling of the swart labour carried on hundreds of fathoms beneath our feet. The country shows little of life upon its surface. The soil is cold and clayey—and trees and hedges, if not stunted, are not luxuriant. The visitor will not fail to observe the net of small, rude, black railways, powdered with coal dust, which overlays the whole country—each line stretching away in the direction of a pit heap, and dotted here and there with a convoy of coal waggons—drawn sometimes by horse, sometimes by steam power—speeding from the pit to the shipping place, at some "staith" which runs into the waters of the Tyne, the Wear, or the Tees. The gushes of steam from the engine-house, and the smoke from furnaces burning in the pit and at the surface, tell us that the mines are in full work beneath, while the stranger will observe a characteristic feature in the hill of small coal which surrounds each work, and the scores of tons of which are blazing away unregarded—the oxygen of the air acting upon certain gases distilled from the crumbling, earthy-looking mineral, and thus causing its spontaneous combustion. This catastrophe is rather encouraged than checked by the coal-owners—seeing that, with the exception of comparatively rare cases, small coal is of little value, and that it is very desirable to keep down the size of the pit heap.

Such, then, being the general characteristics of a coal digging country, we will proceed at once to one of the pits, and minutely examine it both above and below ground. Following a road, very often ankle deep in coal mud—passing strings of carts laden with mineral and driven by men with well-besmirched faces, we come to the rising ground, formed in the first instance of the contents of the shaft, added to by the small-coal accumulations of years, and always known as the "pit heap." Scattered round this, upon the waste ground at the bottom, are frequently clusters of mean houses, stables, store-keeping places, and such like. The eye at once catches the grimy bulk of the engine-house, with its hot steam gushes and clank of working mechanism. On the summit of the heap there rise those massive pieces of scaffolding which I have already alluded to. Look to their highest points, and you will observe two wheels, of some eight feet in diameter, set vertically, and round which run ropes or chains, one rising as the other sinks. These are the cords to which we shall have presently to trust ourselves in descending into the bowels of the earth. We proceed to notice things more minutely, as—by means, generally, of a slippery ladder—we mount to the summit of the heap. We usually find that it is partially roofed in. An irregularly built covering stretches, at divers levels, above us, supported by posts and pillars. There is a great bustle and shouting and hurrying to and fro of full and empty tubs of coal, running upon small iron wheels. Looking over a stout railing upon a lower level beneath, we see great screens or oblong iron gratings, stretching at obtuse angles downwards from the stone-paved flooring on which we stand; while beneath them again, upon a rude uneven railway, stand a row of waggons. Everywhere, upon the lower levels, are masses of small coal and coal dust, in which men are shovelling and digging assiduously—some filling carts, some distributing equally the constantly accumulating heap. In corners, horses and carts stand upon the straw-littered earth. As we watch the proceedings on the upper platform, we see strong hardy fellows, with great flannel jackets and leathern defences for the thighs, hurrying the wheeled square tubs along the clattering pavement to the brink. Here the tub tilts over, being only kept from going bodily down by a strong wooden rail against which it falls, upsetting, however, with the shock its cargo into one of the sloping screens beneath, through which the dust and small coal disappear, while the "knobbly" bits slide down into the waggons prepared to receive them. Nothing can be more admirable than the dexterity and strength with which the "banksman" trundles his tubs along the platform, dashes their contents out in an instant, rights them again with a sudden jerk, and then by a dexterous twist sends them spinning back in the direction whence they came. We follow, and perhaps start back from two dark and oblong pits like black graves, yawning in the strong wooden floor which extends at this part of the platform. We are in fact standing over the mouth of the shaft, which of course is circular in shape, but which is always divided by strong wooden partitions reaching from the top to the bottom, into square or oblong compartments of smaller or greater size (according to circumstances which I shall speedily explain), and down which the "cage" containing the tubs slides, steadied by grooved passages, to the bottom of the mine. When we first catch sight of the openings the tubs are probably passing each other half way down the shaft—one set coming up full, the other going down empty. The two ropes are of course spinning past us—one rising from, the other descending, the black abyss. By the edge of what will be the descending shaft in the next trip, stands one of the banksmen in his flannel dress, close to the empty tubs which it will be his duty to deposit in the cage as soon as a colleague has extricated the full ones. At the edge of the nonascending compartment stands another man, dressed in the usual flannel costume, holding in his hand a piece of iron like a pump-handle, connected with which is a simple apparatus for steadying the different stages of the cage as it arrives at the pit mouth, and thus enabling it conveniently to deliver its two or three tiers of coal-laden tubs. Close behind him is a little wooden office or counting-room, with a weighing apparatus, over which the coal tubs are run, and which tells the clerk inside the exact weight of each, a matter which he at once registers. But there is another process hereabouts. You see upon the wall of the office ranges of pegs or nails, with chalked initials beneath each; and hanging from each are a greater or a smaller number of pieces of strong cord, attached to little wooden labels, upon each of which are deeply carved letters corresponding with the chalked initials. A dirty-faced shrill-voiced boy is darting about; and, watching his motions, you suddenly see him pounce upon a tub, untie one of the little pieces of cord from one of its corners—and then, watching his opportunity, just as the tub is being weighed, he shrieks out the initials and the name for which they stand—thus, "J. S., John Smith." This is the name of the hewer who has filled the tub, and the clerk, close to the register of its weight, books that weight of hewn coals to the credit of the labourer who has wrought them. While we are watching the process, the wheels at the top of the great structure of beams and ladders begin to move slowly. The ascending cage is close to the bank of the pit; the alarum bell, which has notified the fact to the engineer, has tingled among the machinery, and with his hand upon the slowly moving lever, he carefully watches the moment to shut the steam off. It has arrived. Up to the ledge of the gulf, with a clatter and a surge comes the cage. It has a strong iron-bound floor, and iron rails, forming as it were the skeleton of a box. This cage stops with its bottom exactly on a level with the edge of the platform; and the banksman, whose business it is, suddenly seizes the tub which it contains, and lugs it out with a wrench, his colleague substituting an empty one— while the third, by a movement of his lever, permits the second tier of the cage, with a second tub, to ascend to the ledge of the aperture. Upon the top of the coals in this second tub there perhaps lies a little piece of rope. This is "a token" that men are coming up as the next cargo, and the lever-man usually apprises the engineer, with whom he can immediately communicate, of the fact. Presently, if you are attentive, you observe a hammer rise from a block of iron, apparently without a hand, and strike two blows. The lever which moved it has been worked at the bottom of the mine, and sometimes the strokes simultaneously resound in the engine-room and at the mouth of the pit. They form the signal that the men are ready to rise. Three blows in some collieries, and one in others, announce that the cargo is coals. The engineer, upon noting the double stroke, does his spiriting gently. The rope begins to move as easily as if a careful hand stirred it—the top cage slowly sinks into the darkness—then the engine gradually puts on its speed, and in a second or two the living freight is careering up through the strata of the earth. Before they make their appearance we shall describe the old and rude method, still practised in some remote parts of the country, of ascending and descending mines.

At one time the shafts were generally open, and undivided by the wooden partitions which now separate them into square boarded compartments. The coals were then raised, not in tubs placed in cages, but simply in "corves" or round baskets, shaped like pots, and with a pot handle, which was attached to the hook in which the chain terminated. The men, however, seldom went down or came up in these corves—there being a risk of their grazing as they passed each other swinging in the darkness of the shaft. To ascend or descend, the pitmen simply stuck a hook in a link of the chain, and formed a loop. Into this two men inserted their right thighs, grasping the chain with their right hands, and armed with small sticks held in the left hand, for the purpose of steadying the motion by keeping the ends of the rods as much as possible in contact with the walls of the shaft. When men were on the chain no corf was allowed to be attached to the other extremity. Two was the regular number who could be accommodated in the loop; but three, four, and five frequently went down or came up, clinging to each other and to the chain. Signals by blows were not then in use. The regular formula of communication between the top and the bottom was as follows:—

The man at the bottom sung out, "Hi! ho!"

To which the banksman responded, "Hillo!"

The first speaker then shouted, "Men going to ride."

The banksman replied, "Men ride away," and gave notice to the engineer. Meantime the people below had hooked themselves on, and when all were ready they shouted up, "Tee ware." Immediately the engine moved, and off they went.

The coal-pits in the North have generally excellent machinery for ascending and descending the shaft; but the Staffordshire pits are notoriously deficient in this respect. During the year from the 1st of

January, 1848, to the 31st of December, there were killed in Staffordshire no less than 37 men by breakage of ropes and chains, while in all
the Durham and Northumberland pits the number so destroyed was
only six. In Staffordshire common chains are generally made use of. In
the North, wire ropes spun flat are becoming very common, although
hemp has still its advocates. A not uncommon accident, occasioned
almost invariably by pure negligence, is that of men being drawn, not
only out of the pit, but right over the wheel and pulley, through the
engine not being stopped in time. This catastrophe involves almost
certain death, as the men are generally precipitated down the shaft,
in which case their coffins have often to be sent below, as it would be
impossible to remove otherwise the shattered fragments of mortality.

But meantime the cage has reached the surface, freighted with
near half-a-dozen hewers and putters—a cluster of black, smirched
faces, and grimy hands holding on to the chains, and flannel jackets
with here and there faint streaks of a shade somewhat resembling the
original colour of the stuff. They speedily disengage themselves from
the cage, and go blinking along in the sudden glare of the daylight.
There are two classes of them—men and lads. All wear flannel jackets
and coarse warm waistcoating. Some have wooden and tin canteens
swung over their shoulders, and canvass bags protruding from their
pockets. The head-dress is generally a greasy cap. The men mostly
carry small straight pickaxes, and wear sometimes trowsers and sometimes breeches and stockings. These are the hewers, and the lads who
accompany them are the putters. The latter wear short drawers not
reaching further down than the centre of the thigh, and a sort of leg-
ging extending from the ankle to below the knee. A great portion
of the limb is thus, but for its covering of coal dust, left perfectly exposed, and one wonders at the impunity with which they ascend, thus
slightly clad, from the hot regions of the mine into the nipping air of
wintry weather. But putters never think of colds or rheumatism.

All things being now ready, we will ourselves descend. If the visitor be wise he will change his hat for a cap, and envelop himself in
his coarsest and oldest pea-coat. We then take our station in the cage.
We shall be told to stand bolt upright, and keep our hands within the
iron railings. The hammer gives a tap to notify that all is ready below,
the banksman tugs his lever, and the same instant—with a feeling
strictly analogous to that which one experiences aboard a steamer as
she shoots from the calm water of a harbour, and performs her first
plunge into the trough of a seaway—the cage sinks beneath us, the

faces of the people above, the buildings, and the sunlight, disappear as if by magic. For a second or two a faint grey glimmer of light shows the perpendicular walls down which we are shooting with a rapid, noiseless, and perfectly easy motion, and then all is pitchy darkness. The sensation now becomes curious. We are utterly unable to tell whether we are going up or down, but the suspense is speedily over; a minute or two, and our speed is palpably checked. A glimmer of red candlelight shines from below, and almost at the same moment we observe that the cage is descending so slowly as to be, to use the expression, feeling for the bottom; and, as we touch the earth again, we see, by the flicker of three or four rushlights stuck in lumps of clay, a dark uncertain sort of hole, with a dripping as of falling water drops—a row or two of coal-laden tubs, over which we have to clamber—half a dozen black hands put out to help us, half a dozen black faces grinning at our perplexity—a sleek horse or two standing motionless beside the tubs—caverned walls, dark and tunnel-like about us, and a curious warm earthy odour, not at all unpleasant, and mixed somehow up with a smell of stables. One of the pitmen immediately hands us one of the lumps of clay, which serve as candlesticks. The contrivance at first seems rude, but long ere you have traversed the pit you will find its excellence. The candles used are very small, being sometimes 40 to the pound, but they give a wonderfully good light. They are stuck through the clay so as to show about an inch above it, and of course you push them up as they burn away. The clay candlestick can be moulded in a minute so as to stick to any ledge or even roughness in the walls. If it be required, two can be at once joined together, and there is a knack of carrying the lump in the hollow of the hand, so as to shield the flame from the draughts. I have seen a pitman carry an inch of candle thus for miles against the main ventilating current, when I have not been able to keep my light alive for a yard.

The workings where the people are actually digging may be a mile or two from the shaft; and while we are plodding our rough way towards it, through dark tunnels paved with little tramways, I shall endeavour plainly and intelligibly to describe the mode of laying out, ventilating, and working a coal mine.

The spot for digging having been fixed upon, the operations are commenced by gangs of "sinkers," who are to regular pitmen what navvies are to regular railway servants. A sinker will sometimes take employment as a hewer, but only when no sinking work is to be got. As soon as he hears of a new mine he is off with his pickaxe and shovel at once. The work of sinking never ceases after it is begun, until the necessary depth is reached. The sinkers work in three gangs, and relieve each other every four hours, day and night. Their turns are so arranged as to give every man alternate spells of four hours' work and eight hours' rest. Their wages may average about 3s. 8d. per day—the daily work-hours numbering, of course, eight. During the early stages of the process the earth excavated is raised to the surface by a machine called a sack roll—in other words, a large winch. When the rocky strata are reached, a gin or capstan is employed, worked by horses; and when the excavators are down some 50 fathoms in the earth, a steam-engine, which will be used afterwards for the general purposes of the pit, is applied. The bed of coal being attained, operations are continued by excavating roomy passages, called rolley-ways, and which may be described as the principal thoroughfares of the mine—both for the passage of coal and air. By this time another shaft has most probably been sunk some dozen yards, more or less, from the first; and the main passages, or galleries, must always be so arranged as to communicate with both. Without such a disposition of matters there would be no means of forcing a current of air through the mine. Some pits, however, have only one shaft, divided into two air-tight compartments by wooden partitions called brattices. The ventilating principle in both cases is the same, but I shall continue to speak of the double-shafted pits, which are the best and happily the most common. These shafts have, of course, different functions to perform, but in all of them a space is partitioned off for the exclusive purpose of conducting down fresh air into the workings, and letting it escape when it is done with. The shaft through which the ventilating current descends is called the down-cast shaft—that through which the air ascends, the up-cast shaft. Almost immediately under the latter, piled upon a great square block of masonry and surrounded by caverned walls, is heaped a vast roaring furnace, burning night and day. The effect of this furnace is, of course, to rarify to a high degree the air beneath the up-cast shaft, and consequently to produce through all the mine a current setting towards it. Of course the cold air descends the other shaft to supply the vacancy; and it is then, by a system of doors and traps, forced to traverse every foot of every passage of the mine, before it is allowed, in popular terms, to be sucked in by the draught of the furnace. As I have hinted in my last letter, this is rather the principle of the system than the actual plan adopted in all cases; for in many mines the air—moving at the rate of, say 400 feet per minute, in the main passages, and creeping at perhaps only the fourth of that speed through the narrower corridors and workings—would take more than twelve hours to permeate the mine, and would return so impure as to be unfit for supporting healthy existence. The current is therefore by a combination of passages and traps, split into different branches, and sent to different districts of the mine, in proportions depending upon the number of people, hewing and putting, in each group of workings. In all the main passages of the pit the current comes by like the blowing of a steady breeze. In the galleries branching off at right angles from the chief rolley-ways, the atmosphere is hardly felt to move, but the slight flare of the candle reveals that the air is not actually stagnant.

The reader will, then, now keep in mind that, from the two shafts, passages or corridors (all connected with each other) branch away in parallel or different directions, as the case may be; the passages connected with the down-cast shaft being traversed by a fresh breeze running into the mine—those connected with the up-cast, traversed by a breeze nearly as strong, but by no means so fresh. The rolley-ways, of course, are cut in the bed of coal, which may rise on either side nearly to the roof, or which may extend only three or four feet up the wall, like the strip of wainscoting in old-fashioned rooms. The next thing to be done is to work out the coals from the bed. Narrow passages are therefore cut, generally about four feet high, right into the coal, at right angles from the rolley-way. These passages are called "headways." At a certain distance they expand into spaces of greater width, of oblong square shape, formed, of course, by the excavation of the coals. These spaces or chambers are called "boards" or workings, and there the coals are hewn. We will suppose that two "boards" are being wrought at once. The miners are, therefore, excavating two oblong chambers at right angles from the rolley-way, and leaving between each a great mass of solid coal. But the boards must be connected, or they could not well be ventilated. A passage is, therefore, dug from one to the other, parallel with the rolley-way, but at the depth of the board from it. Thus it will be seen that a great square pillar of coal is left untouched, but that there is free communication round it, its boundaries being—the rolley-way on one side, the two oblong rooms with their narrow necks on two others, and the passage parallel to the rolley-way on the fourth. I am anxious that this system of "pillar" working should be fully understood, and, therefore, even at the risk of being tedious, I will add a simple illustration. Suppose two bottles to be inserted parallel to each other, and at the distance of a foot, in a bank of earth; their position horizontal, with their apertures just showing on the face of the bank. Now suppose the bottom of the bottles broken out and a pipe in the earth forming a communication between them, so that if you blew into the mouth of one bottle the air would come out at that of the other. This illustration exactly describes the method in which the mines are worked. Each pillar of coal left entire supports the roof, and the process is carried on, square after square being formed, until the boundary of the mine is reached, or until the difficulty of ventilating the labyrinth of boards puts a stop to progress in that direction. The boards are generally about five yards wide, and the pillars are generally about sixteen by twenty yards. It will be seen, therefore, that the miner at first leaves nearly two-thirds of the coal untouched. The reason of the narrow passage opening into the boards is to facilitate blocking them up after they are exhausted and after a "goaf" has been formed; and also to give conveniences for regulating the supply of air. The hewer is at his labour in the board, cutting down the coal; thus, of course, enlarging every hour the chamber in which he works, and filling from time to time the tubs which stand beside him, and which the putter directly seizes, and pushes upon narrow tramways back out through the boards and narrow necks into the rolley-way. The little trapper opens the door for him to pass—a door, which were it not kept shut, would allow the air-current to escape into the main corridor, instead of forcing it to make its way as it will do, into the next board; and the driver outside in the rolley-way, with his low platform-like train, receives and places upon it the coal-filled tubs which the putter delivers into his hands, and when his freight is complete makes the best of his way with it out to the pit shaft.

Having carried his workings as far as is deemed practicable, the miner returns upon his steps, and attacks the oblong pillars of coal hitherto left untouched. As he digs them away, he inserts strong props, to stay up the roof. This state of things, when a vast hollow in the earth is kept from collapsing by props, is called a "jud." But as not even a prop is lost, if it can be helped, in a coal-pit, the workmen cautiously withdraw them, beginning of course at the furthest end. As the supports are removed, the roof falls in with more or less rapidity. Sometimes tons of earth come tumbling down at once. Sometimes the descent is more gradual. Thus by degrees, successive rows of props are taken away, and the space in which they stood is occupied by a chaos of broken strata, heaped together with more or less solidity, but generally intersected with cracks, crevices, and hollow chambers, formed by the irregular shapes of the fallen rocks and stones. This dreary space is called a "goaf," and every mine which has been for some time worked possesses one, the dimensions of which, of course, are being daily added to. Old mines of great extent have several goafs, and sometimes they each include dozens of acres of space. A mine thoroughly worked out will be all goaf, and probably the majority of pits have a nucleus of fallen and crumbling strata. These goafs are too often the plague-spots of coal-mines. Towards the centre they are supposed to be more solid and compact than nearer the edges; but as a vast quantity of coal has been extracted, and as the surface of the country above seldom sinks, it is evident that there must be a vacant space left beneath. But goafs are seldom or never, indeed they cannot be, ventilated. Very often, in the expressive language of the pitmen, they are "lying dead," without a cubic foot of fresh air circulating through their winding crevices and splintered chambers. They then become the fertile generators of foul gases. The fire-damp rises slowly from these unwholesome recesses, and being one-half lighter than common air, ascends to the caverned roof of the vault. There, of course, it is harmless. No one works near a goaf without a safety-lamp, but occasionally—often on account of fresh falls from the roof—the space occupied by the vapour is lessened, and it struggles to set itself free, and gradually leaks through crack and crevice into the working parts of the pit. The terrible results the public are well acquainted with.

I have thus given a general outline of the nature and arrangement of a coal-pit, with its down-cast and up-cast shafts, its main corridors, or rolley-ways, and its workings branching off in square labyrinths—sometimes from one side, sometimes from both, of the main passages. I shall now therefore proceed, trusting that the reader will find no difficulty in following me, to sketch the actual appearance of a pit, and the nature of the employment of the several classes of workmen. In most respects the labour and the condition of the labourer in all pits are very much the same. The differences lie in the nature of the seam in process of being dug—in the distance which the hewer has to walk underground before he reaches the workings—in the varying degrees of temperature, altering as they do at various depths—and in the efficiency of the ventilating apparatus in sending the air current through the recesses of the pit.

These are subjects upon which I shall afterwards have to touch; at present I proceed with my description of the underground features of a pit. Our progress will be first along the rolley-way, our destination being of course the workings. The path is occupied by a single tramway, the space between the rails being taken up by short sleepers, laid as close as the rounds of a ladder. On one or both sides there trickle down to the well or "sunk," near the shaft, driblets in some cases, and rivulets in others, of salt and muddy water. Presently you may meet a party of pitmen returning from work. You hear their voices, and see the glimmer of their light at a distance; and presently they pass you—in Indian file—a ghastly-looking procession, seen by the flickering light of the single candle half enclosed in the hollows of the leader's hand. You will not go far without hearing the noise of an approaching train of waggons. The sound rumbles and reverberates, so that it requires a practised ear to distinguish in which direction the convoy is proceeding. Presently, however, you see the gleam of a light approaching, and very likely the shrill voice of a boy singing some popular ditty at the top of his voice. You stand aside, squeezing yourself against the damp wall, to allow the train to go by. It is drawn by a single horse at a walking pace, and may convey a dozen or fourteen loaded tubs. The platforms upon which these are placed are not more than two feet from the ground. The driver is usually a lad under eighteen. He always sits just behind the horse, with his legs extended upon the low shafts between which the animal is yoked. He has a single light swinging in a lamp from the top of the foremost tub, but so placed as to be invisible until you are close upon it. These drivers are paid like the trappers, by the day, and their wages may average about 1s. 2d. They enter and leave the mines with the putters. Occasionally considerable portions of the way are inclined planes, where the services of horses are not required. The full waggons running down pull the empty ones up. At either end of the inclined plane, a couple of individuals, generally a man and a boy, are stationed to arrange the waggons. There is a bell wire in many instances running along the roof of the passage, and a vigorous tug at this by the man below announces to his coadjutor above, that he may start the loaded waggons, which come careering down like thunder, in the darkness. The glimmer of light at what may be called the station is commonly afforded by a candle, stuck by means of clay to a post or the wall. We may now be supposed to have advanced some distance into the mine, and a difference is perceived in the atmosphere. The men generally tell you that they are quite comfortable; but, however much they may be accustomed to the comparative closeness, a stranger is apt to feel an unpleasant sense of oppression on the chest, accompanied with a slight degree of nausea. As soon, however, as the heated air produces copious perspiration these unpleasant feelings go off—at least they did so in my case; and I afterwards felt no inconvenience when more than a mile further in, and away altogether from the main channel.

In traversing the Gosforth Pit I was struck with the aspect of a little workshop excavated in the wall near the top of an inclined plane, and tenanted by a single old man, who has charge of all the safety-lamps used in the mine. He sat at a bench with a great jar of oil by his side, busily employed in filling and trimming the lamps, which, when he had finished, he hung upon the wall on ranges of hooks, the initials of the miners being chalked below them. In the passages Davy lamps are not required, but in the distant workings apart from the main stream of air, they are commonly used, whether the existence of gas be suspected or not. I inquired whether the men ever lighted their pipes at the lamps. The old man didn't know but what they might sometimes. It required good suction to get the flame through the gauze, but "some on 'em had a rare twist with the pipes in their cheeks." The old lamp-trimmer sat in his gnome-like workshop nine hours a day. There was a second small chamber off it, in which were placed a vice, hammers, files, and other instruments required for the repair of the metal parts of the lamps.

In following the track of a rolley-way, you often observe examples of the "pitches" and "troubles" with which miners have to contend. Sometimes the seam makes a sudden bend upwards or downwards, involving, unless it speedily returns to its former pitch, the necessity of a change of level in the workings; at other times a band of clayey stone or shale intersects it. It is curious to observe the thin layers of unworkable coal, perhaps two or three inches thick, glancing like a black riband along the lighter-coloured strata through which the passage has been cut. In some points props are fastened to strengthen and support the sides, and in others the corridor is regularly built in with masonry, so as to appear precisely like a railway tunnel. In moving with the current of air you feel its influence in a very small degree, and the reflux and agitation produced by the going by of a train is most refreshing. After having passed, it may be, several stations at the bottoms and tops of inclined planes—at each of which the attendants will probably be sitting upon lumps of coal or rude benches, or on the waggons, waiting for the moment when their services are called into operation—we reach a point whence we can diverge into the workings. A row of waggon frames stands here, opposite an aperture in the wall which may measure, say from three to four feet square, and raised about two feet above the tramway, so as to allow the tubs pushed out of it to glide at once, without change of level, upon the framework. We now come, for the first time, upon the Putters. You hear a shouting and a clattering in the black hole before you, and in a minute a coal-tub emerges, with a crash, upon the locomotive platform—and you perceive a figure, more than half-naked, pouring with perspiration, and, of course, as black as a negro, who has looked out for a moment, exchanged a word with the driver, and then disappeared in the recesses of the "headway," shoving an empty tub before him. This is the Putter, and we shall follow him. Clambering over the waggons we find ourselves in a narrow passage, ruggedly cut among the coals, and the painful stooping position generally necessary to traverse which speedily makes one think of taking to all-fours as a luxury. At all events, you almost envy the putter the tub upon which he leans as he pushes it out and in. Here, as in the rolley-way, there is a tramroad, the rails being necessarily of a very narrow gauge. About half-way to where the board opens up, we pass an air door, attended by a trapper. The poor little fellow sits squatted on the ground in a recess, holding a cord in his hand, with which he chucks-to the door after the putter and his tub have passed. If he can beg or pick up any candle-ends, the trapper has the luxury of light; if not, he must sit quietly in the darkness. The trapper's wages are always 10d. a day. The air is first forced into the boards by means of either a door or barrier in the main passage, and then, as it cannot escape back again towards the furnace by the nearest way, it necessarily courses through every part of the workings. Leaving the trapper behind, we can probably catch at length the faint click of the picks which the hewers are wielding, and presently the passage through which we are crawling opens into a sort of shallow chamber—the "board"—heaped with loose coal, the roof strengthened by short props and cross bars, and at the farther end of it gleam the glowworm-like sparks of the Davy lamps. We are now fairly in the recesses of the pit, and the eye being by this time pretty well accustomed to the darkness, we can watch the hewers at their work. The labour would be toilsome even in the fresh air, but in the deep recesses of a mine it must be very fagging. The short straight pick is the principal implement employed, with iron wedges, and mallets for driving them into the seam when the coal shows a tendency to come away in large lumps. Gunpowder is only employed in the more open parts of the mine. Of course, to fire a train where Davy lamps are habitually requisite would be madness. The toil of the hewer depends greatly upon the thickness of the seam, which prescribes the attitudes in which he is obliged chiefly to labour. Sometimes he stands; sometimes he works on his knees; sometimes he flings himself down on his side, to get at the lower part of the bed. The skill and endurance of the hewer are mostly shown by the facility with which he can accommodate his postures to the nature of the seam, and the vigour and effect with which he can labour in them all. The coal is always pretty compactly lodged, and requires a smart blow to bring down even an ordinary shovel-full; and this is the more felt from the cramping position, often among props and posts, in which the limbs have to be exerted. The men work in flannel shirts and short drawers, with the perspiration washing every now and then a new white streak in their besmirched faces. Close behind the hewer stand one or more empty tubs, which he has to fill. He then attaches to the staple fixed in the corner of each one of the little cords and wooden labels already described, and the putter wheels it out, by main force, through the narrow passages. The hewers of course take down with them as many labels as they expect to fill tubs. Their hours of work are at present eight or nine per day. Here and there a very hard-working man will work somewhat longer. In some pits there are relays of hewers, so as to carry the work on until late at night, but the following plan is more generally adopted:—The hewers enter the pit at two or three in the morning, and set to work; the putters come to their aid two hours from the time they have commenced, so as to find coals hewn and ready to be carried out. In some pits another set of hewers enter at eight or nine o'clock; but this, I repeat, is not a general practice. As the putters arrive two hours later than the hewers, so they remain behind them to accomplish their task. There is one putter to every three or four hewers, and the like proportion of drivers and other labourers employed about the waggons and inclines to every three or four putters. These last are, as has been mentioned, lads generally under twenty. Their work requires constant stooping, and constant and severe muscular exertion. They have generally begun as trappers—then they have been team drivers—after which they have been promoted to putting, and of course look forward to becoming hewers. It is not easy for people who never saw the employment to realize to themselves what putting is. Let them, however, just try to fancy a pitchy dark, oblong hole, just about big enough to contain an ordinary sofa. Then let them fancy the shoving and dragging of waggons holding about 7 cwt. of coal from one end of this hole to the other—the labourer always of course stooping almost double, and the thermometer seldom below 75 degrees. This is what is called "putting coals." Although mere lads are engaged in it I fancied the muscular exertion to be even more than that requisite in the hewer's labour. Both hewers and putters are paid by the quantity of coals extracted, and the latter make nearly as much as the former, their wages averaging from 3s. to 3s. 6d. per day. Of course the amount must depend on the quantity of coal picked by the hewers. The latter will earn, if they do not restrict themselves, something like 3s. 10d. or 4s. per day; and besides this they have certain advantages in the way of house accommodation, which I shall afterwards allude to. The pitmen take what provisions they need during their working hours down with them. They have canteens and bags for the solids, called "bait pokes." No beer or spirits is allowed in any mine whatever, and the men all agree in the reasonableness of the regulation. In the canteens they have coffee, which they drink cold, milk, and water. The putters consume an immensity of water, notwithstanding the heat and perspiration in which they are continually bathed. In many pits casks of the pure fluid are provided for these poor thirsty fellows. I have peeped into several "bait pokes," and generally found their contents to be great hunches of bread, with smaller portions either of meat or of cheese. These small haversacks are hung to nails upon props, until their proprietors feel sufficiently appetised to attack them. The hewers generally labour by threes or fours in the same board. They are, I was told by some good authorities, although the statement was denied by others, by no means fond of working alone, from superstitious considerations. Many of the old-fashioned ideas in this respect are dying away, but the mining population, particularly the hewers, are still very attentive to signs and omens before they commence their day's work. They account it specially unlucky to cross a woman on their way to the pit. Considering the hour at which they leave home, the conjunction does not probably often take place; but many a miner, if he catches a glimpse, or fancies he does so, of the flutter of a female dress, will turn on his heel and go back to bed again. A gentleman informed me that he had once unwittingly stopped the day's working of a pit by passing the "row," when the men were going to their labour, wrapped up in a light-coloured plaid. He afterwards learned that there was a grand consultation held on the bank, and that it was unanimously resolved that nothing could be more rash than going into the pit after several of the party had distinctly seen a ghost. The superstitions of the pitmen, however, form a subject on which I shall afterwards have occasion to touch.

The labour of the putter is at present being considerably infringed upon by the introduction of Shetland ponies small enough to traverse the headways, and strong enough speedily to hurry out the tubs. The horses used in mines, after they are once brought down, seldom see the light again. They are generally in capital condition, the warm air making their coats sleek, and their docility is very striking. Indeed, unruly horses would never do for pit labour. The stables are usually situated close to the down-cast shaft, and, except being a trifle darker, are very like stables above ground. The horses are attended to by stablemen who do not interfere in any other work of the pit.

In returning from the recesses of the mine, which we may do by the up-cast passages, we have an opportunity of seeing the furnace, attended by its solitary watchman. The rush of air close to an efficient furnace forms a current which a sailor would call a topgallant-sail breeze. There are generally two fire-trimmers, who relieve each other night and day. The smoke of the furnace and the impure air escape by the up-cast shaft together. If you stand by its brink, you will observe the vapour rising like a dense steam from the pit. The pumping apparatus may be fixed in either shaft. Every thirty-three feet from top to bottom there is a cistern, inserted in a recess cut in the side of the shaft for the purpose, and the water is raised by different sets of rods, from one cistern to the other, until it is elevated to the surface.

Such, then, is a general view of a coal mine and of the labour of those who work in it. There are many points in this letter slightly touched on, with respect to which I shall afterwards enter into fuller details, but I cannot close without acknowledging the kind attention of Mr. John Mainham, the intelligent and courteous under-viewer of the Gosforth Colliery, to whom I am indebted for facilities for acquiring practical mining information, from which much of this communication has been drawn up.

# LABOUR AND THE POOR.

—◆—

## THE MANUFACTURING DISTRICTS.

[FROM OUR SPECIAL CORRESPONDENT.]

## THE MINING DISTRICTS OF DURHAM AND NORTHUMBERLAND.

## Letter XX.

In this and my next communication I propose to describe with minuteness the daily toil and life of a coal miner in Northumberland and Durham. I shall detail the conditions of his labour—by which I mean the varying terms and discipline under which it is carried on. I shall describe the ordinary dwellings in which he and his family live—their sanitary and material condition; and, recurring to the underground work, I shall give some account of the accidents to which pitmen are exposed, and state, as I am enabled to do, the opinion of a great mass of the mining operatives upon the nature and efficiency of the precautions at present taken against such catastrophes. I shall also detail the grievances chiefly complained of by the mining population, stating likewise the representations upon the other side—of the coal owners. It will be also my duty to give a general view of the moral and educational condition of the pit population—to describe their social state and peculiarities—to sketch their amusements and their superstitions, and, generally, to do what I can towards producing an elaborate picture of the mining population of the north.

The reader having been already informed as to the general nature of the coal trade, its growth, extent, the present population dependent upon it, and the laws affecting it, and having also been presented with a description of what a coal mine is, will, it is hoped, be able to understand and appreciate the details which are now about to be placed before him.

Until 1844, pitmen, and indeed everybody connected with pits, were always hired by the year. The "binding," as it was called, took place at the end of March. The men then assembled at the colliery, and met the proprietor or his agents, who read the bond, detailing the

terms to be paid, and the discipline and regulations of the mine. To
this the labourers affixed their names or marks. Earnest money, called
"arles," was then given. Up to 1804 the arles frequently amounted to
two or three guineas. At that date the sum was reduced to half-a-
crown, and since the strike in 1844 the custom has been totally abolished. The bond, as it is at present drawn out, invariably stipulates
that the engagement on either side is terminable at a month's notice.
The pitmen, I must say, are a class of people not always to be easily
pleased. When the bond held them for a year, they urged that it placed
them under an unduly lengthened thraldom. At present, complaints
are not wanting that the monthly system enables masters to dismiss
their hands without giving sufficient warning. The bond usually commences by binding all the persons hired to hew, work, fill, drive, and
put coals, or to do such other work as they may be directed, and as
shall appear necessary to the owners for carrying on with advantage
the operations of the mine. Thus, at a pinch, any man is bound to
perform any sort of work. The bond next sets forth that the wages are
to be paid fortnightly, and it recounts the rates to be adopted for the
working of different seams—the coals to be in all cases sent to bank
in a clean and mercantile state, and free from all refuse. The method
of working to be pursued is then stipulated, and the allowance, if any,
of gunpowder to the hewers set forth. Since the abolition, however,
of the yearly-binding, powder is very rarely furnished by the owners. The rate of wages payable to the putters is next stated—that rate
differing according to the distance which they will have to push the
tubs. Next, the wages of the day labourers are set forth, and parents
of trap-boys are cautioned against deceiving the managers of the pits
as to their children's ages. Stipulations are also commonly made for
the weighing of the coals sent to bank. The allowance for deficient
weight (if any), and the quantity of refuse permitted in each tub, are
then stated, with the penalties to be incurred if either condition be violated. Articles are then inserted, binding the workpeople to continue
the servants of the proprietors, in the case of the working of the mine
being temporarily discontinued, and binding the proprietors to pay
a certain amount of wages for all such times of abeyance; the men,
meantime, obliging themselves, in consideration of these wages, to
set themselves to any work which the proprietors direct. The day's
work for a hewer is defined to be a day "not exceeding eight hours;"
and the hewers are bound not to leave the pit until they have hewn
and filled a corresponding quantity of coals. The day's work of the

operatives paid a fixed weekly wage is commonly understood to consist of twelve hours—the period commencing with the hour when the engine begins to draw coals to the surface. When the hewers are required to act as putters, they receive a certain extra amount of wages called "furtherance." The bond then commonly goes on to provide that all persons to whom the proprietors assign houses, hold those houses not as tenements, but as part of their wages, and to bind the recipients to give up possession within a certain number of days after the termination of the hiring. The bond sometimes, although by no means invariably, terminated with a clause binding the workmen to keep no horses, donkeys, dogs, poultry, or, in some cases, pigs. This provision is, however, now very generally exploded, or at all events if made, is not enforced. Pigs, dogs, and poultry, in especial abound in most colliery villages.

Such, then, is a general statement of the stipulated terms on which the pitmen descend to their work. I proceed to detail their habits of daily toil and life. The hewer only requires tools. There are drills for boring into the seam when gunpowder is to be used, picks for separating the masses of coal, iron wedges and mells for loosening the mineral, when blasting is not permitted, and shovels for filling the tubs. The picks and drills are usually the property of the hewer; the mells, wedges, and sometimes the shovels, are found him. A hewer possesses at least half a dozen picks. They may cost about 1s. 8d. each. He generally fits the hafts to them himself, and a blacksmith, partially paid by the colliery, keeps the iron part in order. The picks have to be sharpened every day, so each hewer when he ascends goes straight with his implement to the blacksmith's shop, and next morning finds it laid out in readiness for him. The hewer pays 2d. per fortnight to the blacksmith. Gunpowder for blasting is, as I have said, in the great majority of cases, found by the men themselves. Sometimes they are compelled to buy both it and their candles of the overmen, who occasionally supply the articles. The powder, which is very coarse stuff, costs 6d. per lb., and hewers will often use from three to four pounds in a fortnight. They make the cartridges in which it is fired at their leisure. In some collieries the men have a powder and candle magazine established in a detached building, and attended to by one of themselves, whom they pay for the purpose. They are thus supplied with the articles at cost price. As an instance of the too prevalent recklessness of miners, I may mention that I have found men smoking in a magazine with scores of pounds of powder lying in paper bags upon the shelves. The candles used are sometimes thirty, and sometimes forty, and, rarely, sixty to the pound. A hewer will require about two pounds of candles in a fortnight. Like the powder, they cost about 6d. a pound. Out of the fortnight's wages of a hewer are, therefore, to be deducted the price he pays for his gunpowder and candles, amounting probably to about 2s. 6d. a fortnight. Davy lamps are always found and partly kept in order by the colliery. I have described the lamp-trimmer whom I saw in Gosforth Pit. The hewers on returning from work pass the shop—there are such in every pit—and the lamp-man unscrews the bottom part of the lamps to be refilled and trimmed. The men carry the gauze cylinders home with them and clean them carefully, as, should the wire net work become partially clogged with coal dust, the danger of explosion is greatly increased. I have described the excellent pit candlesticks, made of lumps of clay. The clay is generally obtained by the wives or children of the hewers, who will sometimes threaten to "lie idle" unless they are kept well supplied. Men working with Davy's have, in a money point of view, a slight advantage over those labouring with candles, but they carry on their toil by a worse light, and of course in a more dangerous position. Drivers are supplied with lanterns—called, I believe, "mistresses," by the pit. The poor little trap-boys have no such advantage, and light is too expensive a luxury for them to buy. If their parents are indulgent they will give them a couple of candles per day to light them in and out of the pit. These poor little fellows often complain grievously of sitting for twelve hours at a stretch in the dark. After the first few hours, the pitmen have told me that the constant cry of the trappers to all who pass their solitary stations is, "What o'clock is it?" or, "Will it soon be time to call kenner?"—the latter phrase signifying an expression shouted down the shaft by the banksman, and repeated throughout the workings, when the hour has arrived for knocking off and ascending to the surface. As might be expected, the trap-boys are not by any means devoid of superstitious terrors. After an accident they are especially sensitive, and have a great aversion to going near places where the dead bodies have been laid previously to being brought to bank. For all this, however, it rarely happens that the parents have to use any compulsion to force a boy to work. The hewers are in the practice of taking their children very early down into the pit, and habituating them to its repulsive features; while, if a boy has been at school, he is generally delighted to exchange the discipline of the class even for work underground. The number of trap-door boys required at present is, however, far less than it used to be; the doors being now commonly constructed with springs so as to swing-to every time they are opened. As a general rule, a trap-boy is placed as near his father or brothers as is practicable. The putters who pass by the doors are notoriously careless as to whether the trapper does his duty or not. Indeed, this recklessness appears common to almost every workman in coal pits. It is the business of the putters to push their tubs through the doors, and they appear to take no heed whether or no the portals are closed behind them. Indeed, I understand it to be by no means unusual for the putter to run the tub with such precipitancy as to break or disable the door, which will probably remain for several hours in an imperfect state before it is repaired by the deputies.

The last-mentioned class of functionaries I have not yet alluded to. I may therefore now sketch their duties, along with those of another body of *employés*—generally classed with them—the overmen. Both overmen and deputies are ordinarily selected from the hewers. Their wages range from 18s. to 25s. per week, and to them are usually assigned the best houses in the pit village. The overmen in a mine hold analogous positions to boatswains' mates on shipboard, or corporals in a regiment. They are the lowest persons in authority. The deputies are employed in fixing props and brattices, and generally in taking charge of the woodwork of a mine, a department on the efficient discharge of the duties of which the ventilation of the pit entirely depends. When gunpowder is used in safety-lamp works, the deputy always fires the charge. Both classes of officials are nominally, and no doubt often really, selected from the most experienced and most intelligent of the hewers; but an unpopular appointment of the kind is sure to result in a charge against the masters of partiality and favouritism. A number of the deputies, I have been informed by the pit hands, are "blacklegs"—that is, men who have kept aloof from the Union, and generally declined to join in strikes. It is the duty of the overmen and deputies to descend into the pit by midnight, or before it, and to traverse the whole of the workings, in order to see that there is no appearance of dangerous gases or of symptoms of fall from the roof. When anything wrong is apprehended, the inspecting party leave a rude caution, in the shape of a prop or a shovel flung across the path, as a token for the hewers, when they arrive, to go no further. Sometimes they chalk a word of warning upon the blade of a shovel, and stick it upright in the castle; but so profound is the ignorance of many of the pitmen, that an intelligent hewer informs me that shovels have been frequently kept until he made his appearance, when they were presented to him, with a request that he would decipher the mystic hieroglyphics.

There is, generally speaking, a watch kept all night upon the pit heap; and at the proper hours, the sentinel, who is termed from one part of his duties the "callsman," proceeds round the colliery village to rouse the hewers—rapping at every door and proclaiming that it is time to turn out. A great number of the pits are worked by two shifts or sets of hewers—called respectively the fore-shift and the back-shift. In these cases the callsman proceeds on his first round about one o'clock in the morning. The hewers composing the fore-shift thereupon turn out and array themselves in their working dresses, which are generally left roasting before the fire. They let themselves out, falling-to latches being attached to the door, for the purpose of securing them thereafter, and proceed to the shaft, which they de-scend in parties of half-a-dozen or more. About two hours after the hewers have been at work, the callsman makes a second round, and summons the drivers, putters, and trap-boys. By this time the hew-ers have filled a sufficient number of tubs to set their coadjutors to work, and as soon as the engine begins to heave up its first load of coals to the bank, the day's work, so far as regards those who work by the day, is held to have commenced. The back-shift of hewers "go in" about eight or nine o'clock in the morning. The fore-shift come out about ten or eleven a.m., and the back-shift about four or five p.m. The men of each shift change hours every week, the fore-shift of one week being the back-shift of the next.

About eleven o'clock in the forenoon, then, the first party knock off work. They place their picks in the waggons, take them out again at the bottom of the shaft, and, having ascended, proceed with them to the blacksmith's shop. By the time they get home, their well-earned breakfast is waiting them. But instead of sketching in general terms a fore-shift man's method of passing his day, I will transcribe, almost *verbatim*, the statement of one pitman—a statement which, upon very extensive inquiry, I find may be taken as giving a fair specimen of the habits of the body.

"Well, sir, when I get to bank I'm very ready for my breakfast. We're all that. Pitmen have the best of appetites. No one can beat the hewers in that way, except, perhaps, the putters. They've a won-derful swallow, certainly. My mistress knows better nor to keep me waiting when I come to bank. If I expect to ride (ascend the shaft) at ten o'clock, she has the coffee hot by nine o'clock, in case I should be sooner nor I thought. I don't wash until I have my breakfast. I'm two sharp-set for that. Aye, aye, I must have my coffee and bread before I do aught else. 'Refreshment in the pit?' No, sir, I only take in a bit of bread in my bail-poke, or, may-be, wrapped in a bit o' clout, and a drop o' water in the canteen. The drivers and trappers take down more, because they stay longer than us. Well, when I've had my coffee—it used to be porridge, but we've got more genteel now—I warrant you I've a good wash—a wash all over. There's always warm water ready, and soap. Cold won't bring the muck off, and besides, warm's comfortabler like—I get to bed. 'Too tired to wash, and go to bed without it?' Bless you, sir, ask the mistress if she would let me do that. No, no. She has over-much respect for the sheets. Pretty sheets they would be if colliers got into them without washing. Well, sir, I have a sleep of two or three hours, till the afternoon; then I get up, and feel quite ready for dinner. We don't get so much flesh-meat as we could eat, I assure you. What a man has in that way depends on circumstances. If he has a large young family, it's little enough, you may take your oath of it. Still, a man who works like a hewer must have nourishing meat. That's a necessity. He couldn't handle the pick without. A single man gets two or three pound of meat in a week, but we make it go as far as we can. We have often suet puddings and dumplings. They're great things with the pitmen, are suet dumplings. We never have any beer or ale at dinner—only water; but we generally manage to have some ale on Saturday nights, particularly on pay-weeks. Well, after dinner I've generally a lot of little things to do, perhaps about my tools, perhaps about my garden. Maybe I may sit down and make cartridges for the shots, or put new hafts to the picks, or I may dander in and speak to a neighbour, or have a game at quoits, or a walk to breathe the fresh air. Some of us that have a turn that away read books, or make small things in the furniture way, especially bird cages and little chests of drawers for ornament, or we smoke our pipes before the door. Then we have some tea, and go to bed, perhaps about seven o'clock or eight o'clock. Those who go in late in the morning have dinner when they come to bank, and then go to bed. They have tea when they rise again, and can do what they like till night, when they turn in in time enough to get up very well by seven o'clock, or six o'clock; and that, sir, is a very fair account of a pitman's day."

The clothes used for the mine are, as I have said, made entirely of coarse flannel. Sometimes the wives are competent to shape and sew them. Sometimes they are purchased at slop-shops at Newcastle. A hewer's dress consists of a long jacket with large pockets, a waist-coat, a flannel shirt, a pair of short drawers reaching to the middle of the thigh, a pair of stout flannel trowsers worn over them, with worsted stockings or "hoggers"—that is, stockings with the feet cut away. Many of the hewers who wear hoggers envelop their feet in rags to prevent the coal dust getting between the toes. They all wear stout shoes. While at their work, the heat is commonly found so oppres-sive that the hewers often fling off every stitch save the short drawers. They generally, however, come to the pit mouth fully dressed. The putters, on the contrary, make their appearance, as I have already de-scribed, in the short drawers with or without "hoggers." A pit suit of good material and fair workmanship will cost about a pound. In spite of their grimy avocation, there are probably no members of the labouring classes more clean than the pitmen of Northumberland and Durham when above ground. They have a thorough scrubbing with soap and hot water every day of their lives, and they generally dress in far better style than the ordinary run of labouring men. Indeed, it is difficult to believe that the clean, respectably-attired person who ac-costs you is the same begrimed, three-parts naked being, whose white gleaming eyes and teeth you remember as he turned round from the wall of coal, and held up his Davy-lamp for your convenience. I was remarking one day how exceedingly black a putter looked, when, half-an-hour after, I beheld him emerge from his home, his complexion almost as light as that of an Albino, and a profusion of "lint-white locks" streaming in dandified curls down his cheeks.

A pit-row is like nothing whatever in the shape of a collocation of dwelling places that I know of in England. It is neither like a coun-try village, nor a section of the meaner part of a manufacturing town; but it appears to me to possess more than the inconveniences of the one, and more than the ugliness of the other. The shops, if anything worthy of the name exist at all, are of the meanest and most miserable description. From end to end there is not a single large house, a tree, or a church spire to break the shabby uniformity of the pitmen's cot-tages. The general run of chapels, principally belonging to Methodist bodies, which abound, may be distinguished from barns only by being far smaller and more paltry looking. But I shall endeavour to sketch the *tout ensemble.* Fancy, then, in the vicinity of the pit-heap, a suc-cession of rows of one-storied, red-tiled cottages. Sometimes they are arranged in double lines on all sides of a square, leaving a black, dismal vacancy in the centre. But more commonly they fill up an oblong space, the longitudinally running rows being, however, unbroken by cross-streets. Uniform as all the houses at first appear to be, a second glance will show that there are differences. In some rows the ridge of the roof is equi-distant from the eaves—the two surfaces of tiles sloping at similar angles. In others, a series of smaller houses, in the manner of lean-to's, appears to have been added to the original tenements; although, in fact, the whole row was so constructed from the beginning. By this method of building, the houses have a one-sided appearance, fully twice as much of their bulk extending on one side as on the other. These peculiarities of construction produce three distinct classes of houses. The third, or lowest class, is formed by the back house, or lean-to. The second class is formed of the front houses to which the smaller ones are attached; and a house of the first or best class is produced by flinging a front and a back tenement into one dwelling. Opposite the doors, on either side of every row, will be observed small detached buildings with the roof sloping in one way only, and here and there will be scattered little houses like miniature dwellings, but adorned with chimneys from which smoke occasionally issues. The first erections are pantries and larders, one of which is attached to every house; the second are ovens, at which the bread of a dozen families can be baked at once.

Let us now proceed along the streets of the colliery village. Almost without exception they will be found in a miserably filthy condition. Sometimes ash-pits have been formed with singular judgment close to the larders, but most commonly the ashes and all sorts of domestic refuse are flung into the centre of the street. All the way along the dismal thoroughfare runs a sierra of "middens," with here and there a filthy pig-sty. In a few colliery villages there is a feeble attempt at surface-drainage, the liquid refuse in these channels being very frequently stagnant; but in not one pit-row out of the scores I have seen, and in not one pit-row, I am told, in Northumberland and Durham, is there a single foot of underground drainage, calculated, by means of sinks, to carry away domestic slops. And these rows, be it observed, were not built piecemeal by poor men, ignorant of the importance of drainage to health and life; they were, one and all, constructed wholesale by the owners of the neighbouring pits, for the accommodation of their workpeople, and they are the only houses in which these workpeople can possibly live. But I have a more serious charge to bring against the owners of colliery villages even than that involved in lack of drainage. There may be exceptions to the general rule (if there be, I have not seen them); but the general, almost the universal rule in Durham and Northumberland is the construction of little towns—for many pit villages may be so called—without the erection of one single privy or cesspool, either public or private. The few privies which, in rare instances, do exist, are rude constructions of boards, built by the occupants of the houses themselves, and generally located in corners of gardens. I repeat that, to their flagrant disgrace, the owners of the pit villages of the north have made not the slightest provision for public decency or public health in the respect in question. In the worst parts of Manchester and Oldham, I have found some sort of accommodation of the kind, exceedingly defective, and often exceedingly filthy. It was reserved for the pit owners of Northumberland and Durham to set every claim of nature and common self-respect alike at defiance. Of course the consequences of such a state of things may be imagined. I have dwelt upon the point, because I have been over and over again most earnestly entreated by the pitmen to bring the circumstance before the public, as one in which not only the convenience and the health, but the feelings and the morals of the mining population are deeply concerned.

The houses of the pit villages may, as I have stated, be divided into three classes. Those of the lowest grade usually contain only one room; those of the second class contain a large room and an attic. The best houses consist of two rooms on the ground floor, with generally an attic over one of them. In all cases, the sitting-room door is the street-door. It will be obvious that tenements so arranged furnish miserably deficient accommodation. The largest families have only two habitable rooms, the others being wretched lofts, with the tiles left bare, and so low that even beneath the ridge of the roof a man cannot stand upright. But two-roomed houses fall to the lot of perhaps only one-third of the mining population. The dwellings, as I have stated, are accounted part of the wages, and they are apportioned by the proprietor or his agents, not so much according to the family of each pitman as according to the family he has working, or likely to work, in the mine. A young married couple go, after their union, into one of the back or lean-to houses. Here they remain until they have a young family around them. Then they are probably transferred to one of the second-class dwellings, of one room, with an attic, and by the time that the boys begin to work in the pit the father can claim a first-class or double house. If the family consist wholly or principally of girls, they must make shift in the second-rate house. Parents with growing boys have always the preference in obtaining work in a coal-pit, and houses in a pit village: indeed, married men without families are sometimes turned out of their own into inferior houses to make room for the more useful circle of juvenile labourers. Practically, and for all the purposes of living, the attic seems, from all I can gather, to be of small use; and the deplorable consequence is, that more than one half of the pit population virtually live—each family— in a single room. Here is bedroom and kitchen—here the men and boys, on their return from the pit, wash their almost naked bodies, too often in the presence of growing up daughters and sisters—and here, too, the women dress and undress, unless the presence of an absolute stranger compels them to run across the street, in order, as I have over and over again witnessed, to change their attire in the pantry. The men say that they cannot wash up-stairs, as the water would plash through the frequently warped flooring down upon the furniture, and perhaps the bed below; and in the unfrequent cases of two-storied pit houses, complaints are frequently made of the spillage caused by the occupants of the higher room. The best sort of houses in a pit village are always occupied by the deputies, the overmen, and the principal waggon-drivers, and the range is commonly nicknamed "Quality-row." As a general rule, a garden goes with every house, the ground being sometimes attached to it; but by far the most frequent plan is to subdivide a field into patches, wherein each pitman may grow a few pecks of potatoes or cabbages. The miners sometimes take pains with their gardens, but they are more commonly neglected. Besides his house, each miner receives fuel, not quite for nothing, but for 3d. per week, the trifling amount in question being nominally paid, not for the coal, but for the "leading," or carting it to the door. Let us imagine, then, if we would form an idea of a colliery village, some half dozen rows of perfectly uniform one-storied cottages, the intersecting lanes dotted with ash-heaps and "middens," with, in rainy weather, perfect sloughs of mud formed round the hills of refuse. On the outskirts rise one or two modest-looking dissenting chapels, as unadorned as though the line of beauty typified the path to destruction, and about as big as ordinary sized parlours. At one end probably rises the pit heap, at the other extends the garden field, and all around stretches a labyrinth of deep rutted, miry cross roads, through which, in this wintry weather, the wayfarer, as I have had woful experience, wades rather than walks.

We will now enter one of the ordinary class of houses. In one respect, particularly in the cold season, the pitman's dwelling is especially comfortable; it is sure to have a blazing fire, the bright red reflection of which dances cheerfully on everything around. As a general rule, the furniture is decidedly good; some articles are even costly. The visitor's attention will be especially drawn to the bed and the chest of drawers. In a great proportion of cases neither of these would be out of place in a house of some pretensions. The bedstead is very frequently of carved and turned mahogany, and the bed, clean, soft, and comfortable, with white furniture and a quilted coverlid. The chest of drawers is an article which frequently costs from £8 to £10. It commonly rises almost to the ceiling, only leaving room for a few old-fashioned china or stoneware ornaments to be placed upon the top. The chairs are sometimes deal, and sometimes mahogany. The mantelpiece is generally crowded with little ornaments of china and glass; the plates, cups, and saucers, are usually kept in cupboards; but highly polished brass candlesticks, placed on shelves, or hung upon nails, glitter from the wall. Birds and birdcages abound. The songsters are generally fine canaries, or carefully bred mules, and the cages have often been manufactured by the occupant of the cottage. The stock of books is generally very small, but there is almost always a large folio Bible to be found, often accompanied by a few Methodist tracts, and—strange literary jumble—assortments of dream-books, "Oracles of Fate, as consulted by the Emperor Napoleon," and "Little Warblers."

The women are the great agents in getting the houses so well furnished as they are. They strive to outdo each other in the matters of beds and chests of drawers, the two great features of their rooms. When a young couple get married, they generally go to a furniture broker in Newcastle or Sunderland, with perhaps £10 of ready money, obtaining a considerable part of their "plenishing" upon credit, and paying for it by instalments. Like the Manchester mill-hands, the colliery folks have a great notion of clocks; but, unlike the cotton workers, a great proportion of the pitmen's timepieces are regular eight-day clocks with metallic dials. The floors of the houses are seldom or never boarded. Sometimes they are formed of a hard composite, but they are more often paved with red brick—here and there, perhaps, covered with strips of carpeting. Complaints of dampness are very rife, and the chimneys frequently smoke abominably. The attic is invariably gained by a perpendicular flight of steps and a trap-door. The pitmen represent that it is so bare and cold as to render sleeping in it in the cold season a matter of real suffering to people accustomed to the hot air of the mine while at work, or to blazing fires in their living rooms at home. I may add, that I have seen houses of a decidedly superior class to those just sketched, but I have good reason to believe that most industrious pitmen can attain to the state of comparative domestic comfort above described.

I have now to turn for a brief space to the sad subject of accidents in coal mines. It has been stated as matter of regret before several parliamentary committees, that no means exist of getting at, with anything like accuracy, the statistics of the loss of life underground. Except in the case of a catastrophe on a great scale, little or nothing is heard of coal-pit accidents beyond the immediate locality of the mine. Many violent deaths occur underground which the coroner never hears of. An explosion perhaps kills a couple of men. There are numerous persons in authority interested in hushing the matter up. So the proprietors pay for the funeral of the victims—make some small money present to the widows, if there be any—allow them to continue in possession of their houses, and little or nothing more is ever heard on the subject. One evil resulting from this state of things is, the facility which it affords to different parties of under-estimating and over-estimating the probable number of yearly victims. For instance, on the late occasion of the opening of the Coal-Exchange—a placard was extensively circulated in London, one of the statements of which was that since 1800 more than 20,000 human beings had been killed by explosions in coal-pits. This estimate seemed so fearful that I have taken some pains in order to ascertain whether there were any exaggeration involved. There was a small pamphlet published some years ago by a working collier, in which are given the number of fatal accidents, the several causes and results, with the names of the collieries in which they happened, in the counties of Durham and Northumberland, the register embracing the lengthened period between 1756 and 1843. I have gone carefully over this calendar, and the results are, that according to the pamphlet in question, there perished in Durham and Northumberland during 87 years, from explosion, about 1,491 persons, and from all other accidents, common to miners, about 270 persons, making a total of 1,760 violent deaths. Now, taking the fatal accidents of Northumberland and Durham as amounting only to one-fourth of those which occur in Great Britain, the general result would be an estimate far below that given in the placard in question. Let us try it by another test. The number of known deaths by accident and misadventure in 55 mining districts in 1838 was, from all causes, 349. This number taken as an average, and multiplied by 49, would give a total of about 17,000 fatal accidents. But out of the 349 deaths not above one-fourth were caused by explosion; therefore, still taking 1838 as an average year, it would appear that the fair estimate for deaths by explosion for forty-nine years would be about 4,250, instead of 20,000. I have already mentioned the increase in the total number of accidents from explosion which took place in the northern coal-field after the introduction of the safety-lamp. By parliamentary returns connected with that inquiry, it appeared that in thirty-six years the loss of life in the northern coal-district by explosion was 985. The South Shields committee reported that in twenty years 680 miners were destroyed by explosion in the valleys of the Tyne and Wear. These several estimates give approximate results to what is probably the truth of the matter; and although they contradict the exaggerated estimate of 20,000 lives lost by explosion in less than half a century, they still tell a terrible tale—it may be in some cases of carelessness and recklessness—but assuredly in all cases of the defective ventilation, which made that recklessness and that carelessness so widely fatal. But accidents from fire-damp form only one category of those incidental to coal-pits. Mine catastrophes may be divided into three general classes—those in the shaft, those produced by the falling of the roof, and those the result of the presence of diluted carburetted gas. Shaft accidents are perhaps, more frequently than any others, the results of carelessness. Since the introduction of the cage, for ascending and descending pits, the chance of casualties has been much diminished. I have already described the hazardous mode in which men were formerly pulled up from, and let down into the pits, dangling with their thighs in the loop. It was a common thing for a couple of men to descend thus:—Each with a boy upon his knee, while half-a-dozen boys over them, clung one above the other to the chain. These last grasped the rope in succession as it moved downwards into the pit; and of course a false movement, in a moment's nervousness or hesitation might, and often did, cause them to miss their grasp and perish miserably. At present, however, where in the case of almost every pit the men traverse the shaft in cages, the principal danger to be apprehended is the breaking of the rope. To guard against the consequences of this accident an ingenious invention has lately been patented, consisting of a system of springs, attached to the edges of the cage, which, when released from the pressure caused by the weight of the tubs, as they would be by the breaking of the rope, immediately start out in a lateral direction, and, seizing the spears or guides down which the cage glides, arrest its progress, and hold it suspended until a new rope can be attached to it. Experiments, considered by practical men to be satisfactory, have been made with this apparatus, which is the invention of Mr. Foudrinier. At the Usworth colliery, in Durham, the apparatus was affixed to a cage, loaded to the extent of two tons and a-half. The rope suspending this great weight was several times disengaged, and on every occasion the spring clasps leaped forth and held the cage stationary. A certificate setting forth the confidence of the subscribers in the invention, and stating it to be "highly important for the saving of life," was signed upon the spot by 12 viewers, four engineers, and several other gentlemen connected with the scientific management of collieries. On another occasion, four gentlemen actually confided their lives to the working of the apparatus, standing upon upwards of 40 cwt. of coal. An objection started to the invention, upon the ground of the risk from perhaps more than 200 fathoms of heavy rope or chain falling upon the arrested cage, has been met by the fact, that in the Usworth colliery this casualty actually happened. Upwards of 200 fathoms of rope, weighing 37 cwt., did actually, after an accident, fall upon the suspended cage, without overcoming the clutch of the springs, or injuring either cage or shaft—of course the former is strongly roofed in. In talking over the merits of this invention with a very able colliery viewer, he started an objection, which seems unfortunately too characteristic of colliery management. He feared that such an apparatus would have a strong tendency to cause the use of ropes after they had become worn out and unsafe. In other words, the safeguard, in case of accident actually happening, would tend to supersede the means taken for preventing accident. It was so to a certain extent with the Davy. The lamp was intended as a protection when accidentally carried into foul air; but no sooner had it been adopted than it was habitually and knowingly carried into foul air—a policy very like that of wilfully running a ship among breakers because a life boat is known to be at hand.

The falling in of the roof is most commonly caused by parsimony in using supporting timber, or by want of skill and care in withdrawing that timber when a goaf is to be formed. The men state that they have cause to complain in this respect, both from the insufficient quantity of props often employed, and from the lack of skill of the deputies by whom the props and other timber defences are arranged.

But the fearful scourge of the coal mine is the distillation from the mineral of carburetted hydrogen or fire-damp. The pure gas is inexplosive; but when mixed with eight times its volume of air, the fluid acquires powers more terrible than even those of gunpowder. A mine explosion is a thing unhappily often heard of; but its terrible features are not in general correctly realized. A light is brought in contact with the aerial agent. Immediately it bursts, with a smothered roar into a vast sea of scathing flame, flying from passage to passage, and corridor to corridor, wherever the explosive compound exists, and dashing planking, brattices, and doors before it, as though they had been shattered by cannon-balls. In a pit near Newcastle three men were employed close to the bottom of a shaft, coaling up the entrance to an old deserted working. Behind them, at a few paces distance, was a brattice, or partition, extending down and across the shaft, and formed of seasoned three-inch planking. A candle was fetched, the better to survey the masonry. Gas was present—it fired—and the three men were blown right through the three-inch planking, and smashed into pulp on the opposite side of the shaft. In other cases, men have been shot up out of the shaft like bullets out of a gun-barrel, and their blackened limbs picked up scattered in the adjacent fields. But generally, the loss of life from actual flame, or from being dashed against the sides of the mine, is comparatively small. The worst comes after the explosion. No sooner has the sheet of flame spent itself than volumes of carbonic acid—the fatal choke-damp or stythe, one breath of which, in its pure state, is death—come rolling in suffocating fumes along the neighbouring passages. The explosion has frequently blown down the brattices and trap-doors; the ventilation of the mine is, therefore, in a moment suspended, and the stythe works its deadly will. It frequently happens that ten men are killed by stythe for one burnt by the fire-damp. The poor fellows are found unscathed in face and limb, but choked by the suffocating vapour. Several men have given me descriptions of what they witnessed of the effects of explosions taking place in quite a different part of the mine from that in which they were working.

"I remember, sir," said one, "an explosion happening in our pit. It was far from us, and we heard no noise; but all at once the air was chopped off from our mouths. Then we knew what had happened. Not one of us spoke a word to the other, but we cast down our picks, and we ran to the shaft for life! I did not think of death to myself, but I thought of Jane (his wife) and the five little ones. Thank God, we got safe to the bottom of the shaft; but if the stythe had chanced to come across we should have fallen down and died where we lay."

The miners know when they are in foul air by the appearance of the flame in the Davy-lamp. It becomes elongated, and presently, if the gas continues to pour forth, the ordinary flame is, as it were, lipped and haloed by a second bluish-hued fire, formed by the burning of the carburetted hydrogen within the gauze-screen. It used to be not an uncommon practice for miners to continue working in the full consciousness of the atmosphere with which they were thus surrounded, and perfectly aware that their lamps were, as it is called, "afire." Recklessness of this kind is now, however, by no means so common as it was. In such cases as I have mentioned, an accident to the lamp from a fall, or the chance blow of a pick, would have produced an instantaneous explosion. Still, however, men do not scruple to carry the Davy into an atmosphere which they know to be highly inflammable. A scientific gentleman deputed from Government was lately examining the scene of a fatal explosion. He was accompanied by the underviewer of the colliery, and as they were inspecting the edges of a goaf, it was observed that the Davys which they carried were afire.

"I suppose," said the inspector, "that there is a good deal of firedamp hereabouts?"

"Thousands and thousands of cubic feet, all through the goaf," replied his companion, coolly.

"Why," exclaimed the official, "do you mean to say that we have nothing but a shred of wire gauze between us and eternity?"

"Nothing at all," said the under-viewer, very tranquilly—"there's nothing where we stand but the gauze to keep the whole mine from being blown into the air."

The inspector made a wise and precipitate retreat. Occasionally, when the men come to their work, they find, if the ventilation has been defective, a stratum, as it were, of explosive air floating near the roof of the working. A common remedy in such cases is for them to strip off their jackets and brush and sweep the foul air out towards the main passages, where the strong ventilating current carries it harmlessly away. In about eight or ten mines in the north, the Davy has been superseded by the Clanny lamp, a light which I have the testimony of many practical men for asserting to be superior in many respects to the Davy. The general principle, that dependent upon the wire gauze, is the same in both lamps; but in the Clanny apparatus there is an additional glass cylinder to protect the flame against draughts, and matters are so ordered that as soon as the air reaches the explosive point, the flame goes out. The Clanny lamp, besides being in this way safer than the Davy, gives out more than twice as much light. Its drawbacks are, being heavier, and, as I believe, more expensive. While upon this subject I may mention that Dr. Reid Clanny, of Sunderland, the inventor of this lamp, had conceived and carried out the idea of availing himself of the non-passage of flame through wire gauze at least two years before the invention of Sir Humphry Davy. Of course, all gases given out in coal mines are not explosive. Carbonic acid, although generally the product of explosion, is sometimes generated spontaneously. In this shape it is seldom fatal, because its increase is gradual, and it extinguishes the lamps, thus forcing the men to leave the place long before the air becomes absolutely poisonous to breathe. Sometimes carbonic acid causes lamps to burn so dimly that the men are forced to agitate them to improve the flame, and I have heard of cases in which boys have been employed at 1s. 6d. and 1s. 8d. per day to swing the lamps in order to keep them alight. The effect of hard and protracted labour in such an atmosphere must be palpable.

The facts stated above necessitate the conclusion that it is not to the most admirably adapted lamps which science can invent, but to steady and well-regulated ventilation, that we must look for the prevention of explosive accidents in mines. To make things reasonably secure the current ought to play ceaselessly through every nook and winding of the pit. The smallest quantum of air which ought to be sent through the main passages of a fiery colliery is, in the opinion of competent witnesses, from 350 to 400 cubic feet per second; and in the better ventilated pits, upwards of 30,000 cubic feet do actually pass per minute. In this respect the Durham and Northumberland collieries are far in advance of the pits in other districts; but even in many of these there is great room for improvement. Among the working men there exists a very deep and natural feeling upon the subject, which is one of life or death to them. The topic is now under the consideration of Government, and Professor Phillips is at present engaged in inspecting, on the part of Government, certain of the northern coal mines. The method adopted by the Professor has been very freely canvassed by the working miners—who conceived that a list of collieries furnished to him by the viewers, and which he is at present engaged in inspecting, included only the very best ventilated pits in the district, and was not calculated to convey a correct idea of the general condition of the coal mines of the north. Acting upon this persuasion, a deputation of the working miners, appointed at a public meeting of the body, waited upon Professor Phillips, to request that he would also descend and examine an additional number of collieries, a list of which they furnished him. This deputation, composed of delegates from the different pits in question, had an interview with the Professor on the 22d of October last, when he explained to them that the list furnished by the viewers was drawn up in accordance with his own views, as he intended, first, to examine a number of what might be termed model pits, and thus form a standard by which he could afterwards the better judge of the condition of the inferior ones. The deputation then handed to the Professor statements of the condition of things in the mines which they represented, every delegate detailing the condition, as regards ventilation, of his own pit. I have been furnished with copies of these statements, which I subjoin. They are, to a certain extent, *ex parte* documents, and must be viewed in that light, but they are of very considerable interest and importance, as expressing the opinion, rightly or wrongly entertained, by a large body of working men upon matters with respect to which they must be practically, if not scientifically, familiar, and which (at all events) involve their chances of life from hour to hour. I am in possession of the delegates' names, but have been requested to suppress them. The documents put into my hands I transcribe unaltered as regards arrangement and composition:—

STATE AND CONDITION OF THE COLLIERIES IN TYNE, WEAR, AND TEES, WITH RESPECT TO VENTILATION, AS REPRESENTED BY A DEPUTATION OF MINERS TO PROFESSOR PHILLIPS, OCTOBER 22, 1849.

NORTH HETTON COLLIERY.—The ventilation down the staple is very bad; the air is so slack that when men fire their shots (blasting the coal) the smoke from the same stands there all the day, there not being a current of air to carry it away. The staple is about one mile from the main shaft, and is 12 fathoms deep. The Hazard Pit is very bad in the broken or pillar working; the safety lamp will not live, and is necessarily unfit for a man to work in six hours. The brattices are put in for 14 yards to the pillar, which is 24 yards, together with 12 yards of wall, being 22 yards before the air. The waggon and tram ways are insufficiently propped—that is, the timber is too scant; and thus we are exposed to dangers from the falling roof. There are no parties to look after the same. Since the ponies (small horses) came into general use the air is much more soft, and we consider that the said ponies consume more air than was consumed by the putters, and they increase the danger by their superior strength in drawing when the tub, or corf, is fast to the timber or props.—Remarks: The tendency of the powder smoke to still further contaminate the air is obvious and clear; and it is also clear that the constitutions of the workmen must suffer in a corresponding ratio—nothing being more calculated to injure the health than contaminated air. Better to have pure air. Very many fatal accidents have occurred through insufficient timber, and when no one is appointed to inspect the state of the props the danger is increased. £10 per month would remedy all this evil—being but 2d. per score for 60 scores per day, 5 days per week. What a great good for so small a sum as 2d. per score.

WESTERTON COLLIERY.—State of the ventilation on October 16, 1849: The men of the above colliery complain "That the air is not properly conducted in the working places." That there is a great deficiency of trap doors and stoppings, all essential to a proper conducting of the air, and bearing up to where men have to labour. That cases are of frequent occurrence where men have had to leave their work through an excess of the presence of carbonic acid gas, or stythe. We, the workmen of the above colliery, would respectfully request to have a visit from the commissioner, and feel hurt at the Black Boy being chosen as a colliery to be inspected with a view to afford a criterion, which colliery is well known to be a better ventilated one than ours.

WASHINGTON COLLIERY.—State of the ventilation, October 2, 1849; September 25, 1849. Pit fired at a place where a box is placed to convey the foul air out of the working, when it is mixed with the fresh air and sent through the workings of two other districts or flats. The masters blame the leaving open of a door which stood in the headways course, at a place called the far crosscut (angular excavation), and assert that the lad, or boy, expressed his desire to have the door to mind, that the price paid for so doing might add to his scanty wages. Another explosion took place in July, 1849, when George Dang was so severely burnt that he only survived nine days. December last, 16th, 1848, four men were drawn over the pulley. Henry Huchinson and John Forster were killed; the others survived the accident. The coroner's depositions went to find fault with the engineman, he being too young, according to Lord Ashley's Act. The owners have never allowed the friends or relatives of the sufferers recompense; but the case is before a solicitor, to compel proper damages. Examined the pit on the 19th and 20th October; went through the workings and the waste also. Took the west side of the rolleyway first, then the east to the staple, where all the returns meet. The staple is 7 feet diameter. The down-cast shaft is 7 feet, and the up-cast 7 feet also. We are working the Hutton seam and the Low-main. The furnace is in the Mandlin seam, 11 fathoms above the Hutton seam. The height of the

Hutton seam is 3 feet 8 inches, the Low-main the same. We found the furnace slack in the up-cast shaft. Water was falling. There were places wanting brattices. Great improvements since we refused to work on account of the previous accidents. The ponies and asses that are used in the workings consume the air, and otherwise prevent its free circulation. The tubs are 7 cwt.

CASTLE EDEN COLLIERY, NEAR HARTLEPOOL.—State of the ventilation, October, 1849. The owner,—Gladstone, Esq. Viewer, M. B. Robson. Resides on the colliery; is manager at Whitwell Colliery also. The subordinates are chiefly (to the best of my knowledge) selected for their capabilities in being active in getting the work out, and not for their acquirements in the science of ventilation, they not being capable of writing. The mine is worked with candles generally, but sometimes Davy-lamps are used. The seams are the Low-main and Main coal, liable to fire-damp; evolves from the coal and roof also. The weather does not, to my knowledge, influence the discharge of gas. The shaft is twelve feet diameter, and is in three compartments, two of which are down-casts, and the up-cast being about one-third of the whole. The ventilation is by furnace. The pit works double shift, from Monday, at one o'clock, a.m., till Saturday, at twelve, p.m. The hewers work double in walls, where two are turned away at one time, making four men in one board; when the heat from the perspiration of the men and the blasting of the coal renders it almost insupportable to life, and consequent injury to health. The brattices are much neglected, though there are printed rules stating that the brattice is not to exceed six feet from the face, yet they are sometimes ten or twelve yards from the face. There are thirty-six horses or ponies. The air passes through the stables and carries with it most unwholesome effluvia into the workings. There have been repeated solicitations to give a scale of air to the stables, and carry it off to the furnace; yet it has always been refused. Where doors are thought necessary they are swing doors, and often will not fall close. The tubs are left in the face of each working place, &c.; in narrow places the men cannot get out, though in the same mine blowers are very frequent. The quality of the air is mostly complained of as doing serious injury to our health: it is called damp air. The workmen's tools are frequently left in the workings, and are covered with mould or damp; a fungus is always hanging upon the prop of timber. We are exposed to dangers in want of deputies, &c., to prop the place, and when we complain we are told to do it ourselves, and if that does not suit, they (the workmen) may leave. The tubs are 25 pecks or 7½ cwt. The danger from want of timber is of common occurrence; and though representing the case to our employers, they still pay no heed to our solicitations. 170 to the Hutton seam, and 150 to the Low-main.

CROW TREES COLLIERY.—State of the ventilation, October, 1849. Three down-cast shafts and one up-cast, the last 7 feet diameter. There is a split at the bottom, and goes 150 yards along the rolleyway to a main door, takes to the east, where twenty-four men work. No system of conducting the air to these men, there being no brattices; the air returns back through the goaf for about 300 yards, comes again into the waggon-ways, and travels near a mile to another main door, and goes south, where a few men work: no means are taken to convey the air to these men. Then takes over the goaf to another flat; between that flat and another there is a swing door, no other means being employed to convey the air to the men. Very often the men have to return without working for want of air; many are heard to wish there was a little gas. The air is so damp that when we lose our light no lucifer match will strike. The return, in a certain place and for some distance, has to traverse a passage not more than two feet high, indeed men have to creep on all fours. The seam is 3 feet 3 inches high. Mr. John Robson, viewer and manager.

OXCLOSE COLLIERY.—State of the ventilation, Oct. 1849. The diameter of the down-cast shaft is 7 feet 3 inches; the diameter of the up-cast shaft is 8 feet. There is a pumping set of three lifts, 10 inches in the bore, in the up-cast shaft. The men requested to examine the pit; but Mr. Willis, the overman, stated he could not allow that to be done without leave from the head-viewer, Mr. Elliott. He promised to see him on the Friday, but did not; consequently we have not had the opportunity of examining the pit. The seam makes a great quantity of gas of the explosive character, and frequently men have been burnt, one of whom died very lately (September 23, 1849). The boards are partially bratticed, but not wholly so; there is a want of system in that particular. Few doors in the workings, and those are swing-doors. There is deficiency of the known means to render the men's lives safe.

WINGATE GRANGE COLLIERY.—State of the ventilation, October 22, 1849. The workmen of the above colliery sent a man to be examined before Professor Phillips, the commissioner of mines. We send the following cases, to which we can bear witness:—We are compelled to drive the narrow places 5 feet wide, and to drive the boards from 20 to 30 yards to the pillar. The walls from 7 to 14 yards. We are compelled to drive them these distances without brattices or doors, and instead of main or sheth doors, nothing but swing doors, when there are any at all. The air is split six times from the main passage. A headways course is driven on each side of the mothergate board, at each flat. In some instances they convey the air into the workings with a wooden box, 8 or 10 inches square. We frequently have to begin work in the morning with the Davy-lamp, until the deputy thinks the place clear of gas, and then we get the naked light or candle. The gas has frequently to be dusted out in the morning even in the boards near the flat. The height of the seam is 5 feet; under the present mode of working by taking up the bottom stone and leaving the top coal, the height is 4 feet. The tubs are 3 feet 6 inches high, the breadth 3 feet 4 inches. The space for air to travel is but small. This is our condition at present.—The men of Wingate Grange.

CASSOP COLLIERY.—State of the ventilation, October 22, 1849. The shaft is 12 feet diameter, and is divided into three partitions, two of which are down-casts, the other up-cast. The air splits at the bottom of the shaft, the one goes east and the other west. The air courses are driven six feet wide. The height of the seam is 3 feet 4 inches, and it invariably falls from want of wastemen and timber. There are not more than 2 square feet for the return air to the up-cast shaft. In consequence of the want of air before the boards are up to the pillar, the candles will not burn, and even in some cases two or three candles are lighted at the same time in order to get a sufficient light, all of which could be prevented if doors or brattices were provided to conduct the air up into the boards. When the men blast the coal, the powder smoke stands upon them all the future part of the day, which is found very injurious to the men's health. The old colliery has two shafts, one a down-cast and the other one up-cast. The air is split at the bottom of the shaft; after that it is split very often, but we cannot tell the number of splits; but in the workings there is a deficiency of air for the men to work in, which could be entirely obviated if a sufficient quantity of doors and brattices were provided. There is not much hydrogen gas, but chiefly carbonic acid gas, which we feel very injurious to our health. In the broken, or pillars, the Davy-lamp will not burn for want of air.

SOUTH WINGATE COLLIERY.—State of the ventilation, October 22, 1849. Owner, A. Seymour; viewer, Martin Seymour. There is one shaft divided into three compartments. Fire damp prevails. There were no brattices in the pit until a recent explosion, wherein two men and two boys were burnt severely. Brattices are now in the pit. The following particulars are from the mouth of one of the sufferers, and other workmen employed in the colliery. There is one engine on the colliery which draws the coals by day; when the ropes are taken off for the purpose of drawing water by night. The men were sent down on the day in question, and then the ropes were taken off; they then went into the working places, where many were; there being no brattices, no precautions were taken by the officers to inform of the presence of gas; one of them went up a board to get a shovel (a very common occurrence), when the gas ignited, burning him severely and three others. Had the explosion not driven itself out, there can be no doubt, owing to the accumulation of gas in the other places, that all in the pit would have perished. Those who were burnt were brought to the shaft bottom, and the signal given to get them to bank, but without avail; all means were used in their power, by shouting and beating on the iron tubs to make a noise; it is evident they were known to be there, inasmuch as the rapper was muzzled, and coals were thrown down the shaft. The unfortunate sufferers thus lay in agonies 5 hours and 35 minutes before they were got up. The manager knew gas was generated in the mine, previous to the explosion. There is a stone band in the seam: this is thrown behind the workmen; thus the boards are almost choked up, there being only a narrow passage to convey the coals out. Since the explosion, the officers state the sufferers had orders not to go without a lamp; yet in the presence of the witness one of the sufferers denies the assertion, and states he had no such orders. He is not likely to survive.

TRIMDEN GRANGE COLLIERY.—State of the ventilation, October 22, 1849. We, the workmen of the above colliery, will give you a correct statement of Trimden Grange Colliery. The down-cast shaft to the five-quarter seam is 6 feet by 8 feet 9 inches: the down-cast to the main coal seam is the same. There are two engines down the five-quarter seam supplied with steam from bank, with pipes 2¼ inches in diameter; there is a gas pipe in the same shaft, 2 inches in diameter, goes down to the five-quarter seam, which is a great injury to the men's health when they are at work. The air courses are 6 feet wide with waggonway. The return in the waste one way is 4 yards wide, and is just high enough that a man can creep upon his belly, and we state that it is not sufficient to keep the pit in a working state. The men many a time have to leave their work after they have been at it 2 or 3 hours many a time insensible. In many instances they have to light two or three candles to prevent their being in the dark, and we think it injurious to work in such places. The air is split in three different places, and there is nothing but fly doors, with the exception of one or two, and all of them stand open nearly the whole of the day. They are working the whole pillars from 24 to 40 yards, and no brattice in any of them, therefore the air is quite flat, for there is no board-end stoppings.

OUSTON COLLIERY.—State of the ventilation, Oct. 22, 1849. The owners are Mr. Henry Hunt and partners. The old pit is divided into two compartments; the air is split at the bottom, going north and west 1½ miles, going south and east 1½ miles. The pillars are driven from 24 to 30 yards, without brattice or doors, which causes the gas to accumulate. Sometimes the men have to work with their lamps red hot, which endangers their lives very much.

SEATON BURN.—State of the ventilation, Oct. 22, 1849. A great deficiency of air in the working places, in consequence of only one length of brattice (wooden partition) being put in at the board end, and there being no board-end doors. The boards are driven 30 yards to the pillar, the walls are ten yards, making 40 yards before the air.

The walls being 4 yards wide, the current of air is nearly stagnant in the headways course. The air is damp and cold, yet of that sluggish character, that the smoke of gunpowder, with which the men blast the coal, stands upon them all the future part of the day.

LUDWORTH COLLIERY.—State of the ventilation, October 22, 1849. Sir—The men of Ludworth colliery are labouring under vary bad circumstances, which is ruining their health for the want of better ventilation. On Friday, the 19th of October, 1849, the onsetter had to come to bank for the smoke going down the down-cast shaft, which penetrated the brattice when ascending the up-cast. There is also a want of timber to support the roof in the workings, and our lives are in danger therefrom. The boards are driven 26, and some 30 yards, to the pillar. There is but two lengths of brattice in each board, and both sides of the board nearly close. The large tubs (30 pecks) so fill up the narrow places that the workmen cannot get out should anything happen—that is, should the place explode, or should the roof fall. Chief agent, Mr. Thomas Wood, but does not reside on the colliery.

What the miners are almost to a man in favour of is, regular Government inspection of the collieries—the inspector to have the power of enforcing his recommendations. Petitions to this effect have been in former sessions presented to Parliament, and the question will be again agitated next year. Tracts are at present being published upon the subject, under the auspices of the delegate-council of the Pitmen's Union. The men urge that of all classes of labour none has a greater claim upon the paternal vigilance of a Government than a dangerous and little understood toil, surrounded with special causes of peril, and carried on apart from the general eye, in the dark recesses of the earth. They argue that while the factory labourer and the emigrant are officially cared for and protected, and while not a train is allowed to be run upon a new railway until a scientific agent of the Government has minutely inspected and testified to its safety, that vast numbers of people are daily obliged to hazard their lives in an occupation which, for its safe conduct, imperatively demands constant, vigilant, and scientific superintendence—a species of superintendence, moreover, carried on in a different spirit to that now exercised on the part of the owners themselves; and who, the men allege, in the management of coal mines, are very often apt to make the safety of the pit a secondary consideration as compared with its profitable working. For these reasons amongst others, the miners are anxious for the appointment of Government inspectors, men of scientific knowledge and practical skill, able not only to recommend, but empowered to put their recommendations into practice.

———

# LABOUR AND THE POOR.

—◆—

## THE MANUFACTURING DISTRICTS.

[FROM OUR SPECIAL CORRESPONDENT.]

### THE MINING DISTRICTS OF NORTHUMBERLAND AND DURHAM.

### LETTER XXI.

I have stated in a previous communication that the great strike of 1844 paralysed, if it did not temporarily break up, the miners' combination in Durham and Northumberland. More than one of the unionists have informed me that that strike was resolved on in opposition to the earnest counsel of the most able men in the body; and a most intelligent individual, of much authority among the associated workmen, has deplored to me the fact that people always connect unions with strikes. The former he regards as a legitimate and necessary means of enabling labour to hold its own against the power of capital; but a "turn out" he believes to be an expedient which, although sometimes it may be absolutely indispensable, is yet always, and must be always attended with profound human suffering—with a dislocation of the great industrial machine, in the smooth and steady working of which all are interested—and a measure which ought, therefore, never to be adopted unless at the call of a stern and imperative necessity.

Whatever may be its future operations, however, the Miners' Union is now again making head. The association in the north is local, being confined to the counties of Durham and Northumberland. It numbers at present upwards of 7,000 members, of whom a few, and only a few, are boys. It employs six paid labourers to disseminate and enforce its views—comprehends upwards of sixty collieries, many of them among the largest and most important in the district—and holds regular fortnightly meetings, at which a delegate from each pit attends to consult and report progress. As one of these meetings, thus composed of working men, deputed by their brethren to represent their interests in the struggle between capital and labour, was held the other day at Newcastle, I deemed it my duty to attend, and state the nature of my mission in the north, so as to receive from the mouths of the men themselves their own version of their grievances. I am aware that any such statements will be generally regarded as proceeding from sources peculiarly interested in impressing the public with a one-sided idea of alleged wrongs. But I shall take care that both sides of the question are submitted to the world. I shall give the statements of the pitmen, and I shall add the counter representations of gentlemen also practically connected with collieries, but who, in their capacity as viewers or proprietors, are naturally led to regard the same subject from a different point of view. If I shall succeed in fairly and honestly stating the *pros* and *cons* of a disputed matter which has occasioned numberless strikes and a vast degree of bad blood between employers and employed, I shall account my object as so far answered.

Leaving out of view for the present questions as to the rate of wages—always of course a fertile subject of dispute, but one continually changing its phases with fluctuations of the coal market—I proceed at once to state what appears to me to be the chronic source of bad feeling between the colliery operatives and their employers. In working coal-mines there are two sets of fines or forfeitures falling upon the men, which have been enforced more or less rigidly from time immemorial. Hewers are, as the reader knows, paid by the quantity of coals which they send up to the pit-bank. These coals are placed in tubs, and must amount to a certain weight, which, I believe, differs in a slight degree at different collieries. If, upon their arrival at the weighing machine at the pit mouth, they prove to be, by a certain number of pounds (generally fourteen) under weight, then the hewer loses the whole amount due for hewing the tub-full. This custom is called "set out," and earnings thus forfeited are said to be lost by "set out." But even if the weight be found correct, there is another ordeal to be gone through. When the coals are tilted into the screen, a person appointed for the purpose, and called a "keeker," closely examines them, and picks out any stones, splint, and foul and inferior coal, which he can detect. If this refuse amount to more than one quart in some collieries, and two quarts in others, then the hewing of the whole tub is forfeited. This penalty is called "laid out." Beside the screens there are generally placed shallow wooden trays, divided into different compartments, in which the refuse from each tub is "laid out," to be shown to the hewer who sends it up when he comes to bank. These two customs of "laid out" and "set out" are at the bottom of a vast proportion of the disputes between master and man in the coal districts. In estimating the amount of wages lost by the fines in question, the coal-owners and coal-workers usually differ very widely. Much, in the case of "laid out," depends upon the quality of the seam in process of working. Sometimes the coal is pure and easily wrought; at others it is, to a greater or lesser extent, intermingled with different mineral substances, the uniform rejection of which, in filling his tub, requires the constant care and minute attention of the hewer. In the report of Mr. Tremenheere for 1846, there is a calculation of the amount lost in fines in 120 collieries from April 5, 1843, to April 5, 1845. From this estimate the loss would appear to be, on the average, not more than ½d. per day per man. In some of these collieries, it is stated that the amount averages 2¼d. per man—in others it is lower than one farthing.

I referred this statement to the meeting of delegates, and there was at once a unanimous denial of its correctness. They were not prepared, they said, with particulars, at the moment; but the amount of fines lost on an average, they solemnly assured me, was much more serious. A number of cases in support of the general assertion were then adduced. First came the statement put forth by the "Committee of the Seaton Delaval Colliery," giving an account of the "laid out and set out" at that pit for five fortnights, beginning in last February. From this statement it appears, that during the ten weeks in question, there were drawn 35,881 tons 15 cwt. of coals. The united "laid out" and "set out" were 1,302 tons 7 cwt. The average price of working was stated at 1s. 1¼d. per ton; therefore 1,302 tons 7 cwt., at 1s. 1¼d. per ton, makes a "dead loss to the hewers of the sum of £71 17s. 5d." In another colliery I was informed by the delegate representing it that 145 score, at 10s. per score, had been lost to the hewers in nine months. In a third colliery—I refrain from giving names, but they are on my note-book before me—I was assured that as much as 6s., 7s., and 9s. had been lost by one man in a fortnight's pay. Of a fourth colliery— a southern one—the following statement was made:—In one of the seams there are six or eight inches of "grey" or coarse coal. These the men have to "carve out," and if 6 lbs. of this coal be found in one tub the miner forfeits the whole of it. My informant said, that, working "to the greatest extreme"—meaning with the most extreme care—he had frequently lost his tub, which cost him each time 5½d. He added, that it was all but impossible to distinguish the coarse from the good coal in the darkness of the board. This statement was corroborated on all hands; and it has been confirmed to me by working men, both before and since, in several parts of the two counties. They state that, although it is easy in the daylight at the bank to distinguish bad coal or coal stones, yet that in the pit—and more particularly if the hewer is using the Davy—the most practised eye is frequently deceived. As to "set out," I found the complaint general that, particularly in the cases where coals have to be conveyed a long way to the pit mouth, there is frequently a waste occasioned by accidental spillage—principally in descending inclined planes, where the waggons are subjected to shocks and jerks. In fact, the hewer has no one to look after his interests from the time when the putter moves away the full tub until the banksman jerks it out of the cage. At the weighing-house the hewers have, in many collieries, an agent who checks the weight. In their anxiety to avoid the "set out," it of course often happens that the hewers pile up their waggons with more than the standard weight. For this they are paid 1d. for every 14 lbs. of overweight sent up. In a large colliery which I visited to the north of Newcastle, the checksman informed me that, previously to his appointment, the extra earnings had been on an average 1d. per score in every six weeks. Now, the men gained 3d. per score per fortnight. My informant was of course paid by the hewers, at the rate of about 18s. per week.

I return, however, to the statements of the delegates upon the subject. Having heard their representations as to "laid out" and "set out," I inquired whether they thought that the masters ought not to have some check upon the quantity and quality of the coals sent up. To this a unanimous and hearty affirmative was at once given. It was only just and reasonable, they said, that the masters should have a check. The men did not want to be paid for a greater weight than they had worked, or for stones or splent sent up instead of coal. But what they did complain of was the loss of the whole tub for a trifling underweight or a trifling mixture of "foul" coal. It was very hard that for some accidental spillage—perhaps taking place when they had no control over the tub—they should pay so heavy a penalty as its entire forfeiture. This was what they proposed: Let the weight of the foul coal be by all means deducted, and let the hewer be paid for the net quantity of pure coal which he sends up. This arrangement, they argued, would be fair for master and man. They admitted at once that it would be absurd to expect an owner to pay putters and drivers, and keep machinery going in order to bring to the surface a useless material; but they submitted that the men, as their wages would be reduced by every pound of stone or splent with which they loaded their tubs, would have the same interest as the proprietor in keeping stone and splent out of them.

These statements I have laid before several gentlemen connected, as proprietors and viewers, with coal-pits, and their answers to them may be briefly stated as follows. In regard to "set out," they admitted that grievances from spillage might have existed when the old-fashioned corves or baskets were in use, but they were unanimous in declaring that, with the square tub running upon wheels, and drawn to the bank in a cage, no appreciable waste whatever could take place. If, these gentlemen urged, the hewers were paid by the exact amount of coal which they sent up, there would be no check upon their putting the whole lifting mechanism of the mine into operation to raise much smaller quantities than that mechanism was calculated to convey to the surface. If a hewer, they argued, can fill ten tubs in a given time, he can half fill those tubs in half the time. So far as regards his individual labour, he might be fairly paid by the actual weight of coals raised. But there is a great body of putters who are paid by the tub, whatever may be its weight—and a still greater body of drivers, banksmen, &c., who are paid by the day—and an expensive system of machinery, calculated to raise certain weights every time it is put into operation. It is clear, therefore, they argued, that if hewers are paid by the weight at the end of a day's work, and not by the weight of each individual tub, the owners have no check upon their giving to the whole of the remaining working agents of the mine half only of that amount of labour for the performance of which they are arranged and paid.

With respect to "laid out," I was requested to observe that the men are always paid at a higher rate for working seams much intermingled with stones and foul coal, than for excavating seams containing little or nothing save the pure mineral. If they are, therefore, occasionally called upon to work slowly and circumspectly, they are paid accordingly. Besides, I was informed, it is always reckoned the duty of a hewer to clean the coals, and part of his wages are given to him in consideration of that special portion of his work. This statement the hewers themselves at once admitted to be correct. It is, of course, necessary, I was told by viewers and proprietors, that the coals should be cleaned by some one. The common-sense way is to clean them at the bottom of the pit, and so to avoid lifting unmarketable rubbish to the bank. This is, therefore, the plan adopted; and when the hewers send up foul coal, they break their agreement, and are therefore equitably fined. To separate the valuable from the valueless mineral is a work involving a certain degree of time and trouble. If the hewer were therefore, permitted to shirk the task, he would be paid for a smaller quantity of coal in each individual tub, but his wages would not be reduced, because he would have more time to fill tubs—while, as in the case of "set out," the whole machinery of the pit would be working to convey to the bank stuff which was of no use when it got there. The gentleman whose views I am stating observed, that as to the vast majority of men, the penalties were merely nominal. One of them showed me several pit accounts—taken, as I know, perfectly at random—in none of which the amount deducted for laid-out and set-out rose, in a fortnight's pay, higher than two or three shillings; while, in two fortnights, the amounts were respectively 3d. and 9d. out of more than £120. The same gentleman informed me that in a pit belonging to a near relative of his own, there was a seam longitudinally intersected by a seam of inferior coal, which was not worth while bringing to bank. The rule of the colliery was, that if a certain number of pounds of this substance was found in any tub, the hewer forfeited no less than 3s. "The amount seems great," said my informant, "but then the fine is never incurred. The worthless coal can only be shovelled into the tub from sheer carelessness, and that carelessness the fine prevents."

Thus, then, I have stated both sides of the question fully, and I think fairly. It is not my business to decide between the conflicting views. I leave them as I found them, and return in the meantime to the meeting of union delegates, from which I have wandered in order to connect a subject discussed there before me with the replies subsequently entrusted to me to be made public along with the delegates' arguments.

There being representatives present of so many and such important collieries, it occurred to me that I might with advantage seize the opportunity of acquiring some of the educational, moral, and intellectual statistics of the district. At my request, therefore, the acting chairman read, name by name, the list of collieries represented, and called upon the delegate of each to enumerate the number and nature of schools established in connection with his pit, stating by whom they were supported, and whether there existed any news-rooms or libraries for the adults. The required information was given by each delegate succinctly and briefly. The following are the results. I may add that I have appended the population of each colliery the name of which appears in the official documents furnished to the Newcastle Coal Trade-office in 1844.

SEATON DELAVAL.—Male working population, 626. Three schools and one library. Two of the schoolmasters supported entirely by the workmen, and teaching in Methodist chapels; the owners of the colliery finding the school-room of the third.

COWPEN.—Population, 318. Several schools, including an infant school, supported by the men. No library or reading room.

WEST HOLLYWELL.—Population, 143. One National school. The owners were formally in the habit of giving 8s. a week towards the support of the schoolmaster. Recently this allowance was withdrawn, but they furnish a house and school-room free. There was a library which had commenced operations only the previous Monday. The delegate added that for any deficiency in the means of intellectual improvement, the people were much more to blame than the owners.

SEATON BURN.—Population, 296. One school mutually supported—that is, the house accommodation found by the master, and the fees paid by the fathers of the scholars. No library.

WALL'S-END.—Population, 255. Five or six schools mutually supported, and one library.

BUCKWORTH.—One school and a library, mutually supported. The owners give £2 a year to the library.

BRANSPETH.—Population, 111. Only a dame school for the younger children, and a night school, supported by the men, and taught by one of them. No library.

WOODIFIELD.—Population, 76. Three schools, two of them supported by the men, the third in connection with the Established Church. One library.

BEACHBURN.—One infant school. One night school, supported by the men, and taught by one of themselves.

TRIMDON.—Population, 519. One school, mutually supported, and a reading-room established by the owners.

COXHOE.—Population, 368. Two schools, supported by the men, and a library, mutually supported.

NORTH HETTON.—Population, 325. One regular school, mutually supported; two night schools, supported by the men, and taught by members of their own body. No library. House accommodation provided by the owners.

WEST CRAMLINGTON.—Population, 315. One school, mutually supported, the fees of the children being only one penny a week. No news-room, but the owner wishes to erect one. "If the men will take one step, he will take ten."

PITTINGTON.—Population, 580. Three schools—one supported by the owners and two by the men.

WASHINGTON.—Population, 194. One National school. House accommodation free. Fees, 1d. per week. No library.

ELEMORE AND APPLETON.—Two schools, mutually supported. No library.

SHERBURN HILL.—Two National schools, mutually supported. No library.

RAINTON.—Population, 500. One school for boys and girls, supported by the owner. No library.

GREAT HETTON.—One National school, mutually supported. Another school, supported by the men. The owner gives a free house to a schoolmaster and mistress.

MARLEY HILL.—Population, 128. One school, mutually supported. No library.

CASTLE EDEN.—Population, 450. One school, supported by the owners, who will not allow any other school in the colliery. One library, in which the "Liberal newspapers" are allowed. The delegate had himself opened a night school, but was compelled to give it up.

WINGATE GRANGE.—Population, 626. One National school, mutually supported, and a reading-room.

NEW DURHAM.—One good school, supported by fees. The children pay 2d. a week for the elementary classes. No library; but the owner will fit up a room, and "give them a chance" of establishing one.

SHINCLIFFE.—Population, 213. Two schools—one National. The other kept by a working man at night. No library.

HASWELL.—Population, 305. One National school, mutually supported. Two other schools similarly maintained. A library, unhappily allowed to "lie dormant."

CASSOP.—Population, 469. One National school, and two others self-supported. No library.

HEUGH HALL.—Two mutually supported schools. No library.

GRANGE.—A school entirely supported by the men, and a library belonging to the Wesleyan body.

BROOMSIDE.—One National school, mutually supported, and one self-supporting school. No library.

BELMONT.—Population, 185. One mutually supported school. No reading-room.

LITTLE CHILTON.—One school, mutually supported. The owner offered to set a library on foot; but prohibits political publications.

HARTLEY.—Population, 270. One school, supported by the men. No library.

HATHERTON.—Population, 246. One school, mutually supported, and a library on a small scale.

BLACK BOY.—Population, 430. Two schools, mutually supported. House accommodation is provided for both master and mistress.

RODDY MARE.—One school, mutually supported. No library.

WESTERTON.—Population, 184. One school, connected with the Church. The fines go to purchase prizes.

CROPPY CROOKS.—One school. House accommodation provided by owners; fees paid by parents.

DERWENT (coal and iron works).—Eight schools; five for boys, and three for girls. Self supported. The use of the library is restricted to the clerks at the office and the foremen.

LUDWITH.—One National school, mutually supported. Children pay 1d. per week.

SHOTTON.—Population, 676. One mutual National school, and a library, which is well supported. It belongs to the company.

DANTON.—One school, in connection with the Methodist body. House accommodation provided for master and mistress.

EDMONDSLEY.—Population, 275. One school; held in the Methodist chapel. The owners give £50 between master and mistress. Threepence per week is deducted from the wages of those who have children at the school.

CHALAN.—Population, 150. One National school. No library; but the owners are about to establish one. Fifteen pounds has been collected for books.

KIBBLESWORTH.—Population, 129. One school, supported by the men, and one library, supported by the master.

ELSWICK.—Population, 146. One dame school, a library, and a Sunday school, supported by the men.

WOODHOUSE CLOSE.—Neither school nor library.

HUNWICK.—Population, 152. One mutually supported National school. No library.

TANFIELD LEE.—Population, 283. One National school. The pupils pay 2d. a week.

Walker.—Population, 357. Four or five schools. Two of them National. A library connected with the iron works doing well, with 300 members, at 1d. per week each.

Hebburn.—Population, 361. Two schools for males and females. Both are held in chapels, and are self-supporting.

South Hetton.—Population, 518. One National school, mutually supported. A library, supported by the owners.

Eldon.—Population, 218. No school at this colliery.

Mickley.—Population, 194. No school; no library.

Black Prince.—One National school and a library, both mutually supported.

The names of several other collieries were called, but the delegates did not happen to be in the room. Some little confusion was occasioned by the term "mutually supporting" being generally used, only when the owner paid a sum of money to the schoolmaster; but I am given to understand that the rule of the proprietors giving a house, and generally a garden and coals, to the teacher or teachers, is all but universal. The Marquess of Londonderry contributes about £300 a year to the schools upon his estates. They educate upwards of 630 children, each of whom pays 1d. per week.

The list of colliery schools given above, although it doubtless leaves much to be done, still shows that progress in the right direction has, to some extent, been made. A dozen of years ago not one-third of them were in existence. In those portions of Mr. Tremenheere's Reports, devoted to the educational facilities afforded in the colliery districts, the phrase continually occurs when describing a pit seminary—"Until within a late period the only means of instruction for the people were dame schools." Many of the old class of schools, taught by masters, were also wretchedly inefficient—the teachers being frequently disabled workmen, and the number of their scholars forming but a miserable per centage of the workpeople of the colliery. The consequence has been that the mining population are exceedingly low in point of education and intelligence; and yet they contradict the theories generally entertained upon the connection of ignorance with crime, by presenting the least criminal section of the population of England. Indeed, the disproportion between the mining districts of Northumberland, Durham, and the average of England, particularly as regards the more trifling class of offences against property, is very remarkable; and great as this disproportion is, that of female crime in the mining districts, as contrasted with the general average, is still greater. In 1847, the number of persons offending against property in England was 28 out of every 10,000 of the population. In the mining districts, including Northumberland, Durham, Cumberland, and Cornwall, the proportion was only 7 in every 10,000. Again, for the three years ending 1847, there were, in the mining districts, only 9.33 female thieves out of every 10,000 women. The proportion in Middlesex was 34.69; while, throughout England and Wales generally, the proportion was 17.67. The author of "Tactics for the Times," in adducing these results, attempts to account for them on the supposition that the uncertainty of human life, caused by the frequency and terrible nature of accidents in mines, produces a deep and salutary effect on the minds of the people. But the explanation seems very fanciful. A sailor undergoes at least as much risk as a miner; and sailors are not reckoned a particularly thoughtful race. Besides, taking one of the most exclusively coal-mining districts I can find—that of Auckland, Teesdale, and Weardale—the Registrar-General's last Report makes the general value of life within it as 1 in 49—a higher proportion than that of London, and more than 20 per cent. higher than that of Manchester. The fact, to some extent, appears to be, that that naturally sombre and earnest mental temperament which distinguishes the people of the north of England in general, has, in the case of the miners, been fostered and wrought out into strong religious convictions through the agency of the Methodist bodies, who have obtained almost the entire spiritual control of the people; the efforts of the thousands of local and itinerant preachers being greatly aided by the comparatively isolated condition in which the mining population live—seldom or never coming in contact with the members of any industrial class except their own, and little exposed to the influences and excitements of great towns. Let the cause be, however, what it may, the miners are the reverse of a criminal population, and they are also the reverse of an intelligent one. An educational census of the people employed in the collieries of the Earl of Durham was lately instituted; and the results may, I believe, be taken as giving a tolerably fair view of the general state of education and intelligence throughout the coal districts. The number of people directly or indirectly connected with the Earl of Durham's collieries was about 4,500. This estimate includes persons engaged in a variety of occupations having more or less reference to pit labour, embracing waggon-way wrights, waggon fillers, blacksmiths, engineers, banksmen, &c. From the total number, more than 700 was deducted for children below five years of age; of the remainder, numbering 3,716, there were 1,461 who could read and write; 1,339 who could read only; and 916 above the age of five who could neither read nor write. This is the general result, applying to all the workpeople above and under ground; but the details of the inquiry proved that while upwards of one-half of the families—the males of which were not, strictly speaking, pitmen—could read and write, only one-third of the pit families were so far educated. But a pitman's notions of reading and writing, I was informed by an intelligent member of their own body, are very modest. "Many a hewer and a putter," said this individual, "will tell you that they can write; but you would be sorely puzzled to read the specimens they would give you." In a colliery in another part of the district, where an educational investigation was set on foot, the results were, that of 331 persons capable of being educated, only 165 could read the Bible. A schoolmaster with whom I conversed, and who has had a lengthened experience amongst a pit population, estimated that only about 25 per cent. of the children were kept at school so long as to be really benefited. He said that their parents commonly professed to be very anxious about the education of their children, but that they sadly grudged the fees, and the boys were sent down to the pit as soon as they could earn a shilling. At many collieries, the pitmen have been found to prefer sending their children to schools taught by inefficient masters of their own class, rather than to seminaries managed by properly trained instructors. As in the cloth and cotton districts, Sunday-schools have played a principal part in affording to the present generation of pit-labourers what degree of education they do possess. In every pit village there are one or more Wesleyan or Primitive Methodist Chapels, and attached to every one of these there is a Sunday-school. With the exception of what is done in these institutions, the education of a pitman may be said to terminate with the day when he first descends the mine to labour. He begins, perhaps, as a trapper, and sits 12 hours of the day in the dark. Indeed, during a considerable portion of the year, the trappers, drivers, and putters never see daylight except on Sundays. They descend the mine before dawn, and ascend it after nightfall. The work of boys, both in driving and trapping, is, therefore, so drearily monotonous and sombre that they are very unwilling to undergo anything like additional restraint above ground—while the labours of putters and hewers is physically so severe and exhausting, that by the time they ascend to day, there seems to be but little left of that energy and vigour which, in so many instances, prompt the manufacturing operative to visit the lecture or the concert-room. The pitmen, as a body, know little, and care little, about politics. Their ideas are limited to the mine in a far greater degree than the spinner's or the weaver's are confined to the factory. If they have no particular technical grievances to complain of, they seldom disturb themselves about abstract political claims, or abstract political wrongs. I have been in scores of pitmen's houses, and I do not think that I saw a newspaper in one of them. Where there were books, they generally consisted of Methodist religious publications. The Bible is, however, to be found in almost every house, and the religious feelings of the community, if unenlightened, are strong and practically binding. The Church of England is, I believe, from what I have seen, regarded by a large proportion of the mining community with feelings of positive and active enmity. They almost invariably class it with the aristocratic institutions and influences which they believe to be hostile to them. The church clergymen, they say, take part with the masters, but the Ranters take part with the men; in fact, most of the local preachers are themselves working men, addressing their comrades in their own *patois*, and treating every scriptural subject in the peculiarly technical tone of mind which is common to the whole community.

In the mining districts the family tie remains almost invariably unbroken until the marriage of the children. Trappers invariably give their wages to their parents. When a boy comes to be a driver he is allowed a small weekly amount of pocket-money; and when he attains to the dignity of "putting," he either pays his father for his board and lodging, and clothes himself, or hands over the entire amount of his wages, requiring to be found in board, lodging, and clothes, and demanding a certain sum, usually about 2s. 6d., per fortnight, for his *menus plaisirs*. The pitmen do not generally marry until they become hewers, and their wives are almost invariably chosen out of their own community. Whole villages are thus often related by marriage. Occasionally, but not often, a pitman's child will go out to service; but in the vast proportion of cases a hewer's daughter becomes a hewer's wife. Should she be left a widow she still remains in the pit row, sometimes opening a small huckstering shop, and taking in clothes to wash and mangle. A disabled man also occasionally takes to dealing in small wares; and in some cases superannuated hewers will, in addition to what light jobs they can pick up about the pit, occupy themselves in collecting the clay used for the workmen's candles. A hewer is past his prime at forty. Pains and stiffness in the back and loins begin to come on, and he finds, particularly in difficult seams, that he can no longer send to bank the same quantity of coals as he managed ten years before. Old pitmen are very generally supported in whole or in part by their grown-up families—a filial duty, the performance of which is far more common in the mining than in the manufacturing districts.

The amusements of the pit population are, as might be expected, somewhat limited. Dog and cock fighting used to be prevalent, but both of these cruel sports are now dying out. The cocks, when pitted against each other, are always armed *secundum artem* with steel spurs, and a few men still rear bull-dogs for fighting purposes. The fights generally took place in slack times, or upon the Saturday following the fortnightly pay Friday. At present the sports most in use are quoit-playing, foot-racing, and bowling. The latter game, as it is understood in Northumberland and Durham, means simply trundling a ball of stone, iron, or heavy earthenware, along a certain distance, either upon a road or across a moor—the victor being the player whose bowl traverses the space propelled by the fewest number of throws. Foot races are often got up at public-houses, for such stakes as pints of ale. Putters are the usual performers; hewers soon get too stiff in the joints to do much in the running way. A piece of Christmas mummery, now dying out, was formerly much in fashion, and it appears, from the descriptions I got of it, to have very much resembled the chimney-sweeps' antics on May-day. The exhibition is called the sword dance, from five of the performers going through evolutions armed with weapons of the kind. The whole party consisted, generally, of about ten persons; of these five were dancers. One was called the "gunner," another the "clothes carrier." The two principal personages were termed "Tommy" and "Bessy," and a performer on the fiddle usually made up the troupe. All were more or less fantastically dressed. "Tommy" and "Bessy," especially, wore masses of fluttering ribbons of the gayest colours. The part of the lady, be it remarked, was always enacted by a man. The functions of the "clothes carrier" are explained by his title—the party proceeding across the country from colliery to colliery, at each of which they donned their masquerading attire, and were made very welcome. After due obeisances had been paid to Tommy and Bessy, the dancers drew their weapons, and proceeded, in peaceful fashion to use them. They capered about, clashing the cold steel, and as it was necessary in some of the evolutions that every man should grasp the end of his partner's blade with one hand while he held his own with the other, the sharp edges were carefully concealed beneath a lashing of rosined cord. Meantime Tommy and Bessy carried round the hat, and at every fresh largess the report of the gunner's musket saluted the liberality of the donor.

The pitmen are, generally speaking, a decidedly temperate race. Dram-drinking, for instance, is unknown amongst them. Ale is their usual festive beverage; but, except on Saturday nights, they very seldom exceed in it, and often do not touch it. Once a fortnight, however, there is a general *gaudeamus* at the public-houses in or near the colliery village. The men assemble in great sociality at the sign of the "Pit Lad," or the "Davy." Pipes are lit; songs, in the curious *patois* of the district—which sounds like broad Scotch, ill spoken—are roared in chorus; the strong ale does its duty; and the wives who have come to coax their goodmen home find themselves on a bootless errand. Unhappily, however, a very frequent termination of the festivities is, or rather was—for the pitman is improving in that respect as in many others—a quarrel, a scuffle, and a battle royal, fought by the whole of the *dramatis personæ*. Sometimes the apple of discord appears in the shape of money transactions. At others, squabbles and little jealousies between the women are broached and discussed—the husbands, brothers, and sweethearts taking different sides; and occasionally, says my informant (himself a pitman), they begin to boast of each other's personal prowess. "I'se a better mon than thee'st," one self-satisfied gentleman will remark to his compotator. A depreciating rejoinder of course follows. "Debate arising," as the journals of the House of Commons say, a general row is the issue. "Pitmen," remarked my informant, "will fight fair, and mainly with their fists, if they are one to one; but in a general scuffle each will catch up and lay about him with anything handy. I have seen candlesticks, pots, and even chairs flung about; and in one public-house in particular the landlord was obliged to keep the poker chained to the hearth."

It is, however, to be distinctly understood that these descriptions refer to a state of society in rapid process of change for the better. The same remark applies to the superstitions of the mining population. I have had some difficulty in getting at even the traditions of fancies which were once generally and devoutly believed by the coal-workers of the North. The old men, I have been frequently told, have still a lingering faith in the legends of the mine; but the young men only laugh at them. The class of superstitions which still maintains some hold is

that involved in the belief in omens, tokens, dreams, and lucky or unlucky occurrences. I have already mentioned that a pitman dislikes
meeting a woman when he is going to his work. The walk from home
to the pit mouth, often performed in the dead of night, is the period
most rife in warnings of some fatal result which the day's labour is to
bring forth. A supernatural appearance, of a warning character, was
often supposed to cross the miner's path in the shape of a little white
animal like a rabbit. In fact, anything moving and white was held
to be an omen of impending disaster. Mental as well as visual warnings abounded. The miners had frequent presentiments that something was about to go wrong, and the teachings of the inward monitor
were very carefully attended to. The pitmen of the Midland counties
have (or had) a belief, unknown in the North, in aerial whistlings
ringing through the night air, and warning them not to descend the
shaft. Who or what the invisible musicians were, nobody pretended
to know. One therefore feels somewhat surprised at their having been
enumerated and found to consist of seven, thenceforth designated the
"Seven Whistlers." I have only heard of two actual goblins known to
haunt the mine. The one is a mischievous elf, whose presence is only
indicated by the damage which he perpetrates. He is called "Cutty
Soams," and appears to employ himself only on the stupid device of
severing the rope-traces or soams by which an assistant-putter, hon-
oured by the title of the "foal," is yoked to the tub. The strands of
hemp are left all sound in the board at night; in the morning they
are found severed in twain. "Cutty Soams has been at work," says the
putter dolefully, knotting the injured rope. The second goblin was altogether a more sensible, and, indeed, an honest and hard-working
bogle—much akin to the Scotch brownie, or the hairy fiend whom
Milton rather scurvily apostrophises as a "lubber." The supernatural
personage in question was, in fact, a sort of ghostly putter, and his
name was Blue Cap. Sometimes the scared miners would behold a
light blue flame, or "low," flicker through the air, and settle down on
a full coal tub, which immediately moved towards the rolley-way as
though impelled by a stalwart putter. Industrious Blue Cap was at
work. But he required, and rightly, to be paid for his services, which
he modestly rated as those of an ordinary average putter. Therefore
once a fortnight Blue Cap's wages were left for him in a solitary corner of the mine. If they were a farthing below his due, indignant Blue
Cap would not pocket a stiver. If they were a farthing over his due,
conscientious Blue Cap left the surplus revenue where he found it. I

asked my informant whether, if Blue Cap's wages were left out for him now-a-days, he thought they would be appropriated. He sensibly replied that he had no doubt that they would be pocketed by Blue Cap—or somebody else.

# LABOUR AND THE POOR.

———◆———

## THE MANUFACTURING DISTRICTS.

[FROM OUR SPECIAL CORRESPONDENT.]

### THE MINING DISTRICTS OF NORTHUMBERLAND AND DURHAM.

### Letter XXII.

I have already alluded to a combination among the coal-owners for restricting the amount of coals brought to market, and thereby keeping up the prices. This combination, or, as it was called, "Limitation of the Vend," after having existed at intervals for many years, is now extinct. A practical "Limitation of the Vend" still, however, exists as regards a considerable proportion—more than one-third—of the Durham and Northumberland pits. This restriction, or, as its participators prefer calling it, "Regulation," is the work of the men themselves; and although they will not admit that it is an offshoot of the union, and although it may not exist in all pits connected with the union, it never exists save in such pits. This "Regulation" is a rule among the men themselves not to send up to bank more than a given quantity of coals per day per man. The amount is fixed by each colliery for itself, and the arrangement is always spoken of as perfectly voluntary, and one which any hewer may take part in or not as he pleases. The practical consequence, however, is that the regulation, wherever it is introduced into a pit, speedily becomes all but universal. The proprietors do not sanction the arrangement, but I cannot find that they are very violently opposed to it. The fact is, that it stands them in some respect instead of the old "Limitation of the Vend." I have not neglected to make inquiries into the working results of the "Regulation," as well as into the policy of its champions.

The first practical effect of the "Regulation" is of course to curtail, and in some degree to equalize, the rate of pitmen's wages. These wages I have generally reckoned as from 3s. 6d. to 4s. a day, with a free house and garden, and coals at almost a nominal rate. The drawbacks, as I have stated them, may amount to about 1s. 6d. per week.

As in the case of all work paid by the piece, the inquirer into the re-muneration of coal-workers is presented with the most contradictory estimates, but the above calculation I believe to be pretty near the mark. In one of Mr. Tremenheere's reports there is an estimate of the average of wages, as connected with this subject of restriction, which a number of pitmen to whom I have shown it pronounced partial and over-rated; but which these very individuals have given me data for believing to be under, rather than over, the mark. In this calculation the average earnings of the hewers in the Tyne and Blythe Collieries are estimated at 3s. 9¾d. per man per day, those of the Wear at 3s. 7¾d., and those of the Tees at 3s. 9½d. The highest average in the several pits are—in the first district, 4s. 4d. per day paid at Wallsend, 4s. 4½d. at Cramlington, and 4s. 8¼d. at East Holywell and Seghill. On the Wear the highest averages paid are 4s. 3d. at South Hetton, 4s. 3¾d. at Garmondsway-moor, and 4s. 10½d. at Kelloe. On the Tees the highest averages are—4s. 3d. paid at Auckland St. Helens, 4s. 3¼d. paid at Westerton, and 4s. 11¼d. paid at Craggwood. The lowest averages in the same districts are as follows:—On the Tyne, at Lea moor, 3s. 1d. per man per day; at Pelaw Main, 3s. 1½d.; and at Cotlodge, 3s. 1¾d. On the Wear, at Elnet, Washington, and Kerpier Musgrove, 3s.; at Beamish and Crow Tees, 3s. 1d.; and at Shotton, 3s. 1½d. On the Tees, at Hunwick, 3s. 1¼d.; at Greenwood, 3s. 4½d.; and at Brancepeth and Etherley, 3s. 6d. This statement was furnished by the viewers and owners of the different collieries, and, as I have re-marked, was pronounced exaggerated by several practical hewers. In the course of conversation with one of these individuals, he told me of a "hewing match," formerly an ordinary occurrence among pitmen, in which his brother had been one of the competitors, and which he himself had witnessed. The seam of coal performed upon was, as I understood, one of fair average height and hardness. The parties per-formed a regular day's work of eight hours, and at the conclusion of the trial, the winner had hewn 12s. 10d. worth, and the loser 12s. 2d. worth of coal. The average between the two was thus 12s. 6d. Now, subtracting the 6d. for fines and drawbacks, and accounting an ordi-nary eight hours' work as one-third of the labour performed during an eight hours' match—surely no extravagant estimate of the toil which a man can, as a general rule, get through—the product is 4s., a higher amount by 2½d. than Mr. Tremenheere's highest averages. Taking then 3s. 9d. as the average of wages before the restriction came into play, I find, from calculations drawn from the source already indicated, that the average fall on the Tyne has been, including fractions, 7d. per day, each hewer voluntarily muleting himself of that amount. On the Wear, the fall has been 6d., and on the Tees 9d. per day; making the general restricted earnings 3s. 2d. in the first district, 3s. 1d. in the second, and 3s. in the third. At the Wallsend Colliery, one of the men, who had them in his possession, produced a number of packets of pay-bills, showing the amount, all fines deducted, actually received throughout an extended period by the men. From the mass I selected the bills of one fortnight, and, after making a careful average, I found that the wages actually paid during that time amounted to only 2s. 9d. per man per day, counting six days to the week. The average during the existence of the restriction, given for Wallsend in the official documents, is 3s. 4d., showing a wide difference, which, however, may be easily accounted for on the supposition that the colliery was not working full time during the fortnight selected—a state of matters of very frequent occurrence—and also that there may have been one, or perhaps two, Saturdays of broken or of suspended labour during the period in question. In the Thornley Colliery calculations have been made upon a surer basis than those which I was enabled to frame from the data above stated—the gross number of days worked being taken instead of the number of hewers. The figures are, without cavil, those which stand in the books of the colliery and in the pay-bills in possession of the men; and the result of the most extended calculation is, that 22,645 restricted days' work were paid for by £3,816 12s. 7d., or at the rate of 3s. 4½d. per man per day. From this deduct 1¾d. for fines, and the net product is 3s. 2¾d. I may add that the estimate was framed with a view quite different from that of ascertaining the actual amount of wages. I fully believe, then, on all these authorities, and on many other statements derived from *vivâ voce* intercourse with individuals, that good hewers, when working unrestricted, can earn 4s. and more per day, and that inferior hewers can earn 3s. and more per day. It follows from the averages I have given, that the brunt and hardship of the restriction falls upon the best men in each pit. Coal-owners have informed me that it operates advantageously for slow or lazy men, because the fact of their superiors restricting themselves to a certain sum acts as a powerful stimulus upon them to approach that amount as nearly as possible. "Many and many a man," said a hewer to me, and I believe with perfect truth, "is not touched by the restriction at all. He can't come up to it." It would follow that the best men lose by this restriction at the very least 9d., and many of the less skilful more than 4½d. a day. The reasons why they subject themselves to this very serious deduction from wages which they are admittedly capable of earning, were detailed to me by an individual, who, I have good grounds for knowing, possesses the full confidence of the restricting hewers. These reasons were much to the following import:—"The restriction is fixed at the limit of what we consider a fair day's work for a man of ordinary powers and endurance, engaged in the toilsome and exhausting labour of hewing. We believe that working men in this country work too long and too hard, and we would like to see the time and the fatigue both abridged. Besides, we think it fair to stand by each other as a body, and not to go on competing the one with the other. We feel assured that if we worked to the utmost that we are capable of, we should suffer severely in health, and perhaps ultimately in wages. We know that there are more men in the trade than are requisite to raise the amount of coals required for the average vend; but by restricting each individual's work, we compel the masters to employ all, or nearly all of us, and thus to bring into operation what, under the competing system, would be the surplus labour. We conceive that this arrangement, while it benefits the body of hewers, does not injure the masters, because they are only asked to divide the same amount of wages amongst a greater number of men; the only hardship upon them, and we think it a very slight one, is, that there may be the loss of part of the interest of the money laid out upon the machinery, because that machinery does not work every day so long as it was calculated for. But we have also this reason—We think, and so did the masters when they had their limitation of the vend, that this restriction limits the quantity of coals brought to market; and in our opinion, if the quantity be limited, prices will rise, and our wages will—or, at all events, ought to—rise with them. It may be very well to say that if the price of coals rises, so much will not be bought. But we know what we are about; we know that coals must be had. This country could no more go on without coals than without meat. That is our vantage ground. Every steam-engine—in every factory—on every railway—on board every boat and ship—depends upon us, and if we chose to be united we could stop them all. We therefore are of opinion, that, were the restriction universal—and we are trying to make it so—we could not only shorten the hours of our labour, but cause the hours in which we do work to be paid for at a higher rate."

This I believe to be a fair and perfectly uncoloured view of the opinions of an overwhelming proportion of the pitmen—of those of them, at least, who have opinions at all; and this section always leads the remainder, who follow the advice of those of their own class whose abilities they feel to be superior to their own, with the blindest confidence and the most unerring exactitude. I had much conversation with the individual to whom I am indebted for the above explanation of his comrades' views, and I found that he was deeply impressed with the logical truth of the position which they held, notwithstanding the untoward result of several strikes which had been commenced more or less upon the principles above indicated. That there is a considerable quantity of surplus labour existing in the northern coal-field is admitted by masters and men; indeed, one of the objects of the restriction is to provide employment for it. A portion of that surplus labour was of course caused by the population increasing faster than the trade; but a still greater proportion was the consequence of the various great strikes, every one of which introduced a fresh infusion of working men, from the Midland counties or from Wales. In the strike of 1831-32, more than 2,000 strangers were brought into the trade. In the strike of 1844, the Marquess of Londonderry alone imported nearly 200 Irishmen to labour at one of his pits. A great number of Welsh miners were also induced to immigrate, and there can be no doubt that the amount of extra labour introduced was such as seriously to interfere with the balance of industrial supply and demand. But even at the time of the strike there were many more hewers and other labourers than were required for the work to be done. An address to the colliers, drawn up at the time by, as I am assured, a competent authority, estimates that in 1830 there were employed underground, deducting all persons in command, about 12,700 men and boys. In 1844 the number had increased to 22,700, being a rise of 79 per cent. The increase of vend during the period was 53 per cent. But, in 1830, it was contended that even then there was 25 per cent. of surplus labour in the market, so that the surplus labour of 1844 amounted to upwards of 30 per cent.; in other words, there were 22,749 persons employed, while 15,924 were competent to raise all the coals which the masters wished to raise—that is, all for which they could find a profitable sale. This disproportion is now increased. The restriction no doubt prevents it from being felt with such severity as in other circumstances it would be; but I need only hint that the line of policy which degrades the best men to the pay of the worst, and the tendency of which is to crush down all superiority in energy or skill to a dead level of mediocrity, is hardly one of which the long continuance is, or ought to be, expected.

I now pass to a part of the coal system from which springs much bad blood between employers and employed. It is not, as has been already explained, the tendency of the coal-raising trade to create inland towns. Every pit has its village, exclusively inhabited by the people employed in the mine; and almost as a matter of course the dwellings in which they live are erected by the owner of the works, nobody else having any interest to speculate in the building of cottage-villages. These cottages, as I have also stated, are held not as tenements, but as wages. It follows, that on occasions of strikes the payment of wages and the right to the occupancy of houses cease together. Hence frequently arises a system of evictions which I believe not only to be productive of the worst moral consequences to the people, but to be continually sowing seeds of bitter grudges between them and their employers. The mere act of ceasing to pay wages when men cease to work, has in it something so perfectly and obviously natural, that it involves no idea of hardship; but the turning a man out of his house, particularly when, as must happen in the very nature of things in the coal districts, he has much difficulty in finding another roof to get under—such a proceeding is regarded, by those who suffer from it, and by those who sympathise with them, as harsh, if not tyrannical. They do not readily realize an abstract idea of right—and not only of right but even of necessity, on the coal-owners' part—particularly when all their household goods are overturned by its exercise. A strike followed by an eviction has very recently occurred at a colliery called Kepier Grange, a mile or two to the south of Durham. Hearing that the turn-out workpeople were huddled together, principally in the public-houses in the neighbourhood, I proceeded to the spot, and was conducted by several of the hewers to see what they termed the "tender mercies" of the coal-owners. First, however, I requested the workmen to give me their version of the cause of the strike. It was partly for higher wages, partly on account of an alleged grievance in the weighing of the coals. In a handbill published by the men, they state that the price paid them for hewing a tub of coals of the weight of 6 cwt. was 2¼d., and that no allowance whatever was made to them for underweight. They had asked ¼d. per tub more—were refused—and so turned out. In their verbal communications with me they stated that the atmosphere of the pit was exceedingly damp, and that in some places the workings were very wet. For coals hewn in the wet workings they were paid not 2¼d., but 4d. per tub; but the tubs were not weighed when brought to bank, because it was contended that the quantity of moisture which they contained made them apparently heavier than they really were. Thus, they said, although a workman might lose a tub which was a pound under weight, he reaped no advantage from a tub which was ten pounds over weight. They argued that they had lost more in this way than the extra sum which they were paid for working in wet places. They had no grievances in the way of "laid out" to complain of; but they added that the people of an adjoining colliery were paid more than twice as much for a tub as they were. This difference of course resulted from the difference of the seams worked—the fact of there being little or no "laid out," showing that the coal at Kepier Grange was clean and unmixed with refuse, while, as regards the pit referred to, I had subsequently woeful accounts of the difficulty of working its seams owing to their extreme shallowness. I proceeded to inspect the condition of the people who had turned out. In the public-house which I first entered there had been 28 persons accommodated. The back yards and out-houses were crammed with the coarser furniture, while the better articles were stowed away within. In one room three temporary beds were spread, and I was told that others were nightly made up on the floor. The huddling together of families in this way—the sleeping arrangements being quite unscreened each from the others—cannot but produce the worst moral and social effects. In another public-house, close at hand, a similar state of matters prevailed. Three uncurtained beds were placed at the head of a room so close that each touched the other, and in the night time mattresses were laid all along the kitchen floor. Bad as all this was, I was given to understand that things had been even worse, but that the strike having now continued about a fortnight, the people were being gradually absorbed into Durham and the villages round it. In one small house, consisting of one small room, situated close behind one of the empty and evacuated dwellings, I found that eleven persons had taken refuge. The owner of the place was a single old man, who had received a family of ten from the neighbouring cottage. There was but one bedstead in the room, and upon that the mattresses and bedclothes, which served the whole family and their host, were piled nearly as high as my shoulder. At night they covered every available inch of the earthern floor up to the fire-place. The father and mother complained bitterly of the harsh manner in which they stated that they had been evicted. It was already dark, they said, and a cold stormy night, when the police-officers arrived to turn them out. Their furniture was seized and rudely flung in heaps into the muddy road. They pointed out a ditch into which tables and chairs had fallen pell-mell. On the bank of this ditch one of their boys lighted a fire in a pot. A policeman said that they had no business to kindle it, because the coals, as part of their wages, did not belong to them any more than the house—and he kicked the lighted embers into the ditch. The family then attempted to find partial refuge in the recess of the door of their late habitation. The snow was falling fast, and they were in a dreary condition of cold and wet, when their charitable neighbours came forth and took them in.

This was the statement furnished to me. The evicted individual affirmed that he had had no warning that he was to be turned to the door on the day when the catastrophe took place; but all of the miners readily admitted that, in striking work, they knew that they rendered themselves liable to eviction. I had some conversation with one of the leading men amongst them. He said that they did not complain so much of losing their houses, which they admitted were part of their wages, as of the eviction being conducted harshly, and with unnecessary haste. "The houses, too, were standing empty. The owners might as well have let us keep them until they got somebody else to put into possession. It would be no loss to them, and a great favour to us." Without passing judgment upon the reasonableness of this idea, I must mention that the tone adopted in urging it was quite an appeal *ad misericordiam*. With respect to the length of the notice given of intention to evict, I was subsequently informed that it generally depended upon the length of the notice the men gave of their intention to strike—in fact, that the men virtually gave their own notice of ejectment. If they signified their intention of striking in a fortnight's time, they knew that they were liable to be turned out at the end of a fortnight. If they struck without giving notice, the masters could turn them out of the houses without notice. The owners of the deserted colliery were, when I visited it, making great exertions to obtain a supply of labour. "They would employ you for a hewer in a minute if you wanted the job," was remarked to me by one of the turn-outs. A great number of the body seemed to be lounging all day in and about the public-houses, smoking and discussing the chances of the strike. The publicans gave them lodging for nothing, charging only for provisions; and those of their poor neighbours who could, appeared very ready to make room for as many as possible. Whilst I was standing at the door of one of the taverns in question, a man went by, escorted by one of the rural police. The hewers told me that he was a tailor, who had taken employment in the pit, and they laughed at the notion of his pseudo-guardian. "If we wished to injure the man," they said, "it wouldn't be a single policeman who could prevent us."

I have thus stated the case of the men as given to me by themselves, omitting or modifying no particle of it. I applied, however, to the owners of the colliery for their version of the matter, and was courteously furnished by Mr. Sinclair, the viewer, with the following elaborate reply, dated a day or two after my visit to Kepier Grange.

"TO THE SPECIAL CORRESPONDENT OF THE MORNING CHRONICLE.

"SIR—I am very glad to have the opportunity of assisting you in the object you have in view, as expressed in your note of the 12th, which I have just received, the more so that I feel that the more public a true statement of the relative position of the pitmen and their employers can be made, the sooner will a stop be put to those ruinous strikes amongst the pitmen, which have unfortunately been of too frequent occurrence.

"The disagreement between the owners of the Kepier Grange Colliery and their pitmen is a most striking instance of the folly of a body of pitmen giving up employment where they were earning good wages with a moderate amount of labour, and which, after being unemployed for nearly a month, they would now very gladly have if they could obtain it.

"The pitmen sent a written notice to the owners, in which they stated that they were not adequately paid for their labour, and that unless certain additions were made to the different prices, they would cease working at the expiration of a fortnight, which is the length of time required for notice at this colliery when a pitman either leaves or is discharged. The owners, after taking the matter into their consideration, replied, through me, that they could not give any advance of price, but that they thought the men had acted properly in giving the requisite notice, and that they could leave the colliery at the expiration of their term of notice if they thought they could get better employment elsewhere—at the same time giving them notice that if they did so they must leave the cottages they then occupied, which were allowed them as part of their wages, as the cottages would be required for the new pitmen who would be employed. At the expiration of the term of notice the men ceased working, but did not leave their cottages. Other workmen were employed, and on the second night after these men began to work, the window of the cottage in which one of them lived was broken in by a volley of stones; and another man had some of his furniture injured by stones having been thrown into his house. This intimidated the men who were working, and I was obliged to apply to the superintendent of the county constabulary to send some of his force to protect these men and the property belonging to the owners of the colliery. Until this occurred I was unwilling to turn out the pitmen who had ceased working, and I still wished them to remove their own furniture to wherever they might choose to put it; and on consulting with the owners of the colliery, they agreed to give the pitmen a week to remove their furniture, and, if they would not do so, then to turn them out. None of them removed their furniture, and I had to get a sufficient force and remove it for them. This was done so as to give them as little annoyance as possible.

"From that time until yesterday I had no application from the men to be allowed to return to the colliery, and I employed other workmen, who were working as many coals as we wanted. Yesterday they came in a body to my office, and asked if I would again employ them. I told them I could give them no answer as a body of men; but, if they came singly into my office and applied for work, I would employ as many of them as I wanted: this they did, and I have again employed about half of them on the very same terms as they had when they ceased working—whilst the other half will, I believe, find very great difficulty in obtaining employment as pitmen at this season of the year, and would be very glad to have again the employment they have so foolishly lost.

"I will now give you a statement of the earnings of these men before they ceased working, and also of the earnings of the men who have been employed since the others ceased—some of the latter never worked coal before, but were working as labourers eleven hours a day for 2s. 2d. I must also beg you to remember that the pitmen have good cottages with gardens, and firecoal, in addition to what they earn in the pit.

"On referring to the pay-bills I see that during the fortnight ending November 3, before notice was given by the pitmen, that sixteen men, who worked 151 days, earned 34*l.* 5s. 6d., or 4s. 6d. a day; the remainder averaged 3s. 10d. a day, the average of the whole being nearly 4s. a day. During the next fortnight, after they had given notice, twenty men, who worked 184 days, earned 40*l.* 14s., or 4s. 2d. a day, and the remainder 3s. 9d. a day; the average of the whole being about 3s. 10½d. a day. None of these men worked more than six hours a day, and many of them not five hours. During the next fortnight, after the pitmen ceased working, the new men earned as follows:—

|   |   |   |   | £ | s. | d. |   | s. | d. |   |
|---|---|---|---|---|---|---|---|---|---|---|
| 3 men earned in | 30 days | 10 | 8 | 4, or | 6 | $3\frac{3}{4}$ | a day. |
| 2 | „ | 20 | „ | 3 | 18 | 5, or | 3 | 11 | „ |
| 5 | „ | 35 | „ | 6 | 3 | 2, or | 3 | $6\frac{3}{4}$ | „ |
| 4 | „ | 32 | „ | 6 | 15 | 10, or | 4 | 3 | „ |
| 6 | „ | 27 | „ | 6 | 2 | 0, or | 4 | 6 | „ |
| 20 men earned in | 144 days | 33 | 7 | 9, or | 4 | $7\frac{1}{2}$ | a day. |

"These men worked six hours a day. During the present fortnight, which will end to-morrow, we have had more pitmen at work; and though I cannot yet be certain what their earnings will amount to, I am sure it will be above 5s. a day; three of them having in one day, when they worked eight hours, made 1*l*. 14s. 6d., or 11s. 6d. a man a day.

"I have now, I think, given you all the information you require on this matter; but, should you wish for any further information, I shall be happy to give you any that I can.—I am, sir, your very obedient servant,
"EDWARD SINCLAIR,
"Viewer of Keepier Grange Colliery.
"Keepier Grange Colliery, Durham, Dec. 14."

The cases are frequent in which evictions give rise to tumult, and even to bloodshed. On the very day on which I visited Keepier Grange an eviction took place at Charlaw, a colliery not very far distant. In this case there was also a strike, and the men had had repeated warnings that they would be forced to give up possession of their houses. On the Friday they were told that all those who did not begin work on the Monday following must find other homes. A few complied; the rest remained firm; and a body of police were despatched to carry out the ejectment. Before, however, any steps were actually taken, and while the policemen were in the act of descending from the vehicle in which they arrived, a rush was made at them by the miners, prefaced by a shower of stones—and in the scuffle which followed, a policeman was severely hurt about the head, and one of the attacking party had his skull fractured. This seems to have put an end to active opposition. The people left their houses without resistance, but at night I understand that a good many of them broke through the windows and took possession again. They were to be proceeded against for trespass.

Such scenes as these—however justifiable or necessary the evictions (in other words the stoppage of all wages) may be—such scenes, it must be admitted, are very deeply to be lamented. They form one of the most painful features of coal-strikes, and one the remembrance of which rankles longest in the miner's breast. I believe that the cases are very few indeed in which wanton harshness is displayed on the part of the masters; but the very nature of the system, under which wages cannot be stopped without ejection of the recipients from hearth and home, seems painful and unsatisfactory. How it can be remedied is the difficulty. There is no choice of lodgings for the workman; and besides, he finds a free house and garden exceedingly convenient; while, on the other hand, the master will not willingly give up an arrangement by which he possesses so strong a hold over those whom he employs. Some of the pitmen say that the fact of their employers being also their landlords involves the truck system; but they admit that in almost every case there are no houses other than their employers' for them to live in—so that if the arrangement does involve the truck system, it does so from the pure necessity of the case.

I have found few differences in respect to grades of house accommodation, worth noting, in my tour through the colliery villages in Durham and Northumberland. I saw pit-rows attached to old and to (as they are called) "young" mines. The later-built houses were generally more substantial and roomy than the old ones; but the plan continued exactly the same, and the room accommodation was just as deficient. Near the Walker pit there are a few detached houses of two stories, formerly used for the works connected with a deserted shaft, and now patched up into dwellings—each family occupying a single, unventilated, and crazy room. At Framwellgate-moor I found that from the working of the mine being partially discontinued, the owners were letting out a fair row of cottages, after their sort, at the easy rate of 6d. a week. The floors of all these houses were of some composite stuff, in many cases broken away. At a place called New Durham there is a large colliery village, containing a great number of houses, below the average in point of comfort. Outside, the whole place was a perfect waste of filth; and within the houses, the furniture I found to be in many cases meagre in quantity, and poor and shabby in quality. The people complained bitterly of the construction of the chimneys, which, they said, were continually smoking, in spite of all doctoring. In one range of two-roomed houses, fires could only be lighted in one apartment at a time. This range was known in the village as "Smoky-row." The floors of several of the houses were miserably damp, and the whole of the ashes and domestic filth were flung out before the doors. The people in this village were uncomfortable in several respects. The place is an exception to the general rule, in being situated nearly two miles from the shaft. This distance the fore shift and all the putters and drivers have to travel at least once a day in the dark, through miry fields. The workings, again, are fully a mile from the bottom of the shaft—so that the hewers and putters are forced to walk upwards of six miles above and beneath ground, going to and coming from their work. Besides, one at least of the seams now being wrought is an exceedingly severe one, the height of the coal being only nineteen inches, with nine inches additional cut for the behoof of the putters—making a total height of twenty-eight inches in which the hewers work. One of the latter sat down before me on the floor of his house in the attitude in which he laboured. It was an uncomfortable sitting posture, with the right leg extended sideways, the left foot planted on the ground, the knee drawn up, and the head stooped, so as to bring the chin upon a level with the most elevated part of the limb. The hewer sat upon a very low stool, raised hardly two inches, and called a "bracket." His wife said that the work was breaking his back. At Collier-row, on the property of the Marquess of Londonderry, I found some fair cottages, constructed of wood, and double-roomed. The usual ridge of ashes and filth extended along the rows, and across the road by which I reached the place two streams of water were flowing. Middle Rainton, also belonging to the Marquess, has a very favourable *primâ facie* look. One range of houses lines the turnpike-road. These are two-storied structures, most substantially built. They accommodate two families, one on each story, the arrangements being two good rooms and a pantry for each. The lower floor was paved with flags, and altogether the aspect of things in the row was decidedly pleasant. Penetrating, however, to the back, I found quite a different condition of affairs—wretched houses of one small room each, the floors below the level of the refuse-piled streets, and the whole place wearing an aspect of dreary poverty and filth. There are some decidedly good houses in all the Marquess's pit villages, but the majority seem to be very much akin to the general run of pitmen's dwellings—no better and no worse. The people informed me that for certain improvements made, some time ago, they have to thank a visit of the Marchioness. The Marquess, however, is on the whole rather a popular person with the pitmen. In the strike of 1831 he offered himself as a mediator between the labourers and their masters, and was the means of obtaining for the pitmen a concession of their demands.

As I am now approaching the termination of my account of the Durham and Northumberland Coal-field, I may as well devote a paragraph to those miscellaneous facts and morsels of information connected with the subject which from time to time I became acquainted with—frequently after the letters in which they would severally have been most in place had been already despatched.

Hewers are apportioned to different seams, and different parts of seams, by lot; or, as it is technically called, "cavil." The cavil takes place once a quarter. The men's names, written on scraps of paper, are placed in a hat, and the first name drawn settles the place of its owner, and through him the places of his comrades, according to a predetermined arrangement. It not unfrequently happens, under the present system of monthly hiring, particularly if the demand for hewers is brisk, that a workman who has had a "bad cavil"—that is, a place in a hard or difficult seam—gives his month's warning and betakes himself to another colliery, in the hope of meeting with better luck. That the proceeding is obviously unfair does not prevent it from frequently taking place. In cases of removal, the old plan was for the new master to pay the expenses of the "flitting," but this has been discontinued, and the colliers must now transport their goods and chattels from place to place at their own cost. In a great number of collieries within a reasonable distance of Newcastle, the proprietors send in one or more carts every Saturday, to carry out the marketings of the women, who proceed to town to lay in their stock of groceries, &c., for the ensuing week. The carts put up at some central point in the town. Thither the tradesmen send the purchased goods, which are thence conveyed to the doors of their owners without any expense, other than the pence paid by each family to the driver of the vehicle. In cases of fatal accidents in coal-pits, the widows of the men killed are almost invariably allowed to retain houses rent free in the Pit-row— although, if they occupy double tenements, they must often remove to smaller ones. Women placed under these circumstances seldom or never quit the colliery. They set up little huckstering shops, and take in washing. The owners always pay the funeral expenses of men killed in their employment, and make a money present to the surviving relations. One or more benefit societies are in connection with each pit. They grant allowances on their largest scale in cases of accident; on a smaller scale in cases of sickness; and they commonly also afford small superannuation pensions. Generally speaking, some light sort of work about the pit is found for hewers who have grown grey in the service.

The fines from "laid out" and "set out" are sometimes set apart by the owners for charitable purposes. But there are cases—the Haswell Coal Pit afforded a recent one—in which the men have absolutely refused the offer of the proprietors to apportion the fines in this way. "If you take them," said the workmen, "you take them unjustly, and you may keep them." The tone occasionally adopted by the pitmen may be judged of by this reply. The small chapels which abound in colliery villages are "served" three Sundays out of every four by "local preachers," themselves working men. These persons proceed from mine to mine agreeably to a regular printed arrangement, a copy of which may be frequently found suspended from the walls of a hewer's cottage. They officiate gratis, generally dining at the table of any zealous member of the congregation. These local preachers exercise the deepest influence over a very large proportion of the coal-mining population. Their sermons are usually couched in the homeliest *patois*, and are very often full of technical allusions and illustrations.

I have now described, step by step, the raising of coal to the surface—detailing the minutiæ of the daily toil and the daily lives of the population engaged in the process. It only remains that I should sketch the manner in which the great bulk of the mineral so procured is shipped to the various markets. From every pit a tramway runs, either to join a neighbouring railroad or to connect the mine with one of the thousand "staiths" which form so prominent a feature along the banks of the Tyne and Wear. These "staiths" are high wooden jetties, generally running so far into the river as to allow vessels of considerable burden to lie afloat at their extremities, even at low water. The tramway runs from the pit to the end of the staith—the latter usually forming an incline, down which each heaped-up waggon as it descends pulls up an empty one. The ship to be loaded lies of course below. The full waggon, under charge of a brakesman, lodges upon a species of ingeniously balanced framework, calculated to swing down with the weight from the end of the staith, and to come to a rest exactly over the open hatchway of the vessel beneath. The brakesman or rider accompanies the waggon in its descent, and removing a bolt, the bottom of the vehicle gives way in trap-door fashion, and its load sinks into the hold—the well-balanced platform immediately rising as the weight is removed from it, and restoring the waggon to its position at the extremity of the staith, up which it is pulled by the next descending load. There is a brakesman to every waggon, assisted by an off-putter, whose station is at the extremity of the staith, and who keeps an account of the number of waggonfuls shipped. The wages of the waggon-rider are about 15s., those of the off-putter about 18s. or 20s. weekly. The latter frequently goes on board vessels, so as to pilot them to their proper position at the end of the staith.

The largest class of collier loading at a staith will have her cargo aboard in a tide. In the hold there are a gang of "trimmers," whose duty it is to stow away the coals as they are poured under hatches. The trimmers are paid 3s. 6d. for each keel of eight Newcastle chaldrons. The crews of colliers never meddle with the shipping of the cargo. They work the vessel, and do nothing more.

Occasionally, instead of the vessel ascending the river to a staith, she lies at Shields, in the Tyne, or at Sunderland, in the Wear, and has her lading conveyed to her by keels, and shovelled on board by keelmen. These keels are the coal-barges of the North. They are heavily built craft, partially decked, the hatchway being in general so large as to leave the impression that the boat has merely a ledge of deck running inwards from her gunwale. These keels are sloop-rigged, carrying a mainsail and jib, the blackened canvass of which forms one of the characteristics of the northern coal rivers. Each keel has an after-cabin, or "huddick," in which the crew occasionally sleep. The huddick is furnished neither with berths nor hammocks—two or three mattresses and as many blankets, laid on the floor round the stove, affording the necessary accommodation. Keelmen form a sort of cross between hewers and sailors. They wear a peculiar costume, consisting of a large jacket, or rather doublet, with loose breeches, made very wide at the knee, and not descending further. The wearers of this costume are, or at all events were, a proverbially unintelligent, ignorant, and intemperate set of men. One keelman, it used to be said, could drink out three pitmen; and there is a species of traditional story, well known in Newcastle, and which has long passed current as illustrative of the intelligence of those whose duty it is to make the "keel row." According to this legend, a keelman, seeing alongside of his craft a hoop inside of which an unbroken mass of froth had collected, leaped overboard to secure the prize, taking it for a floating grindstone! Having been pulled out, he was narrating his mishap to a comrade, who vastly enjoyed the joke, but gently reprimanded the adventurer, telling him that he ought to have seen at a glance that the floating object was not a grindstone, because, by his own account, it had not a hole in the middle!

Coal Staith on the Tyne

The keel trade has been much injured by the railways, which convey coals to Sunderland and Shields more cheaply and speedily than they can be transported by water carriage. A keelman told me that in the old days he had often made £2 10s. per week. His gains at present are from 15s. to 18s. Sometimes a large colliery maintains a fleet of keels, but generally they are the property of comparatively poor men, each of whom acts as the skipper of his own craft. A keel is paid by the tide, that is, by the trip between the staith and the ship's-side, whatever may be the distance between them. The freight is always one guinea, the keelmen for this shovelling the coals aboard. Formerly each keel was manned by three men and a boy, the latter called the "paydee." The guinea was divided between the three men in nearly equal shares, the skipper having only 8d. per tide over and above the portion of each of his crew. The "paydee" had 1s. 6d. per week and his food. Since the keel trade has been slack, however, his services have been in general dispensed with. Before the period in question a keel not unfrequently made ten tides per week, but a third of that number is now reckoned fair average employment. Sometimes, but not often, the keels venture into the open sea to load vessels which cannot conveniently come over the bar. The seamen who man the coal brigs of Northumberland and Durham are almost all north countrymen. If engaged by the month their pay is 50s. A great proportion of these collier brigs, however, are London traders. They may make from ten to twelve trips back and fore per annum. And the pay of each seaman, his food being found, is always £4 per trip. As I have already stated, he takes no part in loading the cargo in the north. The keelman or the staithman performs that part of the work in the Tyne, or the Wear—the coal-whipper clears the hold in the Port of London.

# LABOUR AND THE POOR.

—◆—

## THE MANUFACTURING DISTRICTS.

[FROM OUR SPECIAL CORRESPONDENT.]

### THE STAFFORDSHIRE COLLIERIES.

## Letter XXIII.

In the southern part of Staffordshire—touching upon the town of Wolverhampton, then running in a north-easterly direction towards Bloxwich, from thence stretching to the south, and comprising within its limits Walsall, Wednesbury, and Tipton, and extending as far as Dudley—lies the South Staffordshire Coal-field. It is a great basin of coal and iron-stone seams, frequently running in alternate strata, and in some places, especially towards the northern skirts of the field, approaching so near the surface as to be capable of excavation by means of rude and inexpensive, though in the end very uneconomical, machinery. This coal and iron bed has been diligently worked for many years. Above, for dozens of miles together, the country is literally a waste of cinders and refuse coal dust, studded with flaming iron-works, countless engine-houses, and thickly clustered groups of dismal, squalid villages, any one of which it is as hard to distinguish from its neighbour as it is to make out the peculiar features of individual pit-men, when their faces are all one black mask of coal-dust and grime. Underneath these iron-works, engine-houses, and swarming villages, the country is absolutely hollow—the rent and cracked walls, and tottering buildings, marking where the superincumbent strata have been crushed down into the caverns gradually formed beneath them.

The vast majority of the inhabitants of this region are engaged in the employment which the nature of the soil has made the staple industry. The working men are exclusively iron smelters and forgers, and colliers. Indeed, the two trades seem hereabouts like branches of one occupation. When the iron trade languishes, the coal trade is depressed; and yet, closely linked as the twin branches of labour are, there are wide social and physical differences between the two classes of labourers.

The Midland iron districts exhibit some of the very worst phases of manufacturing life. The working population are rude and unintelligent beyond those who people either the cotton or the woollen country. In the Wolverhampton district, out of 1,133 marriages which took place in 1846, not less than 649 men and 833 women signed the register with their marks. In the Westbromwich district, out of 827 marriages, 342 men and 398 women signed with marks; and in the Walsall district, out of 327 marriages, 153 men and 218 women similarly attested their want of education. From an estimate, the calculations for which extend over some years, it would appear that in the iron districts generally, 57 per cent. of the women and 39 per cent. of the men are enabled to write their names. In point of criminality, Staffordshire is worse than the average of English counties. It is, indeed, the twelfth in point of immorality, as measured by committals—standing in this respect between the agricultural counties of Bucks and Wilts. A considerable portion of the shire is, however, purely rural, and game-law offences form a large item in the list of convictions. In 1847 the criminality of the mining districts of the north was represented by 6.81; that of the silk districts stood at 10.15; that of the agricultural districts at 14.80; that of the cotton districts at 18.52; and that of the iron districts at 20.24. The average of England and Wales was 15.90. The proportion of female offences in the Staffordshire iron and coal districts is great. The women work at rude and unsexing labour at the pit mouth, partly assuming the habiliments and altogether adopting the coarseness of the men. The houses are far inferior to the ordinary standard of the industrial districts, and they seldom or never have gardens. The people are often both dirty and intemperate. At Bilston it is calculated that 5,000 miners spend annually £50,000 in ale; and at Moxley there is one beer-shop to every 12 dwellings. The value of life at Wolverhampton is about one in 40; at Westbromwich one in 45; and at Walsall one in 43. The population of the district of Wolverhampton, in 1841, was 80,721; that of Westbromwich was 52,578; and that of Walsall, 34,253. The number of illegitimate births in Wolverhampton, in 1846, was 188; in Westbromwich, 100; and in Walsall, 107.

In the Parliamentary borough of Wolverhampton, including the towns of Bilston, Ledgley, Wednesbury, and Willenhall, there was, in 1841, a labouring population of 79,259, including upwards of 30,000 children under fifteen years of age, dependent upon cheap public schools for education. Of these it was estimated that about one-fourth attended day schools of some kind, and that about one-half attended Sunday schools—leaving upwards of 15,000 children in a space of a few square miles growing up in dense and total ignorance.

The principal seam of coal which traverses the Stafford mineral district is no less than ten yards in thickness. The centre of the basin may be near Tipton. At Wolverhampton, to the north-west, the ten-yard seam begins to crop out to the surface, and disappears; and the pits thereabouts principally work the lower lying strata, which run in masses of from three to nine feet in depth. The "new mine" belt of coal lies beneath the ten-yard seam. Where the latter dips deeply, it is almost the only one worked—as at Westbromwich; but when it rises towards the edges of the basin, the pitmen sink their shafts to the inferior strata, which of course heave themselves up towards the surface at a still greater distance from the centre of the field. It is calculated that the gross contents of the ten-yard seam are about 48,000 tons per acre; but, owing in a great measure to the rude style of working practised, the actual yield per acre is at present not much above 16,000 tons.

The change from the collieries of Northumberland and Durham to those of Staffordshire seems like going back at least a century in the art of mine engineering. On the banks of the Tyne and the Wear, science the most profound, and practical skill the most trained and enlightened, are brought to bear upon the excavation of coal. The pits are worked under the constant superintendence of regularly educated viewers, each of whom has a staff of assistants, of more or less scientific and practical skill, to carry his directions into execution. In the Staffordshire coal district, on the contrary, everything seems to be done by the roughest rule of thumb. The pits, as regards depth, are mere scratches, compared with those in the North; and, except in the case of a few of the thick-seam mines, they are ventilated solely by the agency of the vast number of shafts with which the whole coal-field is honeycombed—anything like artificial means for creating a current of air being seldom or never thought of. The workings in such excavations are, of course, very limited. The labourers could not breathe at any considerable distance from one of the shafts; and the consequence of the whole system is, that the coal is worked in the slowest, most dangerous, and least economical fashion.

The appearance of the country around Wolverhampton, Willenhall, and Bilston, where the thin seams principally lie, is strange in the extreme. For miles and miles the eye ranges over wide-spreading masses of black rubbish, hills on hills of shale, and mashed and mudded coal dust, extracted from beneath, and masking, as it were, the whole face of nature. The earth hereabouts seems, as far as the eye can reach, to be literally turned inside out. Here and there a sterile-looking field may chequer the black prospect, but the general landscape may be correctly described as a perfect desert of coal-dusts, mud, and refuse. This uninviting-looking region is honeycombed with pit-shafts, and many of the surface undulations which catch the eye are the result of the earth having fallen in and collapsed on insufficiently propped workings. Dotted thickly over the coal expanse are scores of rudely-built engine-houses with short chimneys, and miserable hovels used as places of shelter for the above-ground workers, with here and there rows of dilapidated cottages; and there is hardly a building or a wall which the continued sinking of the earth has not thrown off the perpendicular. Engine-houses lean this way and that—great cracks and rents opening in their walls; and the visitor is sometimes shown spots where rows of houses have been engulfed altogether in the earth. The tramways which wind through these dreary wastes are of the rudest construction; and here and there, labouring to load the waggons or pile the coals brought to the surface, are groups of swart-faced women—but with every womanly feature and attribute ground out of them by the coarse and filthy toil.

The spectator will observe, that from every engine-house there extends, as from a common centre, a number of chains, sometimes passing over wheels working close to the ground, sometimes supported by means of rude stakes, at varying heights—the altitude becoming greater as the distance from the engine-house increases, until each chain passes over the apex of a triangle of posts, and then sinks perpendicularly down into the shaft beneath. The engine thus works three, four, five, and sometimes as many as seven shafts, all leading into the same pit, and all lying within a circle of a couple of hundred yards or so in diameter. The chains are so arranged that one-half of them wind up while the other half are being let out. The working of this mechanism is wretchedly slow, while the chance of shaft accidents is, of course, immensely increased by the fact that there is often necessarily employed three times the length of chain requisite for simply descending to the bottom. The pit may be but thirty fathoms deep, but probably there are nearly a hundred additional fathoms of chain requisite to stretch from the bank to the engine.

The chains used are generally composed of flat links of iron, and there is always a heavy lump of metal attached to them just above the "skip," which serves to keep the long horizontal extent of iron links from slackening when the load is at the surface. The beautiful contrivances in use in the North for warning the engineman that the tub is near the brink of the shaft, are here unknown. Sometimes a bundle of rags is attached to the chain some half-dozen yards above the skip, and the appearance of this rude token suffices as a signal for the slackening of the engine. In many of the South Staffordshire pits, the engineman does not know whether he is regulating the ascent of men or of coals. "Look at that wire," said one of them to me at a mine near Bilston—pointing to a rusted thread of iron trampled into the coal dust; "it used to be fixed to a bell in the engine-room, and when men were coming up the banksman rung it. But it got broken somehow—nobody will be at the trouble or the expense to repair it, and so I can never tell what sort of cargo there is in the skip." At another pit, a rude telegraphic sign, by the motion of the banksman's arm, announced to the engineman that miners were ascending. I asked how the sign was managed at night. "Oh," said the banksman, "then I wave my arm before the fire here; but we're not very particular." So indeed it appeared.

There are scores of coal-pits scattered through the Wolverhampton district, worked without any steam-engine at all, simply by the aid of a rude gin and a blind old horse. This gin is a species of capstan—the cylinder, on which the rope winds, being usually about six feet in diameter. It is strengthened by a rude but massive scaffolding, and the horse is harnessed to a strong circulating bar. A gin is seldom employed to work more than two shafts. The ropes used are common round hempen ones, and each winds in a different direction upon the cylinder. In these small pits there are usually about ten men under ground, and a couple of men and as many women at bank. In no case which I have seen is the shaft furnished with those wooden partitions and guiding spears down which the cages slide so smoothly in the North. The hole has the appearance of a huge well, and the skip has ample room to oscillate as it swings up or down along the greenish slimy brickwork.

The system of working pursued in Staffordshire depends upon the thickness of the seam. The ten-yard seam is, as its name imports, a vast bed of mineral thirty feet in thickness. In removing this deposit vast pillars are necessarily left to support the roof, and the men frequently work on ladders and stages fixed in the face of the coal. The boards or workings are generally about three yards wide, with a pillar six or eight yards square left between each. At almost every thirty yards a larger pillar, forming an immense block of coal, called a "fire rib," is allowed to stand—each group of workings opening out a cavern of about forty square yards, the roof supported by four pillars, with a fire rib on each side. Efforts are now being made to improve this manner of working, and to dig away great portions of the pillars, leaving the remainder to be crushed down by the weight above, and to form vast gas-breeding goaves. In the mines where the seams worked are not above five feet in height, the pitmen proceed "long-wall fashion." They drive a rolley-way, or, as it is here called, a "gate road," right from the bottom of the shaft to the extent of the boundary—and then, commencing at the furthest extremity, they "howk out" almost the whole of the seam, temporarily supporting the roof with earth and rubbish, but so inefficiently as to make it certain that it will ultimately collapse or "scrounce in" behind them. The iron-stone seams are worked in the same way, although as these last are generally thinner than the coal belts, the work is more severe; and a great number of boys are employed to load the refuse into small iron skips called "dans," and to trundle it out of the way of the excavators to those portions of the pit which, having been hollowed, require, partially at least, to be filled up with supporting masses of rubbish.

The general want of system, and the almost total absence of anything like scientific management, make great portions of the Staffordshire coal-field almost as dangerous to those who live upon the surface as to those who work beneath it. I shall afterwards minutely describe the state of the hundreds of ruinous houses which I have found inhabited, although actually sinking into the moving and crumbling earth. As regards a great part of the district, nothing like authentic marks of the underground excavations are preserved. The workmen proceed partly by guess, partly guided by the position of the old shafts around them. Very often one mine runs beneath another; and it continually happens that the gas accumulating in old deserted workings leaks into pits in the course of excavation, and produces fatal results. Fortunately, however, the thin-coal seams give out very little carburetted hydrogen. On the surface it not uncommonly happens that old shafts are left almost entirely undefended. Some of them, indeed, are walled round—others are built in with circular roofs, looking exactly like gigantic bee-hives—but I have seen many shafts down which an unwary

A Pair of the Earl of Dudley's Thick Coal Pits in the
Black Country

step in a dark night might precipitate the wayfarer. When an open shaft exists near a cluster of houses, the inhabitants frequently dig a drain running into it—the mine, in this case, forming an undeniably handy cesspool. It sometimes happens that when a shaft is deserted, some poor vagrant family squat themselves down in the "hovel" upon its brink, which they are allowed to occupy either rent-free, or for about sixpence a week. This is a practice which has given rise to many accidents, especially those of children falling down the shafts. Occasionally, too, the apparently solid earth gives way—the descent taking place suddenly, and producing a hole, of no great depth perhaps, but a fall into which, when the opening is recent, is exceedingly dangerous, from the volumes of gas which very frequently ascend through the newly-loosened earth. Three people, residents in a hovel, lost their lives in this way a few weeks ago.

The Staffordshire coal mines are almost universally worked upon the "buttie" system. The buttie is a sort of middleman or contractor. Generally speaking, he has been a working man himself, and still preserves the appearance, dress, and style of living of his original condition. The buttie is, in most cases, an entirely uneducated man. He may be, and usually is, a person of practical experience, and often of much natural sagacity; but it frequently happens that he cannot write, and can hardly read—and to this individual the whole working and management of the mine is entrusted. The engine and the machinery belong, in the majority of cases, to the proprietor of the royalty. He pays the buttie a certain sum for every ton of coal extracted, and leaves the mode of working entirely to his agent. The engineman and some few of the people employed above ground are sometimes paid by the proprietor, but all the underground workmen are hired and remunerated by the buttie, who, in fact, is at once a commercial agent and a managing engineer. The buttie has always a foreman called a "doggie," who passes the whole day in the pit, superintending and aiding in the proceedings of the workpeople. The doggie is paid regular wages, generally either 4s. or 4s. 6d. per day. The great mass of the workpeople are either "holers" or "bandsmen." The holer answers in some respects to the northern hewer, but the manner of working the seam is different. The Staffordshire labourer commences operations by hollowing under, or undermining the ledge of coal. Squatting himself on the ground, or lying on his side, he hacks out the supporting strata to the depth of about eighteen inches, extending his operations along the seam, and pausing from time to time to support the coal thus deprived of its resting-place, by means of short props called "sprags." Close to him stand the iron carriages already mentioned, called "skips," and which look like great metal salvers set upon wheels. Upon these skips the coal is piled, the mass being steadied by moveable iron hoops, placed one above the other, so as to girdle and support the lumps of mineral. These carriages are loaded by the bandsman; but our business at present is with his comrade.

The holer is paid by the stint—this stint being the undermining of a certain breadth of coal, differing, of course, with the hardness and difficulty of the seam. The present remuneration for a "stint" is 2s. 3d. Many holers are able to work at least a stint and a half a-day, and are paid accordingly. The greater number, however, I am assured, do not earn, at the present prices of coal, more than 2s. 6d. per day. The holer may ascend as soon as he has completed his stint, or he may remain until the termination of the twelve hours, or twelve hours and a half, of daily toil. The holers who can and do earn their two stints a day are, I am informed, exceptions to the general rule. A few years ago, when the coal and iron trades were in a more prosperous condition than they are now, there were great complaints of the self-restrictive system upon which the pitmen worked. In 1847, Mr. Parker, of the Chillington Iron Works, near Wolverhampton, stated that the colliers were then restricting themselves to eight and nine hours' daily work for only five days in the week, their wages being, upon the average, 4s. 4½d. per day. He added, that if the men would work twelve hours more per week, the difference would suffice to make up the quantity of coal and iron-stone required, and that three pits out of every twenty might be then closed up. I have said enough, however, in a former letter, to show that this is one of the questions on which the men conceive that their interests, and those of their employers, lie in quite opposite directions. At present, however, the trade is too slack for anything like restriction to exist. The men are only over-glad to get what labour their employers can afford them. I have made inquiries in many quarters among the working men, and they all tell me that the coal union is extinct in Staffordshire. "They may get it up again," said one of them, "in the North—but we're people from a great many counties here, and we don't trust each other."

Next in position to the holer comes the bandsman or bonds-man. This functionary completes the work which his comrade began—breaks down with mallets and hammers, and sometimes blows down with gunpowder, the masses of coal already undermined by the holer—and then piles them upon the skip. In the majority of coal-seams no putter is required. The horse which draws the skips comes close up to the workpeople, and from thence tugs his burden to the bottom of the shaft. In very many pits there is only a single horse below ground. It is in the iron-stone mines, where the seams are often very thin, that putters are necessary. They are always mere boys, and the tubs which they "put" or "pitch" are the small skips called "dans." The bandsman is paid by fixed wages, varying in different pits from 4s. to 4s. 3d. per day. For this he remains underground for twelve hours, descending at six a.m. The holer generally keeps beforehand with his work, so as always to leave the bandsman plenty to do. The boy who drives the horse and attends to him is paid from 2s. to 2s. 3d. per day; and about the same amount of wages is earned by the hooker-on, a functionary who attaches the skips to the chain at the bottom of the shaft, and gives the signal for hoisting.

Upon the bank at the mouth of each shaft there are two or more women, superintended in their operations by a man. It is difficult to conceive anything more utterly or coarsely unfeminine than the aspect of these persons. They are lean, haggard, and grisly creatures—their skins engrained with dirt, which is very often never washed off from Saturday to Saturday—while, as for their ages, the great proportion actually seem to be of any age between 20 and 50. They generally wear men's coats buttoned over their dresses, and squab flattened bonnets, often crowned with a wisp of straw done up in a clout, on which to lay the basketfuls of coals which they often choose to carry upon their heads. These women seldom use spades or shovels in emptying the skips into the waggons. They work amongst the lumps of mineral with their bare hands, and they are altogether, in their persons and their minds, melancholy examples of the effect of rude coarse toil in absolutely unsexing the women who are employed in it. The lowness of the wages paid to these individuals is the chief reason why the butties employ them, since frequent shaft accidents occur through their heedlessness. Their pay is sometimes a shilling, but more frequently they have only 10d. or 11d. per day, and many of them assured me that sometimes they do not make more than 3s. per week. As tolerably long intervals take place between the arrival of the different skips, the banksmen and women are unoccupied for a considerable portion of their time. They then retreat into the "hovel," a wretched hut built of loosely piled stones, furnished with a coarse bench, and in the winter time with a brazier of blazing coals. One of those "hovels" stands by the mouth of every shaft. The boys employed in the Staffordshire coal-pits are not numerous. There are few or no traps for them to attend to, and their principal work consists of waiting upon the men, carrying their picks to be sharpened and put in order, and holding and trimming their candles. The provisions of Lord Ashley's act, so far as regards the ages of boys working in coal-pits, are, I have reason to know, habitually set at defiance in South Staffordshire. In none of Mr. Tremenheere's reports which I have by me is the subject alluded to; but when I have inquired of the people themselves, I have almost uniformly been answered by a laugh at the absurdity of the question. "Not till they're ten years old! Ah, sir, they're in the pits long, long before that." The women have never been in the habit of working underground in this district.

There is nothing particularly characteristic in the dress of the Staffordshire miners. It generally consists of coarse loose flannel jackets and trowsers, with thick heavy shoes. At their work both holers and bandsmen labour naked to the waist. The latter set up the props, or "trees" as they are here called; but, as one of them remarked to me, "There isn't much timber used hereabouts; we takes rubbish instead; it's not so good nor timber, but it's much cheaper, and that makes all the difference." The Staffordshire coal workers, behind their northern brethren in most respects, are especially so in point of cleanliness. The aspect of the beds in the cottages is alone sufficient to prove this. I should be loath to suppose that the statement is true generally—but it was asserted to me by a Northumberland pitman, who had passed many years in Staffordshire and Lancashire, that "he knew many a holer and bandsman whose legs were never washed since their mothers washed them." If such things can be, one ceases to wonder at the terrible ravages of cholera in Wednesbury and Bilston—especially when we remember the general intemperance of the working-people hereabouts. The Staffordshire colliers take all their meals, except supper, in the pit. The general dinner time is one o'clock, and an hour is allowed for the meal. The whole "pit's company" then assemble at the bottom of the shaft, while their wives, sisters, and daughters, make their way to the bank with the respective dinners. Each portion is placed in a bowl, tied over with a handkerchief or rag, very often none of the cleanest, and marked by some peculiar token which guides each man to his own mess. "Some people," said a woman to me, "will sew a button on the rag in a particular way; others will pin on a bit of the skirt of a dress which their husband knows the pattern on." The men fetch home the bowls at the end of their day's work. The dinner almost always consists of a portion of meat, with plenty of bread and potatoes. "My husband's dinner," said the wife of a bandsman near Bilston, "is usually half a pound of bread, half a quartern of potatoes, and a piece of meat—bacon very often—more or less of that according to how the money is, and sometimes none at all." "Well—yes—I do generally have meat to dinner," a miner answered to my inquiries, "but it's darned seldom I have so much as I could eat on it. Only on Sundays we does manage a little bit extra." This man showed me his basin, which certainly did contain a rather overwhelming proportion of potatoes. When times are better than they have recently been, the colliers of Staffordshire live well. Their pleasures are essentially animal, and it was said to me by a gentleman who knows the population intimately, that if every man had £5 a week he would spend it in eating and drinking. In Bilston, says Mr. Mosely, the Government inspector of schools, the improvidence of the people may be studied with advantage in the market-place. "No other market is supplied with finer poultry, or, comparatively to the population, in greater abundance; and this is chiefly, if not entirely, for the consumption of the labouring classes—for the resident inhabitants not of those classes are few in number. There, sordid and ill-favoured men may be seen buying on Saturday chickens and ducks and geese, which they eat for supper, and in some instances of which I was informed they drink bottled porter and wine. Yet so little have they beforehand in the world, that if the works were to stop, they would begin within a fortnight to pawn the little furniture of their cottages for subsistence or for drink." This extract applies, perhaps, rather to the iron-workers than to the miners; but to a great degree I believe it at certain times to be true of both. The supply of poultry in Bilston market is a fact which I can corroborate, both from inquiry and from personal observation.

When the dinners of the workpeople are all collected at the mouth of the shaft, they are placed upon a skip and let down *en masse*. The women then fill a basket full of coal, to which each who has a male relation in the pit is entitled, and they walk off very often with more than twenty pounds weight a-piece upon their heads. Soon after noon the Willenhall, the Bilston, and the Dudley roads are lined with these women marching uprightly and steadily under their well-poised burdens. In the northern coal pits the most rigid teetotalism is enforced under ground; but in Staffordshire the butties themselves find their workpeople in beer. I am bound, however, to say, that, from what I hear of the quality of the liquid, not much danger can be apprehended as likely to accrue from it to the sobriety of the consumers. The beer which the workpeople can "command" is, by the custom of the country, that sold at 2d. per quart; but they tell me that the buttie very often sends them down stuff which would make them sick to drink. Adults claim an allowance of a quart, and boys of a pint. The liquor is sent down into the pit in huge wooden bottles, each containing several gallons. The forgemen, however, are the most enormous beer and ale drinkers. The severe muscular fatigue and scorching heat to which they are subjected, are supposed to render a constant consumption of liquid absolutely necessary for them. "There is a 'shingler'" (the appellation will be explained hereafter), said the landlord of a public-house, near Wolverhampton, in answer to my inquiry, "who sometimes comes in here, and drinks eleven quarts of ale at a time. They're capital good customers, them iron-men. Bless you, they're always drinking, and they've got such good pay, a lot of them, that they can afford it. There's several men, at the works nigh here, who spend 3s. in ale every day of their lives." And, indeed, the vast number of beer-shops which abound throughout the district amply corroborate what I heard as to the immense trade driven by the publicans. In Bilston there are eleven churches and chapels—several of them very small—and 142 public-houses. In this parish, I may also add, that although there are hundreds of pit-shafts, and although the whole country is hollowed out, there is not a single resident engineer. The butties and the doggies dig and blast away, each after his own fashion.

A more miserable class even than the bankswomen are the poor creatures who come out to pick coal from the rubbish heaps at the pit mouth. Sometimes they are suffered to make their black gleaning in peace—but at other times, perhaps, if the buttie or the doggie happen to be not in the best of humours, they are given in charge, and hurried off to gaol for stealing coals. "I go to pick at the pit-heaps," said one poor woman to me. "It's the only way I can get fuel to keep me from starving these cold nights; but I must be very careful, and not go too near the shaft. There were two poor creatures committed to Stafford gaol last week for stealing coal, and they were only just picking out a few bits from what the pit people throw away for rubbish." Children are often sent out from Wolverhampton to pick.

There does not seem to be any regular grievance, such as the "laid-out and set-out," rankling in the minds of the Staffordshire coal-workers. Occasionally they summon the butties before the magistrates for stopping part of their wages on account of alleged insufficient work; but the only special hardship which seems to be of a chronic nature is "builtass work." The derivation of the term is curious. Builtass is, or was, an abbey or religious house in Shropshire, which, as tradition states, was constructed by the forced labour or *corvée* of the peasantry. The name has been imported into Staffordshire, and "builtass work" there signifies forced labour. Applied to the coal pits, the phrase implies a day or half a day's work, periodically imposed by the butties, and for which no wages are paid. The toil consists in clearing the mine of those accumulated masses of rubbish which, were they not periodically got rid of, would seriously impede the working of the pit. This gratis labour, whether or not it be objectionable in principle, hardly appears, however, to be very oppressive in practice.

The Staffordshire miner seems to have little superstitious feeling about him. His strongly-developed animal propensities appear to keep him often in a state of actual mental stagnation. If he dreads anything as ominous, it is the appearance, as he goes to his labour, of that unlucky creature—a black cat. But the only strong and general feeling which approaches to superstition is the uniform abandonment of a mine in which a fatal accident has taken place, until the victim shall have been buried. So long as the corpse is above ground, I am assured that nothing will tempt the survivors to resume their labour. The notion that it is unlucky to meet a woman before descending the shaft has no place here. Indeed, the employment of so many women upon the bank effectually neutralizes any idea of the kind.

During my rambles over the coal-field around Wolverhampton, Wednesbury, Bilston, and Bromwich, I have had frequent conversations with the men upon the ventilation of the mines beneath. I find that they trust implicitly to the shallowness of the pits, and to the close collocation of the shafts. "The air is sure to get down some way or other," seemed the grand motto of their engineering; and, in fact, as the heat beneath is generally greater than that of the atmosphere, there is a languid ventilation which renders it possible to exist in the limited excavations in question. The shaft down which the air descends is called the "drawing" and that by which it escapes the "driving" shaft. "Sometimes," I was told at the mine, "if it's very hot close weather, and the pit feels very choky, we light a fire at the bottom of the driving shaft, but in general we can breathe well enough without it." At another pit, worked by a gin and a horse, there was a sort of iron funnel-shaped machine, from which a tube stretched down the shaft, and which, being turned round to face the wind, would no doubt, in a smart breeze, conduct a refreshing current of air below. A second shaft, however, communicating with the pit, had recently been sunk at about 100 yards distance—and the buttie, being of opinion that the new aperture would afford sufficient ventilation, was, while I was on the spot, bargaining to sell his "blower," or ventilating apparatus, as old iron.

I have been more than once overtaken by the night upon the dreary expanse of coal refuse which heaps so many square miles in this part of Staffordshire. A more singular sight than that which is thus presented to the wayfarer it would be difficult to find. The earth, so far as it can be seen, seems like a great black sea of swelling mounds and hollows, dismal and pathless. Neither tree nor shrub, nor aught but crumbling coal ridges, stands up against the sky—but, flaring and flickering close by you, and shining steadily at greater distances, burn hundreds and hundreds of the fires kept alive at the mouths of shafts, showing you by their flashing glare the dismal scaffold-like apparatus of rope and beam which overhangs them, and surrounded by dusky figures, now relieved against the blaze, now retiring into the night. But these are not the only fires which give a character to the scene.

Every mile or two roar the furnaces of great forge and smelting works. The red flames, as they curl up to and over their brickwork barriers, fling into the sky an uncertain lurid glare, which alternately fades and brightens like the quivering of the Northern lights. Girdling those perpetual well-springs of red fire are the dusky outlines of sheds and engine-houses, with a partially illumined streak—the side of the tall chimney next to the furnace light—towering high above them into the air. Over these vast fires, columns of smoke and steam careering by become for a moment visible, and then pass on into the darkness— if, indeed, it can be called darkness, when the whole sky glows with the gleam of the thousand fires beneath. There is something almost terrible in the unwonted aspect of all around—the shale and cinder-covered earth crackling under the tread—the furnaces glowing all around—and the ceaseless murmur of escaping steam and clanking mechanism, borne by every gust of wind over the cinder desert. And almost all this transformation of the natural features of the soil has taken place within the memory of a few old men still living. "I can remember, sir," said an aged person whom I met in the outskirts of Bilston, "when all this country was as green and pleasant as any spot of England. There were coal pits, to be sure; but there were fields, and meadows, and hedges, between them. Now, you see, nothing green will grow, for the level of the country has been changed by these pit heaps, and the sulphur smells, and the bad gases comes up out of the very earth."

# LABOUR AND THE POOR.

—◆—

## THE MANUFACTURING DISTRICTS.

[FROM OUR SPECIAL CORRESPONDENT.]

## THE STAFFORDSHIRE COLLIERIES AND THE TRUCK SYSTEM.

## LETTER XXIV.

Defective as are the dwellings occupied by the pitmen in the North, they are an hundred per cent. superior to the tenements of their brethren in Staffordshire. The coal population in the latter county live, sometimes in poor detached cottages—sometimes in detached rows or clusters of houses, sprinkled here and there amidst the rubbish waste, or along the roads—sometimes in over-grown villages, of each portion or *quartier* of which a smelting or a forging work forms the nucleus. These villages or small towns are, like the northern pit-rows, only to be paralleled by themselves. The Rev. Mr. Owen, the excellent vicar of Bilston, has felicitously sketched one of these joined, yet still disjointed—crowded, yet scattered—collocation of dwellings, describing it as "broken up into thick parenthetical tufts of population in three or four separate faubourgs, baffling the visitor, as he emerges from suburb after suburb, to discover which of them is 'the town,' till he finds that there is no town in particular, and no suburb above another, but that the suburbs are like their inhabitants, all of a class—all of a piece; street after street and man after man—continual duplicates of each other, ... black red bricks and black red men, equally indebted to the everlasting coal and smoke for their hue and complexions." The majority of the houses belong to small proprietors, and fetch, considering their accommodation and construction, high rents. The tendency in building cottages in this part of the country is not only to make the shell very diminutive, but to split the interior up into almost infinitesimal rooms. I have found four chambers in a cottage, the largest of which was not above seven feet by five. The ground floors are hardly ever boarded, being almost always paved with brick, and very commonly sunk beneath the level of the road. Were it not for the cheapness of coal, which allows the people to keep up almost perpetually blazing fires, these rooms would be so damp as to be hardly habitable. As it is, the interstices of the bricks have always a humid, slimy appearance, and the mode of cleansing in use increases the disadvantages of the flooring. Instead of scouring in the ordinary fashion, the people mop their apartments, emptying buckets of water upon the kitchen floor, which, particularly where the level is under that of the road, absorbs through its joints a greater portion of the moisture than the mop can possibly dry up. Excepting the tendency to small rooms, there is no particular phase of cottage construction which seems peculiar to the district. The detached cottages, and rows of cottages, if not generally, have, at all events, not unfrequently, back-doors and yards, the latter usually in a filthy condition. Entrance to the second floor is, in the majority of cases, obtained by a staircase, rising from the principal apartment beneath. The windows are commonly constructed of small lozenge panes in metal frames, the glass often broken and patched with rags, and altogether the interior aspect of the tenements in question is paltry and squalid. I have already learned by ample experience never to expect good furniture in ill-constructed and inconvenient houses. The dwellings of the South Staffordshire colliers confirm the rule. They exhibit neither the well-stocked cupboards, the well-arranged crockery racks and shelves, and the gaily-painted clocks of the Manchester operatives—nor handsome beds, ample and polished chests of drawers, and burnished teapots and candlesticks of the Northumberland and Durham pitmen. In the dwellings of the poor, the degree of comfort of their occupants may be very fairly gauged by the bed and bed linen. In the South Staffordshire cottages, both are very commonly mean, uncomfortable, dirty, and neglected—of course there are exceptions, but I state my general impressions after having visited scores of pitmen's dwellings. The furniture is of a piece—paltry and huddled. There is seldom or ever a carpet, and the accommodations for cooking are very deficient. In many living-rooms I found washing going on, the place reeking with the peculiar fumes of soap and hot water applied to dirty linen, and everything splashed and uncomfortable. I was struck by the almost total absence of newspapers and books—a few dirty tracts, or paltry collections of songs, lying enwreathed with dust on the window sills being the only things literary to be seen. In many of the houses the evidence of slatternliness was just as visible as that of poverty. Dishes lay about unwashed, unswept grates were littered with the grey ashes, and beds were very frequently left unmade, their whitey-brown sheets presenting anything but a pleasant spectacle. The ornaments in the South Staffordshire colliers' houses are few and paltry, consisting almost entirely of little earthenware figures, rudely painted, and the meanest description of plates. In the north, there is hardly a pitman's room but is enlivened by the song of canaries and goldfinches. Cage birds are few in South Staffordshire, and when they do exist, their shabby rushed prisons are quite a contrast to the large and elaborately woven wire receptacles which the northern pitmen themselves delight to fashion for their song birds.

Gardens are quite unknown in the coal and iron districts of Staffordshire. Indeed, for mile after mile, nothing green will grow. Here and there an individual has attempted to form a sort of artificial garden, by bringing soil from a distance, and laying it upon the coal refuse, but the constant smoke kills every bud and sprout. I have already alluded in general terms to the cracked and dilapidated state of immense numbers of the houses, owing to the continued sinking and shifting of the earth. This is one of the worst features of the district. It makes great numbers of the houses uncomfortable—almost uninhabitable—and not a few absolutely dangerous. A visitor to the western outskirts of Bilston, in the direction of the village of Ettingshall, might well imagine that he gazed upon a tract which had been recently convulsed by an earthquake. He will see dozens of dwellings in absolute ruins, the walls partially sunk, and the second floors lying in masses of wet and rotting timber. Other houses, not quite so bad, he would observe torn by great rents from top to bottom, one portion leaning one way—another portion another way; the ground floor, partially collapsed, partially hove up, so as to fix the half-open doors immovably. I measured the crack in one house near Ettingshall—it was seventeen inches in breadth, and surrounded by numerous minor rents. The houses on either side of this one, although far off the perpendicular, and with wavy crevices running all along their walls, were both inhabited. Nothing is more common than to see a couple of windows sloping in different directions, a door broader at bottom than at top, or *vice versâ*—the two gavels leaning towards or from each other, and stacks of chimneys apparently nodding to their fall. Still the people continue to live in these dilapidated dwellings with the coolest indifference.

"Between Birmingham and Kidderminster," says Mr. Mosely, "there are hundreds of paralysed hovels with scarcely a lintel or a door-post in its place. One of them gave a loud crack, and out ran the inmates. It was evidently on the eve of falling; but the husband, on inspecting it, thought 'it would last another week,' and back they all went to stay out the week." In a small grocer's shop which I visited, near Ettingshall, I found I could see daylight shining through the walls from the ceiling to the floor. I called the attention of the proprietor of the place to the fact. He had just been declaiming against the truck system prevalent in the district, and hoping that it would be thoroughly exposed; but, on the dilapidated condition of his own house and those in the vicinity being brought on the *tapis*, he very coolly said that that was quite a different thing, that the cracks made the houses airier and healthier ("they were as good as windows"), and wondered very much what people meant by coming prying about his property, and saying that it was in a dangerous state when it had stood with all its rents and cracks about it for twenty years. The tenants of the rickety houses do not, however, as might be expected, survey the condition of their dwellings with the same complacency. Custom has made many of them reckless to the danger, and in some degree habituated them to the discomfort; but others complained bitterly of the wretched hovels which they were compelled to occupy. One woman in particular, hearing of my errand, ran after me and begged me to come and examine her house. It was one of a row, cracked, distorted, and crumbling from end to end. As I stood by the fireside, I could pass my fingers through a crack into the open air. This crevice was partially stuffed with brown paper, and partially nailed over with rough boards, one of which the woman of the house tore down to let me see the extent of the dilapidation. Up stairs matters were still worse. The inmates could lie in bed and see the sky through half a dozen chinks. Those immediately above the beds—for there were two close to each other, and occupied by two married couples—were partially stuffed with brown paper and rags, while boards, in the fashion of gutters, were fastened so as to lead the rain away from the beds, and let it fall upon the floor. Notwithstanding, however, they often wakened with the bed-clothes drenched. The wall facing the Bilston-road was especially crazy, and the head of the bed in which the woman slept was set close to it. "The bricks have yielded here," she said, "several inches, just a short time ago, and I am sure we never go to sleep without being afraid that in the middle of the night the wall will go altogether, and we shall be pitched out, bed and all, into the road." The rent paid for this place was 1s. 6d. a week. The husband of this woman was a bandsman, in only partial work. The week before my visit he had earned only 6s. 10d. They would leave the house gladly, but they were a little in arrear of rent, and they knew that if they attempted to "flit," their things would be seized on the instant. I proceeded into the next house, which I found in a precisely similar condition. The rain came freely into the living-room and bed-room, and the occupants said that they did not consider their lives safe. The ground beneath them was entirely hollow. The landlord did not expect that the houses would stand much longer, and so he would do nothing for them. There had been two cases of cholera in this house, and the whole row had suffered more or less. It was impossible not to observe that in few or no cases had anything been done in a workmanlike way to keep these rickety houses together, and diminish the danger to their occupants. The brown-paper stuffing and boards were merely intended to keep out the rain and cold. The only instance I saw of architecture suited to the requirements of the locality, was in the case of a most unique-looking church at Ettingshall, which is absolutely bound together by girding timbers and strong iron buttresses. If this building ever sinks into the earth, it will go *en masse*.

Near Wolverhampton, on the Wittenhall road, there is a row of miserable one-storied cottages—the history of which is characteristic of the locality. Where they stand a row of two-storied dwellings formerly existed. These last sank into the earth, and out of the ruins of their upper walls and roofs the present cottages were constructed. This row of houses was severely scourged by cholera. In a short distance along the road, of which the row occupied about one-half, there were more than sixty deaths. The first house I entered was a small detached hovel, not above twelve feet long on the outside, and yet divided into four miserable earthen-floored rooms. There was no ceiling whatever; the bare tiles could be touched by the hand. On the side away from the road, a sort of lean-to was added to the house, forming one of the very worst sleeping-places I ever saw. At its highest pitch the roof was not above five feet from the ground, while at the other side, the face of the furthest over sleeper—and there were two in each of the beds—literally grazed the sloping tiles. In this hole there was neither window nor opening to the outside, but quite enough of cold air penetrated between the loosely laid tiles. Of course the place was pitch dark. The mistress of the house, a haggard, care-worn looking woman, told me that sleeping-places constructed in a similar way were attached to almost every house in the row. In 1832 she had lost her first husband by cholera. Last autumn she had lost her second by the same disease. It raged awfully all around, and many of the people fled and left their friends dying and dead. At that time the houses looked even worse than when I saw them—for they had since been whitewashed, and the windows improved. When the ravages of the cholera there became known in Wolverhampton, the sick people were allowed to want for nothing. They had proper food and medicine; but the close choky air of the small unventilated rooms, and the foul dunghills around, were terrible. The police and the gentlemen from Wolverhampton smashed in the windows and broke holes in the wall to let in light and air. One man came crying into her house for the loan of a hammer to knock some of the bricks out of the wall of the back room where his wife was lying ill. He got the hammer, and while he was breaking a hole to give his wife fresh air, she died. My informant laid out the body. Often and often there was no proper person to prepare the corpses decently for interment. Her son, a young man of twenty, had laid out the bodies of several young women. They were buried in their best gowns. The people got panic-struck when the disease was at its height, and wouldn't go near the bodies. One woman died on the floor. She lay with her cap off and her hair all "staring" about her face, and her legs and arms cramped and drawn up under her. A female went to lay her out; but as soon as she caught sight of the body she rushed back, crying that she had never seen such a corpse, that she couldn't lay it out, or look at it, and that she was a dead woman herself. So indeed it proved—for she was taken ill, and died the same night. In one of the cottages in the neighbouring row, out of a family of eight, a father, mother, and six children, all except one child, were swept away. I proceeded to this house, and found it tenanted by two Irish families, consisting of thirteen or fourteen persons. The damp floor was more than a foot beneath the level of the road. The few articles of furniture—broken old chairs, benches, and crockery-ware lying on the earth—could not be worth half-a-crown. A big navvy-looking fellow had on his knees three or four children, with whom he was sharing a scanty dinner of bread and tea. Some of them slept on rugs upon the floor, and others occupied two wretched beds in an airless hole, similar to that which I have already described, at the back. The rent paid for this place was 2s. a week.

The next house presented a still more miserable scene of poverty. The furniture of the living-room consisted simply of two broken chairs and a pot. The woman who lived here had four children, and expected in two months to be confined again. She looked more than half starved, with pinched-in cheeks, and black livid rings round each of her eyes. Her husband was an engineman, but he had been out of work for twenty-two weeks, mainly in consequence of bad health, produced by the bursting of a blood-vessel when exerting himself to clean a boiler. Before that event they had had a good house of furniture, but they had since lived by selling it piecemeal. Except the two chairs, the pot, and an old worn mattress and rug, they possessed nothing but what they stood upright in. They dared not sleep in the bed-room, it was so damp, but they dragged the mattress into the living-room every night, and laid it down where the heat from the grate had dried the brick flooring. The ceiling was not six feet high, and the floor was a foot beneath the road. They paid 2s. 6d. a week in rent—at least, they had paid it so long as they were able, but now they were in arrears, because they had nothing more to sell. The coals they had she picked at the heaps, but she was continually afraid of being taken up for it. They lived entirely on bread and coffee, but latterly they had sat, children and all, in the house for two whole days without food. It is to be hoped that the fortunes of this poor family are mending. On the day I visited them the husband had gone out to undertake the first work he had been able to get for near five months.

In a third house in the row I heard a story which illustrates the buttie system of working coal. The house was, like all the others, squalid and reeking with moisture. The husband worked in a neighbouring pit; and the wife, a thin, care-worn little woman, was preparing three small Swedish turnips for boiling.

"Ah!" she said, "this has been a bad week with us. We are well nigh clemmed with hunger. My husband came home last Saturday night without even a penny."

I said I feared he had been at the public-house. "No, no, nothing of the kind," replied the wife. "There's not a more sober man in the country than my husband—but he wasn't paid. Not a man in the pit was paid for the week's work."

I inquired the reason.

"Just," she answered, "just because the buttie had a cold and wouldn't go to the pit-mouth. He said that the men could wait till next week, or till he was better. At all events he was too ill to come out of his house; so, after waiting till it was late, all the hands had to go away without getting one farthing."

I inquired if they had had any money in hand to go on with.

"Not a penny," was the reply. "We get too little to save anything from one week to another, and how we're to get on this week I don't know. This is Tuesday, now I'll tell you what I did yesterday. I went out and borrowed a sixpence, and this is the way I spent it. I bought three-halfpence worth of bacon, and a twopenny loaf, a half-ounce of tobacco which cost three-halfpence, one halfpenny worth of beer, and two farthing candles, one of which we burned last night, and one which we have for to-night. I made the sixpence go as far as I could, and to-day I've got these three Swedes (pointing to the turnips), which I'm going to boil; but it's poor watery stuff for a hard working man, that has had no dinner, to make his supper on."

This miserable piece of petty tyranny, or wanton neglect, on the part of the buttie seemed to be taken without anything like indignation, just as a matter of course. The rent cleared by this wretched row, in which not a ceiling is higher than six feet, in which every floor is damp and every wall crasy, and in which the cholera carried off a fearful proportion of its inhabitants, exceeds, for the eight houses of which it is composed, a pound a week, and it has very frequent parallels throughout the district. The cracked and torn house which I have described in detail may be taken as a specimen of the condition of hundreds of dwellings round Wolverhampton, Willenhall, Wednesbury, and Bilston.

The mortality in the latter place from cholera considerably exceeded the proportion of deaths at Paris. Out of a population of about 24,000, more than 700 people died in seven weeks. In the neighbouring district of Cosely the mortality was also great. There had been repeated strikes for wages in the collieries around, and the dietary of the people had consequently been so poor as to render them especially liable to the disease. Bilston is almost exclusively inhabited by colliers and ironworkers. Its population is, as I have stated, about 24,000. Out of these I was informed that about 5,000 persons attend the different churches and chapels, while 11,000 never go near them. There are about 4,000 children connected with the various Sunday and day schools, and upwards of 400 Sunday-school teachers. Out of 5,000 miners in the neighbourhood, it is calculated that 4,000 never attend any place of worship whatever. The prevalent ignorance is, of course, deplorably gross. "Many butties," says the Rev. Mr. Owen, "come to me to prove wills, often to the extent of thousands of pounds, and in nine cases out of ten they affix their marks." Complaints are very rife in the district of the unwillingness of the colliers to make any sacrifice whatever for the education of their children, or even to send them to school gratis. Mr. Parker, the proprietor of very large iron works in the neighbourhood, once offered to pay 2d. a week for any of the children of his workpeople whom their parents would send to school. Out of 1,500 workmen whom he employed, only 30 embraced the offer. The active and enlightened exertions of the Rev. Mr. Owen, of Bilston, to infuse something like intelligence into the population by which he is surrounded ought to be known. The rev. gentleman does not confine himself to religious instruction, but wisely labours to promote the advance of that general intelligence and information without the existence of which the raw mental material can hardly be brought into any shape. Through Mr. Owen's exertions a series of familiar lectures, suitable to the capacities of the audience, have from time to time been given, principally by clergymen of the church. In the list of lectures at present in course of delivery, I find an account of a trip to Snowden, with notices of Wales, and an explanation of the process of floating and hoisting the Menai tubular bridge—a narrative of the escape of Charles II. from Worcester—a history of the American Revolution, and an exposition of "Popular Proverbial Errors." These lectures are, when practicable, illustrated by simple diagrams and dissolving views. When I was at Bilston, I found Mr. Owen actively preparing a lecture on the Bosjesmen, whose presence he had procured from an exhibition-room in Wolverhampton. These lectures are attended on the average by about 600 persons; and here I found, for the first time in the mining districts, the dissenters in a great minority as compared with the church. The clergy of all persuasions, however, work harmoniously together; and, indeed, the field seems amply wide for the labourers. Mr. Owen informed me of the somewhat curious fact, that not one single regular member of the Methodist body at Bilston had died of cholera. This he attributed to the general sober habits of the persons in close communion with and strictly under the discipline of the persuasion in question. The great proportion of deaths at Bilston were amongst the dirtiest and most intemperate of the population. The vast proportion of the town is, however, pitiably behindhand as to sanitary matters. Only about one-third of it is drained, and the sewage of that third flows into an open and filthy brook, which runs through the lower part of Bilston, and on the banks of which more than 100 persons were swept away by the epidemic. Lining this open sewer, for such it is, are groups of small unventilated houses, without back doors, and surrounded by masses of mud and filth. In the brook itself, domestic refuse and the garbage of slaughterhouses abound, and at one part of its course the water is used for the steam-engines of an iron-works, and then partially discharged in a heated condition and sending up the foulest vapours. The cholera was particularly fatal in the vicinity of this dirty pond of steaming water. It is a curious fact that in both visitations the first case at Bilston took place in the same house. I visited it. The building consists of two stories, each of a single room. In the lower chamber there is an oven common to all the neighbours—the place being, in fact, a mere shell, with shattered windows, open to all the winds of heaven. Above it is a small squalid room, for which its female tenant pays 1s. 8d. weekly rent. The brook bathes the walls of the house. All along the banks of this fœtid stream are shallow wells. From any one spot they may be counted in twos and threes. These contain the only water used, for drinking and cooking, by a large proportion of the inhabitants of the poorer part of Bilston. I tasted the fluid, which was mawkish and nasty beyond description, and charged, as was very evident, even to the eye, with solid matter held in suspension. This water is mere surface drainage. The mines have absorbed all the springs in the vicinity. "The wells," said one man, "always rise and fall with the brook." "Aye," added a woman, "and when the brook is dirtiest they're dirtiest." In some of the wells which I looked down, I could see the oily glancing of the scum as it floated upon the top of the water. Only an inconsiderable portion of the public-houses have pipe water, which is brought from Tipton. The local authorities have made efforts to cleanse the dirtiest portions of Bilston-brook; but the nuisance itself, it seems, cannot be suppressed under the existing law. A deputation waited upon the Central Board of Health in London upon the subject, when it was ascertained that no clause in any of the Health of Towns Bills applied to the particular circumstances of the brook, it being a natural stream, and neither a ditch, drain, watercourse, nor sewer.

So intimately connected with the coal districts, collieries, and colliers of South Staffordshire are the ironworks and ironworkers of the county, that a brief incidental notice of the latter is indispensable to a true understanding of a subject to which I shall presently allude—the extensive and disgraceful "Truck System" which prevails in this part of the country. The ironworks are of two general kinds—the smelting or blast furnaces for separating the pure metal from the stone, and the forging-mills, where the former is "puddled," and rolled into sheets, rods, bars, &c. It is calculated that each blast furnace gives employment altogether to upwards of 200 men. Some iron-masters keep their furnaces continually blowing, except when they are obliged to quench them to repair the brickwork. The men are divided into day and night shifts, and on each alternate Sunday the whole twenty-four hours' work is done by one of the shifts, so as to give a fortnightly rest to the others. Some iron-masters occupy their hands upon Sunday in repairing the accidental damage, and wear and tear of the week, and only a few partially suspend operations on the first day of the week, so far as to content themselves with a single instead of a double cast, or extraction of the molten metal. The injury done to the physical powers, as well as to the moral character of the men, by Sunday labour, can be well conceived, and is only too notorious in the district. Many of the iron-masters contend that the system is one of necessity. Others, who do not pursue it, maintain that it is not required by the exigencies of trade, but that, on the contrary, a better week's work is done by labouring in six than by toiling seven days. For Sunday labour extra ale is allowed; and "very often," says a gentleman connected with one of the largest iron-works in the district, "there is much more attention paid to the ale than to the work." The masters who allow their people rest on the Sunday, adds the same authority, have, as a general rule, the steadiest and best hands in the district. Their work, both of repairs and production, is very generally turned out in a better style than that of their Sunday-toiling competitors. The wages of the blast furnace man, in the Staffordshire district, averages about 21s. or 22s. a week, ranging from 18s. to 25s.; but always fluctuating with the state of the iron market. At present, and for some time back, the demand for labour has been slack, and the wages at their lowest point. The consequence has been very general distress amongst the working population.

The iron labourer, it is the concurrent testimony of all who are best acquainted with the Staffordshire district, is improvident to a degree far beyond the average of working men. As a general thing, he and his family live well in the beginning of the week, while the money lasts, although by Saturday a portion of the furniture or the wardrobe may be on the pawnbroker's shelves. There are hundreds of families who habitually pawn their Sunday clothes every Monday

Blast Furnaces.—(Hanley, Staffordshire)

morning, and take them out every Saturday evening, paying, of course, a month's interest upon the loan. A strike of a couple of weeks, or the suspension of work for that period at a forge or mill, always suffices to crowd the pawnbrokers' shops in the vicinity. The men at the forge mills earn higher wages than those at the blast furnaces. In both cases the work is kept up night and day, the shifts changing places every week. The forgemen are exposed to more continuous heat than the blastmen, and their work is on the whole heavier, although by no means unremitting. I abstain here from any description of the labour, as such will appear in its proper place, when iron-forging comes to be more particularly the subject of discussion. I shall merely add that the wages of the forgemen range from 25s. to 30s. per week; those of their boys or "underhands," from 7s. 6d. to 10s. per week; and those of the millmen from 16s. to 25s. per week. A few of the hands will, however, make even still higher wages than those specified. Women of a class similar to those who labour at the pit banks, are employed about the blasting furnaces and the coke ovens. The wages earned by these persons seldom exceeds 1s., and is more frequently only 8d. per day.

I have now to direct attention to the great and flagrant social and industrial evil of the truck system. In many portions of the iron and coal district of South Staffordshire the law upon this subject is so habitually and grossly violated as to be all but a dead letter. Employers of all classes, and of all the staple trades are, in this respect, equal sinners. I found that the very worst "Tommy shops" in this district are kept, not by the ignorant butties, but by great iron-masters—vast capitalists, who employ men by the hundred—and regularly mulct them out of five, six, ten, or even more, per cent. of their wages by paying these wages in goods—the latter, sometimes, but not always, of inferior quality, and in the case of many articles charged at least five per cent. above the market price of the country. I have not, indeed, been more startled by any phenomenon in the course of my researches than the constant and daring violation of the Truck Act in Staffordshire, and the utter helplessness of the people under the oppression of the Tommy masters. I am told that not a few magistrates are themselves notorious truck store-keepers. Of course their names are not openly displayed over the Tommy-shop door, but the fact is just as well known as if they served behind the counter.

The truck system in Staffordshire is part and parcel of what is called the "long-reckoning" system. The iron-masters and coal contractors who practise it have nominal settlements with their hands, sometimes once in three weeks, sometimes once a month, and occasionally not oftener than once in six weeks. This involves the *dodge* by which the law is evaded. They say, "We are obliged to pay in money, but we shall only pay when it suits us. In the meantime you (the men) may have what goods you want to go on with. These are not given in payment of wages, but merely as private arrangements to enable you to keep afloat until pay-day comes round; and when that epoch arrives we shall, of course, settle in money." This is the general principle on which the act is evaded. The details of the contrivances differ widely. Sometimes wages are paid on account by cheques upon distant banks, there being always a clear understanding on either side that the cheque is never to be presented where it is payable. If, indeed, it be cashed at all, the recipient has an immediate notice to quit his employment; and instances, I am told, are not wanting of the district banks, when actually applied to, refusing or delaying, upon the ground of some alleged technical informality, to honour the draft. The cheque system is generally adopted by the truck iron-masters—the order being, of course, intended for presentation at the Tommy-shop, and sometimes there is an understanding that a certain portion of the amount, from ten to twenty per cent., will be paid in money. The butties, however, and some of the iron-masters, give direct orders on the Tommy-shop, the form being a line of intimation that the shop-keeper may trust the bearer to the amount of so-and-so, being the sum standing to the credit of the latter in the pay-books of the concern. This kind of order is always paid entirely in goods. At the large iron works the Tommy-shop is usually on the premises, and the concern is entirely local. A number of butties, on the contrary, will have a Tommy-shop between them. Sometimes the shopkeeper is merely the agent of the employer. In other cases the business is effected in the following manner. The employer agrees with a general shopkeeper to make all his men deal at the establishment of the latter. Then orders are issued for 10s. and 5s. worth of goods each—the cheque of course clearing the master of these amounts of wages, and the shop-keeper giving what quantity and quality of goods he pleases for it—in other words, charging his own price. When the cheques amount to a certain sum—say £100, the shopkeeper makes out his bill, deducting from it 5, 7, or 10 per cent., according to agreement—the deduction, whatever it is, being of course so much clear gain to the master, and so much absolute loss to the men. It is right, however, to state, that in making bargains of this kind, some of the iron-masters stipulate that the goods supplied shall be of fair quality, and shall be retailed at prices not higher than a fixed rate. In the majority of instances, how-ever, the price charged is just sufficiently low to keep the workpeo-ple from breaking out into actual defiance of the system. I ought to mention that it commonly happens that different Tommy-shops sell particular articles cheaper than others. Thus, one establishment will have a comparatively good character for butcher's meat—another for groceries; but, as a rule, the prices range higher than those charged by fair tradesmen—in proportions which may be estimated by the particulars given below.

The ordinary prices of the ordinary articles of consumption in Wolverhampton are as follow:—Mutton, 6½d.; beef, 6d.; pork, 5d.; bacon, of different qualities, 7d., 6½d., 6d., and 5d.; flour, 1s. 9d., 1s. 8d., and 1s. 7d. per peck; cheese, 5d. and 4d. per lb.; salt butter, 10d., 9d., and 8d.; fresh ditto, 1s. 2d.; herrings, 1d. each; potatoes, 10d. or 11d. per peck; oatmeal, 2d. per lb.; tea, 4s. per lb.; the best coffee, 1s. 10d.; inferior kinds, 1s. 6d. and 1s. 8d.; sugar, 4½d.; candles, 5½d. per lb. Those last are made as small as 20 to the pound. Best brown

soap 6d., and inferior soap 5d. per lb. Now, the general assurance I received from the working people who have "tommeyed" was, that the
truck-masters charged from 2d. to 3d. out of every shilling higher
than the fair traders—on some articles a fraction more, on some a
fraction less. A strike, having reference to the truck system, lately
took place at Darlaston, a small town in the district, the staple trade
of which is gun-lock filing. Two statements were published by the
turn-out, purporting to be a fair comparison of truck and ordinary
prices. From the first of these I transcribe the following table:—

| GROCER'S PRICE. | s. | d. | TRUCK-MASTER'S PRICE. | s. | d. |
|---|---|---|---|---|---|
| Cheese, per lb. ...... | 0 | 6 | Cheese, per lb. ...... | 0 | 8 |
| Fresh butter, per 22 oz. | 1 | 0 | Fresh butter, per 16 oz. | 1 | 4 |
| Bacon, per lb. ........ | 0 | 5 | Bacon, per lb. ........ | 0 | 9 |
| Ham, per lb. ........ | 0 | 7 | Ham, per lb. ........ | 0 | 11 |
| Sugar, per lb. ........ | 0 | 5 | Sugar, per lb. ........ | 0 | 7 |
| Salt butter, per lb. ... | 0 | 9 | Salt butter, per lb. ... | 1 | 0 |
| Flour, per strike ..... | 7 | 0 | Flour, per strike ..... | 8 | 4 |
| Total grocer's price | 10 | 8 | Total truck price ... | 13 | 7 |

Taking this statement as correct, the profit realised by the truck
master over and above that of the fair dealer would be more than 27
per cent. A second statement, corroborative of the first, soon made its
appearance, and supplied a numerous list of articles upon which the
alleged profit of the tommy-shop keeper was still higher. As thus:—

| GROCER'S PRICE. | s. | d. | TRUCK-MASTER'S PRICE. | s. | d. |
|---|---|---|---|---|---|
| Tea, per oz. ....... | 0 | 3 | Tea, per oz. ....... | 0 | 5 |
| Coffee, per 2 oz. ... | 0 | 3 | Coffee, per 2 oz. ... | 0 | 5 |
| Rice, per lb. ....... | 0 | 2 | Rice, per lb. ....... | 0 | 4 |
| Soap, per lb. ....... | 0 | 5 | Soap, per lb. ....... | 0 | 7 |
| Candles, per lb. .... | 0 | 5 | Candles, per lb. .... | 0 | 7 |
| Raisins, per lb. ..... | 0 | 5 | Raisins, per lb. ..... | 0 | 7 |
| Currants, per lb. ... | 0 | 5 | Currants, per lb. ... | 0 | 7 |
| Red herrings, per doz. | 1 | 0 | Red herrings, per doz. | 1 | 10 |
| Total grocer's price | 3 | 4 | Total truck price ... | 5 | 4 |

The statement goes on to contrast the prices of the truck materials used by the gun-lock filers when purchased at the fair and at the
tommy shops:—

| WHOLESALE HARDWARE (IRONMONGER). | | | | WHOLESALE HARDWARE (TRUCK). | | | |
|---|---|---|---|---|---|---|---|
| | £ | s. | d. | | £ | s. | d. |
| Iron, per bundle .... | 0 | 3 | 3 | Iron, per bundle .... | 0 | 4 | 6 |
| Steel „ .... | 0 | 17 | 0 | Steel „ .... | 1 | 1 | 0 |
| Files, 11 in., 3-square, per dozen ........ | 0 | 9 | 0 | Files, 11 in., 3-square, per dozen ........ | 0 | 12 | 0 |
| Files, 8 in., 3-square, ½ round, round edge, per dozen ... | 0 | 3 | 6 | Files, 8 in., 3-square, ½ round, round edge, per dozen ... | 0 | 4 | 6 |
| Files, 6 in., 3-square, ½ round, round edge, per dozen ... | 0 | 2 | 4 | Files, 6 in., 3-square, ½ round, round edge, per dozen ... | 0 | 3 | 6 |
| Total fair price .... | £1 | 15 | 1 | Total truck price ... | £2 | 5 | 6 |

The next comparative statement refers to the drapery goods. It is as follows:—

| DRAPER'S PRICE. | | | TRUCK PRICE. | | |
|---|---|---|---|---|---|
| | s. | d. | | s. | d. |
| Good worsted shawls .... | 4 | 6 | Good worsted shawls .... | 9 | 0 |
| Gown pieces ........... | 3 | 6 | Gown pieces ........... | 6 | 0 |
| Half-handkerchief ...... | 0 | 5 | Half-handkerchief ...... | 0 | 9 |
| Stockings, per pair ...... | 0 | 7 | Stockings, per pair ...... | 1 | 0 |
| Total fair price ....... | 9 | 0 | Total truck price ...... | 16 | 9 |

I submitted these figures to several respectable tradesmen—themselves sufferers by the truck system—and they assured me that both sets of figures were in several instances exaggerated—the fair selling prices much too low, and the truck prices much too high. Fifteen per cent. was, however, the amount which two of the authorities in question agreed in rating the truck above the ordinary prices. But, perhaps, the literal truth, both as regards prices and other features of the system, will be best come at by giving *verbatim* the information which I collected from door to door. My informants were uniformly women, the men being, in all cases, at their work.

The first woman I questioned was the wife of a coal bandsman, living in a very dilapidated house on the confines of the parishes of Wolverhampton and Bilston. She spoke nearly as follows:—"My husband is tommeyed. We're nearly all tommeyed hereabouts. I go to the tommy-shop every week with an order. I get half money and half goods. They put down the whole of the money on the counter; but I only take up half of it: or if I do take up the whole, it is only to give it back again. Of course I know that if I do not spend 5s. out of every 10s. my husband will never have another day's work in the pit. But, after all, our tommy-shop is much better than many others. At ——'s (naming an establishment kept by an iron master), the poor people never get one shilling in money—it must be all taken out in goods. I pay 11d. a pound for butter, such as I could get in Wolverhampton for 8d., and 1s. 9d. for a peck of such flour as I could get there for 1s. 7d. At ——'s they won't give you not even one penny to buy barm to bake your bread, if you were to pray for it. Very few of the tommy-shops keep barm. My husband is always paid, when reckoning comes, in a beer-shop. I have heard say that that is unlawful. The buttie keeps the beer-shop. My husband must spend at least 6d. in ale for 'his shot.' The buttie wouldn't like him if he didn't. The reckoning comes once a month. Very often there is not 2s. for us in money. The rest has all been taken out, half in goods and half in cash, from week to week."

Another woman, a neighbour of the first witness, dealt at a similarly conducted tommy-shop. "We spend there 10s. out of every pound my husband earns. I pay 1s. 9d. for flour, and 6d. for the sugar which I could get for 4½d. in Wolverhampton. Every week we have a draw, that is, the men's names are sent in on a list to the tommy-shop, with a sum of money to each, and we have goods for half of it. The women always go for the draw. I think the goods I get are of fair quality, and some things are not dearer than they are at the small shops round. Still I would like that we had our money paid to us direct. I could lay it out far better. I would go in once a week to Wolverhampton, and get the things I wanted. Formerly we dealt at ——'s (naming the place already referred to). That was when my husband was in the employ of ——. Then we had nothing at all but goods from one reckoning to another. My husband was making good wages, but I solemnly declare that for six weeks together I never have had a single penny of ready money. The money we got at the reckonings all went to pay the rent and to get clothing. I have had to borrow a penny to buy barm to bake with." [It will be observed that two women, examined separately, made use of the self-same illustration of the practices of the same tommy shop.]

An engineman whom I talked to at a pit-heap, said that at the tommy-shop kept by the buttie who worked the mine, flour was 4d. a peck and butter 2d. a lb. dearer than at Bilston. He had often heard of men being discharged because they would not deal at the shop. If a man wanted to go to the pit he must go to the shop, that was the rule;

and he reckoned that it was pretty much the same thing with most of the colliers.

A butcher at Swan-hill, West Bromwich, said—"I believe that round this place, within two miles, there are from 2,000 to 3,000 men tommeyed. It is ruination to honest tradespeople. If the masters want to keep shops, why don't they do it fairly, and try to sell better and cheaper than we do? But there's no chance for us; because, whatever price the truckmen ask the workmen must pay. I am now selling ribs of beef for 4½d., and roasting pieces for 3d. The tommy-shops are charging 6½d. and 7d. for the same meat. I sell mutton at from 5d. to 5½d., the tommy-shops sell it at 6½d. a lb. The masters hereabouts say that the reckonings come once a fortnight, and so they do, nominally; but then they are continually being put off, for one reason or another."

At Wednesbury, a master miller informed me that flour was retailed by the truck-masters at 1d., 1¼d., and 1½d. per peck dearer than the ordinary market price. On the western outskirts of the same place, a married woman stated that she dealt at a tommy-shop which she thought was better than most of them. The reckoning was sometimes once a fortnight, and sometimes once in three weeks. She took orders to the shop, and for every pound she got 4s. in ready cash, the rest in goods. Sugar, she thought, was about ½d. in the lb. dearer than at the shops. Cheese was 1d. and 1½d. dearer. She need not go to the Tommy-shop; but then if she didn't her "husband would not be thought so well of." Another woman stated that their reckoning only came about once in five weeks; of course they had to deal at the Tommy-shop. They paid 7s. 4d. a strike for flour, and 9d. a lb. for bacon. She did not think that meat was much dearer than at the shops about. But she could lay out the money much better if she had it all to spend when she liked. "If a man works for money, he ought to get money."

The following is the testimony of a gentleman connected with a large iron-works, and who has taken much interest in the condition of the labourers throughout the district:—"The truck system produces the worst of feelings between the masters and workmen—and no wonder. The iron-masters usually pay in cheques upon distant banks, but if any of the hands dare to cash them their services will very soon be dispensed with. Instead of the bank, they carry their cheques to the Tommy-shops, the masters pretending that the workmen must find the shop handy. I feel quite sure that many of the colliers do not get above 2s. a week in money, and that almost all goes to pay the rent. The reckoning is often delayed for five weeks. In fact, the time of payment is at the caprice of the masters. The people are thus often put to great shifts for money. I have known a woman go to the Tommy-shop—get a pound of sugar at 6d. a pound—and sell it to a neighbour who was not Tommeyed for 4d., just in order to raise the ready cash."

All the clergymen with whom I have conversed bear testimony to the moral and social, as well as physical, evils caused by this system. The working people are cheated, and the fair traders are cheated, by the truck-masters, just as much as they would be by smugglers. That the compulsory paying for labour in goods is fostered and made practicable by the long-reckoning system, is another point upon which all local authority seems to be agreed. It is, indeed, the "long-reckoning" plan which, in a great measure, enables the truck-masters to evade the law. "There is," says the Rev. Mr. Owen, "a text in Deuteronomy which I have more than once publicly referred to;" and certainly the verse in question—the fifteenth of the twenty-fourth chapter—does strikingly apply to South Staffordshire. The employer is thus commanded to treat his labourer—"At his day thou shalt give him his hire; neither shall the sun go down upon it; for he is poor and setteth his heart upon it: lest he cry against thee unto the Lord, and it be a sin to thee." The rev. gentleman is of opinion that no legislative enactment will put down the truck system, until the long-reckonings be abridged by the interference of Parliament. The best class of masters— the "honourable" masters, as those who do not Tommy their men are emphatically called—settle regularly once a fortnight. The butties, as I have said, often pay in beershops, in the face of the law, which enacts that all payments so made are null and void. Prosecutions are sometimes set on foot against the truck-masters, but the difficulty of adducing legal evidence is so great, that the stray convictions now and then obtained have little or no real effect in putting down the system. In Darlaston, I believe that the people are really bestirring themselves, and making head against it; but in Wednesbury, I was told that two new Tommy shops had been very recently opened. The local press is overawed by the iron-masters. The people fret and chafe under the exaction, but are compelled to submit to it; and thus, by notorious, flagrant, and habitual violation of the law, workpeople, tradespeople, and "honourable" masters are alike made subservient, and alike suffer through the cupidity of men who ignore every consideration save that of profit.

# LABOUR AND THE POOR.

—◆—

## THE MANUFACTURING DISTRICTS.

[FROM OUR SPECIAL CORRESPONDENT.]

### NOTTINGHAM AND THE LACE TRADE.

## LETTER XXV.

The industrial staples of the three Midland counties of England, Nottinghamshire, Derbyshire, and Leicester, consist, in a general way, of the manufacture of lace, of silk, and of hosiery, in all its very numerous branches. Of these, the hosiery or framework knitting trade is the oldest, and the most impartially scattered over the three counties. The town of Nottingham is, however, beyond doubt, the metropolis of the Midland lace trade, and as such I give it the first place in describing the district.

Nottingham lies in the very centre of England. It is built on high ground, occupying part of the southern declivity of a long range of hills, running from the north, and which hereabouts fade away into the open champagne country beneath. The town extends over an area of about 2,610 acres. In 1831 it contained 10,642 houses. In 1841 the number had increased to 11,612. In the former year the population was 50,680; in the latter, 53,091. Nottingham presents characteristic features, commercially and socially. To a superficial observer, it appears a handsome, old-fashioned town, full of quaint and quaintly-named streets, narrow and winding, but frequently affording glimpses full of architectural picturesqueness, while so long as the visitor confines himself to the principal thoroughfares, his impression will also be decidedly in favour of the town, as respects the important essentials of good substantial paving and of cleanliness. Both soil and situation facilitate the latter quality. A great portion of the town is built upon the face of such steep declivities as afford natural surface drainage, and the soil, generally of sandstone, is almost as absorbent as a sponge. Notwithstanding these advantages, however, Nottingham is, in one respect, one of the worst built towns in England. Its area is the most crowded in the kingdom. According to Mr. Hawksley's report, there is in Nottingham one individual to "every square of four and a half yards on the side," the calculation including the very large open space of the market-place, while, in one particular part of the town, it has been ascertained by the Poor-law authorities that upwards of 4,200 people dwell in a space not measuring 220 yards square. The inhabitants are thus crowded, because of course the houses are crowded. "In Nottingham, sir," said a framework knitter to me, "the poor live on each other's backs." Out of the 11,000 houses of which the town is composed, more than 8,000 are inhabited by the working classes, and more than 7,000 are built back to back and side to side. Of course a great majority of these open into narrow courts and *cul-de-sacs*, very frequently approached by openings which are rather tunnels than passages, many of them being under eight feet high and three feet wide. "These courts," says Mr. Hawksley, "are almost uniformly closed at both ends." In some of the better class which I have seen, the blocks of buildings are far enough apart to admit of miniature plots of garden ground, each about a couple of yards square, and enclosed by toy palings, a foot or so high. But in many instances the courts in Nottingham are mere grimy slits in the masonry, with broken pavements, and abounding in unsavoury sights and smells. Great quantities of yellowish linen are habitually hung up to dry in these places, stopping the current of what little air might otherwise circulate; and in the lower parts of the town, a similar display is often stretched from window to window across the public thoroughfares. The peculiarly crowded state of Nottingham arose from the land in its vicinity being very extensively held by a peculiar tenure, which permitted the freemen or burgesses to turn out a certain number of cows to pasture upon it annually. The town thus grew up as though girdled by walls, beyond which the mason could not penetrate. The consequence has been that the surplus population, instead of spreading forth into suburbs, has overflowed into many distinct villages and hamlets, such as Carrington and Ison-green. The absurd restriction upon building is now on the eve of being removed. Had it been demolished a score of years ago, it is calculated that Nottingham would have been at least a third larger at the present day.

Of course in a town composed of buildings so closely huddled upon each other, the principles of ventilation and efficient drainage could not have been originally much attended to. Since 1832, however, the successive parochial highway boards have been carrying on a vigorous system of sanitary and structural reform. Previously to that period—and, indeed, as improvements of this sort can proceed but slowly, the description still to a certain extent applies—multitudes of thickly populated streets were utterly unpaved and undrained, pools of stagnant water, and ridges of dung, ashes, and refuse running down their entire length. The privies, where they existed at all, were generally constructed in clusters beneath the houses, and neglected and offensive in the extreme. So late, indeed, as two or three years ago, there existed groups of thirty and forty houses, the occupants of which, since their dwellings were built fifty years ago, had never enjoyed any accommodation of the kind whatever, and "hundreds" of the places actually existing were pronounced by the recently-appointed local sanitary commission to be "unfit for the use of any human being." The supply of water to the town was, at the period in question, scanty and defective. The sewerage which had been formed was also "very defective and unsystematic"—indeed, Mr. Hawksley in his report enumerates more than 61 streets which were undrained as late as 1844. In 1832 the cholera attacked Nottingham, and raged with great severity. There were upwards of 1,100 attacks, of which 289 proved fatal. As usual, the principal ravages of the scourge took place in those wards where the rate of mortality was highest under ordinary circumstances. In the late cholera visitation, however, Nottingham got off almost scot-free. There occurred but eight cases, of which six resulted in death. One of the causes of this comparative immunity may no doubt be found in the sanitary improvements effected since 1832. The water-supply subsequent to that year has been, and is, most abundant; and the work of sewer-making and pavement-making has been steadily progressive. In 1836 a proprietary cemetery of twelve acres in extent was formed in the outskirts, and upwards of 6,600 burials have, up to the present time, taken place there. Another open burial place of seven acres was allotted during the cholera time, and many interments have been effected within it. Still further to stay the plague of intramural sepulture, two public cemeteries have lately been opened without the town, the one connected with the church, the other with dissent. The local authorities, however, not satisfied with the gradual progress of sanitary reform, bestirred themselves, and nearly three years ago the sanitary committee above referred to was appointed. This body seems to have done its duty vigorously. At the instance of the committee, thirty-four dwellings, erected over privies and ash-pits, have been removed, the change in many instances throwing open hitherto unventilated courts and noisome alleys. A great number of foul nuisances of a similar class, including 21 pig-sties and 24 cess-pools, containing "dangerous collections of manure," have been got rid of, and many courts and small streets paved and drained. These improvements will, it is to be hoped, gradually dethrone Nottingham from the head pre-eminence which it occupies in the bills of mortality. By the last returns of the Registrar-General, the proportion of males living to one death was 34.3, of females 39.4, showing a mean rate of about 36 living persons to one death. This is a higher rate of mortality than prevails in any of the cotton towns excepting Manchester, and higher than that existing in any of the woollen towns—not even excepting Leeds. The comparatively great mortality of Nottingham the town owes to a few of its lower districts. There is a difference of nearly 100 per cent. in the value of life in the high and suburban, as compared with the low and crowded, wards of Nottingham. In Park-ward the mean age at death is 37. In a district close to it, composed of courts and back-to-back houses, the mean age at death is less than 18. On the elevated plateaus of the Common, the mean age at death rises to 40. In one part of Castle-ward it sinks to 14.3, and in an adjacent district, an average constructed on 63 deaths, gave a mean age of 14.9 years. In Castle-gate, "open, elevated, and well-drained," with 38½ yards of space for each inhabitant, the mean age at death is 30.6. In Mortimer-street, "crowded, low, and indifferently drained," with only 16 yards of space for each inhabitant, the mean age at death is 17.1. Taken altogether, the mortality of Nottingham is 26 per cent. greater than the mortality of England and Wales, and the mean age at death in Nottingham 22.3 years—just seven years below the average age of death in England and Wales. Some of these results are taken from Mr. Hawksley's report in 1844; but that the general rate of mortality has not diminished is proved by the last tables of the Registrar-General.

About three-fourths of the houses of Nottingham are constructed for and occupied by the working classes, and as a rule they are built in courts and back to back. The general plan of construction divides them into three clear stories, of one room each—a singularly inconvenient and defective arrangement. The staircases are very steep, dark, and narrow, and under them are frequently situated black choky holes of pantries. In many cases coals and provisions are kept in the same recess. The houses have seldom a sub-story, and cellar dwellings are consequently unfrequent. I believe that there are not above 200 in Nottingham. The lower room is in general the living apartment. It is almost always floored with brick, or, if boarded, as it may be in rare cases, sand supplies the place of carpeting. The street door is invariably the room door. In point of furniture, I should say that the living apartments of the Nottingham operatives, particularly those of the framework knitters, are decidedly inferior to the dwellings of the mass of workpeople in the cotton, woollen, and northern coal districts. I have been very frequently struck with the bare appearance of the rooms, and this even in the houses of middlemen in the hosiery trade, who had perhaps a dozen or a score of knitting frames at work. An inferior sort of sofa, however, and a clock are common. The lace-workers' houses are somewhat better furnished. A few of the latter, belonging to operatives earning the higher class of wages, boast a substantial and, occasionally, crowded *ameublement*. The apartment on the first floor is invariably a bedroom; that above it either a bedroom or a workshop, in which knitting machines, and occasionally warp lace frames are set. The central bedroom opens upon the staircase, and is usually patent to the view of the workmen ascending or descending from the shop. In some cases there is a garret above the working room, used occasionally as a lumber receptacle, occasionally as a bedroom, occasionally as both. These places are got at by means of a trap-door and a ladder, and are miserable dark, dog-holes. In houses not constructed in the regular three-storied and three-roomed fashion the apartments are usually very small, and the bed-closets, off the living rooms, are perfectly unlighted and unventilated. The floors of the higher flats in Nottingham are almost universally composed of a layer of coarse plaster of Paris, mixed with ground ashes, and laid about two inches thick. The floors absorb moisture rapidly, and are excessively cold to the feet. I have frequently found them rough, and worn into dusty and flaky cavities. The whole construction of the houses is generally slight, and the roofing particularly so. In crowded cities there must be crowded houses, and in crowded houses crowded rooms. I have frequently found families of five and six living and sleeping in close chambers not more than 12 feet square. The average weekly rent, including parochial taxes, of houses of two stories, containing one living room and one bedroom, is about 1s. 9d.; of those containing a garret in addition, 1s. 11d.; and of those containing a garret and cellar, 2s. 1d. The average weekly rent of a three-storied house, containing a living-room, bed-room, and workshop, is about 2s. 2d.; if a garret be added, 2s. 6d.; and if there be two bed-rooms, as well as the other accommodations, about 2s. 11d.

I have already referred to the water supply of Nottingham, but its abundance, excellence, and cheapness merit further and more detailed notice. Up to within a few years Nottingham was principally served by two companies. The smallest of these, called the Nottingham Old Water Company, has existed upwards of 150 years, but it was not incorporated until 1826. In 1844 it supplied water derived from springs, welling forth at a higher level than that of the town, and about a mile and a half north from it, to from 12,000 to 14,000 of the population. The other company—the Trent Water-works Company—was incorporated in the year 1825. It derived its supply from the Trent, taking the water about a mile south of the town, and filtering it through beds of sand. This company supplied about 36,000 of the inhabitants. Certain minor concerns, deriving the water from wells, accommodated an additional 5,000. In 1845 the two companies amalgamated. The works of both are now kept in action under one general and very economic system of management, with the following results:—Out of the total number of houses, amounting to near 12,000, about 11,500 are supplied in different ways. Of these more than 3,000 are independent tenements, paying the water rates individually, and about 8,500 are small houses, compounded for in groups of not less than three by the landlords, the tenants of course paying the diminished rate as portion of their rents. The dwellings of the poor are supplied at an average charge of about 5s. per annum, or not quite 1¼d. per house per week. The highest charge is calculated at 5 per cent., and the lowest at 3 per cent. on the rent. Houses of £5 are thus charged 5s., and so up to £13, when the rate diminishes to 12s. Houses of £30 are charged 24s.; houses of £50 are charged 35s.; and houses of £100 are supplied for 60s. When landlords compound for their property they are allowed 25 per cent. if they pay poor-rates and parochial charges, and 20 per cent. if they do not. Water-closets in private houses are supplied for 10s. per annum, and private baths at the same charge. Gardens are supplied for 2s. 6d.; and mills, for drinking and washing, per individual employed, at 3d. yearly. When a landlord compounds for a block of tenements, the company conduct the water to the boundary of his property. He may then erect merely stand taps, or lay pipes into every one of the houses at his own pleasure. In Nottingham the water, by day and night, is perpetually "on," and thus all the expensive and cumbrous machinery of tanks and cisterns is avoided. One of the reservoirs being situated at a higher level than the highest houses, there is seldom, in cases of fire, occasion for the engines. Plugs are placed at every hundred yards along the streets, and the hose has only to be screwed on at these apertures to the main. The quantity of water supplied in Nottingham is calculated as amounting to about 450 millions of gallons per annum, or from 18 to 20 gallons per head per day. Previously to the adoption of the present system, a great portion of the poorer part of Nottingham was supplied by carriers. They sometimes charged ¼d. and sometimes ½d. per bucket, according to the situation of the house. The general price was stated to have been three gallons for a farthing. The price is now about ¼d. for 79 gallons, or at a cheaper rate by more than twenty-six times than the charges of yore, the supply too being constantly at hand day and night. The medical men of Nottingham are unanimous in bearing testimony to the excellent sanitary effects of this abundant water supply.

So far as the state of education and sexual morality can be got at through the Registrar-General's returns, I find the condition of matters to be as follows:—In 1846 the number of illegitimate births in Nottingham was 179, or about one to every 160 of the female population. In 1846, out of 642 marriages, 532 were celebrated according to the rites of the Establishment, and 110 in other modes. In 38 cases the man, and in 88 cases the woman, was under age. In 157 cases, or about one-fourth of the whole, the man signed with his mark. In 309 cases, or about one-half of the whole, the woman signed with her mark.

The branch of industry generally known as the lace trade includes two principal departments—the warp process, in which the mechanism is still generally moved by hand labour, and the twist or bobbinnet process, in which the mechanism is now-a-days commonly, although not uniformly, driven by steam. Subordinate to these two principal branches there exist an infinity of minor trade subdivisions in the manufacture—by twist and warp machines, constructed after different fashions—of an endless variety of kinds and qualities of goods. The lace trade, in almost all its ramifications, however, sprung originally from the hosiery manufacture. The first approach to lace weaving by machinery was the fabrication of ornamental stockings, with eyelet holes running up the ankles. Then the stocking frames were used to knit purses, and afterwards, by a peculiar arrangement of their mechanism, to construct point lace. The first great step in advance was the invention of the warp machine, which involved, to a certain extent, the principle of the stocking-frame. The warps were for some time the principal mechanical producers of lace. The jacquard was applied to them, and they were found capable of turning out patterns of a complicated nature. Meantime, however, an apparatus upon a new and improved principle, for the fabrication of the most delicate and elaborately-wrought lace, made its appearance, in the twist or bobbin-net machine—the principal and characteristic feature of the new invention being adopted, it is said, from a contrivance put in use by some ingenious person for the better weaving of cabbage-nets.

Before proceeding to describe the condition of the principal classes of lace-workers, the nature of their toil, and the fashion in which it is carried on, it may be well for me to introduce a brief synoptical statement of the statistics of the manufacture, compiled principally from the results of the elaborate investigation set on foot at two periods, 1831 and 1836, by Mr. Felkin, of Nottingham—a gentleman to whom I am indebted not only for much published but for much personally-communicated information.

The bobbin-net manufacture dates its origin from the year 1811. At that time the population of Nottingham, and of the surrounding districts and villages of Lenton, Beeston, Radford, Basford, Arnold, and Snenton, was 47,300. In 1831, it was calculated that the hosiery trade employed fewer people than it did in 1811; and as the population in question had then increased to 79,000, the augmentation is principally to be ascribed to the rapid growth of the bobbin-net manufacture. By the last census, the population of the area I have mentioned amounted to more than 130,000. In 1831, there were at work in the town of Nottingham upwards of 1,240 lace-making machines, and in the surrounding villages about as many more.

The number of machines then in operation in the kingdom was estimated at 4,500, of which Nottinghamshire, of course, possessed more than half. In 1836, another careful inquiry was set on foot, from which it appeared that the total number of machines had decreased to 3,800. A severe and long-continued depression in the trade had been the cause of upwards of six hundred of them being broken up and sold as old iron. The machinery had also been in a transition state. In many cases, two of the old narrow frames had been joined to make one broader engine, and a few had been exported. The number of machine hands employed had of course decreased with the decrease of the engines upon which they wrought, the number being about 6,000, or less than two to every machine. The number of owners of these machines was stated at about 860. In 1831 there were 1,382 owners. The decrease took place almost entirely in the owners of one or two machines a piece. In 1836, the number of machines in the town of Nottingham was 576; in the subsidiary towns and surrounding district it was about 1,470; showing that the tendency of the manufacture had been to flow from the central point of Nottingham, and to spread itself over the surrounding area. The total number of machines in England, actually at work, in 1836, was 3,547, of which again the county of Nottingham possessed 2,162, or more than one-half. At the period in question, 1836, the number of machines making fancy net in the midland district was increasing, and great improvements were also in the course of being introduced into the mechanism. Indeed, it was then estimated that 1,000 machines had been raised, from the value of from £2 to £10 each, to the value of from £50 to £100 each; while from 1,500 to 2,000 men were employed in making fancy goods, over and above the number to whom work could be given in the manufacture of plain nets.

Since 1836 no census of the number of machines employed in the lace trade has been taken, but I am informed upon the highest authority in the manufacture, that the numerical amount of the machines in use remains pretty stationary but that their productive power has, by the introduction of mechanical improvements, greatly increased. Indeed, the improvement in the machinery employed in lace-making may be conceived from the following extraordinary fact:—In 1810 and 1811 a square yard of a particular kind of lace fetched £5. In 1824 its price was 15s. In 1847 it might have been purchased for 5d. Part of this astounding reduction is owing to the cheapening of the raw material, but of course the great cheapening agent was improved machinery.

The lace of Nottingham is manufactured from cotton and silk threads. These yarns are spun in Manchester and Coventry. For the manufacture of lace it is requisite that they should be loosely doubled. This doubling process is partly performed in Lancashire and Warwickshire, partly in and around the town of Nottingham. The doubling mills are worked principally by women and children, superintended by male overlookers. The processes are simple. The yarn is received from the fine-spinning mills of the North in bundles called cops, and placed on the doubling frame. Spindles are passed longitudinally through these cops, two of the latter being transfixed on each of the former, and the threads are then by power machinery rapidly run off the whirling cops and on to bobbins, each couple of threads being doubled and loosely twisted round each other in the winding process. Women superintend the operation, assisted by children to change and replace the bobbins and cops. The thread is next taken to the clearing-frame, where it is run through delicate metal interstices. The occurrence of any lump or inequality breaks the thread, which it is the workwoman's business to knot again so daintily and delicately as to permit it to run through the testing aperture. If thread of a particularly fine quality be wanted, the filament is next passed several times through the flame of gas, so as to burn off all downy fibre attaching to it. The fourth process consists in unwinding from the bobbins, and reeling the thread into hanks or "slips;" and the final operation is that of the "preparing frame," where the thread is squeezed through cylinders exerting a pressure of from 80 to 100 lbs. weight, in order to smooth and give it gloss. The doubling factories come under the regulations of the Ten Hours Bill, and work daily for that period. They employ about four children for every ten women. The wages of the former range from 3s. to 4s. per week, those of the latter from 6s. 6d. to 7s. 6d. per week.

I proceed to the description of the simplest species of lace-making—that known as the warp trade. The warp machine, as I have stated, sprung directly from the knitting frame. In its uses the former is an extremely flexible apparatus. It is capable of making plain nets, fancy nets, and blonds, with all the tribe of lace "borderings," known as "tattins," "pearlings," "quillings," and so forth. Purses and braces of silk or any other material can be wrought upon the warp-frame. It is used also for the fabrication of strong fleecy hosiery, gloves, stockings, and under garments; and latterly it has been made to weave very good cloth. The jacquard has been applied to the warp, but I understand that the class of fancy goods constructed by its help is now being almost uniformly made by the twist or bobbin-net machine. The warp is, as I have said, generally wrought by hand. Formerly the manufacture was principally domestic; now the machines are very generally being gathered into factories; but as yet factory regulations are by no means uniformly applied to these concentrations of machinery. The system of obliging the workmen to pay rents for their warp-frames is a vestige of the knitting trade, from which the warp manufacture has sprung. The system, however, in this branch of manufacture is not universal. There are, in fact, two scales of wages in use, the journeymen's and the "independent" workmen's rates. In the case of the former, the goods manufactured are paid for according to a certain scale, and no frame-rent is exacted. In the case of the latter, the scale is fixed at higher rates, and a certain stipulated rent is paid weekly. This rent differs with the width and capabilities of the machine, but I am informed that a fair average is about 3s. 6d. A few of the warp-frames are charged as high as 5s. weekly. When the mechanism is not collected in factories, the work is generally received from the manufacturer and given out by middlemen. This is another relic of the frame-work knitting trade, the usages of which, both as respects middlemen and frame-rents, will form the principal subject of my next communication. If a workman be the proprietor of a warp-machine he will frequently purchase the requisite yarns from the large manufacturer and sell the lace in the best market on his own account, but the constant tendency of the trade is to concentrate the machinery in factories, or at all events to concentrate the management of it in the hands of middlemen, each of whom may superintend a dozen frames. The warp-machines are wrought either by jerking a pair of levers, or by a rotatory motion, like turning the handle of a winch. The men frequently have their children to assist them in operating upon the latter class of machines. In the lever frames the feet are used to work treddles, as in a loom. Although the machinery looks heavy, and the frames are sometimes fully twelve feet broad, the mechanism is so nicely balanced, that the toil of putting it in motion cannot be said to be severe. In this respect, however, different frames vary materially. A not unimportant branch of the employment consists in warping, or placing the warp thread in due order for different patterns upon the beam. When a workman labours at home, the middleman furnishes him with the beam ready warped. In factories, there are men engaged upon warping who do nothing else, and are generally paid regular wages, averaging from 16s. to 18s. per week. The girls who do the requisite winding from the skein on to bobbins—always one of the initial processes in textile manufacture—work in the factories generally about eleven hours a day, and are paid about 7s. per week. The warp factory rooms are seldom large. Six or eight frames is an ordinary number to find working together. No artificial heat is required. In some factories the men are charged for candle or gas light; this is when the machines are worked by relays. When only a single hand is employed at a frame, as he labours principally by daylight, no such exaction is usually imposed. The relay system is one which obtains to a very considerable degree, and forms one of the characteristic features of the lace trade. I am informed that, particularly in the case of the bobbin-net machines, the value of the mechanism is so great, as compared with that of the fabric manufactured by it, that to obtain a due return for the capital sunk, it is necessary that the machinery should be kept in motion for a greater number of hours per day than in the instance of any other species of textile mechanism with which I am acquainted. Both bobbin-net and warp-machines are sometimes wrought twenty hours out of the twenty-four. Two men belong to each machine, and relieve each other every four or every six hours. The shifts alternate their task times every week, so as to come in for the bulk of the night-work in turns. One of the principal drawbacks in the warp trade arises from the necessity of occasionally changing the class and pattern of fabrics produced. The process of disposing the myriad threads so as to fit them for being wrought into new combinations, is not only toilsome but tedious. Very often an alteration will keep two men working during a week, and for this they receive no remuneration whatever. They are paid by the piece, and the week which sees no piece produced sees no wages earned. In the silk branch of warp-lace making, the operatives suffer much during the winter season from slackness of work. I have heard many complaints from the men labouring by shifts of the pressure of the night-toil. "After a week of it," said one of them to me, "I'm fit for nothing on the Sunday. I may go and take a little walk, perhaps, after breakfast, and then I go to bed, and sleep the rest of the day." When making alterations, some proprietors allow the men to draw a portion of their wages on account, others will not advance a farthing. The trade, it is right to say, is at present to a great extent in a transition state. The twist machines have taken a considerable portion of the fancy work formerly wrought by the warps; but I understand that some new branches of lace manufacture are likely to infuse fresh life into the warp trade. The bordering fabrics commonly manufactured are wrought upon the warps in broad webs, and the disentanglement of each particular stripe of tattin, or pearling, forms one of the manual employments which occupy children in the lace districts, and to which I shall come speedily. The wages earned by the warp-frame workers vary widely, ranging from 23s. and 25s. down to beneath 10s. A number of workmen to whom I referred the question, after a long consultation, told me, that in their deliberate and candid opinion, the average wages earned by warp-work knitters, clear of all deductions, were from 12s. to 14s. per week.

I now come to the bobbin-net, or twist branch of the lace trade. Here the most complex and expensive machinery is employed in the production of the most delicate and elaborately patterned lace. I have not, the reader will perceive, attempted to explain the mechanism of the warp-frame. I shall still less endeavour to describe that of the twist machine, which of itself is by far the most profoundly complex apparatus existing in the range of textile mechanism; while in many cases ingenious adaptations of the jacquard give the machinery an additional degree of elaborate complication. To build a twist machine requires an outlay of at least £600. As I have already stated, steam power is now being generally applied to the working of these splendid pieces of mechanism—the number of those wrought by hand being daily decreasing. As in the case of the warp trade, the factories are not generally of great size. In fact, nothing like the vast grimy bricken box with which we naturally associate the word "factory" is to be seen in Nottingham. The twist-factory rooms there are generally moderate-sized apartments.

Besides the work of placing the warp upon the beam, which I have already alluded to, there is another set of preliminary processes characteristic of the branch of lace manufacture in question. These are involved in the use of the "bobbins and carriages," which, to employ a very rough, and, in some respects inaccurate analogy, perform one function of the shuttle, and supply the weft to the warp—the machine by its own operations gradually emptying the bobbins of their contents. The charging with the thread, and final preparation of these bobbins, are processes partly performed by women and partly, notwithstanding the dexterous and delicate manipulation requisite, by little imps of boys often under ten years of age. The first thing to be done is the ordinary process of winding the thread from the hank upon common pirns or bobbins. Women or children perform the work, the former getting from 6s. to 8s. a week, the latter from 2s. to 3s. From the bobbins the thread is again wound upon large cylinders called drums, a great many threads from many bobbins being rolled on simultaneously. This operation, requiring more care, is paid for at a rather higher rate, the boys who perform it earning from 4s. to 4s. 6d. weekly. The next process is the first belonging exclusively to the twist trade, and is usually performed by a woman. It consists of putting the thread upon the bobbins used in the machinery. These bobbins are flat circular pieces of brass, each about the size of a small Geneva watch, and so deeply grooved as only to be connected in the centre by a small piece of metal. Round this the thread is wound, sheathed, of course, on each side by its brass case. The way in which the bobbins are filled is ingenious. The operator takes up a number corresponding to the number of threads upon the drum, passes the bobbins by means of a central perforation upon a revolving cylinder, and then, stretching the threads over them, slips each into its respective groove. A few rapid turns to the handle of the winding mechanism, and the bobbins, revolving at great speed, fill themselves from the ample supply of the drum. The operator then slips them off the cylinder, puts on a fresh set, adjusts the threads by passing the full bobbins delicately over the empty ones, then snips the threads in question with her scissors, lays the full bobbins aside, and proceeds again to fill the new batch. The wages earned at this species of work are about 10s. a week. The bobbins being filled, have now to be inserted in the "carriages"—the latter, slight steel frameworks, forming the cases in which the former wheel round. Through a minute hole in one part of the frame or carriage, the other end of the thread upon the bobbin has to be passed. The inserting of the bobbins and threading of the carriages are performed by boys with a rapidity and neatness of manipulation which makes the process almost appear like legerdemain. The wages of these boys are about 3s. 6d. per week. In other respects their condition is by no means a satisfactory one, from the irregularity and frequent length of their hours. Their services are of course only required when the bobbins want refilling; but those periods are very uncertain, and continually vary. A dozen twist machines may start together, making the same pattern, driven by the same steam-engine, and with the same quantity of thread on their bobbins; yet, as accidental delays in greater or less number continually occur, it generally happens that the dozen sets of bobbins become exhausted at different times. Whenever that exhaustion occurs, however, by day or by night, the bobbin-fillers and threaders must be set to work. Sometimes these children are required to be, if not working, at least in attendance from four o'clock in the morning until after midnight. Part of this hardship might be avoided by using a double set of bobbins and carriages, and in some factories this is actually the case. These delicately-fashioned articles are, however, very expensive.

The beams being duly in place, and the bobbins and carriages set in order, the machine is ready for work. In 1835 the average hours of labour in the west of England were 13; in Nottingham, Derby, and Leicester, they were and still are 20 hours per day. The relay system is, therefore, of course requisite. In the first factory I visited the machinery was wrought 18 hours. The first man commenced operations at six a.m., working until nine a.m. The second took his place from nine a.m. until one p.m. The first man again resumed his post from one p.m. until six p.m., and the second superintended the frame from six p.m. until midnight. The shifts equalized their respective working hours by changing turns every week. In another factory, working 20 hours, the following arrangements were adopted:—A wrought from four a.m. until nine a.m.; B from nine a.m. until one p.m. A resumed his post again from one p.m. until six p.m., and B from six p.m. until midnight—an arrangement fairly dividing the 20 hours. So long as the machinery works steadily and without hitch, and there is no breakage in the multitudinous array of threads, the workman may be a mere spectator, but he must always be a vigilant one. His eye must be continually fixed upon the hundred threads, wires, hooks and wheels which throb and quiver before him. The breaking of a single filament of course involving the necessity of stopping the machine, and carefully and delicately repairing the damage. So exquisitely delicate, indeed, is the mechanism, that a few moments' inattention to a single ruptured thread may lead to a smash both amid fabric and machinery which it will cost the workman days and the master pounds to repair. A regular source of delay, and consequently of loss, to the workman is involved in the refitting and shifting of the bobbins, particularly when, as sometimes happens, half-a-dozen machines are exhausted nearly at the same time, and there is but one set of bobbin threaders to supply them. But a still more formidable cause of loss of time is the periodical alterations of the warp, for the purpose of placing on the machine new patterns. These alterations are seldom effected under three days, and sometimes they occupy a fortnight—the average may be something under a week. In some factories the workmen are paid an allowance while "standing for alteration," of from 12s. to 15s. per week. In others they only get an advance, which is repaid by halfcrown instalments, deducted from their subsequent weekly wages. This system of advances and forced repayments is considered by some of the highest authorities in the trade as objectionable, commercially and socially speaking. If any holes or similar imperfections be found in the lace after it is taken off the machine, the men have to pay for the mending by needlework. Sometimes a regular sum is deducted from their wages for mending; in other cases they are mulcted from week to week in proportion to the actual amount of breakage. The former plan is more popular among the men, as they say that under it they at least know what to expect on Saturday night. Lace workers in factories usually pay for lights. If the men work by relays, the sum exacted is 1s. 6d. per week each. If one man only works a machine, he pays 1s. The operatives employed upon hand machines have generally to hire a boy to help them to turn, and who is paid by them about 4s. per week. The net amount of wages paid to good hands in the twist trade is considerable. There are some men at bobbin-net machines who can earn 35s. to 40s. per week. Making allowances for stoppages, a tolerably skilful hand working at fancy goods will make from 25s. to 30s. per week. The average amount may be taken as 18s., or from that to 20s.; and the lowest earned by the youngest hands is about 10s. In the first factory which I visited—one producing exquisitely beautiful fancy goods—the first workman whom I questioned stated that he was earning 27s. or 28s. per week; another, superintending the production of an imitation of Mechlin lace, said he was making 22s. 6d.; and a third, engaged upon a filmy species of silk lace, was receiving about £1. The general run of wages are, however, below these. There is no regular apprenticeship served to the twist trade. Failing eyesight is the great bane of a workman in all branches not only of the lace but the hosiery trade. The vision too often becomes early impaired from the strain to which it is subjected, and men are often compelled to give up the most profitable branches of lace making while enjoying in its fullest powers every other faculty, bodily and mental.

The lace we shall now suppose to be finished and taken from the frame, whether a warp or a twist machine. It has next to undergo the processes which it receives at the hands of the dresser and gasser, and those of the bleacher. The work in a dressing and gassing establishment is carried on almost entirely by women, and is exceedingly simple. The gassing process is similar to one which I have described amid the operations of calico printing. The net, or lace, when taken from the machine is full of downy fibres, which give the mesh-work a dull semi-opaque appearance. To get rid of these, the fabric is passed quickly along cylinders and athwart a thin sheet of gas flame extending along the entire width of the piece. Four girls or women tend the machine; two feeding the revolving cylinders with the lace, two receiving it after the flame has purged off all its superfluous filaments, and extinguishing any sparks which may appear still alive upon the material. These girls are paid 8s. a week, working ten hours a day. They receive 2d. per hour if called upon to work overtime. This rate of 2d. an hour is that very commonly paid for over-time in female labour in many departments of lace making. Having been gassed, the fabric is handed over to the bleacher, who submits it to those processes

common to the blanching of all textile materials, and which therefore
need not be more particularly alluded to here. The fabric is then returned to the dresser's establishment to be stiffened. This operation
is performed by passing the bleached and purified pieces through a
hot mixture of gum and starch boiled together, and then submitting
the reeking lace to the action of revolving cylinders, which squeeze
out the surplus stiffening fluid. The labour requisite here is all but
unskilled. It is generally performed by a man and two or three boys,
the former earning 18s., the latter from 6s. to 8s. per week. The dank
masses of lace, with their folds sticking to each other through the
agency of the clammy mixture, are now hurried away to the stretching-
rooms. These consist of vast extending corridors, down which runs a
frame-work, something like a long skeleton table, the edges bristling
with close set wire points or teeth. The girls employed, each of them
armed with a little bamboo cane, range themselves at the upper end
of the room, on either side of the frame-work, while a boy carrying
the clammy wreathes of lace in a basket walks slowly down the centre.
The upper corners of the piece having been already fastened to the upper corners of the frame-work, the girls, following the boy down the
skeleton table, fasten with nimble fingers the sides of the extending
web to the rows of wire teeth, at the same time switching it with their
canes or "bats," so as to get rid of all the extra starch, and to dislodge
any little impurity which may have clung to the meshes. When the
whole web is fixed, one of the women turns the handle of a winch.
The beams of the frame-work instantly recede from each other, and
the lace is extended out as rigidly as though the threads were iron
wires. The material is now left to dry, while the girls proceed to repeat
the process in another gallery. Matters are sought to be so arranged
that by the time the lace is stretched in the last corridor, it is dry in
the first. Should this not be the case, however, the girls fan it with
light spade-shaped implements, very broad in the blade, the sweeps
of which, wielded by skilful hands, produce powerful currents of air.
When thoroughly dry the lace is disengaged, and folded in readiness
to be sent off to the warehouse. In the stretching and dressing rooms
the women employed are paid 1s. 6d. per day, with 2d. an hour for
over-work. The regular hours are generally from eight o'clock until
one, and from two o'clock until six. The temperature in which the
labour is carried on is extremely high, the thermometer in a stretching room being seldom below 80. In some establishments the heat is

more complained of than in others, and in almost all the girls have a thin, pale look.

I now proceed shortly to describe the different processes in lace manufacture carried on by the manual labour of women and children. Of these the two most important are mending and tambour, or embroidery work. The minor operations are "running," "catching-up," and "drawing." I shall first refer to tambour work. As most of your readers may be aware, it consists of embroidering plain net with flowers or fancy figures by means of a delicate hook, called a crochet needle. Comparatively, little tambour work is done at Nottingham. The manufacturers find it cheaper to disperse the labour throughout the neighbouring counties. There is hardly a hamlet in the midland shires of England where the wives and daughters of cottagers do not eke out the general income by help of the tambour frame. Indeed, the Nottingham lace manufacturers look still further for female labour. The partners of one of the first lace embroidery houses in the town informed me that much of their very best work was performed in Essex. The inferior sorts of tambouring, however, are uniformly executed in the villages around Nottingham, Leicester, and Derby. "I can get," said a warp manufacturer to me—"I can get lace embroidered in the country for 2s. and 3s., for which I would have to pay 4s. or 6s. in Nottingham; and in the country cottages they keep it cleaner too." All round the town, however, the crochet needle is plied in almost every second house. The lace is stretched upon a frame large enough to enable several persons to work upon it at the same time. The occupation, although in one respect graceful and feminine, is of course severe upon the eyes; and from its perfectly sedentary nature, and the stooping position which it demands, is apt to create pulmonary and digestive complaints. The great mass of the embroidery performed round and near Nottingham is managed by middlewomen, or "missuses," who receive the work from the warehouse at a fixed rate, and give it out to whom they please, and take it back when finished. Sometimes the "missuses" give the lace to women to be tamboured at home; sometimes they assemble at their (the missuses') own houses as many girls and children as they can accommodate—the latter thus plying their tasks in the various departments of the trade under their patronesses' immediate superintendence. The wages of the most skilful and most industrious lace tambourer, employed upon the best work, very rarely amount to 10s. a week, and still more rarely exceed that sum. The average may be from 6s. to 7s. per week, but many, especially in the country, do not earn so much. The middlewomen of course pocket a goodly per centage of the wages, amounting, as I am informed, to something like 2d. out of the shilling; and they always endeavour to keep up their influence and their profits by preventing any communication between their *employées* and the manufacturers—keeping the former in ignorance, if possible, of the warehouse for which they are working. A tambourer whom I visited in Nottingham was a married woman, with a family, which prevented her from earning above 3s. a week. If she had no domestic duties to perform, and stuck to the work closely, she might make from 5s. 6d. to 6s. To gain that sum would take twelve hours' labour at the very least. She had her work secondhand, and did not know for what warehouse it was intended. Could she have the lace direct from the manufacturer, she calculated that she could earn at least 7s. per week, but few or none of the warehouses would have anything to do with single hands. The middlewomen saved the former a great deal of trouble, and the workpeople paid for it. This was the substance of the account given, by several tambourers visited, of their situation and earnings. They alternated to a greater or less extent their needle with their household labours. Those girls who met and worked together I generally found assembled in clean and tidy rooms. They gave their earnings at from 10d. to 1s. 3d. per day.

The remaining kinds of lace needlework which I have enumerated are performed partly at the warehouses and partly at the homes of the workpeople. The chief of these employments is "mending," an operation requiring a quick eye and a dexterous and practised hand. The menders fill up any accidental holes in the lace with such neatness that the injured part can hardly, if at all, be recognised. Those who work in the warehouses are paid by the week at rates varying from 6s. to 10s., and extra for over hours. The regular period of labour is from 8 a.m. until 6 p.m., with an hour for dinner, and half an hour for tea. At some warehouses, from 80 to 100 girls are employed in this species of labour. Menders generally begin very young, at five or six years of age. One girl told me that she could not remember the time when she had not been mending. They are frequently shortsighted. Black lace is especially prejudicial to the eyes. The statement of a lace-mender, visited at her home—a very squalid place, consisting of a single room—was as follows:—She was paid 8d. or 1s. per piece, according to the size and number of the holes to be repaired. One week with another, she earned about 6s. or 6s. 6d. She had her house to attend to. Her little girl, eight years old, gave her some trifling help. If she were working in a warehouse she could earn about 8s. Her hours, as a regular thing, were very long—from six in the morning until nine o'clock, and sometimes ten o'clock, at night. She had been mending lace since she was six years old. Another lace-mender stated that she was working at Mechlin lace. The price of the piece was 1s. 6d. To do a piece took her over two days—sometimes more, sometimes less. If she worked at a warehouse she would have about 7s. 6d. per week. She had been a mender since she was five years old. The wages had fallen greatly within her recollection. She remembered receiving 6s. a piece, for mending which she would now get only 1s. 6d. Her hours were from eight o'clock in the morning until ten o'clock or eleven o'clock at night. Her earnings, one week with another, were about 5s.

"Running" consists in circumscribing with a thread the outline of patterns wrought in the net by the machine. The lace is stretched upon a frame, as in tambour work. Four or five "runners" working together estimated their average earnings at 1s. per day each. They worked 14 and sometimes 16 hours. The best hands on the best work could not make more than 1s. 3d. per day, and many, particularly in the country, did not clear above 6d. For the last two years good runners had had plenty of employment. At night they lighted three candles to every four workers. Two runners—a mother and daughter, in another house—calculated that they each made 4s. 6d. per week. They worked in the winter from daylight in the morning until ten at night. They got their work from a middlewoman, and were paid according to the number of figures in the pattern. These poor people were at dinner when I called. The meal consisted of bread and tea, with dripping for butter.

The remaining species of work—"drawing" and "catching up"—are generally performed either at the warehouses or at the houses of the mistresses. The wages are excessively low, and the labour—being perfectly easy, particularly that of drawing, which consists merely in pulling out the thread which unites the stripes of edging material—is chiefly performed by children, who make from 3d. to 6d. a day. These juvenile labourers are set to work at ages sadly early. A gentleman informed me that he has seen a baby, twenty months old, sit in a high chair at a table, and gravely employed in drawing lace.

The missuses, or middlewomen, have generally themselves been embroiderers or menders. They very often have money-lending transactions with their *employées*, and instances are not unfrequent of their carrying on the truck system in a small and modified way, supplying bread, groceries, and candles, and deducting the amount, of course with an additional per centage, from the wages paid at the end of the week. The missuses always, however, profess to supply the articles at market price, and to look to reimbursement and profit from the discount allowed by the tradespeople.

# LABOUR AND THE POOR.

### THE MANUFACTURING DISTRICTS.

[FROM OUR SPECIAL CORRESPONDENT.]

### THE HOSIERY TRADE IN NOTTINGHAM.

## LETTER XXVI.

The manufacture of hosiery is a trade almost exclusively confined to the three Midland counties of Nottingham, Leicester, and Derby. It extends over about 230 parishes—that being the number in each of which, as was ascertained by the industrial census set on foot in 1844 by Mr. Felkin, of Nottingham, not less than six framework-knitting machines were in that year actually at work. The articles of hosiery manufactured—that is to say, knitted upon the frames, and afterwards either seamed or stitched by women—are gloves, stockings, drawers, under-waistcoats, and a variety of small miscellaneous pieces of dress; amongst which may be reckoned the outside woollen jackets sometimes worn by women and children, and for which Leicester has of late acquired some celebrity. The materials used by the framework knitter are—cotton, silk, wool, and various combinations of them. The trade, which may be called a semi-domestic one, is marked by not a few peculiar characteristics. It has been for at least half a century an occupation in which a miserable degree of chronic distress has prevailed, and framework knitting has long been treated as one of the very lowest of textile manufactures. Before, however, proceeding to give a detailed account of the present condition of the hosiery knitters, it may be well that I should introduce it with a brief sketch of the rise and progress and a condensed view of the statistics of the trade. For the facts and figures to which, on this part of my subject, I shall refer, I am very greatly indebted to the extensive researches, already alluded to, of Mr. Felkin.

The knitting-frame, it is commonly known, originated in the county of Nottingham. The somewhat curious account of the invention ordinarily received, is that it was the contrivance of William Lee, a scholar, and the incumbent of Woodborough, early in the time of Elizabeth. The reverend gentleman, finding a lady to whom he was attached generally more intent upon her knitting-needles than interested in his protestations, vowed that he would construct a machine which should revenge him upon the fair one's primitive occupation. The result was the first stocking-frame. It was set up in London, in a house in Bunhill-fields. Queen Elizabeth in person visited the ingenious artist, and accepted a present of hose wrought by the new mechanism. At the outset, Lee met with fame and encouragement; but the tide soon turned. Elizabeth died, and James neglected the claims of the inventor, who, in consequence, accepted the invitation of Sully, and established his manufacture in Rouen. But Henry IV. was assassinated, his minister disgraced, and Lee, sickened with hope deferred, died poor and an alien. His brother returned to England and established the manufacture in London, where it long flourished, and where the Framework Knitters' Company, once a powerful and important guild, still maintains a shadowy existence. Its arms commemorate the inventor of its craft. They display a stocking-frame, supported on one hand by a clergyman, on the other by a woman displaying her useless knitting-needle.

Lee's engine, simplified and improved, spread over many countries of continental Europe, and still plays a conspicuous part in the industry of Saxony. In 1669, there were 660 frames in England—400 of them in London. At that time there were only two frames in the town of Nottingham, and not one hundred in the county. In 1714 there were 2,500 frames in London, 600 in Leicester, and 400 in Nottingham. After this era the trade began to flow steadily from the capital to the central counties, one of the alleged causes being the vexatious tyranny of the Company in London. In 1753 there were only 1,000 frames in London, while the number was as great in Leicester, and half as great again in Nottingham. Up to the end of the first quarter of the last century, silk was the principal material wrought upon the stocking frames. In 1730, cotton hose was first produced. A succession of mechanical improvements and adaptations of the knitting machine followed, rendering the mechanism capable of producing imitations of the pillow-lace then manufactured. Knitting machinery, in fact, was the parent of lace machinery, the one trade grew out of the other, and the elder and the younger branches of industry have long continued close neighbours. In 1782 the number of frames in England was about 20,000, and of these more than 17,000 worked in the

Midland counties. In 1812 the number in Notts, Leicester, and Derby was more than 29,000.

The hosiery trade has frequently been a suffering one. The wages long paid for lace working were amongst the highest—as those earned by hose-knitting were amongst the lowest—of all the branches of textile industry. The general causes of this last phenomenon were stated by Mr. Muggeridge, in his report upon the hosiery trade, to be—the frequent surplus of labour in the market, sometimes occasioned by the very irregular demand for the goods produced, but the perpetual and chronic source of which was the comparative facility with which the process of manufacture could be acquired, and which constantly tempted women and unemployed workpeople of other trades to engage in it—the long-continued custom of compelling the operatives to submit, on various pretexts, to heavy deductions from their ordinary wages—deductions which made it the interest of employers to spread their work over a larger amount of frames than was necessary to its performance; and finally, the exorbitant rents paid by the operatives for their frames—rents which led to the construction of a vast amount of these machines, not by manufacturers engaged in the trade, but as a profitable investment for the capital of private individuals. Mr. Muggeridge concluded his report by stating that the trade can only be maintained by a very marked improvement, not only in the mode of conducting the manufacture, but in the quality of the goods produced.

At the present time the wages of the framework-knitters—partly in consequence of the recent continental turmoil, which has disturbed the foreign-made supply, partly in consequence of an improved and improving demand in the home and the United States markets—are higher than the average amount throughout a long period of years. But the hours of toil are still excessively long, and the remuneration excessively scanty. In the industrial census taken in 1844, already referred to, there are very ample returns of the hosiery wages throughout all the districts in which the trade is carried on. A few of these interesting results I throw into a tabular form—and that the more readily, as I shall presently have to state the prices now paid for framework-knitting in the chief seats of the industry throughout the three counties.

## LEICESTERSHIRE, IN 1844.

ROTHLEY.—Ribbed hose, clear weekly earnings per
    frame ...................................... 4s. 6d.
BURBAGE.—Cotton hose, ditto ................ 5s. 6d.
KIBWORTH.—Wrought worsted hose, ditto ...... 5s. 6d.
HINKLEY.—Cotton and worsted, ditto .......... 5s. 3d.
LEICESTER.—Ditto ......................... 6s. 6d.

## DERBYSHIRE.

ILKESTONE.—Plain fashioned hose, clear weekly
    earnings per frame ........................ 5s. 0d.
ALFRETON.—Plain cotton and silk ............. 5s. 6d.
BELPER. { Hose, ditto ...................... 6s. 9d.
         { Gloves, ditto .................... 8s. 6d.
CHESTERFIELD.—Hose, ditto ................. 5s. 6d.
DERBY.—Silk hose, ditto ................... 6s. 6d.

## NOTTINGHAMSHIRE.

KIRKBY.—Socks and half hose, clear weekly earn-
    ings per frame .......................... 6s. 0d.
EASTWOOD.—Fashioned hose, ditto ............ 5s. 0d.
NEWARK.—Plain cotton hose, ditto ........... 5s. 6d.
BULWELL.—Gloves, ditto ................... 7s. 6d.
NOTTINGHAM.—Hose, ditto ................. 7s. 0d.

The general summing up of wages is given as follows:—"The average net earnings for 60 hours clear labour throughout the counties of Nottinghamshire and Derbyshire in the following subdivisions of employment, are—wrought cotton hose, 6s.; silk hose, 7s. 3d.; silk knitted hose, 8s.; plain silk gloves, 7s. 9d.; wrought cotton gloves, narrow frames, 6s. 6d.; cut-up cotton gloves, 7s. 6d.; cut-up cotton hose, 8s.; drawer and pantaloon branches, 7s. 6d." Appended to the statement, some results of which I have given, are annexed various cases, arranged in a tabular form, detailing the exact amount of wages earned by individuals and families, with the primary and necessary deductions, such as trade expenses and house rent—and showing the actual amount of money weekly available in each family, per head, for food and clothing. From these curious and valuable tables I select the following results:—

|  | s. | d. |
|---|---|---|
| In Belgrave 57 persons had weekly, out of which to feed and clothe themselves, per head ......... | 0 | 10 |
| In Barlestone 35 persons, ditto ................ | 1 | 3¼ |
| In Sheepshead from 2s. to 8¼d.—average ....... | 1 | 0 |
| In Loughborough, 21 persons ................. | 0 | 10 |

From the notes appended it would appear that in many instances the knitters had not had new coats for periods ranging from ten to twenty years—that the clothing purchased was very often obtained from second-hand stalls—and that the families were usually in a state of wretched raggedness.

The statistical work undertaken by Mr. Felkin ascertained with great particularity the number of frames existing and at work in the three counties during the year 1844. The district which is understood to be the area of the hosiery manufacture contains, as I have stated, 230 parishes—the boundary towns being, in a general way, Chesterfield on the north, Newark on the east, Ashby-de-la-Zouch on the west, and Market Harborough on the south. These topographical limits would indicate a space about 70 miles in length and 45 in breadth. Within this area the twist machine and the knitting frame reign preeminent. To proceed to a more detailed topographic allotment of the hosiery trade. There were, in 1844, in the county of Notts, 60 parishes, in each of which there were more than six frames at work. The number of separate shops or working places in the county was ascertained to be 4,621, and the total number of frames 16,382, of which 14,879 were, at the time of the inquiry, in operation. In the county of Leicester there were 100 parishes in each of which more than six frames were at work, and the total number of frames was 20,861, of which 18,558 were in operation. In the county of Derby there were 60 parishes in which more than six frames were at work, and the total number of frames was 6,797, of which 6,005 were in operation. The total number of frames, therefore, in the three counties, may be stated as about 44,000. This was the number in 1844; and as the number of new frames constructed in the three counties, between the years 1833 and 1844, was not above 1,000, it may be assumed that the estimate of 1844 is a tolerably close approximation to the statistics of the trade at the present day. In the last census, the number of individuals employed in framework knitting was reckoned as about 53,000. This estimate, however, gives a false idea. When we reckon not only the men and women—the number of the latter, I may state, is fast diminishing—who actually ply the machines, but the number of women and children directly connected with the trade, and who are occupied in winding the thread, and seaming and stitching the goods after they are removed from the frame, it may be fairly estimated that the number of people closely connected with and dependent upon the hosiery manufacture considerably exceeds 100,000. This mass of population is to a great extent scattered over the three counties, in great numbers of small villages and hamlets, the names of which are only locally known. In the three principal towns of Leicester, Nottingham, and Derby, there were in 1844 only 8,000 frames, forming less than one-fifth of the whole number.

The different branches of the hosiery trade are pretty equally divided throughout the several localities in which they abound. In the town of Nottingham, however, only a small quantity of silk hose is manufactured, the staple in that material being gloves. Cotton drawers and hose are produced to a very considerable extent. In Derby the main hosiery articles manufactured are silk. In Leicester a vast quantity of spun thread gloves, of the kind ordinarily called "Lisle," are knitted, and there is also an important production of woollen and fleecy hosiery. The minute subdivisions into which the manufacture of hosiery is split are almost endless—but one great distinction runs through the whole trade, separating the production of all articles of all materials into two general classes called "fashioned" and "cut-up" goods. Although the definition may not be in all cases technically correct, the phrases may be explained by saying that "fashioned" articles are those which receive their shape during the manufacture of their fabric—which are in fact knitted in the form which they are intended to assume. "Cut-up" pieces, on the contrary, are made in square breadths, often extending across the entire width of the knitting-frame, and afterwards cut into shape with the scissors. In "fashioned" pieces the operative forms a "selvage" along either edge, so as to permit the opposite sides or halves of a garment to be seamed together. In "cut-out," on the contrary, the sides are joined by the more clumsy, and to the wearer less comfortable, fashion of stitching. Of the two modes of manufacture, the "fashioned" is of course the best, requires the most skilful workmen, and commands the highest wages; but a spurious article is sometimes manufactured—a "cut-out" in reality, but a "fashioned" piece in appearance—and of course intended to command the price of the latter in the market, while the knitter only receives the earnings commonly given for the former. This is one of the grievances of the framework knitting trade, and for the removal of which the men contend that all goods prepared upon frames should be sent into market officially stamped with their real quality.

I have described the knitting-frame trade as a semi-domestic one. It is carried on in this way. A very great proportion—more than two-thirds—of the frames belong to the hosiers or manufacturers, who give them out to undertakers or middlemen, these last letting them in turn to the workmen. A middleman may have only two or three, or he may have as many as twenty or thirty frames. These he sets up in his own house—always, in Nottingham, in the highest story, so far as he has room for them. The others, if there be any, he sublets to knitters, who establish them in their own homes. The proportion of frames which do not belong to hosiers are often the property of frame-smiths, or of individuals unconnected with the trade. These machines are called "independent frames," although those who work them are generally the most thoroughly dependent class of individuals in the trade. Very few of the regular knitters possess frames of their own. The work comes so habitually through the channel of the undertakers, that property in machines would be of small use to operatives, who, of course, could never look for a supply of labour so long as one frame belonging to a hosier, or under the patronage of a middleman, was standing idle. Indeed I have heard of repeated instances in which a knitter, who was the proprietor of a frame, had to submit to the usual rent and charges payable by those who use the machinery of others, before he could secure a day's employment.

The middleman, then, receives the yarn to be wrought from the hosier, with the necessary instructions, undertakes the due performance of the labour, and then sets his subordinates to work. He is responsible for the material, and for the safety of the machines intrusted to his care. In respect to the hosier, he acts as a sort of foreman and manager; in respect to the men, he acts as a sort of agent and work collector. Rightly performed and upon a fair footing, there would be evident convenience in the ministration of such a functionary; and I do not find that the frame-work knitters object to the middleman so strongly as they do to certain of the exactions which, by the custom of the trade, he has a right to enforce. The hosiers or warehousemen, on the one hand, state that it would be impossible for them, and inconsistent with their other business, to control and manage the separate accounts of, perhaps, a hundred knitters, working in localities scattered throughout the town and district; while the operatives acknowledge that it is better that one agent should obtain and fetch work for, perhaps, a dozen men at a time, than that each individual should be obliged to repair to the warehouse on his own account as often as the yarn entrusted to him was worked up. The great grievance alleged by the workmen lies in the rent and frame charges. These charges are full of minute shades of difference; indeed, the great difficulty in dealing with this as well as the lace trade is the prevalence of the most puzzling diversities of detail—each slight variation frequently involving a totally different class of trade customs and usages. But, after paying some attention to the subject, I believe I may state that 3s. is a tolerably close approximation to the average sum weekly paid by each frame-work knitter under the name of frame-rent and charges. This amount is made up by the following items:—

| | | |
|---|---|---|
| Frame-rent ...................... | 1s. | 3d. |
| Taking-in ....................... | 0 | 9 |
| Standing room ................... | 0 | 3 |
| Winding ........................ | 0 | 9 |
| | 3 | 0 |

The frame-rent goes of course to the proprietor of the machine. The "taking-in" is the commission paid to the middleman for his trouble in receiving the yarns and orders, taking back the manufactured goods, and keeping the accounts. The "standing room" is the rent paid to the same person for the space taken up by the frame in his house. The winding—that is, of the thread from the hank to the bobbin—is likewise generally, but not always, paid to the middleman, who of course makes a profit upon that also. In the rarer case of a knitter having a frame at his own house, he may keep the charge for winding in his family; but it often happens that even in these instances the workman must pay the middleman for "standing room," quite irrespectively of where the frame may really be. This is especially the case when the middleman allows the knitter as a favour to have his frame in his own house. "If I let you have the frame at your home as a convenience to you, you must pay standing room all the same, as a convenience to me." This is the nature of the understanding usual in such instances. The rent of the frame varies, of course, with the breadth and capability of the instrument, but none that I heard of were let under 1s. weekly. Half a dozen frames are a common number for a middleman to set up in his house. Although virtually a factory in miniature, no sort of factory regulations are enforced in these establishments—the men come and go when they please, and labour as hard or as easily as they like. The middleman commonly, however, stipulates that the work shall be performed within certain reasonable hours—say from five or six in the morning until eleven or twelve at night. Towards the latter end of the week, however, I am informed that the knitters often labour all the night through, in order to get the work ready for the Saturday delivery to the warehouse; and as a general thing, their hours of labour are exceedingly long. In the first frame-shop which I entered, the people stated that they usually worked from six o'clock, a.m., until ten or eleven o'clock, p.m. These they described as very ordinary hours in the trade. The manufacture being carried on was that of drawers and under-waistcoats. In the second shop I visited, a silk glove factory, the hours were described as being from seven in the morning until ten o'clock at night, with an hour for dinner, and half-an-hour for tea. As is more or less the case, however, in all kinds of labour not brought under regular discipline, framework knitters are sometimes given to work by fits and starts. This is especially the case with the quickest hands in the trade; and I have been again and again informed, that in many instances they are among the most intemperate. They will work with unnatural perseverance for two and three days, and then go and drink for the other two and three days, and boast of the money they have earned. "When a master," said a very intelligent workman to me, "talks of our wages, and how much we could earn if we had a mind, it is very often to cases like those that he points."

The frame rent, the standing room, and the taking in, are none of them exacted if the machine has been idle throughout the week. This is the rule, whether the frame belong to a hosier who ordinarily supplies the work, or to a person not in the trade. But if more than one day's work has been performed, the full rent and charges are payable and exacted. This is one of the most palpable anomalies in the frame-rent system, and one naturally and directly leading to the construction of more frames than there is occasion for—not as implements of work, but as implements for bringing in rents. The system occasionally assumes this flagrant form: a middleman will obtain say six frames from a hosier, in addition to six others under the control of, or belonging to, himself. The work which he obtains from the hosier to keep the latter six frames going he will spread over the twelve, and thus pocket a double set of full perquisites, wrung from persons to whom he only gives half work. This, I am assured, is a case of no unfrequent occurrence; and, modified in different ways, it is undoubtedly the tendency of the whole frame-rent system to give rise to similar or analogous evils. Frames are thus often built by persons who never intend to be parties to the production of one inch of knitted stuff. The original cost of a machine of this kind is on the average from £16 to £20, and with ordinary care it will last, without being repaired, for at least a dozen years. One workman assured me that he had worked a frame for nearly twenty-five years ere any repairs became necessary. A very small amount of calculation is requisite to prove what a profitable investment was the capital sunk in such an apparatus, quite apart from the more legitimate profits which it must have realised in the way of fair production. This frame-rent system has, as may be easily understood, always had the effect of leaving a large margin of machinery, the owners of which, except during times of brisk demand, were seldom or never able to obtain regular work for the men whom they nominally employed. It is of course always the interest of a manufacturer owning machinery to keep that machinery as fully employed as possible; but the proprietor of an independent frame has his purpose served if the operative can earn only so much as suffices to pay his rent. Various efforts have been unsuccessfully made by the frame-work knitters to rid themselves of the rent and charges system. First, the point was raised whether the exaction of frame-rent was not illegal under the Truck Act, inasmuch as the workman was compelled to accept the machine, and to pay his employer for the use of it, out of his wages. Westminster Hall decided in favour of the frame rents. A bill was afterwards introduced by Sir Henry Halford to do away with the grievance, but it was thrown out. Measures are, however, at present, as I learn, being taken with a view to the re-opening of the question. A number of remedies have been proposed for the evil—many of them going upon the principle of fixing the minimum of wages. Another proposition is to gather the machines into factories, and to work them under ordinary factory regulations. The workman, so far as I am acquainted with their sentiments, are, however, averse to this plan. They admit that it would be advantageous in many respects, but they state their apprehensions that its tendency would be to prevent work from being obtained by the older and less keen-sighted men (clearness of vision is indispensable to the best paid sorts of frame-work knitting)—a result which, they contend, is at all events prevented by the present rent system. The method most in favour appears to be the payment by the workman, to the owner of the frame, of a per centage upon the work actually performed.

I have said that the principle on which the frame charges are calculated varies as respects different classes of goods. This is especially the case in certain branches of the silk-glove manufacture, in which the deductions are calculated by the dozen of gloves produced. A statement of the items in detail will give a fair notion of the drawbacks to which the wages of the men are subject, and of one of the modes of levying them. For the production of a dozen pair of a common class of gloves, of the cut-up species, 3s. 9d. is the regular price paid by the warehouseman to the undertaker. From the 3s. 9d. are deducted the following charges:—

| | | |
|---|---|---|
| Stitching | 0s. | 8d. |
| Winding | 0 | 1½ |
| Rent of frame | 0 | 2 |
| Standing room | 0 | 0¾ |
| Taking in | 0 | 2¾ |
| | 1 | 3 |

Leaving for the knitter, as his actual earnings, 2s. 6d. Take another class of gloves—one of which great quantities are made, and for the production of a dozen of which the warehouse pays the middleman 4s. 11d. In this department of the manufacture two men are employed with two frames upon each dozen of gloves; one making the hands, the other the fingers. The proportion paid to the latter will be the greatest, seeing that about eight dozen of hands can be made to six dozen of fingers. The knitter's share of the 4s. 11d. will be lessened by the following deductions:—

| | | |
|---|---|---|
| Seaming | 0s. | 10d. |
| Winding | 0 | 1½ |
| Rent of frame | 0 | 4 |
| Standing room | 0 | 2 |
| Taking in | 0 | 5½ |
| | 1 | 11 |

Leaving for the knitters, as their actual earnings, 3s., thus divided: 1s. 1½d. for the hand-maker, 1s. 10½d. for the finger-maker; total, 4s. 11d. It will be seen that in the first estimate the frame-owner's rent was 2d., and in the second 4d. in the respective dozens, while the net profit of the middleman—the taking in and the standing room—in the first transaction was 3½d., and in the second 7½d. I shall now, still keeping in the glove trade, lay before the reader some statements of figures, from which I believe that a fair average of the present rate of wages can be arrived at. That average, taking one season of the year with another, is under 10s. a week; the glove trade representing, so far, pretty accurately the general manufacture—some branches of the former being paid at a higher, and others at a lower rate, than the hose, drawers, and waistcoat departments.

I take again the common glove at 3s. 9d. Of this sum, as I have shown, 2s. 6d. actually goes to the workman. A fair week's work will, I am assured, produce from four to four-and-a-half dozen. The outside of the workman's earnings will therefore be 11s. 3d. per week. Of thread gloves there are seven or eight different qualities. I take the sort called "sixties," for which there is a great demand. The warehouse price for a dozen of these is 2s. 8d., and six dozen can be made in a week. In the manufacture of these gloves, frame rent and standing room are rated at a certain fixed weekly amount, generally 3s. 3d. The case then stands thus:—

```
Six dozen at 2s. 8d. ..................... 16s.  0d.
Deduct frame charges ......... 3s.  3d.
   „    stitching at 7d. per dozen  3s.  6d.
       Total deductions .........  ———  6    9
                                   ————
       Net earnings ...................  9    3
```

The warehouse price for "cotton slights," a species of hosiery made for exportation, is 1s. 11½d., and eight dozen can be made in a week. The following will be the actual remuneration:—

```
Eight dozen at 1s. 11½d. ................ 15s.  8d.
Deduct frame charges ......... 3s.  3d.
   „    stitching at 5½d.  ...... 3s.  8d.
       Total deductions .........  ———  6   11
                                   ————
       Net earnings ...................  8    9
```

The warehouse price of spun silk gloves—of the kind called "38 gauze slights"—is 2s. 4d. per dozen, and about seven dozen is allowed to constitute a fair week's work. The account for their manufacture will stand thus:—

```
Seven dozen at 2s. 4d. ................... 16s.  4d.
Deduct frame rent ............ 3s.  3d.
   „    stitching at 6½d.  ...... 3s.  9½d.
       Total deductions .........  ———  7    0½
                                   ————
       Net earnings ...................  9    3½
```

There are of course many kinds of gloves and other hosiery goods, by the manufacture of which considerably higher wages can be realised; but, taking one man with another, and one season with another, I am assured that the figures given above may be taken as fairly representing the wages of at least the glove-makers in the three counties. In the hosiery, and in the lace trade as well, a man soon becomes too old for the best-paying part of the business. The keen eyesight required often fails long before gray hairs come, and the best workman, so far as manipulation goes, must then sink back into a secondary position. Spectacles of a high magnifying power are often used; but some of the men, more careful than others, employ artificial aid only during the performance of the most delicate portion of the work. Here and there I have heard isolated complaints of a lingering truck system, carried on sometimes by the masters, but more often by the middlemen. The instances reported to me all existed in villages around Nottingham. In one of them the brother of the middleman kept a general shop, and the men were always paid there in a small inner office. After they had received their wages the middleman used to observe, in an off-hand way, "I suppose you'll be going to have some bacon"— or sugar, or coffee, as the case might be—"my brother has some very good; perhaps you observed it when you came into the shop—if not, just take a look at it as you're passing; perhaps you would find it suit you." Of course there was no resisting so considerate an intimation. In instances in which the truck system prevails, the workmen rate the price which the goods are charged as about 10 per cent. higher than the market rates. Two small habitual sources of expense to the framework-knitter, which I have not yet mentioned, are candles and needles. For the former the usual price, which the middleman charges during the winter months, is a penny a day. The "needles" in question are tiny steel hooks, a great number of which are used in a frame, and which are brittle and easily broken. A knitter will estimate his needle expenses at from 2d. to 3d. per week. The repairs requisite for the frame are performed at the expense of the proprietor.

The houses in which framework-knitting is carried on in Nottingham are—as I have already explained, in reference to the town generally—constructed on the principle of a ground-story living-room paved with red brick, a bedroom on the first floor, the workshop on the second, and sometimes a hole of a sleeping garret above it. The windows of the workshop are frequently long glazed strips, such as those used in weavers' houses, and the frames are ranged close to it. In the lower room it is usual to find the wives or children of the knitters engaged in winding. Sometimes old men, whose eyesight has failed them, are obliged to fall back upon this poor resource. With one of the broad knitting frames employed upon a stout fabric, the physical exertion requisite on the part of the workman is by no means inconsiderable. The machine, which, although simple compared with lace mechanism, is still too complicated to be easily explained, is moved by jerking iron levers, to which both hands are applied, and the production of every new row of loops is accompanied by a loud grating noise. There is no apprenticeship served to the knitting-frame. Lads of fourteen and fifteen are frequently found working it. At one time, women as well as men found employment in the trade; but of late years they have been confined almost exclusively to the needlework branch.

There are two classes of needlewomen employed upon goods wrought at the frames; the seamers, whose business is with the fashioned pieces—and the stitchers, who deal with the cuts-up. These women are very commonly the wives and daughters of the knitters; but among them are to be found young girls and widows, who struggle to obtain a livelihood at a toil which is certainly the most miserable that I have seen carried on in connexion with any manufacturing process whatever. The needlework, like the knitting, is chiefly managed through the intervention of a third party—very often the middleman's wife, who naturally undertakes this part of the business. The work is always performed at the residences of the needlewomen. In answer to the first inquiries I made upon the subject, an undertaker in the silk glove branch estimated the earnings of the seamers in that department as from 3s. 6d. to 4s. per week, and to realize this he admitted that they must work, at the very least, twelve hours per day. A "missus"—that is, a female undertaker or middlewoman—in the stocking line, reckoned that 3s. a week was as much as the seamers could well earn, one week with another. The prices which she paid were—

> Seaming fashioned goods according to size, 6d. and 7d. per dozen.
> Seaming half-fashioned goods, ditto, 4d., 4½d. and 5d.
> Stitching cuts-up, 3d., 3½d. and 4d.

The amount of work which a good hand could turn out, she reckoned, was, in seaming fashioned goods, about a dozen pair a day; in seaming half-fashioned goods, about a dozen or rather more; and in stitching, about two dozen; the three classes of earnings being thus—6d. a day for stitching; 5d., or perhaps a fraction more, for half-fashioned seaming; and 7d. per day for full-fashioned seaming. To earn these

amounts a day's unremitting labour of at least twelve hours was absolutely necessary. During our conversation a woman who stitched for
the "missus" entered the room. She stated that she counted herself
a fair hand, and that, labour as she might, she could not earn above
half-a-crown a week. She was receiving parish relief. She could not
live otherwise.

From the "missuses," I proceeded to see some of the seamers and
stitchers in their own homes. The first person of the kind upon whom
I lighted was a young married woman, occupying, with her husband,
a small choky room—paved with the sort of gritty plaster common
in Nottingham, and flanked by a miserable sleeping apartment, cut
in two, as it were, by the slope of the roof, and perfectly lightless and
airless. This species of bedroom, I may here observe, is unhappily too
common in the poorer parts of Nottingham, and so notorious are its
effects upon health, that the poor-law authorities, as a general rule,
refuse out-door relief to persons occupying such dwellings. In the
present case, the living room, though very small, was clean and tidy.
The occupant stated that her husband was a bill-sticker. She stitched
cuts-up. She was paid 3½d. per dozen, and her general earnings were
from 1s. 6d. to 1s. 9d. per week. She could finish a dozen a day if she
stuck to it; but then she had her household work to attend to. On
Monday she did her own and her husband's washing. The other days
she worked as long as she could, and on Friday nights she generally sat
up until midnight, and very often later. She thought that if she had
nothing at all to attend to, she might manage 1½ dozen, and she did
not count herself one of the quickest hands. The stitching was very
easy to do. She could manage it almost without looking at her work.
She had employment generally, but not quite regularly. The rent of
their rooms was 9d. per week.

The next woman I saw was an elderly person, living in a similar
abode to the last. The room was miserably blank—the bed stretched
upon the plaster floor. Two chairs and a tiny round table constituted
the furniture. This woman worked at seaming cotton socks. She was
paid 6d. per dozen. To complete a dozen took her fourteen or fifteen
hours of hard work. She was weak and not well, and she could not
manage above three dozen in a week. If she were strong, she thought
that she could do another dozen. As it was, 1s. 6d. was as much as she
could make per week. Her thread was found her. [The thread is always
found, both in stitching and seaming.] For the seaming of some sorts
of socks 6½d. was paid, and she did not think that they took more

time or trouble than the sixpenny ones. When she first came to Nottingham, in 1810, she used to be paid 1s. a dozen for seaming, and now the price was only 6d., and more work was required to be put into the articles. She had the goods direct from the warehouse—her son, who worked there, fetching them. This woman was receiving parish relief.

The next room into which I found my way was occupied by two elderly women. One was seaming, the other stitching. The seamer said that her eyesight was failing her, and that she could not get through near so much work as she used to do. The price paid her was 7d. per dozen. Half a dozen was as much as she could accomplish, but she knew many hands who could manage the dozen per day. She used to be able to seam nine pair, but not more. The stitcher stated that she was paid 3d. per dozen. Some hands would make two dozen a day, but "more would make less." She had seen a quicker stitcher than she was work very hard to make out her 1½ dozen. The seamer added that thirty years ago she had had 3d. per pair for seaming. She could do many sorts of needlework connected with the hosiery trade, and she had been offered a job at "chenening" gloves, very recently. There were three patterns to be "chenened" in each glove for 3d. a dozen, and she would have nothing to do with it, poor as she was.

"Chenening" is a species of embroidery, consisting in the production of the flower patterns common on the backs of spun silk gloves, and upon the ankles of superior kinds of stockings. A very considerable number of females make their living in Nottingham by chenening, and to a house where this sort of industry was going on I repaired. The cheneners I found to be two sisters. They were working at spun silk gloves. The labour requires considerable skill, and is severe for the eyes. One of the girls, although quite young, wore a pair of huge iron-mounted spectacles. They received 10d. a dozen for the gloves they were chenening, and they could do about a dozen pairs a day. The prices paid in the trade ranged from 2½d. per dozen to 3s. The latter sort, however, required so much work, that the rate of earnings realized by them was not more than could be got by the gloves at 10d. They generally worked ten hours a day, thus earning about 1d. per hour. The silk they used was found them. The best time for cheneners was the winter months. In summer, trade was generally slack, and work very short and uncertain. Chenening was an employment which a woman required great practice in before she could hope to maintain herself. The profit of chenening stockings came to about the same as chenening gloves. My informants had their work from a "missus."

They would be better paid if they had it direct from the warehouse, but that was impossible, because a single hand would give as much trouble and require as long an account as a middlewoman employing fifty workpeople.

The next person I visited was also in the silk spun glove trade. She was both a seamer and stitcher, seaming hands and stitching fingers. The gloves she worked at were "full women's size," and the warehouse for which she laboured paid less for them than any other in Nottingham. The general price was 1s. per dozen, but she only received 9½d. After she had finished the batch in hand she intended to look out for some other work. She had two children, and their father had deserted her. She was sure that these children had not a sufficiency of food. She could not procure it for them. The eldest (a pale little girl of seven years old) helped her with the stitching. Last week, the poor little creature had earned 1s. 6d. This child had been stitching since she was four years of age. She had never been to school. The mother said that she was too poor to send her. If the child went to school she must go without food. Were she an unencumbered woman, she, the mother, could earn about 8s. a week. As it was she generally made from 4s. to 5s. a week. She paid 1s. for rent and 9d. weekly for coals. This left them only 2s. 6d. to live on—2s. 6d. among three. Their food was generally bread and coffee, and sometimes bread without the coffee, and occasionally they had a herring for a treat. The room was miserably poor; the bed clothes of that rug-like texture and that dingy brownish hue which always make their material a matter of some doubt, and which I have been taught by experience invariably to associate with grinding poverty—but things looked, in other respects, tidy and clean, and some humble plants were arranged in pots upon the window-sill.

I may add to this communication—the last which will be dated from Nottingham—that gardening is a favourite amusement with the workpeople, both in the lace and hosiery trades. On the northern outskirts of the town, at a place called the "Stone Waterings," there are many small allotments of garden ground, let to the labouring classes at 1d. or 1¼d. per square yard. It is hoped that one of the consequences of enclosing the land, so long kept common on the outskirts of the town, will be to give facilities for the extension of a taste so rational, and often fraught with so many excellent social results.

*The Morning Chronicle, Wednesday, January 16, 1850.*

To the EDITOR of the MORNING CHRONICLE.

Sir—Seeing in your paper of January 3, a report from your Special Correspondent respecting the Staffordshire Collieries, with your permission I beg to correct a few errors contained therein. Your Correspondent gives a statement from Mr. Barker, of the Chillington iron-works, in 1847, stating that the men were restricting themselves to eight and seven hours' work per day, for five days in the week. It is quite true that the men restricted themselves to five days in the week, but those five days consisted of twelve hours, deducting one hour for dinner. Your Correspondent states that wages averaged 4s. 4½d. per day. But since that time they have fallen more than 40 per cent. in every branch of business connected with the manufacture of iron. Your Correspondent further states that the bandsmen's wages vary in different pits from 4s. to 4s. 3d. per day, whereas upon closer examination he would have found they did not average more than from 2s. 6d. to 3s. 3d. per day. Pikemen, being proficient, get 2s. 10d. per day, when required to work in the band.

Your Correspondent states that, in conversation with a gentleman intimately acquainted with the population, he was told that if every man had 5*l.* per week he would spend it all in eating and drinking. His informant should have stated that such conduct was the exception and not the rule, for there is to be found a large number of as moral men amongst both miners and iron workers as your Correspondent's informant, whoever he might be. That there comes plenty of good poultry to market is quite true, but any reasonable man may judge what portion of it can fall to the working classes, when a man with a family cannot average more than 12s. per week; and the bottled porter and wine alluded to, if drank at all, is by the proprietors and butties, and not by workmen. Some masters even will not allow a workman to smoke a pipe of tobacco while at labour without inflicting a fine upon him. In respect to builtass, it is certainly a grievance any time, when men are called on to perform labour and not partake of the fruits. But there are grievances not mentioned in that letter, such as having to work from six in the morning till one o'clock, or half past, for a-half-day's wage; and the long time from one reckoning to another adopted by many of the employers, in order to compel the men to resort to their truck shop, where they exact a profit of from 20 to 30 per cent. There is, also, another cause that contributes greatly to the immorality of the miners—the butty almost invariably keeps a public-house, and the men who will not drink stand but small chance of much work.

As regards the bankswomen, there are large numbers of them who, after their work is done, would bear comparison, for cleanliness, with any lady in the land.

In justice to working men in general, I hope you will insert these few remarks in your paper, and you will much oblige one of your Correspondent's rude and unintelligent miners.

Yours respectfully,

Bilston, Jan. 14.                                                    * * * *.

# LABOUR AND THE POOR.

—◆—

## THE MANUFACTURING DISTRICTS.

[FROM OUR SPECIAL CORRESPONDENT.]

### DERBY.

### LETTER XXVII.

The pleasant and prosperous town of Derby affords no bad specimen of those third-rate English cities which are at once the seats of an anciently established population, and of a more recently founded industrial importance. It is pleasant to see a town manifestly old and manifestly thriving—a town at once of the present and the past, pervaded by the quaint air of antiquity, and yet instinct with the living energy of an actual and a bustling prosperity. Derby neither looks as if its existence dated from the birth of the steam-engine, nor as if it had lived out its real life in by-gone days, and now lay upon the land little better than a brick-and-mortar skeleton. On the contrary, the fair old Midland town has kept bravely up with the industrial march of the times. As it was the first nursery of the silk manufacture in its infancy, so it has remained one of the principal seats of this branch of industry in its prime. At the same time the industrial resources of the place are fortunately so varied, that although one branch of its trade may occasionally be in a languishing condition, the town, as a whole, enjoys to a high degree a general and continuous degree of prosperity.

Derby lies upon the river Derwent, a stream rising amidst the rocks of the Peak. It was a wool-stapling place in the times of the Plantagenets, the burgesses possessing repeated charters conferring upon them exclusive privileges in the matters of weaving and dyeing woollen cloth. In the sixteenth century numerous fulling-mills stood by the waters of the Derwent, and a thriving trade was for ages carried on in malting and the brewing of humming ale, great quantities of which were drunk in London. It was almost a century and a half ago that Derby suddenly began to rise into importance as a seat of textile industry. The knitting-frame trade, ebbing from London, took up its head-quarters in the three Midland counties, and in the year 1717,

John Lombe, an ingenious and adventurous artisan, returned to his native country from Italy. Carrying with him the secret of the silk-throwing trade, as it was then practised in Piedmont, Lombe settled in Derby. The corporation leased to him, at a low rate, a swampy island in the Derwent. Then he established in the Town-hall certain provisional machinery, and with the profits accruing from its working he erected upon his swampy island a building which still stands there, and which is now, as it was then, designated *par excellence* "The Silk Mill." Within its walls was produced the first silk thread spun by other than hand-labour in England. Lombe, the daring and skilful adventurer, died by poison, but he left the germ of a great trade behind him. The products of the silk spinning machines soon began to be made largely available for the knitting-frames; and improvement after improvement was effected in the latter, each successive step enabling the workmen to grapple with the difficulties of producing new and more elaborate fabrics. Aided by these useful and profitable means of employment, Derby throve apace. Before "the Silk Mill" was erected the town boasted of 700 free burgesses and 4,000 inhabitants. It had fair public walks planted with goodly trees, a well-supplied market-place, many churches, almshouses, fulling-mills, and bleaching grounds. With the growth of improvement in silk-throwing and hosiery-knitting, Derby rose steadily into something like its present importance, trebling its population within thirty-five years. In 1801 the town numbered only about 10,000 inhabitants, in 1811, they had increased to 13,000; in 1821, to 17,500; in 1831, to 23,000; and in 1841, to 35,019. About twenty years ago mechanism for the weaving of piece or broad silk was introduced into Derby, and about the same time the bobbin-net trade was established. At present, then, the principal branches of textile industry pursued are—the throwing of silk, the weaving of it into ribbons and trimmings by steam-power, and into dress pieces by hand, the twisting of boot-laces and sewing silk, and the knitting upon frames of all manner of silk hosiery. The lace trade of the town is not extensive. It is confined to a single factory, producing for the greatest part plain lace. There are about 35 silk manufactories engaged in the various branches of the trade in Derby, and in the different factories it is estimated that about 5,000 people find employment. The town possesses minor resources in its iron-founding establishments. This branch of industry has subsisted for half a century, and there exist at present nine foundries, several of them of great extent. I have stated that the population of the town in 1841 was 35,019. The number of living persons to one annual death appears by the last returns to be—males, 38.4; females, 41.6— giving a mean of somewhat under 40. The total number of marriages in 1840 was 456. Of these, 382 were celebrated according to the rites of the Church, and 74 in other modes. Of the 456 couples married, 105 men and 189 women signed with their marks. The number of illegitimate births during 1846 was 111. The replies returned by Derby to the questions put by the Sanitary Commission are abstracted in one of the reports of that body, much to the following effect:—The local act regulating the construction of new buildings and streets is not attended to; the courts and yards are neglected; the sewers and drains are very defective; refuse accumulates in house drains to a great extent; there are no local regulations for systematic drainage, nor for the amendment and cleansing of drains actually in a foul and offensive condition; there is a regular service of scavengers. The town is supplied with water principally from pumps and wells.

The sanitary and structural state of matters hinted at in the above replies does not seem particularly favourable. Nevertheless, in point of building arrangements, the working population of Derby are very decidedly better off than their neighbours at Nottingham. Derby, in fact, has always had more elbow-room. Its suburbs spread freely forth, and the town exhibits none of that structural piling and huddling, characteristic of the capital of the lace trade. Back-to-back dwellings exist, but they by no means constitute the rule; and towards the suburbs, and in most of the more recently constructed blocks of buildings, the presence of back doors gives facilities for full and free house ventilation. The smallest class of houses contains two apartments, one above another, and the average rent is 2s., although they sometimes fetch 2s. 3d., or, according to situation, 2s. 6d. Tenements of a better order, with two rooms on each floor, are let at rents ranging from 3s. to 3s. 6d. In numerous instances these last houses are occupied by the power-loom ribbon weavers and the hands employed in the foundries. The ground floors are almost invariably paved with brick. As to the generally filthy state of the back yards, I can corroborate the replies returned to the Sanitary Commissioners. It is very common for the workshops of the frame-work knitters to be established in little detached buildings, erected over privies and ash-pits. Courts are very common in the crowded parts of the town. The labouring classes draw their chief supply of water from wells and pumps. The fluid so obtained is clear and tasteless. The present existing waterworks company is indebted to the river Derwent, water from which is forced up into a great tank, situated in a curious locality—namely, at the summit of St. Michael's church—whence the fluid is conveyed by mains and service pipes throughout the town. A sketch of Derby would be incomplete were all mention omitted of the well laid-out public garden or park called the Arboretum, the free gift to the town of Mr. Joseph Strutt, its first mayor after the Reform Bill. As a pleasant place of public summer resort—half a garden, half a park—so planted and arranged as to possess a botanical interest and value, while it furnishes pleasant glimpses of parterre, shrubbery, and woodland—the Arboretum is, probably, unmatched in its way by the pleasure grounds of any other provincial town in England. It is freely open on Wednesdays and Sundays, and considerate arrangements have been made in ornamental lodges for the accommodation of those townsfolk who may propose to pass a day upon the green-sward and bring their own provisions with them. Since its original opening, the Arboretum has been considerably enlarged by the purchase of an adjoining field. There is, I may add, a strong and, I think, reasonable desire in the public mind of Derby, that these pleasure-grounds should be always, instead of periodically, accessible. Derby possesses one extensive cemetery beyond the walls, and arrangements are on foot for the establishment of another. A new water-works company have nearly completed their arrangements, and will commence operations some time this summer. They propose to deliver water in a filtered and perfectly pure state at the top of the highest houses—to establish four reservoirs—to guarantee a supply of 20 gallons per head per day—to keep the pressure continuously on, and to open at least 300 fire-plugs in the streets. Between 1842 and 1848 about 6,600 yards of sewerage have been constructed in Derby by private individuals, and about as many yards more were formed under a local act. Since the latter period, several additional drains have also been constructed, but the majority of those already formed have, says Mr. Cresy, the Superintendent Inspector, been laid down "more with reference to carrying off the street waters than draining the numerous alleys and courts, and freeing them from their pollutions." Adequately to purify the 352 courts and alleys and small streets within the borough, Mr. Cresy calculates that 40,000 yards of tubular drainage, at a cost of about £20,000 will be requisite.

There are in Derby eight Churches of the Establishment, one Unitarian chapel, one Friends' Meeting-house, one Roman Catholic chapel, one Independent chapel, one Congregational, four Baptist, three Wesleyan, one Methodist New Connection, two Primitive Methodist, and one Swedenborgian. With the single exception of the Friends' Meeting-house, Sunday schools are attached to all the above places of worship. The Church schools are attended by about 1,160 boys and 1,430 girls; the Catholic Sunday school by 150 boys and 150 girls; and about 2,845 children attend the different dissenting Sunday schools, making altogether a total of 5,735. The National and Infant schools in the borough are attended by about 1,600 children.

I now proceed to give some account of the several textile branches of manufacture carried on in Derby. I have already, in my letter from Macclesfield, described a silk mill, and detailed the principal processes in the manufacture. The machinery generally in use in Derby, however, is of improved and far more modern construction, as compared with the mechanism employed in the Cheshire town; and the mills in the former place are the largest, and are accounted the most perfectly organized and disciplined of any in the manufacture. Amid the Derby silk-throwing and weaving factories, the principal is the splendid establishment of Messrs. Thomas Bridgett and Co., a mill employing upwards of 1,100 hands. Without professing to give a regularly detailed account of the various departments of the manufacture of silk, as carried on in this great factory, I may advantageously introduce some notices of the process, illustrative of the earnings and the social and industrial position of the workpeople. Mr. Lewis, the managing partner of the firm, introduced the ten-hours system into Nottingham several years before the passing of Lord Ashley's factory bill; and he informed me that the consequence was, that he had, for a considerable period, on that account alone, the pick and choice of the best hands in Derby. Your readers are already aware that in the multitudinous operations of a throwing—that is, a silk-spinning—mill, young women and boys do the work almost exclusively, under the superintendence of male and female adults. In Messrs. Bridgett's establishment the boys and girls are, as far as possible, kept apart. The several winding processes are principally performed by healthy and happy-looking little girls, earning, according to their age and capacity, from 1s. 6d. to 3s. The number working at the former trifling wage is, however, very small—merely a few of the beginners. In the cleaning-rooms elder girls and young women are employed at wages averaging 7s. The spinning-frames are managed entirely by boys, under the superintendence of an overlooker. The spindles in these superb machines make upwards of 4,000 revolutions per minute, and each frame contains 306 spindles. The biggest boys are competent to manage a frame a-piece. The wages in the spinning rooms range from 4s., the lowest point, to 5s. 6d., the highest. In the "staff-room," in which girls of various ages perform a variety of finishing operations on the silk thread, the wages run from 5s. to 6s. In the department in which the sewing-silk is divided into skeins, the wages may average about 7s. 6d. The soft silk winders, *i.e.* the young women who wind the silk after it has been dyed, so as to prepare it for the weavers, make, according to age and capability, from 2s. 8d. up to 9s. 3d. In the dye-works, to which the silk is consigned after leaving the spinning-frame, and before being placed upon the loom, men are of course the operators. The dyers who mix and prepare the colouring compositions receive from 28s. to 30s. per week. The labourers who help them, and whose work is little if at all skilled, are paid 15s., 16s., and 18s.

A peculiar department in most of the silk factories in Derby, and one which exists also to a great extent at Leeds, is the manufacture of sewing silk. I was about to say that the operation is entirely carried on by hand, but I ought rather to describe it as being conducted by foot. The sewing silk-rooms are long sheds or corridors, each 24 yards from end to end. At either extremity—their number depending upon the breadth of the room—are placed wheel machines with hooks, exactly on the same principle as those used in a rope-walk. Opposite these wheels stand frameworks, containing large bobbins, upon which the silk thread has been wound, so as to be easily disengaged by clusters of two, three, or four filaments, as the stoutness of the sewing-silk to be spun may require. The operators consist of a man stationed at each wheel, and two or more boys, his coadjutors. It is the business of these little fellows first to seize the ends of each group of threads upon the bobbins, and run with them to the wheel at the other end of the room. The man then fastens the groups of thread, each of which form the strands to be twisted together, to the hooks on the circumference of the wheel, the boys making successive journeys with the thread until every hook around the wheel is supplied. The man then sets the machine in rapid motion—each hook, of course, firmly twisting together its own contingent of threads. When the process is complete, he breaks the latter off close by the hooks, and attaches the newly-twisted threads to a winding machine, also moved by hand, and upon which the finished silk is rapidly wound— the boy holding in his hands the opposite extremities of the thread, and coming gradually up with them to the winding machine, so as to ensure their being tightly and equably rolled up. I have described in detail a sufficiently commonplace process, because it is one in which there is more muscular motion requisite than in almost any other in the range of textile operations. The actual amount of ground covered at a sharp trot by the boys engaged is calculated at an average of from 20 to 21 miles per day. Mr. Lewis has devoted some attention to the subject, and this is his estimate. The length of the thread twisted is 24 yards, giving the length of every run. There are two or three boys employed at each wheel, and each one has several runs in succession when the threads are being attached to the hooks, and a breathing time when the hoops are being whirled round. The speed at which the little fellows proceeded appeared to me to be nearer six than five miles an hour. The duration of their toil is ten hours per day. Admitting, then, Mr. Lewis's estimate of the extent of ground daily gone over, it would follow that about one-third of the entire time is passed running, and two-thirds resting. The boys, however, running or not, always keep on foot. I watched this novel species of industry for some time, and with some interest; and I am bound to say that the boys appeared to go through it with perfect ease. They were evidently, and no wonder, in fine running order. There was not the slightest perspiration on their faces, nor did there appear anything like a difficulty in breathing. I should add that the day was intensely cold. In warm weather the case is probably different. I tried in vain to distinguish any characteristic peculiarity in the appearance of the boys. Two or three of them certainly had no superfluous flesh on their bones; others, on the contrary, were decidedly stout. A few performed their work barefooted, with handkerchiefs lightly tied round their heads, and in their shirt sleeves. The others wore shoes, caps, and jackets. The floor, I ought to mention, was composed of bricks. None of the boys whom I questioned would admit that the work tired them. They did not go home and go to bed as soon as it was over—they went to play with other lads in the street. Mr. Lewis informed me that the silk-twisting boys had the reputation of being about the most troublesome set of urchins in all Derby. In point of activity and agility, they beat all the other boys hollow. This was a point on which similar testimony was given before Lord Ashley's committee by Mr. Douglas Fox, a medical gentleman of the town. Mr. Fox was asked how he accounted for the phenomenon. The reply was that he only professed to speak to the fact. These lads are gradually broken in to their running duties, beginners being only set to do about half the work of the regular hands, or rather—feet. Curiously enough, they are not necessarily included in the Factory Act, the provisions of which only apply to buildings in which the labour is regulated by a steam-engine. In Leeds there are a great many silk-twisting establishments into which steam-power is not introduced at all, and in which the boys are, therefore, liable to be worked any number of hours that may be thought expedient by their employers. These last are always the men who turn the wheels, each of whom engages and pays as many boys as he thinks proper. Their wages—generally about 3s. 6d. or 4s. a week—the wheel-man pays over to their parents. The actual amount is estimated by the quantity of work done; but it is the custom to give the boys, as pocket-money for themselves, the produce of any labour above a usual fixed amount. The boys thus make from 3d. to 6d. a week on their own account. The wheelman, if he has a family, generally employs his own children. One of the overlookers in Messrs. Bridgett's establishment told me that he had begun by being a running boy. He was then only eight years of age. Boys do not now begin until they are eleven. He did not remember to have ever found the work fatiguing. He was soon too hardened and inured to it for that. In an experience of 33 years, he had never known an instance of a boy breaking down under the fatigue, and giving up the business. In the summer evenings, after work hours, he sometimes walks through the fields as far as Quarner (three or four miles from Derby), and there he often recognizes some of his own "flock," running and jumping, and beating all the other boys at both exercises.

The ribbon-weaving department is the only branch of the silk trade in which the mass of the operatives employed are men. Their earnings are considerable, but often irregular—an irregularity in great part the fault of the men themselves, who are some of them apt to keep their frames longer flung out of gear than is necessary. Mr. Lewis kindly laid before me the wage-book of the firm for this department. I selected the week previous to my visit. It was that before Christmas, and one in which the men commonly exert themselves to get through a good amount of work. On examination I found that 131 power-loom weavers had been paid £144 6s. 9d., or on an average about £1 1s. 11½d. each. The highest amount earned was £2 1s. 10½d., and I was informed that this individual weaver sometimes earned £2 7s. 6d. for weeks together. He was, of course, a skilful and exceedingly careful and industrious workman. I was requested to observe—the steam engine being the real motive labourer—that the earning of the higher amounts of wages depended not upon any increased manual exertion on the part of the workman, but on unremitting attention in keeping his loom as much as possible in gear. In weaving narrow ribbons, the operatives are paid so much per cut. Every man is bound to produce a cut weekly, or he will get nothing at all. A great number of the hands work out just the minimum and no more. Others produce a cut and a half, and a few weave nearly two cuts per week. Broad ribbons are paid for by the half cut. The prices of the cuts and half cuts vary with the breadths of the goods manufactured. I inquired what would be the amount of wages earned if it were possible to keep the engine applied to the loom throughout the whole of the daily ten hours of toil. From the calculations made, at my instance, it appeared that, were the loom kept in gear during the whole of the time the engine is at work, the average produce of the factory would be about doubled. A great many stoppages are, however, requisite for many purposes. In the power ribbon-weaving looms the warp is stitched perpendicularly, in many strips—each of them of course the breadth of the ribbon to be woven, and each of them traversed backwards and forwards by a tiny shuttle. After being taken from the loom the ribbons require to be picked, in order to free them from any little inequalities and thickenings previously existing in the thread. This operation is performed by girls, one of whom picks for about ten weavers—the latter uniting to pay her wages, which are about 8s. per week. The quill-winders, who prepare the shuttles, receive about an equal amount of earnings.

There is a feature in Messrs. Bridgett and Co.'s silk-mills too interesting to pass over unnoticed. It is a most useful and kindly-meant experiment, which Mr. Lewis is engaged in conducting. Fully recognizing the truth that one of the great drawbacks of the factory system is the ignorance in which girls employed in mills almost invariably grow up, in reference to anything like domestic duties—and knowing by long experience that nothing is more common than for a factory girl to marry, without being able even to darn a stocking, make a pudding, or boil a potato—Mr. Lewis is engaged in trying whether he cannot give some of the female children in the mill a domestic as well as a factory education. For this purpose he has selected a number of girls, either orphans or deserted by their parents, from various unions in the neighbourhood of Derby. These girls he boards, clothes, and lodges. They live in a large house suitably fitted up, and under the charge of a schoolmaster, a schoolmistress, and a matron. In the mill they are upon precisely the same footing as the other children, working the same hours, and nominally earning the same wages; and in their leisure hours at home they are taught the elements of a sound education, and instructed in the domestic duties which they will afterwards have to perform. The characteristic peculiarity of this domestic school is, that the girls are instructed naturally, and in the regular course of things, in the work at which they will gain their livelihood, and trained to the habits which will make their future homes comfortable and happy. At the mill they are kept as much as possible together. Mr. Lewis, with a very wise consideration, is careful that the colour and fashion of their dresses may differ, so as to prevent their being marked out and known by anything approaching to a badge of charity. As yet the experiment is too recent to admit of any practical results showing themselves, the institution not having been established more than three years. So far as regards the pecuniary aspect of the affair, I am informed that the children eat more than they work for—and certainly a plumper, chubbier, more perfectly healthy-looking group of girls I never saw. The guardians from the parishes whence they were taken often come to see how they are getting on. I may add that Mr. Lewis's *protegées* go to school one hour and a half in the evening, that they wash and mend their own clothes, and perform part of the culinary duties of the establishment.

A very carefully estimated average of the wages paid in a Derby silk mill, has been handed to me by Mr. Lewis. It is as follows:—

WINDING, CLEANING, REELING, DOUBLING, AND SPINNING.

| | |
|---|---|
| Women employed in winding | 6s. 6d. to 7s. 6d. per week. |
| ditto, in doubling ........ | 6s. 6d. to 7s. 6d. |
| Girls, in doubling ......... | 5s. |
| ditto, in winding —the youngest beginning as learners at 11 years of age .......... | 1s. |
| Then, advancing every three months, until they earn, between 13 and 16 years of age | 3s. 6d. to 5s. |
| Boys—employed in cleaning —the youngest beginning as learners at 11 years of age | 1s. |
| Advancing every three months, until they earn, between 12 and 15 years of age ................... | 3s. to 4s. |
| ditto, in spinning-room .... | 3s. to 5s. |
| Reelers—girls ............ | 5s. |
| ditto, young women ...... | 6s. 6d. to 7s. |

### RIBBON WEAVERS.

| | |
|---|---|
| Men | 20s. 0d. to 21s. 0d. per week. |
| Average of a summer month, with no gas to pay for and good light | 23s. 9d. |
| Average of a winter month, clear earnings | 19s. 0d. |
| Young women—soft silk winders for weavers | 7s. 6d. to 9s. 3d. |
| Girls—ditto, about 13 years of age | 3s. 6d. |
| Warpers—young women | 7s. 6d. to 8s. 6d. |
| Fillers—ditto, of quills for the shuttles | 7s. 6d. to 9s. 0d. |
| Pickers and trimmers | 6s. 6d. to 8s. 0d. |

### DYE-HOUSE.

| | |
|---|---|
| Labourers | 16s. 0d. to 18s. 0d. |
| Dyers | 25s. 0d. to 30s. 0d. |

Over-time paid in proportion. Hours of work, ten.

I have stated that there is in Derby but one lace factory—that of Messrs. Morley and Bouden. As the style of work and the fabric produced differ considerably from those which I have principally had opportunities of seeing in Nottingham, I may advantageously give some account of the establishment in question. It is a power factory, weaving, by means of bobbins and carriages, plain net. There being no patterns or difficult complications of threads primarily to arrange, the machines go on almost continuously. The number of hours wrought per day is eighteen, and to each machine there is a man and a boy. The relay system, in the strict meaning of the phrase, is not practised; the work being so arranged that while one hand alone is engaged at the machine during the first hours in the morning, both are employed together for the bulk of the day, and the second hand is left to work out the last two hours at night. Thus A commences work at four a.m., and tends the machine until eight a.m. At that hour B relieves him, while A has an hour for breakfast. After nine a.m. both are employed together—with the exception, of course, of the dinner hour—until five p.m., when A leaves off for the night, and B, who has also in the meantime had an hour for tea, continues operations until ten p.m. The two colleagues were, as I have said, a man and a boy. During the time that only one is at the frame, he has of course to tent the mechanism; when both are together, the boy always tents, and the man prepares his carriages and bobbins, so as to have them ready for the frame when the supply of shute actually in use is exhausted. In the factory in question, there is a double set of carriages and brass bobbins, so that the threaders and winders are not required to work those irregular and often distressingly long hours which I have alluded to in my communications from Nottingham. It was, indeed, the strong representations made as to the possibility of dispensing with over-long hours of infant labour, by means of using double sets of bobbins and carriages, that prevented the provisions of the Ten-hours Bill being applied to lace factories. As I have said, however, the double mechanism is rather the exception than the rule. The women who fill the brass bobbins perform their work in this factory by a very simple but very neat apparatus, something like a comb, set with teeth exactly corresponding to the clefts in the bobbins. By this means the threads are combed into their respective grooves with the greatest exactness. The women in question work twelve hours a day, and can earn from 9s. to 13s. The wooden bobbin winders make from 5s. 6d. to 9s. The threaders, boys generally, from 12 to 14 years of age, make from 3s. 6d. to 6s. As regards the pay of the higher classes of workmen who tent the machines, the wages-book was submitted to my inspection. I found that the last class of workmen received, upon an average, about 30s. per week; the inferior class of hands from 21s. to 25s. The boys, whose ages vary from 15 upwards, earn from 10s. to 14s. per week. These gradations are the result of different degrees of care and skill bestowed upon different qualities of work. Mr. Bouden informed me that a graduated scale of wages was found of great practical importance, as an inducement to the men to exert themselves, so as to be deemed fit for the best quality of work. The net-weaving rooms I found rather hot—the effect of the working people having a greater aversion to draught than relish for air. I was informed that it was difficult to induce them to allow any of the windows to remain open. In this species of plain lace weaving the task of the workman is easy, the thread being of so strong a texture as seldom to break with the action of the machine. The man and boy, I ought to have mentioned, change hours every week. The trifling amount of embroidered goods wrought in the Messrs. Morley's factory is of an inferior quality, technically known as "rubbishing" fancy lace. It consists of very cheap stripes, used for borders. The wages in this department are the same as in that of the perfectly plain net.

The "mending" is never performed upon the premises. The firm do not encourage the middlewoman system. They prefer to give out work to individual menders. At the same time they are aware that, to a greater or less extent, a mender will frequently get a number of little girls around her, at her own house, and employ them upon the more slightly damaged pieces—work which children are quite capable of performing—and which it would not, in all cases, pay an expert needlewoman to undertake. To this extent it is thought that the middlewoman system is almost inseparable from the lace manufacture. Any running or tambouring practised in Derby is in connection with Nottingham houses. The number of male hands employed in Messrs. Morley and Bouden's factory is about 240.

The broad or piece silk weaving trade is of comparatively recent introduction. The goods woven are of a similar class to those produced at Macclesfield, Middleton, and Spitalfields. Indeed, many of the Middleton weavers, including more than one whose residence I have in a former communication described, work, I find, for Derby houses. The partners of one of the establishments informed me, that their best weavers in Derby were Lancashire men, and that the Middleton people were on the whole better and more industrious workmen than the native midland county weavers. There are a few Irishmen weaving silk in Derby. They have, however, in the majority of cases, been previously employed, either in Macclesfield or London. The broad silk weaving firms in Derby employ their hands either in regularly fitted shops or at their own houses. In the majority of the latter cases, the workmen are scattered through the country in the numerous hamlets within a dozen miles of Derby. The number of looms in shops is about equal to those in the weavers' houses, and the number of jacquards is about equal to that of the plain looms. A few women work in the shops, but the number is decreasing. These shops may each contain a dozen or so of figured and plain looms upon each floor. The looms belong almost invariably to the manufacturers. The ordinary charges paid by the weaver for their use are—6d. weekly for loom rent, 6d. for shop rent, and, in the winter time, 6d. for gas. If a man has a loom at his own house, he, of course, pays merely the rent of the mechanism. The hours commonly worked in the shops are, in summer from six o'clock until dusk, in the winter from seven o'clock until eight o'clock in the evening. The men are not compelled rigidly to attend these hours, but within these limits the shops remain open, and practically they are tolerably closely observed. The domestic weavers work more irregularly, but in the summer they have frequently very long hours, sometimes from three o'clock and four o'clock in the morning until dusk. Contrary to the practice in Middleton, manufacturers here are in the habit of advancing money to their hands before the completion of the pieces on which they are working. And I am informed that it is often difficult to persuade the men not to anticipate almost the whole of their earnings. The weavers who ply the shuttle at their own houses in Derby suffer great inconvenience from the structure of the dwellings, these last being totally unsuitable to the trade. The men are thus obliged to erect the looms either in the principal room or in a bed-chamber. I have repeatedly found the best portion of a house thus occupied. Very often, too, the weavers find it difficult to induce the landlord to allow of the erection of a loom at all, and in some cases the ceiling is too low to admit of the lofty structure of the jacquard. These causes tend to the concentration of the trade in shops, where it can be carried on with greater convenience to all parties. The rural weavers bring in their own work when it is completed, and are frequently visited by the manufacturers or their agents. The following statement of wages paid to handloom-weavers has been handed to me from the firm of Messrs. Stone and Kemp. It is intended to give an idea of the maximum, medium, and minimum wages earned by weavers in their employment during the last six or eight months:—

WAGES OF SILK-WEAVERS IN AND AROUND DERBY.

|  | | | Weekly Earnings. | |
|---|---|---|---|---|
|  | | | s. | d. |
| Man on a jacquard-loom | | | 19 | 0 |
| Do. | do. | do. | 20 | 6 |
| Do. | do. | do. | 20 | 0 |
| Do. | do. | do. | 15 | 0 |
| Do. | do. | do. | 11 | 3 |
| Lad | do. | do. | 14 | 9 |
| Woman | do. | do. | 15 | 0 |
| Do. | do. | do. | 7 | 0 |
| Man on plain work | | | 7 | 0 |
| Do. | do. | do. | 12 | 0 |
| Do. | do. | do. | 10 | 0 |
| Woman | do. | do. | 5 | 0 |
| Man on velvet | | | 13 | 4 |
| Do. | do. | | 15 | 0 |
| Do. | do. | | 11 | 3 |
| Woman | do. | | 5 | 6 |

About seven miles from Derby, situated in a pleasant spot by the waters of the Derwent, is one of the largest and longest-established rural factories in England, and one which, for several reasons, I was anxious to visit. The establishment in question is a cotton mill belonging to the Messrs. Strutt. Under its shadow the best part of the village of Belper has grown up. For considerably more than half a century the factory has given employment to successive generations; while almost all the workpeople live in houses and on ground belonging to the firm.

This mill, which employs more than 1,200 hands, is driven entirely by water. There are no tall chimneys, and no pouring smoke, to disfigure one of the most charming rural spots in England. Just above the factory, which is embowered in shrubbery, and has masses of ivy clinging to its walls, the dammed back waters of the Derwent expand into a shining lakelet—the surplusage tumbling in sparkling volumes over a weir. All round it rise steep, grassy hills, clumped here and there with groups of stately trees, or roughened by brakes of tangled underwood. Cottage and villa buildings are studded here and there. Along the steep high road, amid gardens and sheltering boughs, run broken and irregular rows of old-fashioned houses—a way-side tavern, with its bough-hung sign and horse-trough, many quaint old tenements grouped in picturesque irregularity, with grey ridgy roofs, and cottage lattices opening in the midst of woodbine and ivy. I chanced to be at Belper during one of the few and precious glimpses of the sun which the winter solstice is blest with; and as the red light came sprinkling down upon knoll and brake, on the sparkling frost-bound grass, and the broad shining river—as the smoke from many dwellings swirled perpendicularly up into the still air, and robins and other small birds twittered joyfully from thatch roofs and crisp unstirring branches—I thought I had seldom looked upon a scene more thoroughly and pleasantly rural and peaceful. And yet, from where I stood, I could distinguish the plash of the waterwheels and the murmur of the whirling mechanism of one of the greatest cotton mills in England.

The people in the Messrs. Strutt's factory gave, some years ago, the most thorough trial to the co-operative system of buying provisions and other necessaries which that system has yet received. The plan was abandoned—but more, Mr. J. Strutt informed me, in consequence of the misconduct of some of the conductors of the society, than from any conviction that the association had been a failure. The managers in question began to attend more to the business of the association than to that of the mill, and more to their own interest than either. Nevertheless, for many years the concern flourished. Goods, edible and wearable, were purchased wholesale and for ready money, and year after year the balance of the sums saved to the contributors was paid over to them in proportions sometimes sufficiently large to defray the greater proportion of their house rents. Suspicions, however, gradually arose, and became more or less confirmed. It was found that secretaries and managers were not always proof to the temptation of a bonus from wholesale dealers, and evils were also believed to result from the people giving up the habit of managing their money wages. At length, therefore, after an existence of more than a dozen years, the Co-operative Society of Belper was voluntarily broken up, and has not since been in any degree revived.

Mr. J. Strutt accompanied me to many of the dwellings of his workpeople. These are almost entirely built of substantial blocks of stone, of which there is abundance in the neighbourhood. The smallest class, consisting of two rooms, and generally occupied either by married couples without family, or by widows, are let as low as 15d. and 18d. The highest-rented class come to 4s. per week. In the first house we visited, I found, on the ground-floor, a large roomy kitchen and living room, and up stairs two good bed rooms. The lower rooms were paved with prettily tessellated brick. There was a back door, ensuring thorough ventilation, and decent back accommodations. To every house, large or small, a garden is attached, and every householder may rent an extra garden for about 3d. weekly. The appearance of matters inside denoted decided comfort. There were good cooking utensils, and some mahogany furniture, a sofa and a clock, with ornaments on the chimney-piece and books on the window-sill. The rent was 2s. 5d. In another cottage there were three rooms on the ground-floor—a living room, kitchen, and scullery, two bed-rooms upstairs, and a garret above them. The garden was about twenty yards long, and half as wide. For this house the rent was 3s. 10d. All the upper rooms in all the houses are boarded. In the centre of this pleasant and clean-looking factory village is the boys', girls', and infant school. The children appeared to me to be decidedly cleaner, and under far more perfect control, than is usual in the majority of schools of the class. The girls were getting a knitting and sewing lesson when I visited them. The fees are 2d. per week, and 1d. for the infant school. The children of widows are received into both schools at the latter rate. I should not omit to add that the factory part of the village of Belper is well lighted, paved, and drained; and small flower patches extend before every house, bordered, in several of the streets, by carefully trimmed rows of sycamores.

# LABOUR AND THE POOR.

—◆—

## THE MANUFACTURING DISTRICTS.

[FROM OUR SPECIAL CORRESPONDENT.]

### LEICESTER AND THE WOOLLEN HOSIERY TRADE.

## LETTER XXVIII.

The town of Leicester, like its neighbour, Derby—and to a still greater degree—boasts of having been, in ancient days, a place of note, while it still preserves a considerable commercial importance. A hamlet built where Leicester now stands was a post the possession of which, in the early dawn of our history, was fiercely contended for by Saxon and Dane. In the time of the Heptarchy, a cathedral stood upon the banks of the Soar; and when Duke William attacked the place, so stoutly was it defended that he won nothing save the ruins of the straggling Saxon town. At this early period it is said that there were in Leicester 322 houses, built of clay, timber, and wattles. The town was speedily rebuilt, and in process of time became a Norman stronghold, and a fair abbey and a stately castle rose over the narrow streets. The spirit of trade was, however, even then beginning to spring up in the cold shade of feudalism, and as early as the days of Henry II. there existed in Leicester guilds of handicraftsmen. Throughout the fourteenth century Leicester throve greatly. Churches, hospitals, and gaols were erected; fairs were established, charters granted. During the next age Parliaments met in the ancient religious houses of the borough, and the Leicesterians won the favour of Edward IV. by sending out almost the whole of their male population against the Last of the Barons. In 1485 the burghers of Leicester saw Richard III. pass through the town on his way to Bosworth Field, and, after a short space, his body was brought back and buried in a small church belonging to the Grey Friars. The remains of another great historical personage rest in Leicester. In November, 1530, the once omnipotent Minister of Henry VIII., then "an old man broken with the storms of state," alighted at the Abbey gate, and early in the following month was laid beneath the pavement of "Our Lady's Chapel." In 1563 the still scanty population included no more than 333 families. About half a century afterwards Leicester was erected into a "staple town for the buying and selling of wools." Its growing industry was, however, severely checked by the turmoil of the Civil wars. The Leicesterians were staunch Puritans, forward in insulting the Church and defying the King, so that in 1645 Charles laid siege to the town and stormed it—the stout burgesses fighting from house to house and church to church. The charter of the borough was finally restored by James II.

The eighteenth century saw Leicester rapidly rising to its present position. Many schools, hospitals, and almshouses had already been built, newspapers were established, stage-coaches started, and the knitting of woollen stockings by machinery was increasing rapidly. This manufacture had been commenced in Leicester about the time of the Revolution. It was very unpopular at first, and the few artificers were forced to work their frames in secret places, and by night. They hawked their wares round the country, each manufacturer riding his pannier-laden horse. The trade, however, soon outgrew the prejudices by which it had been at first kept down. In 1712 it was computed that in Leicester 1,000 persons were employed in sorting, combing, and dyeing; 6,000 in spinning, doubling, and throwing; and 6,000 in weaving, seaming, and dressing up the woollen goods. The greatest quantity of these was produced in Leicester—the finest quality in Nottingham. In 1785 the invention of a worsted spinning machine gave the trade an impetus, and in 1792 there were upwards of 70 hosiers in Leicester, employing no less than 3,000 frames. In 1831 the number had doubled; and in 1845 there were in Leicester and the villages around about 10,000 frames employed in making stockings, shirts, drawers, socks, and caps; about 2,000 in making gloves and mitts, and about 750 machines employed in the production of "fancy hosiery." In this department are included figured and coloured scarfs, shawls, cravats, boots and leggings for children, braces, worsted "polka jackets," and so forth. Many of these articles are knitted by hand in the villages of the Midland counties; but the greater portion of the fancy hosiery made is wrought by complicated machinery in Leicester. In this department it was calculated that in 1845 between 7,000 and 8,000 persons were employed. There were also used about 500 stocking frames, ingeniously adapted to the requirements of this new branch of industry—about 150 warp looms, those accommodating engines, which produce every fabric, from the most gossamery lace to the coarsest carpetting—and about 100 machines called grinders, of ingenious and complicated construction. About one half of the fancy hosiery then produced was destined for the foreign, and one half for the home market. In 1845 there were 52 steam-engines employed in propelling the machinery used in the town.

The present condition of the woollen hosiery trade in the town and county of Leicester may be gathered from the following information, furnished to me by Mr. Bigg, a large manufacturer, and a gentleman who has paid great attention to the industrial statistics of the district:—

"There are in the town and county of Leicester about 20,000 frames, employing a manufacturing population of about 35,000 persons. Of these upwards of six-tenths are occupied in the production of common woollen hosiery, two-tenths are engaged in the fancy trade, and the remaining two-tenths in the manufacture of cotton or merino fabrics in the villages of Hinckley and Loughborough. Many frames included in the estimate for the fancy trade produce a particular sort of cloth used by the glovers in Worcester and the west of England. Upwards of seven-tenths of the woollen manufactures of Leicester are now consumed within the United Kingdom. The remaining three-tenths are pretty equally divided between the foreign and the colonial markets. Power is partly applied in the fancy trade, but not in any other department of wool knitting." As regards a general estimate of wages throughout the various branches of the manufacture, I give the following upon the same authority:—"Wages are naturally somewhat higher in the fancy than in other branches, because the work performed requires superior skill for its execution, and because, being partly under factory regulations, the labour goes on steadily and continuously. For a man a fair average would be 20s. per week, for a woman 10s., and for a child 5s. In the glove trade a superior hand may obtain 25s. per week, a middling workman 20s., and an inferior hand 15s. per week. In the manufacture of under clothing, the wages range from 20s. to a much lower sum; the average may be taken as 12s. In knitting 'straight up and down stockings' on broad frames, the remuneration would range from 20s. to 12s. In fashioned stockings the wages are lower, ranging from 10s. to 8s., and 6s. These rates are, in all cases except the last, upwards of 15 per cent. higher than the average of the last seven years." It is Mr. Bigg's decided opinion that the condition of the frame-work knitter will not be permanently improved until the machines are gathered into factories, and something like factory regularity of work established. "At present," he in effect added, "the men often work very long, but as often very irregular hours; sometimes they are idle, sometimes exhausted. Very many of them do no work on Mondays, and not much on Tuesdays." In confirmation of his opinion as to the better wages which might be regularly earned by frame-work knitters were the factory instead of the domestic system adopted, Mr. Bigg handed to me the monetary results of an experiment of the sort, actually tried. Some years ago the firm of which he is a member collected their glove frames, or a great portion of them, into several extensive factories or workshops, insisting upon the observance of regular hours of labour. The experiment was persevered in for several months; and from the tables handed to me of wages actually paid, I take at random the individual amounts for three distinct weeks, earned in two of the shops in question. They were as follows:—

SHOP, NO. I.

| Weeks ending | | Feb. 10. | | Feb. 17. | | Feb. 24. | |
|---|---|---|---|---|---|---|---|
| Wages earned by | | s. | d. | s. | d. | s. | d. |
| Workman, No. 1 | .......... | 20 | 9 | 21 | 8 | 21 | 4 |
| „ 2 | .......... | 21 | 0 | 24 | 10 | 24 | 5 |
| „ 3 | .......... | 24 | 5 | 28 | 9 | 25 | 3 |
| „ 4 | .......... | 15 | 4 | 15 | 9 | 13 | 2 |
| „ 5 | .......... | 11 | 9 | 16 | 7 | 18 | 9 |
| „ 6 | .......... | 14 | 7 | 14 | 6 | 16 | 1 |
| „ 7 | .......... | 16 | 8 | 15 | 9 | 24 | 7 |
| „ 8 | .......... | 18 | 1 | 20 | 3 | 15 | 2 |
| „ 9 | .......... | 29 | 1 | 31 | 3 | 22 | 1 |
| „ 10 | .......... | 11 | 0 | 3 | 8 | 11 | 6 |
| „ 11 | .......... | 16 | 10 | 18 | 7 | 10 | 3 |
| „ 12 | .......... | 20 | 1 | 17 | 4 | 18 | 2 |
| „ 13 | .......... | 20 | 1 | 20 | 6 | 20 | 7 |
| „ 14 | .......... | 24 | 8 | 13 | 7 | 26 | 0 |
| „ 15 | .......... | 18 | 10 | 18 | 10 | 24 | 4 |
| „ 16 | .......... | 12 | 2 | 20 | 6 | 13 | 8 |
| „ 17 | .......... | 23 | 4 | 21 | 10 | 20 | 1 |
| „ 18 | .......... | 16 | 9 | 18 | 2 | 19 | 1 |
| „ 19 | .......... | 19 | 4 | 13 | 5 | 18 | 6 |
| „ 20 | .......... | 17 | 5 | 20 | 1 | 2 | 6 |
| „ 21 | .......... | 18 | 1 | 18 | 10 | 12 | 10 |

SHOP, NO. II.

| Wages earned by | Weeks ending | Feb. 10. | | Feb. 17. | | Feb. 24. | |
|---|---|---|---|---|---|---|---|
| | | s. | d. | s. | d. | s. | d. |
| Workman, No. | 1 | 14 | 1 | ... 11 | 7 | ... 11 | 5 |
| „ | 2 | 15 | 2 | ... 17 | 1 | ... 16 | 1 |
| „ | 3 | 20 | 9 | ... 21 | 4 | ... 17 | 5 |
| „ | 4 | 11 | 6 | ... 15 | 7 | ... 13 | 2 |
| „ | 5 | 18 | 6 | ... 21 | 5 | ... 15 | 2 |
| „ | 6 | 18 | 6 | ... 17 | 4 | ... 14 | 5 |
| „ | 7 | 21 | 6 | ... 21 | 6 | ... 20 | 10 |
| „ | 8 | 23 | 5 | ... 21 | 3 | ... 18 | 6 |
| „ | 9 | 16 | 9 | ... 16 | 3 | ... 14 | 5 |
| „ | 10 | 24 | 4 | ... 21 | 6 | ... 21 | 6 |
| „ | 11 | 18 | 3 | ... 19 | 2 | ... 20 | 5 |
| „ | 12 | 9 | 4 | ... 9 | 5 | ... 9 | 8 |
| „ | 13 | 16 | 3 | ... 18 | 6 | ... 8 | 3 |
| „ | 14 | 10 | 4 | ... 9 | 2 | ... 8 | 7 |
| „ | 15 | 15 | 6 | ... 10 | 4 | ... 14 | 6 |
| „ | 16 | 19 | 10 | ... 17 | 6 | ... 19 | 3 |
| „ | 17 | 21 | 5 | ... 21 | 6 | ... 12 | 2 |
| „ | 18 | 23 | 6 | ... 17 | 4 | ... 16 | 0 |
| „ | 19 | 20 | 2 | ... 20 | 1 | ... 13 | 8 |
| „ | 20 | 14 | 4 | ... 17 | 2 | ... 13 | 4 |
| „ | 21 | 20 | 7 | ... 22 | 0 | ... 16 | 4 |
| „ | 22 | 22 | 4 | ... 21 | 6 | ... 10 | 7 |
| „ | 23 | 14 | 4 | ... 14 | 4 | ... 12 | 9 |
| „ | 24 | 23 | 2 | ... 24 | 7 | ... 17 | 5 |
| „ | 25 | 15 | 6 | ... 20 | 7 | ... 15 | 11 |

So much by way of general history of the town and its trade. Before I proceed to further details it may be advisable that I should sketch the present sanitary and structural condition of the borough.

The town of Leicester lies in a gentle hollow, sheltered, except towards the east, by the undulations of the Dane and Spinney hills—eminences branching from the ridgy range of Charnwood Forest. The sluggish stream of the Soar winds through the town; and in wet weather the adjacent meadows are swampy and often overflowed. The consequence is, the frequent prevalence of fever in the lowest-lying portions of the town. The population of Leicester, in 1831, was 38,904. In 1841, it amounted to 48,167. The number of inhabited houses in 1831 was 8,348—the number in 1841 had increased to 10,046; and in 1848, a local census gave the number of inhabited dwellings at 13,139, and that of the uninhabited as 852, making a total of 13,991 houses. In 1846, there took place in Leicester 587 marriages, in 165 of which the men, and in 273 of which the women, signed with marks. The tables of mortality show that there are annually in Leicester about thirty-six persons living to one death—a proportion indicating no very satisfactory sanitary state of things. Accordingly, I find the local medical authorities examined before Mr. Ranger, the inspector of the Board of Health, pointing out considerable districts of the town as being fruitful in fever cases. In 1846 and 1847, temporary "fever-houses" were obliged to be established, and in one district the medical officer connected with the poor-law administration stated that upwards of one in three of the labouring classes had in 1840 obtained at least one order for medical relief. In 1840, 1841, and 1842, the average mortality of Leicester was 3.0 per cent.; in 1848 it was 2.65 per cent. per annum—the average mortality of England not being above 2.2, and in some great districts not above 2.0 per cent. The mean duration of life in England is 29.11 years. In Leicester it is 25 years, and it is estimated that at least 8,000 of the working-classes in the town annually receive medical assistance from the various charities. The drainage is miserably defective. Out of 242 streets, and 3,417 courts, alleys, and yards, only 112 are entirely culverted, and about 130 partially so. There are nine outfalls of sewers, all situated in the town, and all pouring their contents into the almost stagnant waters of the Soar. The surface drainage is equally defective. There is seldom sufficient fall to carry away the dirty water, which is sometimes obliged to be "swilled" along the kennels for upwards of a quarter of a mile. The entire length of the roads and streets in this condition is nearly 30 miles, occupying an area of more than 113 acres. At the back of each block of the more ordinary class of houses is a common yard, with privies, cesspools, and ash-pits, for the use of the occupants. From these places there is seldom or never any sub-soil drainage. Slops and liquid refuse are left to evaporate, and send up their noisome effluvia. From one of the Health of Towns Commissioners' Reports I transcribe the following very instructive piece of evidence as bearing on the connection between the mortality and insufficient sewerage in parts of Leicester:—

COMPARATIVE MORTALITY IN THE DRAINED AND UNDRAINED
DISTRICTS OF THE TOWN OF LEICESTER.

| Streets. | 1840. | | 1841. | | 1842. | | Average age at Death for the Three Years. |
|---|---|---|---|---|---|---|---|
| | Average Age of Death in Years. | Proportion from Epidemics. | Average Age of Death in Years. | Proportion from Epidemics. | Average Age of Death in Years. | Proportion from Epidemics. | |
| **East District.** | | | | | | | |
| Culverted .... | 23½ | 1-4th | 24 | 1-12th | 26½ | 1-12th | 24⅔ |
| Partly culverted | 17½ | 1-3d | 21 | 1-8th | 21½ | 1-8th | 20 |
| Not culverted .. | 13½ | ½ | 18 | 1-6th | 17½ | 1-7th | 16⅓ |
| **West District.** | | | | | | | |
| Culverted .... | 26 | 1-6th | 30 | 1-14th | 29 | 1-12th | 26⅓ |
| Partly culverted | 21 | 1-5th | 23½ | 1-8th | 22 | 1-11th | 22 |
| Not culverted .. | 14½ | 1-4th | 21 | 1-7th | 17½ | 1-9th | 17⅔ |
| Culverted .... | 25½ | The three years average 21, and rather more. | These years were taken because the year 1840 was remarkable for the increase of disease and the number of deaths throughout the town. | | | | |
| Partly culverted | 21 | | | | | | |
| Not culverted .. | 17 | | | | | | |

Of the 13,991 houses in Leicester only 120 are supplied with water-closets—the average cost of each being £31 10s., a sum equal to half the amount necessary for building a four-roomed house. Many of the cesspools are of great depth; some of them not less than 25 feet; and the consequence is, that, in numerous instances, the water which is found still nearer the surface is poisoned by noxious percolations. The present supply of water is derived from wells, a few public pumps, and from the river Soar. In 1848 it was estimated that the number of wells in Leicester, each furnished with a pump, was 2,800, or about one well to every 4 5-7 houses. Their average depth is about eleven yards, and their cost, including the pumps, about £12 10s. There are besides nearly 3,000 cisterns and tanks for collecting and preserving rain water—the average capacity of these receptacles being 700 gallons, and their average cost £9 10s. The water principally used in Leicester for culinary purposes is exceedingly hard, and by no means pleasantly tasted. Owing, indeed, to the bad quality of the water supply, many dyeing operations require to be sent out of the town for performance to other localities where a purer and softer species of fluid can be obtained. The quantity of soap necessary in washing with Leicester water is most uneconomically great. A water works company exists. They are incorporated by act of Parliament, but a sufficient amount of capital could not be raised, and the scheme remains a dead letter. A large public swimming bath has lately been opened at the charge of 1d. per head, the corporation paying £100 per annum to the proprietor. During the first month 7,026 persons availed themselves of the privilege. There are no parks or gardens in Leicester, nor any space for public recreation, save about four acres used as a cricket-ground, and granted for that purpose by the corporation.

Like Derby, and unlike Nottingham, Leicester is rather a widespread and straggling town. There are very few back-to-back tenements, and not one cellar dwelling. Courts with houses on either hand exist, but in no great numbers. The general plan of building adopted in the construction of houses for the labouring classes is to erect them in blocks, each block perforated by a passage leading to a common back yard, in which are situated the several privies and ash-pits—generally speaking, placed in a cluster. These houses are of two general classes; the better, consisting of four rooms, two above and two on the ground-floor. The inferior class of dwellings consist of two rooms only, one above the other. For a house of the former class the rent charged is from 2s. 3d. to 2s. 6d. per week. For one of the latter it ranges from 1s. 6d. to 2s., according to situation. There are very few of the dwellings of the working-classes cellared. The ground-floors are invariably paved with red brick; the floors of the upper chambers are plastered with gypsum. When there are two first-floor rooms there is always a fire-place in one of them.

The frame-work knitters ply their trade either in shops erected at the back of the middlemen's houses, and frequently forming one side of the common yards above described, or in their own rooms. The shops in question are generally miserable places—mere shells of brick, and rough (yet slight) timber-work; the windows clouded with the dust and dirt of weeks; the bare brick walls and sooty joists festooned with cobwebs, the floors unswept—in most cases I suppose since the structure was built—the frames huddled as closely as possible together, and the whole aspect of things squalid, dirty, and slovenly to the last degree. There may be exceptions, but the foregoing is the general rule. If the frame of a workman stands in his own house, it is usually placed beneath a window in the lower room—never, as is the fashion in Nottingham, in the uppermost apartment.

I now proceed to give some account of the various branches of the staple trade of Leicester, and of the condition of the population engaged in each. As in Derby the factories are almost all devoted to the manufacture of silk thread for weaving and knitting—so those at

Leicester are occupied in the production of woollen yarns for similar purposes. The fleece in Leicester is sorted, carded, combed, and subjected to all the spinning processes requisite to fit the filaments which it produces for the stocking frame, the grinder, or the warp loom. The principal part of the thread thus produced is worked up either in the town or the surrounding district. A few of the factories are introducing the practice of combing wool by power, but the greater part is still combed by hand.

Various kinds of woollen factories—those dealing with the short-stapled wools, as at Huddersfield, and with the long-stapled wools, as at Halifax—have been already described in these letters; and the processes by which yarns fitted for the production of fleecy hosiery are manufactured do not very materially differ from those necessary in preparing the raw material for broad cloth or merinos. The combing by machinery is, however, a feature of the Leicester trade, and one, as may well be believed, by no means popular amongst the hand combers. There are as yet, I think, only two establishments into which the combing mechanism has been introduced, but in these it completely supersedes the labour of skilled adults. Boys and young women only are requisite to superintend the machines, which, to a certain degree, feed themselves. The wages thus earned range from 8s. to 10s. per week. Two girls can manage, if I mistake not, three circular machines, and each machine performs—although, I believe, not quite so delicately—the work of several men. The engines in question are of recent introduction, and not dissimilar in principle to the mechanism used in heckling flax.

Amid the woollen factories of Leicester a large new mill, just opened, is beyond all cavil the most splendid and admirably arranged carding and spinning establishment I have yet seen. The name of the proprietor I withhold at his own request, but it is impossible to describe a factory of this kind without its speedy and accurate local identification. For the first time, I believe, in the history of English textile manufactures, there has been erected a spacious building destined for the labours of the steam-engine, the carding frame, and the spinning frame, in which architectural beauty and symmetry have not been wholly forgotten. "You must," said a Manchester gentleman to one of the partners lately—"you must absolutely have flung hundreds of pounds away in these ornaments, pediments, and entablatures, which are not of the slightest use." But the feeling of the rearers of this noble industrial structure is, that a fair and due sum expended in securing not only the most perfect ventilation and convenience to the workpeople, but in providing a degree of architectural symmetry and grace unhappily too long and too systematically despised by our manufacturers, is money expended in a mode which, in due time, will bear both its pecuniary and its moral harvest. It is the opinion of the gentleman in question—one in which I fully concur—that a well-arranged and well-ordered mill has a powerful tendency in producing in turn well-arranged and well-ordered homes. The habit of constantly seeing, throughout working hours, perfect cleanliness and perfect symmetry upon every side, is a powerful adversary to slatternly and filthy practices out of working hours. In the mill in question the lowest portion of the ceiling of the working rooms is eleven feet from the floor, and as these ceilings are uniformly arched, the mean actual height is still greater. Each room is ventilated quite independently of those above or below it. A rush of air, either hot or cold, can be directed into each chamber through a separate flue, while the foul air constantly escapes through apertures in the ceiling communicating with the chimney. The consequences of these arrangements are, that the atmosphere, even in the carding-rooms, is almost as pleasant as would be desired in a drawing-room. The mill is as yet hardly in working order, but when it is, a functionary will be appointed specially to attend to the ventilation. From the pay books I take the following averages of wages, as earned in a Leicester woollen factory:—

|  |  | s. | d. |  |
|---|---|---|---|---|
| Wool Sorters (men) . . . . . | about | 18 | 0 | per week. |
| Washers (men) . . . . . . . . . | „ | 16 | 0 | „ |
| Boys (their assistants) . . . . | „ | 2 | 0 | „ |
| Carders (women) . . . . . . . | „ | 7 | 0 | „ |
| Preparers (including drawers and rowers—women) . . | about | 6 | 10 | „ |
| Spinners (women) . . . . . . | „ | 7 | 6 | „ |

To give an idea of the working discipline of the mill, I may mention the amount of wages paid for four successive weeks, with the fines deducted from them—it being understood that irregularities of attendance and inattention to work are thus punished:—

| Wages for one week . . . £180 . . . Fines, 1s. 1d. |
| „ another . . . . . . . . 175 . . . Fines, 1s. 1½d. |
| „ „ . . . . . . . . 180 . . . Fines, 3d. |
| „ „ . . . . . . . . 179 13s. . . . . Fines, 5d. |

In laying on these fines, a certain discretionary power is exercised, and a few minutes' absence is excused in a regular hand, but punished in an offender by habit and repute. There is a small library connected with the mill, but the superintendent complains that the girls will read hardly anything save the trash of penny romances.

The wool-combers attached to this establishment work in shops at their own houses. Fully as I have described them in Bradford, there are, however, some peculiarities connected with the combers of the midland counties, which I shall detail as they were recounted to me in the wool-combing establishments which I visited. The first was a shop prepared on purpose for the work, and well ventilated. There was a "pot of four" glowing in the centre, and the same number of men employed. Their answers to my questions may, I think, be condensed much to the following effect:—

"This room we're combing in was intended at first for a kitchen, but as it's an out-house it makes a very good shop. There are few so good in Leicester. Generally the combers work up in the top of the house, but it's very seldom that any one sleeps in the room. There are no charcoal-pots whatever made use of here. If anybody sleeps in the shop-room it's usually the children of the family. The new machine for combing, we fear, will make a great difference to us. We haven't half work in Leicester as it is already. If it wasn't for Yorkshire we could not make a living. The Leicester trade is generally brisk for only four, or at most five months in the year. It begins about the end of August, and if it runs on to Christmas then we call it a good trade, and think that we are well off. After Christmas time it is very common for the Leicester wool-combers to go to Yorkshire—to Bradford generally—in search of work, until the Leicester season comes round again. A great number work regularly in Bradford in the winter and spring, and in Leicester in the summer and autumn. Those who can get work from Yorkshire may, perhaps, stay in Leicester all the year round. If the combers have the means they take their wives and families with them to Bradford; but it is not always that they can. The masters provide no proper shops for the combing. To this rule there is but one exception in Leicester. A great grievance which the midland wool-combers have to complain of is, that the manufacturers are the proprietors of the combs, and that they make the workmen pay regular rent for them, just as in the framework-knitting trade. This rent is generally 3d. a week. If the manufacturer has a pair of combs idle, he will not allow the workmen to labour with their own should they have any. They must use his, and pay rent for them, while their own are lying uselessly by. This is not the case in Yorkshire, and it is not the case in Leicestershire when the men are doing Yorkshire work. In that case they use whatever combs they please." In some instances, I was seriously assured, combs have been given out and paid for, so old and decayed that they were unfit for the work, which was actually executed with other implements—the comber thus paying rent for a double set of tools. "We work"—I continue the epitome of my conversation with the men—"we work what hours we please, but the shop is open for us from five in the morning until nine at night, upon Fridays until ten, and upon Saturdays up to any hour we choose to stay. The pot is never extinguished from Sunday to Sunday. We are paid money for fuel at the rate of 2d. per score. This amounts to about 6d. per week. For shop rent we pay 10d. per week. We estimate our average earnings, when fully employed, as from 10s. to 12s. per week, but wool-combers cannot count on making so much during more than six months in the year."

The second combing shop I visited was situated in a top chamber, approached by a ladder and a trap. The men at work here informed me that in addition to 10d. for shop rent, and 3d. for comb rent, they paid upwards of 1s. weekly for the washing of the wool. In answer to questions as to the original price and actual value of the combs, I was informed that a pair of combs, with four rows of teeth—the implements at present principally in use—might cost about 35s. "When I was a boy," said one of the men, "a pair with three rows cost £2 10s. We have more work to do with the four-rowed combs, and although the price of the article has fallen so much the manufacturers do not reduce one penny of the rent; it is just what it used to be long ago." All the combers whom I questioned agreed in stating that Yorkshire was better than Leicestershire work, being free from several drawbacks incidental to the latter. Still, although they passed one-half of their time in the West Riding, they one and all talked of Leicester as their home.

The fancy branch of the wool-knitting trade is, so far as the altered stocking frames are employed in it, carried on exclusively in shops and factories. The frame-rent system appears more or less to exist in all the branches of the occupation in which the instrument, either in its original or its adapted form, is employed. Indeed, so deeply-rooted in the industrial system of the midland counties is the method of making the textile workman pay a fixed charge for the use of his tools, that, as

I have just shown, it has found its way into the wool-combing trade. It is gratifying, however, to state that the principal fancy houses in Leicester are building new and improved frames, principally for the manufacture of woollen shirts—machines with which they intend to fill factories of their own, and to employ workmen at fixed rates of remuneration, clear of all frame or standing charges whatever. At present the rent and charges payable for a broad frame, suitable for the fancy trade, may amount to 3s., 3s. 6d., and 3s. 9d. weekly. Of this sum 6d. goes to the "second master or middleman" for standing room, and 9d. for winding. The rent paid for the frame varies from 1s. 6d. to about 2s. 6d. As in the plain hosiery trade, the situation of the workman depends in some degree upon the character of the middleman. Occasionally the former may be required to pay a full week's rent when he has received from the second master only a half week's work; but, as a general rule, the machines, being more costly and elaborate than the ordinary stocking-frames, are kept more under the eye of the proprietor, and the men are sometimes provided with work direct, the usual agency being dispensed with. After many conversations with various workmen, I should be inclined to consider the estimate already given of their average earnings as correct. Upon a good job, a good workman may earn as much as £2 per week; upon an inferior one, an inferior hand may receive as little as 10s. One pound is about the average recompense weekly earned by a fancy-work knitter in good work; but taking one month with another, and one person with another, a number of the men warned me against stating a higher average than 15s.

The establishment of Messrs. Harris and Sons, in Leicester, is quite an epitome of the fancy hosiery trade of the town. There machines—of every variety and of every combination of varieties, wrought both by power and by hand—are assembled for the production of every species of figured and coloured worsted goods. Many of these machines are exceedingly complicated and ingenious, working, in frequent cases, with the aid of the jacquard. Men are principally employed in tending this machinery at wages ranging from 18s. to 25s. Boys are engaged in filling and shifting the bobbins and arranging them upon the frames, so as to produce a warp with the requisite diversity of hue, earning at these several occupations from 3s. up to 5s., and even 9s. per week. The men are paid by the pound weight of the fabric which they produce. In the establishment in question every variety of textile manufacture is carried on; goods are knitted, netted, and woven, figured and plain, by hand and by power. I was informed that the quantity of bobbins, in stock and in use, sometimes reached the astounding amount of six or seven millions. A considerable quantity of hand knitting work is given out by the Messrs. Harris. The labour is performed by the wives and daughters of the cottagers throughout the district, who earn from 1s. 6d. and 2s. to 3s. 6d. and 5s., according to their ability, and the time which they are able to bestow upon the manufacture.

The general sketch of the framework knitting trade contained in my second letter from Nottingham forestalls many details that are applicable to Leicester, in common with its two glove and stocking making compeers. I may here, however, be allowed to introduce a brief account of the silk glove and hose makers of Derby, which was accidentally omitted in my communication from that place.

In Derby the silk hosiery knitters generally work in shops belonging to middlemen or second masters. These shops are usually low two-storied buildings, often situated amid dust-heaps and ash-pits in back yards; sometimes, when in the outskirts of the town, more pleasantly located in little gardens. The middleman system is universal. As a rule the frame rent paid is 1s. per week, but some of the masters permit their hands, when work is short, to pay 3d. per dozen on the quantity of articles turned out. This statement, be it remarked, applies only to the glove trade. Standing room is always charged 3d. Cases in which the knitter works at home, and is yet charged by the second master with standing room as though he laboured in the shop, are exceptions to the general rule, but they are exceptions which do occur. Sometimes, if a master has all his frames going, he will employ an independent frame without exacting rent; but it is only when trade is very brisk that the independent machines have much chance in this way. The knitters assured me that they had frequently to complain of being served with old ricketty frames, which they were afraid to work vigorously. They were often, they said, obliged to pay 1s. per week for a piece of mechanism for the fee-simple of which no one would give a pound. To some frames additional works, called "carriers," are added, and for these carriers a separate and additional rent of 2d. is demanded. In answer to my inquiries as to whether the men would in general prefer the factory system to their present irregular and uncertain mode of working, I was informed that the subject was one on which great difference of opinion existed, but that the framework knitters were unanimous in wishing for the substitution of a rent calculated according to the work actually done, instead of the present fixed weekly sum. The estimates of wages with which I was furnished agree precisely with those already published, so far as the glove branch goes. In a large silk-hose knitting shop the men informed me that their charges were 1s. for frame rent, 3d. for standing room, 9d. for winding, 3d. for needles, and about 6d. for fat to burn in lamps. They estimated their wages at about 8s. or 8s. 6d. for a week's full work. On Mondays and Saturdays they generally worked for twelve hours, on other days for fourteen. The amount of rent which they had to pay for broken meshes of work entirely depended upon the character of the second master.

In the plain woollen hosiery trade of Leicester about one-third of the operatives are women. They work at the narrower kind of frames, and earn very much the same amount of wages as are made by the men who labour at the same species of machines. Many of the Leicester middle-men have upwards of thirty frames. The machines are almost universally placed on the ground-floors of the houses or in shops. The average charges are 1s. rent, 6d. winding, 8d. for standing-room, taking in, and preparing work—making a total of 2s. 2d. If the middle-man finds two days' work, he charges half a week or three days' rent. This two middlemen admitted to me themselves—observing at the same time that others made the framework knitters pay rent whether they got work for them or not. Independent frames are sometimes collected in a single shop to the number of a dozen, the workmen stating that individual private frames are hardly worth the working. The highest price paid for knitting the largest size of woollen hose is 2s. 1d. per dozen—the smallest price for the most inferior kind 1s. per dozen; but these last articles, my informant added, and I dare say very truly, "are not worth picking up in the street." The prices rise by twopences, according to the different sizes of the articles produced. One penny three farthings of each of these twopences go to the workman—the remaining farthing to the seamer or stitcher. The lowest price paid for seaming is 4½d. per dozen, and a good seamstress can manage a dozen and a half a day—for stitching, 3d. per dozen, and a skilful hand can turn out about three dozen a day. In the manufacture of ribbed hose, men are almost exclusively employed. The work to a certain extent is of a superior kind, requiring superior hands, and therefore commanding superior prices. The lowest remuneration paid is 1s. 6d. per dozen, and the highest 3s. 6d. per dozen. One person makes the legs—the other the feet. The same division of labour, by-the-way, takes place in the manufacture of some other kinds of plain stockings. In the ribbed stocking shop which I visited, the person knitting the feet was paid 1s. 4d. per dozen, and he could make two dozen a day. The person knitting the legs was paid 2s. 2d. per dozen, and he could make about fourteen pair per day. The leg making is by far the most difficult part of the operation. Apprentices are seldom taken nowadays, the trade being so overcrowded—but when they are they are bound for seven years, during the greater part of which they receive about two-thirds of a journeyman's wages. I ought to add, that from 12s. to 14s. was the highest sum at which the plain woollen hosiery knitters fixed the average of their earnings.

Be the causes what they may, there can be no doubt of the miserably depressed state of the frame-work knitters. They appear to labour without either energy, or hope, or heartiness. Of the different branches of the trade, it appears to me that the Derby silk glove manufacturers are the best off and the most intelligent, and the Nottingham cotton hose makers the worst off, and the most unintelligent. Almost without exception, however, the houses of this class of labourers are squalid and neglected-looking; and in point of personal appearance and decent comfort of attire, the frame-work knitters must take the very lowest rank in the social scale connected with textile industry. Frame rents have been blamed for this result—the middle-man system has been blamed—and irregular semi-domestic labour, as opposed to the industrial discipline of a factory, has been blamed. As to the door at which the fault really lies, it is not my business to try to arrive at any decision. I have pointed out the peculiar industrial conditions under which frame-work knitters labour, and I have stated the low social status which, whether it springs from these conditions or not, at all events co-exists with them.

# LABOUR AND THE POOR.

###### ◆

## THE MANUFACTURING DISTRICTS.

[FROM OUR SPECIAL CORRESPONDENT.]

## THE STAFFORDSHIRE POTTERIES.

## LETTER XXIX.

The case of the Potteries is one of those curious instances so often to be met with in examining the field of British industry, of a certain branch of manufacture setting itself arbitrarily down in a certain locality, without any particular or obvious reason for the selection. It is no doubt impossible to produce crockeryware without an abundant supply of coals. That supply is to be found spread over wide fields in the west, the centre, and the north of England. Yet the trade of the potter is practised, as a staple branch of industry, only in that insignificant stripe of North Staffordshire through which run the infant waters of the River Trent—there a mere brook, fresh from its sources in the Moorlands. Pottery establishments may be scattered here and there over the kingdom; there are several upon the Tyne and the Wear, about Newcastle and Sunderland, but in the trifling strip of Staffordshire called, *par excellence*, "The Potteries," are manufactured nineteen-twentieths of the crockery, coarse and fine, porcelain and earthenware, used in England.

The Pottery district is about ten miles long, and two or three broad, running north and south in the valley of the Trent, and consisting mainly of a chain of large villages, or small towns, or perhaps, to speak more correctly, neither villages nor towns in the ordinary acceptation of the terms, but straggling districts more or less built over—the streets here clustering thickly together—there spreading out in long arms, which just extend far enough to connect the main groups of buildings; the intervening patches of country sometimes consisting of pleasant fields and undulating pastures, sometimes chequered with isolated manufactories and detached rows of smoky houses, surrounded by plots of waste ground, heaped with cinders, scoriæ, and fragments of broken pots which have not stood the fire—the whole being diversified here and there by those black mounds and grimy buildings which denote that a coal shaft is sunk beneath them. The North Staffordshire Railway binds together the range of the Pottery towns like a thread stringing beads. The general sweep of the country is bold and undulating; and from the heights on which the village of Hanley stands, some really fine panoramic glimpses can be caught of green undulating hills, with far spreading breasts, mapped out by tree and hedge-row into arable field and pasture meadow, dotted with the smoky appurtenances of coal pits, the tower-like forms of wind-mills, and here and there by dusky clusters of houses, grouped round a pottery with its tall engine chimney and its bee-hive-like furnaces. As for the Pottery towns, there is hardly more distinctive individuality between them than between the plates and saucers of the well-known willow pattern, which they produce in such abundance. In Hanley alone, there is a market-place, distinguished by some new and handsome ranges of buildings. But you may wander from township to township, and parish to parish, and still imagine, from the aspect of things around, that you have not moved an hundred yards from your starting point. Everywhere there stretch out labyrinths of small, undistinguished, unpaved streets, the houses generally of two stories in height, and built of smoke-grimed brick. Here you will find a new row of cottages, the uniformity of the walls slightly broken by stone facings; hard by may be a cluster of old-fashioned houses, with lead-latticed windows, and perhaps some attempt to cause ivy to train up the wall. Every few steps bring you in sight of a plain brown brick chapel—a Sion, or Ebenezer, or Bethesda—and, numerous as are the Methodist places of worship, I regret to say that the public-houses are more numerous still. I thought that Bilston and Willenhall, in the southern part of the county, were unsurpassable in this respect; but I have repeatedly seen localities in the Potteries where every fourth or fifth house was a tavern. Diverge from the main thoroughfares—into regions of back yards, and little gardens, and outhouses, and waste patches belonging to potter establishments—and you will find yourself in a curious chaos of old tumble-down sheds, littered with crates, broken crockery ware, and straw—of walls and lean-toos, built of old "saggars"—in other words, of great coarse yellow dishes of the commonest ware, used for containing the pots while being burnt—diversified here and there by brick pits, clay pits, smoking engine-houses, and great coal heaps, dismal wastes of muddy ground, more or less strewn with the eternal pavement of broken stone ware, the whole landscape enlivened by glimpses of barges deeply laden with piled-up clay or flints, lying by wharfs, or slowly moving along the narrow canals; for the Potteries are most abundantly supplied with the means of inland navigation. Indeed, had it not been for the genius of Brindley, the white clay of Devon and Cornwall, and the chalk of Kent and Sussex, would never have been worked up into ware in Staffordshire. The great scheme of the Bridgewater canals may be said to have developed itself in the district of the Potteries. It was near Burslem, I think, that the first sod was turned, in breaking ground to join the waters of the Mersey and the Trent; and the first, or one of the first, of the great canal tunnels was cut in the neighbourhood beneath the Air Castle-hill—a somewhat ominous name, which, while the project as yet existed but upon paper, was of great service to the small jokers of the district. Nevertheless the hill is now pierced by two tunnels—the old canal, and the more recent railway one. These excavations run different courses, and at different levels through the earth, crossing each other in the centre of the hill.

In sketching the outward and obvious peculiarities of the Potteries district, I must not forget the significant number of Old Testament names to be seen on every sign-board. Moseses, Jacobs, Seths, Joshuas, Daniels, and Enochs, meet you at every turn. The same peculiarity of nomenclature will be recognized by any one acquainted with the well-known names of many of the principal Pottery firms. Wesley himself planted his church in the district; and at Shelton, near Hanley, is one of the very largest Methodist chapels in the kingdom.

As a whole, the appearance of considerable portions of the Pottery towns, is not very unlike that of the better parts of the iron and coal districts which I have described in the south of the county. The population, however, from the nature of their occupation, look clean and respectable. At meal times, or in the evening, they pour out from the manufactories—men, women, and children—with aprons and sleeves plentifully besprinkled with dashes as of liquid white clay. Here and there, however, you see a symptom of the neighbouring coal-mines, in the appearance of men and boys, in coarse besmirched flannel clothing and wooden clogs, with faces and hands like sweeps.

The Pottery towns are Longton, or Lane-end, Stoke-upon-Trent, Hanley, Shelton, Fenton, Burslem, and Lunstal. The conjoined Stoke and Woolstanton district, which comprehends the greater portion of the Potteries, with a district not strictly belonging to them, is treated as a whole in the Registrar-General's Returns, so that there is no obvious way of ascertaining the separate rates of mortality and the separate educational condition of each individual township. By the general return, it would appear that the number of persons living in and about the Potteries to one death is about 38. The population of the double district in question in 1841 was 81,617. The number of illegitimate births in 1846 was 358. In the same year, out of 933 marriages, 461 men and 632 women—heavy proportions—signed with their marks.

There is little difference between the species of ware manufactured by the different pottery towns. In all of them all the branches of the art are more or less carried on. Longton, locally called Lane-end, was, until lately, to some degree an exception to this rule; the coarser sorts of earthen and stone ware, manufactured in a great degree for the use of hawkers, and sold to them for ready money, having long been almost exclusively produced there; but of late years the finer branches of the trade have been carried on there, as well as the coarser departments. The tone of the population of Lane-end is somewhat behind that of the other pottery towns. The wages of the people are not materially lower, but the strongest local *patois*, the coarsest and roughest manners, and the lowest and most brutalizing amusements, such as dog and cock fighting, still linger in Lane-end to a greater degree, and with a firmer hold, than in the other districts. The locality is also more tinged with colliery population than any other in the Potteries, a circumstance amply sufficient, considering what Staffordshire coal mining and Staffordshire coalmines are, to account for the phenomenon in question.

Having thus briefly sketched the general appearance and most obvious physical characteristic of the Potteries, I proceed to give an account in some detail of the various stages of the most interesting and beautiful manufacture carried on within them. The labour is essentially cleanly, and, in by far the greater portion of its processes, a healthy one. There is a quiet comfortable look about the majority of the rooms in which the work is carried on. The air smells fresh and pure, and even the furnaces are so constructed and managed, as to give out far less heat than the workmen in such kindred establishments, as glasshouses, for instance, are exposed to.

I now proceed to the first process, which consists of grinding and mixing the clayey and flinty ingredients which are to be worked up into stone ware. This clay is of several qualities, suited for coarse or fine pottery—for china or for common ware. The inferior clay is found in Somersetshire and Devonshire, and is known generally as

The Wedgwood Manufactory, Etruria

blue clay. The finer or china clay comes principally from Cornwall. In its dry state, when piled up before grinding and mixing, it exactly resembles whiting. The price of this article of raw material carries with it its exact quality, but it is now much cheaper than formerly. A ton of average purity may cost in the Potteries about £4 4s. Double the money used to be a common price. The task of mixing the different clays so as to produce ware of the exact degree of fineness requisite, is the first skilled labour performed. A personage called, from his grinding duties, a miller, is entrusted with the work. The clays are flung under his directions in proper quantities into great round tubs containing more or less water. In each of these tubs, a wheel—somewhat like a paddle working horizontally with floats, which in their revolutions graze the sides of the vessel, and are turned by steam—continually works, driving the clay and water round and round, and gradually reducing the mixture to an exquisitely fine pulp. More clay of proper degrees of coarseness is added generally once in about two hours. The miller is paid 1s. 8d. per ton, and he can generally prepare about 7 tons a day. Out of these wages he pays the labourers requisite to assist him. With the clay, it is necessary that calcined flint and Cornwall stone—the latter a soft greyish friable mineral—should be mixed. The flint—a great deal of which comes from the Kentish coast, near the mouth of the Thames—is first calcined by means of slack coals. It is then pounded, and finally ground. This last process is similar to the pulping operation undergone by the clay, and the same miller super-intends both. The pounded fragments of flint are flung into capacious circular tubs, round which, as in the former case, revolve great hori-zontal paddle-wheels—what we may call the floats; consisting, how-ever, in this instance, of ponderous square lumps of stone. The process of flint-grinding takes about twenty-four hours, at the expiration of which the stone is reduced into powder as fine as snuff. The bottoms of the flint tubs are paved with stone. The miller makes the necessary changes in the quantity of water or mineral twice a day. The ordinary time which the steam-engine is kept going, is from seven o'clock in the morning until six o'clock at night. Sometimes a day and a fourth, and sometimes a day and a third, are worked; the hours being pro-longed respectively until eight p.m. or nine p.m. The meal times are half an hour for breakfast and an hour for dinner. The appearance of the tubs is very much as though the arms of the revolving wheel were splashing through great cauldrons of blancmange and cream. Of course the steam-engine does the actual work, the tubs being often left unattended for an hour together.

The flint and clay, having each been reduced to a fine pulp, have now to be run through silk sieves, so as to intercept the slightest im-purities, the creamy mixtures, after straining through the silk filter, mingling in a common tank. The process is superintended by a man, with a boy to help him. The wages of the former are about 2s. 2d. per day; hours from seven o'clock a.m. until eight o'clock p.m. The lad has about 4s. a-week, and each receives extra pay for the extra time which they are sometimes called upon to work.

The raw mineral dough has now to undergo its first slack-baking process. The old method—still occasionally practised in the manufac-ture of coarse ware—was to run it into tanks, called air kilns, where, after being well stirred up and agitated, it was left to silth into the requisite consistency. Now, however, the process of evaporation is car-ried on by fire, in what is called a slip kiln. This is a great tank, paved with fire tiles, and with shallow furnaces running beneath. Here the liquid paste is kept at a perpetual slow simmer, until the moisture has evaporated and left the white dough in due consistency. This process is generally accomplished in about two days. During the operation, reeking clouds of steam constantly ascend from the simmering tank, keeping the attendants in some potteries in a constant vapour bath.

In the better ordered establishments, however, the roofs are raised so high, and are so well provided with the means of ventilation, that the great body of steam floats above the level of the attendants. There are generally two men to each slip kiln, each relieving the other in charge of the furnaces and the hot fluid. They are paid severally 1s. 8d. per ton for the clay paste which they produce, the quantity being generally about seven tons per week.

The next process is the squeezing of the paste or dough, in machines something like gigantic coffee-mills, so as to compress out of it any lurking bubbles of air, and finally to crush the mixture into one soft lumpless, gritless mass. Each set of presses are fed and attended to by a man and a boy, who fling huge lumps of clay into the cone-shaped hollow cylinders. Powerful screws, fashioned somewhat on the Archimedian principle, revolve inside, and with a slow and steady certainty crush down the yielding clay, each branch of the screw receiving the substance from that above, and forcibly squeezing it further and further down towards the narrowest part of the cone, from which it emerges in a continuous square shaped flow, of the exact consistence and appearance of putty. The workman, provided with a small brass wire which passes through the solid clay almost as through water, cuts it into oblong blocks, each weighing about one hundredweight, and carries every block into an adjoining warehouse, from whence it is fetched to the workmen whose duty it is to mould the plastic material into shape. The presser makes from 20s. to 22s. per week.

We now come to the first of the plastic processes—that of making round cups or pots, and a beautiful one it is. Each "thrower," as the operator is called, is attended by a woman. He sits upon a stool placed on a table, with his legs stretched out; and between them, fixed upon the top of a perpendicular spindle, there whirls rapidly round in vertical fashion, a circular platter of wood called a "throw block." This whirling platter is, of course, put in motion either by the hand, or by the steam-engine. The principle of the apparatus is exquisitely simple, and as old as pots themselves. The attendant female having broken off from the lump a little round ball of clay dough, hands it to the thrower who places it upon the centre of the revolving platter, urging with gentle and skilful pressure his thumb into the mass, which, impelled by this centrifugal force, and moulded at the same time by the guiding fingers of the operative, straightway assumes the form of a circular vessel within his grasp. If the phrase of an article rising up under the maker's hand can ever be literally applied, it is in this beautiful process of throwing pottery ware. Beneath the skilful fingers of the workman vessels of any shape, so long as the general form be circular, appear as if by magic from the little round dab of clay. The interior of the cup, or pot, is moulded by means of a thin piece of metal, the outline of which shapes the vessel into its required form, while the exact diameter necessary between the opposite rims is obtained by allowing the pot to whirl round until its extreme edge all but touches a guiding wand placed for the purpose. The operator keeps his hands constantly wet, so as to mould the clay with the least possible friction. He is skilful in giving the rims or edges of the basin either an overlapping or a bell shaped form, as may be required; and by a rapid easy motion of the fingers produces the requisite indentations for the reception of spouts and handles. A good thrower in constant work earns considerable wages—the average may be between 30s. and 40s. a week. The woman who hands him the clay is called a "baller." She is paid about 8s. per week. In this, as in all the other skilled branches of the pottery trade, beginners serve an apprenticeship of seven years. The first year they are paid about 2s. per week, the second from 2s. 6d. to 3s., and then they are set to piece work—a consummation which both they and their employers are generally anxious should arrive. Thenceforth until the expiration of their apprenticeship, they are paid half of the regular journeyman's prices. All the pottery which they spoil ere the attainment of requisite skill, they are obliged to work up again without any payment.

The thrower having detached the basin or cup from the wooden platter by means of a very thin iron hoop, it is carried away to the drying oven, there to acquire a certain degree of toughness, amounting to hardness, before the turner operates upon it. The ware comes into the hands of the latter functionary in what potters call a "green" state. The lathe of the turner works much in the same way as the throwing-block in the last described operation. The cup or basin is placed again upon a vertically revolving surface, fastened thereto by a few drops of adhesive liquid, and then the turner applies his chisels just as his brethren do when operating upon wood. The requisite outside mouldings and scoopings are thus quickly and easily given to the vessel. Pottery turners work in large rooms down which there run rows of lathes. Girls and boys are occupied in carrying the vessels from workman to workman. Turners are paid by the piece. A good hand can make his 5s. per day.

It will be obvious, that, as yet, the pots are destitute of handles, or, supposing them to be required, of spouts. The making and fixing on of these appurtenances constitute a separate branch of the trade. Both handles and spouts are formed in moulds. Each of the handles is made in one mould. The operator first rolls out and kneads the clay, gives it the required shape, and fixes it neatly to the cup with no other tools than his wet fingers, a drop of adhesive liquid, and a moist sponge. Spouts are cast in two pieces, joined and stuck on exactly in the same way. The apprentices in this branch are frequently employed in the fabrication of handles for little toy jugs. Journeymen will not find it difficult to earn a pound a week. The rooms, I may add, in which these processes are carried on, are uniformly warm, airy, and cheerful, and the work is light and clean.

Leaving the basins, cups, and tea-pot ready for the first burning, we will now turn for a moment to the plate and dish makers. The plate is formed upon a mould, which whirls round, as in the throwing process. The dish being oblong, and frequently constructed with peculiarly rounded corners, requires a greater degree of skill to fashion it. The clay has in the first place to be batted and mashed so as to render it as plastic as possible when it reaches the hands of the workman. Two men and a boy frequently work at dishmaking together. The boy kneads and mashes the clay, the first workman rolls it out, exactly as a housewife would the cover of a pie, and hands it to his comrade, who proceeds to give the smooth layer of clay paste its requisite form. To accomplish this, he places the plastic substance upon a mould made of plaster of Paris which forms the inside of the dish, and then, giving the mould, which revolves upon a pivot, a series of twirls round, and working the clay at the same time by corresponding jerks of the wrist, he brings the ductile material into a smooth layer exactly corresponding in every respect to the mould beneath. Both are then removed to the drying-oven, half an hour's exposure in which causes the clay to separate readily from the plaster. A good hand at dishmaking will earn from 30s. to 35s. per week. The apprentices are usually set, at the commencement of their labours, to the easier task of plate-making. After the expiration of about three years, as in other branches of the trade, they are employed by the piece, receiving half the amount of journeymen's wages.

No jugs and vessels, not round, can of course come under the hands of either thrower or turner. They are therefore cast in moulds in different pieces, and put together with adhesive liquid so delicately that the mark of the junction can hardly be perceived. A great number of ornamental jugs and vases are thus constructed, the handles, when wanted, being attached to them in the manner already described. The moulders earn from 25s. to 30s. per week.

The next process is the hardening one—of the first or biscuit firing. I have described the outward appearance of the pottery furnaces as that of huge brick beehives. Their internal construction is peculiar. The hive-shaped structure is merely a sort of case built round the real furnace, leaving some four or five feet between them. This case is called an "ovel." It serves to protect the furnace from irregular draughts, which would cause varying degrees of heat, and so spoil the "baking." The ware to be burnt is put into round earthenware tubs, somewhat of the shape of foot-pans, called "saggars"—a word said to be a corruption of "safeguards." These saggars are piled up one above the other in great pillars, reaching to the mouth of the furnace, and smeared with clay at the joints, so as to keep the smoke and soot from the ware inside. The fuel is then kindled beneath them, and the "baking" commences. The furnace is attended to by a principal fireman, who is responsible for the proper burning of the ware, and who employs his own assistants. When in good work, the former can get upwards of £2 a week. Two men can attend to a furnace in operation, but five or six are employed to set and draw it. The ware continues exposed to a white heat for about 48 or 50 hours. The first night, one man only is required to feed the furnace—the fireman and his assistant are both on duty during the second. While the baking is going on, the men generally sleep at the works, and in their clothes, lying down in the most comfortable corners they can find. From time to time the fireman draws a pot to see how the oven is getting on. Of course the entire pile of crockery is at a bright white heat. The fireman's assistant or stoker earns 12s. or 14s. per week.

As soon as the ware is burnt sufficiently hard, the fires are allowed to die out, and the furnace is drawn. The crockery is then in the state of biscuit ware—perfectly white and hard, but still rough and unglazed. It is then transferred to the hands of the "dipper," a workman who performs by far the most unhealthy duty of any connected with pottery labours. To give crockery its glaze it is dipped in a solution, the ingredients of which are various, but the basis of which is white lead. The dipper stands over a tub full of this deleterious wash. He is attended by two boys, the business of one of whom is to take up each article singly as it comes cooled from the furnace and toss it into the tub.

Here the dipper catches it, gives it a plunge into the mixture, and flings it to the second boy, whose duty it is to stack up the dipped utensils in readiness for the glossing over, which fixes and dries the wash. Sometimes the dipper works with his mouth covered, so as to prevent him from inhaling the vapour rising from the constantly agitated mixture. In some potteries, too, the proprietors furnish a species of smock-frock, which envelopes the whole person, and prevents the clothes from being splashed by the deleterious mixture. The diseases, if they take a constitutional form, arising from this work are similar to those common with house painters, but the dippers are in general locally affected. The hands, which are almost constantly immersed in the wash, suffer; the fingers being often distorted and paralysed, and the fore-arm becoming more or less affected. This state of things is sometimes produced in two or three years. Sometimes a man will work at the dip-tub all his life with apparent impunity. The poison affects different constitutions in different ways; but a great deal depends upon strict cleanliness, upon careful washing of the hands, and using means to remove any deposit which may gather under the nails as soon as a man's work is over. Many of the dippers, I am told, are very careless in this respect, and suffer accordingly. The fumes of the white lead, if they act constitutionally, are peculiarly apt to disorder the digestive system, and produce a long train of dyspeptic symptoms. The wages earned by the dipper run as high as £2 2s. per week. The boys are paid 4s. each.

The glazing qualities imparted by the white lead have now to be fixed by the agency of fire, and the ware, for this purpose, is removed to the glossing-oven. Here it remains for about twenty-four hours, subjected to a more moderate degree of heat than that which it has already undergone. Each set of these furnaces and ovens is attended by a fireman and his assistant, who earn about the same amount of wages as those paid for superintending the previous baking.

The ware is now—supposing it to be the finer sort, china or porcelain—ready for the hands of the painters, who trace upon it those bright and beautiful blazonings, the execution of which requires a trained and steady hand and an artistic eye. The painters are both men and women. They work in large *ateliers*, usually oppressive with the strong smell of spirits of turpentine and spirits of tar, with which the pigments are mixed. These artist-operatives find their own brushes and pencils, the paint is provided. They work at long benches. The article to be painted is held in the left hand,

and steadied against the bench and upon the edge of a flat piece of wood propelling at right angles from it. Along this the painter lays his right arm, the support rendering it perfectly steady while he uses the brush, turning at the same time, with his left hand, the article which he is ornamenting, so as to subject every part to the process. Sometimes the pattern is already traced in relief upon the cup or vase, in which case the task of colouring it is simple; but frequently the painter is required to form the outline as well as to supply the filling-up of the design. The patterns principally painted are flowers and leaves, disposed in many flourishes round the moulded forms of the vessels. Artistic skill, in the higher sense of the term, is of course rarely required. The operation requires rather knack than art. To make a good china painter, however, a man must be endowed with an eye susceptible of the grace of form and the harmony of colour, and he must possess a hand skilled in the necessary manipulation and perfectly steady. The circles formed outside and round the rims of vessels, are traced with beautiful steadiness of finger and brush. The apprentices in this branch of the business are frequently employed in painting toy, tea, and dinner sets for children. Painting is at present in a somewhat slack condition in the Potteries, the public taste having, as I was informed for some time back, run upon articles distinguished by beauty of form, rather than by brilliancy of coloured adornment. As a general rule, the most skilled work of this kind is performed by men, who earn wages ranging from 20s. to 50s. per week. Very few, however, are employed at the latter rate—I was informed that the average might be about 30s. The women earn from 9s. to 12s. weekly. The emblazonment of china and porcelain, is an occupation well suited to develop anything like artistic talent amongst those who pursue it. I have accordingly not been surprised to see sundry very fair copies of well known paintings, produced by persons earning their living by tracing glittering adornments on cups and vases. Several of our principal steel engravers were, I believe, brought up as china and porcelain painters.

The ware, gorgeous from the hands of the colourist, has now to undergo a third baking, called the "enamel firing," the effect of which is to fix the paint in the substance of the vessels. The enamel-oven remains lighted only about eight hours, at the expiration of which, if there be gold, as there generally is, traced in the design, the ware is handed over to the burnishers. When they receive it, the gold lines are dim and pale and blurred-looking. It is, therefore, their duty, by friction with agate and bloodstone, to burnish up and bring out in all their glittering richness, the gilded blazonries. The burnishers frequently work in the same room with the painters. They are mostly young women. When the china comes from their hands, it is ready for the warehouse. The burnishers earn about as much as the female painters.

The three last processes described, pertain only to the fine and most expensive species of pottery. The vast mass of ware, after coming from the biscuit furnace, undergoes quite a different set of operations, the designs wherewith it is adorned being printed or stamped instead of painted. The printing process is an ingenious and interesting one. Each set of workpeople consists of one man (the copper-plate printer), two women, and a little girl. Part of the operation is similar to ordinary copper-plate or steel-plate working. The printer stands between his press and a little stove. On the former, he heats the plate engraved with the design or pattern, then spreads his colours upon it—these last being made up with strong spirits of tar—wipes clean the level surface of the plate, and in the usual way takes off an impression upon thin tissue paper, previously dipped in a strong adhesive solution. The design is then handed to the little girl, who dexterously cuts away the superfluous paper—not trenching, however, upon the blanks in the interstices of the pattern—and then hands the latter to one of the women, who immediately applies it to the cup or vessel to be ornamented. The adhesive mixture causes the paper to stick, and it is briskly rubbed and smoothed with a hard roll of flannel, to one end of which the operator presses her shoulder. After being allowed to remain for a few minutes, the cup is flung into a vessel of hot water. The paper instantly peels off, leaving the impression with which it was engraved stamped clearly upon the ware. The work of "transferring," as it is called, is the hardest which devolves upon women in the range of pottery manufacture. The set of operatives whom I have described, generally work in a sort of partnership. The articles printed are usually paid for at the rate of 6d. a dozen. Of this the copper-plate printers have 5¼d., and the transferring girls ¾d. One printer with his coadjutors will produce from 80 to 100 dozens per week. The little girl who cuts, earns about 2s. a week. After the biscuit ware has been printed, it is transferred to the dipper, and from him to the glossing-oven, from whence it emerges hard and glass-like, the colours shining through a coat of transparent glaze.

Besides the operations which I have described, there is another which gives employment in most potteries to a number of women and children. This is the manufacture of variously shaped circlets, triangles, &c., formed of the commoner clay, and afterwards baked, for the purpose of placing between the different articles when they are piled up for firing in the saggars, so as to prevent them from injuring each other. The operators are women and boys. They roll the clay cakes out thin, cut them into long strips, sever these across, and mould them into all manner of skeleton shapes called "stilts," "triangles," "cockspurs," and so forth, so as to suit the requirements of any species of crockery. The boys are usually paid one halfpenny a gross for these little pieces of clay frame-work, in other words, they make twelve dozen for a single halfpenny, and can generally earn about 6d. a day.

The ornamented vases and pieces of porcelain and china, enriched with figures and flowers and star-work in relief, are, if not cast altogether in a mould, supplied with their adornments by manual labour—the projecting ornaments being cast in small separate moulds, and fixed on bit by bit by means of strong adhesive composition. The operatives are men who make from £1 to 30s. per week. A vast number of small ornamental articles are got up in this way.

The production of small pieces of statuary is another semi-artistic kind of labour, practised to a great extent in the Potteries. The method adopted is exclusively that of moulds, and the operatives earn from £1 to 36s. per week. The work bears about the same relation to sculpture, as china-colouring or pattern-drawing does to painting. But it struck me very forcibly that the influence of the humanizing and elevating art spirit, even in its faintest development, as distinguished from proficiency in mere manual labour, could be very plainly traced in the looks, bearing, and species of intelligence of the operatives, even although their money wages were in many cases not higher than, nor even so high as, those of cup-throwers and dish-makers.

The modeller who is attached to the larger pottery establishments, has claims to be considered an artist, in the fair meaning of the word. He prepares the shapes by means of which the mould-makers construct their useful fabrics. He is competent to model clay from drawings, and works with sculptor's tools. In fact, he is a copying sculptor. One modeller, to whom I was introduced, was engaged in preparing a very beautiful Mercury, from a design by Flaxman. A new bust of Shakspere from his hand was in readiness for publication. Amongst other artistic matters in the room, were the pretty statuettes of Locke and Newton, evidently modelled from the portraits in Hampton-court. These figures I have since repeatedly seen in many houses in the district. We talked of popular works of the kind. Two nude figures of children, one of them reading, the other writing, with his legs crossed—figures which, I presume, most of your readers will remember—were, I was told, amongst the most popular which were issued from the Potteries. The "Praying Samuel," another very well known cast, was and is in immense vogue; tens of thousands of these were sold, as was also the case with another *morceau* of statuary described to me as, "Good Night, a companion to Samuel."

"But here—see here!" said my companion, observing my looks wandering back to Flaxman's Mercury, "see this," and he produced a well-known figure—exhibiting in full canonicles the not very graceful form, and the long peculiar countenance of John Wesley. "Here is the man that sells. Here is the statuette they buy down here. Flaxman is all very well, but, in a commercial point of view, one Wesley is worth a dozen Mercurys!"

Little china-ware ornaments are, as may be conceived, profusely scattered through the cottages in the pottery districts. A curious use to which I observed small busts of the Queen and Prince Albert put, was placing them under the legs of sofas, like caryatides, so as to raise the article of furniture from a damp brick-paved floor. A vast number of copies of the Portland vase, the clay fired so as to exhibit the exact colours of the original, are yearly manufactured in the potteries. You meet them, though rarely, in the homes of the workpeople. The first *fac similes* of this famous vase, made in Staffordshire, were managed in a true spirit of monopoly. Fifty copies were cast, and then the mould was destroyed. Now-a-days, the vase is reproduced by thousands, carrying into as many homes a memorial and an example of that sincere and perfect art-spirit, conceived and developed by the exquisite mental organization of the antique races of southern Europe. In the case of the potteries of Staffordshire, however, as in the calico-printing districts of Lancashire, the art-creative faculty seems all but torpid. "The French," said the modeller already alluded to, "do all these things far better than we can. For good, well-made, and well-burned serviceable pottery, we can compete with the world; but when we come to art-manufacture, we are compelled to acknowledge our inferiority. Our statuettes, for instance, with some few exceptions, are far inferior in grace, and in freedom of handling and design, to those of the French."

For the greater part of the information embodied in this letter, I am indebted to the facilities most courteously afforded to me by the Messrs. Wedgwood for inspecting their extensive works at Etruria—works in which every process appertaining to the pottery manufacture is carried on.

*The Morning Chronicle, Thursday, January 24, 1850.*

To the EDITOR of the MORNING CHRONICLE.

Sir—Your impression of yesterday contains an interesting statement, having reference particularly to "Leicester and the woollen hosiery trade," written by your "Special Correspondent."

After giving a general history of the town and its trade, your correspondent refers to "a large new mill, just opened;" and gives, "extracted from the pay-books, the following averages of wages" as being earned therein:—

| | | | |
|---|---|---|---|
| Wool sorters (men) ......... about | 18s | 0d | per week |
| Washers (men) ............. „ | 16 | 0 | „ |
| Boys (their assistants) ........ „ | 2 | 0 | „ |
| Carders (women) .......... „ | 7 | 0 | „ |
| Preparers, including drawers and rovers (women) ........... „ | 6 | 10 | „ |
| Spinners (women) ......... „ | 7 | 6 | „ |

As the proprietors of the mill in question, we feel it desirable to state that your intelligent correspondent has, by some means (doubtless most unintentionally), given an incorrect account, in some respects, of the wages paid to our workpeople.

Instead of the amounts, as stated above, we find, on a careful examination, that the following are as nearly as possible the wages we pay:—

| | | | |
|---|---|---|---|
| Wool sorters (men) ............... | £1 | 9 10 | per week |
| Washers (men) ................... | | 16 0 | „ |
| Boys (their assistants) ............. | | 3 9 | „ |
| Carders (girls and women) ......... | | 7 0 | „ |
| Preparers (including drawers and rovers, girls and women) ............... | | 6 10 | „ |
| Spinners (girls and women) ........ | | 10 6 | „ |

We are persuaded that we have but to make the request, to insure the insertion of this correction in your next paper,

And are, most respectfully yours,

JOHN WHITMORE AND CO.

Leicester, Jan. 22, 1850.

# LABOUR AND THE POOR.

—◆—

## THE MANUFACTURING DISTRICTS.

[FROM OUR SPECIAL CORRESPONDENT.]

### THE POTTERIES.

### LETTER XXX.

The exact local population of each of the Pottery towns appears by the last census to be as follows:—

| | |
|---|---:|
| Stoke-on-Trent, and the immediately surrounding villages | 8,391 |
| Hanley | 10,185 |
| Shelton | 11,836 |
| Longton | 12,407 |
| Fenton | 4,923 |
| Burslem and district | 16,090 |
| Tunstall | 6,945 |
| Total | 70,777 |

I have said that the Longton district is that most behind in the tone of its population. The house accommodation there is also inferior to the standard of most others. Filthy and crowded courts— ill-arranged, undrained, and irregular streets—and expanses of half-waste land, covered with rubbish and cinder heaps, patched with neglected gardens, piled up with broken saggars and smashed fragments of pottery, all bear testimony to a hastily, ill-built, and ill-laid-out town. Perhaps the best specimen of a pottery village is to be found in Etruria. This characteristically named hamlet, which is indebted for its classic appellation to the founder of the great pottery firm of Wedgwood, is situated in the township of Shelton, upon the banks of the canal which connects the waters of the Trent and Mersey. The village is entirely the property of the Messrs. Wedgwood, and is almost wholly occupied by the working people in their employment. The manufactory faces the canal—indeed, a branch of the latter runs through it—so that barges float beneath gateways into inner quadrangles, and deliver their cargoes at the threshold of the store houses; and the regularly built streets of the village extend behind the pottery. The houses are of several classes, affording more or less accommodation, at different rents. I visited and minutely inspected several of each grade, and never was I more pleased with the appearance of operatives' dwellings. The abundance of furniture, the hearty air of comfort which reigned in them, one and all, was pleasant to see. The first house which I entered was one of the largest class. It contained no less than six rooms—a comfortable living chamber, a small back kitchen, and a parlour upon the ground floor; upstairs were three bedrooms. The lower apartments were paved with bricks, the upper were floored with boarding. The living room, I could see, was generally used for cooking, the kitchen being appropriated to the purposes of a scullery. There was a capital range, containing boilers, ovens, and apparatus for roasting, all as clean as hard brushes and blacklead could make them. I may mention, also, that in the case of a great number of these cottages the door-step was brightly blackleaded. In almost every house in the village a handsome eight-day clock ticked in a corner, and one side of the living-room was occupied by a sofa, perhaps not very elegantly shaped, but ample, and covered with glazed calico. In the kitchen was a good store of pots, pans, and tea and dinner ware; and behind the house was a garden about twenty yards by six or seven. The rent of this dwelling, garden included, was £7 10s. The local rates formed a separate burden. The next house into which I proceeded was even more comfortable than that which I had just left. In the latter there was a large family of young children, turning everything topsy-turvy. In the other there were no such juvenile demonstrations, and the appearance of plain, substantial, unpretending comfort was complete. A carpet was spread over the brick floor, a roaring fire danced and flickered upon the perfectly polished range and fire-irons; there was a clock and a large and handsome chest of drawers in the room, a central table, and several smaller ones, a sofa, and a comfortable easy chair, in which the man of the house was snugly ensconced, while his wife prepared tea. Upon the several ledges and ridges of the old-fashioned chimney-piece were set a profusion of little chinaware ornaments—dogs, vases, and shepherdesses tending their flocks beneath very green crockery trees. There was also a bookcase, very fairly stocked, and newspapers and cheap serial publications lay in the broad window-sill. The occupant of this abode, one of the workmen in Messrs. Wedgwood's employment, told me that he had been born in the house; and hoped never to leave it. Indeed, the place was in many respects just what an operative's house ought to be: warm, comfortable, and almost crammed with substantial furniture. In the next house I visited there were two rooms on each floor. The rent was £6. Here, also, the floor was at least partially carpetted, and a horse covered with good white crisp linen was airing before the fire. Among a number of portraits and engravings hanging upon the walls was a very fair copy, executed in oil, of David's picture (I think it is) of Napoleon crossing the Alps. The brass candlesticks which were ranged upon cupboard and shelf were as bright as a Dutch housewife could wish them; and at the end of the garden was a small greenhouse. These gardens were one and all provided with proper private accommodations. The fences were formed of old "saggars;" and a fair quantity of kitchen vegetables were, as I was informed, produced by each patch of land. Indeed, I heartily wished, as I was going over these nice, warm, substantial houses, peeping into their bed-rooms and their generally well-stocked pantries, that all the manufacturing operatives, or, indeed, all the Pottery operatives, were as well off—for the houses in Etruria are, unhappily, not by any means to be considered as typical of the entire district, although in Stoke, Hanley, Shelton, and Burslem, there are many streets inhabited by the working population, in which the houses are just as well built and as well furnished as those belonging to the Messrs. Wedgwood.

I examined with some attention the worst parts of Hanley and Shelton. The houses are very seldom built back to back, and there are scarcely any cellar dwellings. With very few exceptions, each tenement has its means of thorough ventilation. Courts, however, abound. The older houses are sometimes built on all sides of a small airless square, with a narrow passage leading to the street. Occasionally the common ash-pits and conveniences are erected in this delectable quadrangle. More generally, each house has its back yard—these places being too often, however, in a filthy state of dirt and neglect—frequently piled up with broken saggars, articles which the people seem wonderfully prone to collect and treasure. The occupants of the worst class of houses I often found to be widows, with miserable, dirty, unkempt-looking children, picking up a livelihood by washing, and depending upon its being eked out by parish relief. Even in the poorest class of dwellings it was curious to observe how the fashion in furniture prevailing in the district was perceptible; wretched imitations of sofas—all ricketty boards, and torn and dirty calico—were often drawn near the fire. In more than one instance these served as day beds, and probably night beds too, for sick children. I examined several of the houses in Hanley in which deaths from cholera had taken place. The disease, when it broke out, produced an absolute panic amongst the poor people. In the first house which I inspected in which a cholera case had taken place, the patient, a labouring man, had been left to die unattended. It was a damp squalid place, with a mere strip of a back-yard, shared with the adjacent tenements. The privies, which had been placed close to the back doors, were removed to a more suitable situation by the Poor-law and sanitary authorities of Stoke. The house in question consisted of three poor rooms, and the rent paid was 2s. per week. In a small yard, close to another house, I found a ragged, patient-looking donkey, standing listlessly to be snowed upon. The woman whom I found within—the occupant of a cold, damp, and squalid room, with little furniture, and that of the most crazy description—said that the donkey slept in the yard all night. I suspected, however, by the very marked odour of the apartment, that Dobbin formed one of the domestic circle, at all events during the long cold winter nights—an opinion which was shared by my companion and guide, a gentleman connected with the Poor-law administration at Stoke. The husband in this case was a labouring man out of work. The place, I was informed, had been a perfect miracle of dirt until, before the advent of the cholera, the Poor-law authorities took it in hand. It is, indeed, probably, to the active and timely measures adopted by the officers of the Stoke Union that the district owed its comparative escape from cholera, which was excessively severe a couple of miles off, at Newcastle-under-Lyme. Since October, 1848, an energetic system of house-to-house visitation for the discovery and removal of sanitary nuisances has been carried on, and although no official records have been preserved of the actual number of foul places cleansed or improved, I am assured that the change effected is a very considerable and important one. As in South Staffordshire, although by no means to the same extent, the earth in some districts of the Potteries has partially collapsed over deserted mine workings, and played the usual havoc with the houses above. I saw in Hanley and Shelton many crushed and deserted dwellings; in some cases contiguous houses leaning away from each other, and in others smashed-down lintels and riven walls. I was told that in more instances than one these movements of the earth had been productive of most afflicting consequences to honest and industrious workmen, who had invested their hard-earned savings in small building speculations, and whose property was thus virtually destroyed. The possession of house property is much coveted by the better class of operatives in the Pottery districts. There are several flourishing building societies, and I was gratified to learn that instances were very common of working men living in their own houses. Rows of newly-erected cottages, upon a plan infinitely superior to the old class of houses, are very common in many districts. In some of these the stone facings, well-kept door steps, and smart window blinds, give the streets quite a jaunty appearance. The old and wide-spread fault of making the entrance door the living-room door is, however, still generally persevered in. Public bakeries are common throughout the Potteries, and are mostly open at fixed hours every day. A great proportion of the bread consumed is home-made, and baked at these ovens. The charge for baking is generally 1d. a lot—the lot to consist of not more than four quartern loaves. I was told that it was only the most improvident among the working classes who purchased their bread at the baker's. Home-making insures a cheaper and a more unadulterated article.

The water supply of Hanley and the surrounding districts is partly derived from wells, partly from the North Staffordshire Water-works Company, which conducts the water in its pipes from springs welling out in the high moorland ranges near Leek. Stand taps are common in the poorer localities, the charge to each cottage benefiting by them being generally 2d. a week. I presume that the inhabitants are not very punctual with their rates; for in several instances, in the course of my wanderings through back courts and unpaved alleys, I found the supply "cut off." In many cases, however, the ingenious defaulters, fertile in expedients, had managed to perforate the leaden pipe, or partially to wrench open the metal lips at the place where the sides of the tube had been crushed together, and so to ensure a small but continuous dribble. In one instance the pipe had either burst or been broken below ground, and so furnished the supply of a small well which came bubbling up, not in the clearest condition, in the centre of a muddy unpaved court. The regular wells seemed to me for the most part forbidding receptacles for mere surface water. Those sunk deeper and provided with pumps yielded a somewhat purer supply. Before leaving the subject of house and street architecture I may be permitted to observe upon the constant recurrence of a phenomenon which I have remarked in many industrial districts of England. In the houses of the worst class—in those the inhabitants of which are obviously at once slatternly and poor—the seldom failing pictorial decoration upon the walls is derived, with significant frequency, from the illustrations of some penny highwayman novel. In more comfortable dwellings, although occupied, perhaps, by individuals of the same nominal rank in the social scale, you may find a stiff family portrait or two—probably a crown or half-crown's worth—from some vagrant artist; or, perchance, there are engravings of some Chartist or Radical leader belonging to the political school of the *pater familias*. But enter the dirty untidy dwelling, where the hearth is unswept, the bed unmade, and everything betokens want and squalor—and almost to a certainty you find, stuck by pins or wafers to the wall, a coarse woodcut showing Claude du Val with his face masked, prancing in a laced coat beneath a gallows, or Dick Turpin, on Black Bess, with a cocked pistol in either hand, clearing the turnpike-gate, on his famous ride to York.

The coal pits about the Potteries are managed very much after the fashion of those in the Wolverhampton and Bilston district of the same county. A few pits are worked by gins and horse power. The buttie system flourishes as in South Staffordshire, but I think upon the whole that the above-ground apparatus is more efficient and less rude. A great many of the coal mines hereabout are rented by the Earl Granville from the Duchy of Cornwall, to whom it seems that the royalty belongs. The principal seam worked—as I was told at a shaft mouth—is one six or seven feet high. The men work from six in the morning until different hours in the afternoon. There is none or very little "tommying" in this part of the county, but the wages of the colliers are seldom paid, as working men's wages ought to be—weekly.

The accusations of improvidence and of a tendency to waste an over proportion of their money upon eating and drinking, which I heard so often urged against the working men in the south of Staffordshire, I find re-echoed and applied to the potters of the north. Upon a point of this sort, all I say must rest on the authority of informants who, living in the district and intimately acquainted with the habits of the people, can base their statements upon far-extended and long-continued observation. A gentleman connected with the Poor-law administration of Stoke observed that in many cases there was "nothing but roasting, and broiling, and frizzing in the houses on the Saturday nights, the Mondays, and the Tuesdays, after which time the families had too often to pinch for it until pay-day came round again." The favourite beverage is ale—the newer and sweeter the better. With the exception of a little cricketing the people are not much in the habit of engaging in manly games. "The public-house is in general," I was told, "the greatest attraction when the day's work is over." The principal supporters of Mechanics' Institutes among the pottery population are the painters and the figure moulders, who may be supposed to belong to a higher class than the ordinary run of workmen; but in North Staffordshire, as almost everywhere else, the institutions in question are practically for the benefit of shopmen and clerks. Dog fighting and cock fighting are both dying out. You see, however, a great number of ferocious-looking bull-terriers still lurking about. In many instances, I was informed, that when a dog or a cock fight is got up, its patrons and supporters are not working-men, but individuals moving in a better rank of life. The vigilance of the police, however, has all but suppressed these miserable exhibitions. Very little out-door relief is granted by the Poor-law administrators in the district, except in cases of widows and old and disabled men. Almost all relief to able-bodied persons, given out of doors, is in the form of food, or necessaries. The workhouse test is sometimes put in force, by requiring able-bodied paupers to pick oakum, or break stones within doors all day, and then permitting them to return to their homes with food, or perhaps a trifle of money, at night.

There is no employment connected with the pottery trade carried on at the homes of the people, with the exception of an instance here and there, in which small ornaments may be fabricated after the regular work hours—and excepting, too, the cases of a few individuals who make and paint boys' marbles. In Burslem a considerable number of these are made, and in a little back-street in Shelton I came upon a household in which the painting of "alleys" and "commoneys" formed the staple industry. The operators were a young woman and a girl. The mother of the elder—an old infirm woman—was sitting by the fire-side, propped up in an arm-chair. She told me that she had been a marble-painter for sixty years, and that her daughter now carried on the trade. At my request, the latter—an intelligent woman—explained the process from first to last. The maker first rolls the lump of clay into a tolerably round form, in his hands. By the help of a common thimble, he then brings it into a perfectly globular shape, and smooths away all surface asperities. The marbles have then to be baked, to be brought into the biscuit-ware condition, just like any other description of pottery. They are burnt in large dishfulls, at an ordinary furnace, the maker paying 1½d. per dish. He then sells them to the manufacturer, who pays him 8d., 10d., or 1s. per thousand, according to the size and quality of the clay. The women who paint and beautify the articles purchase at the same rates, and after finishing them off with the brush and the glazing dish sell them again at 2s., 2s. 6d., and 3s. per thousand. Large marbles, the size of plums, are paid for by the hundred. The process of painting these clay pellets is neat and expeditious. A flat platter of wood, revolving vertically on a spindle, just as in the case of the throwing block, carries round the marble, which is placed upon its centre. The "painting" generally consists of a succession of rings, something like equators and arctic and antartic circles upon globes. The operator holds her camel-hair pencil to the clay, and the revolving marble in some sort paints itself. It is then placed to dry in a little oven or dish by the fireside; and is next dipped into a bowl of the same composition with the lead used for glazing the ordinary biscuit ware. The woman was quite sensible of the deleterious nature of the mixture; but she was not, she said, long over the bowl at a time, and she was very careful in thoroughly washing and cleaning her hands. For the subjection of the dipped marbles to a glossing furnace she paid 1½d. per dish. This of course came out of her profits, as above stated. She was not able to tell me how much she thought she earned, because she worked irregularly. The painting process soon fatigued the eye, so that she could not make the circles true, and then she had to rest.

*The Morning Chronicle, Monday, February 4, 1850.*

*The WAGES of PROTECTED INDUSTRY.*

———◆———

To the EDITOR of the MORNING CHRONICLE.

Sir—Without for a moment intruding in the field of politico-economic controversy, and solely anxious for the recognition of truth, I beg to call your attention to certain circumstances stated in my letters on the hosiery and lace trades of Nottingham, in connection with certain arguments and representations favourable to industrial protection lately made use of both in and out of Parliament.

It is stated with truth that duties are still levied upon the import of certain manufactured articles—these articles being mainly cotton, woollen, and silk goods partially or wholly "made up," that is stitched or seamed together by the needlewoman. These and other cognate branches of industry are chiefly carried on in the midland counties and towns of Nottingham, Leicester, and Derby. The fact of the existence of the duty in question was referred to by the mover of the amendment to the Address in the House of Commons—that honourable gentleman expressing no surprise at the reported prosperity of "protected" trades.

Now, sir, the circumstances to which I wish to call your attention are those set forth in my Nottingham letters, and on the authority of which I now state that the women engaged in the making up of cotton, woollen, and silk articles, are incomparably the most wretchedly underpaid and overworked class with which I became acquainted during a minute investigation extending from one end of the manufacturing districts to the other.

This result I arrived at from personal inquiries, establishing the following facts:—

That the average earnings of the women employed in seaming and stitching different kinds of silk gloves amount respectively to about 5d., 6d., and 7d. a-day of twelve hard-working hours.

That the average earnings of women employed in chenening gloves is somewhat higher, the needlework required being more skilled; but that the most dexterous cheneners cannot earn above 10d. a-day.

That the average earnings of women stitching "cut ups" (in the stocking trade) is not above 5d. per day, and that to obtain that sum requires from twelve to fourteen hours of hard labour.

That the average earnings of women seaming wrought goods (also in the stocking trade) is, in the case of the best hands, not above 7d. a-day; the great majority not earning so much.

That the general prices paid for stitching and seaming various kinds of gloves and stockings, range from 3½d. to 7d. per dozen, and for a few exceptional kinds of goods, to as much as 1s. per dozen; but that the general average of wages over all these trades is certainly not above 6d. per day.

In the different departments of the needlework, plain or ornamental, performed upon lace, the average of wages is far beneath those earned by females in cotton or woollen factories. Tambourers and menders are best paid; but their average earnings are under rather than above 5s. 6d. per week. For "running," "drawing," and "catching up," the wages paid to the young women and children (many of the latter mere babies), run from 1s. 6d. to 3s. per week.

A great number of the stitchers and seamers of Nottingham, particularly those who are not partially supported by the male members of their families, receive parish relief. They could not live else.

I may add, as an all but universal rule, that the hours worked for the pittances mentioned above are very considerably longer than the hours worked in factories, and that the demands made upon the eyesight and upon the endurance of the workwoman are out of all proportion greater.

These facts with reference to "protected" trades are, I think, worthy of being remembered.

I remain, &c. &c.

YOUR CORRESPONDENT FOR THE MANUFACTURING DISTRICTS.

# LABOUR AND THE POOR.

———◆———

## THE MANUFACTURING DISTRICTS.

[FROM OUR SPECIAL CORRESPONDENT.]

## THE POTTERIES.

## Letter XXXI.

About six years ago the working men of the Potteries set on foot a scheme which presented some features of novelty, and which has, so far as I can ascertain the facts, been to a certain degree successful. This was no other than the establishment of a "Potters' Joint-Stock Emigration Society and Savings Fund." Although apparently instituted for a two-fold purpose, the grand and predominating object of the scheme was to provide a home beyond the Atlantic for members of the trade. The Society has since been opened to persons following other occupations; but to the energy and enterprise of the potters, the original idea and its practical working are due. The rules, progress, and condition of this Emigration Society, I shall detail as fully as the data furnished to me will permit.

The Association was established in May, 1844, and was duly enrolled under act of Parliament. Its operations were at first strictly confined to potters and their families. The entrance fee was, and is, £1 1s. 6d., with an extra 1s. for rules, certificate, and card of membership. The weekly regular contribution was, and is, 6d. The society was thrown open about eight months ago. Before that period it had purchased and peopled an estate of 1,600 acres, called "Pottersville," situated at Columbia, in the State of Wisconsin, in North America—a portion of the district called, "The Oak Openings—" a region, by the way, which supplied Cooper with the name of one of his recent novels. The present number of the inhabitants of Pottersville is stated at 134. The association, having extended its means, is now in treaty for a tract of 50,000 acres, situated upon the Fox River, near Fort Winnebago. The preliminary arrangements for the purchase have indeed, I believe, been completed. The land will be formally made over in October, 1850, and in the meantime it is held by what is called "squatters' right." 250 families are either already located upon this land, or are on their way thither. The association has erected on its 50,000 acre estate "two good stores, seven miles apart, stocked with every variety of food, clothing, domestic utensils, farming implements, and live-stock—the whole" (I am quoting from a printed document, furnished to me by one of the secretaries)—"to be purchased by the colonists for a little moderate labour on the reserved land of the society." Of the reserved land in question, 300 acres are stated to be in cultivation; a ferry, with a proper boat, has been established; a blacksmith's shop is at work; and subscriptions are being raised in order to send out a grist-mill.

The beauties and advantages of the transatlantic Paradise are, of course, very glowingly set forth in all the manifestoes of the society; and it is to be hoped that the picture is as faithful as it is flattering. The soil is pronounced "surpassingly rich," and minerals, "it is expected," abound beneath the surface. The average crop of wheat is stated to be thirty bushels to the acre, and the average price of the bushel 3s. Indian corn, we are told, yields sixty or seventy bushels per acre. Grapes grow wild in the woods, and such game as deer and prairie hens are alleged to be abundant. The advantageous situation of Pottersville and the larger estate are then insisted upon. Milwaukei, a "most flourishing town" on Lake Michigan, is 90 miles distant from Pottersville. Fort Winnebago is on the Portage between the Fox and Wisconsin rivers, "on a great route between the Lakes and the Mississippi," and "sixteen oxen conveyances of new emigrants pass through Pottersville daily in the spring, summer, and autumn of the year." The prospectus goes on to state the cost at which an emigrant may be provided with house accommodation. A log dwelling of two rooms may be erected for about £10; a frame dwelling, with oaken floors, cement plaster to make the walls wind-and-water-tight—each room fourteen feet by twelve, with locks, doors, and latches complete—may be had for £12 10s. The cost of breaking up and sowing five acres—in the "openings," I presume—is stated at £5, and the average passage-money of an adult from an English port to Pottersville as about £8.

The mode in which the society works has now to be explained. It comprises an unlimited number of shares, the price of each being £1 1s. 6d., with the weekly payment of 6d. The possessor of a share has a right to the occupancy of 20 acres of land, but not to the permanent possession, until he has paid £5 10s. to the society—thus fixing the absolute cost of the allotments at 5s. 2½d. per acre. A person having become a shareholder, may immediately emigrate at his own expense, carrying with him his certificates. Upon each estate, or each department of the larger tract, estate stewards are resident, who are bound, upon the production of a certificate, to supply the bearer with a land allotment. The unappropriated allotments are balloted for, each emigrant drawing the number of his farm from a bag. So far as is possible, the allotments are so parcelled out as to contain each a "fair share of clear and wooded land." The emigrant, being put in possession, has a right to the store provisions of the society, and to the use of agricultural implements. These, I presume, include oxen for ploughing—the document from which I quote stating that a team of five oxen and a strong plough are requisite to break up the virgin prairie sod. "The frost of one winter turns the broken land into the richest soil." Until the emigrant clears accounts with the society, he holds his land only by a deed of lease duly signed. He may, if he be willing and able, pay the entire amount down before leaving home, in which case he is furnished with proper title deeds, conferring on him the freehold of the land; and he may also become entitled, by paying at the same time an additional £23, to a free passage, to a log hut when he arrives, and to the cultivation and fencing of one-fourth of his twenty-acre allotment; in short, the society professes to take up a working man, and upon the receipt of about £30, to settle him comfortably on his own land in Wisconsin. Emigrants not in command of the ready money may proceed on the terms which I have before described, and they are allowed six years after taking possession to repay the society for all advances made on their behoof. For the money no interest is charged; the exact sum expended is alone required to be returned, and the repayments may be made in wheat. In general the land is expected to be paid for by the weekly "levy" of sixpence. Thus a man who has been a member for a year has already paid nearly one-half of the purchase money of the twenty acres. A failure in the weekly instalment does not preclude the defaulter from the advantages of the money which he has already paid in. He may at any subsequent period renew his contributions, as if no lapse had taken place; but in the interim he will lose his right to ballot—an important privilege in the list of those which the society offers.

This balloting is in fact a sort of lottery—success in which entitles the winner to claim his land, outfit, and passage from the society, becoming bound to repay the whole within ten years. The process of balloting takes place at stated times, and every individual holding a share has a chance of being chosen. The ballot may be held at any place—in the rooms of any branch of the parent society—but its effect is always general. The mechanical plan adopted is peculiar. Each shareholder is distinguished by a number—these numbers being enrolled in duplicate on the central and branch books. They are also inscribed round the edge of the ballot-table—a circular apparatus four feet in diameter, every number being divided by "raised brass-work as sharp as the edge of a knife." By means of a large wheel moving on a pivot, and some other mechanical contrivances, a chance number is indicated, the possessor of which can claim the whole emigrating expenses of himself, wife, and all the members of his family under eighteen years of age, as well as the other advantages purchasable, as already stated, by less lucky members, at about £23. Two acres of his land he receives sown with Indian corn, and three with wheat. He is provided with agricultural implements and provisions for the first year of his settlement. The latter advantages he pays for in labour on the reserved land of the society, and the money actually laid out for him is repaid in ten yearly instalments of wheat. A winner at the ballot, if he is not prepared to proceed across the Atlantic, may sell his privilege to whom he pleases. I was informed that "ballots" have fetched as much as £18 and £20 a piece, the value of the claim to the original shareholder depending very much upon the number of his family. Loss of right to benefit by the chances of the ballot occurs when a member is four weeks in arrear with his sixpences, but he recovers his claim if he can prove that the deficiency in payments was caused either by sickness or unavoidable loss of work. For every additional £1 1s. 6d. paid in to the society a member obtains a right to an additional chance of the ballot, without, however, incurring any further weekly responsibility than the original sixpences. As to the land purchased by the society, the scheme proposes its ultimate division into separate estates of 2,000 acres each. Each of these will comprehend 100 allotments of 20 acres each. One half of these allotments are reserved for sale purposes, their cultivation being effected by the labour due to the society in payment for provisions and the use of agricultural implements. At any future time which may seem most advisable for the interests of the society, these cleared and cultivated allotments will be offered for sale, the colonists having the preference. Should the latter not purchase, the land will be sold to strangers. Things are so managed that the reserved patches alternate, in position, with the allotted ones. The acre, I should mention, is reckoned at 4,840 square yards. One of the allegations put forth by the society is, that in Wisconsin all kinds of farming stock—live stock is meant, I presume—are 400 per cent. cheaper than in England; and among the inducements to working men to emigrate, the political franchise of the United States, acquired on the easy terms of a six months residence in the territory, is not forgotten. A somewhat singular undertaking which the society professes to accomplish is, in case of the death of the head of a family incapacitating its surviving members from continuing the yearly instalments of repayment, to "take such family under its care, and protect it in its adversity until the said family be equal to the honest discharge of its liabilities." In all the estates, save that of Pottersville, the salaries of the land-stewards are to be paid by means of a commission on the sale of store goods. It is expressly stipulated that no particular allotment will be reserved for a shareholder who does not choose to take possession at once. The land-steward, or local manager, is bound to find land for a member presenting his certificate, and, if no allotment remain unoccupied, "a new purchase must be made." No money paid into the coffers of the society is to be returned, except in case of a dissolution of the association, or when a member is emigrating on his own resources, in which event the money he has paid up is of course expended upon him.

In the document from which I have mainly gathered the foregoing facts, an appeal is made to trades to connect themselves *en masse* with the society. It is urged that they would thus secure a quick and cheap means of providing for their unemployed brethren, and of course lessening the burden of competition upon themselves. They are reminded that for the money advanced from the trade funds for the purchase of membership, the payment of passage, and the erection of a log-hut, there will be landed security—the sum being entered in the deed of lease, and the annual repayments being made to the estate-steward, and finally to the trade through the parent society. The exponents of the Potters' Emigration scheme, in developing their views in this respect, venture a little on delicate ground. How superior, they plead, would the adoption of some such means of rapid emigration be to the "common plan of strikes and turn-outs—to the supporting of willing labourers in a state of pernicious idleness;" and then the writer proceeds to put this query—"Could not a new system of strikes be established, by clearing a work, at once—by making farmers of the turn-outs—and then dictating terms for a new complement of hands?" The spirit of this proposition does not seem peculiarly conciliating. "Dictating" is a harsh word on either side; but, absurd in some respects as the scheme may be, the idea is worth noting as one of the moving straws in the atmosphere of our social and industrial system.

In the last published report of the affairs of the society I see it stated that about £1,690 has actually been remitted to America for the purchase of land, stores, &c. The estate of Pottersville is represented as being worth four times its original purchase-money; but it is regretted that "a great portion of the money and provisions advanced to the colonists on that estate still remains unsettled." Payment, it is announced, however, "can and will be" enforced. It seems that matters had fallen into some confusion at the time when the society was thrown open to all trades, but the accounts have been audited, and things are now stated to be advancing prosperously. The number of land certificates sent out has been 350—each, in almost every case, representing a family. The number of members now connected with the society is 3,500. The treasurer and committee seem to be recompensed on a scale of laudable economy; the amount paid to the former being 5s. weekly, and to each member of the latter 1s. for each meeting. The Potters' Trade Union was dissolved in June last, when the scheme was made general. In one of the documents before me, there is a list of the branch clubs or associations scattered throughout the chief towns of Great Britain, in connection with the parent body. The number of those enumerated is 105, and the amount of money received from them, from the 8th of June, 1840, to the 8th of September, 1849, is about £2,871. The names of some of these local clubs are not without their significance. I transcribe a few. "The Home in the West," Crewe; "The Emigrant's Castle," Newcastle; "The Land of the Free," Preston; "The Washington," Manchester; "The Emancipation," Manchester; "The Liberty," Leek; "The People's Hope," Macclesfield; "The Star in the West," Warrington; "The Land of Liberty," Manchester; "The Hope in the West," Farnworth; "The Workman's Resource," Manchester; "The Labourer's Refuge," Oldham; "The Hope of Independence," Manchester; "The New Paradise," Ashton; "The Poor Man's Hope," Duckinfield; "The Spinner's Home," Preston; "The Republican," Halifax; "The Rights of Labour," Kilbirnie; "The United Labour," Oldham; "The Hope of Freedom," Bury; "The Tree of Liberty," Birmingham; "The Slave's Hope," Hull; "The Stripes and Stars," London; "The Prairie," Manchester; "The American Prospect," Dundee; "The New Ark," Dale Hill. There is one foreign branch—"The Abbeville," in the town of the same name.

A feature in the constitution of this association is that they have established a small weekly newspaper, the *Potters' Examiner*, published in Shelton, and exclusively devoted to promoting the objects and gaining the necessary publicity for the schemes in view. The printing apparatus and premises are the property of the association, and much of the typographical work of the various working men's societies throughout the district is performed at their office. The paper itself is published at one penny, and is usually filled with reports of the proceedings of branch clubs, and with copious extracts of letters received from the emigrants. Some of them have also been published in a separate shape. In the numbers of the *Potters' Examiner* which I had an opportunity of seeing, the letters published from the settlers in Wisconsin appeared to me to have been fairly enough selected. The general tone was by no means that of men suddenly finding themselves in an earthly paradise. There was nothing, in short, of a claptrap character about the documents. The various obstacles and hardships encountered were set down candidly enough. Many cases of the quarrel and split-up of parties were narrated, and the grand chorus was, "Let no one come out here who is afraid of rough living and hard work." In a few instances, "home sickness" was ominously alluded to, and *àpropos* of one of these, the writer adds—"The London men are the worst of all."

I have now given as detailed and minute an account as possible of the "Potters' Emigration Society," not because of any intrinsic importance possessed by the institution, but because it was the first—and is, so far as I can learn, the only—association of working men for the avowed purpose of facilitating emigration. Respecting the ability of the body to accomplish the work which it professes to undertake, I know nothing. I have described its plan of operations, not as the grand scheme of an all-potent corporation, but simply as a phenomenon constituting an instructive sign of the times. To a certain extent the principle of the Building Societies would seem, in this instance, to have been applied to emigration. And, so far as I can see, there is nothing unreasonable in the supposition that, if association and small weekly payments can provide a man with a home in England, the same agency may be employed in securing for him a freehold in the United States.

About a couple of miles from Hanley, lying to the west of the line of Pottery towns, is the ancient borough of Newcastle-under-Lyme. The latter portion of the name refers to what was once a tract of forest land, skirting the eminences above the town. A brook, called the Lyme, not many degrees removed from the status of a common sewer, runs through the place. The population in 1841 amounted to 19,489; and the number of living persons to one death during the seven years from 1838 to 1844, was rather more than 40. Newcastle-under-Lyme, although lying on the outskirts of the Pottery district, has nothing in common with it. The town is ancient and quaint—the houses frequently exhibiting high peaked gables, and the bye streets being narrow, old-fashioned, and tortuous. The massive square tower surmounting the church is of vast and obvious antiquity. A casual glimpse of the borough reveals little to distinguish it from scores of common-place English country towns. The visitor from the Potteries will look in vain for any sign of the industry which he has just left. No piles of smashed pottery ware lie mouldering in yards and corners. A few tall chimneys are visible, but the chances are that they will be smokeless; and the spectator may, perhaps, in connection with this ominous symptom, observe men with aprons, having the appearance of operatives in some textile branch of industry, lounging listlessly about the street corners.

Newcastle-under-Lyme is, in fact, the seat of a dying—almost a dead trade—that of the manufacture of beaver hats. Factories which once gave constant employment to hundreds of hands now provide fitful jobs for perhaps a dozen or a score; and workmen, who were once engaged in the production of the most expensive hats, now think themselves lucky if they can earn a pittance by the manufacture of coarse felt "wide awakes," locally called "caps." The introduction of silk hats has been, as I understand, the cause of this revulsion in the trade. The old beavers have all but gone out of use. The cheap silk hats manufactured in London, in Lancashire, and abroad, have completely supplanted the more expensive article, and ruined the staple trade of Newcastle.

Without much difficulty I found out an intelligent operative hatter—one of the few still lingering about the scene of their former prosperity, and striving, by the profits of uncertain and ill-paid labour, to make both ends meet. His account of the state of the hatting trade in Newcastle-under-Lyme was nearly as follows:—

"Out of the multitude of people engaged in the hatting business twenty years ago there are now, I should say, hardly a hundred left in Newcastle. The trade is gone away and ruined. Since the cheap silk hats came in, hardly anything else is made. If an order does come, the wages are a mere nothing to what they used to be. The men struggle for the job, and so bring wages down. I mean the few of us who are left. The great body of the Newcastle hatters are gone long since. There was not a living for them here. They had to take to all manner of trades—to do anything for a living. Some of them went to work in the clay-pits; others went to the brick-fields. Some got to be potters; lots went to be cotton-spinners in Lancashire; others turned railway navvies; and a good many went to London to work at silk-hatting if they could, or to do anything which might turn up. In fact, they're all broken up and away. A good many of those who had the means went off to America, and some had to go to the workhouse. Of the hundred or so who are still here, the most are making felt caps, and some few have turned their hands to silk hats; but the silk is quite a different trade from the beaver; and it is hard for a grown-up man, who has served an apprenticeship, to set to and learn another craft. In the good days of the beaver trade, the hatters used to work, the most of them, in factory, and a smaller number at their own homes, or in shops attached to them. These shops were principally at the backs of the houses. The owners of them were generally piece-masters, as they were called, and they had the privilege of taking apprentices. I am a piece-master; but of course there are no apprentices now. That is all over. The piece-masters worked for a factory. They got the materials from the manufacturer, and took back the finished goods. Besides the beavers, there was a common sort of hat manufactured to a very great extent in Newcastle. They were called 'stuff hats.' I have known a single firm here have upwards of 32,000 dozen of these hats on stock. They were exported to America and the West Indies for the slaves. Thirty years ago the prices paid for making the bodies of stuff hats were 8s., 9s., and 10s. per dozen. The same work is done now-a-days for 2s. 9d. The old prices for making the body of a beaver hat were 2s. 6d. and 3s. a-piece; they are now made for 14d. and 15d., and sometimes for even less than that. When the hat trade was fairly broken up, and the people gone, a great swarm of Irish came, and took possession of the houses. In a district called the Blue-buildings, three-fourths of the people used to be English hatters, and now three-fourths, and more than that, are Irish. A few, but only a very few, of these Irish try to work at hatting; the great bulk of them go strolling about, begging, and collecting bones, rags, bottles, and the like. The few who work at hatting have been regularly brought up in the trade. The wages that a man can earn at cap-making are very low; he might almost as well be idle. The bulk of that trade is in Lancashire. I have said that a body-maker is now paid 2s. 9d. per dozen. It takes a good week's work to make four dozen, and a very hard week's work to make four dozen and a half. But there is little work even at this price. I have had only two dozen for the last 15 weeks, and there are many as ill off as I am. A 'rougher' would be paid about 5s. 6d. per dozen, and he would 'rough' from three dozen to four dozen a week. A finisher would have about 3s. per dozen, and he might turn out about seven dozen, or rather more, a week. The men who have learned silk hatting can't make a pound a week. These are about the prices when there is work. We hope there will be some potteries started here soon. They talk about it, as soon as a new branch railway is opened. Then perhaps we should have a chance of turning our hands to something new, for there's no use in talking about making a living in the hat trade any longer."

I proceeded to several small shops where the caps, or wide-awakes, were manufactured, but found only one open. It was merely a miserable, crazy shed, crusted over with dirt from long neglect. Four or five men were at work within it. They made any sort of hats for which they could get an order; but the wide-awakes formed their staple trade. Working twelve hours a day, when they could get work, they assured me that they hardly earned 10s. a week. The hours some of the men laboured, when an order came in, were excessive—sometimes from three in the morning until ten at night. "But, as I might well conceive," they added, "it is not from over-work we suffer."

*The Derby Mercury, Wednesday, February 6, 1850.*

## LEICESTER AND ITS NEIGHBOURHOOD.

The report which appeared in the Morning Chronicle, has created quite a stir among the operatives of the Borough, they having been shown as earning a greater amount of wages than is really the fact; full three-fourths of the glove, wrought hose, straight-down, shirt and drawers, and other weaving branches, and the wool-combing hands, not receiving weekly scarcely half the amount as is in that statement represented.

It appears that, from nearly all the manufactories or factories in Leicester, a "middle man," or by some called a "bagman," is employed to receive the materials for working up from the master hosiers, &c.— taking home the work when finished. Some of those, for instance, take for 12 frames on a Monday morning, which during the day is given out to different weavers; this middle-man making those materials supply in addition to the 12 represented to the manufacturer six other independent frames of his own. Those articles, on being finished, are collected and taken home by this bagman at the close of the week, and given in as being the work of only 12 hands—when it is, in fact, that of 18. He is paid for them as 12 hands, and such are entered only as 12 hands he (the middle-man) receives, and the payer conceives that the amount given out has to be divided only among 12 men, it is entered in the master's books as such. These, on being shewn to a reporter, perhaps ignorant of such deception, he is led to believe and to publish it to the world that the working-men of Leicester, and in the county throughout, are earning good and remunerative wages; when, in truth, they are generally suffering the most intense poverty and deprivation.

Fancy hands, when in full work, do earn fair wages; but then it appears, from the statement made by the operatives, that the good season is only for about four months in the year, at two different seasons, viz., in February and March and about two months just before Christmas: during the other eight months they seldom earn more than from 5s. to 7s. per week, and are then subject to the same expenses for hire of frame, &c.

Being anxious to arrive at the simple and clear facts, we appointed to meet some of the most expert and intelligent hands; each speaker was requested to make his statement as concise as possible, and to confine himself to simple matter of facts, as what they said would no doubt be published in the public London and country newspapers, and, if wrong, would certainly be replied to, and contradicted. All present declared that nothing should be said but what they were prepared to prove and abide by.

The first who spoke was a 24 glove branch hand. The names of all were taken, but for obvious reasons it is not deemed prudent to publish them. This man stated as follows:—I am a married man—have no children—have worked at the glove trade for the last five years. The highest wages I earn is 20s. per week; some weeks 15s., others not more than 10s.; at times, when on short work, not above 9s. Mine is a four handed frame. I am charged weekly—*work or play*—4s. 9d. for frame, winding, and standing, and have also to pay 2s. per week for the rent of a two-roomed dwelling. Many weeks, after deducting expenses, I have not more than from 4s. to 5s. left, to keep myself and wife through the whole week. In the same shop that I work in, it is no uncommon thing for the middle-man to send the poor framework-knitter to the relieving officer, to solicit from him a small pittance to add to his small earnings, to enable him to buy bread for his famishing family. The work at this branch of trade is good about six months in the year, the remaining part very flat. My earnings do not exceed 8s. per week, generally working 16 hours each day, in the best of the year, after deducting the various expenses. I know those making fine gloves out of factories, whose earnings are quite as scanty.

The next who spoke was one employed in the *wrought hose branch*, whose statement was authenticated by a fellow workman. He said—I think there are about ten thousand hands now working at this branch of the trade in and around Leicester, the majority not earning more than from 6s. to 7s. per week, and neat hands too; perhaps some may make occasionally 9s. per week, but of those very few. All have to pay 1s. per week for hire of frame, 6d. for winding, 6d. for standing and taking in, besides for seaming, needles, candles, fire, &c., amounting in the winter to 1s. per week, and in the summer to about 3d. They are paid by the dozen, at from 2s. 3d. up to 4s. per dozen. At the highest price, ready hands may make from two to two dozen and a half in a week of six days, 15 to 16 hours each day; those at 2s. 3d. per dozen, fair hands, will turn out from three to four dozen in a week; but aged, and inferior hands, will not make more than from two to two dozen and a half of the commonest sorts.

The next who gave a statement was a man employed in the *Straight-down branch*, viz., on those hose where there is no narrowing in the legs nor heels. He said—I am a married man, with a wife and nine children; seven at home earning nothing; myself, wife, and those seven children have to be supported from my small earnings; I have also to pay 2s. 6d. per week as rent for my dwelling; I am considered to be as good a hand as most men at my trade, and lose as little time, yet my average earnings, throughout the year, do not exceed from 16s. to 17s. a week; my frame is 4-hose; I am charged 5s. 9d. per week for the hire of it, and other expenses; if in some weeks I earn but 10s., I am still charged the 5s. 9d.; or should it be but as much as would cover that charge, all would be stopped; in the winter it costs me a further 1s. per week for needles, candles, and extra firing; I work in a regular way from 14 to 16 hours each day, viz., from 5 in the morning till 11 o'clock at night; I work at what is known as out journey work; I do not go home from morning till night; frequently take my little food I have, and eat it at the frame, without stopping my work; some weeks my earnings are not more than from 5s. to 6s., yet, on the Monday morning, in comes the landlord for his 2s. 6d. rent, and will not leave till he has got it.

The next, a *shirt* and *drawer* workman, said—I have worked at this branch for the last five or six years, labouring generally six days, 14 hours each day if I can get it to do; am paid by the dozen, prices vary materially, from 6s. as high as 15s. per dozen; a good hand may make a dozen in a week of those at 15s. a dozen, and perhaps two dozen of the lower priced sorts, out of such earnings has to be paid 3s. 8d. per week for hire of frame, winding, taking-in, and standing; and about 9d. a dozen for needles, candles, &c. This part of the Leicester trade is looked upon as being as regular as most branches, yet if the average earnings, the year round, is 10s. per week, it is considered good, as many first-rate hands do not make more than from 7s. to 8s. per dozen.

We next heard from one of two *woolcombers* present the following—We are both married men, with families. We work by the piece, on our master's premises. We have the wool given out by the score pounds to comb, earning, when in full six days' work, about 12s. We have to pay 1s. each for comb rent and firing. Work is pretty good for from six to eight months in the year; during the other four months often very slack; then we often do not earn more than from 6s. to 8s. per week. We have to pay each 2s. per week as rent for tenement under our master; work or not, it is charged, and we dare not grumble. The master they worked for employed about 70 hands, and has eight carding machines, each machine doing as much in one day as four men formerly did in a week by the old system. It is said that the various carding machines now working in Leicester have deprived at least 800 hands of work in that branch of trade, each machine carding five packs of wool, of 240 lbs. weight each, in six days.

A large meeting of the operatives was held on Tuesday night last, at Mr. Gisborne's King and Crown Inn, Town Hall-lane, Leicester, at which the above written statements were confirmed by the different deputations from the committees deputed from the different operative associations existing in the borough.—*From a Correspondent of Payne's Leicester and Midland Counties Advertiser.*

# LABOUR AND THE POOR.

—◆—

## THE MANUFACTURING DISTRICTS.

[FROM OUR SPECIAL CORRESPONDENT.]

### SHEFFIELD.

### Letter XXXII.

Around a spot in the West Riding of Yorkshire, only a few miles from the borders of Derbyshire, where five streams unite—one of them a deep, sedgy, and slow-flowing brook, the others shallow, brawling, and rapid rivulets—stands the town of Sheffield. These

Five rivers, like the fingers of a hand,"

as the Corn-law Rhymer calls them, do not actually unite at a single point, but they mingle their waters within the area covered by the buildings of the great cutlery emporium. Their names are the Sheaf, the Don, the Loxeley, the Porter, and the Reviling. Of these the Sheaf flows most quietly, although the most liable to sudden and overwhelming floods. The Don pours down the most continuously ample volumes, and the others, losing themselves in his waters and his name, form the river which flows through the broad champagne country about Doncaster, to swell, first, the Ouse, and afterwards the Humber.

Sheffield stands about the point where the wild hilly country—in part wooded, in part moorland—amongst which its rivers rise, begins to fine away into the smooth expanse of the south-easterly plains of Yorkshire. The precipitous and picturesque district, stretching westward from the town, gradually rises into the great heathery ridge, the northern continuation of which I have so frequently had occasion to allude to under the local title which in various places it bears, of the "backbone of England." To the south, this long mountain range loses itself in the expanses of what was once Charnwood Forest. Dodworth calls the ridge the "English Appenines," because the "rain-water which there falleth sheddeth from sea to sea." Above

Sheffield, the steep glens cleaving its sides, and down which descend the five streamlets I have mentioned, are full of picturesque and woodland glimpses. There lies gloriously piled a far-stretching panorama of forest, and knoll, and cliff. Oaks of vast girth and spread are common in the district: grey scaurs of naked rock rise grimly from the foliage. The streams come dancing downwards with many a foaming rapid and sparkling fall. In addition to the natural ledges and weirs of rock which stretch across the current there are scores of artificial dams—the water-power thus obtained and regulated turning many a grindstone, and moving many a forging-hammer upon the banks.

In this wild woodland district the ancient forest game of England long lingered. The significant appellation of "Chace" is still applied to widespread regions of glade and pasture; and Hunter says, in his History of Hallamshire, published in 1819, that one of these, "Loxeley Chace, was in the memory of man wholly unenclosed and uncultivated." The name of Loxeley, although the ancient spelling is not preserved, will awaken many memories. It was the "Locksley" of old—the birth-place of Robin Hood, and the district from which he derived his real name. It is only within the present generation that the ruins of a house, in which tradition said that the stout yeoman was born, have disappeared; but a fountain of pure water in the vicinity is still reverenced by the peasants as "Robin Hood's Well." On the sylvan sports and sylvan fare of Wharncliffe Chace, Taylor, the Water-poet, dilates with great gusto, in his well-known northern tour, in which, with a greater regard for alliteration than for sense, he professes to give "News from Hell, Hull, and Halifax." Taylor was the guest of "Sir Francis Wortley," one of whose ancestors, in the time of Henry VIII., built a hunting-lodge on one of the highest peaks of the then green-wood wildernesses, "for his pleasure," as a beautifully quaint inscription still testifies—"for his pleasure to hear the hart's bell." In this same house, by the way, Lady Mary Wortley passed several years after her marriage. In after years, writing from Avignon, she describes a landscape in the South of Europe as the finest she had ever seen— "except Wharncliffe Chace."

Sheffield, as most people are aware, has more than a five-hundred-years-old reputation for cutlery. Of the jovial miller in the "Canterbury Pilgrimage" we have this graphic picture:—

> " A Shefeld thwytel bare he in his hose,
> Ronde was his face and camysed was his nose."

It has been remarked as singular, that in the earliest enumerations we have of steel articles manufactured in Sheffield, there is no mention made of warlike weapons—unless, indeed, the "thwytel" or "whittle"—a knife worn down to the time of Charles I. by those whose rank did not permit them to bear more honourable arms—be taken as an instrument of offence. Still it is to be presumed that among the knives, reaping-hooks, and shears, manufactured upon the banks of the five rivers, there were also blades for daggers and swords, and steel heads for lances and cloth-yard shafts. The arms of the church burgesses of Sheffield are, indeed, a sheaf of arrows. In its early days, however, the town by no means enjoyed a monopoly in the production of cutting steel implements. Up to the time of Elizabeth, knives of France and "Almayne" were regular articles of import. London, Godalming, Salisbury, and Woodstock had also their cutlery manufactures—the bulk of the knives made in Sheffield being "for the common use of the common people," and sold to them for 1d. a piece. There were then—I speak of the times of Elizabeth and James—no great cutlery establishments in or around Sheffield. The trade was carried on by a great number of small masters, whose grinding wheels were wrought by the rapid waters of the Loxeley and the Reviling. The rules existing in 1590 for the government of the craft are, as might be expected, conceived in the narrowest spirit of restriction, and contain several stipulations curious for their very absurdity. The first article, indeed, provides that no master, servant, or apprentice shall perform any work "appertayneing to the scyence or mysterye of cutlers" for eight-and-twenty days next ensuing the 28th of August in each year, nor from Christmas to the 23d of January—but shall apply themselves to other labours, under the "payne of forfeyture of twentye shillings" to the lord of the manor, then one of the Earls of Shrewsbury. The regulations went on to stipulate that each master should be entitled to only one apprentice, and that no person should presume to exercise the craft unless he had learned it within the lordship. These bye-laws were, no doubt, framed with the honest intention of benefiting the neighbourhood, according to the notions of economical science then current; and the last clause declares that the ordinances preceding shall be made null and void in case that they are not found to benefit the "poorer sort." That a large proportion of the cutlers of Sheffield came under the latter denomination, is proved by an exceedingly curious document, copies of which are common in the town. I transcribe it entire, conceiving it to throw a striking light upon a portion of the good old times:—

> "By a survaie of the town of Sheffield, made the second day of January, 1615, by twenty-four of the most sufficient inhabitants there, it appeareth that there are in the town of Sheffield 2,207 people; of which there are—
> 725 which are not able to live without the charity of their neighbours. These are all begging poore.
> 100 householders which relieve others. These (though the beste sort) are but poore artificers; among them there is not one which can keep a teame on his own land, and not above tenn who have grounds of their owne that wille keep a cow.
> 160 householders not able to relieve others. These are such (though they beg not) as are not able to abide the storme of one fortnight's sicknesse, but would be therebye driven to beggary.
> 1,222 servants and children of the said householders, the greatest part of which are such as live of small wages, and are constrained to work sore to provide them necessaries."

From this document, the authenticity of which I am informed is undoubted, it would appear that in the early part of the seventeenth century nearly one-third of the inhabitants of Sheffield were habitual begging paupers; that nearly one-fourth of the remainder were living from hand to mouth, in a condition only one degree removed from pauperism; that not one-twentieth of the whole number of house-holders were able to rent the patch of land (then no doubt to be had cheaply enough) sufficient to support a cow; and that the great majority of the entire population, young and old, were compelled to "work sore to provide them with necessaries."

Such was the pauperised state of Sheffield two centuries ago; and from the terms of the account we have no right to come to any other conclusion than that the condition indicated was the chronic, if not the normal, state of things. Let us now glance at the pauper statistics of the town in modern days:—

| Year Ending Easter, | Population. | Valuation for Poor-Rate. | Number in Workhouse. |
|---|---|---|---|
| 1825 | 47,335 | £50,000 | not known |
| 1830 | 57,565 | 55,000 | 334 |
| 1831 | 59,011 | 56,500 | 319 |
| 1832 | 60,440 | 59,000 | 315 |
| 1833 | 61,951 | 61,500 | 374 |
| 1834 | 63,326 | 63,800 | 328 |
| 1835 | 64,569 | 65,000 | 312 |
| 1836 | 65,704 | 66,800 | 227 |
| 1837 | 66,725 | 71,520 | 252 |
| 1838 | 67,628 | 152,340 | 353 |
| 1839 | 68,408 | 157,240 | 349 |
| 1840 | 69,062 | 156,200 | 352 |
| 1841 | 69,587 | 161,142 | 460 |

The above table extends over a period of great prosperity and rampant speculation, and into a period of great depression and distress. The latter cycle commenced about 1836, and has, with some slight alleviations, continued, as regards this town, till within a year or two. At the period when the distress was most profound, the number of persons in receipt of relief amounted to upwards of one-eleventh of the entire population. The difference thus visible between a modern period of depression and the ancient ordinary condition of things, is striking and instructive. At present the trade of the town is fast recovering from its long-continued lethargy. The improvement which has taken place since this time last year, as well as the actually existing state of things, is palpably shown by the following abstract of returns lately made from the Sheffield Union. They contain a statement of the relief given in four corresponding weeks in 1848 and 1849 to destitute able-bodied workmen—most of them, of course, operatives engaged in the staple occupations of the town.

SHEFFIELD UNION.

| EMPLOYMENT OR OCCUPATION. | Number of each Class relieved in your District, in the four last weeks of the Quarter ended Dec. 25, 1848. | Number of each Class relieved in your District, in the four last weeks of the Quarter ended Dec. 25, 1849. | Average rate of wages at Christmas, 1848. | Average rate of wages at Christmas, 1849. |
|---|---|---|---|---|
| | | | s.   s. | s.   s. |
| Agricultrual & other Labourers | 13 | 4 | 12 to 15 | 12 to 15 |
| Carpenters and Joiners ...... | 2 | — | 20 to 24 | 20 to 24 |
| Moulders ............... | 3 | 1 | 18 to 25 | 18 to 25 |
| Surgeon ................. | 1 | — | — | — |
| Draper .................. | 1 | — | — | — |
| Rod Roller ............. | 1 | — | 18 to 25 | 18 to 25 |
| File Hardeners ........... | 1 | — | 15 to 20 | 15 to 20 |
| File Cutters ............. | 3 | — | 18 to 30 | 18 to 30 |
| Scissors Grinders ......... | 5 | — | 18 to 22 | 18 to 22 |
| Ditto Forgers ............ | 4 | 2 | 16 to 20 | 16 to 20 |
| Edge-Tool Forgers ........ | 6 | 2 | 20 to 30 | 20 to 30 |
| Table Knife Cutlers ....... | 8 | — | 8 to 16 | 8 to 16 |
| Ditto Grinders ........... | 9 | 1 | 10 to 16 | 10 to 16 |
| Spring Knife Cutlers ...... | 6 | 1 | 12 to 18 | 12 to 18 |
| Pearl Cutters ........... | 1 | — | 15 | 15 |
| Silversmiths ............. | 1 | — | 25 | 25 |
| Engravers ............... | 1 | — | 15 to 30 | 15 to 30 |
| Smiths ................. | 1 | — | 18 | 18 |
| Button Makers ........... | 2 | — | 10 to 12 | 10 to 12 |
| Razor Grinders .......... | 7 | 2 | 14 to 22 | 14 to 22 |
| Glass Grinders ........... | 1 | — | 16 to 20 | 16 to 20 |
| Colliers ................. | 3 | — | 15 to 30 | 15 to 30 |
| Whitesmiths ............ | — | 1 | — | — |
| File Forgers ............ | 1 | — | 32 to 36 | 32 to 36 |
| File Grinders ............ | 3 | — | 28 to 40 | 28 to 40 |
| Table Knife Hafters ....... | 4 | — | 8 to 16 | 8 to 16 |
| Edge-Tool Grinders ....... | 1 | — | 20 to 30 | 20 to 30 |
| Spindle Turners .......... | 1 | — | 16 to 18 | 16 to 18 |
| Steel Millers ............. | 1 | 1 | 20 to 30 | 20 to 30 |
| Wire Workers ............ | 1 | — | — | — |
| Scissors Filers ........... | 1 | — | 16 to 20 | 16 to 20 |
| Razor-Blade Strikers ...... | 1 | — | 16 | 16 |
| Auger Makers ........... | 1 | — | 15 to 20 | 15 to 20 |
| Fender Makers ........... | 1 | — | 28 | 28 |
| Edge-Tool Hardeners ..... | — | 1 | 24 | 24 |
| Anvil Makers ............ | 1 | — | 20 | 20 |

| Is the amount of reduction in wages, where reduction has taken place, comparatively greater or less than the reduction in the price of provisions? | State whether the demand for labour in each class is greater or less at the present time than at the same period of last year. |
|---|---|

Though there has been but little variation as to the prices paid to artisans in most of the trades, yet there is no doubt but the demand for labour in each class has been much greater at Christmas, 1849, than 1848. This has been clearly proved both by the difference in the amount of wages paid by the manufacturers, and the increased receipts by the retail shopkeepers, in the week preceding the 25th of December last. The difference in the price of provisions also, viz., meat, flour, potatoes, and groceries, between the two years, has been in favour of the consumer.

I have before me a similar return from the Ecclesall Bierlow Union, comprehending three of the townships—urban, suburban, and rural—of Sheffield. The number of able-bodied persons relieved was, in the two periods of 1848 and 1849 respectively, 74 and 6. The number of agricultural labourers relieved in the four weeks of 1848 was 10; in the corresponding period of 1849 it was 1. The number of persons connected with the staple trade relieved at each period was respectively 58 and 3.

I continue my notices of the gradual growth of the town and trade of Sheffield. In 1624 the cutlers were incorporated by act of Parliament; the necessity for such a guild having arisen from the old regulations having fallen into disuse, whereby various interlopers untaught in the mystery were "likely to have wrought scandal upon the cutlers of that lordship and liberty, and disgrace and hindrance of the sale of cutlery." By this charter the letter of the old by-laws was altered, and their spirit relaxed. Masters were allowed, under certain conditions, to take two apprentices, and the use of distinctive marks upon the wares of each workman was strictly enjoined. The managers of the guild were a corporation of thirty-three persons—the "Master Cutler"—a title still surviving—being at their head.

About 360 persons were immediately enrolled members of the company, and in 1638 a hall was built. By the beginning of the next century the incorporated cutlers of Sheffield and its neighbourhood amounted to about 6,000 persons, and several thousand more were engaged in occupations allied to the cutlery manufacture. The value of the goods then produced was estimated at about £100,000 per annum, half of which was exported. About 1,500 tons of Sheffield goods were yearly forwarded to Hull. Still there were no great establishments, with the exception of some few of the converting and smelting furnaces. The cutlers were almost entirely small masters, supplying the agents of London houses, and seldom sending their wares on their own account from forge or grinding-wheel, except now and then when they might risk a small venture to the fairs of Chester or Bristol.

The Sheffield manufacturers formed then a rude and unlettered populace. A very small number of books, kept in the vestry of the parish church, was the only library in the town; and it is said that the severe labour then necessary in certain processes of the staple manufacture, and now performed by machinery and steam, was wont to produce a melancholy proportion of injured and distorted limbs. The only communication between Sheffield and London was conducted by packhorses traversing dangerous and miry ways. The streets were formed of plain substantial stone houses, and the only structural adornment to be seen was here and there a rude carving of the town's emblem—the arrow-sheaf. About the end of the first half of the last century, the Don was made navigable for barges nearly up to Sheffield; not, however, until after a long and fierce battle fought with the squires, whose lands were benefited by the improved means of communication, but who considered the undertaking as an attack upon their privacy. In 1742 the process of silver plating was introduced, and it has grown up to be an important branch of trade; and soon afterwards the inhabitants, eager for "Latest Intelligence," made a spirited arrangement, by which the *Northampton Mercury*, published in that town on Saturday, was circulated in Sheffield upon the Monday. A curious account of the advance towards politeness of the burgesses of Sheffield about this period is to be found in "Hunter's History of Hallamshire"—how the neighbouring gentry began to resort to the annual cutlers' feast—and how the inhabitants, having set on foot assemblies, danced gaily in a charity school beneath the light of tallow candles stuck in sconces of tin.

It was not until the commencement of the era of merchants as well as of manufacturers—of warehouses as well as of grinding-mills and forges—that Sheffield rapidly advanced upon the track which has brought it to its present eminence. Then new streets sprung up fast—new roads were opened—old roads improved—banks, libraries, and a newspaper established—valuable shops and ample hotels opened—and all the paraphernalia of a great modern town created. Immense local improvements, structural and architectural, were effected, one by one, and despite the shocks given to its trade by successive American and French wars, the cutlery of Sheffield rapidly attained that pre-eminence which it still holds in the markets of the world.

In 1796 the population of the town was 9,095, and of the parish of Sheffield, 14,105. In 1821 they were respectively 31,314 and 45,758. In 1831 they were 42,157 and 65,275; and by the last census they were 69,587 and 112,492. During the ten years previous to 1841, the number of occupied houses had increased by 4,691, and the number of the population by 20,800. Of that decennial period, three years—those of 1834, 1835, and 1836—were characterised by extraordinary prosperity. New streets and manufactories sprung up as if by magic, and "five joint-stock banks," says Dr. Holland, "fiercely competed with each other for the privilege and honour of giving credit."

Sheffield Saw Manufacture.—Grinding

In 1836 the value of the hardware exports of Great Britain—to which Sheffield of course contributed a great share—rose from £1,833,043 to £2,271,313, the amounts for 1833 and 1834 having been about £1,400,000. In the year succeeding the panic of 1837, the value had sunk to about its old level of £1,400,000. From that time until very recently the trade of Sheffield has languished, year by year.

| | | |
|---|---|---|
| In the year ending March 1837, the total amount of relief was | | £10,548 |
| Ditto | 1838 | 14,084 |
| Ditto | 1839 | 15,516 |
| Ditto | 1840 | 18,065 |
| Ditto | 1841 | 23,806 |
| Ditto | 1842 | 23,716 |

On March 1, 1843, there were in the receipt of outdoor relief upwards of 720 able-bodied workmen, connected with the different staple branches of the town's industry. As will be seen by future statements which I have to make, the rates even at this period of great and universal distress would have pressed in a still heavier proportion upon the solvent population, had it not been for the accumulated funds of many of the Trades Unions, which were lavishly dispensed during the period of depression. Without following any further the history of the long and dreary cycle of distress, I may at once state the gratifying fact, that at present there are but few workmen connected with any branch of the cutlery trade who cannot obtain fairly remunerative employment.

The remark is, I think, made by Mr. Porter in one of his statistical works, that the operatives of Sheffield possess superior house accommodation to that enjoyed by the great bulk of our manufacturing population. To this part of the subject I shall in a future communication* devote attention; in this preliminary sketch of the town, some general statements upon the point may suffice. There are in Sheffield many old, crowded, and filthy localities, and a very considerable proportion of the operatives' dwellings are constructed back to back. They usually open either upon streets, or, according to Dr. Holland's "Vital Statistics of Sheffield," into "moderately spacious yards." Generally speaking, the cottage houses contain a small cellar, a living room about twelve feet square, a chamber of the same size above, and, in perhaps one-half of the entire number, an attic about seven feet high over the chamber. Cases are rare in which more than one artisan's family inhabit the same house, and cellar-dwellings are totally unknown. The rents run from 1s. 6d. to 3s. 6d. per week. Some years since building speculation was greatly in vogue in Sheffield, and many hundreds of cottages were run up in an exceedingly slight and flimsy style. One speculator alone, who was stated to be "destitute of capital," erected upwards of 200 cottage houses in the course of a few months. The consequence at first was the existence of a vast proportion of uninhabited houses; but the increasing population is now tending to their almost uniform occupancy. In 1841 there were in the township of Sheffield 206 inhabited houses to each thousand residents, the number of empty houses to the thousand inhabitants being 32. In 1831 there were in the parish of Sheffield about 200 inhabited cottage houses to each 1,000 of the population, the empty houses being 10. It results that the amount of house accommodation,

---

* No further Letters from the Manufacturing Districts have been found.

as compared with the requirements of the population, has increased in a slight but perceptible degree during the decennial period. The number of inhabited houses to each thousand of the population throughout England, was, in 1841, about 184; in Scotland, 191; in Lancashire, 173. The number in Bolton was 185; in Liverpool, 148; in Manchester, 168; in Rochdale, 185. Manchester and Liverpool are thus far beneath the average of England, while Sheffield is considerably above the average of Scotland. Every thousand persons in Liverpool live in fewer houses by 57—and in Manchester by 37—than the population of Sheffield; there being in Liverpool about 7, in Manchester about 6, and in Sheffield hardly 5 individuals to each house.

The supply of water in Sheffield, provided by the Waterworks Company, is good. The total surface area of the several reservoirs amounts to about 63 acres. The principal of these lies seven miles west from the town. The supply is originally derived from the surface-drainage of a tract of moorland high up among the hills. From the main the water is conducted by means of an open conduit, lined with stone, into the service reservoir at Crookes, about a mile from the town, whence it can be conducted without propulsive power to the tops of the highest houses. There are nearly fifty miles of cast-iron pipes employed to conduct the supply through the town.

The sewerage of Sheffield is partial and insufficient. Few towns are more favourably situated for being drained of their liquid refuse; the fall towards the rivers being, except at the very lowest levels, considerable. Inconvenience has of late been experienced in consequence of the sewers, in the oldest and lowest part of the town, being found insufficient to convey the increased volume poured into them by the enlargement and extension of the drains in the upper and better portions of Sheffield. All the sewers recently built have been made sufficiently capacious to admit men without inconvenience to cleanse and repair them. In 1843 the total length of the public sewers was about ten miles and a half. The private sewers do not extend above two miles. The most recent educational statistics of Sheffield showed the number of children attending Sunday-schools, connected both with the Church and dissent, to be 11,212. The number attending public day-schools was 6,188; the number attending private day-schools (including dame-schools), 4,459. Further statistical tables proved that of the whole number of scholars attending day-schools, more than 26 per cent. were continually absent, and that the average period of the children's stay in school is only thirteen months. Deducting the habitual amount of absentees, the number receiving the poor thirteen-months' education will be only about 8,000; and as there are nearly 25,000 boys and girls in a state of pupillage in Sheffield, the result would seem to be that two-thirds of the juvenile population receive no week-day instruction whatever.

With reference to the physical and sanitary condition of the population of Sheffield, I cannot at the outset do better than append the following instructive table, prepared by direction of the Commissioners for the Health of Towns:—

DIFFERENT RATES OF MORTALITY PREVALENT AMONG CLASSES OF PERSONS ENGAGED IN THE MANUFACTURES OF SHEFFIELD, AND RESIDENT IN THE TOWNSHIPS OF ECCLESALL BIERLOW, AND NORTHERN DIVISION OF NETHER HALLAM.

Population, 26,280.

| | Average Age at Death of all who have Died. | Average Age at Death of all who have Died above 21. | Proportion per Cent. of Deaths from Epidemics. | Proportion per Cent. of Deaths under 15 to Total Deaths. | Average premature Loss of Life to each Class by Death below the experience of Carlisle, or a healthy Agricultural County. | | Total Deaths, 1839, 1840, and 1841. |
|---|---|---|---|---|---|---|---|
| | | | | | At all Ages. | All who Die above 21. | |
| Class 1. Gentry and Professional Persons | 45.90 | 60.36 | 10.78 | 1.29 | . | 1.64 | 102 |
| Class 2. Tradesmen | 27.01 | 51.12 | 15.74 | 5.88 | 11.99 | 10.88 | 216 |
| General Trades | 20.57 | 54.31 | 24.88 | 14.33 | 18.43 | 7.69 | 414 |
| Silver & Plated Workers | 18.69 | 63. | 24.39 | 1.62 | 20.31 | . | 41 |
| White Metal Smiths | 17.75 | 34. | . | .22 | 21.25 | 28. | 8 |
| Saw Makers | 13.94 | 44.33 | 29.63 | .9 | 25.06 | 17.67 | 27 |
| Edge Tool Forgers & Strikers | 21.86 | 59.08 | 2.78 | 1.29 | 17.14 | 2.92 | 36 |
| Table Knife Forgers & Strikers | 19.43 | 56. | 2.26 | 1.18 | 19.57 | 6. | 31 |
| File Forgers, Cutlers, and Hardeners | 16.08 | 45.36 | 28.05 | 3.02 | 22.92 | 16.64 | 82 |
| Table Knife Hafters | 14.68 | 37.66 | 17.86 | 1.96 | 24.32 | 24.34 | 56 |
| Spring Knife Cutlers | 22.49 | 53.36 | 18.28 | 3.81 | 16.51 | 8.64 | 116 |
| Razor Smiths | 17.91 | 55. | 22.22 | 1.06 | 21.09 | 7. | 27 |
| Scissors Smiths | 15.86 | 38.43 | 21.05 | .62 | 23.14 | 23.57 | 19 |
| Fork Grinders | 24.25 | 48. | . | .11 | 14.75 | 14. | 4 |
| Other Grinders | 18.15 | 44.09 | 23.46 | 6.04 | 20.85 | 17.91 | 179 |
| Comb Makers | 15.23 | 64.16 | 33.33 | .67 | 23.77 | . | 15 |
| Various | 19.20 | 49.89 | 23.68 | 4.03 | 19.80 | 12.11 | 114 |
| Class 4. Undescribed Persons | 27.98 | 48.6 | 14.06 | 5.20 | 11.02 | 13.4 | 128 |
| Class 5. Paupers in Workhouse | 35.51 | 63.38 | 23.44 | 1.51 | 3.49 | . | 64 |
| Class 6. { Agricultural } Farmers | 38.09 | 55.63 | 12.20 | .73 | .91 | 6.37 | 41 |
| Population } Farm Labourers | 26.10 | 56.71 | 19.40 | 2.01 | 12.90 | 5.29 | 67 |
| Totals | 22.58 | 52.70 | 20.82 | 57.53 | 16.42 | 9.30 | 1787 |

*Class 3. Artisans and Labourers.* — *Sheffield Manufacturing Trades.*

The number of persons living to one death is, taking the whole population of the Sheffield district, nearly 37. The number of deaths of children under five years of age is about 506 to every 1,000 deaths, of all ages. The number in Manchester is 517—that in London 401; and the average over England and Wales, 393. The mortality of children in Sheffield is thus nearly as great as that in Manchester. Typhus prevails to a less extent than in many larger and more crowded towns, as the following table will testify:—

DEATHS FROM TYPHUS IN 100,000 DEATHS.

| | |
|---|---|
| Sheffield, mean of three years ....... | 1.551 |
| London ....................... | 7.855 |
| Manchester and Salford ............ | 7.530 |
| Liverpool ..................... | 10.833 |
| Leeds ......................... | 4.688 |
| Birmingham .................... | 5.338 |

Diseases of the lungs and air-passages are, it is well known, the most fatal and characteristic complaints of Sheffield. Several of the grinding processes, by the quantities of excessively fine steel-dust flung into the atmosphere, are frequently and rapidly fatal to those engaged in them; while the bending or stooping postures necessary in all grinding, wet as well as dry, have necessarily their more gradually prejudicial effect. As a body, the grinders are stated to be the most depressed, dissipated, and reckless of all the Sheffield operatives. Of 200 cases of disease—the patients being, with few exceptions, connected with the staple manufactures of Sheffield—the following was ascertained to be the nature of their respective complaints:—

| | |
|---|---|
| Diseases of the air passages .......... | 60 cases. |
|       „     „    digestive apparatus .... | 25 |
|       „     „    urinary organs ....... | 7 |
|       „     „    nervous system ....... | 19 |
|       „     „    heart .............. | 3 |
|       „     „    skin .............. | 3 |
| Diarrhœa and dysentry ............ | 26 |
| Rheumatism ................... | 25 |
| Fever ........................ | 10 |
| Debility ...................... | 3 |
| Miscellaneous ................. | 19 |

Amongst the diseases of the air-passages are reckoned cases of bronchitis, pleuritis, asthma, catarrh, and phthisis. By the table already inserted, it will be seen that while the average age of the gentry and professional persons is 45.90, that of the sawmakers is only 13.94, and that of various grinders, 18.15. In the deaths occurring after the age of 21, the average age of the first class is 60.36, while that of scissor-smiths is only 38.43—of white metal smiths, 34.0—and of grinders, 44.0. The fork branch is the most prejudicial of all the dry-grinding operations; and the average age attained by the men who work at it is under 30. In 1830, the number of persons engaged in the fatal process was 80, and the deaths in the five years following were 20; 17 deaths being those of persons under 34 years of age. At this period one-fourth of the whole number of working fork-grinders died every five years. Out of 55 operatives of this class who died between 1825 and 1840, only one had attained his 48th year, four were under 22, thirteen under 26, seven under 28, nine under 34, and seven under 38; and of the longest livers—that is, of the fourteen above 36 years of age—it was ascertained that four had either entered the business late in life, or had discontinued it during long intervals of time.

*The Morning Chronicle, Tuesday, February 26, 1850.*

### ADVANCE OF WAGES AT LEICESTER.

———◆———

To the EDITOR of the MORNING CHRONICLE.

Sir—Hearing that you have been at great expense and trouble in endeavouring to ascertain the condition of the working classes of this country, and of vindicating their cause, for which we return our sincere thanks, we beg the insertion of the following in your valuable paper.

The straight-down hose branch middle-gauges of Leicester have received an advance of wages during the last week, for which they return their sincere thanks to the manufacturers; and they trust that the exertions you have used, and the good feeling at present manifested by the manufacturers, will tend to the amelioration and improvement of the working classes throughout the country.

THOMAS BENT, Secretary, 25, York-street.

Leicester, Feb. 23.

# Angus B. Reach

Angus Bethune Reach (Scottish Highland name, "ch" pronounced "k") was born in Inverness in 1821 and became a prolific writer, journalist and dramatist. In his early twenties, after a short period working for the Inverness Courier newspaper, he followed his family when they moved to London where his long association with *The Morning Chronicle* would begin.

Charles Mackay, another contributor to the "Labour and the Poor" series, was sub-editor at the time and they became firm friends thereafter. His initial application for employment was unsuccessful due to his lack of short-hand skills, a prerequisite for working as a reporter on a newspaper. This he would soon rectify as Charles Mackay in his Forty Years' Recollections notes in his half-chapter dedicated to Angus Reach:—

> Prior to the year 1841 the business of newspaper reporting was not to be considered among the fine arts, or one that required much literary ability. The great things needful for a reporter were quickness, facility in short-hand, and the faculty of abridgment so as to omit judiciously from the speech of a long-winded orator, all irrelevant matter, and all needless repetitions, to give if necessary the spirit without the form of a speech, and to be able to finish in print the sentences which too many public speakers are unable to complete when addressing an audience. The reporter was never called upon to describe anything he saw or to indulge in language of his own. His business was to hear and not to see, to reproduce the meaning and the language of others, whether in Parliament, in the Courts of Law, or in public meetings. Some of the best reporters of that and a previous time were short-hand writers only, and had no more pretensions to literature than a scene-shifter had to tragic or to comic power. To obtain a connection with journals of the highest class it was of course an advantage to a man to be something better than a short-hand writer, for the Parliamentary reporters being for the most part engaged by the year, and Parliament being in recess at least half that time, he who in the Parliamentary vacation could review books or write notices of new pieces or new actors at the theatres, was of greater value to his employers than he who was but an echo of what he heard. But beyond these two spheres of usefulness, the reporter was seldom or never required to travel. His work was almost purely mechanical, and matters of description were left to a very inferior class of men known

as "penny-a-liners," who were paid by the job, and often personally unknown to the editors to whose journals they contributed. It was their
interest to spin out their reports to the greatest possible length, and
to tell the story of accidents, fires, robberies, murders, and executions
which formed the specialties of their business with a plethora of words
and phrases that was always wearisome and often abominable. But a
change was approaching. In the year 1841, a young Scottish gentleman named Angus Bethune Reach arrived in London from Inverness,
and presented a letter of introduction at the *Morning Chronicle* office.
He was just of age, and, finding his native town in the Highlands too
small for the exercise of his literary talents, determined to launch into
the wider sea of London, and try his fortune on the daily press. He
had had some little experience on the *Inverness Courier*, and the letter he brought addressed to myself was from Mr. Robert Carruthers,
the accomplished editor of that journal. It was a desperate venture on
which he had entered, but he had a strong heart to surmount strong obstacles. And his very obstacles did him good service. His father, once
the leading solicitor in Inverness, had fallen upon evil days, from the
exercise—it was reported—of a too generous hospitality in the enter-
tainment of distinguished strangers, who arrived in the "capital of the
highlands," and in his old age had found it necessary to break up his
home and with his wife to accompany his son to London. It is usually
hard work for a young man in the metropolis without other profession than literature to maintain himself; but poor Angus Reach had a
threefold burden—to him no burden because his love, his hope, and
his consciousness of genius supported him. There was unluckily no vacancy for him on the *Chronicle*. If there had been, he was too young
and inexperienced for political work, and for the work of reporting in
Parliament (for which there was always a demand in those days when
every London morning paper had its own staff of reporters) he was
disqualified because he was unable to write short-hand. This disqual-
ification he immediately set himself to remove, and in the meantime,
thanks to one sympathising spirit who knew his worth, and had the
means in a humble way of pushing him forward—he procured occasional employment—in describing those events of minor importance,
but of general interest which the public liked to read, and very speedily
played havoc with the small penny-a-liners on whom the *Chronicle* as
well as other papers had formerly been compelled to rely. His father,
too—Mr. Roderick Reach—a shrewd and able man, with an excellent
literary style, found employment as the London correspondent of the
*Inverness Courier*, of which he was once the proprietor. Mr. Roderick
Reach was among the first to enter into this walk of journalism, which
has since been so largely trodden, and by means of the wayfarers in
which the public of the provinces are kept so much more fully informed

of the minor doings of the notabilities of the metropolis, and of all the gossip and small talk of fashion than the Londoners themselves. There was at last a vacancy in the reporting department of the *Chronicle*, consequent upon the death of the gentleman who attended the Central Criminal Court, and Angus Reach, pre-informed by myself, was the first candidate in the field. The office was not one of great emolument, but it was a certainty; and Reach, to the great joy of himself and family, obtained it. He had now got his foot on the first rung of the literary ladder, and his upward progress was both steady and rapid. A fortunate accident led to his advancement to the Parliamentary gallery, where he acquitted himself with distinction. One of the ordinary staff had been suddenly called upon to leave London on business of importance to remain absent for two or three weeks, but had begged hard to be excused for domestic and other reasons, to the great annoyance of the editor. The difficulty was to procure a substitute during the day, and it so happened that Reach was in the writing room busy in transcribing his notes. His name was suggested and found acceptance. Being asked how long it would take him to get ready, he promptly replied, "half an hour or less." "That's a man to get on!" said Mr. (afterwards Sir John) Easthope, "a true Scotsman, always ready."

This fortunate circumstance raised him at once from a subordinate to a superior station, and secured him the favour of those who had power to advance him still higher.

In the capacity of a narrator of events which largely interested the public, he was constantly employed; and introduced a style till then unpractised, except in the editorial articles, by means of which he brought before the reader's mind a vivid picture, such as a novelist would paint, of every occurrence that passed under his eye—rapid, correct, graphic, and full of life and animation. Under his influence the reader could but see what he saw, hear what he heard, and share all the emotions and excitements of an actual spectator of the scene. This was an immense advance upon the old reporting style. It immediately found imitators in other journals, and picturesque reporting became thenceforward the fashion, and has so remained to this day, when the picturesque threatens to be swallowed up by the sensational.

Following his work on the "Labour and the Poor" series he travelled to France to report on rural life in connection with *The Morning Chronicle's* extended investigation into "Agriculture and the Rural Population Abroad". He would go on to publish "Claret and Olives" based on these travels in France. He became a great friend of Shirley Brooks who also worked for *The Morning Chronicle* on their "Labour and the Poor" and "Agriculture and the Rural Population Abroad" investigations and who would go on to become editor of *Punch*. This friendship continued during Angus Reach's prolonged and debilitating illness, Shirley Brooks undertaking Angus Reach's writing commitments and handing the payment for these to his wife for their ongoing support. Other writers such as William Makepeace Thackeray would give benefit lectures on their behalf. In 1856 Angus Bethune Reach died, his life and his untimely death recorded in the following obituary piece published by his early employer:—

Inverness Courier, Thursday, December 4, 1856.

## DEATH OF MR ANGUS B. REACH.

We have this week to record the death of our townsman, friend, and long our valued correspondent—Mr Angus Bethune Reach. This event took place at London, on Tuesday afternoon, the 29th ult., after a long illness, the circumstances of which have been of so sad a nature, that we cannot call the final catastrophe by any but a friendly name. These circumstances are already known to our readers; Mr Reach could not long cease to delight the public with his happy, genial essays, and the cause remain concealed; and for nearly two years his familiar name has been missed, where it was once so often seen and so much respected. Let us not seek to examine too closely the gradual eclipse of so bright and gentle a spirit; although our friend is now no more, we are permitted to think of him as the living, lively, warm-hearted associate and distinguished man of letters that he used to be.

Mr Reach was but thirty-five years of age when he died, having been born on the 23d of January 1821. Yet it is sixteen or seventeen years since he became a contributor to this journal. He was then a lad at college, fresh from the classes of the Inverness Royal Academy, devotedly attached to literary studies, and already a proficient in the art of catching those phases of character or events which are transferable to paper, and he was a master of expression. Of all the juvenile compositions which have been submitted to us as journalists, Mr Reach's required the least "licking into shape"—to use a Virgilian phrase—and though, as he grew in years, he added reflection and observation to his writings, his style underwent very little change. If we remember rightly, Mr Macaulay was the theme of Mr Reach's first printed essay; the illustrious reviewer was then in the hey-day of his popularity at Edinburgh, and naturally attracted the attention of the young litterateur. Sketches of Professor Wilson and other Edinburgh celebrities followed, and on returning to Inverness to spend the holidays at his father's house, he became all but a regular member of the slender literary staff of the *Courier*. This was in the year 1840. His father, Mr Roderick Reach—an eminent solicitor in Inverness, and a man of rare intellectual parts—afterwards removed from the North to London, where he commenced the world *de novo*. His warm interest in the Highlands, which no transfer of abode could alienate, led him to become our first London correspondent, and so highly were his admirable letters appreciated, that, in a very few years, almost every paper in Scotland followed our example, and added to their original matter a weekly letter from the metropolis. Mr Angus Reach, however, remained in Scotland, and devoted a small sum of money of his own to the prosecution of his studies at the University of Edinburgh. In 1842 he repaired to London, with the intention of attaching himself to the public press. The only introduction which he brought with him was a letter which had been written by Dr Charles Mackay to ourselves, acknowledging a friendly critique, by Mr Reach, in the *Courier*, of Dr Mackay's poem the Salamandrine—a slender basis, indeed, on which to trust for earning the means of livelihood! Dr Mackay was then, however, sub-editor of the *Morning Chronicle*, and having tested his young critic's capacity for ordinary newspaper work and for shorthand reporting, procured an engagement for him as what is called an "outsider," or reporter of general public meetings, as distinguished from the meetings of Parliament. The connection once formed was never broken as long as Mr Reach could wield his pen, and it is to the credit of the managers of the *Morning Chronicle*, that they continued to regard him as one of their staff until long after all hope of his recovery was banished. Thirteen or fourteen years does not seem a long period for a young man to have been employed on a leading journal; but it is significant of the uncertainty of the London press as a profession, that several years ago there was not a single contributor to the *Morning Chronicle* whose connection with it was not formed subsequently to that of Mr Reach.

Our townsman had not been long in London when he formed additional literary engagements. His frank manner and genial disposition soon won the friendship of all with whom he came in contact, and they readily led him into those fields where they themselves reaped reputation and profit. The London miscellanies of the day opened their columns to him, and starting, as he did, with the general principle of affixing his name to all his productions—the name or initials of Angus B. Reach, in a very few years, became familiar to every reader of the current magazine literature of England. His facility in dashing off readable, even instructive, papers on almost any subject was something marvellous. We have known him frequently to sit down after breakfast, and write the greater part, if not the whole, of a quiet reflective article for a magazine—then visit some new exhibition or novelty in London, about which a paragraph had to be written for the *Chronicle*—block out the points of a review, or, if the book was one of no great note, actually write the critique as it was to appear—and finish the day by producing half a column of lively and graphic criticism on the opera of that evening. This facility of composition was fatal to him. The bent of the mind became fixed in that direction, and it was with great difficulty afterwards that he could apply his mind to a long-sustained effort. In striking contrast to his career was that of a fellow-townsman, an attached friend, and a collaborateur on the *Chronicle*—Mr Alexander Mackay, the author of "The Western World," who was also prematurely called away some years ago. They commenced their life in London nearly together, and both were men of fine intellect and indefatigable industry; but while the one was winning a fleeting celebrity in periodicals that were cast aside as soon as read, the other was making a long-sustained effort for rewards of a more lasting character. Both have had their reward; and though it is to be regretted that Mr Reach devoted himself so exclusively to periodical literature, every one who has read his many genial essays, dashed as they were by a fine love of all that is poetical and true and lovely, must give him credit for many hours of pure and elevated enjoyment. It would be wrong, however, to say that Mr Reach made no effort at success in a higher range of literature. In 1848-49 he published, in monthly parts, a romance which has gone through several editions—Clement Lorimer. The story is a wild one of Italian revenge, and the treatment of it is singularly bold and striking. Some passages may rank in the highest class of animated descriptive writing, and the work promises to be long a favourite. In 1850 appeared a still more ambitious work—Leonard Lindsay, or a Story of the Buccaneers—a two-volume novel, which displays the same remarkable power of description, and greater skill in conducting narrative and dialogue than the first. The only other volume which he lived to produce, and which may be ranked in a superior category to the hurried shilling miscellanies constantly issuing from his pen, is his popular work on Southern France, "Claret and Olives." It contains the essence of a very careful examination of the vine-counties of France, conducted in 1850 on behalf of the *Morning Chronicle*, in connection with their celebrated inquiry into the state of labour and the poor in England and Europe. Mr Reach took a large share in this great work, having reported specially on the manufacturing and coal districts of the north of England, as well as on France. Dr Charles Mackay, Mr Alexander Mackay, Mr Henry Mayhew, and Mr Chevalier, were among those employed along with Mr Reach in this gigantic undertaking. Mr Reach meditated two other works, springing partly from this inquiry: one a companion to "Claret and Olives," which he thought of calling the "Rhone and the Garonne;" and the other, an essay on the manufactures and manufacturing population of the North of England. On the latter subject he wrote a long and very interesting pamphlet, which was published by the Messrs Chambers.

It would be endless to enumerate the publications to which Mr Reach's ready pen periodically contributed. Latterly, besides his duty as musical and art critic, and the principal reviewer of the *Morning Chronicle*, which he never sacrificed to his other avocations, Mr Reach was one of the regular writers in a great many magazines and newspapers. He wrote largely for the Messrs Chamber's publications, *Bentley's Miscellany*, and a great number of London periodical magazines—the *Illustrated London News*, to which he gave a weekly summary of gossip called "Town Talk and Table Talk," besides frequent literary articles and Christmas tales; the *Era*, the *Atlas*, the *Britannia*, the *Sunday Times*, a weekly paper in Sheffield, and one in Durham—were all recipients of his productions; he was for some time the London correspondent of the *Glasgow Citizen*, and from the date of his father's death, in 1853, until successive paralytic strokes had prostrated his powers, he was the correspondent of this paper. In an intermediate position between these contributions to the weekly and daily press, and the more important works alluded to above, are those amusing miscellanies which some years ago were so popular, such as "The Natural History of the Bore," and "of the Humbug," the monthly serial "The Man in the Moon," which he conducted along with Mr Albert Smith; "A Story with a Vengeance," written jointly with Mr Shirley Brooks, &c., &c. One and all, they are sparkling, pleasant, readable works, containing a great deal of shrewd observation and good sense, and seldom surpassed in pointed epigrammatic expression. Had the same power been devoted to the production of only two or three works in the course of Mr Reach's brief career in London, few names would have stood higher in the estimation of the world, among the authors of the present day. Personally Mr Reach was one of the most amiable and generous men that ever came before the public as a man of letters. We say this in all soberness, and from, we believe, a competent knowledge of the circumstances of his career, and of his private character. When his life comes to be written, it will be seen that there have been few more touching scenes in the republic of letters than the self-sacrifice and filial devotion of Mr Angus B. Reach. Nor will it be easy to find an example of an author who wrote so much and said so few unkind things of his contemporaries. Living as he did for a while in the very heat of an uninterrupted fire of wit, this is great praise. He threw off squibs and pasquinades as profusely as any one; but it would be hard to find a bitter one, and impossible to find a malicious one among them all. Hence all who knew, loved the man; and their friendship grew with their knowledge of him; and when the clouds gathered round his chamber at last, it was cheering to see with what heart and unanimity friends rallied to his side, and fought his battle to the end. Conspicuous among these were Mr Shirley Brooks, an old and a fast friend, Dr Charles Mackay, Mr Albert Smith, Mr Thackeray, and Mr Munro, sculptor. These and many others interested themselves to the last in Mr Reach's circumstances—they got up amateur theatrical performances, delivered lectures, and laid siege to Downing Street in his behalf. They never laboured in a worthier cause, and they showed themselves thereby disciples of the same school of which he was a conspicuous ornament. Let us hope that their efforts will not be relaxed now that he is removed from among us, until his widow, who has watched over Mr Reach during his protracted illness with the most devoted care and attention, be placed in a position of comparative comfort and independence.

Yesterday Mr Reach's remains were to have been laid beside those of his late father in the cemetery at Norwood, and the chief mourners named are Mr Shirley Brooks, Mr A. Munro, Mr Albert Smith, Mr T. Holmes, and Mr Carruthers of Inverness. It was not expected that Dr Mackay would be able to attend.

# Index

# Titles Available in the Series

## LABOUR AND THE POOR

### Volumes I to IV: The Metropolitan Districts
*Henry Mayhew*

ISBN 978-1-913515-11-9, 978-1-913515-12-6, 978-1-913515-13-3, 978-1-913515-14-0

### Volume V: The Manufacturing Districts
*Angus B. Reach*

ISBN 978-1-913515-15-7

### Volumes VI & VII: The Rural Districts
*Alexander Mackay & Shirley Brooks*

ISBN 978-1-913515-16-4, 978-1-913515-17-1

### Volume VIII: Wales
*Special Correspondent*

ISBN 978-1-913515-18-8

### Volume IX: Birmingham
*Charles Mackay*

ISBN 978-1-913515-19-5

### Volume X: Liverpool
*Charles Mackay*

ISBN 978-1-913515-20-1

For information on these and other titles available please visit:

DittoBooks.co.uk